College Writing Skills
with Readings

Seventh Edition

College Writing Skills with Readings

John Langan
Atlantic Cape Community College

Boston   Burr Ridge, IL   Dubuque, IA   Madison, WI   New York   San Francisco   St. Louis
Bangkok   Bogotá   Caracas   Kuala Lumpur   Lisbon   London   Madrid   Mexico City
Milan   Montreal   New Delhi   Santiago   Seoul   Singapore   Sydney   Taipei   Toronto

The McGraw·Hill Companies

McGraw Hill Higher Education

3 4 5 6 7 8 9 0 DOC/DOC 0 9 8

ISBN 978-0-07-338408-5 (student edition)
MHID 0-07-338408-9 (student edition)
ISBN 978-0-07-334393-8 (instructor's edition)
MHID 0-07-334393-5 (instructor's edition)

Editor in Chief: *Emily Barrosse*
Sponsoring Editor: *John Kindler*
Developmental Editor: *Alyson Watts*
Editorial Coordinator: *Jesse Hassenger*
Marketing Manager: *Tamara Wederbrand*
Production Editor: *Karol Jurado*
Production Service: *Newgen–Austin*
Project Manager: *Shirley Michels*
Manuscript Editor: *Mary Ann Short*
Photo Research: *Emily Tietz*
Media Project Manager: *Ron Nelms, Jr.*
Media Producer: *Alex Rohrs*
Production Supervisor: *Tandra Jorgensen*
Art Director: *Jeanne M. Schreiber*
Design Manager: *Preston Thomas*
Text Designer: *Maureen McCutcheon*
Cover Illustration: *Tom White Illustrations*
Composition: *11/13 Times by Newgen*
Printing: *45# Pub Matte, R. R. Donnelley & Sons*

Library of Congress Cataloging-in-Publication Data

Langan, John
   College writing skills with readings / John Langan.—7th ed.
      p. cm.
   Includes index.
   ISBN-13: 978-0-07-338408-5 (alk. paper)
   ISBN-10: 0-07-338408-9 (alk. paper)
   1. English language—Rhetoric. 2. English language—Grammar. 3. College readers. I. Title.
PE1408.L3178 2008
808′.042—dc22   2007022814

The Internet addresses listed in the text were accurate at the time of publication. The inclusion of a Web site does not indicate an endorsement by the authors or McGraw-Hill, and McGraw-Hill does not guarantee the accuracy of the information presented at these sites.

www.mhhe.com

Praise for the Langan series

"There can be no legitimate comparison between John Langan's McGraw-Hill developmental composition text series and any other texts available. Other texts are simply not as clear, precise, interesting, or comprehensive."
—Candace C. Mesa, Dixie College

"John Langan's pedagogical approach makes all kinds of sense to me. The emphasis on reading and structured writing provides students with a solid foundation in composition."
—Kristine Anderson, Riverside Community College

"The writing style, tone, and level are perfect for my target student audience: the explanations are clear, the reading choices are varied and thought-provoking, and the amount of examples and exercises is just enough to help students but not so much that they feel overwhelmed."
—Marcie Sims, Green River Community College

"The down-to-earth, believable student samples demonstrate the process of writing absolutely clearly, from a simple prewriting effort into a finished product. A student can identify not only with the content but see concrete examples of the process of writing."
—Gloria Jean Kirby, Lincoln Land Community College

"I appreciate the concise and clear presentation of grammar and the grammar review tests. Students have ample examples, yet the grammar pages don't overtake the text."
—Lisa Windham, McLennan Community College

"Langan does a wonderful job of reflecting the nontraditional as well as the traditional student, and of providing readings that appeal to a diverse audience."
—Pamela Arlov, Macon State College

"The Langan books truly provide the clearest explanations of grammar rules."
—Lisa Moreno, Los Angeles Trade Technical College

About the Author

John Langan has taught reading and writing at Atlantic Cape
Community College near Atlantic City, New Jersey, for more than
25 years. The author of a popular series of college textbooks on both
writing and reading, John enjoys the challenge of developing materials
that teach skills in an especially clear and lively way.
Before teaching, he earned advanced degrees in writing at
Rutgers University and in reading at Rowan University. He
also spent a year writing fiction that, he says, "is now at the
back of a drawer waiting to be discovered and acclaimed
posthumously." While in school, he supported himself by
working as a truck driver, a machinist, a battery assembler, a
hospital attendant, and an apple packer. John now lives with
his wife, Judith Nadell, near Philadelphia. In addition to his wife
and Philly sports teams, his passions include reading and turning on
nonreaders to the pleasure and power of books. Through Townsend
Press, his educational publishing company, he has developed the
nonprofit "Townsend Library"—a collection of more than 50 new and
classic stories that appeal to readers of any age.

Contents

Part 3: Special Skills 374

Part 4: Handbook of Sentence Skills 446

SECTION 1: Grammar 448

Readings Listed by Rhetorical Mode

Note: Some selections are cross-listed because they illustrate more than one rhetorical method of development.

DESCRIPTION

NARRATION

EXEMPLIFICATION

PROCESS

CAUSE AND EFFECT

COMPARISON OR CONTRAST

DEFINITION

DIVISION-CLASSIFICATION

ARGUMENT

To the Instructor

College Writing Skills with Readings is a rhetoric with readings that will help students master the traditional five-paragraph essay and variations of this essay. It is a very practical book with a number of unique features designed to aid instructors and their students.

Key Features of the Book

- *Four principles are presented as keys to effective writing.* These four principles—unity, support, coherence, and sentence skills—are highlighted on the inside back cover and reinforced throughout the book.

  Part One focuses on the first three principles and to some extent on sentence skills.

  Parts Two and Three show, respectively, how the four principles apply in the different patterns of essay development and in specialized types of writing.

  Part Four serves as a concise handbook of sentence skills.

  Finally, the professional readings in **Part Five** are followed by questions and assignments that encourage students to apply the four principles in a variety of well-developed essays.

  The ongoing success of *College Writing Skills with Readings* is evidence that the four principles are easily grasped, remembered, and followed by students.

- *Writing is treated as a process.* The first chapter introduces writing as both a skill and a process of discovery. The second chapter, "The Writing Process," explains and illustrates the sequence of steps in writing an effective essay. In particular, the chapter focuses on prewriting and revision as strategies to use with any writing assignment. Detailed suggestions for prewriting and revision then accompany many of the writing assignments in Part Two.

- *Activities and assignments are numerous and varied.* For example, Part One contains more than 90 activities to help students apply and master the four principles, or bases, of effective writing. The entire book has over 250 activities and tests. A variety of writing assignments follow each pattern of essay development in Part Two and each reading in Part Five. Some topics are highly structured, for students who are still learning the steps in the writing process; others are open-ended. Instructors thus have the option of selecting those assignments most suited to the individual needs of their students.

- *Clear thinking is stressed throughout.* This emphasis on logic starts with the opening pages of the book. Students are introduced to the two principles that are the bedrock of clear thinking: *making a point* and *providing support to back up that point.* The focus on these principles then continues throughout the book, helping students learn that clear writing is inseparable from clear thinking.

- *The traditional essay is emphasized.* Students are asked to write formal essays with an introduction, three supporting paragraphs, and a conclusion. Anyone who has tried to write a solidly reasoned essay knows how much work is involved. A logical essay requires a great deal of mental discipline and close attention to a set of logical rules. Writing an essay in which there is an overall thesis statement and in which each of the three supporting paragraphs begins with a topic sentence is more challenging for many students than writing a free-form or expressive essay. The demands are significant, but the rewards are great.

    At the same time that students learn and practice the rules of the five-paragraph essay, professional essays representing the nine patterns of development show them variations possible within the essay form. These essays provide models if instructors decide that their students will benefit from moving beyond the traditional essay form.

- *Lively teaching models are provided.* The book includes two high-interest student essays and one engaging professional essay with each chapter in Part Two. Students then read and evaluate these essays in terms of the four bases: unity, support, coherence, and sentence skills. Instructors can also refer their students to appropriate essays from the collection of professional readings in Part Five. After reading vigorous papers by other students as well as papers by professional authors and experiencing the power that good writing can have, students will be encouraged to aim for a similar honesty, realism, and detail in their own work.

- *The book is versatile.* Since no two people use an English text in exactly the same way, the material has been organized in a highly accessible manner. Each of the five parts of the book deals with a distinct area of writing. Instructors can therefore turn quickly and easily to the skills they want to present.

- *Nineteen professional essays appear in Part Five.* These essays, like the nine professional readings in Part Two, deal with both contemporary and timeless concerns. They will stimulate lively class discussions and individual thought as well as serve as a rich source of material for a wide range of writing assignments.

  Part Five has three special features. First is the emphasis placed on helping students become stronger readers. An introductory section offers tips on effective reading, and questions after each selection help students practice skills in both reading comprehension and critical thinking. A second feature of Part Five is a set of questions about structure and technique so that students can analyze and learn from a writer's craft in developing an essay. Finally, a series of writing assignments include suggestions and guidelines that will help students think about and proceed with an assignment.

Changes in the Seventh Edition

Here is an overview of what is new in the seventh edition of the book:

- *Among several changes in this seventh edition is its new, more contemporary design.* The enhanced four-color design adds visual appeal for students while highlighting key material for them and helping them make connections and find the information they need.

- *Over 70 images have been added throughout the text.* Because today's students respond so readily to visual images, and must learn to evaluate such images critically, this text features more than seventy new images, each chosen and used for a pedagogical purpose.

  - ✔ Every part now opens with an image (or images) accompanied by a writing prompt that introduces students to the lessons that section of the text will cover.

  - ✔ Every chapter in Parts One through Three opens with a compelling visual or visuals, all of which are accompanied by writing prompts related to the particular chapter. In addition, every section in Part Four features a visual opener with accompanying writing prompt.

  - ✔ Part Five, Readings for Writers, now includes writing prompts for featured images, which are linked thematically to the readings.

- *Key features have been added to make the book easier to use for instructors and students.*

  - ✔ Every part and chapter now opens with an outline of its contents, preparing students for the lessons to follow.

✔ Tip, Hint, and Explanation Boxes throughout the text offer advice about grammar rules, hints for students on how to complete selected activities, and explanations of why the answers to sample activities are correct.

✔ Marginal technology icons have been simplified to include just one easily recognizable icon directing students to the book's Online Learning Center, where they can find expanded coverage of a particular topic or hone their skills through completing additional exercises.

✔ A new Collaborative Learning icon highlights all student activities that can be assigned as collaborative activities, either in or outside of class.

✔ Teaching Tips are available in the margins throughout the Annotated Instructor's Edition.

✔ ESL Tips, which offer specific advice for instructing multilingual writers, are also featured in the margins of the Annotated Instructor's Edition.

• *New checklists reinforce the importance of the four bases during revision.* Every chapter in Part Two: Patterns of Essay Development now features a specialized checklist of the four bases that students can use when revising essays written in the different patterns of development. Each checklist is tailored to the particular pattern of writing the students are working on in that chapter.

• *The book features two new readings.* Chosen for their appeal and relevance to today's students, these new essays address the effects of sleep deprivation and what to do about it and the increasing amount of sexuality in the media that is targeted at teens.

• *A new appendix, "A Writer's Journal,"* has been added to encourage students to keep a writing journal and to give them room to start recording ideas.

Helpful Learning Aids Accompany the Book

Supplements for Instructors

• The *Annotated Instructor's Edition* (ISBN 0-07-334393-5) consists of the student text complete with answers to all activities and tests, followed by an Instructor's Guide featuring teaching suggestions and a model syllabus. The Annotated Instructor's Edition of *College Writing Skills with Readings* also includes three diagnostic or achievement tests: two 40-question tests

(A and B), and, for added flexibility, a single 60-question test (C) derived from tests A and B. These tests, along with their scoring keys, are included in print form in the back of the book. The tests are also available via the *College Writing Skills with Readings* Online Learning Center (**www.mhhe .com/langan**). Instructors directing students to take the tests online can have students' scores and assessments e-mailed to them directly. (Students taking these tests will receive their final scores and an assessment, but not the correct answers to individual responses.)

- An *Online Learning Center* (**www.mhhe.com/langan**) offers a host of instructional aids and additional resources for instructors, including a comprehensive computerized test bank, the *Instructor's Manual and Test Bank*, online resources for writing instructors, and more.

- *PageOut* helps instructors create graphically pleasing and professional Web pages for their courses, in addition to providing classroom management, collaborative learning, and content management tools. PageOut is **FREE** to adopters of McGraw-Hill textbooks and learning materials. Learn more at **www.mhhe.com/pageout.**

- *The McGraw-Hill Virtual Workbook* offers interactive activities and exercises that reinforce the skills students learn in Part Four of *College Writing Skills with Readings*. Authored by Donna T. Matsumoto, Leeward Community College, and powered by Quia, each interactive, Web-based activity corresponds to a key section or chapter in Part Four, giving students additional opportunities for practice in grammar, punctuation, and mechanics. This online workbook is supported by a powerful array of Web-based instructor's tools, including an automated online gradebook.

Supplements for Students

- An *Online Learning Center* (**www.mhhe.com/langan**) includes self-correcting exercises, writing activities for additional practice, a PowerPoint grammar tutorial, guides to doing research on the Internet and avoiding plagiarism, useful Web links, and more.

- *The McGraw-Hill Virtual Workbook* offers interactive activities and exercises that reinforce the skills students learn in Part Four of *College Writing Skills with Readings*. Authored by Donna T. Matsumoto, Leeward Community College, and powered by Quia, each interactive, Web-based activity corresponds to a key section or chapter in Part Four, giving students additional opportunities for practice in grammar, punctuation, and mechanics.

Dictionary and Vocabulary Resources

- *Random House Webster's College Dictionary* (ISBN 0-07-240011-0) This authoritative dictionary includes over 160,000 entries and 175,000 definitions. The most commonly used definitions are always listed first, so students can find what they need quickly.

- *The Merriam-Webster Dictionary* (ISBN 0-07-310057-9) Based on the best-selling Merriam-Webster's Collegiate Dictionary, the paperback dictionary contains over 70,000 definitions.

- *The Merriam-Webster Thesaurus* (ISBN 0-07-310067-6) This handy paperback thesaurus contains over 157,000 synonyms, antonyms, related and contrasted words, and idioms.

- *Merriam-Webster's Vocabulary Builder* (ISBN 0-07-310069-2) This handy paperback introduces 3,000 words, and includes quizzes to test progress.

- *Merriam-Webster's Notebook Dictionary* (ISBN 0-07-299091-0) An extremely concise reference to the words that form the core of English vocabulary, this popular dictionary, conveniently designed for three-ring binders, provides words and information at students' fingertips.

- *Merriam-Webster's Notebook Thesaurus* (ISBN 0-07-310068-4) Conveniently designed for three-ring binders, this thesaurus helps students search for words they might need today. It provides concise, clear guidance for over 157,000 word choices.

- *Merriam-Webster's Collegiate Dictionary and Thesaurus, Electronic Edition* (ISBN 0-07-310070-6) Available on CD-ROM, this online dictionary contains thousands of new words and meanings from all areas of human endeavor, including electronic technology, the sciences, and popular culture.

You can contact your local McGraw-Hill representative or consult McGraw-Hill's Web site at **www.mhhe.com/english** for more information on the supplements that accompany *College Writing Skills with Readings*, Seventh Edition.

Acknowledgments

Reviewers who have contributed to this edition through their helpful comments include

Kristine R. Anderson, Riverside Community College

Ben DeSure, Pittsburgh Technical Institute

Carolyn E. Gordon, Cuyahoga Community College

Laura Hope-Aleman, Chaffey College

Teresa S. Irvin, Columbus State University

Gloria Jean Kirby, Lincoln Land Community College

Gail K. L. Levy, Leeward Community College

Donna T. Matsumoto, Leeward Community College

Christina Putney, Mott Community College

Judi Salsburg, Monroe Community College

Midge Shaw, Rogue Community College

Marcie L. Sims, Green River Community College

Julia L. Smith, Kennedy-King College

J. Christian Tatu, Warren County Community College

Eileen Thompson, Edison Community College

Dennielle True, Manatee Community College

Lisa Windham, McLennan Community College

I am also grateful for the talented support of my McGraw-Hill editors, John Kindler and Alyson Watts. Editorial/marketing team members Jesse Hassenger and Tamara Wederbrand also made valuable contributions to this text. Many thanks to the skilled production and design team—Karol Jurado, Shirley Michels at Newgen–Austin, Preston Thomas, Maureen McCutcheon, Emily Tietz, and Tandra Jorgensen. Also, I'd like to thank Ron Nelms, Jr. and Alex Rohrs for producing the text's media component.

Joyce Stern, Assistant Professor at Nassau Community College, contributed the ESL Tips to the Annotated Instructor's Edition of *College Writing Skills with Readings.* Professor Stern is also Assistant to the Chair in the department of Reading and Basic Education. An educator for over thirty years, she holds an advanced degree in TESOL from Hunter College, as well as a New York State Teaching Certificate in TESOL. She is currently coordinating the design, implementation, and recruitment of learning communities for both ESL and developmental students at Nassau Community College and has been recognized by the college's Center for Students with Disabilities for her dedication to student learning.

Donna T. Matsumoto, Assistant Professor of English and the Writing Discipline Coordinator at Leeward Community College in Hawaii (Pearl City), wrote the Teaching Tips for the Annotated Instructor's Edition of *College Writing Skills with Readings.* Professor Matsumoto has taught writing, women's studies, and American studies for a number of years throughout the University of Hawaii system, at Hawaii Pacific University, and in community schools for adults. She received a 2005 WebCT Exemplary Course Project award for her online writing course and is the author of *The McGraw-Hill Virtual Workbook,* an online workbook featuring interactive activities and exercises.

John Langan

PART 1

Essay Writing

Preview

Have yourself a merry little Christmas
It may be your last
Next year we may all be living in the past
Have yourself a merry little Christmas
Pop the champagne cork
Next year we may all be living in New York.
No good times like the olden days,
Happy golden days of yore,
Faithful friends who were dear to us
Will be near to us no more.
But at least we all will be together
If the Lord allows.
From now on we'll have to muddle through somehow.
So have yourself a merry little Christmas now.

Have Yourself a Merry Little Christmas,
Let your heart be light
From now on, our troubles will be out of sight
Have yourself a merry little Christmas
Make your yuletide gay
From now on our troubles will be miles away.
Here we are as in olden days,
Happy golden days of yore.
Faithful friends who were dear to us
Gather be near to us once more.
Through the years we all will be together
If the fates allow.
Until then, we'll have to muddle through somehow
So have yourself a merry little Christmas now.

Even songwriters often have to write several drafts of lyrics before producing an effective song. Compare this excerpted draft of "Have Yourself a Merry Little Christmas" by Hugh Martin with its final version; what has changed? Choose one revision and explain why and how it makes the lyrics more effective.

1

An Introduction to Writing

This chapter will explain and illustrate

- the importance of supporting a point in writing

- the structure of the traditional essay

- the benefits of writing the traditional essay

This chapter also

- presents writing as both a skill and a process of discovery

- suggests keeping a journal

© Stock Image/SuperStock

What is your ideal job? Write two or more paragraphs about what your ideal job would be and what your daily activities on the job would entail. Be sure to include your reasons for wanting such a job.

The experience I had writing my first college essay helped shape this book. I received a C− for the essay. Scrawled beside the grade was the comment "Not badly written, but ill-conceived." I remember going to the instructor after class, asking about his comment as well as the word *Log* that he had added in the margin at various spots. "What are all these logs you put in my paper?" I asked, trying to make a joke of it. He looked at me a little wonderingly. "Logic, Mr. Langan," he answered, "logic." He went on to explain that I had not thought out my paper clearly. There were actually two ideas rather than one in my thesis, one supporting paragraph had nothing to do with either idea, another paragraph lacked a topic sentence, and so on. I've never forgotten his last words: "If you don't think clearly," he said, "you won't write clearly."

I was speechless, and I felt confused and angry. I didn't like being told that I didn't know how to think. I went back to my room and read over my paper several times. Eventually, I decided that my instructor was right. "No more logs," I said to myself. "I'm going to get these logs out of my papers."

My instructor's advice was invaluable. I learned that clear, disciplined thinking is the key to effective writing. *College Writing Skills* develops this idea by breaking down the writing process into a series of four logical, easily followed steps. These steps, combined with practical advice about prewriting and revision, will help you write strong papers.

Here are the four steps in a nutshell:

1. Discover a clearly stated point, or thesis.
2. Provide logical, detailed support for your thesis.
3. Organize and connect your supporting material.
4. Revise and edit so that your sentences are effective and error-free.

Part One of this book explains each of these steps in detail and provides many practice materials to help you master them.

Point and Support

An Important Difference between Writing and Talking

In everyday conversation, you make all kinds of points or assertions. You say, for example, "My boss is a hard person to work for," "It's not safe to walk in our neighborhood after dark," or "Poor study habits keep getting me into trouble." The points that you make concern personal matters as well as, at times, outside issues: "That trade will be a disaster for the team," "Lots of TV commercials are degrading to women," "Students are better off working for a year before attending college."

The people you are talking with do not always challenge you to give reasons for your statements. They may know why you feel as you do, or they may already agree with you, or they simply may not want to put you on the spot; and so they do not always ask why. But the people who read what you write may not know you, agree with you, or feel in any way obliged to you. If you want to communicate effectively with readers, you must provide solid evidence for any point you make. An important difference, then, between writing and talking is this: *In writing, any idea that you advance must be supported with specific reasons or details.*

Think of your readers as reasonable people. They will not take your views on faith, but they are willing to accept what you say as long as you support it. Therefore, remember to support with specific evidence any point that you make.

Point and Support in a Paragraph

In conversation, you might say to a friend who has suggested a movie, "No, thanks. Going to the movies is just too much of a hassle. Parking, people, everything." From shared past experiences, your friend may know what you are talking about so that you will not have to explain your statement. But in writing, your point would have to be backed up with specific reasons and details.

Below is a paragraph, written by a student named Diane Woods, on why moviegoing is a nuisance. A *paragraph* is a short paper of around 150 to 200 words. It usually consists of an opening point, called a *topic sentence,* followed by a series of sentences that support that point.

The Hazards of Moviegoing

Although I love movies, I've found that there are drawbacks to moviegoing. One problem is just the inconvenience of it all. To get to the theater, I have to drive for at least fifteen minutes, or more if traffic is bad. It can take forever to find a parking spot, and then I have to walk across a huge parking lot to the theater. There I encounter long lines, sold-out shows, and ever-increasing prices. And I hate sitting with my feet sticking to the floor because of other people's spilled snacks. Another problem is my lack of self-control at the theater. I often stuff myself with unhealthy calorie-laden snacks. My choices might include a bucket of popcorn, a box of Milk Duds, a giant soda, or all three. The worst problem is some of the other moviegoers. Kids run up and down the aisle. Teenagers laugh and shout at the screen. People of all ages drop soda cups and popcorn tubs, cough and burp, and talk to one another. All in all, I would rather stay home and watch a DVD in the comfort of my own living room.

Notice what the supporting evidence does here. It provides you, the reader, with a basis for understanding *why* the writer makes the point that is made. Through this specific evidence, the writer has explained and successfully communicated the idea that moviegoing can be a nuisance.

The evidence that supports the point in a paper often consists of a series of reasons followed by examples and details that support the reasons. That is true of the paragraph above: three reasons are provided, with examples and details that back up those reasons. Supporting evidence in a paper can also consist of anecdotes, personal experiences, facts, studies, statistics, and the opinions of experts.

The paragraph on moviegoing, like almost any piece of effective writing, has two essential parts: (1) a point is advanced, and (2) that point is then supported. Taking a minute to outline "The Hazards of Moviegoing" will help you understand these basic parts. Write in the following space the point that has been advanced in the paragraph. Then add the words needed to complete the paragraph's outline.

Activity

1

Point
Support

_____

1. _____

   a. Fifteen-minute drive to theater

   b. _____

   c. Long lines, sold-out shows, and increasing prices

   d. _____

2. Lack of self-control

   a. Often stuff myself with unhealthy snacks

   b. Might have popcorn, candy, soda, or all three

3. _____

   a. _____

   b. _____

   c. People of all ages make noise.

Point and Support in an Essay

An excellent way to learn how to write clearly and logically is to practice the traditional college *essay*—a paper of about five hundred words that typically consists of an introductory paragraph, two to four supporting paragraphs (the norm in this book will be three), and a concluding paragraph. The central idea, or point, developed in any essay is called a *thesis statement* (rather than, as in a paragraph, a topic sentence). The thesis appears in the introductory paragraph, and the specific support for the thesis appears in the paragraphs that follow. The supporting paragraphs allow for a fuller treatment of the evidence that backs up the central point than would be possible in a single-paragraph paper.

Structure of the Traditional Essay

A Model Essay

www.mhhe.com/langan

The following model will help you understand the form of an essay. Diane Woods, the writer of the paragraph on moviegoing, later decided to develop her subject more fully. Here is the essay that resulted.

The Hazards of Moviegoing

Introductory paragraph

I am a movie fanatic. My friends count on me to know movie trivia (who was the pigtailed little girl in E.T.: The Extra-Terrestrial? Drew Barrymore) and to remember every big Oscar awarded since I was in grade school (Best Picture, 1994? Forrest Gump). My friends, though, have stopped asking me if I want to go out to the movies. While I love movies as much as ever, the inconvenience of going out, the temptations of the concession stand, and the behavior of some patrons are reasons for me to wait and rent the DVD.

First supporting paragraph

To begin with, I just don't enjoy the general hassle of the evening. Since small local movie theaters are a thing of the past, I have to drive for fifteen minutes to get to the nearest multiplex. The parking lot is shared with several restaurants and a supermarket, so it's always jammed. I have to drive around at a snail's pace until I spot another driver backing out. Then it's time to stand in an endless line, with the constant threat that tickets for the show I want will sell out. If we do get tickets, the theater will be so crowded that I won't be able to sit with my friends, or we'll have to sit in a front row gaping up at a giant screen. I have to shell out a ridiculous amount of money—up to $11—for a ticket. That entitles me to sit while my shoes seal themselves to a sticky floor coated with spilled soda, bubble gum, and crushed Raisinets.

Second supporting paragraph

Second, the theater offers tempting snacks that I really don't need. Like most of us, I have to battle an expanding waistline. At home I do pretty well by simply not buying stuff that is bad for me. I can make do with snacks like celery and carrot sticks because there is no ice cream in the freezer. Going to the theater, however, is like spending my evening in a 7-Eleven that's been equipped with a movie screen and comfortable seats. As I try to persuade myself to just have a Diet Coke, the smell of fresh popcorn dripping with

(continued)

butter soon overcomes me. Chocolate bars the size of small automobiles seem to jump into my hands. I risk pulling out my fillings as I chew enormous mouthfuls of Milk Duds. By the time I leave the theater, I feel disgusted with myself.

Many of the other patrons are even more of a problem than the concession stand. Little kids race up and down the aisles, usually in giggling packs. Teenagers try to impress their friends by talking back to the screen, whistling, and making what they consider to be hilarious noises. Adults act as if they were at home in their own living room. They comment loudly on the ages of the stars and reveal plot twists that are supposed to be a secret until the film's end. And people of all ages create distractions. They crinkle candy wrappers, stick gum on their seats, and drop popcorn tubs or cups of crushed ice and soda on the floor. They also cough and burp, squirm endlessly in their seats, file out for repeated trips to the restrooms or concession stands, and elbow me out of the armrest on either side of my seat.

Third supporting paragraph

After arriving home from the movies one night, I decided that I was not going to be a moviegoer anymore. I was tired of the problems involved in getting to the theater, resisting unhealthy snacks, and dealing with the patrons. The next day, I arranged to have premium movie channels added to my cable TV service, and I also got a Netflix membership. I may now see movies a bit later than other people, but I'll be more relaxed watching box office hits in the comfort of my own living room.

Concluding paragraph

Parts of an Essay

"The Hazards of Moviegoing" is a good example of the standard short essay you will write in college English. It is a composition of over five hundred words that consists of a one-paragraph introduction, a three-paragraph body, and a one-paragraph conclusion. The roles of these paragraphs are described and illustrated below.

Introductory Paragraph

The introductory paragraph of an essay should start with several sentences that attract the reader's interest. It should then advance the central idea, or *thesis,* that will be developed in the essay. The thesis often includes a *plan of development*—a preview of the major points that will support the thesis. These supporting points should be listed in the order in which they will appear in the essay. In some cases, the plan of development is presented in a sentence separate from the thesis; in other cases, it is omitted.

1. In "The Hazards of Moviegoing," which sentence or sentences are used to attract the reader's interest?

    a. First sentence

    b. First two sentences

    c. First three sentences

2. In which sentence is the thesis of the essay presented?

    a. Third sentence

    b. Fourth sentence

3. Does the thesis include a plan of development?

    a. Yes

    b. No

4. Write the words in the thesis that announce the three major supporting points in the essay:

    a. _____

    b. _____

    c. _____

Body: Supporting Paragraphs

Most essays have three supporting points, developed at length over three separate paragraphs. (Some essays have two supporting points, others four or more. For the purposes of this book, your goal will be three supporting points unless your instructor indicates otherwise.) Each of the supporting paragraphs should begin with a *topic sentence* that states the point to be detailed in that paragraph. Just as a thesis provides a focus for an entire essay, a topic sentence provides a focus for a supporting paragraph.

1. What is the topic sentence for the first supporting paragraph of the model essay?

    _____

    _____

2. The first topic sentence is then supported by the following details (fill in the missing details):

    a. Have to drive fifteen minutes

    b. _____

   c. Endless ticket line

   d. _____

   e. _____

   f. Sticky floor

3. What is the topic sentence for the second supporting paragraph of the essay?

   _____

   _____

4. The second topic sentence is then supported by the following details:

   a. At home, only snacks are celery and carrot sticks.

   b. Theater is like a 7-Eleven with seats.

      (1) fresh popcorn

      (2) _____

      (3) _____

5. What is the topic sentence for the third supporting paragraph of the essay?

   _____

   _____

6. The third topic sentence is then supported by the following details:

   a. _____

   b. _____

   c. Adults talk loudly and reveal plot twists.

   d. People of all ages create distractions.

Concluding Paragraph

The concluding paragraph often summarizes the essay by briefly restating the thesis and, at times, the main supporting points. In addition, the writer often presents a concluding thought about the subject of the paper.

1. Which two sentences in the concluding paragraph restate the thesis and supporting points of the essay?

   a. First and second

   b. Second and third

   c. Third and fourth

Activity

4

2. Which sentence in the concluding paragraph contains the final thought of the essay?

    a. Second

    b. Third

    c. Fourth

Diagram of an Essay

The following diagram shows you at a glance the different parts of a standard college essay, also known as a *one-three-one essay*. This diagram will serve as a helpful guide when you are writing or evaluating essays.

TITLE OF THE ESSAY

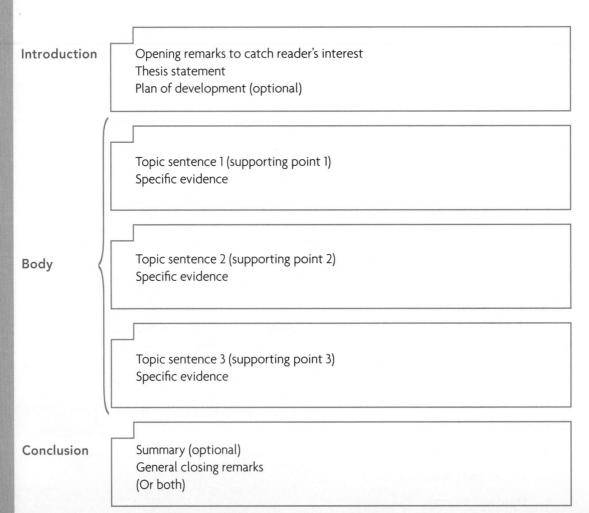

Introduction

Opening remarks to catch reader's interest
Thesis statement
Plan of development (optional)

Topic sentence 1 (supporting point 1)
Specific evidence

Body

Topic sentence 2 (supporting point 2)
Specific evidence

Topic sentence 3 (supporting point 3)
Specific evidence

Conclusion

Summary (optional)
General closing remarks
(Or both)

You now have an overview of the traditional form of the essay. In Chapter 2, you will learn *how* to go about writing an effective essay. First, though, it will be helpful to consider the following: the benefits of writing traditional essays, the advantage of seeing writing as both a skill and a process of discovery, the value of keeping a journal, and the ways a computer can enhance the writing process.

Benefits of Writing the Traditional Essay

Learning to write a traditional essay offers at least three benefits. First of all, mastering the traditional essay will help make you a better writer. For other courses, you'll often compose papers that will be variations on the essay form—for example, examination essays, reports, and research papers. Becoming comfortable with the basic structure of the traditional essay, with its emphasis on a clear point and well-organized, logical support, will help with almost every kind of writing that you have to do.

Second, the discipline of writing an essay will strengthen your skills as a reader and listener. As a reader, you'll become more critically aware of other writers' ideas and the evidence they provide (or fail to provide) to support those ideas. Essay writing will also help you become a better speaker. You'll be more prepared to develop the three basic parts of an effective speech—an appealing introduction, a solidly developed body, and a well-rounded conclusion—because of your experience writing three-part essays.

Most important, essay writing will make you a stronger thinker. Writing a solidly reasoned traditional essay requires mental discipline and close attention to a set of logical rules. Creating an essay in which there is an overall thesis statement and in which each of three supporting paragraphs begins with a topic sentence is more challenging than writing a free-form or expressive paper. Such an essay obliges you to carefully sort out, think through, and organize your ideas. You'll learn to discover and express just what your ideas are and to develop those ideas in a logical, reasoned way. Traditional essay writing, in short, will train your mind to think clearly, and that ability will prove to be of value in every phase of your life.

Writing as a Skill

A realistic attitude about writing must build on the idea that *writing is a skill,* not a "natural gift." It is a skill like driving, typing, or cooking; and, like any skill, it can be learned. If you have the determination to learn, this book will give you the extensive practice needed to develop your writing skills.

People often fear they are the only ones for whom writing is unbearably difficult. They believe that everyone else finds writing easy or at least tolerable. Such people typically say, "I'm not any good at writing," or "English was not one of my good subjects." They imply that they simply do not have a talent for writing, while others do. Often, the result of this attitude is that people try to avoid writing, and when they do write, they don't try their best. Their attitude becomes a self-fulfilling prophecy: their writing fails chiefly because they have brainwashed themselves into thinking that they don't have the "natural talent" needed to write.

Many people find it difficult to do the intense, active thinking that clear writing demands. It is frightening to sit down before a blank sheet of paper or computer screen and know that an hour later, nothing on it may be worth keeping. It is frustrating to discover how much of a challenge it is to transfer thoughts and feelings from one's head onto the page. It is upsetting to find that an apparently simple subject often turns out to be complicated. But writing is not an automatic process: we will not get something for nothing—and we should not expect to. For almost everyone, competent writing comes from plain hard work—from determination, sweat, and head-on battle. The good news is that the skill of writing can be mastered, and if you are ready to work, you will learn what you need to know.

Writing as a Process of Discovery

In addition to believing that writing is a natural gift, many people falsely believe that writing should flow in a simple, straight line from the writer's head onto the written page. But writing is seldom an easy, one-step journey in which a finished paper comes out in a first draft. The truth is that *writing is a process of discovery* involving a series of steps, and those steps are very often a zigzag journey. Look at the following illustrations of the writing process:

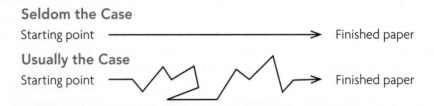

Seldom the Case

Starting point ——————————————————▶ Finished paper

Usually the Case

Starting point ⟍⟋\⟋\⟍⟋\⟋\⟍——▶ Finished paper

Very often, writers do not discover just what they want to write about until they explore their thoughts in writing. For example, Diane Woods (the author of the paragraph and essay on moviegoing) had been assigned to write about an annoyance in everyday life. She did not know what annoyance she would choose; instead, she just began writing about annoyances in general, in order to discover a topic. One of those annoyances was traffic, which seemed promising, so she began putting down ideas and details that came to her about traffic. One detail was the traffic she had to deal with in going to the movies. That made her think of the traffic in the parking lot at the theater complex. At that point, she realized that moviegoing itself was an annoyance. She switched direction in midstream and began writing down ideas and details about moviegoing.

As Diane wrote, she realized how much other moviegoers annoyed her, and she began thinking that other movie patrons might be her main idea in a paper. But when she was writing about patrons who loudly drop popcorn tubs onto the floor, she realized how much all the snacks at the concession stand tempted her. She changed direction again, thinking now that maybe she could talk about patrons and tempting snacks. She kept writing, just putting down more and more details about her movie experiences, still not having figured out exactly how she would fit both patrons and snacks into the paper. Even though her paper had not quite jelled, she was not worried, because she knew that if she kept writing, it would eventually come together.

The point is that writing is often a process of continuing discovery; as you write, you may suddenly switch direction or double back. You may be working on a topic sentence and realize suddenly that it could be your concluding thought. Or you may be developing a supporting idea and then decide that it should be the main point of your paper. Chapter 2 will treat the writing process more directly. What is important to remember here is that writers frequently do not know their exact destination as they begin to write. Very often they discover the direction and shape of a paper during the process of writing.

Writing as a Way to Communicate with Others

When you talk, chances are you do not treat everyone the same. For example, you are unlikely to speak to your boss in the same way that you chat with a young child. Instead, you adjust what you say to suit the people who are listening to you—your *audience.* Similarly, you probably change your speech each day to suit whatever *purpose* you have in mind when you are speaking. For instance, if you wanted to tell someone how to get to your new apartment, you would speak differently than if you were describing your favorite movie.

To communicate effectively, people must constantly adjust their speech to suit their purpose and audience. This same idea is true for writing. When you write for others, it is crucial to know both your purpose for writing and the audience who will be reading your work. The ability to adjust your writing to suit your purpose and audience will serve you well not only in the classroom, but also in the workplace and beyond.

TIP Purpose and audience, further explained on page 172, are special focuses of each of the nine patterns of essay development in Part Two.

Keeping a Journal

Because writing is a skill, it makes sense that the more you practice writing, the better you will write. One excellent way to get practice in writing, even before you begin composing essays, is to keep a daily or almost daily journal. Writing in a journal will help you develop the habit of thinking on paper and will show you how ideas can be discovered in the process of writing. A journal can make writing a familiar part of your life and can serve as a continuing source of ideas for papers.

At some point during the day—perhaps during a study period after your last class of the day, or right before dinner, or right before going to bed—spend fifteen minutes or so writing in your journal. Keep in mind that you do not have to plan what to write about, or be in the mood to write, or worry about making mistakes as you write; just write down whatever words come out. You should write at least one page in each session.

© Jamie Grill/Corbis

You may want to use a notebook that you can easily carry with you for on-the-spot writing. You can also use the journal provided in Appendix A of this book. Or you may decide to write on loose-leaf paper that can be transferred later to a journal folder on your desk. Many students choose to keep their journals on their home computer or laptop. No matter how you proceed, be sure to date all entries.

Your instructor may ask you to make journal entries a specific number of times a week, for a specific number of weeks. He or she may have you turn in your journal every so often for review and feedback. If you are keeping the journal on your own, try to make entries three to five times a week every week of the semester.

Tips on Using a Computer

www.mhhe.com/langan

- If you are using your school's computer center, allow enough time. You may have to wait for a computer or printer to be free. In addition, you may need several sessions at a computer and printer to complete your paper.

- Every word-processing program allows you to save your writing by pressing one or more keys. Save your work frequently as you write your draft. A saved file is stored safely on the computer or network. A file that is not saved will be lost if the computer crashes or if the power is turned off.

- Keep your work in two places—the hard drive or network you are working on and a backup USB drive. At the end of each session with a computer, copy your work onto the USB drive or e-mail a copy to yourself. Then, if the hard drive or network fails, you'll have the backup copy.

- Print out your work at least at the end of every session. Then you will have not only your most recent draft to work on away from the computer but also a copy in case something should happen to your electronic file.

- Work in single spacing so that you can see as much of your writing on the screen at one time as possible. Just before you print out your work, change to double spacing.

- Before making major changes in a paper, create a copy of your file. For example, if your file is titled "Worst Job," create a file called "Worst Job 2." Then make all your changes in that new file. If the changes don't work out, you can always go back to the original file.

Using a Computer at Each Stage of the Writing Process

Following are some ways to make word processing a part of your writing. Note that this section may be more meaningful *after* you have worked through Chapter 2 of this book.

Prewriting

If you're a fast typist, many kinds of prewriting will work well on a computer. With freewriting in particular, you can get ideas onto the screen almost as quickly as they occur to you. A passing thought that could be productive is not likely to get lost. You may even find it helpful, when freewriting, to dim the monitor screen so that you can't see what you're typing. If you temporarily can't see the screen, you won't have to worry about grammar or spelling or typing errors (all of which do not matter in prewriting); instead, you can concentrate on getting down as many ideas and details as possible about your subject.

After any initial freewriting, questioning, and list-making on a computer, it's often very helpful to print out a hard copy of what you've done. With a clean print-out in front of you, you'll be able to see everything at once and revise and expand your work with handwritten comments in the margins of the paper.

If you have prepared a list of items, you may be able to turn that list into an outline right on the screen. Delete the ideas you feel should not be in your paper (saving them at the end of the file in case you change your mind), and add any new ideas that occur to you. Then use the cut and paste functions to shuffle the supporting ideas around until you find the best order for your paper.

Word processing also makes it easy for you to experiment with the wording of the point of your paper. You can try a number of versions in a short time. After you have decided on the version that works best, you can easily delete the other versions—or simply move them to a temporary "leftover" section at the end of the paper.

Writing Your First Draft

Like many writers, you may want to write out your first draft by hand and then type it into the computer for revision. Even as you type your handwritten draft, you may find yourself making some changes and improvements. And once you have a draft on the screen, or printed out, you will find it much easier to revise than a handwritten one.

If you feel comfortable composing directly on a computer, you can benefit from its special features. For example, if you have written an anecdote in your freewriting that you plan to use in your paper, simply copy the story from your freewriting file and insert it where it fits in your paper. You can refine it then or later. Or if you discover while typing that a sentence is out of place, cut it out from where it is and paste it wherever you wish. And if while writing you realize that an earlier sentence can be expanded, just move your cursor back to that point and type in the additional material.

Revising

It is during revision that the virtues of word processing really shine. All substituting, adding, deleting, and rearranging can be done easily within an existing file. All changes instantly take their proper places within the paper, not scribbled above the line or squeezed into the margin. You can concentrate on each change you want to make, because you never have to type from scratch or work on a messy draft. You can carefully go through your paper to check that all your supporting evidence is relevant and to add new support as needed here and there. Anything you decide to eliminate can be deleted in a keystroke. Anything you add can be inserted precisely where you choose. If you change your mind, all you have to do is delete or cut and paste. Then you can sweep through the paper, focusing on other changes, such as improving word choice, increasing sentence variety, and eliminating wordiness.

> **TIP** If you are like many students, you might find it convenient to print out a hard copy of your file at various points throughout the revision. You can then revise in longhand—adding, crossing out, and indicating changes— and later quickly make those changes in the document.

Editing and Proofreading

Editing and proofreading also benefit richly from word processing. Instead of crossing out mistakes, using correction fluid, or rewriting an entire paper to correct numerous errors, you can make all necessary changes within the most recent draft. If you find editing or proofreading on the screen hard on your eyes, print out a copy. Mark any corrections on that copy, and then transfer them to the final draft.

If the word-processing program you're using includes spelling and grammar checks, by all means use them. The spell-checker function tells you when a word is not in the program's dictionary. Keep in mind, however, that the spell-checker cannot tell you how to spell a name correctly or when you have mistakenly used, for example, *their* instead of *there*. To a spell-checker, *Thank ewe four the complement* is as correct as *Thank you for the compliment*. Also, use the grammar-checker with caution. Any errors it doesn't uncover are still your responsibility.

A word-processed paper, with its clean appearance and handsome formatting, looks so good that you may feel it is in better shape than it really is. Do not be fooled. Take sufficient time to review your grammar, punctuation, and spelling carefully.

Even after you hand in your paper, save the computer file. Your teacher may ask you to do some revising, and then the file will save you from having to type the paper from scratch.

Review Activities

Answering the following questions will help you evaluate your attitude about writing.

Activity

5

1. How much practice were you given writing compositions in high school?

   _____ Much   _____ Some   _____ Little

2. How much feedback (positive or negative comments) from teachers were you given on your compositions?

   _____ Much   _____ Some   _____ Little

3. How did your teachers seem to regard your writing?

    _____ Good   _____ Fair   _____ Poor

4. Do you feel that some people simply have a gift for writing and others do not?

    _____ Yes   _____ Sometimes   _____ No

5. When do you start writing a paper?

    _____ Several days before it is due

    _____ About a day before it is due

    _____ At the last possible minute

EXPLANATION: Many people who answer *Little* to questions 1 and 2 often answer *Poor, Yes,* and *At the last possible minute* to questions 3, 4, and 5. On the other hand, people who answer *Much* or *Some* to questions 1 and 2 also tend to have more favorable responses to the other questions. The point is that people with little practice in the skill of writing often have understandably negative feelings about their writing ability. They need not have such feelings, however, because writing is a skill that they can learn with practice.

---

6. Did you learn to write traditional essays (introductory paragraph, supporting paragraphs, concluding paragraph) in high school?

    _____ Yes   _____ No

7. If so, did your teacher explain to you the benefits of writing such essays?

    _____ Yes, very clearly

    _____ Maybe, but not that I remember

    _____ No

EXPLANATION: If you answered *Maybe* or *No* to question 7, you may not be looking forward to taking the course in which you are using this book. It will be worth your while to read and consider again (on page 13) the enormous benefits that can come from practice in writing traditional essays.

8.　In your own words, explain what it means to say that writing is often a zigzag journey rather than a straight-line journey.

_____

_____

_____

_____

_____

Following is an excerpt from one student's journal. As you read, look for a general point and supporting material that could be the basis for an interesting paper.

Activity

6

September 6

　　My first sociology class was tonight. The parking lot was jammed when I got there. I thought I was going to be late for class. A guard had us park on a field next to the regular lot. When I got to the room, it had the usual painted-cinder-block construction. Every school I have ever been in since first grade seems to be made of cinder block. The students all sat there without saying anything, waiting for the instructor to arrive. I think they were all a bit nervous like me. I hoped there wasn't going to be a ton of work in the course. I think I was also afraid of looking foolish somehow. This goes back to grade school, when I wasn't a very good student and teachers sometimes embarrassed me in class. I didn't like grade school, and I hated high school. Now here I am six years later—in college, of all places. Who would have thought I would end up here? The instructor appeared—a woman who I think was a bit nervous herself. I think I like her. Her name is Barbara Hanlin. She says we should call her Barbara. We got right into it, but it was interesting stuff. I like the fact that she asks questions but then she lets you volunteer. I always hated it when teachers would call on you whether you wanted to answer or not. I also like the fact that she answers the questions and doesn't just leave you hanging. She takes the time to write important ideas on the board. I also like the way she laughs. This class may be OK.

1.　If the writer of the journal entry above was looking for ideas for an essay, he could probably find several in this single entry. For example, he might write a story about the apparently roundabout way he wound up in college. See if you can find in the entry an idea that might be the basis for an interesting essay, and write your point in the space below.

_____

2. Take fifteen minutes now to write a journal entry on this day in your life. On a separate sheet of paper, just start writing about anything that you have seen, said, heard, thought, or felt today, and let your thoughts take you where they may.

Using This Text

Here is a suggested sequence for using this book if you are working on your own.

1. After completing this introduction, read Chapters 2 through 6 in Part One and work through as many of the activities as you need to master the ideas in these chapters. By the end of Part One, you will have covered all the basic theory needed to write effective papers.

2. Work through some of the chapters in Part Two, which describes a number of traditional patterns for organizing and developing essays. You may want to include "Exemplification," "Process," "Comparison or Contrast," and "Argument." Each chapter opens with a brief introduction to a specific pattern, followed by two student essays and one professional essay written in that pattern. Included are a series of questions so that you can evaluate the essays in terms of the basic principles of writing explained in Part One. Finally, a number of writing topics are presented, along with hints about prewriting and revising to help you plan and write an effective paper.

3. Turn to Part Three as needed for help with types of writing you will do in college: exam essays, summaries, reports, the résumé and cover letter, and the research paper. You will see that these kinds of writing are variations of the essay form you have already learned.

4. In addition, refer to Part Four as needed for review and practice in the skills needed to write effective, error-free sentences.

5. Finally, if you are using the alternate version of this book—*College Writing Skills with Readings*—then read some of the selections in Part Five and respond to the activities that follow the selections.

For your convenience, the book includes the following:

•   On the inside back cover, there is a checklist of the four basic steps in effective writing.

•   On page 632, there is a list of commonly used correction symbols.

Get into the habit of regularly referring to these guides; they'll help you produce clearly thought-out, well-written essays.

College Writing Skills will help you learn, practice, and apply the thinking and writing skills you need to communicate effectively. But the starting point must be your own determination to do the work needed to become a strong writer. The ability to express yourself clearly and logically can open doors of opportunity for you, both in school and in your career. If you decide—and only you can decide—that you want such language power, this book will help you reach that goal.

The Writing Process

This chapter will explain and illustrate

- the sequence of steps in writing an effective essay
- prewriting
- revising
- editing

Think about an electronic device you use every day. It could be your cell phone, radio, computer, iPod, Palm Pilot, etc. See if you can write for ten minutes about why you couldn't live without it. Don't worry about spelling and punctuation; just get your thoughts down on paper.

Chapter 1 introduced you to the essay form and to some basics of writing. This chapter explains and illustrates the sequence of steps in writing an effective essay. In particular, the chapter focuses on prewriting and revising—strategies that can help with every essay you write.

For many people, writing is a process that involves the following steps:

1. Discovering a thesis—often through prewriting.
2. Developing solid support for the thesis—often through more prewriting.
3. Organizing the thesis and supporting material and writing it out in a first draft.
4. Revising and then editing carefully to ensure an effective, error-free essay.

Learning this sequence will help give you confidence when the time comes to write. You'll know that you can use prewriting as a way to think on paper and to gradually discover just what ideas you want to develop. You'll understand that there are four clear-cut goals—unity, support, organization, and error-free sentences—to aim for in your writing. You'll realize that you can use revision to rework an essay until it is a strong and effective piece of writing. And you'll be able to edit your writing so that your sentences are clear and error free.

Prewriting

If you are like many people, you may have trouble getting started with writing. A mental block may develop when you sit down before a blank sheet of paper. You may not be able to think of an interesting topic or thesis. Or you may have trouble coming up with relevant details to support a possible thesis. And even after starting an essay, you may hit snags—moments when you wonder, What else can I say? or Where do I go next?

The following pages describe five prewriting techniques that will help you think about and develop a topic and get words on paper: (1) freewriting, (2) questioning, (3) making a list, (4) clustering, and (5) preparing a scratch outline. These techniques help you think about and create material, and they are a central part of the writing process.

Technique 1: Freewriting

Freewriting means jotting down in rough sentences or phrases everything that comes to mind about a possible topic. See if you can write nonstop for ten minutes or more. Do not worry about spelling or punctuating correctly, about erasing mistakes, about organizing material, or about finding exact words. Instead, explore

www.mhhe.com/langan

an idea by putting down whatever pops into your head. If you get stuck for words, repeat yourself until more words come. There is no need to feel inhibited, since mistakes *do not count* and you do not have to hand in your freewriting.

Freewriting will limber up your writing muscles and make you familiar with the act of writing. It is a way to break through mental blocks about writing. Since you do not have to worry about mistakes, you can focus on discovering what you want to say about a subject. Your initial ideas and impressions will often become clearer after you have gotten them down on paper, and they may lead to other impressions and ideas. Through continued practice in freewriting, you will develop the habit of thinking as you write. And you will learn a helpful technique for getting started on almost any writing you have to do.

Freewriting: A Student Model

Diane Woods's essay "The Hazards of Moviegoing" on page 6 was developed in response to an assignment to write about some annoyance in everyday life. Diane began by doing some general freewriting and thinking about things that annoy her. Here is her freewriting:

> There are lots of things I get annoyed by. One of them that comes to mind is politishans, in fact I am so annoyed by them that I don't want to say anything about them the last thing I want is to write about them. Another thing that bothers me are people who keep complaining about everything. If you're having trouble, do something about it just don't keep complaining and just talking. I am really annoyed by traffic. There are too many cars in our block and its not surprising. Everyone has a car, the parents have cars and the parents are just too induljent and the kids have cars, and theyre all coming and going all the time and often driving too fast. Speeding up and down the street. We need a speed limit sign but here I am back with politiks again. I am really bothered when I have to drive to the movies all the congestion along the way plus there are just so many cars there at the mall. No space even though the parking lot is huge it just fills up with cars. Movies are a bother anyway because the people can be annoying who are sitting there in the theater with you, talking and dropping popcorn cups and acting like they're at home when they're not.

At this point, Diane read over her notes and, as she later commented, "I realized that I had several potential topics. I said to myself, 'What point can I make that I can cover in an essay? What do I have the most information about?' I decided that maybe I could narrow my topic down to the annoyances involved in going to the movies. I figured I would have more details for that topic." Diane then did more focused freewriting to accumulate details for an essay on problems with moviegoing:

I really find it annoying to go see movies anymore. Even though I love films. Traffic to Cinema Six is awful. I hate looking for a parking place, the lot isn't big enough for the theaters and other stores. You just keep driving to find a parking space and hoping someone will pull out and no one else will pull in ahead of you. Then you don't want there to be a long line and to wind up in one of the first rows with this huge screen right in front of you. Then I'm in the theater with the smell of popcorn all around. Sitting there smelling it trying to ignore it and just wanting to pour a whole bucket of popcorn with melted butter down my throat. I can't stop thinking about the choclate bars either. I love the stuff but I don't need it. The people who are there sometimes drive me nuts. Talking and laughing, kids running around, packs of teens hollaring, who can listen to the movie? And I might run into my old boyfriend—the last thing I need. Also sitting thru all the previews and commercals. If I arrive late enough to miss that junk the movie may be selled out.

Notice that there are errors in spelling, grammar, and punctuation in Diane's freewriting. Diane is not worried about such matters, nor should she be. At this stage, she just wants to do some thinking on paper and get some material down on the page. She knows that this is a good first step, a good way of getting started, and that she will then be able to go on and shape the material.

You should take the same approach when freewriting: explore your topic without worrying at all about being correct. Figuring out what you want to say and getting raw material down on the page should have all of your attention at this early stage of the writing process.

To get a sense of the freewriting process, take a sheet of paper and freewrite about some of the everyday annoyances in your life. See how much material you can accumulate in ten minutes. And remember not to worry about mistakes; you're just thinking on paper.

Activity

1

Technique 2: Questioning

In *questioning,* you generate ideas and details by asking questions about your subject. Such questions include *why, when, where, who,* and *how.* Ask as many questions as you can think of.

www.mhhe.com/langan

Questioning: A Student Model

Here are some questions that Diane Woods might have asked while developing her essay.

Questions	Answers
Why don't I like to go to a movie?	*Just too many problems involved.*
When is going to the movies a problem?	*Could be any time—when a movie is popular, the theater is too crowded; when traffic is bad, the trip is a drag.*
Where are problems with moviegoing?	*On the highway, in the parking lot, at the concession stand, in the theater itself.*
Who creates the problems?	*I do by wanting to eat too much. The patrons do by creating disturbances. The theater owners do by not having enough parking space and showing too many commercials.*
How can I deal with the problem?	*I can stay home and watch movies on DVD or cable TV.*

Asking questions can be an effective way of getting yourself to think about a topic from a number of different angles. The questions can really help you generate details about a topic.

Activity

2

To get a sense of the questioning process, use a sheet of paper to ask yourself a series of questions about a good or bad experience that you have had recently. See how many details you can accumulate in ten minutes. And remember again not to be concerned about mistakes, because you are just thinking on paper.

Technique 3: Making a List

www.mhhe.com/langan

In *making a list*, also known as *brainstorming*, you collect ideas and details that relate to your subject. Pile these items up, one after another, without trying to sort out major details from minor ones or trying to put the details in any special order. Your goal is just to make a list of everything about your subject that occurs to you.

Making a List: A Student Model

After Diane did her freewriting about moviegoing, she made up the following list of details.

Traffic is bad between my house and theater

Noisy patrons

Don't want to run into Jeremy

Hard to be on a diet

Kids running in aisles

I'm crowded into seats between strangers who push me off armrests

Not enough parking

Parking lot needs to be expanded

Too many previews

Can't pause or fast-forward as you can with a DVD

Long lines

High ticket prices

Too many temptatons at snack stand

Commercials for food on the screen

Can prepare healthy snacks for myself at home

Tubs of popcorn with butter

Huge choclate bars

Candy has always been my downfall

Movie may be sold out

People who've seen movie before talk along with actors and give away plot twists

People coughing and sneezing

Icky stuff on floor

Teenagers yelling and showing off

One detail led to another as Diane expanded her list. Slowly but surely, more details emerged, some of which she could use in developing her paper. By the time she was done with her list, she was ready to plan an outline of her paragraph and then to write her first draft.

To get a sense of list-making, list on a sheet of paper a series of realistic goals, major or minor, that you would like to accomplish between today and one year from today. Your goals can be personal, academic, or career-related.

www.mhhe.com/langan

Technique 4: Clustering

Clustering, also known as *diagramming* or *mapping,* is another strategy that can be used to generate material for an essay. This method is helpful for people who like to do their thinking in a visual way. In clustering, you use lines, boxes, arrows, and circles to show relationships among the ideas and details that occur to you.

Begin by stating your subject in a few words in the center of a blank sheet of paper. Then, as ideas and details come to you, put them in boxes or circles around the subject and draw lines to connect them to each other and to the subject. Put minor ideas or details in smaller boxes or circles, and use connecting lines to show how they relate as well.

Clustering: A Student Model

Keep in mind that there is no right or wrong way of clustering or diagramming. It is a way to think on paper about how various ideas and details relate to one another. Below is an example of what Diane might have done to develop her ideas.

> **TIP** In addition to helping generate material, clustering can give you an early sense of how ideas and details relate to one another. For example, the cluster for Diane's essay suggests that different kinds of noisy people could be the focus of one paragraph and that different kinds of temptations could be the focus of another paragraph.

Use clustering (diagramming) to organize the list of year-ahead goals that you created for the previous activity (page 30).

Activity

4

www.mhhe.com/langan

Technique 5: Preparing a Scratch Outline

A *scratch outline* is an excellent sequel to the first four prewriting techniques. A scratch outline often follows freewriting, questioning, list-making, or diagramming; or it may gradually emerge in the midst of these strategies. In fact, trying to make a scratch outline is a good way to see if you need to do more prewriting. If you cannot come up with a solid outline, then you know you need to do more prewriting to clarify your main point or its several kinds of support.

In a scratch outline, you think carefully about the point you are making, the supporting items for that point, and the order in which you will arrange those items. The scratch outline is a plan or blueprint to help you achieve a unified, supported, well-organized essay.

When you are planning a traditional essay consisting of an introduction, three supporting paragraphs, and a conclusion, a scratch outline is especially important. It may be only a few words, but it will be the framework on which your whole essay will be built.

Scratch Outline: A Student Model

As Diane was working on her list of details, she suddenly realized what the plan of her essay could be. She could organize many of her details into one of three supporting groups: (1) annoyances in going out, (2) too many tempting snacks, and (3) other people. She then went back to the list, crossed out items that she now saw did not fit, and numbered the items according to the group where they fit. Here is what Diane did with her list:

1   Traffic is bad between my house and the theater

3   Noisy patrons

~~Don't want to run into Jeremy~~

(continued)

2   *Hard to be on a diet*

3   *Kids running in aisles*

3   *I'm crowded into seats between strangers who push me off armrests*

1   *Not enough parking*

1   *Parking lot needs to be expanded*

1   *Too many previews*

~~*Can't pause or fast-forward as you can with a DVD*~~

1   *Long lines*

1   *High ticket prices*

2   *Too many temptatons at snack stand*

~~*Commercials for food on the screen*~~

2   *Can prepare healthy snacks for myself at home*

2   *Tubs of popcorn with butter*

~~*Candy has always been my downfall*~~

2   *Huge choclate bars*

1   *Movie may be sold out*

3   *People who've seen movie before talk along with actors and give away plot twists*

3   *People coughing and sneezing*

1   *Icky stuff on floor*

3   *Teenagers yelling and showing off*

Under the list, Diane was now able to prepare her scratch outline:

Going to the movies offers some real problems.

1. *Inconvenience of going out*

2. *Tempting snacks*

3. *Other moviegoers*

After all her prewriting, Diane was pleased. She knew that she had a promising essay—one with a clear point and solid support. She saw that she could organize the material into a traditional essay consisting of an introduction, several supporting paragraphs, and a conclusion. She was now ready to write the first draft of her essay, using her outline as a guide.

> **TIP** Chances are that if you do enough prewriting and thinking on paper, you will eventually discover the point and support of your essay.

Create a scratch outline that could serve as a guide if you were to write an essay about your year-ahead goals.

Activity

5

Writing a First Draft

When you write a first draft, be prepared to put in additional thoughts and details that did not emerge during prewriting. And don't worry if you hit a snag. Just leave a blank space or add a comment such as "Do later" and press on to finish the essay. Also, don't worry yet about grammar, punctuation, or spelling. You don't want to take time correcting words or sentences that you may decide to remove later. Instead, make it your goal to state your thesis clearly and develop the content of your essay with plenty of specific details.

Writing a First Draft: A Student Model

Here is Diane's first draft:

Even though I love movies, my friends have stopped asking me to go. There are just too many problems involved in going to the movies.

There are no small theaters anymore, I have to drive fifteen minutes to a big multaplex. Because of a supermarket and restarants, the parking lot is filled. I have to keep driving around to find a space. Then I have to stand in a long line. Hoping that they do not run out of tickets. Finally, I have to pay too much money for a ticket. Putting out that much money, I should not have to deal with a floor that ~~is sticky~~ seems coated with rubber cement. By the end of a movie, my shoes are often sealed to a mix of spilled soda, bubble gum, and other stuff.

(continued)

The theater offers temptatons in the form of snacks I really don't need. Like most of us I have to worry about weight gain. At home I do pretty well by simply watching what I keep in the house and not buying stuff that is bad for me. I can make do with healthy snacks because there is nothing in the house. Going to the theater is like spending my evening in a ~~market~~ 7-Eleven that's been equiped with a movie screen and there are seats which are comfortable. I try to persuade myself to just have a diet soda. The smell of popcorn soon overcomes me. My friends are as bad as I am. Choclate bars seem to jump into your hands, I am eating enormous mouthfuls of milk duds. By the time I leave the theater I feel sick and tired of myself.

Some of the other moviegoers are the worst problem. There are teenagers who try to impress their friends in one way or another. Little kids race up and down the aisles, gigling and laughing. Adults act as if they're watching the movie at home. They talk loudly about the ages of the stars and give away the plot. Other people are droping popcorn tubs or cups of soda crushed ice and soda on the floor. Also coughing a lot and doing other stuff—bms!

I decided one night that I was not going to be a moviegoer anymore. I joined Netflix, and I'll watch movies comfortable in my own living room.

TIP After Diane finished the first draft, she was able to put it aside until the next day. You will benefit as well if you can allow some time between finishing a draft and starting to revise.

Activity 6

Team up with someone in your class and see if you can fill in the missing words in the following explanation of Diane's first draft.

1. Diane has a very brief introduction—no more than an opening sentence and a second sentence that states the _____. She knows she can develop the introduction more fully in a later draft.

2. Of Diane's three supporting paragraphs, only the _____ paragraph lacks a topic sentence. She realizes that this is something to work on in the next draft.

3. There are some misspellings—for example, _____. Diane doesn't worry about spelling at this point. She just wants to get down as much of the substance of her paper as possible.

4. There are various punctuation errors, such as the run-on sentences in the

    _____ paragraphs. Again, Diane is focusing on content; she knows
    she can attend to punctuation and grammar later.

5. At several points in the essay, Diane revises on the spot to make images more

    _____: she changes "is sticky" to "seems coated with rubber ce-
    ment," "market" to "7-Eleven," and "cups of soda" to "cups of crushed ice and
    soda."

6. Near the end of her essay, Diane can't think of added details to insert so she

    simply puts the letters "_____" at that point to remind herself to
    "be more specific" in the next draft. She then goes on to finish her first draft.

7. Her _____ is as brief as her introduction. Diane knows she can
    round off her essay more fully during revision.

Revising

Revising is as much a stage in the writing process as prewriting, outlining, and doing the first draft. *Revising* means rewriting an essay, building on what has already
been done, to make it stronger. One writer has said about revision, "It's like cleaning house—getting rid of all the junk and putting things in the right order." But it
is not just "straightening up"; instead, you must be ready to roll up your sleeves and
do whatever is needed to create an effective essay. Too many students think that
the first draft *is* the essay. They start to become writers when they realize that revising a rough draft three or four times is often at the heart of the writing process.

Here are some quick hints that can help make revision easier. First, set your
first draft aside for a while. A few hours will do, but a day or two would be better.
You can then come back to the draft with a fresh, more objective point of view.
Second, work from typed or printed text. You'll be able to see the essay more im-
partially in this way than if you were just looking at your own familiar handwriting. Next, read your draft aloud. Hearing how your writing sounds will help you
pick up problems with meaning as well as with style. Finally, as you do all these
things, add your thoughts and changes above the lines or in the margins of your essay. Your written comments can serve as a guide when you work on the next draft.

There are three stages to the revising process:

- revising content

- revising sentences

- editing

Revising Content

To revise the content of your essay, ask these questions:

www.mhhe.com/langan

1. Is my essay **unified**?
    *   Do I have a thesis that is clearly stated or implied in the introductory paragraph of my essay?
    *   Do all my supporting paragraphs truly support and back up my thesis?
2. Is my essay **supported**?
    *   Are there three separate supporting points for the thesis?
    *   Do I have specific evidence for each of the three supporting points?
    *   Is there plenty of specific evidence for each supporting point?
3. Is my essay **organized**?
    *   Do I have an interesting introduction, a solid conclusion, and an accurate title?
    *   Do I have a clear method of organizing my essay?
    *   Do I use transitions and other connecting words?

Chapters 3 and 4 will give you practice in achieving **unity, support,** and **organization** in your writing.

Revising Sentences

To revise sentences in your essay, ask yourself the following questions:

1. Do I use parallelism to balance my words and ideas?
2. Do I have a consistent point of view?
3. Do I use specific words?
4. Do I use active verbs?
5. Do I use words effectively by avoiding slang, clichés, pretentious language, and wordiness?
6. Do I vary my sentences?

Chapter 5 will give you practice in revising sentences.

Editing

After you have revised your essay for content and style, you are ready to *edit*—check for and correct—errors in grammar, punctuation, and spelling. Students often find it hard to edit their writing carefully. They have put so much, or so little, work into their writing that it's almost painful for them to look at the essay one more time. You may simply have to *will* yourself to perform this important closing step in the writing process. Remember that eliminating sentence-skill mistakes will improve an average essay and help ensure a strong grade on a good essay. Further, as you get into the habit of checking your writing, you will also get into the habit of using the sentence skills consistently. They are an integral part of clear and effective writing.

Chapter 5 and Part Four of this book will serve as a guide while you are editing your essay for mistakes in **sentence skills.**

www.mhhe.com/langan

An Illustration of the Revising and Editing Processes

Revising with a Second Draft: A Student Model

Since Diane Woods was using a word-processing program on a computer, she was able to print out a double-spaced version of her essay about movies, leaving her plenty of room for revisions. Here is one of her revised paragraphs:

> Second,
> The theater offers ~~temptatons in the form of~~ snacks I really don't
>   tempting
> need. Like most of us I have to ~~worry about weight gain.~~ At home I do
>   battle an expanding waistline.
>
> pretty well by simply ~~watching what I keep in the house and~~ not buying
>
> stuff that is bad for me. I can make do with ~~healthy~~ snacks because
>   like celery and carrot sticks
> there is ~~nothing~~ in the freezer. Going to the theater is like spending
>   no ice cream   however
>
> my evening in a 7-Eleven that's been equiped with a movie screen
>
> and ~~there are seats which are comfortable.~~ I try to persuade myself to
>   comfortable   As
> just have a diet soda, The smell of fresh popcorn soon overcomes me.
>   t   dripping with butter
>
> *(continued)*

> *My friends are as bad as I am.* Choclate bars seem to jump into ~~your~~ ^my^
> ^risk pulling out my fillings as I chew^
> hands. I ~~am eating~~ enormous mouthfuls of milk duds. By the time I
> ^disgusted^
> leave the theater I feel ~~out of sorts~~ with myself.

Diane made her changes in longhand as she worked on the second draft. As you will see when you complete the activity below, her revision serves to make the paragraph more unified, better supported, and better organized.

Activity

7

Fill in the missing words.

1. To achieve better organization, Diane adds at the beginning of the paragraph the transitional phrase "_____," making it very clear that her second supporting idea is tempting snacks.

2. Diane also adds the transition "_____" to show clearly the difference between being at home and being in the theater.

3. In the interest of (*unity, support, organization*) _____, Diane crosses out the sentence "_____." She realizes this sentence is not a relevant detail but really another topic.

4. To add more (*unity, support, organization*) _____, Diane changes "healthy snacks" to "_____"; she changes "nothing in the freezer" to "_____"; she adds "_____" after "popcorn"; and she changes "am eating" to "_____."

5. In the interest of eliminating wordiness, she removes the words "_____ _____" from the third sentence.

6. In the interest of parallelism, Diane changes "and there are seats which are comfortable" to "_____."

7. For greater sentence variety, Diane combines two short sentences, beginning the first sentence with the subordinating word "_____."

8. To create a consistent point of view, Diane changes "jump into your hands" to "_____."

9. Finally, Diane replaces the vague "out of sorts" with the more precise "_____."

Editing: A Student Model

After typing into her word-processing file all the changes in her second draft, Diane printed out another clean draft of the essay. The paragraph on tempting snacks required almost no more revision, so Diane turned her attention mostly to editing changes, illustrated below with her work on the second supporting paragraph:

> Second, the theater offers tempting snacks I really don't need. Like most
>
> of us, I have to battle an expanding waistline. At home I do pretty well by
>
> simply not buying stuff that is bad for me. I can make do with snacks
>
> like celery and carrot sticks because there is no ice cream in the freezer.
>
> Going to the theater, however, is like spending my evening in a 7-Eleven
>
> *equipped*
> that's been ~~equiped~~ with a movie screen and comfortable seats. As I try
>
> *Coke*
> to persuade myself to just have a Diet ~~soda~~, the smell of fresh popcorn
>
> *Chocolate* *the size of small automobiles*
> dripping with butter soon overcomes me. ~~Choclate~~ bars seem to jump into
>
> my hands. I risk pulling out my fillings as I chew enormous mouthfuls of
>
> *M   D*
> milk duds. By the time I leave the theater, I feel disgusted with myself.

Once again, Diane makes her changes in longhand right on the printout of her essay. To note these changes, complete the activity below.

Fill in the missing words.

1. As part of her editing, Diane checked and corrected the _____ of two words, *equipped* and *chocolate*.

2. She added _____ to set off two introductory phrases ("Like most of us" in the second sentence and "By the time I leave the theater" in the final sentence) and also to set off the interrupting word *however* in the fifth sentence.

3. She realized that "milk duds" is a brand name and added _____ to make it "Milk Duds."

4. And since revision can occur at any stage of the writing process, including editing, she makes one of her details more vivid by adding the descriptive words
"_____."

Activity

8

Review Activities

You now have a good overview of the writing process, from prewriting to first draft to revising to editing. The remaining chapters in Part One will deepen your sense of the four goals of effective writing: unity, support, organization or coherence, and sentence skills.

To reinforce the information about the writing process that you have learned in this chapter, you can now work through the following activities:

- taking a writing inventory
- prewriting
- outlining
- revising

Taking a Writing Inventory

Activity

9

Answer the questions below to evaluate your approach to the writing process. This activity is not a test, so try to be as honest as possible. Becoming aware of your writing habits will help you realize changes that may be helpful.

1. When you start work on an essay, do you typically do any prewriting?

   _____ Yes   _____ Sometimes   _____ No

2. If so, which prewriting techniques do you use?

   _____ Freewriting   _____ Diagramming

   _____ Questioning   _____ Scratch outline

   _____ List-making   _____ Other (please describe)

3. Which prewriting technique or techniques work best for you, or which do you think will work best for you?

4. Many students say they find it helpful to handwrite a first draft and then type that draft on a computer. They then print the draft out and revise it by hand. Describe the way you proceed in drafting and revising an essay.

5. After you write the first draft of an essay, do you have time to set it aside for a while so that you can come back to it with a fresh eye?

   _____ Yes   _____ No

6. How many drafts do you typically write when working on an essay? _____

7. When you revise, are you aware that you should be working toward an essay that is unified, solidly supported, and clearly organized? Has this chapter given you a better sense that unity, support, and organization are goals to aim for?

8. Do you revise an essay for the effectiveness of its sentences as well as for its content?

   _____ Yes   _____ No

9. Do you typically do any editing of the almost-final draft of an essay, or do you tend to "hope for the best" and hand it in without careful checking?

   _____ Edit   _____ Hope for the best

10. What (if any) information has this chapter given you about *prewriting* that you will try to apply in your writing?

11. What (if any) information has this chapter given you about *revising* that you will try to apply in your writing?

12. What (if any) information has this chapter given you about *editing* that you will try to apply in your writing?

Prewriting

On the following pages are examples of how the five prewriting techniques could be used to develop the topic "Problems of Combining Work and College." Identify each technique by writing F (for freewriting), Q (for questioning), L (for list-making), C (for clustering), or SO (for the scratch outline) in the answer space.

Activity

10

_____ Never enough time

Miss campus parties

Had to study (only two free hours a night)

Give up activities with friends

No time to rewrite papers

Can't stay at school to play video games or talk to friends

Friends don't call me to go out anymore

Sunday no longer relaxed day—have to study

Missing sleep I should be getting

Grades aren't as good as they could be

Can't watch favorite TV shows

Really need the extra money

Tired when I sit down to study at nine o'clock

_____ What are some of the problems of combining work and school?	Schoolwork suffers because I don't have time to study or rewrite papers. I've had to give up things I enjoy, like sleep and touch football. I can't get into the social life at college, because I have to work right after class.
How have these problems changed my life?	My grades aren't as good as they were when I didn't work. Some of my friends have stopped calling me. My relationship with a girl I liked fell apart because I couldn't spend much time with her. I miss TV.
What do I do in a typical day?	I get up at 7 to make an 8 a.m. class. I have classes till 1:30, and then I drive to the supermarket where I work. I work till 7 p.m., and then I drive home and eat dinner. After I take a shower and relax for a half hour, it's about 9. This gives me only a couple of hours to study—read textbooks, do math exercises, write essays. My eyes start to close well before I go to bed at 11.
Why do I keep up this schedule?	I can't afford to go to school without working, and I need a degree to get the accounting job I want. If I invest my time now, I'll have a better future.

_____ Juggling a job and college has created major difficulties in my life.

1. Little time for studying
   a. Not reading textbooks
   b. No rewriting papers
   c. Little studying for tests

2. Little time for enjoying social side of college
   a. During school
   b. After school

3. No time for personal pleasures
   a. Favorite TV shows
   b. Sunday football games
   c. Sleeping late

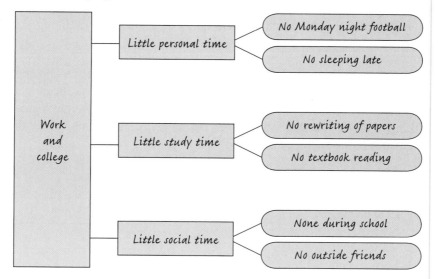

_____ It's hard working and going to school at the same time. I never realized how much I'd have to give up. I won't be quitting my job because I need the money. And the people are friendly at the place where I work. I've had to give up a lot more than I thought. We used to play touch football games every Sunday. They were fun and we'd go out for drinks afterwards. Sundays now are for catch-up work with my courses. I have to catch up because I don't get home every day until 7, I have to eat dinner first before studying. Sometimes I'm so hungry I just eat cookies or chips. Anyway, by the time I take a shower it's 9 p.m. or later and I'm already feeling tired. I've been up since 7 a.m. Sometimes I write an English paper in twenty minutes and don't even read it over. I feel that

I'm missing out on a lot in college. The other day some people I like were sitting in the cafeteria listening to music and talking. I would have given anything to stay and not have to go to work. I almost called in sick. I used to get invited to parties, I don't much anymore. My friends know I'm not going to be able to make it, so they don't bother. I can't sleep late on weekends or watch TV during the week.

Outlining

As already mentioned (see page 31), outlining is central to writing a good essay. An outline lets you see, and work on, the bare bones of an essay, without the distraction of a clutter of words and sentences. It develops your ability to think clearly and logically. Outlining provides a quick check on whether your essay will be *unified*. It also suggests right at the start whether your essay will be adequately *supported*. And it shows you how to plan an essay that is *well organized*.

The following two exercises will help you develop the outlining skills so important to planning and writing a solid essay.

Activity

11

One key to effective outlining is the ability to distinguish between major ideas and details that fit under those ideas. In each of the four lists below, major and supporting items are mixed together. Working in pairs, put the items into logical order by filling in the outline that follows each list. In items 3 and 4, one of the three major ideas is missing and must be added.

1. Thesis: My high school had three problem areas.

    Involved with drugs   a. _____
    Leaky ceilings
                                    (1) _____
    Students
    Unwilling to help after class   (2) _____
    Formed cliques
    Teachers   b. _____
    Buildings
                                    (1) _____
    Ill-equipped gym
    Much too strict   (2) _____

                                    c. _____

                                    (1) _____

                                    (2) _____

2. Thesis: Working as a dishwasher in a restaurant was my worst job.

    Ten-hour shifts   a. _____
    Heat in kitchen
    Working conditions   (1) _____

                                    (2) _____

Minimum wage
Hours changed every week
No bonus for overtime
Hours
Pay
Noisy work area

b. _____

   (1) _____

   (2) _____

c. _____

   (1) _____

   (2) _____

3. Thesis: Joining an aerobics class has many benefits.

Make new friends
Reduces mental stress
Social benefits
Strengthens heart
Improves self-image
Mental benefits
Tones muscles
Meet interesting instructors

a. _____

   (1) _____

   (2) _____

b. _____

   (1) _____

   (2) _____

c. _____

   (1) _____

   (2) _____

4. Thesis: My favorite times in school were the days before holiday vacations.

Lighter workload
Teachers more relaxed
Pep rallies
Less work in class
Friendlier atmosphere
Less homework
Holiday concerts
Students happy about vacation

a. _____

   (1) _____

   (2) _____

b. _____

   (1) _____

   (2) _____

c. _____

   (1) _____

   (2) _____

Read the following essay and outline it in the spaces provided. Write out the central point and topic sentences, and summarize in a few words the supporting material that fits under each topic sentence. One item is summarized for you as an example.

Activity

12

Losing Touch

Steve, a typical American, stays home on workdays. He logs onto his e-mail. Evenings, he listens to his iPod, watches a DVD, or surfs the Internet. On many days, Steve doesn't talk to any other human beings, and he doesn't see any people except those on television. Steve is imaginary, but his lifestyle is very common. More and more, the inventions of modern technology seem to be cutting us off from contact with our fellow human beings.

Thesis: _____

_____

The world of business is one area in which technology is isolating us. Many people now work alone at home. With access to a large central computer, employees such as secretaries, insurance agents, and accountants do their jobs at display terminals in their own homes. They no longer have to actually see the people they're dealing with. In addition, employees are often paid in an impersonal way. Workers' salaries are automatically credited to their bank accounts, eliminating the need for paychecks. Fewer people stand in line with their coworkers to receive their pay or cash their checks. Finally, personal banking is becoming a detached process. Customers interact with machines rather than people to deposit or withdraw money from their accounts. Even some bank loans are approved or rejected, not in an interview with a loan officer, but by a computer program.

First topic sentence: _____

_____

Support: 1. Many people now work alone at home.

2. _____

_____

3. _____

_____

   a. _____

_____

   b. _____

_____

Another area that technology is changing is entertainment. Music, for instance, was once a group experience. People listened to music in concert halls or at small social gatherings. For many people now, however, music is a solitary experience. Walking along the street or sitting in their living rooms, they wear headphones to build a wall of music around them. Movie entertainment is changing, too. Movies used to be social events. Now, some people are not going out to see a movie. Some are choosing to wait for a film to appear on cable television or DVD. Instead of being involved with the laughter, applause, or hisses of the audience, viewers watch movies in the isolation of their own living rooms.

Second topic sentence: _____

_____

Support: 1. _____

_____

        2. _____

_____

Education is a third important area in which technology is separating us from others. From elementary schools to colleges, students spend more and more time sitting by themselves in front of computers. The computers give them feedback, while teachers spend more time tending the computers and less time interacting with their classes. A similar problem occurs in homes.

(continued)

As more families buy computers, increasing numbers of students practice their math and reading skills with software programs instead of with their friends, brothers and sisters, and parents. Last, alienation is occurring as a result of DVDs. People are buying DVDs on subjects such as cooking, real estate investment, speaking, and speed-reading. They then practice their skills at home rather than by taking group classes in which a rich human interaction can occur.

Third topic sentence: _____

_____

Support: 1. _____

           _____

        2. _____

           _____

        3. _____

           _____

Technology, then, seems to be driving human beings apart. Soon, we may no longer need to communicate with other human beings to do our work, entertain ourselves, or pursue an education. Machines will be the coworkers and companions of the future.

Revising

Activity

13

Following is the second supporting paragraph from an essay called "Problems of Combining School and Work." The paragraph is shown in four different stages of development: (1) first full draft, (2) revised second draft, (3) edited next-to-final draft, (4) final draft. The four stages appear in scrambled order. Write the number 1 in the answer blank for the first full draft, and number the remaining stages in sequence.

_____ I have also given up some personal pleasures in my life. On sundays for example I used to play softball or football, now I use the entire day to study. Good old-fashioned sleep is another lost pleasure for me now. I never get as much as I like because their just isn't time. Finally I miss having the chance to just sit in front of the TV, on weeknights. In order to watch the whole lineup of movies and sports that I used to watch regularly. These sound like small pleasures, but you realize how important they are when you have to give them up.

_____ I've had to give up pleasures in my life. I use to spend sundays playing games, now I have to study. Im the sort of person who needs a lot of sleep, but I dont have the time for that either. Sleeping nine or ten hours a night woul'dnt be unusual for me. Psycologists say that each individual need a different amount of sleep, some people need as little as five hours, some need as much as nine or ten. So I'm not unusual in that. But Ive given up that pleasure too. And I can't watch the TV shows I use to enjoy. This is another personal pleasure Ive lost because of doing work and school. These may seem like small things, but you realize how good they are when you give them up.

_____ Besides missing the social side of college life, I've also had to give up some of my special personal pleasures. I used to spend Sunday afternoons, for example, playing lob-pitch softball or touch football depending on the season. Now I use Sunday as a catch-up day for my studies. Another pleasure I've lost is sleeping late on days off and weekends. I once loved mornings when I could check the clock, bury my head in the pillow, and drift off for another hour. These days I'm forced to crawl out of bed the minute the alarm lets out its piercing ring. Finally, I no longer have the chance to just sit watching the movies and sports programs that I enjoy. A leisurely night of <u>Monday Night Football</u> or a network premiere of a Tom Hanks movie is a pleasure of the past for me now.

_____ Besides missing the social side of college life, I've also had to give up some of my special personal pleasures. I used to spend sunday afternoons, for example playing lob-pitch softball or touch football depending on the season. Now I use the day as a catch-up day for my studies. Another pleasure I've lost is sleeping late on days off and weekends. I once loved mornings when I could check the clock, then burying my head in the pillow, and you drift off to sleep for another hour. These days I'm forced to get out of bed the minute the alarm lets out it's ring. Finally I no longer have the chance to just sit watching the movies and also programs with sports that I enjoy. A leisurely night of Monday Night Football or a network premiere of a Tom Hanks movie is a pleasure of the past for me now.

The First and Second Steps in Essay Writing

3

This chapter will show you how to

- start an essay with a point, or thesis

- support that point, or thesis, with specific evidence

© Jiang Jin/SuperStock

Describe a favorite childhood place that made you feel secure, safe, private, or in a world of your own. Begin with a thesis statement, something like this: "_____ was a place that made me feel _____ when I was a child." Remember to keep the point of your thesis statement in mind as you describe this place. Include only details that will support the idea that your place was one of security, safety, privacy, or the like.

Chapter 2 emphasized how prewriting and revising can help you become an effective writer. This chapter focuses on the first two steps in writing an effective essay:

1. Begin with a point, or thesis.
2. Support the thesis with specific evidence.

The chapters that follow will focus on the third and fourth steps in writing:

3. Organize and connect the specific evidence (pages 80–104).
4. Write clear, error-free sentences (pages 105–138).

www.mhhe.com/langan

Step 1: Begin with a Point, or Thesis

Your first step in writing is to discover what point you want to make and to write that point out as a single sentence. There are two reasons for doing this. You want to know right from the start if you have a clear and workable thesis. Also, you will be able to use the thesis as a guide while writing your essay. At any stage you can ask yourself, Does this support my thesis? With the thesis as a guide, the danger of drifting away from the point of the essay is greatly reduced.

Understanding Thesis Statements

In Chapter 1, you learned that effective essays center around a thesis, or main point, that a writer wishes to express. This central idea is usually presented as a *thesis statement* in an essay's introductory paragraph.

A good thesis statement does two things. First, it tells readers an essay's *topic*. Second, it presents the writer's *attitude, opinion, idea,* or *point* about that topic. For example, look at the following thesis statement:

Owning a pet has several important benefits.

In this thesis statement, the topic is *owning a pet;* the writer's main point is that owning a pet *has several important benefits.*

Activity

1

For each thesis statement below, single-underline the topic and double-underline the main point that the writer wishes to express about the topic.

EXAMPLES Our company president should be fired for three main reasons.

The Internet has led to new kinds of frustration in everyday life.

1. Our cafeteria would be greatly improved if several changes were made.
2. Celebrities are often poor role models because of the ways they dress, talk, and behave.
3. My first night as a security guard turned out to be one of the most frightening experiences of my life.

4. SUVs are inferior to cars because they are harder to control, more expensive, and dangerous to the environment.

5. The twentieth century produced three inventions that dramatically changed the lives of all Americans.

6. Stress in the fast-food workplace has led to serious physical, psychological, and emotional problems for employees.

7. Advertisers target young people when marketing cigarettes, alcohol, and adult movies.

8. Living in the city has certain advantages over living in the suburbs.

9. Before moving away from home, every person should have mastered certain key skills.

10. Independent mom-and-pop stores are superior to larger chain stores for a number of reasons.

Writing a Good Thesis I

Now that you know how thesis statements work, you can begin writing your own. To start, you need a topic that is neither too broad nor too narrow. Suppose, for example, that an instructor asks you to write a paper on marriage. Such a subject is too broad to cover in a five-hundred-word essay. You would have to write a book to support adequately any point you might make about the general subject of marriage. What you would need to do, then, is limit your subject. Narrow it down until you have a thesis that you can deal with specifically in about five hundred words. In the box that follows are (1) several general subjects, (2) a limited version of each general subject, and (3) a thesis statement about each limited subject.

www.mhhe.com/langan

General Subject	Limited Subject	Thesis
Marriage	Honeymoon	A honeymoon is perhaps the worst way to begin a marriage.
Family	Older sister	My older sister helped me overcome my shyness.
Television	TV preachers	TV evangelists use sales techniques to promote their messages.
Children	Disciplining of children	My husband and I have several effective ways of disciplining our children.

(continued)

Sports	Players' salaries	Players' high salaries are bad for the game, for the fans, and for the values our children are developing.

Sometimes a subject must go through several stages of limiting before it is narrow enough to write about. Below are four lists reflecting several stages that writers went through in moving from a general subject to a narrow thesis statement. Number the stages in each list from 1 to 5, with 1 marking the broadest stage and 5 marking the thesis.

List 1

_____ Teachers

_____ Education

_____ Math teacher

_____ My high school math teacher was incompetent.

_____ High school math teacher

List 2

_____ Bicycles

_____ Dangers of bike riding

_____ Recreation

_____ Recreational vehicles

_____ Bike riding in the city is a dangerous activity.

List 3

_____ Retail companies

_____ Supermarkets

_____ Dealing with customers

_____ Working in a supermarket

_____ I've learned how to handle unpleasant supermarket customers.

List 4

_____ Camping

_____ First camping trip

_____ Summer vacation

_____ My first camping trip was a disastrous experience.

_____ Vacations

Later in this chapter, you will get more practice in narrowing general subjects to thesis statements.

Writing a Good Thesis II

When writing thesis statements, people often make mistakes that undermine their chances of producing an effective essay. One mistake is to simply announce the subject rather than state a true thesis. A second mistake is to write a thesis that is too broad, and a third is to write a thesis that is too narrow. A fourth error is to write a thesis containing more than one idea. Here are tips for avoiding such mistakes and writing good thesis statements.

1 Write Statements, Not Announcements

The subject of this paper will be my parents.

I want to talk about the crime wave in our country.

The baby-boom generation is the concern of this essay.

In this first group, the sentences are not thesis statements but announcements of a topic. For instance, "The subject of this paper will be my parents" does not make a point about the parents but merely tells, in a rather weak and unimaginative way, the writer's general subject. Remember, a thesis statement must make a point about a limited subject. Effective thesis statements based on the above sentences could be as follows:

My parents each struggled with personal demons.

The recent crime wave in our city has several apparent causes.

The baby-boom generation has changed American society in key ways.

2 Avoid Statements That Are Too Broad

Disease has shaped human history.

Insects are fascinating creatures.

Men and women are very different.

www.mhhe.com/langan

In the preceding examples, each statement is too broad to be supported adequately in a student essay. For instance, "Disease has shaped human history" would require far more than a five-hundred-word essay. In fact, there are many lengthy books written on the exact same topic. Remember, your thesis statement should be focused enough that it can be effectively supported in a five-paragraph essay. Revised thesis statements based on the topics in the above sentences could be as follows:

In the mid-1980s, AIDS changed people's attitudes about dating.

Strength, organization, and communication make the ant one of nature's most successful insects.

Men and women are often treated very differently in the workplace.

3 Avoid Statements That Are Too Narrow

Here are three statements that are too narrow:

The speed limit near my home is sixty-five miles per hour.

A hurricane hit southern Florida last summer.

www.mhhe.com/langan

A person must be at least thirty-five years old to be elected president of the United States.

In this third group, there is no room in any of the three statements for support to be given. For instance, "The speed limit near my home is sixty-five miles per hour" is too narrow to be expanded into a paper. It is a simple fact that does not require any support. Such a statement is sometimes called a *dead-end statement:* there is no place to go with it. Remember, a thesis statement must be broad enough to require support in an essay. Successful thesis statements based on the preceding sentences are as follows:

The speed limit near my home should be lowered to fifty-five miles per hour for several reasons.

Federal officials made a number of mistakes in their response to the recent Florida hurricane.

The requirement that a U.S. president must be at least thirty-five years old is unfair and unreasonable.

4 Make Sure Statements Develop Only One Idea

Here are three statements that contain more than one idea:

One of the most serious problems affecting young people today is bullying, and it is time more kids learned the value of helping others.

Studying with others has several benefits, but it also has drawbacks and can be difficult to schedule.

Teachers have played an important role in my life, but they were not as important as my parents.

In this fourth group, each statement contains more than one idea. For instance, "One of the most serious problems affecting young people today is bullying, and it is time more kids learned the value of helping others" clearly has two separate ideas ("One of the most serious problems affecting young people today is bullying" *and* "it is time more kids learned the value of helping others"). The reader is asked to focus on two separate points, each of which more logically belongs in an essay of its own. Remember, the point of an essay is to communicate a *single* main idea to readers. To be as clear as possible, then, try to limit your thesis statement to the single key idea you want your readers to know. Revised thesis statements based on each of the examples above are as follows:

One of the most serious problems affecting young people today is bullying.

Studying with others has several benefits.

Teachers have played an important role in my life.

Write TN in the space next to the two statements that are too narrow to be developed in an essay. Write TB beside the two statements that are too broad to be covered in an essay. Then, in the spaces provided, revise one of the too-narrow statements and one of the too-broad statements to make them each an effective thesis.

_____ 1. The way our society treats elderly people is unbelievable.

_____

_____ 2. Up to 70 percent of teenage marriages end in divorce.

_____

_____ 3. Action must be taken against drugs.

_____

_____ 4. I failed my biology course.

_____

Step 2: Support the Thesis with Specific Evidence

www.mhhe.com/langan

The first essential step in writing a successful essay is to formulate a clearly stated thesis. The second basic step is to support the thesis with specific reasons or details.

To ensure that your essay will have adequate support, you may find an informal outline very helpful. Write down a brief version of your thesis idea, and then work out and jot down the three points that will support the thesis.

Here is the scratch outline that was prepared by the author of the earlier essay on moviegoing:

> *Moviegoing is a problem.*
> 1. *Inconvenience of going out*
> 2. *Tempting snacks*
> 3. *Other moviegoers*

A scratch outline like this one looks simple, but developing it often requires a great deal of careful thinking. The time spent on developing a logical outline is invaluable, though. Once you have planned the steps that logically support your thesis, you will be in an excellent position to go on to write an effective essay.

Activities in this section will give you practice in the crucial skill of planning an essay clearly.

Following are ten informal outlines. Working with a partner, complete any five of them by adding a third logical supporing point (*c*) that will parallel the two already provided (*a* and *b*).

1. The first day on a new job can be nerve-racking.

    a. Meeting new people

    b. Finding your way around a new place

    c. _____

2. My stepmother has three qualities I admire.

    a. Patience

    b. Thoughtfulness

    c. _____

3. The neighborhood grocery store is poorly managed.

    a. The checkout lines are always long.

    b. The aisles are dirty and understocked.

    c. _____

4. College students should live at home.

    a. Stay in touch with family

    b. Avoid distractions of dorm or apartment life

    c. _____

5. _____ is the worst job I've ever had.

    a. Difficult boss

    b. Poor pay

    c. _____

6. College is stressful for many people.

    a. Worry about grades

    b. Worry about being accepted

    c. _____

7. My landlord adds to the stress in my life.

   a. Neglects repairs

   b. Ignores phone calls

   c. _____

8. Our neighborhood park is an unsafe place to visit.

   a. Aggressive dogs

   b. Broken glass

   c. _____

9. Buying a used car is better than buying a new one.

   a. Used cars are less likely to be stolen than new cars.

   b. Used cars don't lose their value as quickly as most new cars.

   c. _____

10. Many companies use annoying practices to increase sales.

    a. Junk mail

    b. Spam e-mail

    c. _____

The Importance of *Specific* Details

Just as a thesis must be developed with three supporting points, each supporting point must be developed with specific details. Specific details are valuable in two key ways. First, details excite the reader's interest. They make writing a pleasure to read, for we all enjoy learning particulars about people, places, and things. Second, details serve to explain a writer's points. They give the evidence needed for us to see and understand general ideas.

All too often, the body paragraphs in essays contain only vague generalities, rather than the specific supporting details that are needed to engage and convince a reader. Here is what one of the paragraphs in "The Hazards of Moviegoing" would have looked like if the writer had not detailed her supporting evidence vividly:

> Some of the other patrons are even more of a problem than the theater itself. Many people in the theater often show themselves to be inconsiderate. They make noises and create disturbances at their seats. Included are people in every age group, from the young to the old. Some act as if they were at home in their own living room watching TV. And people are often messy, so that you're constantly aware of all the food they're eating. People are also always moving around near you, creating a disturbance and interrupting your enjoyment of the movie.

The following box contrasts the vague support in the preceding paragraph with the specific support in the essay.

Vague Support	Specific Support
1. Many people in the theater show themselves to be inconsiderate. They make noises and create disturbances at their seats. Included are people in every age group, from the young to the old. Some act as if they were at home in their own living room watching TV.	1. Little kids race up and down the aisles, usually in giggling packs. Teenagers try to impress their friends by talking back to the screen, whistling, and making what they consider to be hilarious noises. Adults act as if they were at home in their own living room and comment loudly on the ages of the stars or why movies aren't as good anymore.
2. And people are often messy, so that you're constantly aware of all the food they're eating.	2. And people of all ages crinkle candy wrappers, stick gum on their seats, and drop popcorn tubs or cups of crushed ice and soda on the floor.
3. People are also always moving around near you, creating a disturbance and interrupting your enjoyment of the movie.	3. They also cough and burp, squirm endlessly in their seats, file out for repeated trips to the restrooms or concession stand, and elbow you out of the armrest on either side of your seat.

The effective paragraph from the essay provides details that make vividly clear the statement that patrons are a problem in the theater. The writer specifies the exact age groups (little kids, teenagers, and adults) and the offenses of each (giggling, talking and whistling, and loud comments). She specifies the various food excesses (crinkled wrappers, gum on seats, dropped popcorn and soda containers). Finally, she provides concrete details that enable us to see and hear other disturbances (coughs and burps, squirming, constant trips to restrooms, jostling for elbow room). The ineffective paragraph asks us to guess about these details; the effective paragraph describes the details in a specific and lively way.

In the strong paragraph, then, sharp details capture our interest and enable us to share the writer's experience. They provide pictures that make us feel we are there. The particulars also enable us to understand clearly the writer's point that patrons are a problem. Aim to make your own writing equally convincing by providing detailed support.

Write S in front of the two selections below that provide specific evidence to support the opening point. Write X in front of the two selections in which the opening point is followed by vague, general, wordy sentences.

Activity

5

_____ 1. The people who have moved in beside us are unpleasant neighbors.

They barely say hi when we're in our neighboring yards. When we invited them to a neighborhood barbecue, they said they were going to be busy. They sometimes turn loud music on late at night, and we have to close our window to shut out the noise. To top it off, they own a dog, which they let roam free in our street.

_____ 2. My mother was a harsh disciplinarian.

When I did something wrong, no matter how small, she would inflict serious punishment. She had expectations that I was to live up to, and she never changed her attitude. When I did not behave as I should, I was dealt with severely. There were no exceptions as far as my mother was concerned.

_____ 3. Some things are worse when they're "improved."

A good cheesecake, for one thing, is perfect. It doesn't need pineapple, cherries, blueberries, or whipped cream smeared all over it. Plain old American blue jeans, the ones with five pockets and copper rivets, are perfect too. Manufacturers only made them worse when they added flared legs, took away the pockets, tightened the fit, and plastered white logos and designers' names all over them.

_____ 4. Pets can be more trouble than children.

My dog, unlike my children, has never been completely housebroken. When he's excited or nervous, he still has an occasional problem. My dog, unlike my children, has never learned how to take care of himself when we're away, despite the fact that we've given him plenty of time to do so. We don't have to worry about our grown children anymore. However, we still have to hire a dog-sitter.

The Importance of *Adequate* Details

One of the most common and most serious problems in students' writing is inadequate development. You must provide *enough* specific details to fully support the point in a body paragraph of an essay. You could not, for example, include a paragraph about a friend's unreliability and provide only a one- or two-sentence example. You would have to extend the example or add several other examples showing your friend as an unreliable person. Without such additional support, your paragraph would be underdeveloped.

Students may try to disguise unsupported paragraphs through repetition and generalities. Do not fall into this "wordiness trap." Be prepared to do the plain hard work needed to ensure that each paragraph has solid support.

Activity

6

Both of the following body paragraphs were written on the same topic, and each has a clear opening point. Which paragraph is adequately developed? Which one has only several particulars and uses mostly vague, general, wordy sentences to conceal that it is starved for specific details?

Eternal Youth?—No, Thanks

I wouldn't want to be a teenager again, first of all, because I wouldn't want to worry about talking to girls. I still remember how scary it was to call up a girl and ask her out. My heart would race, my pulse would pound, and perspiration would trickle down my face, adding to my acne by the second. I never knew whether my voice would come out deep and masculine, like a television anchorman's, or squeaky, like a little boy's. Then there were the questions: Would she be at home? If she was, would she want to talk to me? And if she did, what would I say? The one time I did get up the nerve to take a girl in my homeroom to a movie, I was so tongue-tied that I stared silently at the box of popcorn in my lap until the feature finally started. Needless to say, I wasn't very interesting company.

Terrors of My Teenage Years

I wouldn't want to be a teenager again, first of all, because I wouldn't want to worry about talking to girls. Calling up a girl to ask her out was something that I completely dreaded. I didn't know what words to express or how to express them. I would have all the symptoms of nervousness when I got on the phone. I worried a great deal about how I would sound, and I had a lot of doubts about the girl's reaction. Once, I managed to call up a girl to go out, but the evening turned out to be a disaster. I was too unsure of myself to act in a confident way. I couldn't think of anything to say and just kept quiet. Now that I look back on it, I really made a fool of myself. Agonizing over my attempts at relationships with the opposite sex made adolescence a very uncomfortable time.

The first paragraph offers a series of well-detailed examples of the author's nerve-racking experiences, as a teenager, with girls. The second paragraph, on the other hand, is underdeveloped. For instance, the second paragraph makes only the general observation "I would have all the symptoms of nervousness when I got on the phone," but the first paragraph states, "My heart would race, my pulse would pound, and perspiration would trickle down my face."

The second paragraph makes the general statement "I worried a great deal about how I would sound," but in the first paragraph the author wonders if his voice will "come out deep and masculine, like a television anchorman's, or squeaky, like a little boy's." And the second paragraph has no specific description of the evening that turned into a disaster. In summary, the second paragraph lacks the full, detailed support needed to develop its opening point convincingly.

Take a few minutes to write a paragraph supporting the point "My room is a mess." Afterward, you and your classmates, perhaps working in small groups, should read your paragraphs aloud. The best-received paragraphs are almost sure to be those with plenty of specific details.

Activity

7

Practice in Advancing and Supporting a Thesis

You now know the two most important steps in competent essay writing: (1) advancing a point, or thesis, and (2) supporting that thesis. The purpose of this section is to expand and strengthen your understanding of these two basic steps. You will first work through a series of activities on *developing* a thesis:

- identifying the parts of an essay
- evaluating thesis statements
- completing thesis statements
- writing a thesis statement
- limiting a topic and writing a thesis

You will then sharpen your understanding of how to *support* a thesis effectively by working through the following activities:

- providing specific evidence
- identifying adequate supporting evidence
- adding details to complete an essay

Identifying the Parts of an Essay

Activity

8

Each cluster below contains one topic, one thesis statement, and two supporting sentences. In the space provided, label each item as follows:

> T—topic
> TH—thesis statement
> S—supporting sentence

Group 1

_____ a. TV has forced politicians to focus more on appearance than substance.

_____ b. Television has had a massive impact on politics in the United States.

_____ c. The expense of producing and airing ads has made politicians worry more about fund-raising than serving their public.

_____ d. Television

Group 2

_____ a. Community colleges are much more affordable than most four-year colleges.

_____ b. There are several advantages to attending a community college instead of a four-year school.

_____ c. Community colleges

_____ d. Community colleges typically offer more convenient and more flexible scheduling than traditional schools.

Group 3

_____ a. Medicine

_____ b. Antibiotics have enabled doctors to control many diseases that were once fatal.

_____ c. Organ transplants have prolonged the lives of tens of thousands of people.

_____ d. Advances in modern medicine have had great success in helping people.

Group 4

_____ a. Reading

_____ b. Parents can take steps to encourage their children to enjoy reading.

_____ c. The adults' own behavior can influence children to become readers.

_____ d. Parents can make sure the physical environment of the home encourages reading.

Group 5

_____ a. Insects perform many helpful functions for human beings.

_____ b. Insects are essential to the growth of many important crops.

_____ c. Insects

_____ d. Insects protect the environment by removing wastes and controlling disease-causing germs.

This activity will sharpen your sense of the parts of an essay. The essay that follows, "Coping with Old Age," has no indentations starting new paragraphs. Read this essay carefully, and then double-underline the thesis and single-underline the topic sentence for each of the three supporting paragraphs and the first sentence of the conclusion. Write the numbers of those sentences in the spaces provided at the end.

Activity

9

Coping with Old Age

[1]I recently read about an area of the former Soviet Union where many people live to be well over a hundred years old. [2]Being 115 or even 125 isn't considered unusual there, and these old people continue to do productive work right up until they die. [3]The United States, however, isn't such a healthy

(continued)

place for older people. ⁴Since I retired from my job, I've had to cope with the physical, mental, and emotional stresses of being "old." ⁵For one thing, I've had to adjust to physical changes. ⁶Now that I'm over sixty, the trusty body that carried me around for years has turned traitor. ⁷Aside from the deepening wrinkles on my face and neck, and the wiry gray hairs that have replaced my brown hair, I face more frightening changes. ⁸I don't have the energy I used to. ⁹My eyes get tired. ¹⁰Once in a while, I miss something that's said to me. ¹¹My once faithful feet seem to have lost their comfortable soles, and I sometimes feel I'm walking on marbles. ¹²In order to fight against this slow decay, I exercise whenever I can. ¹³I walk, I stretch, and I climb stairs. ¹⁴I battle constantly to keep as fit as possible. ¹⁵I'm also trying to cope with mental changes. ¹⁶My mind was once as quick and sure as a champion gymnast. ¹⁷I never found it difficult to memorize answers in school or to remember the names of people I met. ¹⁸Now, I occasionally have to search my mind for the name of a close neighbor or favorite television show. ¹⁹Because my mind needs exercise, too, I challenge it as much as I can. ²⁰Taking a college course like this English class, for example, forces me to concentrate. ²¹The mental gymnast may be a little slow and out of shape, but he can still do a backflip or turn a somersault when he has to. ²²Finally, I must deal with the emotional impact of being old. ²³Our society typecasts old people. ²⁴We're supposed to be unattractive, senile, useless leftovers. ²⁵We're supposed to be the crazy drivers and the cranky customers. ²⁶At first, I was angry and frustrated that I was considered old at all. ²⁷And I knew that people were wrong to stereotype me. ²⁸Then I got depressed. ²⁹I even started to think that maybe I was a castoff, one of those old animals that slow down the rest of the herd. ³⁰But I have now decided to rebel against these negative feelings. ³¹I try to have friends of all ages and to keep up with what's going on in the world. ³²I try to remember that I'm still the same person who sat at a first-grade desk, who fell in love, who comforted a child, who got a raise at work. ³³I'm not "just" an old person. ³⁴Coping with the changes of old age has become my latest full-time job. ³⁵Even though it's a job I never applied for, and one for which I had no experience, I'm trying to do the best I can.

Thesis statement in "Coping with Old Age": _____

Topic sentence of first supporting paragraph: _____

Topic sentence of second supporting paragraph: _____

Topic sentence of third supporting paragraph: _____

First sentence of the conclusion: _____

Evaluating Thesis Statements

As was explained on pages 54–55, some writers announce a subject instead of stating a true thesis idea. Others write a dead-end thesis statement that is too narrow to need support or development. Contrasting with such a dead-end statement is the statement that is wide open—too broad to be adequately supported in the limited space of a five-hundred-word essay. Other thesis statements are vague or contain more than one idea. They suggest that the writer has not thought out the main point sufficiently.

Write A beside each sentence that is an announcement rather than a thesis statement. Write OK beside the statement in each pair that is a clear, limited point that could be developed in an essay.

1. _____ a. This essay will discuss the people you meet in exercise class.

   _____ b. The kinds of workout clothes worn in my aerobics class identify "jocks," "strugglers," and "princesses."

2. _____ a. I made several mistakes in the process of trying to win the respect and affection of my teenage stepson.

   _____ b. My thesis in this paper is relationships between stepparents and stepchildren.

3. _____ a. A period of loneliness can teach you to use your creativity, sort out your values, and feel empathy for others.

   _____ b. Loneliness is the subject of this paper.

4. _____ a. This paper will be about sharing housework.

   _____ b. Deciding who will perform certain unpleasant household chores can be the crisis that makes or breaks a marriage.

5. _____ a. My concern here is to discuss near-death experiences reported by some patients.

   _____ b. There are several possible explanations for the similar near-death experiences reported by some patients.

Write TN beside each statement that is too narrow to be developed in an essay. Write OK beside the statement in each pair that is a clear, limited point.

1. _____ a. I had squash, tomatoes, and corn in my garden last summer.

   _____ b. Vegetable gardening can be a frustrating hobby.

2. _____ a. The main road into our town is lined with billboards.

   _____ b. For several reasons, billboards should be abolished.

3. _____ a. There are now more single-parent households in our country than ever before.

_____ b. Organization is the key to being a successful single parent.

4. _____ a. My first job taught me that I had several bad work habits.

_____ b. Because I was late for work yesterday, I lost an hour's pay and was called in to see the boss.

5. _____ a. Americans abuse alcohol because it has become such an important part of our personal and public celebrations.

_____ b. Consumption of wine, beer, and hard liquor increases in the United States every year.

Activity 12

Write TB beside each statement that is too broad to be developed in an essay. Write OK beside the statement in each pair that is a clear, limited point.

1. _____ a. In many ways, sports are an important part of American life.

_____ b. Widespread gambling has changed professional football for the worse.

2. _____ a. Modern life makes people suspicious and unfriendly.

_____ b. A frightening experience in my neighborhood has caused me to be a much more cautious person in several ways.

3. _____ a. Toy ads on television teach children to be greedy, competitive, and snobbish.

_____ b. Advertising has bad effects on all of society.

4. _____ a. Learning new skills can be difficult and frustrating.

_____ b. Learning to write takes work, patience, and a sense of humor.

5. _____ a. I didn't get along with my family, so I did many foolish things.

_____ b. Running away from home taught me that my parents weren't as terrible as I thought.

Activity 13

For each pair, write 2 beside the statement that contains more than one idea. Write OK beside the statement that is a clear, limited point.

1. _____ a. Working with old people changed my stereotypical ideas about the elderly.

_____ b. My life has moved in new directions since the rewarding job I had working with older people last summer.

2. _____ a. The new architecture on this campus is very unpleasant, although the expansion was desperately needed.

   _____ b. Our new college library building is ugly, intimidating, and inefficient.

3. _____ a. Among the most entertaining ads on TV today are those for mail-order products.

   _____ b. Although ads on TV for mail-order products are often misleading, they can still be very entertaining.

4. _____ a. My roommate and I are compatible in most ways, but we still have conflicts at times.

   _____ b. My roommate has his own unique systems for studying, writing term papers, and cleaning our room.

5. _____ a. Although some good movies have come out lately, I prefer to watch old movies because they're more interesting.

   _____ b. Movies of the 1930s and 1940s have better plots, sets, and actors than movies made today.

Completing Thesis Statements

Complete the following thesis statements by adding a third supporting point that will parallel the two already provided. You might want to first check the section on parallelism in Chapter 5 (page 106) to make sure you understand parallel form.

Activity

14

1. Because I never took college preparatory courses in high school, I entered college deficient in mathematics, study skills, and _____.

2. A good salesperson needs to like people, to be aggressive, and _____ _____.

3. Rather than blame myself for failing the course, I blamed the instructor, my adviser, and even _____.

4. Anyone who buys an old house planning to fix it up should be prepared to put in a lot of time, hard work, and _____.

5. Our old car guzzles gas, makes funny noises, and _____ _____.

6. My mother, my boss, and my _____ are three people who are very important in my life right now.

7. Getting married too young was a mistake because we hadn't finished our education, we weren't ready for children, and _____
_____.

8. Some restaurant patrons seem to leave their honesty, their cleanliness, and their _____ at home.

9. During my first semester at college, I had to learn how to manage my time, my diet, and _____.

10. Three experiences I wish I could forget are the time I fell off a ladder, the time I tried to fix my parents' lawn mower, and _____
_____.

Writing a Thesis Statement

Activity

15

Write a thesis for each group of supporting statements. This activity will give you practice in writing an effective essay thesis—one that is neither too broad nor too narrow. It will also help you understand the logical relationship between a thesis and its supporting details.

1. Thesis: _____

   a. My first car was a rebellious-looking one that matched the way I felt and acted as a teenager.

   b. My next car reflected my more mature and practical adult self.

   c. My latest car seems to tell me that I'm aging; it shows my growing concern with comfort and safety.

2. Thesis: _____

   a. All the course credits that are accumulated can be transferred to a four-year school.

   b. Going to a two-year college can save a great deal of money in tuition and other fees.

   c. If the college is nearby, there are also significant savings in everyday living expenses.

3. Thesis: _____

   a. First, I tried simply avoiding the snacks aisle of the supermarket.

   b. Then I started limiting myself to only five units of any given snack.

c. Finally, in desperation, I began keeping the cellophane bags of snacks in a padlocked cupboard.

4. Thesis: _____

a. The holiday can be very frightening for little children.

b. Children can be struck by cars while wearing vision-obstructing masks and dark costumes.

c. There are always incidents involving deadly treats: fruits, cookies, and candies that contain razor blades or even poison.

5. Thesis: _____

a. First of all, I was a typical type A personality: anxious, impatient, and hard-driving.

b. I also have a family history of relatives with heart trouble.

c. My unhealthy lifestyle, though, was probably the major factor.

Limiting a Topic and Writing a Thesis Statement

The following two activities will give you practice in distinguishing general from limited subjects and in writing a thesis.

Look carefully at the ten general subjects and ten limited subjects below. Then write a thesis statement for any five of them.

Activity

16

> **HINT** To create a thesis statement for a limited subject, ask yourself, What point do I want to make about _____ (*my limited subject*)?

General Subject	Limited Subject
1. Apartment	1. Sharing an apartment with a roommate
2. Self-improvement	2. Behavior toward others
3. Family	3. My mother
4. Eating	4. Fast-food restaurants
5. Automobiles	5. Bad driving habits
6. Health	6. Regular exercise
7. Owning a house	7. Do-it-yourself home repairs
8. Baseball	8. Free-agent system

9. Parenthood   9. Being a single parent

10. Pollution   10. Noise pollution

Thesis statements for five of the limited subjects:

_____

_____

_____

_____

_____

_____

_____

_____

_____

_____

_____

_____

_____

Activity

17

Here is a list of ten general subjects. Limit five of the subjects. Then write a thesis statement about each of the five limited subjects.

General Subject	Limited Subject
1. Pets	_____
2. Teenagers	_____
3. Television	_____
4. Work	_____
5. College	_____
6. Doctors	_____
7. Vacations	_____
8. Cooking	_____
9. Money	_____
10. Shopping	_____

Thesis statements for five of the limited subjects:

_____

_____

_____

_____

_____

_____

_____

_____

_____

_____

_____

_____

Providing Specific Evidence

Provide three details that logically support each of the following points. Your details can be drawn from your own experience, or they can be invented. In each case, the details should show *specifically* what the point expresses only generally. State your details briefly in several words rather than in complete sentences.

Activity

18

EXAMPLE

We quickly spruced up the apartment before our guest arrived.

1. _Hid toys and newspapers in spare closet_

2. _Vacuumed pet hairs off sofa_

3. _Sprayed air freshener around living room_

1. The dinner was a disaster.

   _____

   _____

   _____

2. My seven-year-old nephew has some disgusting habits.

_____

_____

_____

3. There are several reasons why I put off studying.

_____

_____

_____

4. My parents never allowed me to think for myself.

_____

_____

_____

5. I have several ways to earn extra cash.

_____

_____

_____

6. My car needs repairs.

_____

_____

_____

7. Friday evening, I didn't sit still for a minute.

_____

_____

_____

8. Mr. (or Ms.) _____ was the worst teacher I ever had.

_____

_____

_____

Identifying Adequate Supporting Evidence

The following body paragraphs were taken from student essays. Two of the paragraphs provide sufficient details to support their topic sentences convincingly. Write AD for *adequate development* beside those paragraphs. Three paragraphs use vague, wordy, general, or irrelevant sentences instead of real supporting details. Write U for *underdeveloped* beside those paragraphs.

Activity

19

_____ 1.   Another consideration in adopting a dog is the cost. Initial fees for shots and a license might add up to $50. Annual visits to the vet for heartworm pills, rabies and distemper shots, and general checkups could cost $100 or more. Then there is the cost of food. A twenty-five-pound bag of dry food (the cheapest kind) costs around $15. A large dog can eat that much in a couple of weeks.

_____ 2.   People can be cruel to pets simply by being thoughtless. They don't think about a pet's needs, or they simply ignore those needs. It never occurs to them that their pet can be experiencing a great deal of discomfort as a result of their failure to be sensitive. The cruelty is a result of the basic lack of attention and concern—qualities that should be there, but aren't.

_____ 3.   If I were in charge of the nighttime programming on a TV network, I would make changes. I would completely eliminate some shows. In fact, all the shows that proved to be of little interest would be canceled. Commercials would also change so that it would be possible to watch them without wanting to turn off the TV. I would expand the good shows so that people would come away with an even better experience. My ideal network would be a great improvement over the average lineup we see today on any of the major networks.

_____ 4.   A friend's rudeness is much more damaging than a stranger's. When a friend says sharply, "I don't have time to talk to you just now," you feel hurt instead of angry. When a friend shows up late for lunch or a shopping trip, with no good reason, you feel that you're being taken for granted. Worst, though, is when a friend pretends to be listening to you but his or her wandering eyes show a lack of attention. Then you feel betrayed. Friends, after all, are supposed to make up for the thoughtless cruelties of strangers.

_____ 5.   Giving my first shampoo and set to a real person, after weeks of practicing on wigs, was a nerve-racking experience. The customer was a woman who acted very sure about what she came for. She tried to describe what she wanted, and I tried without much success to understand what she had in mind. Every time I did something, she seemed to be indicating in one way or another that it was not what she wanted. I got more and more nervous as I worked on her hair, and the nervousness showed. The worst part of the ordeal happened at the very end, when I added the final touches. Nothing, to this woman, had turned out right.

Activity
20

Adding Details to Complete an Essay

The following essay needs specific details to back up the ideas in the supporting paragraphs. Using the spaces provided, add a sentence or two of clear, convincing details for each supporting idea. This activity will give you practice at supplying specific details and an initial feel for writing an essay.

Introduction

Life without Television

When my family's only television set went to the repair shop the other day, my parents, my sister, and I thought we would have a terrible week. How could we get through the long evenings in such a quiet house? What would it be like without all the shows to keep us company? We soon realized, though, that living without television for a while was a stroke of good fortune. It became easy for each of us to enjoy some activities alone, to complete some postponed chores, and to spend rewarding time with each other and friends.

First supporting paragraph

First of all, with no television to compete for our time, we found plenty of hours for personal interests. We all read more that week than we had read during the six months before. _____

_____

_____

We each also enjoyed some hobbies we had ignored for ages. _____

_____

_____

_____

In addition, my sister and I both stopped procrastinating with our homework. _____

_____

_____

_____

_____

    Second, we did chores that had been hanging over our heads for too long. There were many jobs around the house that had needed attention for some time._____

_____

_____

We also had a chance to do some long-postponed shopping. _____

_____

_____

_____

And each of us also caught up with e-mail and did paperwork that was long overdue. _____

_____

_____

Second supporting paragraph

    Finally, and probably most important, we spent time with each other. Instead of just being in the same room together while we stared at a screen, we actually talked for many pleasant hours. _____

_____

_____

Moreover, for the first time in years, my family played some games together. _____

_____

_____

Third supporting paragraph

(continued)

And because we didn't have to worry about missing this or that show, we had some family friends over on a couple of evenings and spent an enjoyable time with them._____

_____

_____

Conclusion

Once our television returned, we were not prepared to put it in the attic. But we had a sense of how it can take over our lives if we are not careful. We are now more selective. We turn on the set for our favorite shows, certain sports events, and the news, but we don't leave it running all evening. As a result, we find we can enjoy television and still have time left over for other activities and interests.

© Comstock Select/Corbis

What are some ways besides watching TV that you and your family or friends spend quality time together? Write about one of these activities and why you enjoy it.

The Third Step in
Essay Writing

4

© Tim Pannell/Corbis

This chapter will show you how to

- organize and connect specific evidence in the body paragraphs of an essay

- begin and end an essay with effective introductory and concluding paragraphs

In the previous chapter, you helped complete one student's essay about life without television. Without television, the student had time to enjoy a host of other activities he or she otherwise would not have had time to do. Write an essay about what, in your life, keeps you from completing tasks or doing what you enjoy. Also include what you would do with your time if this obstacle was removed.

You know from Chapter 3 that the first two steps in writing an effective essay are advancing a thesis and supporting it with specific evidence. This chapter deals with the third step: organizing and connecting the supporting information in a paper. You'll also learn how to start an essay with a suitable introductory paragraph and how to finish it with a well-rounded concluding paragraph.

Step 3: Organize and Connect the Specific Evidence

As you are generating the specific details needed to support a thesis, you should be thinking about ways to organize and connect those details. All the details in your essay must *cohere,* or stick together, so that your reader will be able to move smoothly from one bit of supporting information to the next. This section shows you how to organize and connect supporting details by using (1) common methods of organization, (2) transitions, and (3) other connecting words.

Common Methods of Organization

Two common methods used to organize the supporting material in an essay are time order and emphatic order. (You will learn more specific methods of development in Part Two of this book.)

 Time order, or *chronological order,* simply means that details are listed as they occur in time. *First* this is done; *next* this; *then* this; *after* that, this; and so on. Here is an outline of an essay in this book that uses time order:

www.mhhe.com/langan

Thesis

> *To exercise successfully, you should follow a simple plan consisting of arranging the time, making preparations, and warming up properly.*
>
> 1. *To begin with, set aside a regular hour for exercise.*
> 2. *Next, prepare for your exercise session.*
> 3. *Finally, do a series of warm-up activities.*

Fill in the missing words: The topic sentences in the essay use the words or phrases

_____, _____, and _____ to help show time order.

Here is one supporting paragraph from the essay:

Next, prepare for your exercise session. You do this, first, by not eating or drinking anything for an hour before the session. Why risk an upset stomach? Then, dress comfortably in something that allows you to move freely. Because you'll be in your own home, there's no need to invest in a high-fashion dance costume. A loose T-shirt and shorts are good. A bathing suit is great in summer, and in winter long underwear is warm and comfortable. If your hair tends to flop in your eyes, pin it back or wear a headband or scarf. After dressing, prepare the exercise area. Turn off the phone and lock the door to prevent interruptions. Shove the coffee table out of the way so that you won't bruise yourself on it. Finally, get out the simple materials you'll need to exercise on.

Fill in the missing words: The paragraph uses the following words to help show time order: _____, _____, _____, _____, and _____.

Emphatic order is sometimes described as "saving the best till last." It is a way to put *emphasis* on the most interesting or important detail by placing it in the last part of a paragraph or in the final supporting paragraph of an essay.

www.mhhe.com/langan

> **TIP** In cases where all the details seem equal in importance, the writer should impose a personal order that seems logical or appropriate.

The last position in a paper is the most emphatic position because the reader is most likely to remember the last thing read. *Finally, last of all,* and *most important* are typical words or phrases showing emphasis. Here is an outline of an essay in this book that uses emphatic order:

Celebrities lead very stressful lives.   Thesis

1. *For one thing, celebrities don't have the privacy an ordinary person does.*

2. *In addition, celebrities are under constant pressure.*

3. *Most important, celebrities must deal with the stress of being in constant danger.*

Fill in the missing words: The topic sentences in the essay use the words or phrases _____, _____, and _____ to help show emphatic order.

Here is the third supporting paragraph from the essay:

> Most important, celebrities must deal with the stress of being in constant danger. The friendly grabs, hugs, and kisses of enthusiastic fans can quickly turn into uncontrolled assaults on a celebrity's hair, clothes, and car. Celebrities often get strange letters from people who become obsessed with their idols or from people who threaten to harm them. Worst of all, threats can turn into deeds. The attempt to kill Ronald Reagan and the murder of John Lennon came about because two unbalanced people tried to transfer the celebrity's fame to themselves. Famous people must live with the fact that they are always fair game—and never out of season.

Fill in the missing phrase: The words _____ are used to mark the most emphatic detail in the paragraph.

Some essays use a combination of time order and emphatic order. For example, the essay on moviegoing in Chapter 1 (page 6) includes time order: the writer first describes getting to the theater, then the theater itself, and finally the behavior of audience members during the movie. At the same time, the writer uses emphatic order, ending with the most important reason for her dislike of moviegoing: "Some of the other patrons are even more of a problem than the theater itself."

Activity 1

Part A Read the essays listed below (page numbers are in parentheses) and identify their method of organizing details—time order, emphatic order, or a combination of both.

1. "Adopting a Handicap" (page 203)

    _____

2. "A Vote for McDonald's" (page 290)

    _____

3. "Everyday Cruelty" (page 223)

    _____

Part B Now see if you can complete the explanations that follow.

The essay titled "Adopting a Handicap" uses (*add the missing word*)

_____ order. The author begins with the challenge of learning to sit properly in the wheelchair, then moves on to learning to move in the wheelchair, and ends with several problems that occurred next, during the church service. "A

Vote for McDonald's" uses (*add the missing word*) _____ order. The writer presents three advantages of eating at McDonald's and ends with the most important one: reasonable prices. "Everyday Cruelty" uses a combination of

(*add the missing words*) _____ and _____ order. It moves from the beginning to the end of a particular workday. It also ends with the "worst incident of mean-spiritedness" that the writer witnessed that day.

Transitions

Transitional Words

Transitions signal the direction of a writer's thoughts. They are like the road signs that guide travelers. In the box that follows are some common transitions, grouped according to the kind of signal they give to readers. Note that certain words provide more than one kind of signal.

www.mhhe.com/langan

Common Transitions

Addition signals: one, first of all, second, the third reason, also, next, another, and, in addition, moreover, furthermore, finally, last of all

Time signals: first, then, next, after, as, before, while, meanwhile, soon, now, during, finally

Space signals: next to, across, on the opposite side, to the left, to the right, above, below, near, nearby

Change-of-direction signals: but, however, yet, in contrast, although, otherwise, still, on the contrary, on the other hand

Illustration signals: for example, for instance, specifically, as an illustration, once, such as

Conclusion signals: therefore, consequently, thus, then, as a result, in summary, to conclude, last of all, finally

Activity

2

1. Underline the three *addition* signals in the following selection:

> To create the time you need to pass difficult courses, find some easy courses. These are the ones that combine the least amount of work with the fewest tests and the most lenient professors. One way to find such courses is to ask friends and classmates about courses in which they received A's after attending only 25 percent of the classes. Also, inquire around to see which instructors lecture with the same notes every year and give the same tests. Photocopies of the class notes are usually cheap and widely available. Another great way of finding simple courses is to pick up a copy of the master schedule and study it carefully. Find the telltale course titles that signal an easy glide through a painless subject. Look for titles like "History of the Animated Cartoon," "Arts and Crafts for Beginners," and "Rock Music of the 1950s."

2. Underline the four *time* signals in the following selection:

> After you've snagged the job of TV sports reporter, you have to begin working on the details of your image. First, invest in two or three truly loud sports jackets. Look for gigantic plaid patterns in odd color combinations like purple and green or orange and blue. These should become familiar enough to viewers so that they will associate that crazy jacket with that dynamic sportscaster. Next, try to cultivate a distinctive voice that will be just annoying enough to be memorable. A nasal whine or a gravelly growl will do it. Be sure to speak only in tough, punchy sentences that seem to be punctuated with imaginary exclamation points. Finally, you must share lots of pompous, obnoxious opinions with your viewers. Your tone of voice must convey the hidden message "I dare anyone to disagree with me." If the home teams lose, call them bums. If players strike, talk sarcastically about the good old days. If a sports franchise leaves town, say, "Good riddance."

3. Underline the three *space* signals in the following selection:

The vegetable bin of my refrigerator contained an assortment of weird-looking items. Next to a shriveled, fuzz-coated lemon were two oranges covered with blue fuzz. To the right of the oranges was a bunch of carrots that had begun to sprout points, spikes, knobs, and tendrils. The carrots drooped into U shapes as I picked them up with the tips of my fingers. Near the carrots was a net bag of onions; each onion had sent curling shoots through the net until the whole thing resembled a mass of green spaghetti. The most horrible item, though, was a head of lettuce that had turned into a pool of brown goo. It had seeped out of its bag and coated the bin with a sticky, evil-smelling liquid.

4. Underline the two *change-of-direction* signals in the following selection:

Taking small children on vacation, for instance, sounds like a wonderful experience for the entire family. But vacations can be scary or emotionally overwhelming times for children. When children are taken away from their usual routine and brought to an unfamiliar place, they can become very frightened. That strange bed in the motel room or the unusual noises in Grandma's spare bedroom may cause nightmares. On vacations, too, children usually clamor to do as many things in one day as they can and to stay up past their usual bedtime. And since it is vacation time, parents may decide to give in to the children's demands. A parental attitude like this, however, can lead to problems. After a sixteen-hour day of touring the amusement park, eating in a restaurant, and seeing a movie, children can experience sensory and emotional overload. They become cranky, unhappy, or even rebellious and angry.

5. Underline the two *illustration* signals in the following selection:

Supermarkets also use psychology to encourage you to buy. For example, in most supermarkets, the milk and the bread are either at opposite ends of the store or located far away from the first aisle. Even if you've stopped at the market only for staples like these, you must pass hundreds of items to reach them. The odds are that, instead of leaving with just a quart of milk, you'll leave with additional purchases as well. Special displays, such as a

(continued)

pyramid of canned green beans in an aisle and a large end display of cartons of paper towels, also increase sales. Because you assume that these items are a good buy, you may pick them up. However, they may not even be on sale! Store managers know that the customer is automatically attracted to a display like this, and they will use it to move an overstocked product.

6. Underline the two *conclusion* signals in the following selection:

Finally, my grandmother was extremely thrifty. She was one of those people who hoard pieces of used aluminum foil after carefully scrubbing off the cake icing or beef gravy. She had a drawer full of old eyeglasses that dated back at least thirty years. The lens prescriptions were no longer accurate, but Gran couldn't bear to throw away "a good pair of glasses." She kept them "just in case," but we could never figure out what situation would involve a desperate need for a dozen pairs of old eyeglasses. We never realized the true extent of Gran's thriftiness, though, until after she died. Her house was to be sold, and therefore we cleaned out its dusty attic. In one corner was a cardboard box filled with two- and three-inch pieces of string. The box was labeled, in Gran's spidery hand, "String too short to be saved."

Transitional Sentences

Transitional sentences, or *linking sentences,* are used between paragraphs to help tie together the supporting paragraphs in an essay. They enable the reader to move smoothly from the idea in one paragraph to the idea in the next paragraph.

Here is the linking sentence used in the essay on moviegoing:

Many of the other patrons are even more of a problem than the concession stand.

The words *concession stand* remind us of the point of the first supporting paragraph, while *Many of the other patrons* presents the point to be developed in the second supporting paragraph.

Activity

3

Following is a brief sentence outline of an essay. The second and third topic sentences serve as transitional, or linking, sentences. Each reminds us of the point in the preceding paragraph and announces the point to be developed in the current paragraph. In the spaces provided, add the words needed to complete the second and third topic sentences.

The most helpful values I learned from my parents are the importance of family support, of hard work, and of a good education.

Thesis

First, my parents taught me that family members should stick together, especially in times of trouble. . . .

First supporting paragraph

In addition to teaching me about the importance of _____,
_____,
my parents taught me the value of _____
_____. . . .

Second supporting paragraph

Along with the value of _____,
my parents emphasized the benefits of _____
_____. . . .

Third supporting paragraph

Other Connecting Words

In addition to transitions, there are three other kinds of connecting words that help tie together the specific evidence in a paper: *repeated words, pronouns,* and *synonyms.*

www.mhhe.com/langan

Repeated Words

Many of us have been taught—correctly—not to repeat ourselves in writing. However, repeating *key* words helps tie together the flow of thought in a paper. Below, repeated words remind readers of the selection's central idea.

One reason for studying <u>psychology</u> is to help you deal with your children. Perhaps your young daughter refuses to go to bed when you want her to and bursts into tears at the least mention of "lights out." A little knowledge of <u>psychology</u> comes in handy. Offer her a choice of staying up until 7:30 with you or going upstairs and playing until 8:00. Since she gets to make the choice, she does not feel so powerless and will not resist.

(continued)

> Psychology is also useful in rewarding a child for a job well done. Instead of telling your ten-year-old son what a good boy he is when he makes his own bed, tell him how neat it looks, how happy you are to see it, and how proud of him you are for doing it by himself. The psychology books will tell you that being a good boy is much harder to live up to than doing one job well.

Pronouns

Pronouns (*he, she, it, you, they, this, that,* and others) are another way to connect ideas. Also, using pronouns in place of other words can help you avoid needless repetition. (Note, however, that pronouns should be used with care to avoid the problems described on pages 504–506.) Here is a selection that makes good use of pronouns:

> Another way for people to economize at an amusement park is to bring their own food. If they pack a nourishing, well-balanced lunch of cold chicken, carrot sticks, and fruit, they will avoid having to pay high prices for hamburgers and hot dogs. They will also save on calories. Also, instead of filling up on soft drinks, they should bring a thermos of iced tea. Iced tea is more refreshing than soda, and it is a great deal cheaper. Every dollar that is not spent at a refreshment stand is one that can be spent on another ride.

Synonyms

Synonyms are words alike in meaning. Using synonyms can also help move the reader easily from one thought to the next. In addition, the use of synonyms increases variety and interest by avoiding needless repetition.

Note the synonyms for *method* in the following selection:

> Several methods of fund-raising work well with small organizations. One technique is to hold an auction, with everyone either contributing an item from home or obtaining a donation from a sympathetic local merchant. Because all the merchandise and the services of the auctioneer have been donated, the entire proceeds can be placed in the organization's treasury. A second fund-raising procedure is a car wash. Club members and their children get together on a Saturday and wash all the cars in the neighborhood for a few dollars apiece. A third, time-tested way to raise money is to hold a
> *(continued)*

bake sale, with each family contributing homemade cookies, brownies, layer cakes, or cupcakes. Sold by the piece or by the box, these baked goods will satisfyingly fill both the stomach and the pocketbook.

Read the selection below and then answer the questions about it that follow.

[1]When I think about my childhood in the 1930s, life today seems like the greatest of luxuries. [2]In our house, we had only a wood-burning cookstove in the kitchen to keep us warm. [3]In the morning, my father would get up in the icy cold, go downstairs, and light a fire in the black iron range. [4]When he called us, I would put off leaving my warm bed until the last possible minute and then quickly grab my school clothes. [5]The water pitcher and washing basin in my room would be layered with ice, and my breath would come out as white puffs as I ran downstairs. [6]My sisters and I would all dress—as quickly as possible—in the chilly but bearable air of the kitchen. [7]Our schoolroom, once we had arrived, didn't provide much relief from the cold. [8]Students wore woolen mitts that left their fingers free but covered their palms and wrists. [9]Even with these, we occasionally suffered chilblains. [10]The throbbing swellings on our hands made writing a painful process. [11]When we returned home in the afternoon, we spent all our indoor hours in the warm kitchen. [12]We hated to leave it at bedtime to make the return trip to those cold bedrooms and frigid sheets. [13]My mother made up hot-water bottles and gave us hot bricks to tuck under the covers, but nothing could eliminate the agony of that penetrating cold when we first slid under the bedclothes.

1. How many times is the key word *cold* used? _____

2. Write here the pronoun that is used for *father* (sentence 4): _____

3. Write here the words in sentence 3 that are used as a synonym for *cookstove:*

    _____; write in the words in sentence 10 that are used as a synonym

    for *chilblains:* _____; write in the word in sentence 12 that

    is used as a synonym for *cold:* _____.

Introductions, Conclusions, and Titles

So far, this chapter has discussed ways to organize and connect the supporting paragraphs of an essay. A well-organized essay, however, also needs a strong introductory paragraph, an effective concluding paragraph, and a good title.

www.mhhe.com/langan

Introductory Paragraph

Functions of the Introduction

A well-written introductory paragraph performs four important roles:

1. It attracts the reader's interest, encouraging him or her to continue reading the essay.

2. It supplies any background information that the reader may need to understand the essay.

3. It presents a thesis statement. This clear, direct statement of the main idea of the paper usually appears near the end of the introductory paragraph.

4. It indicates a plan of development. In this preview, the major supporting points for the thesis are listed in the order in which they will be presented. In some cases, the thesis and plan of development appear in the same sentence. However, writers sometimes choose not to describe the plan of development.

Common Methods of Introduction

Here are some common methods of introduction. Use any one method, or a combination of methods, to introduce your subject to the reader in an interesting way.

- **Begin with a broad, general statement of your topic and narrow it down to your thesis statement.** Broad, general statements ease the reader into your thesis statement by first introducing the topic. In the example below, the writer talks generally about diets and then narrows down to comments on a specific diet.

> Bookstore shelves today are crammed with dozens of different diet books. The American public seems willing to try any sort of diet, especially the ones that promise instant, miraculous results. And authors are more than willing to invent new fad diets to cash in on this craze. Unfortunately, some of these fad diets are ineffective or even unsafe. One of the worst fad diets is the Palm Beach plan. It is impractical, doesn't achieve the results it claims, and is a sure route to poor nutrition.

- **Start with an idea or a situation that is the opposite of the one you will develop.** This approach works because your readers will be surprised, and then intrigued, by the contrast between the opening idea and the thesis that follows it.

When I decided to return to school at age thirty-five, I wasn't at all worried about my ability to do the work. After all, I was a grown woman who had raised a family, not a confused teenager fresh out of high school. But when I started classes, I realized that those "confused teenagers" sitting around me were in much better shape for college than I was. They still had all their classroom skills in bright, shiny condition, while mine had grown rusty from disuse. I had to learn how to locate information in a library, how to write a report, and even how to speak up in class discussions.

- **Explain the importance of your topic to the reader.** If you can convince your readers that the subject in some way applies to them, or is something they should know more about, they will want to keep reading.

Diseases like scarlet fever and whooping cough used to kill more young children than any other cause. Today, however, child mortality due to disease has been almost completely eliminated by medical science. Instead, car accidents are the number-one killer of our children. And most of the children fatally injured in car accidents were not protected by car seats, belts, or restraints of any kind. Several steps must be taken to reduce the serious dangers car accidents pose to children.

- **Use an incident or a brief story.** Stories are naturally interesting. They appeal to a reader's curiosity. In your introduction, an anecdote will grab the reader's attention right away. The story should be brief and should be related to your main idea. The incident in the story can be something that happened to you, something you have heard about, or something you have read about in a newspaper or magazine.

Early Sunday morning, the young mother dressed her little girl warmly and gave her a candy bar, a picture book, and a well-worn stuffed rabbit. Together, they drove downtown to a Methodist church. There the mother told the little girl to wait on the stone steps until children began arriving for Sunday school. Then the young mother drove off, abandoning her five-year-old because she couldn't cope with being a parent anymore. This incident is one of thousands of cases of child neglect and abuse that occur annually.

(continued)

> Perhaps the automatic right to become a parent should no longer exist. Would-be parents should be forced to apply for parental licenses for which they would have to meet three important conditions.

- **Ask one or more questions.** You may simply want the reader to think about possible answers, or you may plan to answer the questions yourself later in the paper.

> What is love? How do we know that we are really in love? When we meet that special person, how can we tell that our feelings are genuine and not merely infatuation? And, if they are genuine, will these feelings last? Love, as we all know, is difficult to define. But most people agree that true and lasting love involves far more than mere physical attraction. Love involves mutual respect, the desire to give rather than take, and the feeling of being wholly at ease.

- **Use a quotation.** A quotation can be something you have read in a book or an article. It can also be something that you have heard: a popular saying or proverb ("Never give advice to a friend"), a current or recent advertising slogan ("Can you hear me now?"), or a favorite expression used by friends or family ("My father always says . . ."). Using a quotation in your introductory paragraph lets you add someone else's voice to your own.

> "Fish and visitors," wrote Benjamin Franklin, "begin to smell after three days." Last summer, when my sister and her family came to spend their two-week vacation with us, I became convinced that Franklin was right. After only three days of my family's visit, I was thoroughly sick of my brother-in-law's lame jokes, my sister's endless complaints about her boss, and their children's constant invasions of our privacy.

Activity 5

The box that follows summarizes the six kinds of introductions. Read the introductions that come after it and, in the space provided, write the letter of the kind of introduction used in each case.

A. General to narrow	D. Incident or story
B. Starting with an opposite	E. Questions
C. Stating importance of topic	F. Quotation

_____ 1. The ad, in full color on a glossy magazine page, shows a beautiful kitchen with gleaming counters. In the foreground, on one of the counters, stands a shiny new food processor. Usually, a feminine hand is touching it lovingly. Around the main picture are other, smaller shots. They show mounds of perfectly sliced onion rings, thin rounds of juicy tomatoes, heaps of matchstick-sized potatoes, and piles of golden, evenly grated cheese. The ad copy tells you how wonderful, how easy, food preparation will be with a processor. Don't believe it. My processor turned out to be expensive, difficult to operate, and very limited in its use.

_____ 2. My father stubbornly says, "You can often tell a book by its cover," and when it comes to certain paperbacks, he's right. When you're browsing in the drugstore or supermarket and you see a paperback featuring an attractive young woman in a low-cut dress fleeing from a handsome dark figure in a shadowy castle, you know exactly what you're getting. Every romance novel has the same elements: an innocent heroine, an exotic setting, and a cruel but fascinating hero.

_____ 3. We Americans are incredibly lazy. Instead of cooking a simple, nourishing meal, we pop a frozen dinner into the oven. Instead of studying a daily newspaper, we are contented with the capsule summaries on the network news. Worst of all, instead of walking even a few blocks to the local convenience store, we jump into our cars. This dependence on the automobile, even for short trips, has robbed us of a valuable experience—walking. If we drove less and walked more, we would save money, become healthier, and discover fascinating things about our surroundings.

Concluding Paragraph

A concluding paragraph is your chance to remind the reader of your thesis idea and bring the paper to a natural and graceful end.

www.mhhe.com/langan

Common Methods of Conclusion

You may use any one of the methods below, or a combination of methods, to round off your paper.

- **End with a summary and final thought.** When army instructors train new recruits, each of their lessons follows a three-step formula:

  1. Tell them what you're going to tell them.
  2. Tell them.
  3. Tell them what you've told them.

An essay that ends with a summary is not very different. After you have stated your thesis ("Tell them what you're going to tell them") and supported it ("Tell them"), you restate the thesis and supporting points ("Tell them what you've told them"). However, don't use the exact wording you used before. Here is a summary conclusion:

> Online shopping at home, then, has several advantages. Such shopping is convenient, saves you money, and saves you time. It is not surprising that growing numbers of people are doing the majority of their shopping on the Internet, for everything from turnip seeds to televisions.

Note that the summary is accompanied by a final comment that rounds off the paper and brings the discussion to a close. This combination of a summary and a final thought is the most common method of concluding an essay.

- **Include a thought-provoking question or short series of questions.**
  A question grabs the reader's attention. It is a direct appeal to your reader to think further about what you have written. A question should follow logically from the points you have already made in the paper. A question must deal with one of these areas:

  1. Why the subject of your paper is important
  2. What might happen in the future
  3. What should be done about this subject
  4. Which choice should be made

In your conclusion, you may provide an answer to your question. Be sure, though, that the question is closely related to your thesis. Here is an example:

> What, then, will happen when most of the population will be over sixty years old? Retirement policies could change dramatically, with the age-sixty-five testimonial dinner and gold watch postponed for five or ten years. Even television would change as the Red Bull generation replaces the Pepsi generation. Glamorous gray-haired models would sell everything from toilet paper to televisions. New soap operas and situation comedies would reveal the secrets of the "sunset years." It will be a different world indeed when the young find themselves outnumbered.

- **End with a prediction or recommendation.** Like questions, predictions and recommendations also involve your readers. A prediction states what may happen in the future:

> If people stopped to think before acquiring pets, there would be fewer instances of cruelty to animals. Many times, it is the people who adopt pets without considering the expense and responsibility involved who mistreat and neglect their animals. Pets are living creatures. They do not deserve to be treated as carelessly as one would treat a stuffed toy.

A recommendation suggests what should be done about a situation or problem:

> Stereotypes such as the ditzy blonde, harried executive, and annoying in-law are insulting enough to begin with. In magazine ads or television commercials, they become even more insulting. Now these unfortunate characters are not just being laughed at; they are being turned into hucksters to sell products to an unsuspecting public. Consumers should boycott companies whose advertising continues to use such stereotypes.

In the space provided, note how each concluding paragraph ends: with a summary and final thought (write S in the space), with a prediction or recommendation (write P/R), or with a question (write Q).

Activity

6

_____ 1. Disappointments are unwelcome, but regular, visitors in everyone's life. We can feel depressed about them, or we can try to escape from them. The best thing, though, is to accept a disappointment and then try to use it somehow: step over the unwelcome visitor and then get on with life.

_____ 2. Holidays, it is clear, are often not the fulfilling experience they are supposed to be. They can, in fact, be very stressful. But would we rather have a holiday-free calendar?

_____ 3. Some people dream of starring roles, their names in lights, and their pictures on the cover of People magazine. I'm not one of them, though. A famous person gives up private life, feels pressured all the time, and is never completely safe. So let someone else have that cover story. I'd rather lead an ordinary, but calm, life than a stress-filled one.

Titles

A title is usually a very brief summary of what your paper is about. It is often no more than several words. You may find it easier to write the title *after* you have completed your paper.

Following are the introductory paragraphs for two of the essays in this text, along with the titles of the essays.

Introductory paragraph

I'm not just a consumer—I'm a victim. If I order a product, it is sure to arrive in the wrong color, size, or quantity. If I hire people to do repairs, they never arrive on the day scheduled. If I owe a bill, the computer is bound to overcharge me. Therefore, in self-defense, I have developed the following consumer's guide to complaining effectively.

Title: How to Complain

Introductory paragraph

Schools divide people into categories. From first grade on up, students are labeled "advanced" or "deprived" or "remedial" or "antisocial." Students pigeonhole their fellow students, too. We've all known the "brain," the "jock," the "dummy," and the "teacher's pet." In most cases, these narrow labels are misleading and inaccurate. But there is one label for a certain type of college student that says it all: "zombie."

Title: Student Zombies

Note that you should not underline the title. Nor should you put quotation marks around it. On the other hand, you should capitalize all but small connecting words in the title. Also, you should skip a space between the title and the first line of the text. (See "Manuscript Form," page 534.)

Activity

7

Write an appropriate title for each of the introductory paragraphs that follow.

1. For my birthday this month, my wife has offered to treat me to dinner at the restaurant of my choice. I think she expects me to ask for a meal at the Chalet, the classiest, most expensive restaurant in town. However, I'm going to eat my birthday dinner at McDonald's. When I compare the two restaurants, the advantages of eating at McDonald's are clear.

    Title: _____

2. I've been in lots of diners, and they've always seemed to be warm, busy, friendly, happy places. That's why, on a recent Monday night, I stopped at a diner for a cup of coffee. I was returning home after an all-day car trip and needed something to help me make the last forty-five miles. A diner at midnight, however, was not the place I had expected. It was different—and lonely.

    Title: _____

3. If you see punk-rock-concert audiences only on television or in newspaper photos, the people at these events may all seem to be excited teenagers. However, if you attended a few punk-rock shows, you would see that several kinds of people make up the crowd. At any concert, you would find the typical fan, the out-of-place person, and the troublemaker.

    Title: _____

© Topham/The Image Works

Peace Lily, 2001 (oil on canvas) by Copeland, Mark (b.1956) (Contemporary Artist) © Private Collection/ © Portal Gallery Ltd/ The Bridgeman Art Library

For further practice in writing titles, write an appropriate title for each image pictured here.

Practice in Organizing and Connecting Specific Evidence

You now know the third step in effective writing: organizing the specific evidence used to support the thesis of a paper. This closing section will expand and strengthen your understanding of the third step in writing. You will work through the following series of activities:

- organizing through time or emphatic order

- providing transitions

- identifying transitions and other connecting words

- completing transitional sentences

- identifying introductions and conclusions

Organizing through Time or Emphatic Order

Use time order to organize the scrambled lists of supporting ideas below. Write *1* beside the supporting idea that should come first in time, *2* beside the idea that logically follows, and *3* beside the idea that comes last in time.

1. Thesis: When I was a child, Disney movies frightened me more than any other kind.

    _____   As a five-year-old, I was terrified by the movie *Pinocchio,* about a puppet transformed into a boy.

    _____   Although I saw *Bambi* when I was old enough to begin poking fun at "baby movies," the scene during which Bambi's mother is killed has stayed with me to this day.

    _____   About a year after *Pinocchio*, I gripped my seat in fear as the witches and goblins of *Fantasia* flew across the screen.

2. Thesis: There are techniques to help you overcome three common pitfalls in making a cheesecake.

    _____   There's only one way to remove the cake cleanly and easily from its pan.

    _____   Plan in advance to have your equipment ready and the ingredients at room temperature.

    _____   Remember to time the baking process and regulate the oven temperature while the cake is baking.

3. Thesis: Applying for unemployment benefits was a confusing, frustrating experience.

    _____   It was difficult to find both the office and a place to park.

    _____   When I finally reached the head of the line after four hours of waiting, the clerk had problems processing my claim.

    _____   There was no one to direct or help me when I entered the large office, which was packed with people.

Use emphatic order (order of importance) to arrange the following scrambled lists of supporting ideas. For each thesis, write 1 in the blank beside the point that is perhaps less important or interesting than the other two, 2 beside the point that appears more important or interesting, and 3 beside the point that should be most emphasized.

Activity 9

1. Thesis: My part-time job has been an invaluable part of my life this year.

    _____   Better yet, it has taught me how to get along with many kinds of people.

    _____   Since it's in the morning, it usually keeps me from staying up too late.

    _____   Without it, I would have had to drop out of school.

2. Thesis: We received some odd gifts for our wedding.

    _____   The winner in the odd-gift category was a large wooden box with no apparent purpose or function.

    _____   Someone gave us a gift certificate for a massage.

    _____   Even stranger, my uncle gave me his favorite bowling ball.

3. Thesis: Donna is my most loyal friend.

    _____   She has taken time to do special favors for me.

    _____   She's always there in real emergencies or emotional crises.

    _____   She once lent me her favorite necklace to wear on a date.

Providing Transitions

In the spaces provided, add appropriate transitions to tie together the sentences and ideas in the following essay. Draw from the words given in the boxes above the paragraphs. Use each word only once.

Activity 10

Annoying People

President Richard Nixon used to keep an enemies list of all the people he didn't especially like. I'm ashamed to confess it, but I, too, have an enemies list—a mental one. On this list are all the people I would gladly live without, the ones who cause my blood pressure to rise to the boiling point. The top three places on the list go to people with annoying nervous habits, people

(continued)

who talk in movie theaters, and people who talk on cell phones while driving.

For example	First of all	Another	However

_____, there are the people with annoying nervous habits.

_____, there are the ones who make faces. When in deep thought, they twitch, squint, and frown, and they can be a real distraction when

I'm trying to concentrate during an exam. _____ type of nervous character makes useless designs. These people bend paper clips into abstract sculptures or string the clips into necklaces as they talk.

_____, neither of these groups is as bad as the people who make noises. These individuals, when they are feeling uncomfortable, bite their fingernails or crack their knuckles. If they have a pencil in their hands, they tap it rhythmically against whatever surface is handy—a desk, a book, a head. Lacking a pencil to play with, they jingle the loose change or keys in their pockets. These people make me wish I were hard of hearing.

On the contrary	Then	As a result	After	Second

A _____ category of people I would gladly do away with is the ones who talk in movie theaters. These people are not content to sit back, relax, and enjoy the film they have paid to see. _____, they feel compelled to comment loudly on everything from the hero's hairstyle to the appropriateness of the background music. _____, no one hears a word of any dialogue except theirs. _____ these people have been in the theater for a while, their interest in the movie may fade. _____ they will start discussing other things, and the people around them will be treated to an instant replay of the latest family scandal or soap-opera episode. These stories may be entertaining, but they don't belong in a movie theater.

In addition	But	Last of all

_____, there are the people who talk on the phone while they're driving. One of the things that irritates me about them is the way they seem to be showing off. They're saying, "Look at me! I'm so important I have to make phone calls in my car." _____, such behavior is just plain dangerous. Instead of concentrating on adjusting carefully to ever-changing traffic conditions, they're weaving all over the road or getting much too close to the car in front of them as they gossip with a friend, make an appointment with a doctor, or order a pizza.

So long as murder remains illegal, the nervous twitchers, movie talkers, and cell-phone users of the world are safe from me. _____ if ever I am granted the power of life or death, these people had better think twice about annoying me. They might not have long to live.

Identifying Transitions and Other Connecting Words

The following sentences use connecting words to help tie ideas together. The connecting words you are to identify are set off in italics. In the space, write T for *transition*, RW for *repeated word*, S for *synonym*, or P for *pronoun*.

Activity

11

_____   1. Kate wears a puffy, quilted, down-filled jacket. In this *garment*, she resembles a stack of inflated inner tubes.

_____   2. Plants like poinsettias and mistletoe are pretty. *They* are also poisonous.

_____   3. A strip of strong cloth can be used as an emergency fan-belt replacement. *In addition,* a roll of duct tape can be used to patch a leaky hose temporarily.

_____   4. I'm always losing my soft contact lenses, which resemble little circles of thick Saran Wrap. One day I dropped both of *them* into a cup of hot tea.

_____   5. The molded plastic chairs in the classrooms are hard and uncomfortable. When I sit in one of these *chairs*, I feel as if I were sitting in a bucket.

_____   6. One way to tell if your skin is aging is to pinch a fold of skin on the back of your hand. If *it* doesn't smooth out quickly, your skin is losing its youthful tone.

_____   7. I never eat sloppy joes. *They* look as if they've already been eaten.

_____   8. Clothing intended just for children seems to have vanished. *Instead,* children wear scaled-down versions of everything adults wear.

_____   9. Some successful salespeople use voice tones and hand gestures that are almost hypnotic. Customers are not conscious of this *hypnotic* effect but merely feel an urge to buy.

_____   10. The giant cockroaches in Florida are the subject of local legends. A visitor, according to one tale, saw one of the *insects,* thought it was a Volkswagen, and tried to drive it away.

_____   11. Some thieves scour garbage cans for credit-card receipts. *Then* they use the owner's name and card number to order merchandise by phone.

_____   12. When the phone rang, I dropped the garden hose. *It* whipped around crazily and squirted water through the kitchen screen door.

_____   13. There are many phobias other than the ones described in psychology textbooks. I have *phobias,* for instance, about toasters and lawn mowers.

_____   14. My mother believes that food is love. *Therefore,* when she offers homemade cookies or cupcakes, I hate to hurt her feelings by refusing them.

Completing Transitional Sentences

Activity 12

Following are brief sentence outlines from two essays. In each outline, the second and third topic sentences serve as transitional, or linking, sentences. Each reminds us of the point in the preceding paragraph and announces the point to be developed in the current paragraph. In the spaces provided, add the words needed to complete the second and third topic sentences.

Thesis 1

  To set up a day care center in your home, you must make sure your house conforms to state regulations, obtain the necessary legal permits, and advertise your service in the right places.

First supporting paragraph

  First of all, as a potential operator of a home day care center, you must make sure your house conforms to state regulations. . . .

Second supporting paragraph

  After making certain that _____

  _____ ,

  you must obtain _____ . . . .

Finally, once you have the necessary _____,
you can begin to _____.

| Third supporting paragraph |

Cheaper cost, greater comfort, and superior electronic technology make watching football at home more enjoyable than attending a game at the stadium.

| Thesis 2 |

For one thing, watching the game on TV eliminates the cost of attending the game. . . .

| First supporting paragraph |

In addition to saving me money, watching the game at home is more _____ than sitting in a stadium. . . .

| Second supporting paragraph |

Even more important than _____ and _____, though, is the _____ that makes a televised game better than the "real thing." . . .

| Third supporting paragraph |

Identifying Introductions and Conclusions

The following box lists six common kinds of introductions and three common kinds of conclusions. Read the three pairs of introductory and concluding paragraphs that follow. Then, in the space provided, write the letter of the kind of introduction and conclusion used in each paragraph.

Activity

13

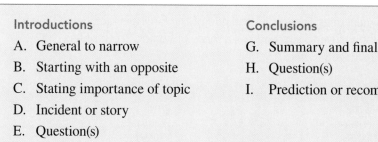

Introductions

A. General to narrow
B. Starting with an opposite
C. Stating importance of topic
D. Incident or story
E. Question(s)
F. Quotation

Conclusions

G. Summary and final thought
H. Question(s)
I. Prediction or recommendation

Pair 1

_____   Shortly before Easter, our local elementary school sponsored a fund-raising event at which classroom pets and their babies—hamsters, guinea pigs, and chicks—were available for adoption. Afterward, as I was driving home, I saw a hand drop a baby hamster out of the car ahead of me. I couldn't avoid running over the tiny creature. One of the parents had taken the pet, regretted the decision, and decided to get rid of it. Such people have never stopped to consider the several real obligations involved in owning a pet.

_____   A pet cannot be thrown onto a trash heap when it is no longer wanted or tossed into a closet if it begins to bore its owner. A pet, like us, is a living thing that needs attention and care. Would-be owners, there-fore, should think seriously about their responsibilities before they acquire a pet.

Pair 2

_____   What would life be like if we could read each other's minds? Would communications be instantaneous and perfectly clear? These questions will never be answered unless mental telepathy becomes a fact of life. Until then, we will have to make do with less perfect means of commu-nication. Letters, telephone calls, and e-mail messages do have serious drawbacks.

_____   Neither letters, phone calls, nor e-mails guarantee perfect commu-nication. With all our sophisticated skills, we human beings often com-municate less effectively than howling wolves or chattering monkeys. We always seem to find some way to foul up the message.

Pair 3

_____   "Few things are harder to put up with," said Mark Twain, "than the annoyance of a good example." Twain obviously knew the problems faced by siblings cursed with older brothers or sisters who are models of per-fection. All our lives, my older sister Shelley and I have been compared. Unfortunately, in competition with my sister's virtues, my looks, talents, and accomplishments always ended up on the losing side.

_____   Although I always lost in the sibling contests of looks, talents, and accomplishments, Shelley and I have somehow managed not to turn into deadly enemies. Feeling like the dud of the family, in fact, helped me to develop a drive to succeed and a sense of humor. In our sibling rivalry, we both managed to win.

The Fourth Step in Essay Writing

This chapter will show you how to

- revise so that your sentences flow smoothly and clearly

- edit so that your sentences are error free

What differences do you notice about the two students in the photograph above? Most likely, you can identify with both of them. Thinking about your own experiences in the classroom, write an essay about one or more teachers or instructors who have conducted classes that made you glad to learn or, alternatively, left you daydreaming in class. Once you have written your first draft, read it aloud to make sure all your sentences flow smoothly and clearly.

Up to now, this book has emphasized the first three goals in effective writing: unity, support, and coherence. This chapter focuses on the fourth goal of writing effectively: sentence skills. You'll learn how to revise an essay so that your sentences flow smoothly and clearly. Then you'll review how to edit a paper for mistakes in grammar, punctuation, and spelling.

Revising Sentences

These strategies will help you to revise your sentences effectively:

- Use parallelism.
- Use a consistent point of view.
- Use specific words.
- Use active verbs.
- Use concise words.
- Vary your sentences.

Use Parallelism

www.mhhe.com/langan

Words in a pair or a series should have parallel structure. By balancing the items in a pair or a series so that they have the same kind of structure, you will make the sentence clearer and easier to read. Notice how the parallel sentences that follow read more smoothly than the nonparallel ones.

Nonparallel (Not Balanced)

My job includes checking the inventory, initialing the orders, and *to call* the suppliers.

The game-show contestant was told to be cheerful, charming, and *with enthusiasm.*

Grandmother likes to read mystery novels, to do needlepoint, and *browsing* the Internet.

Parallel (Balanced)

My job includes checking the inventory, initialing the orders, and calling the suppliers.
(A balanced series of *-ing* words: *checking, initialing, calling*)

The game-show contestant was told to be cheerful, charming, and enthusiastic.
(A balanced series of descriptive words: *cheerful, charming, enthusiastic*)

Grandmother likes to read mystery novels, to do needlepoint, and to browse the Internet.
(A balanced series of *to* verbs: *to read, to do, to browse*)

We painted the trim in the living room; *the wallpaper was put up by a professional.*	We painted the trim in the living room; a professional put up the wallpaper. (Balanced verbs and word order: *We painted . . . ; a professional put up . . .*)

Balanced sentences are not a skill you need worry about when writing first drafts. But when you rewrite, you should try to put matching words and ideas into matching structures. Such parallelism will improve your writing style.

Cross out and revise the unbalanced part of each of the following sentences.

EXAMPLE   Chocolate makes me gain weight, lose my appetite, and ~~breaking~~ *break* out in hives.

1. The novelty store sells hand buzzers, plastic fangs, and insects that are fake.

2. Many people share the same three intense fears: being in high places, working with numbers, and speeches.

3. To decide on a career, students should think closely about their interests, hobbies, and what they are skilled at.

4. At the body shop, the car was sanded down to the bare metal, painted with primer, and red enamel was sprayed on.

5. To become a dancer, Lola is taking lessons, working in amateur shows, and auditioned for professional companies.

6. Juan's last job offered security; a better chance for advancement is offered by his new job.

7. People in today's world often try to avoid silence, whether on the job, in school, or when relaxing at home.

8. Because the dying woman was dignified and with courage, she won everyone's respect.

9. The politician trusted no one, rewarded loyalty, and was dependent only on his own instincts.

10. If we're not careful, we'll leave the next generation polluted air, contaminated water, and forests that are dying.

Activity

1

www.mhhe.com/langan

Use a Consistent Point of View

Consistency with Verbs

Do not shift verb tenses unnecessarily. If you begin writing a paper in the present tense, do not shift suddenly to the past. If you begin in the past, do not shift without reason to the present. Notice the inconsistent verb tenses in the following example:

Incorrect Jean *punched* down the risen yeast dough in the bowl. Then she *dumps* it onto the floured worktable and *kneaded* it into a smooth, shiny ball.

The verbs must be consistently in the present tense:

Correct Jean *punches* down the risen yeast dough in the bowl. Then she *dumps* it onto the floured worktable and *kneads* it into a smooth, shiny ball.

Or the verbs must be consistently in the past tense:

Correct Jean *punched* down the risen yeast dough in the bowl. Then she *dumped* it onto the floured worktable and *kneaded* it into a smooth, shiny ball.

Activity

2

Make the verbs in each sentence consistent with the *first* verb used. Cross out the incorrect verb and write the correct form in the space at the left.

EXAMPLE

___*ran*___ Aunt Flo tried to kiss her little nephew, but he ~~runs~~ out of the room.

_____ 1. An aggressive news photographer knocked a reporter to the ground as the movie stars arrive for the Academy Awards.

_____ 2. The winning wheelchair racer in the marathon slumped back in exhaustion and asks for some ice to soothe his blistered hands.

_____ 3. On the commercial for mail-order kitchen knives, an actor cuts a tree branch in half and sliced an aluminum can into ribbons.

_____ 4. "My husband is so dumb," said Martha, "that when he went to Las Vegas, he tries to play the soda machines."

_____ 5. The Jeep swerved around the corner, went up on two wheels, and tips over on its side.

_____ 6. In a zero-gravity atmosphere, water breaks up into droplets and floated around in space.

_____ 7. Ralph ripped open the bag of cheese puffs with his teeth, grabs handfuls of the salty orange squiggles, and stuffed them into his mouth.

_____ 8. From his perch high up on the rocky cliff, the eagle spots a white-tailed rabbit and swooped down toward his victim.

_____ 9. Several times a year, I like to take a day off, go away by myself, and recharged my mental batteries.

_____ 10. When the great earthquake struck San Francisco in 1906, the entire city burns to the ground in less than twenty-four hours.

Consistency with Pronouns

When writing a paper, you should not shift your point of view unnecessarily. Be consistent in your use of first-, second-, or third-person pronouns.

Point of View

	Singular	Plural
First-person pronouns	I (my, mine, me)	we (our, us)
Second-person pronouns	you (your)	you (your)
Third-person pronouns	he (his, him)	they (their, them)
	she (her)	
	it (its)	

TIP Any person, place, or thing, as well as any indefinite pronoun such as *one, anyone, someone,* and so on (page 505), is a third-person word.

For instance, if you start writing in the first person, *I,* do not jump suddenly to the second person, *you.* Or if you are writing in the third person, *they,* do not shift unexpectedly to *you.* Look at the following examples.

Inconsistent

One of the fringe benefits of my job is that *you* can use a company credit card for gasoline.

(The most common mistake people make is to let *you* slip into their writing after they start with another pronoun.)

Though *we* like most of *our* neighbors, there are a few *you* can't get along with.

(The writer begins with the first-person pronouns *we* and *our* but then shifts to the second-person *you*.)

Consistent

One of the fringe benefits of my job is that *I* can use a company credit card for gasoline.

Though *we* like most of *our* neighbors, there are a few *we* can't get along with.

Activity

3

Cross out inconsistent pronouns in the following sentences, and revise with the correct form of the pronoun above each crossed-out word.

EXAMPLE   When I examined the used car, ~~you~~ *I* could see that one of the front fenders had been replaced.

1. Many people are ignorant of side effects that diets can have on your health.

2. When I buy lipstick or nail polish, you never know how the color will actually look.

3. It is expensive for us to take public transportation to work every day, but what choice do you have if you can't afford a car?

4. During the border crisis, each country refused to change their aggressive stance.

5. If you want to do well in this course, one should plan on attending every day.

6. One of the things I love about my new apartment is that you can own a pet.

7. Toni refuses to eat pepperoni pizza because she says that it gives you indigestion.

8. It's hard for us to pay for health insurance, but you don't dare go without it.

9. People often take a first-aid course so that we can learn how to help choking and heart attack victims.

10. There are several ways you can impress your new boss. For example, one should dress well, arrive at work on time, and complete tasks efficiently.

Use Specific Words

To be an effective writer, you must use specific words rather than general words. Specific words create pictures in the reader's mind. They help capture interest and make your meaning clear. Compare the following sentences:

www.mhhe.com/langan

General	Specific
She walked down the street.	Anne wandered slowly along Rogers Lane.
Animals came into the place.	Hungry lions padded silently into the sawdust-covered arena.
The man signed the paper.	The biology teacher hastily scribbled his name on the course withdrawal slip.

The specific sentences create clear pictures in our minds. The details *show* us exactly what has happened.

Here are four ways to make your sentences specific.

1. Use exact names.

   He sold his *camper.*

   Luke sold his *Winnebago.*

2. Use lively verbs.

   The flag *moved* in the breeze.

   The flag *fluttered* in the breeze.

3. Use descriptive words (modifiers) before nouns.

   A man strained to lift the crate.

   A *heavyset, perspiring* man strained to lift the *heavy wooden* crate.

4. Use words that relate to the senses—sight, hearing, taste, smell, touch.

   That woman jogs five miles a day.

   That *fragile-looking, gray-haired* woman jogs five miles a day. (*sight*)

   A noise told the crowd that there were two minutes left to play.

   A *piercing whistle* told the *cheering* crowd that there were two minutes left to play. (*hearing*)

   When he returned, all he found in the refrigerator was bread and milk.

   When he returned, all he found in the refrigerator was *stale* bread and *sour* milk. (*taste*)

Neil stroked the kitten's fur until he felt its tiny claws on his hand.

Neil stroked the kitten's *velvety* fur until he felt its tiny, *needle-sharp* claws on his hand. (*touch*)

Fran placed a sachet in her bureau drawer.

Fran placed a *lilac-scented* sachet in her bureau drawer. (*smell*)

Activity

4

Revise the following sentences, replacing vague, indefinite words with sharp, specific ones.

EXAMPLE   *Several of our appliances* broke down at the same time.

Our washer, refrigerator, and television broke . . .

1. *Salty snacks* are my diet downfall.

_____

_____

_____

2. I swept aside the *things* on my desk to spread out the road map.

_____

_____

_____

3. Our neighbor's family room has *a lot of electronic equipment.*

_____

_____

_____

4. *Several sections* of the newspaper were missing.

_____

_____

_____

5. The doctor examined *various parts of my body* before diagnosing my illness as bronchitis.

_____

_____

_____

Again, you will practice changing vague, indefinite writing into lively, image-filled writing that helps capture the reader's interest and makes your meaning clear. With the help of the methods described on page 111, add specific details to the five sentences that follow. Note the two examples.

EXAMPLES   The person got off the bus.

The teenage boy bounded down the steps of the shiny yellow school bus.

She worked hard all summer.

All summer, Eva sorted peaches and blueberries in the hot, noisy canning factory.

1. The car would not start.

    _____

    _____

    _____

2. The test was difficult.

    _____

    _____

    _____

3. The boy was tired.

    _____

    _____

    _____

4. My room needs cleaning.

    _____

    _____

    _____

5. A vehicle blocked traffic.

    _____

    _____

    _____

Rewrite the sign pictured here using lively, image-filled writing that will grab people's attention.

www.mhhe.com/langan

Use Active Verbs

When the subject of a sentence performs the action of the verb, the verb is in the *active voice*. When the subject of a sentence receives the action of a verb, the verb is in the *passive voice*.

Passive voice uses a form of the verb *to be* (*am, is, are, was, were*) and the past participle of the main verb (usually the same as its past-tense form). Look at the following active and passive forms.

Passive	Active
The computer *was turned on* by Hakim.	Hakim *turned on* the computer.
The car's air conditioner *was fixed* by the mechanic.	The mechanic *fixed* the car's air conditioner

In general, active verbs are more effective than passive verbs. Active verbs give your writing a simpler and more vigorous style.

Revise the following sentences, changing verbs from the passive to the active voice and making any other word changes necessary.

Activity

6

EXAMPLE   Fruits and vegetables are painted often by artists.

Artists often paint fruits and vegetables.

1. Many unhealthy foods are included in the typical American diet.

    _____

2. The family picnic was invaded by hundreds of biting ants.

    _____

3. Antibiotics are used by doctors to treat many infections.

    _____

4. The fatal traffic accident was caused by a drunk driver.

    _____

5. Final grades will be determined by the instructor on the basis of class performance.

    _____

Use Concise Words

Wordiness—using more words than necessary to express a meaning—is often a sign of lazy or careless writing. Your readers may resent the extra time and energy they must spend when you have not done the work needed to make your writing direct and concise.

www.mhhe.com/langan

Here are two examples of wordy sentences:

In this paper, I am planning to describe the hobby that I enjoy of collecting old comic books.

In Ben's opinion, he thinks that cable television will change and alter our lives in the future.

Wordy

Omitting needless words improves these sentences:

I enjoy collecting old comic books.

Ben thinks that cable television will change our lives.

Clear

Following is a list of some wordy expressions that could be reduced to single words.

Wordy Form	Short Form
at the present time	now
in the event that	if
in the near future	soon
due to the fact that	because
for the reason that	because
is able to	can
in every instance	always
in this day and age	today
during the time that	while
a large number of	many
big in size	big
red in color	red
five in number	five
return back	return
good benefit	benefit
commute back and forth	commute
postponed until later	postponed

Activity 7

Revise the following sentences, omitting needless words.

1. In conclusion, I would like to end my essay by summarizing each of the major points that were covered within my paper.

    _____

    _____

2. Controlling the quality and level of the television shows that children watch is a continuing challenge to parents that they must meet on a daily basis.

    _____

    _____

3. In general, I am the sort of person who tends to be shy, especially in large crowds or with strangers I don't know well.

    _____

    _____

4. Someone who is analyzing magazine advertising can find hidden messages that, once uncovered, are seen to be clever and persuasive.

_____

_____

5. My greatest mistake that I made last week was to hurt my brother's feelings and then not to have the nerve to apologize and say how sorry I was.

_____

_____

6. In today's uncertain economic climate, it is clear that people, namely, average middle-class working people, have great difficulty saving much money or putting anything aside for emergencies.

_____

_____

7. We thought the television program that was on last night was enjoyable, whereas our parents reacted with dislike to the content of the show.

_____

_____

8. Because of the bad weather, the school district felt it would be safer to cancel classes and let everyone stay home than to risk people having accidents on the way to school.

_____

_____

9. Out of all the regrets in my life so far, one of my greatest ones to the present time is that I did not take additional art classes when I was still in high school and had a chance to do so.

_____

_____

10. It seems obvious to me, and it should be to everyone else, too, that people can be harmed as much by emotional abuse as by physical abuse, even if you don't lay a hand on them.

_____

_____

Vary Your Sentences

One part of effective writing is to vary the kinds of sentences you write. If every sentence follows the same pattern, writing may become monotonous to read. This section explains four ways you can create variety and interest in your writing style. It also describes coordination and subordination—two important techniques for achieving different kinds of emphasis in writing.

The following are four methods you can use to revise simple sentences, making them more complex and sophisticated:

- Add a second complete thought (coordination).

- Add a dependent thought (subordination).

- Begin with a special opening word or phrase.

- Place adjectives or verbs in a series.

Revise by Adding a Second Complete Thought

When you add a second complete thought to a simple sentence, the result is a *compound* (or double) sentence. The two complete statements in a compound sentence are usually connected by a comma and a joining or coordinating word (*and, but, for, or, nor, so, yet*).

A compound sentence is used to give equal weight to two closely related ideas. The technique of showing that ideas have equal importance is called *coordination*. Following are some compound sentences. In each case, the sentence contains two ideas that the writer considers equal in importance.

Greg worked on the engine for three hours, but the car still wouldn't start.

Bananas were on sale this week, so I bought a bunch for the children's lunches.

We laced up our roller blades, and then we moved cautiously onto the rink.

Activity

8

Combine the following pairs of simple sentences into compound sentences. Use a comma and a logical joining word (*and, but, for, so*) to connect each pair of statements.

> **HINT** If you are not sure what *and, but, for,* and *so* mean, review pages 472–473.

EXAMPLE   The weather was cold and windy.
             Al brought a thick blanket to the football game.

The weather was cold and windy, so Al brought a thick blanket to the

football game.

1. My son can't eat peanut butter snacks or sandwiches.
   He is allergic to peanuts.

   _____

   _____

2. I tried to sleep.
   The thought of tomorrow's math exam kept me awake.

   _____

   _____

3. This diner has its own bakery.
   It has take-out service as well.

   _____

   _____

4. The cardboard storage boxes were soggy.
   Rainwater had seeped into the basement during the storm.

   _____

   _____

5. I didn't have enough money to buy my parents an anniversary present.
   I offered to mow their lawn for the whole summer.

   _____

   _____

Revise by Adding a Dependent Thought

When you add a dependent thought to a simple sentence, the result is a *complex* sentence.* A dependent thought begins with one of the following subordinating words:

_____

*The two parts of a complex sentence are sometimes called an *independent clause* and a *dependent clause*. A *clause* is simply a word group that contains a subject and a verb. An independent clause expresses a complete thought and can stand alone. A dependent clause does not express a complete thought in itself and depends on the independent clause to complete its meaning. Dependent clauses always begin with a dependent or subordinating word.

www.mhhe.com/langan

> ## Subordinating Words
>
> | | | |
> |---|---|---|
> | after | if, even if | when, whenever |
> | although, though | in order that | where, wherever |
> | as | since | whether |
> | because | that, so that | which, whichever |
> | before | unless | while |
> | even though | until | who |
> | how | what, whatever | whose |

A complex sentence is used to emphasize one idea over another. Look at the following complex sentence:

Although the exam room was very quiet, I still couldn't concentrate.

The idea that the writer wishes to emphasize here—*I still couldn't concentrate*—is expressed as a complete thought. The less important idea—*Although the exam room was very quiet*—is subordinated to the complete thought. The technique of giving one idea less emphasis than another is called *subordination*.

Following are other examples of complex sentences. In each case, the part starting with the dependent word is the less emphasized part of the sentence.

Even though I was tired, I stayed up to watch the horror movie.

Before I take a bath, I check for spiders in the tub.

When Ivy feels nervous, she pulls on her earlobe.

Activity	Use logical subordinating words to combine the following pairs of simple sentences into sentences that contain a dependent thought. Place a comma after a dependent statement when it starts the sentence.
9	

EXAMPLE   Rita bit into the hard taffy.
            She broke a filling.

When Rita bit into the hard taffy, she broke a filling.

_____

1.   I had forgotten to lock the front door.
     I had to drive back to the house.

_____

_____

2. The bear turned over the rotten log.
   Fat white grubs crawled in every direction.

_____

_____

3. Kevin had ordered a set of tools.
   He changed his mind about spending the money.

_____

_____

4. Some people are allergic to wool.
   They buy sweaters made only from synthetic fibers.

_____

_____

5. An older woman in my typing class can type almost one hundred words a minute.
   She is having trouble landing a secretarial job.

_____

_____

Revise by Beginning with a Special Opening Word or Phrase

Among the special openers that can be used to start sentences are *-ed* words, *-ing* words, *-ly* words, *to* word groups, and prepositional phrases. Here are examples of all five kinds of openers:

-ed word

Concerned about his son's fever, Paul called a doctor.

-ing word

Humming softly, the woman browsed through the rack of dresses.

-ly word

Hesitantly, Sue approached the instructor's desk.

to **word group**

To protect her hair, Eva uses the lowest setting on her blow dryer.

Prepositional phrase

During the exam, drops of water fell from the ceiling.

Activity

10

Combine each of the following pairs of simple sentences into one sentence by using the opener shown at the left and omitting repeated words. Use a comma to set off the opener from the rest of the sentence.

EXAMPLE   *-ing* word   The pelican scooped small fish into its baggy bill. It dipped into the waves.

Dipping into the waves, the pelican scooped small fish into its baggy bill.

1. Shirley signed the repair contract.
    She was reluctant.

-ly word

_____

_____

to word group

2. The interns volunteered to work overtime.
    They wanted to improve their chances of promotion.

_____

_____

Prepositional phrase

3. The accused murderer grinned at the witnesses.
    He did this during the trial.

_____

_____

-ed word

4. The vet's office was noisy and confusing.
    It was crowded with nervous pets.

_____

_____

-ing word

5. Barry tried to find something worth watching.
    He flipped from channel to channel.

_____

_____

Revise by Placing Adjectives or Verbs in a Series

Various parts of a sentence may be placed in a series. Among these parts are adjectives (descriptive words) and verbs. Here are examples of both in a series:

Adjectives

I gently applied a *sticky new* Band-Aid to the *deep, ragged* cut on my finger.

Verbs

The truck *bounced* off a guardrail, *sideswiped* a tree, and *plunged* down the embankment.

Combine the simple sentences into one sentence by using adjectives or verbs in a series and by omitting repeated words. Use a comma when necessary between adjectives or verbs in a series.

Activity

11

EXAMPLE   Jesse spun the basketball on one finger.
He rolled it along his arms.
He dribbled it between his legs.

Jesse spun the basketball on one finger, rolled it along his arms, and

dribbled it between his legs.

1. The baby toddled across the rug.
He picked up a button.
He put the button in his mouth.

_____

_____

2. Water dribbled out of the tap.
The water was brown.
The water was foul-tasting.
The tap was rusty.
The tap was metal.

_____

_____

3. By 6 a.m., I had read the textbook chapter.
    I had taken notes on it.
    I had studied the notes.
    I had drunk eight cups of coffee.

    _____

    _____

4. The exterminator approached the wasps' nests hanging under the eaves.
    The nests were large.
    The nests were papery.
    The eaves were old.
    The eaves were wooden.

    _____

    _____

5. Reeds bordered the pond.
    The reeds were slim.
    The reeds were brown.
    The pond was green.
    The pond was stagnant.

    _____

    _____

Editing Sentences

After revising sentences in a paper so that they flow smoothly and clearly, you need to edit the paper for mistakes in grammar, punctuation, mechanics, usage, and spelling. Even if a paper is otherwise well-written, it will make an unfavorable impression on readers if it contains such mistakes. To edit a paper, check it against the agreed-upon rules, or conventions, of written English—simply called *sentence skills* in this book. Here are the most common of these conventions:

> ✓   Write complete sentences rather than fragments.
> ✓   Do not write run-on sentences.
> ✓   Use verb forms correctly.
> ✓   Make sure that subject, verbs, and pronouns agree.
>
> *(continued)*

✓ Eliminate faulty modifiers.

✓ Use pronoun forms correctly.

✓ Use capital letters where needed.

✓ Use the following marks of punctuation correctly: apostrophe, quotation marks, comma, semicolon, colon, hyphen, dash, parentheses.

✓ Use correct manuscript form.

✓ Eliminate slang, clichés, and pretentious words.

✓ Check for possible spelling errors.

✓ Eliminate careless errors.

These sentence skills are treated in detail in Part Four of this book, and they can be referred to easily as needed. Both the list of sentence skills on the inside back cover of this book and the correction symbols on page 632 include page references so that you can turn quickly to any skill you want to check.

Hints about Editing

These hints can help you edit the next-to-final draft of a paper for sentence-skill mistakes:

1. Have at hand two essential tools: a good dictionary and a grammar handbook (you can use the one in this book beginning on page 446).

2. Use a sheet of paper to cover your essay so that you will expose only one sentence at a time. Look for errors in grammar, spelling, and typing. It may help to read each sentence out loud. If a sentence does not read clearly and smoothly, chances are something is wrong.

3. Pay special attention to the kinds of errors you tend to make. For example, if you tend to write run-ons or fragments, be especially on the lookout for those errors.

4. Try to work on a typewritten or word-processed draft, where you'll be able to see your writing more objectively than you can on a handwritten page; use a pen with colored ink so that your corrections will stand out.

> **TIP** A series of editing tests appears on pages 604–617. You will probably find it most helpful to take these tests after reviewing the sentences skills in Part Four.

www.mhhe.com/langan

Proofreading

Proofreading means closely checking the final, edited draft of your paper for typos and other careless errors. A helpful strategy is to read your paper backward, from the last sentence to the first. This helps keep you from getting caught up in the flow of the paper and missing small mistakes. Here are six helpful proofing symbols:

Proofing Symbol	Meaning	Example
∧	insert missing letter or word	ach*i*eve
⎯⎯℮	omit	draw two ~~two~~ conclusions
⌒⌒	reverse order of words or letters	lived happily after ever
#	add space	all#right
⌒	close up space	base ball
cap, lc	Add a capital (or a lowercase) letter	(cap) My english Class (lc)

If you make many corrections, retype the page or enter corrections into your word-processor file and reprint the page.

Activity

12

In the spaces below this paragraph, write the numbers of the ten word groups that contain fragments or run-ons. Then, in the spaces between the lines, edit by making the necessary corrections. One is done for you as an example.

A unique object in my family's living room is an ashtray. Which I made in second grade. I can still remember the pride I felt. When I presented it to my mother. Now, I'm amazed that my parents didn't hide it away at the back of a shelf it is a remarkably ugly object. The ashtray is made out of brown clay that I had tried to mold into a perfect circle, unfortunately my class was only forty-five minutes long. The best I could do was to shape it into a lopsided oval. Its most distinctive feature, though, is the grooves carved into its rim. I had theorized that each groove could hold a cigarette or cigar, I made at least fifty of them.   I somehow failed to consider that the only person who smoked in my family was my father.   Who smoked about five cigars a year.   Further, although our living room is decorated in sedate tans and blues, my ashtray is bright purple,   My favorite color at the time.

 For variety, it has stripes around its rim they are colored neon green.   My parents have proudly displayed my little masterpiece on their coffee table for the past ten years.   If I ever wonder if my parents love me,   I look at that ugly ashtray, the answer is plain to see.

1. __2__   3. _____   5. _____   7. _____   9. _____

2. _____   4. _____   6. _____   8. _____   10. _____

Practice in Revising Sentences

You now know the fourth step in effective writing: revising and editing sentences. You also know that practice in *editing* sentences is best undertaken after you have worked through the sentence skills in Part Four. The focus in this section, then, will be on *revising* sentences—using a variety of methods to ensure that your sentences flow smoothly and are clear and interesting. You will work through Review Tests on the following:

- using parallelism
- using a consistent point of view
- using specific words
- using active verbs
- using concise words
- varying your sentences

Using Parallelism

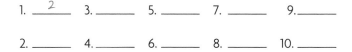

Cross out the unbalanced part of each sentence. In the space provided, revise the unbalanced part so that it matches the other item or items in the sentence.

EXAMPLE   Cigarette smoking is expensive, disgusting, and ~~a health risk~~. *unhealthy*

1. Jesse prefers books that are short, scary, and filled with suspense.

   _____

2. A sale on electrical appliances, furniture for the office, and stereo equipment begins this Friday.

   _____

3. To escape the stresses of everyday life, I rely on watching television, reading books, and my kitchen.

   _____

4. The keys to improving grades are to take effective notes in class, to plan study time, and preparing carefully for exams.

   _____

5. Qualities that I look for in friends are a sense of humor, being kind, and dependability.

   _____

6. My three favorite jobs were veterinary assistant, gardener, and selling toys.

   _____

7. Housekeeping shortcuts will help you speed up doing laundry, cleaning rooms, and food on the table.

   _____

8. Studying a little every day is more effective than to cram.

   _____

9. The chickens travel on a conveyor belt, where they are plucked, washed, rinsed, and bags are put on them.

   _____

10. The speaker impressed the audience because of his clear, reasonable presentation with friendliness as well.

   _____

Review Test   2

Cross out the unbalanced part of each sentence. In the space provided, revise the unbalanced part so that it matches the other item or items in the sentence.

1. Paying college tuition and not studying is as sensible as to buy tickets to a movie and not watching it. _____

2. The best programming on television includes news coverage, shows on science, and children's series. _____

3. Curling overgrown vines, porch furniture that was rotted, and sagging steps were my first impressions of the neglected house. _____

4. The little girl came home from school with a tear-streaked face, a black eye, and her shirt was torn. _____

5. There are two ways to the top floor: climb the stairs or taking the elevator. _____

6. While waiting for the exam to start, small groups of nervous students glanced over their notes, drank coffee, and were whispering to each other. _____

7. In many ways, starting college at forty is harder than to start at eighteen. _____

8. Interesting work is as important to me as pay that is good. _____

9. The homeless woman shuffled along the street, bent over to pick something up, and was putting it in her shopping bag. _____

10. A teamsters' strike now would mean interruptions in food deliveries, a slowdown in the economy, and losing wages for workers. _____

Using a Consistent Point of View

Review Test   3

Change verbs as needed in the following selection so that they are consistently in the past tense. Cross out each incorrect verb and write the correct form above it, as shown in the example. You will need to make ten corrections.

My uncle's shopping trip last Thursday was discouraging to him. First of

        found
all, he had to drive around for fifteen minutes until he finds a parking space.

There was a half-price special on paper products in the supermarket, and every spot is taken. Then, when he finally got inside, many of the items on his list were not where he expected. For example, the pickles he wanted are not on the same shelf as all the other pickles. Instead, they were in a refrigerated case next to the bacon. And the granola was not on the cereal shelves but in the health-food section. Shopping thus proceeds slowly. About halfway through his list, he knew there would not be time to cook dinner and decides to pick up a barbecued chicken. The chicken, he learned, was available at the end of the store he had already passed. So he parks his shopping cart in an aisle, gets the chicken, and came back. After adding half a dozen more items to his cart, he suddenly realizes it contained someone else's food. So he retraced his steps, found his own cart, transfers the groceries, and continued to shop. Later, when he began loading items onto the checkout counter, he notices that the barbecued chicken was missing. He must have left it in the other cart, certainly gone by now. Feeling totally defeated, he returned to the deli counter and says to the clerk, "Give me another chicken. I lost the first one." My uncle told me that when he saw the look on the clerk's face, he felt as if he'd flunked Food Shopping.

Review Test   4

Cross out inconsistent pronouns in the following sentences, and revise with the correct form of the pronoun above each crossed-out word.

EXAMPLE   Dog owners should put tags on their dogs in case ~~you~~ *they* lose their pets.

1. These days, people never seem to get the recognition they deserve no matter how hard you work.

2. All you could hear was the maddening rattle of the heating register, even though I buried my face in the pillow.

3. When we answer the telephone at work, you are supposed to say the company's name.

4. Each year I pay more money for my college tuition. But despite the cost, one must complete college to get a better, more meaningful job.

5. Gary bought the used car from a local dealership. The car was so clean and shiny that you could not tell that the engine needed to be replaced.

6. I would like to go to a school where one can meet many people who are different from me.

7. When I first began to work as a waitress, I was surprised at how rude some customers were to you.

8. When you drive on the highway, I get disgusted at the amount of trash I see.

9. Students may not leave the exam room unless you have turned in the exam.

10. Nina wanted to just browse through the store, but in every department a salesperson came up and asked to help you.

Using Specific Words

Review Test   5

Revise the following sentences, changing vague, indefinite words to sharp, specific ones.

1. When my marriage broke up, I felt *various emotions*.

   _____

   _____

   _____

2. The *food choices* in the cafeteria were unappetizing.

   _____

   _____

   _____

3. *Bugs* invaded our kitchen and pantry this summer.

   _____

   _____

   _____

4. All last week, *the weather was terrible.*

    _____

    _____

    _____

5. In the car accident, our teacher suffered *a number of injuries.*

    _____

    _____

    _____

Review Test   6

With the help of the methods described on page 111, add specific details to the sentences that follow.

1. The salesperson was obnoxious.

    _____

    _____

    _____

2. The child started to cry.

    _____

    _____

    _____

3. The game was exciting.

    _____

    _____

    _____

4. The lounge area was busy.

    _____

    _____

    _____

5. A passenger on the bus was acting strangely.

_____

_____

_____

Using Active Verbs

Review Test   **7**

Revise the following sentences, changing verbs from the passive to the active voice and making any other necessary word changes.

EXAMPLE   Soccer is played by children all over the world.

Children all over the world play soccer. _____

1. The pizza restaurant was closed by the health inspector.

_____

2. Huge stacks of donated books were sorted by the workers in the library.

_____

3. My computer was infected by a virus.

_____

4. Gasoline prices will not be increased by oil companies this winter.

_____

5. High-powered bombs were dropped by our airplanes onto enemy bases.

_____

6. An additional charge was placed on our phone bill by the telephone company.

_____

7. The community center was damaged by a group of vandals.

_____

8. Stress is relieved by physical activity, meditation, and relaxation.

_____

9. Taxes will be raised by the federal government to pay for highway improvements.

_____

10. Studies show that violent behavior among young children is increased by watching violent TV programs.

_____

Using Concise Words

 **8**

Revise the following sentences, omitting needless words.

1. I finally made up my mind and decided to look for a new job.

_____

_____

2. Due to the fact that the printer was out of paper, Renee went to the store for the purpose of buying some.

_____

_____

3. Tamika realized suddenly that her date had stood her up and was not going to show up.

_____

_____

4. Our teacher does not know at this point in time whether she will return to our school next year.

_____

_____

5. The salesperson advised us not to buy the laptop at this time because it was going to have a drop in price in the very near future.

_____

_____

Review Test 9

Revise the following sentences, omitting needless words.

1. The policy at our company at the present time is that there are two coffee breaks, with each of them being fifteen minutes long.

    _____

    _____

2. Permit us to take this opportunity to inform you that your line of credit has been increased.

    _____

    _____

3. I have a strong preference for candy over fruit, which, in my opinion, doesn't taste as good as candy does.

    _____

    _____

4. Lynn is one of those people who rarely admits being wrong, and it is very unusual to hear her acknowledge that she has made a mistake.

    _____

    _____

5. Many people are of the opinion that children should be required by law to attend school until they reach the age of sixteen years old.

    _____

    _____

Varying Your Sentences

Review Test 10

Combine each of the following groups of simple sentences into one longer sentence. Omit repeated words. Various combinations are often possible, so try to find the combination in each group that flows most smoothly and clearly.

1. Sophie had repaired her broken watchband with a paper clip.
    The clip snapped.
    The watch slid off her wrist.

    _____

    _____

2. The physical therapist watched.
    Julie tried to stand on her weakened legs.
    They crumpled under her.

    _____

    _____

3. There were parking spaces on the street.
    Richard pulled into an expensive garage.
    He did not want to risk damage to his new car.

    _____

    _____

4. The truck was speeding.
    The truck was brown.
    The truck skidded on some ice.
    The truck almost hit a police officer.
    The police officer was startled.
    The police officer was young.

    _____

    _____

5. The rainstorm flooded our basement.
    The rainstorm was sudden.
    The rainstorm was terrible.
    It knocked slates off the roof.
    It uprooted a young tree.

    _____

    _____

Review Test 11

Combine each of the following groups of simple sentences into two longer sentences. Omit repeated words. Various combinations are often possible, so try to find combinations in each group that flow most smoothly and clearly.

1. A sudden cold front hit the area.
    Temperatures dropped thirty degrees in less than an hour.
    My teeth began to chatter.
    I was not wearing a warm jacket.

_____

_____

_____

2.   Vern works as a model.
He has to look his best.
He gained ten pounds recently.
He had to take off the extra weight.
He would have lost his job.

_____

_____

_____

3.   The ball game was about to begin.
A dog ran onto the field.
The dog began nipping the infielders' ankles.
The game had to be delayed.
The dog was chased away.

_____

_____

_____

4.   The lion was hungry.
It watched the herd of gazelle closely.
A young or sick animal wandered away from the group.
The lion would move in for the kill.

_____

_____

_____

5.   My aunt decided to find a helpful form of exercise.
She was suffering from arthritis.
She learned that swimming is very healthful.
It works every muscle group in the body without straining the muscles.

_____

_____

_____

Review Test 12

Combine the sentences in the following paragraph into four sentences. Omit repeated words. Try to find combinations in each case that flow as smoothly and clearly as possible.

Lena and Miles wanted a vacation. They wanted a vacation that was nice. They wanted one that was quiet. They wanted one that was relaxing. They rented a small lakeside cabin. Their first day there was very peaceful. The situation quickly changed. A large family moved into a nearby cabin. They played music at top volume. They raced around in a speedboat with a loud whining engine. Lena and Miles were no longer very relaxed. They packed up their things. They drove off. They returned to their quiet apartment.

_____

_____

_____

_____

_____

_____

_____

_____

_____

_____

Four Bases for Revising Essays

6

This chapter will show you how to evaluate an essay for

- unity
- support
- coherence
- sentence skills

© Michael Ainsworth/Dallas Morning News/Corbis

What emotions come to mind as you look at this photograph taken in the aftermath of Hurricane Katrina? Write an essay about a tragedy you have experienced in your own life. What was the experience like and how did it change you—for better or worse? After writing the first draft of your essay, check that you have covered the four bases of writing: unity, support, coherence, and sentence skills.

In the preceding chapters, you learned four essential steps in writing an effective paper. The box below shows how the steps lead to four standards, or bases, you can use in revising an essay.

Four Steps ⟶	Four Bases
1 If you advance a single point and stick to that point,	your paper will have *unity*.
2 If you support the point with specific evidence,	your paper will have *support*.
3 If you organize and connect the specific evidence,	your paper will have *coherence*.
4 If you write clear, error-free sentences,	your paper will demonstrate effective *sentence skills*.

This chapter discusses these four bases—unity, support, coherence, and sentence skills—and shows how the four bases can be used to evaluate and revise a paper.

Base 1: Unity

Understanding Unity

The following student essays are on the topic "Problems or Pleasures of My Teenage Years." Which one makes its point more clearly and effectively, and why?

Essay 1

Teenage Pranks

Looking back at some of the things I did as a teenager makes me break   1
out in a sweat. The purpose of each adventure was fun, but occasionally
things got out of hand. In my search for good times, I was involved in three
notable pranks, ranging from fairly harmless to fairly serious.

The first prank proved that good, clean fun does not have to be dull. As   2
a high school student, I was credited with making the world's largest dessert.
With several friends, I spent an entire year collecting boxes of Jell-O. Entering
our school's indoor pool one night, we turned the water temperature up as

(continued)

high as it would go and poured in box after box of the strawberry powder. The next morning, school officials arrived to find the pool filled with thirteen thousand gallons of the quivering, rubbery stuff. No one was hurt by the prank, but we did suffer through three days of a massive cleanup.

Not all my pranks were harmless, and one involved risking my life. As soon as I got my driver's license, I wanted to join the Fliers' Club. Membership in this club was limited to those who could make their cars fly a distance of at least ten feet. The qualifying site was an old quarry field where friends and I had built a ramp made of dirt. I drove my battered Ford Pinto up this ramp as fast as it would go. The Pinto flew ten feet, but one of the tires exploded when I landed. The car rolled on its side, and I luckily escaped with only a bruised arm.   3

Risking my own life was bad enough, but there was another prank where other people could have been hurt, too. On this occasion, I accidentally set a valley on fire. Two of my friends and I were sitting on a hill sharing a few beers. It was a warm summer night, and there was absolutely nothing to do. The idea came like a thunderclap. We collected a supply of large plastic trash bags, emergency highway flares, and a half tank of helium left over from a science-fair experiment. Then we began to construct a fleet of UFOs. Filling the bags with helium, we tied them closed with wire and suspended several burning flares below each bag. Our UFOs leaped into the air like an army of invading Martians. Rising and darting in the blackness, they convinced even us. Our fun turned into horror, though, as we watched the balloons begin to drop onto the wooded valley of expensive homes below. Soon, a brushfire started and, quickly sobered, we hurried off to call the fire department anonymously.   4

Every so often, I think back on the things that I did as a teenager. I chuckle at the innocent pranks and feel lucky that I didn't harm myself or others with the not-so-innocent ones. Those years were filled with wild times. Today I'm older, wiser—and maybe just a little more boring.   5

Problems of My Adolescence   Essay 2

In the unreal world of television situation comedies, teenagers are carefree, smart, funny, wisecracking, secure kids. In fact, most of them are more "together" than the adults on the shows. This, however, isn't how I   1

(continued)

recall my teenage years at all. As a teen, I suffered. Every day, I battled the terrible physical, family, and social troubles of adolescence.

For one thing, I had to deal with a demoralizing physical problem—acne. **2** Some days, I would wake up in the morning with a red bump the size of a taillight on my nose. Since I worried constantly about my appearance anyway, acne outbreaks could turn me into a crying, screaming maniac. Plastering on a layer of (at the time) orange-colored Clearasil, which didn't fool anybody, I would slink into school, hoping that the boy I had a crush on would be absent that day. Within the last few years, however, treatments for acne have improved. Now, skin doctors prescribe special drugs that clear up pimples almost immediately. An acne attack could shatter whatever small amount of self-esteem I had managed to build up.

In addition to fighting acne, I felt compelled to fight my family. As a **3** teenager, I needed to be independent. At that time, the most important thing in life was to be close to my friends and to try out new, more adult experiences. Unfortunately, my family seemed to get in the way. My little brother, for instance, turned into my enemy. We are close now, though. In fact, Eddie recently painted my new apartment for me. Eddie used to barge into my room, make calls on my cell phone, and read my e-mail. I would threaten to tie him up and leave him in a garbage dumpster. He would scream, my mother would yell, and all hell would break loose. My parents, too, were enemies. They wouldn't let me stay out late, wear the clothes I wanted to wear, or hang around with the friends I liked. So I tried to get revenge on them by being miserable, sulky, and sarcastic at home.

Worst of all, I had to face the social traumas of being a teenager. **4** Things that were supposed to be fun, like dates and dances, were actually horrible. On the few occasions when I had a real date, I agonized over everything—my hair, my weight, my pimples. After a date, I would come home, raid the kitchen, and drown my insecurities in a sea of junk food. Dances were also stressful events. My friends and I would sneak a couple of beers just to get up the nerve to walk into the school gym. Now I realize that teenage drinking is dangerous. I read recently that the number-one killer of teenagers is drunk driving. At dances, I never relaxed. It was too important to look exactly right, to act really cool, and to pretend I was having fun.

I'm glad I'm not a teenager anymore. I wouldn't ever want to feel so **5** unattractive, so confused, and so insecure again. I'll gladly accept the crow's-feet and stomach bulge of adulthood in exchange for a little peace of mind.

Fill in the blanks.

Activity

1

Essay _____ makes its point more clearly and effectively because _____

_____

_____

EXPLANATION: Essay 1 is more effective because it is unified. All the details in this essay are on target; they support and develop each of its three topic sentences ("The first prank proved that good, clean fun does not have to be dull"; "Not all my pranks were harmless, and one involved risking my life"; and "Risking my own life was bad enough, but there was another prank where other people could have been hurt, too").

On the other hand, essay 2 contains some details irrelevant to its topic sentences. In the first supporting paragraph (paragraph 2), for example, the sentences "Within the last few years, however, treatments for acne have improved. Now, skin doctors prescribe special drugs that clear up pimples almost immediately" do not support the writer's topic statement that she had to deal with the physical problem of acne. Such details should be left out in the interest of unity.

The difference between these first two essays leads us to the first base, or standard, of effective writing: *unity*. To achieve unity is to have all the details in your paper related to your thesis and to your three supporting topic sentences. Each time you think of something to put into your paper, ask yourself whether it relates to your thesis and your supporting points. If it does not, leave it out. For example, if you were writing a paper about the problems of being unemployed and then spent a couple of sentences talking about the pleasures of having a lot of free time, you would be missing the first and most essential base of good writing.

www.mhhe.com/langan

Revising for Unity

Go back to essay 2 and cross out the two sentences in the second supporting paragraph (paragraph 3) and the two sentences in the third supporting paragraph (paragraph 4) that are off target and do not support their topic sentences.

Activity

2

Base 2: Support

Understanding Support

The following essays were written on "Dealing with Disappointment." Both are unified, but one communicates more clearly and effectively. Which one, and why?

Essay 1

Dealing with Disappointment

One way to look at life is as a series of disappointments. Life can   1
certainly appear that way because disappointment crops up in the life of
everyone more often, it seems, than satisfaction. How disappointments are
handled can have a great bearing on how life is viewed. People can react
negatively by sulking or by blaming others, or they can try to understand the
reasons behind the disappointment.

Sulking is one way to deal with disappointment. This attitude—Why   2
does everything always happen to me?—is common because it is easy to
adopt, but it is not very productive. Everyone has had the experience of
meeting people who specialize in feeling sorry for themselves. A sulky
manner will often discourage others from wanting to lend support, and it
prevents the sulker from making positive moves toward self-help. It becomes
easier just to sit back and sulk. Unfortunately, feeling sorry for oneself does
nothing to lessen the pain of disappointment. It may, in fact, increase the
pain. It certainly does not make future disappointments easier to bear.

Blaming others is another negative and unproductive way to cope with   3
disappointment. This all-too-common response of pointing the finger at
someone else doesn't help one's situation. This posture will lead only to
anger, resentment, and, therefore, further unhappiness. Disappointment in
another's performance does not necessarily indicate that the performer is
at fault. Perhaps expectations were too high, or there could have been a
misunderstanding as to what the performer actually intended to accomplish.

A positive way to handle disappointment is to try to understand   4
the reasons behind the disappointment. An analysis of the causes of
disappointment can have an excellent chance of producing desirable results.
Often understanding alone can help alleviate the pain of disappointment
and can help prevent future disappointments. Also, it is wise to try to
remember that what would be ideal is not necessarily what is reasonable to
expect in any given situation. The ability to look disappointment squarely in
the face and then go on from there is the first step on the road back.

Continuous handling of disappointment in a negative manner can lead   5
to a negative view of life itself. Chances for personal happiness in such a

(continued)

---

state of being are understandably slim. Learning not to expect perfection in an imperfect world and keeping in mind those times when expectations were actually surpassed are positive steps toward allowing the joys of life to prevail.

Reactions to Disappointment   Essay 2

1. Ben Franklin said that the only sure things in life are death and taxes. He left something out, however: disappointment. No one gets through life without experiencing many disappointments. Strangely, though, most people seem unprepared for disappointment and react to it in negative ways. They feel depressed or try to escape their troubles instead of using disappointment as an opportunity for growth.

2. One negative reaction to disappointment is depression. For example, Helen, a woman trying to win a promotion, works hard for over a year in her department. Helen is so sure she will get the promotion, in fact, that she has already picked out the car she will buy when her salary increase comes through. However, the boss names one of Helen's coworkers to the spot. The fact that all the other department employees tell Helen that she is the one who really deserved the promotion doesn't help her deal with the crushing disappointment. Deeply depressed, Helen decides that all her goals are doomed to defeat. She loses her enthusiasm for her job and can barely force herself to show up every day. Helen tells herself that she is a failure and that doing a good job just isn't worth the work.

3. Another negative reaction to disappointment, and one that often follows depression, is the desire to escape. Jamal fails to get into the college his brother is attending, the college that was the focus of all his dreams, and decides to escape his disappointment. Why worry about college at all? Instead, he covers up his real feelings by giving up on his schoolwork and getting completely involved with friends, parties, and "good times." Or Carla doesn't make the varsity basketball team—something she wanted very badly—and so refuses to play sports at all. She decides to hang around with a new set of friends who get high every day; then she won't have to confront her disappointment and learn to live with it.

4. The positive way to react to disappointment is to use it as a chance for growth. This isn't easy, but it's the only useful way to deal with an inevitable part of life. Helen, the woman who wasn't promoted, could have handled her disappointment by looking at other options. If her boss doesn't

(continued)

recognize her talent and hard work, perhaps she could transfer to another department. Or she could ask the boss how to improve her performance so that she would be a shoo-in for the next promotion. Jamal, the boy who didn't get into the college of his choice, should look into other schools. Going to another college may encourage him to be his own person, step out of his brother's shadow, and realize that being turned down by one college isn't a final judgment on his abilities or potential. Rather than escape into drugs, Carla could improve her basketball skills for a year or pick up another sport—like swimming or tennis—that would probably turn out to be more useful to her as an adult.

Disappointments are unwelcome but regular visitors to everyone's life.   5
We can feel depressed about them, or we can try to escape from them. The best thing, though, is to accept a disappointment and then try to use it somehow: step over the unwelcome visitor on the doorstep and get on with life.

Activity 3

Fill in the blanks.

Essay _____ makes its point more clearly and effectively because _____

_____

_____

EXPLANATION: Here, essay 2 is more effective, for it offers specific examples of the ways people deal with disappointment. We see for ourselves the kinds of reactions people have to disappointment.

Essay 1, on the other hand, gives us no specific evidence. The writer tells us repeatedly that sulking, blaming others, and trying to understand the reasons behind a disappointment are the reactions people have to a letdown. However, the writer never *shows* us any of these responses in action. Exactly what kinds of disappointments is the writer talking about? And how, for instance, does someone analyze the causes of disappointment? Would a person write a list of causes on a piece of paper, or review the causes with a concerned friend, or speak to a professional therapist? In an essay like this, we would want to see *examples* of how sulking and blaming others are negative ways of dealing with disappointment.

Consideration of these two essays leads us to the second base of effective writing: *support*. After realizing the importance of specific supporting details, one student writer revised a paper she had done on being lost in the woods as the worst

experience of her childhood. In the revised paper, instead of talking about "the terror of being separated from my parents," she referred to such specifics as "tears streamed down my cheeks as I pictured the faces I would never see again" and "I clutched the locket my parents had given me as if it were a lucky charm that could help me find my way back to the campsite." All your papers should include such vivid details.

Revising for Support

On a separate sheet of paper, revise one of the three supporting paragraphs in "Dealing with Disappointment" by providing specific supporting examples.

Activity

4

Base 3: Coherence

Understanding Coherence

The following two essays were written on the topic "Positive or Negative Effects of Television." Both are unified, and both are supported. However, one communicates more clearly and effectively. Which one, and why?

Harmful Effects of Watching Television   Essay 1

In a recent cartoon, one character said to another, "When you think of   1
the awesome power of television to educate, aren't you glad it doesn't?"
It's true that television has the power to educate and to entertain, but
unfortunately, these benefits are outweighed by the harm it does to
dedicated viewers. Television is harmful because it creates passivity,
discourages communication, and presents a false picture of reality.

Television makes viewers passive. Children who have an electronic   2
babysitter spend most of their waking hours in a semiconscious state.
Older viewers watch tennis matches and basketball games with none
of the excitement of being in the stands. Even if children are watching
Sesame Street or Barney & Friends, they are being educated passively. The
child actors are going on nature walks, building crafts projects, playing
with animals, and participating in games, but the little viewers are simply
watching. Older viewers watch guests discuss issues with Oprah Winfrey, but
no one will turn to the home viewers to ask their opinion.

Worst of all, TV presents a false picture of reality that leaves viewers   3
frustrated because they don't have the beauty or wealth of the characters on

(continued)

---

television. Viewers absorb the idea that everyone else in the United States owns a lavish apartment, a suburban house, a sleek car, and an expensive wardrobe. Every detective, police officer, oil baron, and lawyer, male or female, is suitable for a pinup poster. The material possessions on TV shows and commercials contribute to the false image of reality. News anchors and reporters, with their perfect hair and makeup, must fit television's standard of beauty. From their modest homes or cramped apartments, many viewers tune in daily to the upper-middle-class world that TV glorifies.

Television discourages communication. Families watching television do   4
very little talking except for brief exchanges during commercials. If Uncle Bernie or the next-door neighbors drop in for a visit, the most comfortable activity for everyone may be not conversation but watching ESPN. The family may not even be watching the same set; instead, in some households, all the family members head for their own rooms to watch their own sets. At dinner, plates are plopped on the coffee table in front of the set, and the meal is wolfed down during NBC Nightly News. During commercials, the only communication a family has all night may consist of questions like "Do we have any popcorn?" and "Where's TV Guide?"

Television, like cigarettes or saccharin, is harmful to our health. We   5
are becoming isolated, passive, and frustrated. And, most frightening, the average viewer now spends more time watching television than ever before.

The Benefits of Television

Essay 2

We hear a lot about the negative effects of television on the viewer.   1
Obviously, television can be harmful if it is watched constantly to the exclusion of other activities. It would be just as harmful to listen to CDs all the time or to eat constantly. However, when television is watched in moderation, it is extremely valuable, as it provides relaxation, entertainment, and education.

First of all, watching TV has the value of sheer relaxation. Watching   2
television can be soothing and restful after an eight-hour day of pressure, challenges, or concentration. After working hard all day, people look forward to a new episode of a favorite show or yet another showing of Casablanca or Anchorman. This period of relaxation leaves viewers refreshed and ready to take on the world again. Watching TV also seems to reduce stress in some people. This benefit of television is just beginning to be recognized. One doctor, for example, advises his patients with high blood pressure to relax in the evening with a few hours of television.

(continued)

In addition to being relaxing, television is entertaining. Along with the standard comedies, dramas, and game shows that provide enjoyment to viewers, television offers a variety of movies and sports events. Moreover, viewers can pay a monthly fee and receive special cable programming or Direct TV. Viewers can watch first-run movies, rock and classical music concerts, and specialized sports events, like international soccer and Grand Prix racing. Viewers can also buy or rent movies and TV shows on DVD. Still another growing area of TV entertainment is video games. PlayStation, Xbox, and Nintendo consoles allow the owner to have a video-game arcade in the living room.

3

Most important, television is educational. Preschoolers learn colors, numbers, and letters from public television programs, like Sesame Street, that use animation and puppets to make learning fun. On the Discovery Channel, science shows for older children go on location to analyze everything from volcanoes to rocket launches. Adults, too, can get an education (college credits included) from courses given on television. Also, television widens our knowledge by covering important events and current news. Viewers can see and hear presidents' speeches, state funerals, natural disasters, and election results as they are happening.

4

Perhaps because television is such a powerful force, we like to criticize it and search for its flaws. However, the benefits of television should not be ignored. We can use television to relax, to have fun, and to make ourselves smarter. This electronic wonder, then, is a servant, not a master.

5

Fill in the blanks.

Essay _____ makes its point more clearly and effectively because _____

_____

_____

Activity

5

EXPLANATION: In this case, essay 2 is more effective because the material is organized clearly and logically. Using emphatic order, the writer develops three positive uses of television, ending with the most important use: television as an educational tool. The writer includes transitional words that act as signposts, making movement from one idea to the next easy to follow. The major transitions include *First of all*, *In addition*, and *Most important;*

(continued)

transitions within paragraphs include such words as *Moreover, Still another, too,* and *Also.* And this writer also uses a linking sentence ("In addition to being relaxing, television is entertaining") to tie the first and second supporting paragraphs together clearly.

Although essay 1 is unified and supported, the writer does not have any clear and consistent way of organizing the material. The most important idea (signaled by the phrase *Worst of all*) is discussed in the second supporting paragraph instead of being saved for last. None of the supporting paragraphs organizes its details in a logical fashion. The first supporting paragraph, for example, discusses older viewers, then goes to younger viewers, then jumps back to older people again. The third supporting paragraph, like the first, leaps from an opening idea (families talking only during commercials) to several intervening ideas and then back to the original idea (talking during commercials). In addition, essay 1 uses practically no transitional devices to guide the reader.

www.mhhe.com/langan

These two essays lead us to the third base of effective writing: *coherence.* All the supporting ideas and sentences in a paper must be organized so that they cohere, or "stick together." As has been discussed in Chapter 4, key techniques for tying together the material in a paper include a clear method of organization (such as time order or emphatic order), transitions, and other connecting words.

Revising for Coherence

Activity

6

On a separate sheet of paper, revise one of the three supporting paragraphs in "Harmful Effects of Watching Television" by providing a clear method of organizing the material and transitional words.

Base 4: Sentence Skills

Understanding Sentence Skills

Following are the opening paragraphs from two essays. Both are unified, supported, and organized, but one version communicates more clearly and effectively. Which one, and why?

"revenge"

[1]Revenge is one of those things that everyone enjoy. [2]People don't like to talk about it, though. [3]Just the same, there is nothing more tempting, more satisfying, or with the reward of a bit of revenge. [4]The purpose is not to harm your victims. [5]But to let them know that you are upset about something they are doing. [6]Careful plotting can provide you with relief from bothersom coworkers, gossiping friends, or nagging family members.

[7]Coworkers who make comments about the fact that you are always fifteen minutes late for work can be taken care of very simply. [8]The first thing that you should do is to get up extra early one day. [9]Before the sun comes up, drive to each coworker's house, reach under the hood of his car, and disconnected the center wire that leads to the distrib. cap. [10]The car will be unharmed, but it will not start, and your friends at work will all be late for work on the same day. [11]If your lucky, your boss might notice that you are the only one there and will give you a raise. [12]Later if you feel guilty about your actions you can call each person anonymously and tell them how to get the car running. . . .

Essay 1, First Part

A Bit of Revenge

Revenge is one of those things that everyone enjoys. People don't like to talk about it, though. Just the same, there is nothing more tempting, more satisfying, or more rewarding than a bit of revenge. The purpose is not to harm your victims but to let them know that you are upset about something they are doing to you. Careful plotting can provide you with relief from bothersome coworkers, gossiping friends, or nagging family members.

Coworkers who make comments about the fact that you are always fifteen minutes late for work can be taken care of very simply. The first thing that you should do is to get up extra early one day. Before the sun comes up, drive to each coworker's house. Reach under the hood of your coworker's car and disconnect the center wire that leads to the distributor cap. The car will be unharmed, but it will not start, and your friends at work will all be late for work on the same day. If you're lucky, your boss might notice that you are the only one there and will give you a raise. Later, if you feel guilty about your actions, you can call your coworkers anonymously and tell them how to get their cars running again. . . .

Essay 2, First Part

Fill in the blanks.

Essay _____ makes its point more clearly and effectively because _____

_____

_____

EXPLANATION: Essay 2 is more effective because it uses *sentence skills,* the fourth base of competent writing. Here are the sentence-skills mistakes in essay 1:

- The title should not be set off in quotation marks.
- The first letter of the title should be capitalized.
- The singular subject *everyone* in sentence 1 should have a singular verb: *enjoy* should be *enjoys.*
- There is a lack of parallelism in sentence 3: *with the reward of* should be *more rewarding.*
- Word group 5 is a fragment; it can be corrected by attaching it to the previous sentence.
- The word *bothersom* in sentence 6 is misspelled; it should be *bothersome.*
- The word *disconnected* in sentence 9 should be *disconnect* to be consistent in tense with *reach,* the other verb in the sentence.
- The word *distrib.* in sentence 9 should be spelled out in full: *distributor.*
- The first *your* in sentence 11 stands for *you are;* an apostrophe and an *e* must be added: *you're.*
- Commas must be added in sentence 12 to set off the interrupting words.
- The words *each person* and *the car* in sentence 12 need to be changed to plural forms to agree with *them.*

Revising for Sentence Skills

Here are the final three paragraphs from the two essays. Edit the sentences in the first essay to make the corrections needed. Note that comparing essays 1 and 2 will help you locate the mistakes. This activity will also help you identify some of the sentence skills you may want to review in Part Four.

... [13]Gossiping friends at school are also perfect targets for a simple act of revenge. [14]A way to trap either male or female friends are to leave phony messages on their lockers. [15]If the friend that you want to get is male, leave a message that a certain girl would like him to stop by her house later that day. [16]With any luck, her boyfriend will be there. [17]The girl won't know what's going on, and the victim will be so embarrassed that he probably won't leave his home for a month. [18]The plan works just as well for female friends, too.

[19]When Mom and Dad and your sisters and brothers really begin to annoy you, harmless revenge may be just the way to make them quite down for a while. [20]The dinner table, where most of the nagging probably happens, is a likely place. [21]Just before the meal begins, throw a handful of raisins into the food. [22]Wait about 5 minutes and, after everyone has began to eat, clamp your hand over your mouth and begin to make odd noises. [23]When they ask you what the matter is, point to a raisin and yell, "Bugs!" [24]Dumping the food in the disposal, the car, will head quickly for mcdonald's [25]That night, you'll have your first quiet, peaceful meal in a long time.

[26]Well-planned revenge does not have to hurt anyone. [27]The object is simply to let other people know that they are beginning to bother you. [28]You should remember, though, to stay on your guard after completing your revenge. [29]The reason for this is simple,. coworkers, friends, and family can also plan revenge on you.

3

4

5

Essay 1, Last Part

... Gossiping friends at school are also perfect targets for a simple act of revenge. A way to trap either male or female friends is to leave phony messages on their lockers. If the friend that you want to get is male, leave a message that a certain girl would like him to stop by her house later that day. With any luck, her boyfriend will be there. The girl won't know what's going on, and the victim will be so embarrassed that he probably won't leave his home for a month. The plan works just as well for female friends, too.

(continued)

3

Essay 2, Last Part

When Mom and Dad and your sisters and brothers really begin to annoy   4
you, harmless revenge may be just the way to make them quiet down for a
while. The dinner table, where most of the nagging probably happens, is a
likely place. Just before the meal begins, throw a handful of raisins into the
food. Wait about five minutes and, after everyone has begun to eat, clamp
your hand over your mouth and begin to make odd noises. When they ask you
what the matter is, point to a raisin and yell, "Bugs!" They'll all dump their food
in the disposal, jump into the car, and head quickly for McDonald's. That night,
you'll have your first quiet, peaceful meal in a long time.

Well-planned revenge does not have to hurt anyone. The object is   5
simply to let other people know that they are beginning to bother you.
You should remember, though, to stay on your guard after completing your
revenge. The reason for this is simple. Coworkers, friends, and family can also
plan revenge on you.

www.mhhe.com/langan

Practice in Using the Four Bases

You are now familiar with four standards, or bases, of effective writing: *unity, support, coherence,* and *sentence skills.* In this section you will expand and strengthen your understanding of the four bases as you evaluate and revise essays for each of them.

Revising Essays for Unity

Activity

9

Both of the following essays contain irrelevant sentences that do not relate to the thesis of the essay or support the topic sentence of the paragraph in which they appear. Cross out the irrelevant sentences and write the numbers of those sentences in the spaces provided.

Essay 1

Playing on the Browns

¹For the past three summers, I have played first base on a softball team   1
known as the Browns. ²We play a long schedule, including playoffs, and
everybody takes the games pretty seriously. ³In that respect, we're no different
from any other of the thousand or so teams in our city. ⁴But in one respect,
we are different. ⁵In an all-male league, we have a woman on the team—me.
⁶Thus I've had a chance to observe something about human nature by seeing

(continued)

how the men have treated me. ⁷Some have been disbelieving; some have been patronizing; and, fortunately, some have simply accepted me.

⁸One new team in the league was particularly flabbergasted to see me start the game at first base. ⁹Nobody on the Comets had commented one way or the other when he saw me warming up, but playing in the actual game was another story. ¹⁰The Comets' first-base coach leaned over to me with a disbelieving grin and said, "You mean, you're starting, and those three guys are on the bench?" ¹¹I nodded and he shrugged, still amazed. ¹²He probably thought I was the manager's wife. ¹³When I came up to bat, the Comet pitcher smiled and called to his outfielders to move way in on me. ¹⁴Now, I don't have a lot of power, but I'm not exactly feeble. ¹⁵I used to work out on the exercise machines at a local health club until it closed, and now I lift weights at home a couple of times a week. ¹⁶I wiped the smirks off their faces with a line drive double over the left fielder's head.

The number of the irrelevant sentence: _____

¹⁷The next game, we played another new team, the Argyles, and their attitude was patronizing. ¹⁸The Argyles had seen me take batting practice, so they didn't do anything so rash as to draw their outfield way in. ¹⁹They had respect for my ability as a player. ²⁰However, they tried to annoy me with phony concern. ²¹For example, a redheaded Argyle got on base in the first inning and said to me, "You'd better be careful, hon. ²²When you have your foot on the bag, somebody might step on it. ²³You can get hurt in this game." ²⁴I was mad, but I have worked ou several mental techniques to control my anger because it interferes with my playing ability. ²⁵Well, this delicate little girl survived the season without injury, which is more than I can say for some of the he-men on the Argyles.

The number of the irrelevant sentence: _____

²⁶Happily, most of the teams in the league have accepted me, just as the Browns did. ²⁷The men on the Browns coached and criticized me (and occasionally cursed me) just like anyone else. ²⁸Because I'm a religious person, I don't approve of cursing, but I don't say anything about it to my

(continued)

teammates. [29]They are not amazed when I get a hit or stretch for a wide throw. [30]My average this year was higher than the averages of several of my teammates, yet none of them acted resentful or threatened. [31]On several occasions I was taken out late in a game for a pinch runner, but other slow players on the team were also lifted at times for pinch runners. [32]Every woman should have a team like the Browns!

The number of the irrelevant sentence: _____

[33]Because I really had problems only with the new teams, I've concluded   5
that it's when people are faced with an unfamiliar situation that they react defensively. [34]Once a rival team has gotten used to seeing me on the field, I'm no big deal. [35]Still, I suspect that the Browns secretly feel we're a little special. [36]After all, we won the championship with a woman on the team.

Essay 2

How to Con an Instructor

[1]Enter college, and you'll soon be reminded of the old saying "The   1
pen is mightier than the sword." [2]That person behind the instructor's desk holds your future in his or her ink-stained hands. [3]So your first important assignment in college has nothing to do with required readings, examinations, or even the hazards of registration. [4]It is, instead, how to con an instructor.

[5]The first step in conning an instructor is to use body language. [6]You   2
may be able to convince your instructor that you are special without even saying a word. [7]When you enter the classroom, be sure to sit in the front row. [8]That way, the instructor can't possibly miss you. [9]Then, as the instructor lectures, take notes frantically. [10]The instructor will be flattered that you think so much of his or her words that you want to write them all down. [11]A felt-tip pen is superior to a pen or pencil; it will help you write faster and prevent aching wrists. [12]While you are writing, be sure to smile at the instructor's jokes and nod violently in agreement with every major point. [13]Most important, as class continues, sit with your body pitched forward and your eyes wide open, fixed firmly, as if hypnotized, on your instructor's face. [14]Make your whole body suggest that you are watching a star.

The number of the irrelevant sentence: _____

---

[15]Once you have mastered body language, it is time to move on to the second phase of conning the instructor: class participation. [16]Everyone knows that the student who is most eager to learn is the one who responds to the questions that are asked and even comes up with a few more. [17]Therefore, be sure to be responsive. [18]Questions such as "How does this affect the future of the United States?" or "Don't you think that someday all this will be done by computer?" can be used in any class without prior knowledge of the subject matter. [19]Many students, especially in large classes, get lost in the crowd and never do anything to make themselves stand out. [20]Another good participation technique is to wait until the instructor has said something that sounds profound and then ask him or her to repeat it slowly so you can get it down word for word in your notes. [21]No instructor can resist this kind of flattery.

3

The number of the irrelevant sentence: _____

---

[22]However, the most advanced form of conning an instructor happens after class. [23]Don't be like the others who slap their notebooks closed, snatch up their books, and rush out the door before the echoes of the final bell have died away. [24]Did you ever notice how students begin to get restless about five minutes before class ends, even if there's no clock on the wall? [25]Instead, be reluctant to leave. [26]Approach the instructor's desk hesitantly, almost reverently. [27]Say that you want to find out more about the topic. [28]Is there any extra reading you can do? [29]Even better, ask if the instructor has written anything on the topic—and whether you could borrow it. [30]Finally, compliment your instructor by saying that this is the most interesting course you've ever taken. [31]Nothing beats the personal approach for making an instructor think you care.

4

The number of the irrelevant sentence: _____

---

[32]Body language, questions, after-class discussions—these are the secrets of conning an instructor that every college student should know. [33]These kinds of things go on in high school, too, and they're just as effective on that level. [34]Once you master these methods, you won't have to worry about a thing—until the final exam.

5

The number of the irrelevant sentence: _____

Revising Essays for Support

Activity

10

Both of the essays below lack supporting details at certain key points. In each essay, identify the spots where details are needed.

Essay 1

Formula for Happiness

¹Everyone has his or her own formula for happiness. ²As we go through life, we discover the activities that make us feel best. ³I've already discovered three keys to happiness. ⁴I depend on karate, music, and self-hypnosis.   **1**

⁵Karate helps me feel good physically. ⁶Before taking karate lessons, I was tired most of the time, my muscles felt like foam rubber, and I was twenty pounds overweight. ⁷After three months of these lessons, I saw an improvement in my physical condition. ⁸Also, my endurance has increased. ⁹At the end of my workday, I used to drag myself home to eat and watch television all night. ¹⁰Now, I have enough energy to play with my children, shop, or see a movie. ¹¹Karate has made me feel healthy, strong, and happy.   **2**

The spot where supporting details are needed occurs after sentence _____.

---

¹²Singing with a chorus has helped me achieve emotional well-being by expressing my feelings. ¹³In situations where other people would reveal their feelings, I would remain quiet. ¹⁴Since joining the chorus, however, I have an outlet for joy, anger, or sadness. ¹⁵When I sing, I pour my emotions into the music and don't have to feel shy. ¹⁶For this reason, I most enjoy singing certain kinds of music, since they demand real depth of feeling.   **3**

The first spot where supporting details are needed occurs after sentence _____.

The second spot occurs after sentence _____.

---

¹⁷Self-hypnosis gives me peace of mind. ¹⁸This is a total relaxation technique, which I learned several years ago. ¹⁹Essentially I breathe deeply and concentrate on relaxing all my muscles. ²⁰I then repeat a key suggestion to myself. ²¹Through self-hypnosis, I have gained control over several bad habits that have long been haunting me. ²²I have also learned to reduce the stress that goes along with my secretarial job. ²³Now I can handle the boss's demands or unexpected work without feeling tense.   **4**

The first spot where supporting details are needed occurs after sentence _____.

The second spot occurs after sentence _____.

> [24]In short, my physical, emotional, and mental well-being have been greatly increased through karate, music, and self-hypnosis. [25]These activities have become important elements in my formula for happiness.
>
> **5**

Problems of a Foreign Student

Essay 2

[1]About ten months ago I decided to leave my native country and come to the United States to study. [2]When I got here, I suddenly turned into someone labeled "foreign student." [3]A foreign student, I discovered, has problems. [4]Whether from Japan, like me, or from some other country, a foreign student has to work twice as hard as Americans do to succeed in college.   **1**

[5]First of all, there is the language problem. [6]American students have the advantage of comprehending English without working at it. [7]But even they complain that some professors talk too fast, mumble, or use big words. [8]As a result, they can't take notes fast enough to keep up, or they misunderstand what was said. [9]Now consider my situation. [10]I'm trying to cope with a language that is probably one of the hardest in the world to learn. [11]Dozens of English slang phrases—"mess around," "hassle," "get into"—were totally new to me. [12]Other language problems gave me trouble, too.   **2**

The spot where supporting details are needed occurs after sentence _____.

> [13]Another problem I face has to do with being a stranger to American culture. [14]For instance, the academic world is much different in Japan. [15]In the United States, instructors seem to treat students as equals. [16]Many classes are informal, and the relationship between instructor and student is friendly; in fact, students call some instructors by their first names. [17]In Japan, however, the instructor-student relationship is different. [18]Lectures, too, are more formal, and students show respect by listening quietly and paying attention at all times. [19]This more casual atmosphere occasionally makes me feel uncomfortable in class.   **3**

The spot where supporting details are needed occurs after sentence _____.

> ²⁰Perhaps the most difficult problem I face is social. ²¹American   **4**
> students may have some trouble making new friends or may feel lonely at
> times. ²²However, they usually manage to find other people with the same
> background, interests, or goals. ²³It is twice as hard to make friends, though,
> if a person has trouble making the small talk that can lead to a relationship.
> ²⁴I find it difficult to become friends with other students because I don't
> understand some aspects of American life. ²⁵Students would rather talk to
> someone who is familiar with these things.

The spot where supporting details are needed occurs after sentence _____.

> ²⁶Despite all the challenges that I, as a foreign student, have to   **5**
> overcome, I wouldn't give up this chance to go to school in the United
> States. ²⁷Each day, the problems seem a little bit less overwhelming. ²⁸Like a
> little child who is finally learning to read, write, and make sense of things,
> I am starting to enjoy my experience of discovering a brand-new world.

Revising Essays for Coherence

Activity

11

Both of the essays that follow could be revised to improve their coherence. Answer
the questions about coherence that come after each essay.

Essay 1

> ### Noise Pollution
>
> ¹Natural sounds—waves, wind, birdsong—are so soothing that companies   **1**
> sell recordings of them to anxious people seeking a relaxing atmosphere at
> home or in the car. ²One reason why "environmental sounds" are big business
> is that ordinary citizens, especially city dwellers, are bombarded by noise
> pollution. ³On the way to work, on the job, and on the way home, the typical
> urban resident must cope with a continuing barrage of unpleasant sounds.
>
> ⁴The noise level in an office can be unbearable. ⁵From nine to   **2**
> five o'clock, phones and fax machines ring, computer keyboards chatter,
> intercoms buzz, and copy machines thump back and forth. ⁶Every time the
> receptionists can't find people, they resort to a nerve-shattering public
> address system. ⁷And because the managers worry about the employees'
> morale, they graciously provide the endless droning of canned music. ⁸This
> effectively eliminates any possibility of a moment of blessed silence.
>
> *(continued)*

⁹Traveling home from work provides no relief from the noisiness of the office. ¹⁰The ordinary sounds of blaring taxi horns and rumbling buses are occasionally punctuated by the ear-piercing screech of car brakes. ¹¹Taking a shortcut through the park will bring the weary worker face to face with chanting religious cults, freelance musicians, screaming children, and barking dogs. ¹²None of these sounds can compare with the large radios many park visitors carry. ¹³Each radio blasts out something different, from heavy-metal rock to baseball, at decibel levels so strong that they make eardrums throb in pain. ¹⁴If there are birds singing or wind in the trees, the harried commuter will never hear them.

3

¹⁵Even a trip to work at 6 or 7 a.m. isn't quiet. ¹⁶No matter which route a worker takes, there is bound to be a noisy construction site somewhere along the way. ¹⁷Hard hats will shout from third-story windows to warn their coworkers below before heaving debris out and sending it crashing to earth. ¹⁸Huge front-end loaders will crunch into these piles of rubble and back up, their warning signals letting out loud, jarring beeps. ¹⁹Air hammers begin an earsplitting chorus of rat-a-tat-tat sounds guaranteed to shatter sanity as well as concrete. ²⁰Before reaching the office, the worker is already completely frazzled.

4

²¹Noise pollution is as dangerous as any other kind of pollution. ²²The endless pressure of noise probably triggers countless nervous breakdowns, vicious arguments, and bouts of depression. ²³And imagine the world problems we could solve, if only the noise stopped long enough to let us think.

5

1. In "Noise Pollution," what is the number of the sentence to which the transition word *Also* could be added in paragraph 2? _____

2. In the last sentence of paragraph 2, to what does the pronoun *This* refer?

_____

3. What is the number of the sentence to which the transition word *But* could be added in paragraph 3? _____

4. What is the number of the sentence to which the transition word *Then* could be added in paragraph 4? _____

5. What is the number of the sentence to which the transition word *Meanwhile* could be added in paragraph 4? _____

6. What word is used as a synonym for *debris* in paragraph 4? _____

7. How many times is the key word *sounds* used in the essay? _____

8. The time order of the three supporting paragraphs is confused. What is the number of the supporting paragraph that should come first? _____ Second? _____ Third? _____

Essay 2

Weight Loss

¹The big fraternity party turned out to be the low point of my first year at college. ²I was in heaven until I discovered that my date with handsome Greg, the fraternity vice president, was a hoax: he had used me to win the "ugliest date" contest. ³I ran sobbing back to the dorm, wanting to resign from the human race. ⁴Then I realized that it was time to stop kidding myself about my weight. ⁵Within the next two years, I lost forty-two pounds and turned my life around. ⁶Losing weight gave me self-confidence socially, emotionally, and professionally.

1

⁷I am more outgoing socially. ⁸Just being able to abandon dark colors, baggy sweaters, and tent dresses in favor of bright colors, T-shirts, and designer jeans made me feel better in social situations. ⁹I am able to do more things. ¹⁰I once turned down an invitation for a great camping trip with my best friend's family, making up excuses about sun poisoning and allergies. ¹¹Really, I was too embarrassed to tell them that I couldn't fit into the bathroom in their Winnebago! ¹²I made up for it last summer when I was one of the organizers of a college backpacking trip through the Rockies.

2

¹³Most important, losing weight helped me seek new professional goals. ¹⁴When I was obese, I organized my whole life around my weight, as if it were a defect I could do nothing about. ¹⁵With my good grades, I could have chosen almost any major the college offered, but I had limited my goal to teaching kindergarten because I felt that little children wouldn't judge how I looked. ¹⁶Once I was no longer fat, I realized that I love working with all sorts of people. ¹⁷I became a campus guide and even had small parts in college theater productions. ¹⁸As a result, last year I changed my major to public relations. ¹⁹The area fascinates me, and I now have good job prospects there.

3

²⁰I have also become more emotionally honest. ²¹Rose, at the college counseling center, helped me see that my "fat and jolly" personality had been false. ²²I was afraid others would reject me if I didn't always go along with their suggestions. ²³I eventually put Rose's advice to the test. ²⁴My roommates were planning an evening at a Greek restaurant. ²⁵I loved the restaurant's atmosphere, but there wasn't much I liked on the menu. ²⁶Finally, in a shaky voice I said, "Actually, I'm not crazy about lamb. ²⁷How about Chinese food?" ²⁸They scolded me for not mentioning it before, and we had dinner at a Chinese restaurant. ²⁹We all agreed it was one of our best evenings out.

4

(continued)

---

³⁰Fortunately, the low point of my first year turned out to be the turning 5
point, leading to what promises to be an exciting senior year. ³¹Greg's cruel
joke became a strange sort of favor, and I've gone from wanting to resign
from the human race to welcoming each day as a source of fresh adventure
and self-discovery.

---

1. In "Weight Loss," what is the number of the sentence to which the transition words *For one thing* could be added in paragraph 2? _____

2. What is the number of the sentence to which the transition word *Also* could be added in paragraph 2? _____

3. What is the number of the sentence to which the transition word *But* could be added in paragraph 2? _____

4. In sentence 11, to what does the pronoun *them* refer? _____
_____

5. What is the number of the sentence to which the transition word *However* could be added in paragraph 3? _____

6. What word is used as a synonym for *obese* in paragraph 3? _____

7. How many times is the keyword *weight* used in the essay? _____

8. What is the number of the supporting paragraph that should be placed in the emphatic final position? _____

Revising Essays for All Four Bases: Unity, Support, Coherence, and Sentence Skills

In this activity, you will evaluate and revise two essays in terms of all four bases: unity, support, coherence, and sentence skills. Comments follow each supporting paragraph. Circle the letter of the statement that applies in each case.

Activity

12

Essay 1

Chiggers

I had lived my whole life not knowing what chiggers are. I thought they 1
were probably a type of insect Humphrey Bogart encountered in The African
Queen. I never had any real reason to care, until one day last summer. Within

(continued)

twenty-four hours, I had vividly experienced what chigger bites are, learned how to treat them, and learned how to prevent them.

First of all, I learned that chiggers are the larvae of tiny mites found in   2
the woods and that their bites are always multiple and cause intense itching. A beautiful summer day seemed perfect for a walk in the woods. I am definitely not a city person, for I couldn't stand to be surrounded by people, noise, and concrete. As I walked through the ferns and pines, I noticed what appeared to be a dusting of reddish seeds or pollen on my slacks. Looking more closely, I realized that each speck was a tiny insect. I casually brushed off a few and gave them no further thought. I woke up the next morning feeling like a victim staked to an anthill by an enemy wise in the ways of torture. Most of my body was speckled with measlelike bumps that at the slightest touch burned and itched like a mosquito bite raised to the twentieth power. When antiseptics and calamine lotion failed to help, I raced to my doctor for emergency aid.

a.   Paragraph 2 contains an irrelevant sentence.

b.   Paragraph 2 lacks supporting details at one key spot.

c.   Time order in paragraph 2 is confused.

d.   Paragraph 2 contains two run-ons.

Healing the bites of chiggers, as the doctor diagnosed them to be, is not   3
done overnight. It seems that there is really no wonder drug or commercial product to help. The victim must rely on a primitive home remedy and mostly wait out the course of the painful bites. First, the doctor explained, the skin must be bathed carefully with warm soapy water. An antihistamine spray applied several hours later will not cure the bites but will soothe the intense itching and help prevent infection. A few days after the treatment, the bites finally healed. Although I was in pain, and desperate for relief, I followed the doctor's instructions.

a.   Paragraph 3 contains an irrelevant sentence.

b.   Paragraph 3 lacks supporting details at one key spot.

c.   Time order in paragraph 3 is confused.

d.   Paragraph 3 contains one fragment.

Most important of all, I learned what to do to prevent getting   4
chigger bites in the future. Mainly, of course, stay out of the woods in the summertime. But if the temptation is too great on an especially beautiful day, I'll be sure to wear the right type of clothing, like a long-sleeved shirt, long pants, knee socks, and closed shoes. In addition, I'll cover myself with clouds of superstrength insect repellent. I will then shower thoroughly as

(continued)

soon as I get home, I also will probably burn all my clothes if I notice even one suspicious red speck.

a.   Paragraph 4 contains an irrelevant sentence.

b.   Paragraph 4 lacks supporting details at one key spot.

c.   Paragraph 4 lacks transitional words.

d.   Paragraph 4 contains a run-on and a fragment.

I will never forget my lessons on the cause, cure, and prevention of 5 chigger bites. I'd gladly accept the challenge of rattlesnakes and scorpions in the wilds of the West but will never again confront a siege of chiggers in the pinewoods.

The Hazards of Being an Only Child

Essay 2

Many people who have grown up in multichild families think that being 1 an only child is the best of all possible worlds. They point to such benefits as the only child's annual new wardrobe and the lack of competition for parental love. But single-child status isn't as good as people say it is. Instead of having everything they want, only children are sometimes denied certain basic human needs.

Only children lack companionship. An only child can have trouble 2 making friends, since he or she isn't used to being around other children. Often, the only child comes home to an empty house; both parents are working, and there are no brothers or sisters to play with or to talk to about the day. At dinner, the single child can't tell jokes, giggle, or throw food while the adults discuss boring adult subjects. An only child always has his or her own room but never has anyone to whisper to half the night when sleep doesn't come. Some only children thrive on this isolation and channel their energies into creative activities like writing or drawing. Owing to this lack of companionship, an only child sometimes lacks the social ease and self-confidence that come from being part of a close-knit group of contemporaries.

a.   Paragraph 2 contains an irrelevant sentence.

b.   Paragraph 2 lacks supporting details at one key spot.

c.   Paragraph 2 lacks transitional words.

d.   Paragraph 2 contains one fragment and one run-on.

(continued)

Second, only children lack privacy. An only child is automatically the 3 center of parental concern. There's never any doubt about which child tried to sneak in after midnight on a weekday. And who will get the lecture the next morning. Also, whenever an only child gives in to a bad mood, runs into his or her room, and slams the door, the door will open thirty seconds later, revealing an anxious parent. Parents of only children sometimes don't even understand the child's need for privacy. For example, they may not understand why a teenager wants a lock on the door or a personal telephone. After all, the parents think, there are only the three of us, there's no need for secrets.

a.   Paragraph 3 contains an irrelevant sentence.

b.   Paragraph 3 lacks supporting details at one key spot.

c.   Paragraph 3 lacks transitional words.

d.   Paragraph 3 contains one fragment and one run-on.

Most important, only children lack power. They get all the love; but if 4 something goes wrong, they also get all the punishment. When a bottle of perfume is knocked to the floor or the television is left on all night, there's no little sister or brother to blame it on. Moreover, an only child has no recourse when asking for a privilege of some kind, such as permission to stay out late or to take an overnight trip with friends. There are no other siblings to point to and say, "You let them do it. Why won't you let me?" With no allies their own age, only children are always outnumbered, two to one. An only child hasn't a chance of influencing any major family decisions, either.

a.   Paragraph 4 contains an irrelevant sentence.

b.   Paragraph 4 lacks supporting details at one key spot.

c.   Paragraph 4 lacks transitional words.

d.   Paragraph 4 contains one fragment and one run-on.

Being an only child isn't as special as some people think. It's no fun being 5 without friends, without privacy, and without power in one's own home. But the child who can triumph over these hardships grows up self-reliant and strong. Perhaps for this reason alone, the hazards are worth it.

PART 2

Patterns of Essay Development

Preview

What do all of the images shown here have in common? They can all be classified as news sources. Think about the many different formats available for getting the news today. Then select three formats and write an essay in which you discuss the unique qualities of each.

7

Introduction to Essay Development

This chapter will

- introduce you to nine patterns of essay development

- explain the importance of understanding the nature and length of an assignment

- explain the importance of knowing your subject, your purpose, and your audience

- explain the three different points of view used in writing

- show you how to conduct a peer review and personal review

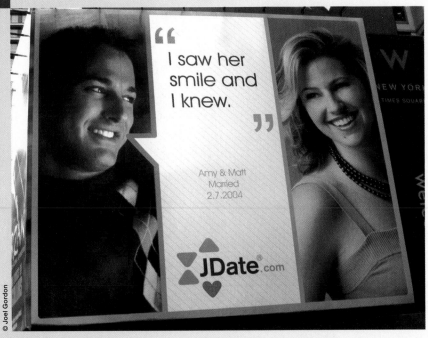

© Joel Gordon

Who is the intended audience of this advertisement? Write a description of the intended audience.

Important Considerations in Essay Development

When you begin work on particular types of essays, keep in mind several general considerations about writing; they are discussed in the following pages.

Understanding the Nature and Length of an Assignment

In all likelihood, your college writing assignments will have a good deal of variety. Sometimes you will be able to write on a topic of your own choosing or on a point you discover within a given topic; at other times you may be given a very specific assignment. In any case, do not start writing a paper until you know exactly what is expected.

First of all, be clear about *what kind of paper* the instructor has in mind. Should it be primarily a research paper summarizing other people's ideas? Should it consist entirely of your own ideas? Should it consist of a comparison of your ideas with those of a given author? Should it be something else? If you are not sure about the nature of an assignment, other students may be confused as well. Do not hesitate, then, to ask an instructor about an assignment. Most instructors are more than willing to provide an explanation. They would rather spend a few minutes of class time explaining an assignment than spend hours reading student essays that miss the mark.

Second, find out right at the start *how long* a paper is expected to be. Many instructors will indicate the approximate length of the papers they assign. Knowing the expected length of a paper will help you decide exactly how detailed your treatment of a subject should be.

Knowing Your Subject

Whenever possible, try to write on a subject that interests you. You will then find it easier to put more time into your work. Even more important, try to write on a subject that you already know something about. If you do not have direct experience with the subject, you should at least have indirect experience—knowledge gained through thinking, reading, or talking about the subject as well as from prewriting.

If you are asked to write on a topic about which you have no experience or knowledge, do whatever research is required to gain the background information you may need. Chapter 21, "Using the Library and the Internet," will show you how to look up relevant information. Without direct or indirect experience, or the information you gain through research, you may not be able to provide the specific evidence needed to develop an essay.

Knowing Your Purpose and Audience

The three most common purposes of writing are *to inform, to persuade,* and *to entertain.* As noted previously, much of the writing you do in this book will involve some form of argumentation or persuasion. You will advance a point or thesis and then support it in a variety of ways. To some extent, also, you will write papers to inform—to provide readers with information about a particular subject. And since, in practice, writing often combines purposes, you might also find yourself at times providing vivid or humorous details to entertain your readers.

Your audience will be primarily your instructor and sometimes other students. Your instructor is really a symbol of the larger audience you should see yourself writing for—educated adult readers who expect you to present your ideas in a clear, direct, organized way. If you can learn to write to persuade or inform such a general audience, you will have accomplished a great deal.

It will also be helpful for you to write some papers for a more specific audience. By doing so, you will develop an ability to choose words and adopt a tone and point of view that are just right for a given audience. This part of the book includes assignments asking you to write with very specific purposes in mind and for very specific audiences.

www.mhhe.com/langan

Determining Your Point of View

When you write, you can take any of three approaches, or points of view: first person, second person, or third person.

First-Person Approach

In the first-person approach—a strongly individualized point of view—you draw on your own experience and speak to your audience in your own voice, using pronouns like *I, me, mine, we, our,* and *us.*

The first-person approach is most common in narrative essays based on personal experience. It also suits other essays where most of the evidence presented consists of personal observation.

Here is a first-person supporting paragraph from an essay on camping:

> First of all, I like comfort when I'm camping. My motor home, with its completely equipped kitchen, shower stall, toilet, double bed, and flatscreen television, resembles a mobile motel room. I can sleep on a real mattress, clean sheets, and fluffy pillows. Next to my bed are devices that make me feel at home: a Bose radio, an alarm clock, and a remote control. Unlike the poor campers huddled in tents, I don't have to worry about cold, rain, heat,
>
> *(continued)*

> or annoying insects. After a hot shower, I can slide into my best nightgown, sit comfortably on my down-filled quilt, and read the latest best seller while a thunderstorm booms outside.

Second-Person Approach

In the second-person approach, the writer speaks directly to the reader, using the pronoun *you.* The second-person approach is considered appropriate for giving direct instructions and explanations to the reader. That is why *you* is used throughout this book.

You should plan to use the second-person approach only when writing a process essay. Otherwise, as a general rule, never use the word *you* in writing.

> **TIP** If using *you* has been a common mistake in your writing, you should review the rule about pronoun point of view on pages 109–110.

Third-Person Approach

The third-person approach is by far the most common point of view in academic writing. In the third person, the writer includes no direct references to the reader (*you*) or the self (*I, me*). Third person gets its name from the stance it suggests—that of an outsider or "third person" observing and reporting on matters of public rather than private importance. In this approach, you draw on information achieved through observation, thinking, or reading.

Here is a similar paragraph on camping, recast in the third person. Note the third-person pronouns *their, them,* and *they,* which all refer to *campers* in the first sentence.

> First of all, modern campers bring complete bedrooms with them. Winnebagos, Airstream motor homes, and fleetwood recreational vehicles lumber into America's campgrounds every summer like mobile motel rooms. All the comforts of home are provided inside. Campers sleep on real mattresses with clean sheets and fluffy pillows. Next to their beds are the same gadgets that litter their night tables at home—Bose radios, alarm
>
> *(continued)*

clocks, and remote controls. It's not necessary for them to worry about annoyances like cold, heat, rain, or buzzing insects, either. They can sit comfortably in bed and read the latest best sellers while a thunderstorm booms outside.

Using Peer Review

In addition to having your instructor as an audience for your writing, you will benefit from having other students in your class as an audience. On the day a paper is due, or on a day when you are writing papers in class, your instructor may ask you to pair up with another student (or students). That student will read your paper, and you will read his or her paper.

Ideally, read the other paper aloud while your peer listens. If that is not practical, read it in a whisper while your peer looks on. As you read, both you and your peer should look and listen for spots where the paper does not read smoothly and clearly. Check or circle the trouble spots where your reading snags.

Your peer should then read your paper, marking possible trouble spots. Then each of you should do three things.

1 Identification

At the top of a separate sheet of paper, write the title and author of the paper you have read. Under it, write your name as the reader of the paper.

2 Scratch Outline

"X-ray" the paper for its inner logic by making up a scratch outline. The scratch outline need be no more than twenty words or so, but it should show clearly the logical foundation on which the essay is built. It should identify and summarize the overall point of the paper and the three areas of support for the point.

Your outline can look like this:

Point: _____

Support:

(1) _____

(2) _____

(3) _____

For example, here is a scratch outline of the essay on moviegoing on page 6:

Point: _____

Support:

(1) _____

(2) _____

(3) _____

3 Comments

Under the outline, write a heading: "Comments." Here is what you should comment on:

- Look at the spots where your reading of the paper snagged. Are words missing or misspelled? Is there a lack of parallel structure? Are there mistakes with punctuation? Is the meaning of a sentence confused? Try to figure out what the problems are and suggest ways to fix them.

- Are there spots in the paper where you see problems with *unity, support,* or *organization*? (You'll find it helpful to refer to the Four Bases checklist on the inside back cover of this book.) If so, offer comments. For example, you might say, "More details are needed in the first supporting paragraph," or, "Some of the details in the last supporting paragraph don't really back up your point."

- Finally, note something you really liked about the paper, such as good use of transitions or an especially realistic or vivid specific detail.

After you have completed your evaluation of the paper, give it to your peer. Your instructor may give you the option of rewriting a paper in light of the feedback you get. Whether or not you rewrite, be sure to hand in the peer-evaluation form with your paper.

Doing a Personal Review

1. While you're writing and revising an essay, you should be constantly evaluating it in terms of *unity, support,* and *coherence.* Use as a guide the detailed checklist on the inside back cover of the book.

2. After you've finished the next-to-final draft of an essay, check it for the *sentence skills* listed on the inside back cover. It may also help to read the paper out loud. If a given sentence does not sound right—that is, if it does

not read clearly and smoothly—chances are something is wrong. Then revise or edit as needed until your paper is error-free.

Patterns of Essay Development

Traditionally, essay writing has been divided into the following patterns of development:

- Description
- Narration
- Exposition

    Exemplification   Comparison or contrast

    Process   Definition

    Cause and effect   Division-classification

- Argument

A *description* is a verbal picture of a person, place, or thing. In *narration,* a writer tells the story of something that happened.

In *exposition,* the writer provides information about and explains a particular subject. Patterns of development within exposition include giving examples (*exemplification*), detailing a *process* of doing or making something, analyzing *causes and effects, comparing or contrasting, defining* a term or concept, and *dividing* something into parts or *classifying* it into categories.

Finally, in *argument,* a writer attempts to support a controversial point or to defend a position on which there is a difference of opinion.

The pages ahead present individual chapters on each pattern. You will have a chance, then, to learn nine different patterns or methods for organizing material in your papers. Each pattern has its own internal logic and provides its own special strategies for imposing order on your ideas. As you practice each pattern, keep these two points in mind:

- **While each essay that you write will involve one predominant pattern, very often one or more additional patterns may be involved.** For example, consider the two student essays in Chapter 10, "Exemplification." The first essay there, "Everyday Cruelty" (page 223), is developed through a series of *examples.* But there is also an element of *narration,* because the writer presents examples that occur as he proceeds through his day. In the second essay, "Altered States" (page 225), *exemplification* is again the predominant pattern, but in a lesser way the author is also explaining the *causes* of altered states of mind.

- **No matter which pattern or patterns you use, each essay will probably involve some form of argumentation.** You will advance a point and then go on to support that point. In "Everyday Cruelty," for instance, the author uses *exemplification* to support his point that people inflict little cruelties on each other. In "The Diner at Midnight," a writer supports the point that a particular diner is depressing by providing a number of *descriptive details* (see page 180). In "A Night of Violence," another writer claims that a certain experience in his life was frightening and then uses a *narrative* to persuade us of the truth of this statement (see page 205). Yet another author states that a fast-food restaurant can be preferable to a fancy one and then supplies *comparative information* about both to support his statement (see page 296, "A Vote for McDonald's"). Much of your writing, in short, will have the purpose of persuading your reader that the idea you have advanced is valid.

The Progression in Each Chapter

In Chapters 8 through 16, after each type of essay development is explained, student essays and a professional essay illustrating that pattern are presented, followed by questions about the essays. The questions relate to unity, support, and coherence—principles of effective writing explained earlier in this book and outlined on the inside back cover. You are then asked to write your own essay. In most cases, the first assignment is fairly structured and provides a good deal of guidance for the writing process. The other assignments offer a wide choice of writing topics. In each case, one assignment involves writing an essay with a specific purpose and for a specific audience. And in three instances (exemplification, cause and effect, and comparison or contrast), the final assignments require outside reading of literary works; a student model is provided for each of these assignments.

8

Description

This chapter will explain and illustrate how to

- develop a descriptive essay
- write a descriptive essay
- revise a descriptive essay

In addition, you will read and consider

- two student descriptive essays
- one professional descriptive essay

© Photographers Choice RF/SuperStock

Think about your college graduation day and write an essay about what you imagine it will be like. How will you feel? What sights and sounds will surround you? Will your family and friends be there to congratulate you? Describe the day and bring it to life in your essay.

When you describe someone or something, you give your readers a picture in words. To make the word picture as vivid and real as possible, you must observe and record specific details that appeal to your readers' senses (sight, hearing, taste, smell, and touch). More than any other type of essay, a descriptive paper needs sharp, colorful details.

Here is a sentence in which there is almost no appeal to the senses: "In the window was a fan." In contrast, here is a description rich in sense impressions: "The blades of the rusty window fan clattered and whirled as they blew out a stream of warm, soggy air." Sense impressions in this second example include sight (*rusty window fan, whirled*), hearing (*clattered*), and touch (*warm, soggy air*). The vividness and sharpness provided by the sensory details give us a clear picture of the fan and enable us to share the writer's experience.

In this chapter, you will be asked to describe a person, place, or thing sharply, by using words rich in sensory details. To prepare for this assignment, first read the student essays and the professional essay that follow and work through the questions that accompany each piece of writing.

Student Essays to Consider

Family Portrait

My great-grandmother, who is ninety-five years old, recently sent me a photograph of herself that I had never seen before. While cleaning out the attic of her Florida home, she came across a studio portrait she had had taken about a year before she married my great-grandfather. This picture of my great-grandmother as a twenty-year-old girl and the story behind it have fascinated me from the moment I began to consider it.

The young woman in the picture has a face that resembles my own in many ways. Her face is a bit more oval than mine, but the softly waving brown hair around it is identical. The small, straight nose is the same model I was born with. My great-grandmother's mouth is closed, yet there is just the slightest hint of a smile on her full lips. I know that if she had smiled, she would have shown the same wide grin and down-curving "smile lines" that appear in my own snapshots. The most haunting feature in the photo, however, is my great-grandmother's eyes. They are an exact duplicate of my own large, dark brown ones. Her brows are plucked into thin lines, which are like two pencil strokes added to highlight those fine, luminous eyes.

I've also carefully studied the clothing and jewelry in the photograph. Although the photo was taken seventy-five years ago, my great-grandmother is wearing a blouse and skirt that could easily be worn today. The blouse is made of heavy eggshell-colored satin and reflects the light in its folds and

(continued)

hollows. It has a turned-down cowl collar and smocking on the shoulders and below the collar. The smocking (tiny rows of gathered material) looks hand-done. The skirt, which covers my great-grandmother's calves, is straight and made of light wool or flannel. My great-grandmother is wearing silver drop earrings. They are about two inches long and roughly shield-shaped. On her left wrist is a matching bracelet. My great-grandmother can't find this bracelet now, despite our having spent hours searching through the attic for it. On the third finger of her left hand is a ring with a large, square-cut stone.

The story behind the picture is as interesting to me as the young woman   4 it captures. Great-Grandmother, who was earning twenty-five dollars a week as a file clerk, decided to give her boyfriend (my great-grandfather) a picture of herself. She spent almost two weeks' salary on the skirt and blouse, which she bought at a fancy department store downtown. She borrowed the earrings and bracelet from her older sister, Dorothy. The ring she wore was a present from another young man she was dating at the time. Great-Grandmother spent another chunk of her salary to pay the portrait photographer for the hand-tinted print in old-fashioned tones of brown and tan. Just before giving the picture to my great-grandfather, she scrawled at the lower left, "Sincerely, Beatrice."

When I study this picture, I react in many ways. I think about the trouble   5 that my great-grandmother went to in order to impress the young man who was to be my great-grandfather. I laugh when I look at the ring, which was probably worn to make him jealous. I smile at the serious, formal inscription my great-grandmother used at this stage of the budding relationship. Sometimes, I am filled with a mixture of pleasure and sadness when I look at this frozen long-ago moment. It is a moment of beauty, of love, and— in a way—of my own past.

The Diner at Midnight

I've been in lots of diners, and they've always seemed to be warm, busy,   1 friendly, happy places. That's why, on a recent Monday night, I stopped in a diner for a cup of coffee. I was returning home after an all-day car trip and needed something to help me get through the last forty-five miles. I'd been visiting my cousins, whom I try to get together with at least twice a year. A diner at midnight, however, was not the place I had expected—it was different, and lonely.

Even the outside of the diner was uninviting. My Focus pulled to a halt   2 in front of the dreary gray aluminum building, which looked like an old

(continued)

railroad car. A half-lit neon sign sputtering the message "Fresh baked goods daily," reflected on the surface of the rain-slick parking lot. Only half a dozen cars and a battered pickup were scattered around the lot. An empty paper coffee cup made a hollow scraping sound as it rolled in small circles on one cement step close to the entrance. I pulled hard at the balky glass door, and it banged shut behind me.

The diner was quiet when I entered. As there was no hostess on duty, only the faint odor of stale grease and the dull hum of an empty refrigerated pastry case greeted me. The outside walls were lined with vacant booths that squatted back to back in their black vinyl upholstery. On each black-and-white checkerboard-patterned table were the usual accessories—glass salt and pepper shakers, ketchup bottle, sugar packets—silently waiting for the next morning's breakfast crowd. I glanced through the round windows on the two swinging metal doors leading to the kitchen. I could see only part of the large, apparently deserted cooking area, with a shiny stainless-steel range and blackened pans of various sizes and shapes hanging along a ledge.   3

I slid onto one of the cracked vinyl seats at the Formica counter. Two men in rumpled work shirts also sat at the counter, on stools several feet apart, smoking cigarettes and staring wearily into cups of coffee. Their faces sprouted what looked like a day-old stubble of beard. I figured they were probably shift workers who, for some reason, didn't want to go home. Three stools down from the workers, I spotted a thin young man with a mop of curly black hair. He was dressed in new-looking jeans and a black polo shirt, unbuttoned at the neck. He wore a blank expression as he picked at a plate of limp french fries. I wondered if he had just returned from a disappointing date. At the one occupied booth sat a middle-aged couple. They hadn't gotten any food yet. He was staring off into space, idly tapping his spoon against the table, while she drew aimless parallel lines on her paper napkin with a bent dinner fork. Neither said a word to the other. The people in the diner seemed as lonely as the place itself.   4

Finally, a tired-looking waitress approached me with her thick order pad. I ordered the coffee, but I wanted to drink it fast and get out of there. My car, and the solitary miles ahead of me, would be lonely. But they wouldn't be as lonely as that diner at midnight.   5

About Unity

1. In which supporting paragraph of "The Diner at Midnight" does the topic sentence appear at the paragraph's end, rather than the beginning?

   a. paragraph 2

   b. paragraph 3

   c. paragraph 4

Questions

1

2. Which sentence in paragraph 1 of "The Diner at Midnight" should be eliminated in the interest of paragraph unity? *(Write the opening words.)*

_____

3. Which of the following sentences from paragraph 3 of "Family Portrait" should be omitted in the interest of paragraph unity?

   a. Although the photo was taken fifty years ago, my great-grandmother is wearing a blouse and skirt that could easily be worn today.

   b. It has a turned-down cowl collar and smocking on the shoulders and below the collar.

   c. My great-grandmother can't find this bracelet now, despite our having spent hours searching the attic for it.

   d. On the third finger of her left hand is a ring with a large, square-cut stone.

About Support

4. How many separate items of clothing and jewelry are described in paragraph 3 of "Family Portrait"?

   a. four

   b. five

   c. seven

5. Label as sight, touch, hearing, or smell all the sensory details in the following sentences taken from the two essays. The first one is done for you as an example.

   a. "As there was no hostess on duty, only the faint *odor of stale grease* [smell] and the *dull hum* [hearing] of an *empty refrigerated pastry case* [sight] greeted me." (labeled: sight, smell, hearing, sight)

   b. "He was staring off into space, idly tapping his spoon against the table, while she drew aimless parallel lines on her paper napkin with a bent dinner fork."

   c. "The blouse is made of heavy eggshell-colored satin and reflects the light in its folds and hollows."

   d. Her brows are plucked into thin lines, which are like two pencil strokes added to highlight those fine, luminous eyes.

6. What are three details in paragraph 3 of "The Diner at Midnight" that reinforce the idea of "quiet" expressed in the topic sentence?

_____

_____

_____

About Coherence

7. Which method of organization does paragraph 2 of "Family Portrait" use?

   a. Time order

   b. Emphatic order

8. Which sentence in paragraph 2 of "Family Portrait" suggests the method of organization? *(Write the opening words.)*

_____

9. The last paragraph of "The Diner at Midnight" begins with a word that serves as which type of signal?

   a. time

   b. addition

   c. contrast

   d. illustration

About the Introduction and Conclusion

10. Which statement best describes the introduction to "The Diner at Midnight"?

    a. It starts with an idea that is the opposite of the one then developed.

    b. It explains the importance of the topic to its readers.

    c. It begins with a general statement of the topic and narrows it down to a thesis statement.

    d. It begins with an anecdote.

Developing a Descriptive Essay

Considering Purpose and Audience

The main purpose of a descriptive essay is to make readers see—or hear, taste, smell, or feel—what you are writing about. Vivid details are the key to descriptive essays, enabling your audience to picture and, in a way, experience what you describe.

As you start to think about your own descriptive essay, choose a topic that appeals strongly to at least one of your senses. It's possible to write a descriptive essay, maybe even a good one, about a boiled potato. But it would be easier (not to mention more fun) to describe a bowl of potato salad, with its contrasting textures of soft potato, crisp celery, and spongy hard-boiled egg: the crunch of the diced onion, the biting taste of the bits of pickle, the salad's creamy dressing and its tangy seasonings. The more senses you involve, the more likely your audience is to enjoy your paper.

Also, when selecting your topic, consider how much your audience already knows about it. If your topic is a familiar one—for instance, potato salad—you can assume your audience already understands the general idea. However, if you are presenting something new or unfamiliar to your readers—perhaps a description of one of your relatives or a place where you've lived—you must provide background information.

Once you have selected your topic, focus on the goal or purpose of your essay. What message do you hope to convey to your audience? For instance, if you chose as your topic a playground you used to visit as a child, decide what dominant impression you want to communicate. Is your goal to make readers see the park as a pleasant play area, or do you want them to see it as a dangerous place? If you choose the second option, focus on conveying that sense of danger to your audience. Then jot down any details that support that idea. You might describe broken beer bottles on the asphalt, graffiti sprayed on the metal jungle gym, or a pack of loud teenagers gathered on a nearby street corner. In this case, the details support your overall purpose, creating a threatening picture that your audience can see and understand.

Development through Prewriting

When Cindy, the author of "Family Portrait," sat down to think about a topic for her essay, she looked around her apartment for inspiration. First she thought about describing her own bedroom. But she had moved into the apartment only recently and hadn't done much in the way of decorating, so the room struck her as too bare and sterile. Then she looked out her window, thinking of describing the view. That seemed much more promising: she noticed the sights and sounds of children playing on the sidewalks and a group of older men playing cards, as well as smells—neighbors' cooking and exhaust from passing traffic. She was jotting down some details for such an essay when she glanced up at the framed portrait of her great-grandmother on her desk. "I stopped and stared at it, as I often do, wondering again about this twenty-year-old girl who became my great-grandmother," she said. "While I sat there studying it, I realized that the best topic of all was right under my nose."

As she looked at the photograph, Cindy began to freewrite. This is what she wrote:

Great-Grandma is twenty in the picture. She's wearing a beautiful skirt and blouse and jewelry she borrowed from Dorothy. Looks a lot like me—nose, eyes, mouth. She's shorter than I am but you really can't tell in picture. Looks a lot like old photos I've seen of Grandma too—all the Diaz women resemble each other. Earrings and bracelet are of silver and they match.

(continued)

Ring might be amber or topaz? We've laughed about the "other man" who gave it to her. Her brown hair is down loose on her shoulders. She's smiling a little. That doesn't really look like her—her usual smile is bigger and opens her mouth. Looking at the photo makes me a little sad even though I really like it. Makes me realize how much older she's getting and I wonder how long she'll be with us. It's funny to see a picture of your great-grandmother at a younger age than you are now—stirs up all kinds of weird feelings. Picture was taken at a studio in Houston to give to Great-Grandpa. Signed "Sincerely, Beatrice." So serious! Hard to imagine them being so formal with each other.

Cindy looked over her notes and thought about how she might organize her essay. First she thought only of describing how the photograph *looked*. With that in mind, she thought her main points might be (1) what her great-grandmother's face looked like and (2) what her great-grandmother was wearing. But she was stuck for a third main point.

Studying her notes again, Cindy noticed two other possible main points. One was her own emotional reaction to the photo—how it made her feel. The other was the story of the photo—how and why it was taken. Not sure which of those two she would use as her third main point, she began to write. Her first draft follows.

First Draft

Family Portrait

I have a photograph of my great-grandmother that was taken seventy-five years ago, when she was only twenty. She sent it to me only recently, and I find it very interesting.

In the photo, I see a girl who looks a good deal like I do now at twenty-two. Like most of the women in her family, including me, the girl in the picture has the Diaz family nose, waving brown hair, and large brown eyes. Her mouth is closed and she is smiling slightly. That isn't my great-grandmother's usual big grin that shows her teeth and her "smile lines."

In the photo, Great-Grandmother is wearing a very pretty skirt and blouse. They look like something that would be fashionable today. The blouse is made of heavy satin. The satin falls in lines and hollows that reflect the light. It has a turned-down cowl collar and smocking on the shoulders and under the collar. Her skirt is below her knees and looks like it is made of light wool. She is wearing jewelry. Her silver earrings and bracelet match.

(continued)

She had borrowed them from her sister. Dorothy eventually gave them both to her, but the bracelet has disappeared. On her left hand is a ring with a big yellow stone.

When I look at this photo, I feel conflicting emotions. It gives me pleasure to see my great-grandmother as a pretty young woman. It makes me sad, too, to think how quickly time passes and realize how old she is getting. It amuses me to read the inscription to my great-grandfather, her boyfriend at the time. She wrote, "Sincerely, Beatrice." It's hard for me to imagine them ever being so formal with each other.

My great-grandmother had the photograph taken at a studio near where she worked in Houston. She spent nearly two weeks' salary on the outfit she wore for it. She must have really wanted to impress my great-grandfather to go to all that trouble and expense.

Development through Revising

Cindy showed this first draft to her classmate Elena, who read it and returned it with these notes jotted in the margin:

Reader's Comments

Was this the first time you'd seen it? Where's it been? And "very interesting" doesn't really say anything. Be more specific about why it interests you.

The "Diaz family nose" isn't helpful for someone who doesn't know the Diaz family—describe it!

Nice beginning, but I still can't quite picture her. Can you add more specific detail? Does anything about her face really stand out?

Color?

Family Portrait

I have a photograph of my great-grandmother that was taken seventy-five years ago, when she was only twenty. She sent it to me only recently, and I find it very interesting.

In the photo, I see a girl who looks a good deal like I do now at twenty-two. Like most of the women in her family, including me, the girl in the picture has the Diaz family nose, waving brown hair, and large brown eyes. Her mouth is closed and she is smiling slightly. That isn't my great-grandmother's usual big grin that shows her teeth and her "smile lines."

In the photo, Great-Grandmother is wearing a very pretty skirt and blouse. They look like something that would be

(continued)

This is nice—I can picture the material.

What is smocking?

How—what are they like?

It'd make more sense for the main points of the essay to be about your great-grandma and the photo. How about making this—your reaction—the conclusion of the essay?

This is interesting stuff—she really did go to a lot of trouble to have the photo taken. I think the story of the photograph deserves to be a main point.

fashionable today. The blouse is made of heavy satin. The satin falls in lines and hollows that reflect the light. It has a turned-down cowl collar and smocking on the shoulders and under the collar. Her skirt is below her knees and looks like it is made of light wool. She is wearing jewelry. Her silver earrings and bracelet match. She had borrowed them from her sister. Dorothy eventually gave them both to her, but the bracelet has disappeared. On her left hand is a ring with a big yellow stone.

When I look at this photo, I feel conflicting emotions. It gives me pleasure to see my great-grandmother as a pretty young woman. It makes me sad, too, to think how quickly time passes and realize how old she is now. It amuses me to read the inscription to my great-grandfather, her boyfriend at the time. She wrote, "Sincerely, Beatrice." It's hard for me to imagine them ever being so formal with each other.

My great-grandmother had the photograph taken at a studio near where she worked in Houston. She spent nearly two weeks' salary on the outfit she wore for it. She must have really wanted to impress my great-grandfather to go to all that trouble and expense.

Making use of Elena's comments and her own reactions upon rereading her essay, Cindy wrote the final draft that appears on page 179.

A Professional Essay to Consider

Read the following professional essay. Then answer the questions and read the comments that follow.

Lou's Place
by Beth Johnson

Imagine a restaurant where your every whim is catered to, your every want 1
satisfied, your every request granted without hesitation. The people on the staff live
to please you. They hover anxiously as you sample your selection, waiting for your
judgment. Your pleasure is their delight, your dissatisfaction their dismay.

Lou's isn't that kind of place. 2

At Lou's Kosy Korner Koffee Shop, the mock abuse flows like a cup of spilled 3
Folgers. Customers are yelled at, lectured, blamed, mocked, teased, and ignored.
They pay for the privilege of pouring their own coffee and scrambling their own
eggs. As in a fond but dysfunctional family, Lou displays his affection through
criticism and insults, and his customers respond in kind. If Lou's had a slogan, it
might be, "If I'm polite to you, ask yourself what's wrong."

Lou's is one of three breakfast joints located in the business district of a small 4
mid-Atlantic town. The county courthouse is nearby, supplying a steady stream of
lawyers, jurors, and office workers looking for a bite to eat. A local trucking firm
also provides Lou with customers as its drivers come and go in town. Lou's is on
the corner. Beside it is a jewelry shop ("In Business Since 1946—Watch Repairs
Our Speciality") and an upscale home accessories store that features bonsai trees
and hand-painted birdhouses in its window. There's a bus stop in front of Lou's.
Lou himself has been known to storm out onto the sidewalk to shoo away people
who've dismounted from the bus and lingered too long on the corner.

The sign on Lou's front door says "Open 7 a.m.–3 p.m." But by 6:40 on a 5
brisk spring morning, the restaurant's lights are on, the door is unlocked, and Lou
is settled in the booth nearest the door, with the *Philadelphia Inquirer* spread
over the table. Lou is sunk deep into the booth's brown vinyl seat, its rips neatly
mended with silver duct tape. He is studying the box scores from the night before
as a would-be customer pauses on the sidewalk, unsure whether to believe the sign
or her own eyes. She opens the door enough to stick her head in.

"Are you open?" she asks. 6

Without lifting his eyes from the paper, Lou answers. "I'm here, aren't I?" 7

Unsure how to interpret this remark, the woman enters and sits at a booth. Lou 8
keeps studying the paper. He begins to hum under his breath. The woman starts
tracing a pattern on the glass-topped table with her fingernail. She pulls out her
checkbook and pretends to balance it. After a few long minutes, Lou apparently
reaches a stopping point in his reading. He rises, his eyes still on the folded newspaper he carries with him. His humming breaks into low-volume song as he trudges
behind the counter. "Maaaaaaaake someone happy . . . Make-make-maaaaaaake
someone happy," he croons as he lifts the steaming pot that has infused the room

with the rich aroma of freshly brewed coffee. He carries it to the woman's table, fills her cup, and drops two single-serving containers of half-and-half nearby. He then peers over the tops of his reading glasses at his customer. "You want anything else, dear?" he asks, his bushy gray eyebrows rising with the question.

She shakes her head. "I'm meeting someone. I'll order when he gets here." 9

Lou nods absently, his eyes back on his paper. As he shuffles back to his seat, 10 he mutters over his shoulder, "Hope he shows up before three. I close then."

Lou reads his paper; the woman drinks her coffee and gazes around the room. 11 It's a small restaurant: just an eight-seat counter and seven padded booths. A grill, coffeepots, and a huge stainless-steel refrigerator line the wall behind the counter. Under the glass top of the tables is the breakfast menu: it offers eggs, pancakes, home fries, bacon, and sausage. A wall rack holds Kellogg's Jumbo Packs of single-serving cereals: smiling toucans and cheerful tigers offer Froot Loops and Frosted Flakes.

Two poster-size photographs hang side by side at the far wall. One is of Lou 12 and his wife on their wedding day. They appear to be in their midtwenties. He is slim, dark-haired, beaming; his arm circles the shoulders of his fair-haired bride. The other photo shows the same couple in an identical pose—only in this one, Lou looks much as he is today. His short white hair is parted at the side; a cropped white beard emphasizes his prominent red mouth. His formerly slim figure now expands to take up much of the photograph. But the smile is the same as he embraces his silver-haired wife.

The bell at the door tinkles; two sleepy-eyed men in flannel shirts, work boots, 13 and oil-company caps walk in. Lou glances up and grunts at them; they nod. One picks up an *Inquirer* from the display stand and leaves two quarters on the cash register. They drop onto seats at the counter, simultaneously swivel to look at the woman in the booth behind them, and then turn back. For a few minutes, they flip through the sports section. Lou doesn't move. One man rises from his seat and wanders behind the counter to find cups and the coffeepot. He fills the cups, returns to his seat, and immerses himself in the paper. There is no noise but the occasional slurping of men sipping hot coffee.

Minutes pass. Finally one of the men speaks. "Lou," he says. "Can I maybe 14 get some breakfast?"

"I'm reading the paper," says Lou. "Eggs are in the refrigerator." 15

The man sighs and lumbers behind the counter again. "In some restaurants, 16 they actually cook for ya," he says, selecting eggs from the carton.

Lou doesn't raise his eyes. "In some restaurants, they wouldn't let a guy with 17 a face like yours in."

The room falls silent again, except for the splatter of grease on the grill and 18 the scrape of the spatula as the customer scrambles his eggs. He heaps them onto his plate, prepares some toast, and returns to his seat. The bell at the door begins tinkling as the breakfast rush begins—men, mostly, about half in work clothes and the rest in suits. They pour in on a wave of talk and laughter. Lou reluctantly rises and goes to work behind the counter, volleying comments with the regulars:

"Three eggs, Lou," says one.   19

"Three eggs. One heart attack wasn't enough for you? You want some bacon   20 grease on top of that?"

A large red-haired man in blue jeans and a faded denim shirt walks in with   21 a newspaper, which he reads as he waits for his cup of takeout coffee. "Anything good in the paper, Dan?" Lou asks.

"Not a thing," drawls Dan. "Not a *damn* thing. The only good thing is that the   22 machine down the street got my fifty cents instead of you."

Lou flips pancakes as the restaurant fills to capacity. The hum of voices fills   23 the room as the aromas of coffee, bacon, eggs, and toasting bread mingle in the air. A group of suits* from the nearby courthouse slide into the final empty booth. After a moment one rises, goes behind the counter, and rummages in a drawer.

"Whatcha need, Ben?" Lou asks, pouring more batter.   24

"Rag," Ben answers. He finds one, returns to the booth, and wipes crumbs off   25 the tabletop. A minute later he is back to drop a slice of ham on the hot grill. He and Lou stand side by side attending to their cooking, as comfortable in their silence as an old married couple. When the ham is sizzling and its rich fragrance reaches the far corners of the room, Ben slides it onto a plate and returns to his booth.

Filled plate in hand, Lou approaches a woman sitting at the counter. Her   26 golden hair contrasts with her sunken cheeks and her wrinkled lips sucking an unfiltered Camel. "You wanna I put this food in your ashtray, or are you gonna move it?" Lou growls. The woman moves the ashtray aside.

"Sorry, Lou," she says.   27

"I'm not really yelling at you, dear," he answers.   28

"I know," says the woman. "I'm glad *you're* here this morning." She lowers her   29 voice. "That girl you've got working here sometimes, Lou—she doesn't *like* me." Lou rolls his eyes, apparently at the poor taste of the waitress, and moves down to the cash register. As he rings up a bill, a teenage girl enters and walks by silently. Lou glares after her. "Start the day with a 'Good morning,' please," he instructs.

"Good morning, Lou," she replies obediently.   30

"*Very* nice," he mutters, still punching the cash-register buttons. "Thank you   31 *so* much for your concern. I get up at the crack of dawn to make your breakfast, but don't bother saying 'good morning' to *me*."

The day's earliest arrival, the woman in the booth, has been joined by a com-   32 panion. They order eggs and hash browns. As Lou slides the filled plates before them, he reverts briefly to the conventional manners he saves for first-timers. "Enjoy your meal," he says.

---

suits: business executives or professionals (people wearing business suits).

"Thank you," says the woman. "May I have some hot sauce?" 33

Lou's reserve of politeness is instantly exhausted. "Hot sauce. Jeez. She wants 34 *hot sauce!*" he announces to the room at large. "Anything else? Some caviar on the side, maybe?" He disappears behind the counter, reemerging with an enormous red bottle. "Here you are. It's a new bottle. Don't use it all, please. I'd like to save a little for other customers. Hey, on second thought, use it all if you want. Then I'll know you'll like my chili." Laughing loudly at his own joke, he refills the woman's coffee cup without being asked. Golden-brown coffee splashes into her saucer. Lou ignores it.

Lou's waitress, Stacy, has arrived, and begins taking orders and delivering 35 meals. Lou alternates between working the grill and clearing tables. Mid-stride, he halts before the golden-haired woman at the counter, who has pushed her plate aside and is lighting another cigarette. "What? What is this?" he demands.

"Looouuu . . . " she begins soothingly, a stream of smoke jetting from her 36 mouth with the word.

"Don't 'Lou' me," he retorts. "You don't eat your toast, you don't eat your po- 37 tatoes, you barely touch your eggs. Whatcha gonna live on? Camels?"

"Awww, Lou," she says, but she pulls her plate back and eats a few more bites. 38

As the rush of customers slows to a trickle, Lou returns to the register, mak- 39 ing change and conversation, talking Phillies and the weather. One of the flannel-shirted men rises from his counter seat and heads for the door, dropping his money on the counter. "'Bye, Stacy," he says to the waitress. "Have a nice day."

"'Bye, Mel," she replies. "You too." 40

"What about me?" Lou calls after Mel. 41

Mel doesn't pause. "Who cares what kind of a day *you* have?" 42

Mel disappears into the morning sunshine; the Camel lady pulls a crossword 43 puzzle out of her purse and taps an unlit cigarette rapidly against the counter. Stacy wipes the tables and empties a wastebasket of its load of dark, wet coffee grounds. Lou butters a piece of toast and returns to his favorite booth. He spreads out his newspaper again, then glances up to catch the eye of the hot-sauce woman. "Where's your friend?" he asks.

"He left," she replies. 44

"He left you, eh?" Lou asks. 45

"No, he didn't *leave* me. He just had to go to work . . ." 46

"Dump him," Lou responds automatically. "And now, if you don't mind *very* 47 much, I would like to finish my newspaper."

About Unity

1. What is the thesis of Johnson's essay? If it is stated directly, locate the relevant sentence or sentences. If it is implied, state the thesis in your own words.

Questions

2

2. Which statement would best serve as a topic sentence for paragraph 13?

    a. Many of Lou's customers are, like him, interested in the Philadelphia sports teams.

    b. Lou doesn't mind if customers serve themselves coffee.

    c. Lou apparently disliked the two men in oil-company caps who came into the restaurant.

    d. Regular customers at Lou's are used to taking care of themselves while Lou reads his paper.

About Support

3. In paragraph 3, Johnson claims that Lou and his customers are fond of one another. How does she support that claim in the case of the golden-haired woman who is first mentioned in paragraph 26?

    _____

    _____

4. Which of these sentences from "Lou's Place" best supports the idea that customers enjoy the unusual atmosphere at the coffee shop?

    a. "The bell at the door tinkles; two sleepy-eyed men in flannel shirts, work boots, and oil-company caps walk in."

    b. "He and Lou stand side by side attending to their cooking, as comfortable in their silence as an old married couple."

    c. "As [Lou] rings up a bill, a teenage girl enters and walks by silently."

    d. "Mid-stride, [Lou] halts before the golden-haired lady at the counter, who has pushed her plate aside and is lighting another cigarette."

5. Check each sense appealed to in the passage below from "Lou's Place."

    "Maaaaaaaake someone happy . . . Make-make-maaaaaaake someone happy," he croons as he lifts the steaming pot that has infused the room with the rich aroma of freshly brewed coffee. He carries it to the woman's table, fills her cup, and drops two single-serving containers of half-and-half nearby.

    Sight _____ Hearing _____ Taste _____ Smell _____ Touch _____

About Coherence

6. Which of the following sentences contains a change-of-direction signal?

    a. "'You want anything else, dear?' he asks, his bushy gray eyebrows rising with the question."

    b. "'In some restaurants, they wouldn't let a guy with a face like yours in.'"

c. "After a moment one rises, goes behind the counter, and rummages in a drawer."

d. " 'I get up at the crack of dawn to make your breakfast, but don't bother saying "good morning" to *me*.' "

7. Which sentence in paragraph 23 begins with a time signal? *(Write the opening words of that sentence.)*

_____

8. The sentence that makes up paragraph 38 includes which of the following types of transition?

a. time

b. addition

c. change of direction

d. conclusion

About the Introduction and Conclusion

9. Which statement describes the style of Johnson's introduction?

a. It presents a situation that is the opposite of the one that will be developed.

b. It explains the importance of the topic to the reader.

c. It asks a question.

10. Which statement describes the conclusion of "Lou's Place"?

a. It summarizes its description of the coffee shop.

b. It ends with a comment of Lou's that characterizes the mood of his shop.

c. It ends with a prediction of the future of the coffee shop.

Writing a Descriptive Essay

Writing Assignment

1

Write an essay about a particular place that you can observe carefully or that you already know well. You might choose one of the following or another place that you think of:

Pet shop

Doctor's waiting room

Laundromat

Bar or nightclub

Video arcade

Library study area

Your bedroom or the bedroom of someone you know

Locker room after the winning or losing of an important game

Waiting room at train station, bus terminal, or airport

Antique shop or some other small shop

Prewriting

a. Remember that, like all essays, a descriptive paper must have a thesis. Your thesis should state a dominant impression about the place you are describing. Write a short single sentence in which you name the place you want to describe and the dominant impression you want to make. Don't worry if your sentence doesn't seem quite right as a thesis—you can refine it later. For now, you just want to find and express a workable topic. Here are some examples of such sentences:

The study area was noisy.

The bedroom was well-organized.

The pet shop was crowded.

The restaurant was noisy.

The bus terminal was frightening.

The locker room was glum.

The exam room was tense.

b. Once you have written your sentence, make a list of as many details as you can to support that general impression. For example, this is the list made by the writer of "The Diner at Midnight":

Tired workers at counter

Rainy parking lot

Vacant booths

Quiet

Few cars in lot

Dreary gray building

Lonely young man

Silent middle-aged couple

Out-of-order neon sign

No hostess

Couldn't see anyone in kitchen

Tired-looking waitress

c. Organize your paper according to one or a combination of the following:

Physical order—move from left to right or from far to near, or follow some other consistent order.

Size—Begin with large features or objects and work down to smaller ones.

A special order—Use an order that is appropriate to your subject.

For example, the writer of "The Diner at Midnight" builds his essay around the dominant impression of loneliness. The paper is organized in terms of physical order (from the parking lot to the entrance to the interior); a secondary method of organization is size (large parking lot to smaller diner to still smaller people).

d. Use as many senses as possible in describing a scene. Chiefly you will use sight, but to some extent you may be able to use touch, hearing, smell, and perhaps even taste. Remember that it is through the richness of your sense impressions that the reader will gain a picture of the scene.

e. Proceed to write the first draft of your essay.

Revising

After you have completed the first draft of the paper, set it aside for a while—if possible, until the next day. When you review the draft, try to do so as critically as you would if it were not your own work. Ask yourself these questions:

FOUR BASES Checklist for Description

About *Unity*

☑ Does my essay have a clearly stated thesis, including a dominant impression?

☑ Is there any irrelevant material that should be eliminated or rewritten?

About *Support*

☑ Have I provided rich, specific details that appeal to a variety of senses (sight, hearing, smell, taste, touch)?

About *Coherence*

☑ Have I organized my essay in some consistent manner—physical order, size, time progression, or another way that is appropriate to my subject?

☑ Have I used transition words to help readers follow my train of thought?

☑ Do I have a concluding paragraph that provides a summary, a final thought, or both?

About *Sentence Skills*

☑ Have I used a consistent point of view throughout my essay?

☑ Have I used specific rather than general words?

☑ Have I avoided wordiness and used concise wording?

☑ Are my sentences varied?

☑ Have I proofread my essay for spelling and other sentence skills, as listed on the inside back cover of the book?

As you revise your essay through one or more additional drafts, continue to refer to this checklist until you can answer yes to each question.

Writing Assignment

2

Write an essay about a family portrait. (The picture may be of an individual or a group.)

Prewriting

a. Decide how you will organize your essay. Your decision will depend on what seems appropriate for the photograph. Two possibilities are these:

> As in "Family Portrait," you might use the first supporting paragraph to describe the subjects' faces, the second to describe their clothing and jewelry, and the third to describe the story behind the picture.

> Another possible order might be, first, the people in the photograph (and how they look); second, the relationships among the people (and what they are doing in the photo); and third, the story behind the picture (time, place, occasion, other circumstances).

b. Make a scratch outline for your essay, based on the organization you have chosen.

c. Using your scratch outline as a guide, make a list of details that support each of your main points. As practice in doing this, complete the following list of details based on "Family Portrait":

A. Great-Grandmother's face

Small, straight nose

Slight smile on her full lips

Large, dark eyes

_____

_____

_____

B. Great-Grandmother's clothing and jewelry

Blouse of heavy satin

Blouse is eggshell-colored

Cowl collar

(continued)

> *Smocking on blouse*
> *Light wool skirt*
>
> _____
>
> _____
>
> _____
>
> C. *Story behind the photo*
>   *Great-Grandmother spent two weeks' salary on clothing*
>   *Borrowed jewelry from sister*
>
> _____
>
> _____

d. Use your scratch outline and list of details to write your first draft.

Revising

HINT Refer to the FOUR BASES Checklist for Description provided on page 196 with Writing Assignment 1.

Writing Assignment

3 Write an essay describing a person. First, decide on your dominant impression of the person, and then use only those details that will add to it. Here are some examples of interesting types of people you might want to write about:

Campus character	Competitor
Employer	Clergyman
TV or movie celebrity	Clergywoman
Close friend	Teacher
Rival	Child
White-collar crook	Relative

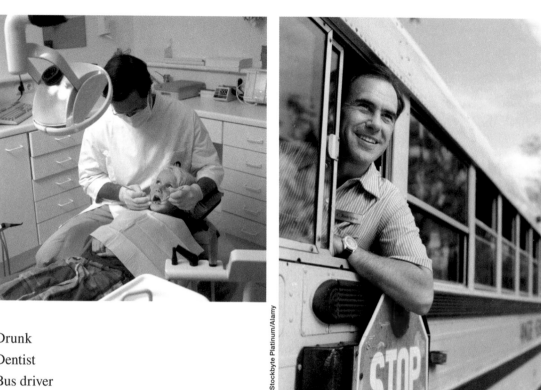

Drunk

Dentist

Bus driver

Homeless person

Older person

Hero

Writing Assignment

Writing for a Specific Purpose and Audience

4

In this descriptive essay, you will write with a specific purpose and for a specific audience. Imagine that you have subscribed to an online dating service. Clients of the service are asked to create a detailed profile and submit photographs. Write a paper in which you describe yourself. Your goal is to give interested members of the dating service a good sense of what you are like.

Prewriting

a. Decide how you will organize your profile. What aspects of yourself will you describe? Remember, your profile will include photos, so viewers of the site will see for themselves what you look like. Therefore, it won't be necessary to describe your appearance.

You might organize your profile in terms of describing your attitudes and beliefs, your interests, and your personal habits. Other ideas you might use as main points could be your hopes for the future, how you spend a typical day, or your imaginary perfect date.

b. Focus on each of the main points you've decided to write on, and ask yourself questions to generate details to support each one. For example, if you were going to write about your perfect date, you would ask questions like these:

> Where would I go?
>
> What would I do?
>
> What time of day would the date occur?
>
> Why would I enjoy this date so much?
>
> How would I travel to my destination?

Continue questioning until you have a number of rich, specific, sensory details to support each of your main points.

c. Plan a brief introductory paragraph that will indicate how you'll organize your profile. For instance, one student might write, "I'm Terry Jefferson. I'm going to tell you something about what I believe, what I enjoy doing, and what I hope to accomplish in the future."

d. Write the first draft of your profile.

Revising

Once you have the first draft of your paper completed, read it to a partner who will give you honest feedback. You and your partner should consider these questions:

FOUR BASES Checklist for Description

About *Unity*

☑   Does my introduction indicate a clear plan of development?

About *Support*

☑   Have I filled each of my supporting paragraphs with rich, descriptive details that help potential dates vividly imagine me?

About *Coherence*

☑   Is my profile clearly organized according to three main points?

(continued)

☑ Have I rounded off my profile with an appropriate concluding paragraph?

About *Sentence Skills*

☑ Have I used a consistent point of view throughout?

☑ Have I used specific rather than general words?

☑ Have I avoided wordiness and used concise wording?

☑ Are my sentences varied?

☑ Have I proofread my profile, referring to the list of sentence skills on the inside back cover?

www.mhhe.com/langan

9

Narration

This chapter will explain and illustrate how to

- develop a narrative essay
- write a narrative essay
- revise a narrative essay

In addition, you will read and consider

- two student narrative essays
- one professional narrative essay

© James Leynse/Corbis

Imagine that you are the owner of your own very successful company, which you have built from the ground up. You have been asked to share your experience with a group of young entrepreneurs who have hopes of owning their own businesses someday. Write a narrative of your success story, including the type of business you own, how you came up with the idea, and how you managed to make it a success.

Children beg to hear a beloved story read again and again. Over dinner, tired adults tell each other about their day. A restless class is hushed when a teacher says, "Let me tell you something strange that happened to me once." Whatever our age, we never outgrow our hunger for stories. Just as our ancestors entertained and instructed each other with tales of great hunts and battles, of angry gods and foolish humans, we still love to share our lives and learn about others through storytelling.

Narration is storytelling, whether we are relating a single story or several related ones. Through narration, we make a statement clear by relating in detail something that has happened to us. In the story we tell, we present the details in the order in which they happened. A person might say, for example, "I was really embarrassed the day I took my driver's test," and then go on to develop that statement with an account of the experience. If the story is sharply detailed, we will be able to see and understand just why the speaker felt that way.

In this chapter, you'll be asked to tell a story that illustrates a specific point. To prepare for this assignment, first read the student essays and the professional essay that follow and work through the questions that accompany each piece of writing. All three essays use narratives to develop their points.

www.mhhe.com/langan

Student Essays to Consider

Adopting a Handicap

My church recently staged a "Sensitivity Sunday" to make our congregation more aware of the problems faced by people with physical disabilities. We were asked to "adopt a disability" for several hours one Sunday morning. Some members, like me, chose to use wheelchairs. Others wore sound-blocking earplugs, hobbled around on crutches, or wore blindfolds. **1**

Just sitting in the wheelchair was instructive. I had never considered before how awkward it would be to use one. As soon as I sat down, my weight made the chair begin to roll. Its wheels were not locked, and I fumbled clumsily to correct that. Another awkward moment occurred when I realized I had no place to put my feet. I fumbled some more to turn the metal footrest into place. I felt psychologically awkward as well, as I took my first uneasy look at what was to be my only means of transportation for several hours. I realized that for many people, "adopting a wheelchair" is not a temporary experiment. That was a sobering thought as I sank back into my seat. **2**

(continued)

3

Once I sat down, I had to learn how to cope with the wheelchair. I shifted around, trying to find a comfortable position. I thought it might be restful, even kind of nice, to be pushed around for a while. I glanced around to see who would be pushing me and then realized I would have to navigate the contraption by myself! My palms reddened and my wrist and forearm muscles started to ache as I tugged at the heavy metal wheels. I realized, as I veered this way and that, that steering and turning were not going to be easy tasks. Trying to make a right-angle turn from one aisle to another, I steered straight into a pew. I felt as though everyone was staring at me and commenting on my clumsiness.

4

When the service started, other problems cropped up to frustrate me further. Every time the congregation stood up, my view was blocked. I could not see the minister, the choir, or the altar. Also, as the church's aisles were narrow, I seemed to be in the way no matter where I parked myself. For instance, the ushers had to squeeze by me to pass the collection plate. This made me feel like a nuisance. Thanks to a new building program, however, our church will soon have the wide aisles and well-spaced pews that will make life easier for the disabled. After the service ended, when people stopped to talk to me, I had to strain my neck and look up at them. This made me feel like a little child being talked down to and added to my sense of powerlessness.

5

My wheelchair experiment was soon over. It's true that it made an impression on me. I no longer resent large tax expenditures for ramp-equipped buses, and I wouldn't dream of parking my car in a space marked "Handicapped Only." But I also realize how little I know about the daily life of a truly disabled person. A few hours of voluntary "disability" gave me only a hint of the challenges, both physical and emotional, that people with handicaps must overcome.

A Night of Violence

1

According to my history instructor, Adolf Hitler once said that he wanted to sign up "brutal youths" to help him achieve his goals. If Hitler were still alive, he wouldn't have any trouble recruiting the brutal youths he wanted; he could get them right here in the United States. I know, because

(continued)

I was one of them. As a teenager, I ran with a gang. And it took a frightening incident for me to see how violent I had become.

The incident was planned one Thursday night when I was out with my   2
friends. I was still going to school once in a while, but most of my friends weren't. We spent our days on the streets, talking, showing off, sometimes shoplifting a little or shaking people down for a few dollars. My friends and I were close, maybe because life hadn't been very good to any of us. On this night, we were drinking wine and vodka on the corner. For some reason, we all felt tense and restless. One of us came up with the idea of robbing one of the old people who lived in the high-rise close by. We would just knock him or her over, grab the money, and party with it.

The robbery did not go as planned. After about an hour, and after more   3
wine and vodka, we spotted an old man. He came out of the glass door of the building and started up the street. Pine Street had a lot of antique stores as well as apartment buildings. Stuffing our bottles in our jacket pockets, we closed in behind him. Suddenly, the old man whipped out a homemade wooden club from under his jacket and began swinging. The club thudded loudly against Victor's shoulder, making him yelp with pain. When we heard that, we went crazy. We smashed our bottles over the old man's head. Not content with that, Victor kicked him savagely, knocking him to the ground. As we ran, I kept seeing him sprawled on the ground, blood from our beating trickling into his eyes. Victor, the biggest of us, had said, "We want your money, old man. Hand it over."

Later, at home, I had a strong reaction to the incident. My head would   4
not stop pounding, and I threw up. I wasn't afraid of getting caught; in fact, we never did get caught. I just knew I had gone over some kind of line. I didn't know if I could step back, now that I had gone so far. But I knew I had to. I had seen plenty of people in my neighborhood turn into the kind of people who hated their lives, people who didn't care about anything, people who wound up penned in jail or ruled by drugs. I didn't want to become one of them.

That night, I realize now, I decided not to become one of Hitler's "brutal   5
youths." I'm proud of myself for that, even though life didn't get any easier and no one came along to pin a medal on me. I just decided, quietly, to step off the path I was on. I hope my parents and I will get along better now, too. Maybe the old man's pain, in some terrible way, had a purpose.

About Unity

1. Which essay lacks an opening thesis statement?

   _____

2. Which sentence in paragraph 4 of "Adopting a Handicap" should be omitted in the interest of paragraph unity? *(Write the opening words.)*

   _____

3. What sentence in paragraph 3 of "A Night of Violence" should be omitted in the interest of paragraph unity? *(Write the opening words.)*

   _____

4. What sentence in the final paragraph of "A Night of Violence" makes the mistake of introducing a new topic and so should be eliminated? *(Write the opening words.)*

   _____

   _____

About Support

5. Label as *sight, touch, hearing,* or *smell* all the sensory details in the following sentences taken from the essays.

   a. "My palms reddened and my wrist and forearm muscles started to ache as I tugged at the heavy metal wheels."

   b. "I could not see the minister, the choir, or the altar."

   c. "The club thudded loudly against Victor's shoulder, making him yelp with pain."

   d. "As we ran, I kept seeing him sprawled on the ground, blood from our beating trickling into his eyes."

6. In a narrative, the main method of organization is time order. Which sentence in paragraph 3 of "A Night of Violence" is placed out of order? *(Write the opening words.)*

   _____

7. In "Adopting a Handicap," how many examples support the topic sentence of paragraph 4, "When the service started, other problems cropped up to frustrate me further"? _____

About Coherence

8. The first stage of the writer's experience in "Adopting a Handicap" might be called *sitting down in the wheelchair.* What are the other two stages of the experience?

   _____

   _____

9. List three time transitions used in the third paragraph of "A Night of Violence."

   _____   _____   _____

About the Introduction and Conclusion

10. What method of introduction forms the first paragraph of "A Night of Violence"? Circle the appropriate letter.

    a. Broad, general statement narrowing to a thesis

    b. Idea that is the opposite of the one to be developed

    c. Questions

Developing a Narrative Essay

Considering Purpose and Audience

The main purpose of a narrative essay is to make a point by telling your audience a story. Colorful details and interesting events that build up to a point of some kind make narrative essays enjoyable for readers and writers alike.

At one time or another, you have probably listened to someone tell a rambling story that didn't seem to go anywhere. You might have impatiently wondered, Where is this story going? or Is there a point here? Keep such questions in mind as you think about your own narrative essay. To satisfy your audience, your story must have some overall purpose and point.

Also keep in mind that your story should deal with an event or a topic that will appeal to your audience. A group of young children, for example, would probably be bored by a narrative essay about your first job interview. They might, however, be very interested if you wrote about a time you were chased by a pack of mean dogs or when you stood up to a bully in your school. In general, narrative essays that involve human conflict—internal or external—are entertaining to readers of all ages.

Development through Prewriting

Freewriting is a particularly helpful prewriting technique as you're planning your narrative essay. As you think about the story you want to relate, many ideas will crowd into your mind. Simply writing them down in free-form style will jog loose details you may have forgotten and also help you determine what the central point of your story really is.

> TIP For more about freewriting, see pages 25–27.

Lisa, the writer of "Adopting a Handicap," spent a half hour freewriting before she wrote the first draft of her essay. Here is what she came up with:

Our church was planning a building renovation to make the church more accessible to handicapped people. Some people thought it was a waste of money and that the disabled could get along all right in the church the way it was. Not many disabled people come to our church anyway. Pastor Henry gave a sermon about disabilities. He suggested that we spend one Sunday pretending to be disabled ourselves. We got to choose our disability. Some people pretended to be blind or deaf or in need of crutches. I chose to use a wheelchair. I thought it might be fun to have someone push me around. It was a lot scarier and more disturbing than I expected. We borrowed wheelchairs and crutches from the local nursing home. I didn't like sitting down in the wheelchair. I didn't know how to work it right.

(continued)

It rolled when I didn't want it to. I felt clumsy trying to make it move. I even ran into a pew. I felt silly pretending to be disabled and also sort of disrespectful because for most people sitting in a wheelchair isn't a choice. It also bothered me to think what it'd be like if I couldn't get up again. It turned out that nobody was going to push me around. I thought Paula would, but instead she put on a blindfold and pretended to be blind. She knocked over a cup of coffee before the morning was over. She told me later she felt really panicky when that happened. Sitting down so low in the wheelchair was weird. I couldn't see much of anything. People ignored me or talked to me like I was a little kid. I was glad when the morning was over. Making the wheels turn hurt my hands and arms.

As Lisa read over her freewriting passage, she decided that the central point of her story was her new realization of how challenging it would be to be truly disabled. To support that central point, she realized, she would need to concentrate on details that demonstrated the frustrations she felt. She created a scratch outline for the first draft of her essay:

Thesis statement: A church experiment led to my spending the morning in a wheelchair.

1. Sitting in the wheelchair

   a. Awkward because it rolled

(continued)

        b.   Awkward because footrest was out of place

        c.   Psychologically awkward

   2. Moving the wheelchair

        a.   I thought someone would push me.

        b.   It was hard to make the chair move and it hurt my hands.

        c.   It was difficult to steer.

   3. Ways the wheelchair affected me

        a.   I couldn't see.

        b.   I felt in the way.

        c.   I felt funny talking to people as they bent down over me.

Lisa based her first draft on her scratch outline. Here is the draft:

First Draft

Adopting a Handicap

The pastor at our church suggested that we each "adopt a disability" for a few hours on Sunday morning. Some members, like me, chose to use wheelchairs. Others wore earplugs, used crutches, or wore blindfolds.

It surprised me that I felt nervous about sitting down in my wheelchair. I'm not sure why I felt scared about it. I guess I realized that most people who use wheelchairs don't do it by choice—they have to.

When I sat down, I thought my friend Paula would push me around. We had talked about her doing that earlier. But she decided instead to "adopt" her own disability and she pretended to be blind. I saw her with a blindfold on, trying to fix herself a cup of coffee and knocking it off the table as she stirred it. So I had to figure out how to make the chair move by myself. It wasn't so easy. Pushing the wheels made my hands and arms sore. I also kept bumping into things. I felt really awkward. I even had trouble locking the wheels and finding the footrest.

I couldn't see well as I sat down low in my chair. When the rest of the congregation stood up, I could forget about seeing entirely. People would nod or chuckle at something that had happened up at the front of the church and I could only guess what was going on. Instead of sitting in the pew with everyone else, I was parked out in the aisle, which was really too narrow for

(continued)

the chair. The new building program our church is planning will make that problem better by widening the aisles and making the pews farther apart. It's going to be expensive, but it's a worthwhile thing. Another thing I disliked was how I felt when people talked to me. They had to lean down as though I was a kid, and I had to stare up at them as though I was too. One person I talked to who seemed to understand what I was experiencing was Don Henderson, who mentioned that his brother-in-law uses a wheelchair.

Development through Revising

Lisa read over her first draft. Then she showed it to her roommate. After hearing her roommate's comments, Lisa read the essay again. This time she made a list of comments about how she thought it could be improved:

- The introduction should explain <u>why</u> the pastor wanted us to adopt disabilities.
- The second paragraph is sort of weak. Instead of saying, "I'm not sure why I felt scared," I should try to put into specific words what was scary about the experience.
- The stuff about Paula doesn't really add to my main point. The story is about me, not Paula.
- Maybe I shouldn't talk so much about the new building program. It's related to people with disabilities, but it doesn't really support the idea that my morning in a wheelchair was frustrating.
- Eliminate the part about Don Henderson. It doesn't contribute to my feeling frustrated.
- The essay ends too abruptly. I need to wrap it up with some sort of conclusion.

With that list of comments in hand, Lisa returned to her essay. She then wrote the version that appears on pages 203–204.

A Professional Essay to Consider

Read the following professional essay. Then answer the questions and read the comments that follow.

The Yellow Ribbon
by Pete Hamill

They were going to Fort Lauderdale, the girl remembered later. There were six 1 of them, three boys and three girls, and they picked up the bus at the old terminal on 34th Street, carrying sandwiches and wine in paper bags, dreaming of golden beaches and the tides of the sea as the gray cold spring of New York vanished behind them. Vingo was on board from the beginning.

As the bus passed through Jersey and into Philly, they began to notice that 2 Vingo never moved. He sat in front of the young people, his dusty face masking his age, dressed in a plain brown ill-fitting suit. His fingers were stained from cigarettes and he chewed the inside of his lip a lot, frozen into some personal cocoon of silence.

Somewhere outside of Washington, deep into the night, the bus pulled into a 3 Howard Johnson's, and everybody got off except Vingo. He sat rooted in his seat, and the young people began to wonder about him, trying to imagine his life: Perhaps he was a sea captain, maybe he had run away from his wife, he could be an old soldier going home. When they went back to the bus, the girl sat beside him and introduced herself.

"We're going to Florida," the girl said brightly. "You going that far?"   4

"I don't know," Vingo said.   5

"I've never been there," she said. "I hear it's beautiful."   6

"It is," he said quietly, as if remembering something he had tried to forget.   7

"You live there?"   8

"I did some time there in the Navy. Jacksonville."   9

"Want some wine?" she said. He smiled and took the bottle of Chianti and 10 took a swig. He thanked her and retreated again into silence. After a while, she went back to the others, as Vingo nodded into sleep.

In the morning they awoke outside another Howard Johnson's, and this time 11 Vingo went in. The girl insisted that he join them. He seemed very shy and ordered black coffee and smoked nervously, as the young people chattered about sleeping on the beaches. When they went back on the bus, the girl sat with Vingo again, and after a while, slowly and painfully and with great hesitation, he began to tell his story. He had been in jail in New York for the last four years, and now he was going home.

"Four years!" the girl said. "What did you do?" 12

"It doesn't matter," he said with quiet bluntness. "I did it and I went to jail. If 13 you can't do the time, don't do the crime. That's what they say and they're right."

"Are you married?" 14

"I don't know." 15

"You don't know?" she said. 16

"Well, when I was in the can I wrote to my wife," he said. "I told her, I said, 17 Martha, I understand if you can't stay married to me. I told her that. I said I was gonna be away a long time, and that if she couldn't stand it, if the kids kept askin' questions, if it hurt her too much, well, she could just forget me. Get a new guy—she's a wonderful woman, really something—and forget about me. I told her she didn't have to write me or nothing. And she didn't. Not for three and a half years."

"And you're going home now, not knowing?" 18

"Yeah," he said shyly. "Well, last week, when I was sure the parole was com- 19 ing through I wrote her. I told her that if she had a new guy, I understood. But if she didn't, if she would take me back she should let me know. We used to live in this town, Brunswick, just before Jacksonville, and there's a great big oak tree just as you come into town, a very famous tree, huge. I told her if she would take me back, she should put a yellow handkerchief on the tree, and I would get off and come home. If she didn't want me, forget it, no handkerchief, and I'd keep going on through."

"Wow," the girl said. "Wow." 20

She told the others, and soon all of them were in it, caught up in the approach 21 of Brunswick, looking at the pictures Vingo showed them of his wife and three children, the woman handsome in a plain way, the children still unformed in a cracked, much-handled snapshot. Now they were twenty miles from Brunswick and the young people took over window seats on the right side, waiting for the ap- proach of the great oak tree. Vingo stopped looking, tightening his face into the ex-con's mask, as if fortifying himself against still another disappointment. Then it was ten miles, and then five and the bus acquired a dark hushed mood, full of silence, of absence, of lost years, of the woman's plain face, of the sudden letter on the breakfast table, of the wonder of children, of the iron bars of solitude.

Then suddenly all of the young people were up out of their seats, screaming 22 and shouting and crying, doing small dances, shaking clenched fists in triumph and exaltation. All except Vingo.

Vingo sat there stunned, looking at the oak tree. It was covered with yel- 23 low handkerchiefs, twenty of them, thirty of them, maybe hundreds, a tree that stood like a banner of welcome blowing and billowing in the wind, turned into a gorgeous yellow blur by the passing bus. As the young people shouted, the old con slowly rose from his seat, holding himself tightly, and made his way to the front of the bus to go home.

About Unity

1. The thesis of Hamill's essay is implied rather than stated directly. See if you can state the thesis in your own words.

   _____

   _____

2. Which statement best expresses the implied point of paragraph 2?

   a. Vingo sat very still in his seat.

   b. Something about Vingo made the young people curious.

   c. Vingo appeared to be a nervous person.

   d. Vingo was the most unusual person the young people had ever seen.

3. Which statement would best serve as a topic sentence for paragraph 11?

   a. The girl's friendliness finally caused Vingo to confide in her.

   b. The group woke up outside of a Howard Johnson's.

   c. Vingo had been in jail for four years.

   d. The girl persisted in being friendly to Vingo.

About Support

4. His fingers were stained from cigarettes and he chewed the inside of his lip a lot, frozen in some personal cocoon of silence. This line from paragraph 2 supports the idea that

   a. Vingo had been drinking.

   b. Vingo was nervous.

   c. Vingo was a hostile person.

   d. Vingo knew the young people were watching him.

5. Hamill writes in paragraph 11 that Vingo seemed very shy. Find at least two pieces of evidence in the essay to support the idea that Vingo was shy.

   _____

   _____

   _____

6. Hamill implies that despite his crime, Vingo was an honorable man. Find evidence that supports that point.

   _____

   _____

About Coherence

7. The story in this essay takes place on a trip, so it's especially appropriate that Hamill uses geographical and place names to signal the passing of time and miles. List at least four of the specific places named.

_____   _____

_____   _____

8. What sentence in paragraph 19 begins with a transition word that indicates contrast? *(Write the opening words.)*

_____

About the Introduction and Conclusion

9. The introductory paragraph indicates that Hamill
   a. was one of the young people on the bus.
   b. heard the story from Vingo years later.
   c. was a friend of Vingo's wife.
   d. interviewed one of the young girls who'd been on the bus.

10. Hamill has concluded his narrative with
    a. a summary.
    b. a thought-provoking question.
    c. a recommendation.
    d. the last event of his narrative.

Writing a Narrative Essay

Writing Assignment

1

Write an essay narrating an experience in which a certain emotion was predominant. The emotion might be disappointment, embarrassment, happiness, frustration, any of the following, or some other:

Fear	Shock	Nervousness	Loss
Pride	Love	Hate	Sympathy
Jealousy	Anger	Surprise	Violence
Sadness	Nostalgia	Shyness	Bitterness
Terror	Relief	Silliness	Envy
Regret	Greed	Disgust	Loneliness

© Rachel Epstein/PhotoEdit

The experience should be limited in time. Note that each of the three essays presented in this chapter describes an experience that occurred within a relatively short period. One writer described her frustration in acting like a disabled person at a morning church service; another detailed the terror of a minute's mugging that had lifelong consequences; Pete Hamill described an overnight bus trip and its thrilling conclusion.

Prewriting

a. Think of an experience or event in your life in which you felt a certain emotion. Then spend at least ten minutes freewriting about that experience. Do not worry at this point about such matters as spelling or grammar or putting things in the right order; instead, just try to get down as many details as you can think of that seem related to the experience.

b. This preliminary writing will help you decide whether your topic is promising enough to continue working on. If it is not, choose another emotion. If it is, do three things:

First, write out your thesis in a single sentence, underlining the emotion you will focus on. For example, "My first day in kindergarten was one of the scariest days of my life."

Second, think about just what creates the conflict—the source of tension—in your story. What details can you add that will build up enough tension to "hook" readers and keep them interested?

Third, make up a long list of all the details involved in the experience. Then arrange those details in chronological (time) order.

c. Using your list as a guide, prepare a rough draft of your paper.

Revising

Once you have a first draft of your essay completed, consider the following checklist as you work on a second draft:

FOUR BASES Checklist for Narration

About *Unity*

Do I state the thesis of my narrative in the introductory paragraph?

If not in the introductory paragraph, is the thesis cleary implied somewhere in the essay?

Are there any portions of the essay that do not support the thesis and should therefore be eliminated or rewritten?

About *Support*

Do I have enough details, including dialogue?

Have I included enough vivid, exact details that will help my readers experience the event as it actually happened?

About *Coherence*

Have I included time signals such as *first, then, next, after, while, during,* and *finally* to help connect details as you move from the beginning to the middle to the end of the narrative?

About *Sentence Skills*

Have I used a consistent point of view throughout my essay?

Have I used specific rather than general words?

Have I avoided wordiness and used concise wording?

Are my sentences varied?

Have I checked for spelling and other sentence skills, as listed on the inside back cover of the book?

Writing Assignment

2

Think of an experience in your life that supports one of the statements below:

> *If you never have a dream, you'll never have a dream come true.*—popular saying
>
> *For fools rush in where angels fear to tread.*—Alexander Pope

Before I got married I had six theories about bringing up children; now I have six children and no theories.—John Wilmot, Earl of Rochester

There are some things you learn best in calm, and some in storm.—Willa Cather

Success is 99 percent perspiration and 1 percent inspiration.—Thomas Edison

Lying is an indispensable part of making life tolerable.—Bergen Evans

What a tangled web we weave / When first we practice to deceive.—Walter Scott

There's a sucker born every minute.—P. T. Barnum

We lie loudest when we lie to ourselves.—Eric Hoffer

All marriages are happy. It's the living together afterward that causes all the trouble.—Raymond Hull

Hoping and praying are easier but do not produce as good results as hard work.—Andy Rooney

A little learning is a dangerous thing.—Alexander Pope

Nothing is as good as it seems beforehand.—George Eliot

You don't like weak women / You get bored too quick / And you don't like strong women / 'Cause they're hip to your tricks.—Joni Mitchell

Give a pig a finger, and he'll take the whole hand.—folk saying

Life shrinks or expands in proportion to one's courage.—Anaïs Nin

When I got to the end of my long journey in life / I realized I was the architect of my own destiny.—Amado Nervo

A fool and his money are soon parted.—popular saying

From what we get, we can make a living; what we give, however, makes a life.—Arthur Ashe

No matter how lovesick a woman is, she shouldn't take the first pill that comes along.—Dr. Joyce Brothers

Fear not those who argue but those who dodge.—Marie von Ebner-Eschenback

Trust in Allah, but tie your camel.—old Muslim proverb

Think of an experience you have had that demonstrates the truth of one of the above statements or another noteworthy saying—perhaps one that has been a guidepost for your life. Then, using one of these statements as your thesis, write a narrative essay about that experience. As you develop your essay, refer to the suggestions in the following prewriting strategies and rewriting strategies.

Prewriting

The key to the success of your essay will be your choice of an incident from your life that illustrates the truth of the statement you have chosen. Here are some guidelines to consider as you choose such an incident:

- The incident should include a *conflict,* or a source of tension. That conflict does not need to be dramatic, such as a fistfight between two characters. Equally effective is a quieter conflict, such as a conflict between a person's conscience and desires, or a decision that must be made, or a difficult situation that has no clear resolution.
- The incident should be limited in time. It would be difficult to do justice in such a brief essay to an experience that continued over several weeks or months.
- The incident should evoke a definite emotional response in you so that it might draw a similar response from your reader.
- The incident must *fully support* the statement you have chosen, not merely be linked by some of the same ideas. Do not, for example, take the statement "We lie loudest when we lie to ourselves" and then write about an incident in which someone just told a lie. The essay should demonstrate the cost of being untruthful to oneself.

Here is how one student tested whether her plan for her narrative essay was a good one:

- What statement have I chosen as my thesis?

    The chains of habit are too weak to be felt until they are too strong to be broken.—Samuel Johnson

- Does the incident I have chosen include some kind of tension?

    Yes. I am going to write about a day when I overheard my little daughter make a remark that made me realize she was aware of my alcohol abuse. The tension is between my fantasy, which was that my drinking was a secret, and the truth, which was that even a little child knew about it.

- Is the incident limited in time?

    Yes. I am going to write about events that happened in one afternoon.

- Does the incident evoke an emotional response in me?

    Yes. I was ashamed, embarrassed, and angry at myself.

- Does the incident support the statement I have chosen?

    Yes. My "habit" was drinking, and I did not realize I was caught in its "chains" until I was unable to stop without help.

Revising

After you have put your essay away for a day, read it to a friend or classmate who will give you honest feedback. You and your reader should consider these questions:

FOUR BASES Checklist for Narration

About *Unity*

- Have I included the essay's thesis (my chosen statement) in my introductory paragraph, or is it clearly implied?

- Does each paragraph, and each sentence within that paragraph, help either to keep the action moving or to reveal important things about the characters?

- Are there portions of the essay that do not support my thesis and therefore should be eliminated or rewritten?

About *Support*

- Do I have enough details, including dialogue?

- Have I included enough vivid, exact details that will help my readers experience the event as it actually happened?

About *Coherence*

- Do transitional words and phrases, and linking sentences between paragraphs, help make the sequence of events clear?

- Should I break up the essay by using bits of interesting dialogue instead of narration?

About *Sentence Skills*

- Have I used a consistent point of view throughout my essay?

- Have I used specific rather than general words?

- Have I avoided wordiness and used concise wording?

- Are my sentences varied?

- Have I checked for spelling and other sentence skills, as listed on the inside back cover of the book?

Continue revising your work until you and your reader can answer "yes" to each question.

Writing Assignment

Writing for a Specific Purpose and Audience

3

In this narrative essay, you will write with a specific purpose and for a specific audience.

Option 1 Imagine that you are in a town fifty miles from home, that your car has broken down several miles from a gas station, and that you are carrying no money. You're afraid you are going to have a terrible time, but the friendly people who help you turn your experience into a positive one. It is such a good day, in fact, that you don't want to forget what happened.

Write a narrative of the day's events in your journal so that you can read it ten years from now and remember exactly what happened. Begin with the moment you realize your car has broken down and continue until you're safely back home. Include a thesis at either the beginning or the end of your narration.

Option 2 Imagine that a friend or sister or brother has to make a difficult decision of some kind. Perhaps he or she must decide how to deal with a troubled love affair, or a problem with living at home, or a conflict with a boss or coworker. Write a narrative from your own experience that will teach him or her something about the decision that must be made.

www.mhhe.com/langan

10

Exemplification

This chapter will explain and illustrate how to

- develop an exemplification essay

- write an exemplification essay

- revise an exemplification essay

In addition, you will read and consider

- two student exemplification essays

- one professional exemplification essay

© AP Photo/James Nachtwey/VII

Did the events of 9/11 bring people in the United States together or are we a more divided nation? Use examples found in the media, in this photograph, or in your own daily observations to support your point.

In our daily conversations, we often provide examples—details, particulars, and specific instances—to explain statements that we make. Here are several statements and supporting examples:

Statement	Examples
The first day of school was frustrating.	My sociology course was canceled. Then, I couldn't find the biology lab. And the lines at the bookstore were so long that I went home without buying my textbooks.
That washing machine is unreliable.	The water temperature can't be predicted; it stops in midcycle; and it sometimes shreds my clothing.
My grandfather is a thrifty person.	He washes and reuses aluminum foil. He wraps gifts in newspaper. And he's worn the same Sunday suit for twenty years.

In each case, exemplification helps us see for ourselves the truth of the statement that has been made. In essays, too, explanatory examples help your audience fully understand your point. Lively, specific examples also add interest to your paper.

In this chapter, you will be asked to use exemplification to support your thesis. First read the student essays and the professional essay that follow and work through the questions that accompany the essays. All three essays use exemplification to develop their points.

www.mhhe.com/langan

Student Essays to Consider

Everyday Cruelty

Last week, I found myself worrying less about problems of world politics and national crime and more about smaller evils. I came home one day with a bad taste in my mouth, the kind I get whenever I witness the little cruelties that people inflict on each other. On this particular day, I had seen too much of the cruelty of the world.

Every day I walk from the bus stop to the office where I work. This walk is my first step away from the comforts of home and into the tensions

(continued)

1

2

of the city. For me, a landmark on the route is a tiny patch of ground that was once strewn with rubbish and broken glass. The city is trying to make a "pocket park" out of it by planting trees and flowers. Every day this spring, I watched the skinny saplings put out tiny leaves. When I walked past, I always noted how big the tulips were getting and made bets with myself on when they would bloom. To pass time as I walk, I often make silly little bets with myself, such as predicting that the next man I see will be wearing a blue tie. But last Wednesday, as I reached the park, I felt sick. Someone had knocked the trees to the ground and trampled the budding tulips into the dirt. Someone had destroyed a bit of beauty for no reason.

At lunchtime on Wednesday, I witnessed more meanness. Along with   3
dozens of other hungry, hurried people, I was waiting in line at McDonald's. Also in line was a young mother with two tired, impatient children clinging to her legs. The mother was trying to calm the children, but it was obvious that their whining was about to give way to full-fledged tantrums. The lines barely moved, and the lunchtime tension was building. Then, one of the children began to cry and scream. As people stared angrily at the helpless mother, the little boy's bloodcurdling yells resounded through the restaurant. Finally, one man turned to her and said, "Lady, you shouldn't bring your kids to a public place if you can't control them." A young woman chimed in with another piece of cruel criticism. The mother was exhausted and hungry. Someone in line could have helped her by kneeling down to interact on eye level with one of the kids. Instead, even though many of the customers in the restaurant were parents themselves, they treated her like a criminal.

The worst incident of mean-spiritedness that I saw that day happened   4
after I left work. As I walked to the bus stop, I approached an old woman huddled in a doorway. She was wrapped in a dirty blanket and clutched a cheap vinyl bag packed with her belongings. She was one of the "street people" our society leaves to fend for themselves. Approaching the woman from the opposite direction were three teenagers who were laughing and talking in loud voices. When they saw the old woman, they began to shout crude remarks at her. Then they did even more cruel things to torment her. The woman stared helplessly at them, like a wounded animal surrounded by hunters. Then, having had their fun, the teenagers went on their way.

I had seen enough of the world's coldness that day and wanted to leave   5
it all behind. At home, I huddled in the warmth of my family. I wondered why we all contribute to the supply of petty cruelty. There's enough of it already.

Altered States

Most Americans are not alcoholics. Most do not cruise seedy city streets looking to score crack cocaine or heroin. Relatively few try to con their doctors into prescribing unneeded mood-altering medications. And yet, many Americans are traveling through life with their minds slightly out of kilter. In its attempt to cope with modern life, the human mind seems to have evolved some defense strategies. Confronted with inventions like television, the shopping center, and the Internet, the mind will slip—all by itself—into an altered state.

Never in the history of humanity have people been expected to sit passively for hours, staring at moving pictures emanating from an electronic box. Since too much exposure to flickering images of police officers, detectives, and talk-show hosts can be dangerous to human sanity, the mind automatically goes into a state of TV hypnosis. The eyes see the sitcom or the dog-food commercial, but the mind goes into a holding pattern. None of the televised images or sounds actually enter the brain. This is why, when questioned, people cannot remember commercials they have seen five seconds before or why the TV cops are chasing a certain suspect. In this hypnotic, trancelike state, the mind resembles an armored armadillo. It rolls up in self-defense, letting the stream of televised information pass by harmlessly.

If the TV watcher arises from the couch and goes to a shopping mall, he or she will again cope by slipping into an altered state. In the mall, the mind is bombarded with the sights, smells, and sounds of dozens of stores, restaurants, and movie theaters competing for its attention. There are hundreds of questions to be answered. Should I start with the upper or lower mall level? Which stores should I look in? Should I bother with the sweater sale at J.Crew? Should I eat fried chicken or try the healthier-sounding Pita Wrap? Where is my car parked? To combat this mental overload, the mind goes into a state resembling the whiteout experienced by mountain climbers trapped in a blinding snowstorm. Suddenly, everything looks the same. The shopper is unsure where to go next and cannot remember what he or she came for in the first place. The mind enters this state deliberately so that the shopper has no choice but to leave. Some kids can be in a shopping mall for hours, but they are exceptions to the rule.

But no part of everyday life so quickly triggers the mind's protective shutdown mode as that favorite pastime of the new millennium: cruising the Internet. A computer user sits down with the intention of briefly checking his or her e-mail or looking up a fact for a research paper. But once tapped into the immense storehouse of information, entertainment, and seemingly

(continued)

intimate personal connections that the Internet offers, the user loses all sense of time and priorities. Prospects flood the mind: Should I explore the rise of Nazi Germany? Play a trivia game? Hear the life story of a lonely stranger in Duluth? With a mind dazed with information overload, the user numbly hits one key after another, leaping from topic to topic, from distraction to distraction. Hours fly by as he or she sits hunched over the keyboard, unable to account for the time that has passed.

Therefore, the next time you see TV viewers, shoppers, or Internet   5
surfers with eyes as glazed and empty as polished doorknobs, you'll know these people are in a protective altered state. Be gentle with them. They are merely trying to cope with the mind-numbing inventions of modern life.

Questions

1

About Unity

1. Which sentence in paragraph 3 of "Altered States" should be omitted in the interest of paragraph unity? *(Write the opening words.)*

   _____

2. Which supporting paragraph in one of the essays lacks a topic sentence?

   _____

3. Which sentence in paragraph 2 of "Everyday Cruelty" should be omitted in the interest of paragraph unity? *(Write the opening words.)*

   _____

About Support

4. Which sentence in paragraph 4 of "Everyday Cruelty" needs to be followed by more supporting details? *(Write the opening words.)*

   _____

5. In paragraph 3 of "Everyday Cruelty," what sentence should be followed by supporting details? *(Write the opening words.)*

   _____

6. What three pieces of evidence does the writer of "Altered States" offer to support the statement that the Internet is an "immense storehouse of information, entertainment, and seemingly intimate personal connections"?

   _____

   _____

   _____

About Coherence

7. In paragraph 3 of "Everyday Cruelty," which four *time* signals does the author begin sentences with? *(Write the four signals here.)*

_____ _____ _____ _____

8. What sentence in "Altered States" indicates that the author has used emphatic order, saving his most important point for last? *(Write the opening words.)*

_____

About the Introduction and Conclusion

9. Of the two student essays, which indicates in its introduction the essay's plan of development? *(Write the title of the essay and the opening words of the sentence that indicates the plan.)*

_____

10. Which statement best describes the concluding paragraph of "Altered States"?

a. It contains a prediction.

b. It combines a summary with a recommendation of how to treat people in an altered state.

c. It refers to the point made in the introduction about alcohol and drugs.

d. It contains thought-provoking questions about altered states.

Developing an Exemplification Essay

Considering Purpose and Audience

If you make a statement and someone says to you, "Prove it," what do you do? Most likely, if you can, you will provide an example or two to support your claim. An exemplification essay has the same purpose: to use specific instances or actual cases to convince an audience that a particular point is true.

In an exemplification essay, you support your point by *illustrating* it with examples. If, for instance, you decide to write an essay that claims capital punishment is immoral, you might cite several cases in which an innocent person was executed. Keep in mind that your examples should connect clearly to your main point so that readers will see the truth of your claim.

The number of examples you choose to include in your essay may vary depending, in part, on your audience. For a group already opposed to the death penalty, you would not need detailed examples to support your belief that capital punishment is immoral. However, if you were writing to a group undecided about capital punishment, you would need more instances to get your point across—and even then, some readers would not believe you. Still, when used well, examples make writing more persuasive, increasing the chances readers will understand and believe your point.

Development through Prewriting

When Cedric, the student author of "Altered States," was considering a topic for his exemplification essay, he looked around his dorm for inspiration. He first considered writing about examples of some different types of people: jocks, dorks, goths. Then he thought about examples of housekeeping in dorm rooms: the Slob Kingdom, the Neat Freak Room, and the Packrat's Place.

"But that evening I was noticing how my roommate acted as he was cruising the Internet," Cedric said. "He sat down to write his brother a brief e-mail, and three hours later he was still there, cruising from Web site to Web site. His eyes were glassy and he seemed out of touch with reality. It reminded me of how spaced out I get when I go to a busy shopping mall. I began to think about how our minds have to adjust to challenges that our grandparents didn't grow up with. I added 'watching television' as the third category, and I had a pretty good idea what my essay would be about."

Cedric had his three categories, but he needed to do some more work to generate supporting details for each. He used the technique of clustering, or diagramming, to help inspire his thinking. Here is what his diagram looked like:

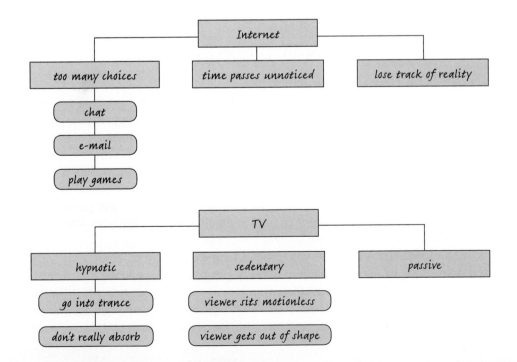

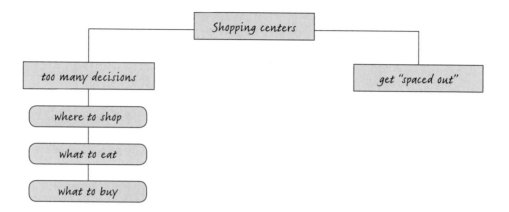

Looking at his diagram, Cedric saw that he would have no trouble supporting the thesis that people's minds go into an "altered state" when they watch TV, go to shopping centers, or use the Internet. As he quickly jotted down details in cluster form, he had easily come up with enough ideas for his essay. He started writing and produced this first draft.

Altered States

First Draft

Modern life makes demands on the human mind that no other period of history has made. As society becomes more and more complex, the mind has developed some defense mechanisms. Confronted with inventions like the Internet, television, and the shopping center, the mind will slip—all by itself—into an altered state.

Cruising the Internet can quickly make the mind slip into a strange state. A computer user sits down to check his e-mail or look up something. But once tapped into the Internet, the user loses all sense of time. He can chat with strangers, research any topic, play a game, or shop for any product. Some people begin to think of the online world and online friends as more real than the people in their own homes. While my roommate is absorbed in the Internet, he can even have brief conversations with people who come into our room, yet not be able to remember the conversations later. He sits there in a daze from information overload. He seems numb as he hits key after key, going from Web site to Web site.

Then there's TV. Growing up, our grandparents could not have imagined the idea of sitting passively for hours, staring at moving pictures emanating from a box. It's not a normal state of affairs, so the mind goes into something like a hypnotic trance. You see the sitcom or the dog-food commercial, but your mind goes into a holding pattern. You don't really absorb the pictures or sounds. Five minutes after I watch a show I can't remember commercials I've seen or why the TV cops are chasing a certain suspect.

(continued)

If the TV watcher arises from the couch and journeys into the real world, he often goes to the shopping center. Here, the mind is bombarded with the sights, smells, and sounds of dozens of stores, restaurants, and movie theaters competing for its attention. Dazed shoppers begin to feel like mountain climbers trapped in a blinding snowstorm. Suddenly, everything looks the same. My father is the worst of all when it comes to shopping in an altered state. He comes back from the mall looking like he'd been through a war. After about fifteen minutes of shopping, he can't concentrate enough to know what he's looking for.

Internet surfers, TV viewers, and shoppers all have one thing in common. They're just trying to cope with the mind-numbing inventions of modern life. I hope that someday we'll turn away from such inventions and return to a simpler and more healthy way of life.

Development through Revising

Cedric showed his first-draft essay to a classmate for her critique. She returned his essay with these comments:

Altered States

Modern life makes demands on the human mind that no other period of history has made. As society becomes more and more complex, the mind has developed some defense mechanisms. Confronted with inventions like the Internet, television, and the shopping center, the mind will slip—all by itself—into an altered state.

Cruising the Internet can quickly make the mind slip into a strange state. A computer user sits down to check his e-mail or look up something. But once tapped into the Internet, the user loses all sense of time. He can chat with strangers, research any topic, play a game, or shop for any product. Some people begin to think of the online world and online friends as more real than the people in their own homes. While my roommate is absorbed in the Internet, he can even have brief conversations with people who come into our room, yet not be able to remember

Reader's Comments

This seems to me like a separate topic—people's relationships with people they meet on the Internet.

Sometimes you write about "a user," other times about "you," and then about "my roommate." It's confusing. Also, is the paragraph about your roommate on the Internet or what people in general are like?

the conversations later. He sits there in a daze from information overload. He seems numb as he hits key after key, going from Web site to Web site.

Then there's TV. Growing up, our grandparents could not have imagined the idea of sitting passively for hours, staring at moving pictures emanating from a box. It's not a normal state of affairs, so the mind goes into something like a hypnotic trance. You see the sitcom or the dog-food commercial, but your mind goes into a holding pattern. You don't really absorb the pictures or sounds. Five minutes after I watch a show I can't remember commercials I've seen or why the TV cops are chasing a certain suspect.

If the TV watcher arises from the couch and journeys into the real world, he often goes to the shopping center. Here, the mind is bombarded with the sights, smells, and sounds of dozens of stores, restaurants, and movie theaters competing for its attention. Dazed shoppers begin to feel like mountain climbers trapped in a blinding snowstorm. Suddenly, everything looks the same. My father is the worst of all when it comes to shopping in an altered state. He comes back from the mall looking like he'd been through a war. After about fifteen minutes of shopping, he can't concentrate enough to know what he's looking for.

Internet surfers, TV viewers, and shoppers all have one thing in common. They're just trying to cope with the mind-numbing inventions of modern life. I hope that someday we'll turn away from such inventions and return to a simpler and more healthy way of life.

These last two sentences are good. I'd like to read more about this "altered state" you think people go into.

The idea of the "hypnotic trance" is interesting, but you need more details to back it up.

The point of view is a problem again. You skip from "you" to "I."

Good image!

I don't think this works. The essay isn't about your father. It should be about modern shoppers, not just one man.

This final sentence seems to introduce a new topic—that we shouldn't get caught up in TV and the Internet, etc.

Cedric read his classmate's comments and reviewed the essay himself. He agreed with her criticisms about point of view and the need for stronger supporting details. He also decided that the Internet was his strongest supporting point and should be saved for the last paragraph. He then wrote the final version of his essay, the version that appears on page 225.

A Professional Essay to Consider

Read the following professional essay. Then answer the questions and read the comments that follow.

Dad

by Andrew H. Malcolm

The first memory I have of him—of anything, really—is his strength. It was in 1 the late afternoon in a house under construction near ours. The unfinished wood floors had large, terrifying holes whose yawning darkness I knew led to nowhere good. His powerful hands, then age thirty-three, wrapped all the way around my tiny arms, then age four, and easily swung me up to his shoulders to command all I surveyed.

The relationship between a son and his father changes over time. It may grow and 2 flourish in mutual maturity. It may sour in resented dependence or independence. With many children living in single-parent homes today, it may not even exist.

But to a little boy right after World War II, a father seemed a god with strange 3 strengths and uncanny powers enabling him to do and know things that no mortal could do or know. Amazing things, like putting a bicycle chain back on, just like that. Or building a hamster cage. Or guiding a jigsaw so it formed the letter F; I learned the alphabet that way in those pretelevision days, one letter or number every other evening plus a review of the collection. (The vowels we painted red because they were special somehow.)

He seemed to know what I thought before I did. "You look like you could use 4 a cheeseburger and a chocolate shake," he would say on hot Sunday afternoons. When, at the age of five, I broke a neighbor's garage window with a wild curveball and waited in fear for ten days to make the announcement, he seemed to know about it already and to have been waiting for something.

There were, of course, rules to learn. First came the handshake. None of those 5 fishy little finger grips, but a good firm squeeze accompanied by an equally strong gaze into the other's eyes. "The first thing anyone knows about you is your hand-shake," he would say. And we'd practice it each night on his return from work, the serious toddler in the battered Cleveland Indians cap running up to the giant father to shake hands again and again until it was firm enough.

When my cat killed a bird, he defused the anger of a nine-year-old with a little 6 chat about something called "instinked." The next year, when my dog got run over and the weight of sorrow was just too immense to stand, he was there, too, with his big arms and his own tears and some thoughts on the natural order of life and death, although what was natural about a speeding car that didn't stop always escaped me.

As time passed, there were other rules to learn. "Always do your best." "Do 7 it now." "NEVER LIE!" And, most important, "You can do whatever you have to do." By my teens, he wasn't telling me what to do anymore, which was scary and heady at the same time. He provided perspective, not telling me what was around the great corner of life but letting me know there was a lot more than just today and the next, which I hadn't thought of.

When the most important girl in the world—I forget her name now—turned 8 down a movie date, he just happened to walk by the kitchen phone. "This may be hard to believe right now," he said, "but someday you won't even remember her name."

One day, I realize now, there was a change. I wasn't trying to please him so 9 much as I was trying to impress him. I never asked him to come to my football games. He had a high-pressure career, and it meant driving through most of Friday night. But for all the big games, when I looked over at the sideline, there was that familiar fedora. And, by God, did the opposing team captain ever get a firm hand-shake and a gaze he would remember.

Then, a school fact contradicted something he said. Impossible that he could 10 be wrong, but there it was in the book. These accumulated over time, along with personal experiences, to buttress[1] my own developing sense of values. And I could tell we had each taken our own, perfectly normal paths.

I began to see, too, his blind spots, his prejudices, and his weaknesses. I never 11 threw these up at him. He hadn't to me, and, anyway, he seemed to need protection. I stopped asking his advice; the experiences he drew from no longer seemed rel-evant to the decisions I had to make. On the phone, he would go on about politics at times, why he would vote the way he did or why some incumbent was a jerk. And I would roll my eyes to the ceiling and smile a little, though I hid it in my voice.

He volunteered advice for a while. But then, in more recent years, politics and 12 issues gave way to talk of empty errands and, always, to ailments—his friends', my mother's, and his own, which were serious and included heart disease. He had a bedside oxygen tank, and he would ostentatiously[2] retire there during my visits, asking my help in easing his body onto the mattress. "You have very strong arms," he once noted.

From his bed, he showed me the many sores and scars on his misshapen body 13 and all the bottles of medicine. He talked of the pain and craved much sympathy. He got some. But the scene was not attractive. He told me, as the doctor had, that his condition would only deteriorate. "Sometimes," he confided, "I would just like to lie down and go to sleep and not wake up."

After much thought and practice ("You can do whatever you have to do"), one 14 night last winter, I sat down by his bed and remembered for an instant those ter-rifying dark holes in another house thirty-five years before. I told my father how much I loved him. I described all the things people were doing for him. But, I said, he kept eating poorly, hiding in his room, and violating other doctors' orders. No amount of love could make someone else care about life, I said: it was a two-way street. He wasn't doing his best. The decision was his.

He said he knew how hard my words had been to say and how proud he was 15 of me. "I had the best teacher," I said. "You can do whatever you have to do." He smiled a little, and we shook hands, firmly, for the last time.

Several days later, at about 4 a.m., my mother heard Dad shuffling about their 16 dark room. "I have some things I have to do," he said. He paid a bundle of bills. He

---

[1]*buttress:* strengthen and support.
[2]*ostentatiously:* dramatically.

composed for my mother a long list of legal and financial what-to-do's "in case of emergency." And he wrote me a note.

Then he walked back to his bed and laid himself down. He went to sleep, **17** naturally. And he did not wake up.

About Unity

1. In the story about Malcolm and his father, which sentence expresses Malcolm's thesis?

    a. The last sentence of paragraph 1

    b. The first sentence of paragraph 2

    c. The last sentence of paragraph 2

    d. The first sentence of paragraph 3

2. Which statement would best serve as a topic sentence for paragraph 6?

    a. My dad loved my dog as much as I did.

    b. Pets were a subject that drew my dad and me together.

    c. My dad helped me make sense of life's tragedies.

    d. I was angry at my cat for killing a bird.

3. Which statement would best serve as a topic sentence for paragraph 10?

    a. School set the author against his father.

    b. The author came to see more and more that his father was usually wrong.

    c. It is best for father and son to see eye to eye.

    d. Some of the author's ideas gradually came to differ from those of his father.

About Support

4. How many details does the author use in paragraph 3 to support the idea that his father "seemed a god with strange strengths and uncanny powers"?

    a. one

    b. two

    c. three

5. With which sentence does Malcolm support his statement in paragraph 14 that his father "wasn't doing his best"? (*Write the opening words.*)

    _____

6. Which of these points is supported by the anecdote in paragraph 8?

    a. "As time passed, there were other rules to learn."

    b. "He provided perspective . . . letting me know there was a lot more than just today and the next . . ."

   c. "One day, I realize now, there was a change."

   d. "I wasn't trying to please him so much as I was trying to impress him."

About Coherence

7. Initially, Malcolm saw his father as all-wise and all-powerful. Which paragraph in the essay signals the turning point at which he began seeing his father in more realistic, less idealized terms? _____

8. In paragraph 6, find each of the following:

   a. two time transition signals

   _____ _____

   b. one addition transition signal

   _____

   c. one change-of-direction transition signal

   _____

9. Which method of organization does Malcolm use in his essay?

   a. Time

   b. Emphatic

About the Conclusion

10. The conclusion of "Dad" is made up of

   a. a summary of the narrative and a final thought.

   b. a question about fatherhood.

   c. the last event of the story about Malcolm and his father.

   d. a prediction of what kind of father Malcolm hopes to be himself.

Writing an Exemplification Essay

Writing Assignment

1

For this assignment, you will complete an unfinished essay by adding appropriate supporting examples. Here is the incomplete essay:

Problems with My Apartment

   When I was younger, I fantasized about how wonderful life would be when I moved into my own apartment. Now I'm a bit older and wiser, and my dreams have turned into nightmares. My apartment has given me nothing but headaches. From the day I signed the lease, I've had to deal with an uncooperative landlord, an incompetent janitor, and inconsiderate neighbors.

First of all, my landlord has been uncooperative. . . .

I've had a problem not only with my landlord but also with an incompetent janitor. . . .

Perhaps the worst problem has been with the inconsiderate neighbors who live in the apartment above me. . . .

Sometimes, my apartment seems like a small, friendly oasis surrounded by hostile enemies. I never know what side trouble is going to come from next: the landlord, the janitor, or the neighbors. Home may be where the heart is, but my sanity is thinking about moving out.

© Journal-Courier/Steve Warmowski/ The Image Works

If you do not have experience with living in an apartment, write instead about problems of living in a dormitory or problems of living at home. Revise the introduction and conclusion so that they fit your topic. Problems of living in a dorm might include these:

Restrictive dorm regulations

Inconsiderate students on your floor

A difficult roommate

Problems of living at home might be these:

Lack of space

Inconsiderate brothers and sisters

Conflict with your parent or parents

Prewriting

a. Generate details for your paper by using questioning as a prewriting technique. Write answers to the following questions. *(Use separate paper.)*

How has the landlord been uncooperative?

In what ways have you been inconvenienced?

Has he (or she) been uncooperative more than once?

How have you reacted to the landlord's lack of cooperation?

What has been the landlord's reaction?

What kinds of things have you said to each other?

What is the most uncooperative thing the landlord has done?

Who is the janitor?

What has he (or she) tried to fix in the apartment?

In what ways has the janitor been incompetent?

How has the janitor inconvenienced you?

Has the janitor's incompetence cost you money?

What is the worst example of the janitor's incompetence?

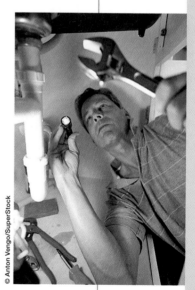

Who are the neighbors?

How long have they lived upstairs?

What kind of problems have you had with them?

Have these problems occurred more than once?

If you have spoken to the neighbors about the problems, how did they respond?

What is the worst problem with these neighbors?

b. Use the details generated by your questioning to flesh out the three paragraphs with details and examples. Remember that you may use one extended example in each paragraph (as in "Everyday Cruelty") or several brief examples (as in "Altered States").

© Anton Vengo/SuperStock

   c.   As you write your first draft, keep asking yourself these questions:

   Do my examples truly show my landlord as *uncooperative?*

   Do my examples truly show the janitor as *incompetent?*

   Do my examples truly show my neighbors as *inconsiderate?*

   d.   Write the first draft of your essay.

Revising

After you have completed the first draft of the paper, set it aside for a while if you can. When you review it, try to do so as critically as you would if it were not your own work. Better yet, read it aloud to a friend or classmate whose judgment you trust. Read the essay with these questions in mind:

FOUR BASES Checklist for Exemplification

About *Unity*

☑   Do I have a clearly stated (or implied) thesis?

About *Support*

☑   Have I provided *relevant* specific details for the landlord's uncooperativeness, the janitor's incompetence, and the neighbors' inconsiderateness?

☑   Have I provided *enough* specific details to support each of the three qualities?

About *Coherence*

☑   Have I used transitions, including transitions between paragraphs, to help readers follow my train of thought?

☑   Do I have a concluding paragraph that provides a summary or final thought or both?

About *Sentence Skills*

☑   Have I used a consistent point of view throughout my essay?

☑   Have I used specific rather than general words?

☑   Have I avoided wordiness and used concise wording?

☑   Are my sentences varied?

☑   Have I proofread my essay for sentence skills, as listed on the inside back cover of the book?

As you revise your essay through one or more additional drafts, continue to refer to this checklist until you can answer yes to each question.

Writing Assignment

2

Write an exemplification essay on the outstanding qualities (good or bad) of a person you know well. This person might be a member of your family, a friend, a roommate, a boss, a neighbor, an instructor, or someone else.

You may approach this assignment in one of two ways. You may choose to write about three related qualities of one person. For example, "My brother is stubborn, bad-tempered, and suspicious." Or you may write about one quality that is apparent in three different aspects of a person's life. For example, "My sister's patience is apparent in her relationships with her students, her husband, and her teenage son."

Just to jog your thinking, here are some descriptive words that can be applied to people. You are *not* restricted to writing about these qualities. Write about whatever qualities the person you choose possesses.

Honest	Persistent	Flirtatious	Spineless
Bad-tempered	Shy	Irresponsible	Good-humored
Ambitious	Sloppy	Stingy	Cooperative
Prejudiced	Hardworking	Aggressive	Disciplined
Considerate	Outgoing	Trustworthy	Sentimental
Argumentative	Supportive	Courageous	Defensive
Softhearted	Suspicious	Compulsive	Dishonest
Energetic	Lazy	Jealous	Insensitive
Patient	Cynical	Modest	Neat
Reliable	Independent	Sarcastic	
Generous	Stubborn	Self-centered	

Prewriting

a. Ask yourself questions to come up with supporting details for your thesis. For instance, if you are writing about your sentimental father, you would ask questions like these:

> Why do I think of Dad as being sentimental?
>
> When have I seen him be sentimental?
>
> What sort of occasions make him sentimental?
>
> Where are some places he's become sentimental about?
>
> Whom does Dad become sentimental about?
>
> What are some memorable examples of Dad's acting sentimental?

b. Look over the material generated by your questioning and decide what your three main points will be.

c. Decide on the order of your supporting paragraphs. If one of your main points seems stronger than the others, consider making it the final point in the body of the essay.

d. Decide whether to use one extended example or two or three brief examples to support each main point.

e. Prepare a scratch outline for your essay. To find your main points and supporting examples, draw on details generated by your questioning.

f. Write the first draft of your essay.

Revising

Refer to the guidelines for revising provided on page 238.

Writing | Assignment

3   Write an exemplification essay based on an outside reading. It might be a selection recommended by your instructor, or it might be a piece by one of the following authors, all of whom have written books of essays that should be available in your college library.

Annie Dillard	David Sedaris
Malcolm Gladwell	Amy Tan
Ellen Goodman	Deborah Tannen
Molly Ivins	Henry David Thoreau
Maxine Hong Kingston	Calvin Trillin
George Orwell	Alice Walker
Anna Quindlen	E. B. White
Richard Rodriguez	Marie Winn
Andy Rooney	

Base your essay on some idea in the selection you have chosen, and provide a series of examples to back up your idea. A student model follows.

Paying Attention to a Death

In "A Hanging," George Orwell describes the execution of a man in a   1
Burmese prison. The prisoner, a Hindu, is marched from his cell, led to a
gallows, and killed when the drop opens and the noose tightens. The entire
procedure takes eight minutes. As he depicts this incident, Orwell uses a series
of details that make us sharply aware of the enormity of killing a human being.

(continued)

The moments leading up to the hanging are filled with tension. Six tall guards, two of them armed with rifles, surround the prisoner, "a puny wisp of a man." The guards not only handcuff the man but also chain his handcuffs to their belts and lash his arms to his sides. The guards, nervous about fulfilling their duty, treat the Hindu like "a fish which is still alive and may jump back into the water." Meanwhile, the jail superintendent prods the head jailer to get on with the execution. The superintendent's irritability is a mask for his discomfort. Then, the procession toward the gallows is interrupted by the appearance of a friendly dog, "wagging its whole body, wild with glee at finding so many human beings together." This does not ease the tension but increases it. The contrast of the lively dog licking the doomed man's face momentarily stuns the guards and arouses in the superintendent a sense of angry urgency.

Next, in the gallows scene, Orwell uses vivid details that emphasize the life within the man who is about to die. The condemned prisoner, who has been walking steadily up to this point, moves "clumsily" up the ladder. And until now, he has been utterly silent. But, after the noose is placed around his neck, he begins "crying out to his god." The repeated cry of "Ram! Ram! Ram!" is "like the tolling of a bell," a death knell. The dog begins to whine at the sound, and the guards go "gray," their bayonets trembling. It is as if the hooded, faceless man on the wooden platform has suddenly become a human being, a soul seeking aid and comfort. The superintendent, who has been hiding his emotions behind a stern face, gives the execution order "fiercely." The living man of moments ago simply ceases to be.

After the hanging, Orwell underscores the relief people feel when the momentous event is over. The jail superintendent checks to be sure that the prisoner is dead and then blows out "a deep breath" and loses his "moody look." "One felt an impulse," Orwell says, "to sing, to break into a run, to snigger." Suddenly, people are talking and chattering, even laughing. The head jailer's story about a condemned prisoner who clung to the bars of his cell so tightly that it took six men to move him sets off a gale of laughter. On the road outside the prison, everyone who participated in the execution has a whiskey. The men, having been so close to death, need to reassure themselves of the fact that they are alive. They must laugh and drink, not because they are insensitive, but because they are shaken. They must try to forget that the dead man is only a hundred yards away.

"A Hanging" sets out to create a picture of death in the midst of life. Orwell tries to make us see, through the details he chooses, that killing a person results in "one mind less, one world less." Such an act—"cutting a life short when it is in full tide"—violates the laws of life and nature.

Writing | Assignment

4 Writing for a Specific Purpose and Audience

In this exemplification essay, you will write with a specific purpose and for a specific audience. Imagine that you have completed a year of college and have agreed to take part in your college's summer orientation program for incoming students. You will be meeting with a small group of new students to help them get ready for college life.

Prepare a presentation to the new students in which you make the point that college is more demanding than high school. Make vividly clear—using several hypothetical students as examples—just what the consequences of being unprepared for those demands can be. Focus on three areas of college and the demands of each. Some areas you might consider are these: instructors, class attendance, time management, class note-taking, choosing courses, studying a textbook, work habits, balancing work and social life, and getting help when it is needed. Each of the areas you choose should be developed in a separate paragraph. Each paragraph should have its own detailed examples.

www.mhhe.com/langan

Process

© Mike Watson Images/Corbis

Write an essay that informs a reader how to perform a particular hobby or activity you enjoy. Depending on the hobby or activity you are writing about, you may prefer to use a humorous approach.

11

This chapter will explain and illustrate how to

- develop a process essay
- write a process essay
- revise a process essay

In addition, you will read and consider

- two student process essays
- one professional process essay

Every day we perform many activities that are *processes,* that is, series of steps carried out in a definite order. Many of these processes are familiar and automatic: for example, loading film into a camera, diapering a baby, or making an omelet. We are thus seldom aware of the sequence of steps making up each activity. In other cases—for example, when someone asks us for directions to a particular place, or when we try to read and follow directions for a new table game that someone has given us—we may be painfully conscious of the whole series of steps involved in the process.

In this chapter, you will be asked to write a process essay—one that explains clearly how to do or make something. To prepare for this assignment, you should first read the student process papers and the professional essay and then answer the questions that follow them.

Student Essays to Consider

Successful Exercise

Regular exercise is something like the weather—we all talk about it,   1
but we tend not to do anything about it. Exercise classes on television and exercise programs on DVDs—as well as instructions in books, magazines, and pamphlets—now make it easy to have a low-cost personal exercise program without leaving home. However, for success in exercise, you should follow a simple plan consisting of arranging time, making preparations, and starting off at a sensible pace.

Everyone has an excuse for not exercising: a heavy schedule at work   2
or school; being rushed in the morning and exhausted at night; too many other responsibilities. However, one solution is simply to get up half an hour earlier in the morning. Look at it this way: if you're already getting up too early, what's an extra half hour? Of course, that time could be cut to fifteen minutes earlier if you could lay out your clothes, set the breakfast table, fill the coffeemaker, and gather your books and materials for the next day before you go to bed.

Next, prepare for your exercise session. To begin with, get yourself   3
ready by not eating or drinking anything before exercising. Why risk an upset stomach? Then, dress comfortably in something that allows you to move freely. Since you'll be in your own home, there's no need to invest in a high-fashion dance costume. A loose T-shirt and shorts are good. A bathing suit is great in summer, and in winter long underwear is warm and comfortable. If your hair tends to flop in your eyes, pin it back or wear a headband or scarf. Prepare the exercise area, too. Turn off the phone and lock the door

(continued)

to prevent interruptions. Shove the coffee table out of the way so you won't bruise yourself on it or other furniture. Then get out the simple materials you'll need to exercise with.

Finally, use common sense in getting started. Common sense isn't so 4 common, as anyone who reads the newspapers and watches the world can tell you. If this is your first attempt at exercising, begin slowly. You do not need to do each movement the full number of times at first, but you should try each one. After five or six sessions, you should be able to do each one the full number of times. Try to move in a smooth, rhythmic way; this will help prevent injuries and pulled muscles. Pretend you're a dancer and make each move graceful, even if it's just getting up off the floor. After the last exercise, give yourself five minutes to relax and cool off—you have earned it. Finally, put those sore muscles under a hot shower and get ready for a great day.

Establishing an exercise program isn't difficult, but it can't be achieved by 5 reading about it, talking about it, or watching models exercise on television. It happens only when you get off that couch and do something about it. As my doctor likes to say, "If you don't use it, you'll lose it."

How to Complain

I'm not just a consumer—I'm a victim. If I order a product, it is sure to 1 arrive in the wrong color, size, or quantity. If I hire people to do repairs, they never arrive on the day scheduled. If I owe a bill, the computer program is bound to overcharge me. Therefore, in self-defense, I have developed the following consumer's guide to complaining effectively.

The first step is getting organized. I save all sales slips and original boxes. 2 Also, I keep a special file for warranty cards and appliance guarantees. This file does not prevent a product from falling apart the day after the guarantee runs out. One of the problems in our country is the shoddy workmanship that goes into many products. However, these facts give me the ammunition I need to make a complaint. I know the date of the purchase, the correct price (or service charge), where the item was purchased, and an exact description of the product, including model and serial numbers. When I compose my letter of complaint, I find it is not necessary to exaggerate. I just stick to the facts.

The next step is to send the complaint to the person who will get 3 results quickly. My experience has shown that the president of the company

(continued)

is the best person to contact. I call the company to find out the president's name and make sure I note the proper spelling. Then I write directly to that person, and I usually get prompt action. For example, the head of AMF arranged to replace my son's ten-speed "lemon" when it fell apart piece by piece in less than a year. Another time, the president of a Philadelphia department store finally had a twenty-dollar overcharge on my bill corrected after I had spent three months arguing uselessly with a computer program.

If I get no response to a written complaint within ten days, I follow   4
through with a personal telephone call. When I had a new bathtub installed a few years ago, the plumber left a gritty black substance on the bottom of the tub. No amount of scrubbing could remove it. I tried every cleanser on the supermarket shelf, but I still had a dirty tub. The plumber shrugged off my complaints and said to try Comet. The manufacturer never answered my letter or e-mail. Finally, I made a personal phone call to the president of the firm. Within days a well-dressed executive showed up at my door. In a business suit, white shirt, striped tie, and rubber gloves, he cleaned the tub. Before he left, he scolded me in an angry voice, "You didn't have to call the president." The point is, I did have to call the president. No one else cared enough to solve the problem.

Therefore, my advice to consumers is to keep accurate records, and   5
when you have to complain, go right to the top. It has always worked for me.

Questions

1

About Unity

1. The (*fill in the correct answer:* first, second, third) _____ supporting paragraph of "Successful Exercise" lacks a topic sentence. Write a topic sentence that expresses its main point:

    _____

    _____

2. Which of the following sentences from paragraph 4 of "Successful Exercise" should be omitted in the interest of paragraph unity?

    a. "Finally, use common sense in getting started."

    b. "Common sense isn't so common, as anyone who reads newspapers and watches the world can tell you."

    c. "If this is your first attempt at exercising, begin slowly."

    d. "You do not need to do each movement the full number of times at first, but you should *try* each one."

3. Which sentence in paragraph 2 of "How to Complain" should be omitted in the interest of paragraph unity? *(Write the opening words.)*

_____

About Support.

4. Which sentence in paragraph 3 of "Successful Exercise" needs to be followed by more supporting details? *(Write the opening words.)*

_____

5. Which supporting paragraph in "How to Complain" uses one extended example? Write the number of that paragraph and tell (in just a few words) what the example was about.

_____

_____

6. Which supporting paragraph in "How to Complain" depends on two short examples? Write the number of that paragraph and tell (in just a few words) what each example was about.

_____

_____

About Coherence

7. Read paragraph 3 of "Successful Exercise" and find the four sentences that begin with time signals. Write those four signals here.

_____   _____

_____   _____

8. In "How to Complain," which time transition word is used in the topic sentence of paragraph 2?_____ In the topic sentence of paragraph 3?

_____

About the Introduction and Conclusion

9. Which statement best describes the introduction of "Successful Exercise"?

   a. It begins with a couple of general points about the topic and then narrows down to the thesis.

   b. It explains the importance of daily exercise to the reader.

   c. It uses a brief story about the author's experience with exercise.

   d. It asks a question about the role of exercise in life.

10. Which method of conclusion is used in both "Successful Exercise" and "How to Complain"?

   a. Summary

   b. Thought-provoking question

   c. Prediction

   d. Recommendation

Developing a Process Essay

Considering Purpose and Audience

Glance at a newsstand and you'll see magazine cover stories with titles such as "How to Impress Your Boss," "How to Seduce Anyone," or "How to Dress Like a Celebrity." These articles promise to give readers directions or information they can follow, and they are popular versions of process essays.

In general, the purpose of a process essay is to explain the steps involved in a particular action, process, or event. Some process essays focus on giving readers actual instructions, while others concentrate on giving readers information. The type of essay you write depends on the specific topic and purpose you choose.

As you prepare to write your process essay, begin by asking yourself what you want your readers to know. If, for example, you want your audience to know how to make the ultimate chocolate chip cookie, your process essay would include directions telling readers exactly what to do and how to do it. On the other hand, if you want your audience to know the steps involved in the process of digesting a chocolate chip cookie, you would instead detail the events that happen in the body as it turns food into energy. In this second instance, you would not be giving directions; you would be giving information.

No matter what your main point, keep your audience in mind as you work. As with any essay, select a topic that will interest readers. A group of college students, for example, might be interested in reading an essay on how to get financial aid but be bored by an essay on how to prepare for retirement. In addition, consider how much your readers already know about your topic. An audience unfamiliar with financial aid may need background information in order to understand the process you have chosen to describe. Also, be sure to follow a clear sequence in your essay, putting events or steps in an order that readers can easily follow.

> **TIP** Typically, steps in a process essay should be presented in time order, though not always. For more information about words that signal time, see page 84.

A final consideration for writing a process essay is point of view. If you are writing specific directions to readers (something done in this book), it is acceptable to write in *second person,* directly addressing your audience as "you." However, if you are presenting information, as in the example about digestion above, it is better to write in the more formal *third person.* In all cases, the goal is to choose the point of view that best suits your audience of readers and increases the likelihood that they will understand your main point.

TIP For more information about point of view, see pages 172–174.

Development through Prewriting

A process essay requires the writer to think through the steps involved in an activity. As Marian, the author of "How to Complain," thought about possible topics for her essay, she asked herself, What are some things I do methodically, step by step? A number of possibilities occurred to her, including getting herself and her children ready for school in the morning, shopping for groceries (from preparing a shopping list to organizing her coupons), and the one she finally settled on: effective complaining. "People tell me I'm 'so organized' when it comes to getting satisfaction on things I buy," Marian said. "I realized that I do usually get results when I complain because I go about complaining in an organized way. To write my essay, I just needed to put those steps into words."

Marian began by making a list of the steps she follows when she makes a complaint. This is what she wrote:

> Save sales slips and original boxes
>
> Engrave items with ID number in case of burglary
>
> Write or e-mail letter of complaint
>
> Save or make photocopy of letter
>
> Create file of warranties and guarantees
>
> Send complaint letter directly to president
>
> Call company for president's name
>
> Follow through with telephone call if no response
>
> Make thank-you call after action is taken

Next, she numbered those steps in the order in which she performs them. She struck out some items she realized weren't really necessary to the process of complaining:

1   Save sales slips and original boxes

~~Engrave items with ID number in case of burglary~~

4   Write or e-mail letter of complaint

~~Save or make photocopy of letter~~

2   Create file of warranties and guarantees

5   Send complaint letter directly to president

3   Call company for president's name

6   Follow through with telephone call if no response

~~Make thank-you call after action is taken~~

Next, she decided to group her items into three steps: (1) getting organized, (2) sending the complaint to the president, and (3) following up with further action.

With that preparation done, Marian wrote her first draft.

First Draft

How to Complain

Because I find that a consumer has to watch out for herself and be ready to speak up if a product or service isn't satisfactory, I have developed the following consumer's guide to complaining effectively.

The first step is getting organized. I save all sales slips, original boxes, warranty cards, and appliance guarantees. This file does not prevent a product from falling apart the day after the guarantee runs out. One of the problems in our country is the shoddy workmanship that goes into many products. That way I know the date of the purchase, the correct price, where the item was purchased, and an exact description of the product.

The next step is to send the complaint to the person who will get results quickly. I call the company to find out the president's name and then I write directly to that person. For example, the head of AMF arranged to replace my son's bike. Another time, the president of a Philadelphia department store finally had a twenty-dollar overcharge on my bill corrected.

If I get no response to a written complaint within ten days, I follow through with a personal telephone call. When I had a new bathtub installed a few years ago, the plumber left a gritty black substance on the bottom of the tub. I tried everything to get it off. Finally, I made a personal phone call

(continued)

> to the president of the firm. Within days a well-dressed executive showed up at my door. In a business suit, white shirt, striped tie, and rubber gloves, he cleaned the tub. Before he left, he said, "You didn't have to call the president."
>
> Therefore, my advice to consumers is to keep accurate records, and when you have to complain, go right to the top. It has always worked for me.

Development through Revising

After she had written the first draft, Marian set it aside for several days. When she reread it, she was able to look at it more critically. These are her comments:

> *I think this first draft is OK as the "bare bones" of an essay, but it needs to be fleshed out everywhere. For instance, in paragraph 2, I need to explain <u>why</u> it's important to know the date of purchase etc. And in paragraph 3, I need to explain more about <u>what happened</u> with the bike and the department store overcharge. In paragraph 4, especially, I need to explain <u>how</u> I tried to solve the problem with the bathtub before I called the president. I want to make it clear that I don't immediately go to the top as soon as I have a problem—I give the people at a lower level a chance to fix it first. All in all, my first draft looks as if I just rushed to get the basic ideas down on paper. Now I need to take the time to back up my main points with better support.*

With that self-critique in mind, Marian wrote the version of "How to Complain" that appears on page 245.

A Professional Essay to Consider

Read the following professional essay. Then answer the questions and read the comments that follow.

How to Do Well on a Job Interview
by Glenda Davis

Ask a random selection of people for a listing of their least favorite activities, 1 and right up there with "getting my teeth drilled" is likely to be "going to a job interview." The job interview is often regarded as a confusing, humiliating, and

www.mhhe.com/langan

nerve-racking experience. First of all, you have to wait for your appointment in an outer room, often trapped there with other people applying for the same job. You sit nervously, trying not to think about the fact that only one of you may be hired. Then you are called into the interviewer's office. Faced with a complete stranger, you have to try to act both cool and friendly as you are asked all sorts of questions. Some questions are personal: "What is your greatest weakness?" Others are confusing: "Why should we hire you?" The interview probably takes about twenty minutes but seems like two hours. Finally, you go home and wait for days and even weeks. If you get the job, great. But if you don't, you're rarely given any reason why.   2

The job-interview "game" may not be much fun, but it is a game you *can* win if you play it right. The name of the game is standing out of the crowd—in a positive way. If you go to the interview in a Bozo the Clown suit, you'll stand out of the crowd, all right, but not in a way that is likely to get you hired.   3

Here are guidelines to help you play the interview game to win: 4

Present yourself as a winner. Instantly, the way you dress, speak, and move gives the interviewer more information about you than you would think possible. You doubt that this is true? Consider this: a professional job recruiter, meeting a series of job applicants, was asked to signal the moment he decided *not* to hire each applicant. The thumbs-down decision was often made *in less than forty-five seconds—even before the applicant thought the interview had begun.*   5

How can you keep from becoming a victim of an instant "no" decision?

- *Dress appropriately.* This means business clothing: usually a suit and tie or a conservative dress or skirt suit. Don't wear casual student clothing. On the other hand, don't overdress: you're going to a job interview, not a party. If you're not sure what's considered appropriate business attire, do some spying before the interview. Walk past your prospective place of employment at lunch or quitting time and check out how the employees are dressed. Your goal is to look as though you would fit in with that group of people.

- *Pay attention to your grooming.* Untidy hair, body odor, dandruff, unshined shoes, a hanging hem, stains on your tie, excessive makeup or cologne, a sloppy job of shaving—if the interviewer notices any of these, your prospect of being hired takes a probably fatal hit.

- *Look alert, poised, and friendly.* When that interviewer looks into the waiting room and calls your name, he or she is getting a first impression of your behavior. If you're slouched in your chair, dozing or lost in the pages of a magazine; if you look up with an annoyed "Huh?"; if you get up slowly and wander over with your hands in your pockets, he or she will not be favorably impressed. What *will* earn you points is rising promptly and walking briskly toward the interviewer. Smiling and looking directly at that person, extend your hand to shake his or hers, saying, "I'm Lesley Brown. Thank you for seeing me today."

- *Expect to make a little small talk.* This is not a waste of time; it is the interviewer's way of checking your ability to be politely sociable, and it is your opportunity to cement the good impression you've already made. The key is to follow the interviewer's lead. If he or she wants to chat about the weather for a few minutes, do so. But don't drag it out; as soon as you get a signal that it's time to talk about the job, be ready to get down to business.

Be ready for the interviewer's questions. The same questions come up again 6 and again in many job interviews. *You should plan ahead for all these questions!* Think carefully about each question, outline your answer, and memorize each outline. Then practice reciting the answers to yourself. Only in this way are you going to be prepared. Here are common questions, what they really mean, and how to answer them:

- *"Tell me about yourself."* This question is raised to see how organized you are. The *wrong* way to answer it is to launch into a wandering, disjointed response or—worse yet—to demand defensively, "What do you want to know?" or "What do you mean?" When this question comes up, you should be prepared to give a brief summary of your life and work experience—where you grew up, where your family lives now, where you went to school, what jobs you've had, and how you happen to be here now looking for the challenge of a new job.

- *"What are your strengths and weaknesses?"* In talking about your strong points, mention traits that will serve you well in this particular job. If you are well-organized, a creative problem-solver, a good team member, or a quick learner, be ready to describe specific ways those strengths have served you in the past. Don't make the mistake of saying, "I don't have any real weaknesses." You'll come across as more believable if you admit a flaw—but make it one that an employer might actually like. For instance, admit that you are a workaholic or a perfectionist.

- *"Why should we hire you?"* Remember that it is up to *you* to convince the interviewer that you're the man or woman for this job. If you just sit there and hope that the interviewer will magically discern your good qualities, you are likely to be disappointed. Don't be afraid to sell yourself. Tell the recruiter that from your research you have learned that the interviewer's company is one you would like to work for, and that you believe the company's needs and your skills are a great match.

- *"Why did you leave your last job?"* This may seem like a great opportunity to cry on the interviewer's shoulder about what a jerk your last boss was or how unappreciated you were. It is not. The experts agree: never bad-mouth *anyone* when you are asked this question. Say that you left in order to seek greater responsibilities or challenges. Be positive, not negative. No matter how justified you may feel about hating your last job or boss, if you give voice to those feelings in an interview, you're going to make the interviewer suspect that you're a whiner and hard to work with.

• *"Do you have any questions?"* This is the time to stress one last time how interested you are in this particular job. Ask a question or two about specific aspects of the job, pointing out again how well your talents and the company's needs are matched. Even if you're dying to know how much the job pays and how much vacation you get, don't ask. There will be time enough to cover those questions after you've been offered the job. Today, your task is to demonstrate what a good employee you would be.

Send a thank-you note. Once you've gotten past the interview, there is one 7 more chance for you to make a fine impression. As soon as you can—certainly no more than one or two days after the interview—write a note of thanks to your interviewer. In it, briefly remind him or her of when you came in and what job you applied for. As well as thanking the interviewer for seeing you, reaffirm your interest in the job and mention again why you think you are the best candidate for it. Make the note courteous, businesslike, and brief—just a paragraph or two. If the interviewer is wavering between several equally qualified candidates, such a note could tip the scales in your favor.

No amount of preparation is going to make interviewing for a job your favorite 8 activity. But if you go in well-prepared and with a positive attitude, your potential employer can't help thinking highly of you. And the day will come when you are the one who wins the job.

About Unity

Questions 2

1. Either of two sentences in "How to Do Well on a Job Interview" might serve as the thesis. Write the opening words of either of these sentences:

_____

_____

_____

2. Which statement would make the best topic sentence for paragraph 4?
   a. Beauty is only skin-deep.
   b. Interviewers care only about how applicants dress.
   c. Professional job recruiters meet many applicants for a single job.
   d. You should present yourself as a winner because first impressions count a lot.

3. In paragraph 6, which statement would best serve as a topic sentence for the list item about strengths and weaknesses?

a. A quality such as perfectionism or workaholism can be seen as both a strength and a weakness.

b. As you talk about your strengths and weaknesses, tailor what you say to the job you're applying for.

c. Claiming to be a "creative problem-solver" is a good idea as you apply for almost any position.

d. The interviewer is not likely to be impressed if you claim to have no major weaknesses.

About Support

4. In paragraph 5, the supporting details for the list item "dress appropriately" are

    a. reasons for dressing appropriately.

    b. quotations of experts on how to dress for job interviews.

    c. ideas on how to dress appropriately.

    d. statistics on how people who are interviewed dress and how well they succeed.

5. Which sentence from paragraph 7 best provides a *reason* for the author's suggestion about sending a thank-you note?

    a. "As soon as you can—certainly no more than one or two days after the interview—write a note of thanks to your interviewer."

    b. "In it, briefly remind him or her of when you came in and what job you applied for."

    c. "Make the note courteous, businesslike, and brief—just a paragraph or two."

    d. "If the interviewer is wavering between several equally qualified candidates, such a note could tip the scales in your favor."

About Coherence

6. In paragraph 1, what three transitional words or phrases are used to begin sentences as the author describes the process of interviewing?

    _____   _____   _____

7. The main method of organization of paragraph 1 is

    a. time order.

    b. emphatic order.

8. In paragraph 5, find the "change of direction" signal that begins a sentence in the first list item. Write the opening words of that sentence here.

    _____

About the Introduction and Conclusion

9. Which statement best describes the introductory paragraph of "How to Do Well on a Job Interview"?

   a. It begins with a broad, general statement about job interviews and narrows it down to the thesis statement.

   b. It describes a typical job interview and its aftermath.

   c. It explains the importance of doing well on a job interview.

   d. It asks a series of questions that encourage readers to think about how they prepare for a job interview.

10. Which statement best describes the concluding paragraph of "How to Do Well on a Job Interview"?

   a. It ends with a summary of the article.

   b. It ends with a prediction of what will happen if advice in the article is followed.

   c. It ends with a series of questions that prompt the reader to think further about what's been written.

Writing a Process Essay

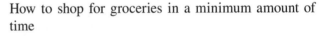

Writing | Assignment

1   Choose a topic from the list below to use as the basis for a process essay.

How to shop for groceries in a minimum amount of time

How to choose a car, rent an apartment, or buy a house

How to do household cleaning efficiently

How to gain or lose weight

How to get over a broken heart

How to plan an event (party, wedding, garage sale, etc.)

How to choose a pet

How to quit smoking (or another bad habit)

© WoodyStock/Alamy

Prewriting

a. Freewrite for ten minutes on the topic you have tentatively chosen. Don't worry about spelling, grammar, organization, or anything other than getting your thoughts down on the page. If ideas are still flowing at the end of ten minutes, keep on writing. This freewriting will give you a base of raw material that you can draw on in the next phase of your work. Judging from your freewriting, do you think you have enough material to support a process essay? If so, keep following the steps below. If not, choose another topic and freewrite about *it* for ten minutes.

b. Develop a single clear sentence that will serve as your thesis. Your thesis can either (1) say it is important that your readers know about this process ("Knowing how to choose a pet wisely can ensure that the two of you have a happy relationship") or (2) state your opinion of this process ("Quitting smoking is the most important single thing you can do for your health").

c. Make a list of the steps you are describing. Here, for example, is the list prepared by the author of "Successful Exercise."

Wear comfortable, loose clothing

Clear an area for exercise

Lock the door and turn off the phone

Tie hair back

Move smoothly and gracefully

Start slowly

Take hot shower afterward

Make time—get up early, give up a TV show

Get out weights or other equipment

Turn on music

Cool down

d. Number your items in time order. Strike out items that do not fit in the list; add others as they occur to you. Thus:

---

2 Wear comfortable, loose clothing

4 Clear an area for exercise

6 Lock the door and turn off the phone

3 Tie hair back

8 Move smoothly and gracefully

7 Start slowly

10 Take hot shower afterward

1 Make time—get up early, give up a TV show

5 Get out weights or other equipment

~~Turn on music~~

9 Cool down

---

e. After making the list, decide how the items can be grouped into a minimum of three steps. For example, with "Successful Exercise," you might divide the process into (1) setting a regular time, (2) preparing for exercise, and (3) doing the exercise. With a topic like "How to Quit Smoking," you might divide the process into (1) keeping a journal of your smoking, (2) preparing mentally and physically, and (3) getting through the first days.

f. Use your list as a guide to write the first rough draft of your paper. Do not expect to finish your paper in one draft. You should be ready to write a series of drafts as you work toward the goals of unity, support, and coherence.

Revising

After you have completed the first draft of the paper, set it aside for a while if you can. Then read the paper out loud to a friend or classmate whose judgment you respect. Keep these points in mind as you hear your own words, and ask your friend to respond to them as well:

FOUR BASES Checklist for Process

About *Unity*

> Does my essay describe the steps in a clear, logical way?

About *Support*

> Does the essay describe the necessary steps so that a reader could perform the task described, or is essential information missing?

About *Coherence*

> Have I used transitions such as *first, next, also, then, after, now, during,* and *finally* to make the essay move smoothly and clearly from one step to another?

> Do I have a concluding paragraph that provides a summary or final thought or both?

About *Sentence Skills*

> Have I used a consistent point of view throughout my essay?

> Have I used specific rather than general words?

> Have I avoided wordiness and used concise wording?

> Are my sentences varied?

> Have I proofread my essay for spelling and other sentence skills, as listed on the inside back cover of the book?

As you revise your essay through one or more additional drafts, continue to refer to this list until you can answer yes to each question.

Writing Assignment

2

Everyone is an expert at something. Write a process essay on some skill that you can perform very well. Write from the point of view that "This is how _____ *should* be done." Remember that your skill need not be unusual. It can be anything from making a perfect pie crust to hooking up a car stereo to dealing with unpleasant customers to using a digital camcorder.

Prewriting

a. If possible, perform the task and, as you go along, take notes on what you're doing. If that's not possible (as when dealing with unpleasant customers), think through a particular time you had to deal with such a task and make notes about just what you did.

b. Look over your notes and make a list of the steps you followed.

c. Considering your list, decide how you can divide the items listed into at least three steps. For instance, look at the following list of items for the process of "Cooking a Pot Roast." Then fill in the blanks in the scratch outline that follows:

1   Marinate the roast for thirty minutes with Adolph's Marinade.

2   Sprinkle the roast with seasoned flour.

3   Heat oil in a heavy pot.

4   Brown roast on all sides in the hot oil.

5   Cover the roast with one-third water, one-third beef broth, and one-third red wine.

6   Bring roast and liquid to boil.

7   Cover pot.

8   Turn down heat and simmer for an hour.

9   Taste broth and add seasonings as desired—salt, pepper, Worcestershire sauce.

10 Peel potatoes and carrots and cut into chunks.

11 Cut onions into chunks.

12 Add vegetables to pot for the last half hour of cooking.

13 Cook until meat flakes easily when you stick a fork in it.

14 Remove meat and vegetables from broth.

15 Dissolve two tablespoons of flour in half-cup cold water.

16 Stir flour mixture into boiling broth to thicken into gravy.

17 Serve gravy with the meat and vegetables.

Step 1: Preparing and cooking the meat

       Items   _____   through   _____

Step 2: Preparing and cooking the vegetables

       Items   _____   through   _____

Step 3: Preparing the gravy and serving

       Items   _____   through   _____

d. Prepare such a scratch outline of your main points. Use it as your guide as you write the rough draft of your paper.

Revising

As you read through your first draft and subsequent drafts, ask yourself these questions:

FOUR BASES Checklist for Process

About *Unity*

☑ Have I introduced my essay with either a statement of the importance of the process or my opinion of the process?

About *Support*

☑ Have I provided a clear step-by-step description of the process?

About *Coherence*

☑ Have I divided the items in the process into at least three logical steps (main points of the essay)?

☑ Have I used transitions such as *first, next, also, then, during,* and *finally* to help readers follow my train of thought?

About *Sentence Skills*

☑ Have I used a consistent point of view throughout my essay?

☑ Have I used specific rather than general words?

☑ Have I avoided wordiness and used concise wording?

☑ Are my sentences varied?

☑ Have I checked for spelling and other sentence skills, as listed on the inside back cover of the book?

As you revise your essay through one or more additional drafts, continue to refer to this checklist until you can answer yes to each question.

Writing | Assignment

3   Any one of the topics below can be written as a process paper. Follow the steps suggested for Writing Assignment 1. Note that some of these topics invite a humorous point of view.

© Bloomimage/Corbis

How to cook a favorite dish

How to break a bad habit

How to live with a two-year-old, a teenager, or a parent

How to make someone like you

How to make excuses

How to fall out of love

How to improve your reading skills

How to care for an aging relative

How to improve a school or a place of work

Writing Assignment

Writing for a Specific Purpose and Audience

4

In this process essay, you will write with a specific purpose and for a specific audience. Imagine that you have a younger brother or sister who has asked you to be a guest editor of his or her high school paper. Prepare an informal essay in which you summarize, in your own words, the steps involved in successfully managing your time in college or in preparing for and taking an essay exam.

www.mhhe.com/langan

Cause and Effect

12

This chapter will explain and illustrate how to

- develop a cause-and-effect essay

- write a cause-and-effect essay

- revise a cause-and-effect essay

In addition, you will read and consider

- two student cause-and-effect essays

- one professional cause-and-effect essay

Write an essay in which you discuss the causes or effects of our society's fascination with reality TV. An essay on the causes would discuss why Americans are so intrigued with reality television shows. An essay on the effects would show how this fascination with reality TV has affected American society.

Why did Gail decide to move out of her parents' house? What made you quit a well-paying job? Why are horror movies so popular? Why has Ben acted so depressed lately? Why did our team fail to make the league play-offs?

Every day we ask questions like these and look for answers. We realize that many actions do not occur without causes, and we realize also that a given action can have a series of effects—good or bad. By examining the causes or effects of an action, we seek to understand and explain things that happen in our lives.

You will be asked in this chapter to do some detective work by examining the cause of something or the effects of something. First read the student essays and the professional essay that follow and work through the questions that accompany the essays. All three essays support their thesis statements by explaining a series of causes or a series of effects.

Student Essays to Consider

The Joys of an Old Car

Some of my friends can't believe that my car still runs. Others laugh when they see it parked outside the house and ask if it's an antique. But they aren't being fair to my twenty-year-old Toyota Corolla. In fact, my "antique" has opened my eyes to the rewards of owning an old car. 1

One obvious reward of owning my old Toyota is economy. Twenty years ago, when my husband and I were newly married and nearly broke, we bought the car—a shiny red year-old leftover—for a mere $4,200. Today it would cost four times as much. We save money on insurance, since it's no longer worthwhile for us to have collision coverage. Old age has even been kind to the Toyota's engine, which has required only three major repairs in the last several years. And it still delivers twenty-eight miles per gallon in the city and forty-one on the highway—not bad for a senior citizen. 2

I've heard that when a Toyota passes the twenty-thousand-mile mark with no problems, it will probably go on forever. I wouldn't disagree. Our Toyota breezed past that mark many years ago. Since then, I've been able to count on it to sputter to life and make its way down the driveway on the coldest, snowiest mornings. When my boss got stuck with his brand-new BMW in the worst snowstorm of the year, I sauntered into work on time. The single time my Toyota didn't start, unfortunately, was the day I had a final exam. The Toyota may have the body of an old car, but beneath its elderly hood hums the engine of a teenager. 3

Last of all, having the same car for many years offers the advantage of familiarity. When I open the door and slide into the driver's seat, the soft 4

(continued)

vinyl surrounds me like a well-worn glove. I know to the millimeter exactly how much room I have when I turn a corner or back into a curbside parking space. When my gas gauge points to "empty," I know that 1.3 gallons are still in reserve, and I can plan accordingly. The front wheels invariably begin to shake when I go more than fifty-five miles an hour, reminding me that I am exceeding the speed limit. With the Toyota, the only surprises I face come from other drivers.

I prize my twenty-year-old Toyota's economy and dependability, and   5
most of all, its familiarity. It is faded, predictable, and comfortable, like a well-worn pair of jeans. And, like a well-worn pair of jeans, it will be difficult to throw away.

Stresses of Being a Celebrity

A woman signing herself "Wants the Truth in Westport" wrote to Ann   1
Landers with a question she just had to have answered. "Please find out for sure," she begged the columnist, "whether or not Oprah Winfrey has had a face-lift." Fortunately for Ms. Winfrey's privacy, Ann Landers refused to answer the question. But the incident was disturbing. How awful it would be to be a celebrity, always in the public eye. Celebrities lead very stressful lives, for no matter how glamorous or powerful they are, they have too little privacy, too much pressure, and no safety.

For one thing, celebrities don't have the privacy an ordinary person has.   2
The most personal details of their lives are splashed all over the front pages of US Weekly and the Globe so that bored supermarket shoppers can read about "Leonardo DiCaprio's Awful Secret" or "The Heartbreak Behind Jessica Simpson's Smile." Even a celebrity's family is hauled into the spotlight. A teenage son's arrest for pot possession or a wife's drinking problem becomes the subject of glaring headlines. Photographers hound celebrities at their homes, in restaurants, and on the street, hoping to get a picture of Halle Berry in curlers or Vince Vaughn guzzling a beer. When celebrities try to do the things that normal people do, like eat out or attend a football game, they run the risk of being interrupted by thoughtless autograph hounds or mobbed by aggressive fans.

In addition to the loss of privacy, celebrities must cope with the   3
constant pressure of having to look great and act right. Their physical appearance is always under observation. Famous women, especially, suffer from the spotlight, drawing remarks like "She really looks old" or "Boy, has she put on weight." Unflattering pictures of celebrities are photographers'

(continued)

prizes to be sold to the highest bidder; this increases the pressure on celebrities to look good at all times. Famous people are also under pressure to act calm and collected under any circumstances. Because they are constantly observed, they have no freedom to blow off steam or to do something just a little crazy.

Most important, celebrities must deal with the stress of being in constant **4** danger. The friendly grabs, hugs, and kisses of enthusiastic fans can quickly turn into uncontrolled assaults on a celebrity's hair, clothes, and car. Most people agree that photographers bear some responsibility for the death of one of the leading celebrities of the 1990s—Princess Diana. Whether or not their pursuit caused the crash that took her life, it's clear she was chased as aggressively as any escaped convict by bloodhounds. And celebrity can even lead to deliberately lethal attacks. The attempt to kill Ronald Reagan and the murder of John Lennon came about because two unbalanced people became obsessed with these world-famous figures. Famous people must live with the fact that they are always fair game—and never out of season.

Some people dream of starring roles, their name in lights, and their **5** picture on the cover of People magazine. But the cost is far too high. A famous person gives up private life, feels pressured to look and act certain ways all the time, and is never completely safe. An ordinary, calm life is far safer and saner than a life of fame.

About Unity

1. Which supporting paragraph in "The Joys of an Old Car" lacks a topic sentence?

   a. 2

   b. 3

   c. 4

2. Which sentence in paragraph 3 of "The Joys of an Old Car" should be omitted in the interest of paragraph unity? *(Write the opening words.)*

   _____

3. Rewrite the thesis statement of "The Joys of an Old Car" to include a plan of development.

   _____

   _____

   _____

About Support

4. In paragraph 4 of "Stresses of Being a Celebrity," the author supports the idea that "celebrities must deal with the stress of being in constant danger" with *(circle the letters of the two answers that apply)*

   a. statistics.

   b. an explanation.

   c. a quotation by an expert.

   d. examples.

5. After which sentence in paragraph 3 of "Stresses of Being a Celebrity" are more specific details needed? *(Write the opening words.)*

   _____

6. In "The Joys of an Old Car," how many examples are given to support the topic sentence "One obvious reward . . . is economy"?

   a. two

   b. three

   c. four

   d. five

About Coherence

7. Which topic sentence in "Stresses of Being a Celebrity" functions as a linking sentence between paragraphs? *(Write the opening words.)*

   _____

8. Paragraph 3 of "Stresses of Being a Celebrity" includes two main transition words or phrases. List those words or phrases.

   _____   _____

9. What are the two transition words or phrases in "The Joys of an Old Car" that signal two major points of support for the thesis?

   _____   _____

About the Introduction and Conclusion

10. Which method is used in the conclusion of "The Joys of an Old Car"?

    a. Summary and final thought

    b. Thought-provoking question

    c. Recommendation

Developing a Cause-and-Effect Essay

Considering Purpose and Audience

The main purpose of a cause-and-effect essay is to explain to your audience (1) the causes of a particular event or situation; (2) the effects of an event or a situation; or more rarely, (3) a combination of both.

The type of cause-and-effect essay you write will depend on the topic you choose and the main point you wish to communicate. If, for example, your purpose is to tell readers about the impact a special person had on your life, your essay would focus mainly on the *effects* of that person. However, if your purpose is to explain why you moved out of your family home, your essay would focus on the *causes* of your decision.

As with all essays, try to pick a topic that will appeal to your audience of readers. An essay on the negative effects of steroids and other drugs on professional athletes may be especially interesting to an audience of sports fans. On the other hand, this same topic might not be as appealing to people who dislike sports. In addition to selecting a lively topic, be sure to make your main point clear so that your audience can follow the cause-and-effect relationship you've chosen to develop. In the preceding instance, you might even announce specific causes or effects by signaling them to readers: "One effect drug use has on athletes is to . . ."

Development through Prewriting

The best essays are often those written about a topic that the author genuinely cares about. When Janine, the author of "The Joys of an Old Car," was assigned a cause-and-effect essay, she welcomed the assignment. She explains, "My husband and I believe in enjoying what we have and living simply, rather than 'keeping up with the Joneses.' Our beat-up old car is an example of that way of life. People often say to me, 'Surely you could buy a nicer car!' I enjoy explaining to them why we keep our old 'clunker.' So when I heard 'cause-and-effect essay,' I immediately thought of the car as a topic. Writing this essay was just an extension of a conversation I've had many times."

Although Janine had often praised the virtues of her old car to friends, she wasn't sure how to divide what she had to say into three main points. To get started, she made a list of all the good things about her car. Here is what she wrote:

> *Starts reliably*
>
> *Has needed few major repairs*
>
> *Reminder of Bill's and my first days of marriage*
>
> *Gets good gas mileage*
>
> *(continued)*

Don't need to worry about scratches and scrapes

I know exactly how much room I need to turn and park

Saves money on insurance

I'm very comfortable in it

No car payments

Cold weather doesn't seem to bother it

Don't worry about its being stolen

Uses regular gas

Can haul anything in it—dog, plants—and not worry about dirt

Know all its little tics and shimmies and don't worry about them

When Janine reviewed her list, she saw that the items fell into three major categories. There was (1) the car's economy, (2) its familiarity, and (3) its dependability. She went back and noted which category each of the items best fit. Then she crossed out those items that didn't seem to belong in any of the categories.

3   Starts reliably

1   Has needed few major repairs

~~Reminder of Bill's and my first days of marriage~~

1   Gets good gas mileage

~~Don't need to worry about scratches and scrapes~~

2   I know exactly how much room I need to turn and park

1   Saves money on insurance

2   I'm very comfortable in it

1   No car payments

3   Cold weather doesn't seem to bother it

~~Don't worry about its being stolen~~

(continued)

1   *Uses regular gas*

   Can haul anything in it—dog, plants—and not worry about dirt

2   *Know all its little tics and shimmies and don't worry about them*

Now Janine had three main points and several items to support each point. She produced this as a first draft:

First Draft

The Joys of an Old Car

When people see my beat-up old car, they sometimes laugh at it. But I tell them that owning a twenty-year-old Toyota has its good points.

One obvious reward is economy. My husband and I bought the car when we were newly married. We paid $4,200 for it. That seemed like a lot of money then, but today we'd spend four times that much for a similar car. We also save money on insurance. In the twenty years we've had it, the Toyota has needed only a few major repairs. It even gets good gas mileage.

I like the familiar feel of the car. I'm so used to it that driving anything else feels very strange. When I visited my sister recently, I drove her new Prius to the grocery store. Everything was so unfamiliar! I couldn't even figure out how to turn on the radio. I was relieved to get back to my own car.

Finally, my car is very dependable. No matter how cold and snowy it is, I know the Toyota will start quickly and get me where I need to go. Unfortunately, one day it didn't start, and naturally that day I had a final exam. But otherwise it just keeps on going and going.

My Toyota reminds me of a favorite piece of clothing that you wear forever and can't bear to throw away.

Development through Revising

Janine traded first drafts with a classmate, Sharon, and each critiqued the other's work before it was revised. Here is Janine's first draft again, with Sharon's comments in the margins.

The Joys of an Old Car

When people see my beat-up old car, they sometimes laugh at it. But I tell them that owning a twenty-year-old Toyota has its good points.

One obvious reward is economy. My husband and I bought the car when we were newly married. We paid $4,200 for it. That seemed like a lot of money then, but today we'd spend four times that much for a similar car. We also save money on insurance. In the twenty years we've had it, the Toyota has needed only a few major repairs. It even gets good gas mileage.

I like the familiar feel of the car. I'm so used to it that driving anything else feels very strange. When I visited my sister recently, I drove her new Prius to the grocery store. Everything was so unfamiliar! I couldn't even figure out how to turn on the radio. I was relieved to get back to my own car.

Finally, my car is very dependable. No matter how cold and snowy it is, I know the Toyota will start quickly and get me where I need to go. Unfortunately, one day it didn't start, and naturally that day I had a final exam. But otherwise it just keeps on going and going.

My Toyota reminds me of a favorite piece of clothing that you wear forever and can't bear to throw away.

Reader's Comments

How? Is the insurance less expensive just because the car is old?

Here would be a good place for a specific detail—how good is the mileage?

This topic sentence doesn't tie in with the others—shouldn't it say "Second," or "Another reason I like the car . . ."?

This is too much about your sister's car and not enough about yours.

This is a good comparison. But draw it out more—how is the car like comfortable old clothes?

Making use of Sharon's comments, Janine wrote the final version of "The Joys of an Old Car" that appears on page 265.

A Professional Essay to Consider

Read the following professional essay. Then answer the questions and read the comments that follow.

Taming the Anger Monster
by Anne Davidson

Laura Houser remembers the day with embarrassment.   1

"My mother was visiting from Illinois," she says. "We'd gone out to lunch and   2
done some shopping. On our way home, we stopped at an intersection. When the

light changed, the guy ahead of us was looking at a map or something and didn't move right away. I leaned on my horn and automatically yelled—well, what I generally yell at people who make me wait. I didn't even think about what I was doing. One moment I was talking and laughing with my mother, and the next I was shouting curses at a stranger. Mom's jaw just dropped. She said, 'Well, I guess *you've* been living in the city too long.' That's when I realized that my anger was out of control."

Laura has plenty of company. Here are a few examples plucked from the head- 3 lines of recent newspapers:

- Amtrak's Washington–New York train: When a woman begins to use her cell phone in a designated "quiet car," her seatmate grabs the phone and smashes it against the wall.

- Reading, Mass.: Arguing over rough play at their ten-year-old sons' hockey practice, two fathers begin throwing punches. One of the dads beats the other to death.

- Westport, Conn.: Two supermarket shoppers get into a fistfight over who should be first in a just-opened checkout line.

Reading these stories and countless others like them which happen daily, it's hard to escape the conclusion that we are one angry society. An entire vocabulary has grown up to describe situations of out-of-control fury: road rage, sideline rage, computer rage, biker rage, air rage. Bookstore shelves are filled with authors' advice on how to deal with our anger. Court-ordered anger management classes have become commonplace, and anger-management workshops are advertised in local newspapers.

Human beings have always experienced anger, of course. But in earlier, more 4 civil decades, public displays of anger were unusual to the point of being aberrant. Today, however, whether in petty or deadly forms, episodes of unrepressed rage have become part of our daily landscape.

What has happened to us? Are we that much angrier than we used to be? Have 5 we lost all inhibitions about expressing our anger? Are we, as a society, literally losing our ability to control our tempers?

Why Are We So Angry?

According to Sybil Evans, a conflict-resolution expert in New York City, there 6 are three components to blame for our societal bad behavior: time, technology and tension.

What's eating up our time? To begin with, Americans work longer hours and 7 are rewarded with less vacation time than people in any other industrial society. Over an average year, for example, most British employees work 250 hours less than most Americans; most Germans work a full 500 hours less. And most Europeans are given four to six weeks vacation every year, compared to the average American's two weeks. To make matters worse, many Americans face long stressful commutes at the beginning and end of each long workday.

Once we Americans finally get home from work, our busy day is rarely done. 8
We are involved in community activities; our children participate in sports, school
programs, and extra-curricular activities; and our houses, yards and cars cry out
for maintenance. To make matters worse, we are reluctant to use the little bit of
leisure time we do have to catch up on our sleep. Compared with Americans of
the nineteenth and early twentieth centuries, most of us are chronically sleep-
deprived. While our ancestors typically slept nine-and-a-half hours a night, many
of us feel lucky to get seven. We're critical of "lazy" people who sleep longer, and
we associate naps with toddlerhood. (In doing so, we ignore the example of successful people including Winston Churchill, Albert Einstein, and Napoleon, all of
whom were devoted to their afternoon naps.)

The bottom line: we are time-challenged and just plain tired—and tired peo- 9
ple are cranky people. We're ready to blow—to snap at the slow-moving cashier,
to tap the bumper of the slowpoke ahead of us, or to do something far worse.

Technology is also to blame for the bad behavior so widespread in our culture. 10
Amazing gadgets were supposed to make our lives easier—but have they? Sure,
technology has its positive aspects. It is a blessing, for instance, to have a cell
phone on hand when your car breaks down far from home or to be able to "instant
message" a friend on the other side of the globe. But the downsides are many.
Cell phones, pagers, fax machines, handheld computers and the like have robbed
many of us of what was once valuable downtime. Now we're *always* available to
take that urgent call or act on that last-minute demand. Then there is the endless
pressure of feeling we need to keep up with our gadgets' latest technological developments. For example, it's not sufficient to use your cell phone for phone calls.
Now you must learn to use the phone for text-messaging and downloading games.
It's not enough to take still photos with your digital camera. You should know how
to shoot ultra high-speed fast-action clips. It's not enough to have an enviable CD
collection. You should be downloading new songs in MP3 format. The computers
in your house should be connected by a wireless router, and online via high-speed
DSL service. In other words, if it's been more than ten minutes since you've updated your technology, you're probably behind.

In fact, you're not only behind; you're a stupid loser. At least, that's how most 11
of us end up feeling as we're confronted with more and more unexpected technologies: the do-it-yourself checkout at the supermarket, the telephone "help center"
that offers a recorded series of messages, but no human help. And feeling like
losers makes us frustrated and, you guessed it, angry. "It's not any one thing but
lots of little things that make people feel like they don't have control of their lives,"
says Jane Middleton-Moz, an author and therapist. "A sense of helplessness is what
triggers rage. It's why people end up kicking ATM machines."

Her example is not far-fetched. According to a survey of computer users in 12
Great Britain, a quarter of those under age 25 admitted to having kicked or punched
their computers on at least one occasion. Others confessed to yanking out cables in
a rage, forcing the computer to crash. On this side of the Atlantic, a Wisconsin man,
after repeated attempts to get his daughter's malfunctioning computer repaired,

took it to the store where he had bought it, placed it in the foyer, and attacked it with a sledgehammer. Arrested and awaiting a court appearance, he told local reporters, "It feels good, in a way." He had put into action a fantasy many of us have had—that of taking out our feelings of rage on the machines that so frustrate us.

Tension, the third major culprit behind our epidemic of anger, is intimately 13 connected with our lack of time and the pressures of technology. Merely our chronic exhaustion and our frustration in the face of a bewildering array of technologies would be enough to cause our stress levels to skyrocket, but we are dealing with much more. Our tension is often fueled by a reserve of anger that might be the result of a critical boss, marital discord, or (something that many of today's men and women experience, if few will admit it) a general sense of being stupid and inadequate in the face of the demands of modern life. And along with the challenges of everyday life, we now live with a widespread fear of such horrors as terrorist acts, global warming, and antibiotic-resistant diseases. Our sense of dread may be out of proportion to actual threats because of technology's ability to so constantly bombard us with worrisome information. Twenty-four hours a day news stations bring a stream of horror into our living rooms. As we work on our computers, headlines and graphic images are never more than a mouseclick away.

The Result of Our Anger

Add it all together—our feeling of never having enough time; the chronic ag- 14 gravation caused by technology; and our endless, diffuse sense of stress—and we become time bombs waiting to explode. Our angry outbursts may be briefly satisfying, but afterwards we are left feeling—well, like jerks. Worse, flying off the handle is a self-perpetuating behavior. Brad Bushman, a psychology professor at Iowa State University, says, "Catharsis is worse than useless." Bushman's research has shown that when people vent their anger, they actually become more, not less, aggressive. "Many people think of anger as the psychological equivalent of the steam in a pressure cooker. It has to be released, or it will explode. That's not true. The people who react by hitting, kicking, screaming, and swearing just feel more angry."

Furthermore, the unharnessed venting of anger may actually do us physical 15 harm. The vigorous expression of anger pumps adrenaline into our system and raises our blood pressure, setting the stage for heart attack and strokes. Frequently-angry people have even been shown to have higher cholesterol levels than even-tempered individuals.

How to Deal with Our Anger

Unfortunately, the culprits behind much of our anger—lack of time, frustrat- 16 ing technology, and mega-levels of stress—are not likely to resolve themselves anytime soon. So what are we to do with the anger that arises as a result?

According to Carol Tavris, author of *Anger: The Misunderstood Emotion,* 17 the keys to dealing with anger are common sense and patience. She points out that almost no situation is improved by an angry outburst. A traffic jam, a frozen computer, or a misplaced set of car keys are annoying. To act upon the angry feelings those situations provoke, however, is an exercise in futility. Shouting, fuming, or leaning on the car horn won't make traffic begin to flow, the screen unlock, or keys materialize.

Patience, on the other hand, is a highly practical virtue. People who take the **18** time to cool down before responding to an anger-producing situation are far less likely to say or do something they will regret later. "It is as true of the body as of arrows," Tavris says, "that what goes up must come down. Any emotional arousal will simmer down if you just wait long enough." When you are stuck in traffic, in other words, turn on some soothing music, breathe deeply, and count to ten—or thirty or forty, if need be.

Anger-management therapist Doris Wild Helmering agrees. "Like any feeling, **19** anger lasts only about three seconds," she says. "What keeps it going is your own negative thinking." As long as you focus on the idiot who cut you off on the expressway, you'll stay angry. But if you let the incident go, your anger will go with it. "Once you come to understand that you're driving your own anger with your thoughts," adds Helmering, "you can stop it."

Experts who have studied anger also encourage people to cultivate activities **20** that effectively vent their anger. For some people, it's reading the newspaper or watching TV, while others need more active outlets, such as using a treadmill, taking a walk, hitting golf balls, or working out with a punching bag. People who succeed in calming their anger can also enjoy the satisfaction of having dealt positively with their frustrations.

For Laura Houser, the episode in the car with her mother was a wake-up **21** call. "I saw myself through her eyes," she said, "and I realized I had become a chronically angry, impatient jerk. My response to stressful situations had become habitual—I automatically flew off the handle. Once I saw what I was doing, it really wasn't that hard to develop different habits. I simply decided I was going to treat other people the way I would want to be treated." The changes in Laura's life haven't benefited only her former victims. "I'm a calmer, happier person now," she reports. "I don't lie in bed at night fuming over stupid things other people have done and my own enraged responses." Laura has discovered the satisfaction of having a sense of control over her own behavior—which ultimately is all any of us can control.

About Unity

Questions

2

1. Which of the following statements best represents the implied thesis of "Taming the Anger Monster"?

   a. People today have lost their ability to control their anger and to behave in a civil fashion.

   b. Anger would last only a few seconds if we didn't keep it going with negative thinking.

   c. While technology has its positive aspects, it has made us constantly available to others and frustrates us with the need to master its endless new developments.

   d. Our out-of-control anger has understandable causes, but common sense and patience are more satisfying than outbursts of rage.

2. Which statement would best serve as a topic sentence for paragraphs 3 and 4?

   a. Anger has become an increasingly common problem in our society.

   b. People should be more thoughtful and tolerant of those around them.

   c. Displays of anger frequently lead to physical violence and even death.

   d. Anger is a natural response to irritating situations.

3. Which statement is the best topic sentence for paragraphs 16–18?

   a. "Unfortunately, the culprits behind much of our anger—lack of time, frustrating technology, and mega-levels of stress—are not likely to resolve themselves anytime soon."

   b. "According to Carol Tavris, author of *Anger: The Misunderstood Emotion,* the keys to dealing with anger are common sense and patience."

   c. "Patience, on the other hand, is a highly practical virtue."

   d. "People who take the time to cool down before responding to an anger-producing situation are far less likely to say or do something they will regret later."

About Support

4. The essay is about one main effect and three possible causes. What is the one main effect? What are the three causes?

   Effect: _____

   Three causes: _____

5. What are some examples cited to support the idea that technology has contributed to America's anger problem?

   _____

   _____

About Coherence

6. What is the best description of the organization of this essay?

   a. Introduction, Thesis, Three Supporting Parts, Conclusion

   b. Introduction, Thesis, Four Supporting Parts, Conclusion

   c. Introduction, Thesis, Five Supporting Parts

   d. Thesis, Six Supporting Parts, Conclusion

7. As shown by the outline below, "Taming the Anger Monster" bears a general resemblance to the traditional one-three-one essay model. Fill in the missing paragraph numbers.

Introduction:	Paragraphs:	_1–5_
Supporting Point 1:	Paragraph(s)	_____
Supporting Point 2:	Paragraph(s)	_____
Supporting Point 3:	Paragraph(s)	_____
Supporting Point 4:	Paragraphs	_____
Supporting Point 5:	Paragraphs	_____
Conclusion:	Paragraph:	_____

8. What are the three addition signals used to introduce the three causes of anger?

_____   _____   _____

About the Introduction and Conclusion

9. What method best describes the introduction to "Taming the Anger Monster"?

   a. Quotation

   b. Broad, general statement narrowing to thesis

   c. Idea that is the opposite of the one to be developed

   d. Anecdote and questions

10. What is the relationship between the essay's first paragraph and its concluding paragraph?

   _____

   _____

Writing a Cause-and-Effect Essay

Writing Assignment

1   In scratch-outline form, on a separate piece of paper, provide brief causes *or* effects for at least *four* of the ten statements below. The first is done for you as an example. Make sure that you have three *separate* and *distinct* items for each statement—don't provide two rewordings that say essentially the same thing. Also, indicate whether the items you have listed are causes or effects.

When you have finished your four scratch outlines, decide which of them would provide the best basis for a cause-and-effect essay that you will write.

1. Many youngsters are terrified of school.

   Causes:

   a. _____

   b. _____

   c. _____

2. Having more mothers in the workforce has changed the way many kids grow up.

© Greg Hinsdale/Corbis

3. Americans tend to get married later in life than they used to.

4. Society would benefit if nonviolent criminals were punished in ways other than jail time.

5. Among winners of prestigious academic awards, a high percentage are children of immigrant families who recently arrived in this country.

6. My relationship with (*name a relative or friend*) _____ has changed over time.

7. Growing up in my family has influenced my life in significant ways.

8. A bad (or good) teacher can have long-lasting impact on a student.

© Bubbles Photolibrary/Alamy

9. The average workweek should be no more than thirty hours.

10. It is easy to fall into an unhealthy diet in our society.

Prewriting

a. Look at the outline you produced in the previous step. You will now use it as the basis for a cause-and-effect essay. The statement will serve as your thesis, and the three causes or effects will function as your main points. Make sure that each of your main points is a *separate* and *distinct* point, not a restatement of one of the other points.

b. Decide whether you will support each of your main points with several short examples or with one extended example. You may want to freewrite about each of these examples for a few minutes, or you may want to make up a list of as many details as you think of that would go with each of the examples.

c. Write a first draft of an introduction that attracts the reader's interest, states your thesis, and presents a plan of development.

Revising

After you have completed the first draft of the paper, set it aside for a while (if possible). Then read it aloud to a friend or classmate. As you listen to your words, you should both keep these questions in mind:

FOUR BASES Checklist for Cause and Effect

About *Unity*

☑ Does the essay have a clearly stated thesis?

☑ Is there any irrelevant material that should be eliminated or rewritten?

About *Support*

☑ Have I backed up each main point with one extended example or several shorter examples?

☑ Do I have enough detailed support?

About *Coherence*

☑ Have I used transition words to help readers follow my train of thought?

☑ Have I provided a concluding paragraph to wrap up the essay?

About *Sentence Skills*

☑ Have I used a consistent point of view throughout my essay?

☑ Have I used specific rather than general words?

☑ Have I avoided wordiness and used concise wording?

☑ Are my sentences varied?

☑ Have I checked for spelling and other sentence skills, as listed on the inside back cover of the book?

As you revise your essay through one or more additional drafts, continue to refer to this list until you can answer yes to each question.

Writing Assignment

2

If friendly aliens from a highly developed civilization decided to visit our planet, they would encounter a contradictory race of beings—us. We humans would have reasons to feel both proud and ashamed of the kind of society the aliens would encounter. Write an essay explaining whether you would be proud or ashamed of the state of the human race today. Give reasons for your feelings.

Prewriting

a. You will probably have an instant gut reaction to the question *Am I more proud of or ashamed of the human race?* Go with that reaction; you will find it easier to come up with supporting points for the thesis that occurred to you immediately.

b. Generate supporting details for your thesis by making a list. Title it "Reasons I am proud of the human race" or "Reasons I am ashamed of the human race." Then list as many items as you can think of. Don't worry about whether the reasons are important or silly, significant or trivial. Just write down as many as possible.

c. Review your list and ask yourself if some of the items could be grouped into one category. For instance, a list of reasons to be proud of humanity might include items such as "We've come up with cures for major diseases," "We've developed the computer," and "We've invented wonderful communication devices like the cellular telephone, the Internet, movies, and TV." All of these could be grouped into a category called "Important inventions." That category, in turn, could serve as a main supporting point in your essay.

d. As described in step *c,* decide on three supporting points. Write a scratch outline that includes those points and the examples (one extended example or several shorter ones). The point described in step *c* would be outlined like this:

Point: The human race has come up with wonderful inventions that benefit all society.
1. Cures for diseases
2. Computers
3. Communication devices, including cell phones, the Internet, and TV

e. Using your scratch outline, write a first draft of the paper. Include an introduction that states your thesis and plan of development, and a conclusion that reminds readers of your thesis and leaves them with a final point to consider.

Revising

As you work through subsequent drafts, ask yourself these questions:

FOUR BASES Checklist for Cause and Effect

About *Unity*

☑ Have I introduced my essay with a clearly stated thesis and plan of development?

About *Support*

☑ Is each of my main points supported by solid, specific details?

About *Coherence*

☑ Have I used transition words such as *first, another, in addition,* and *also*?

About *Sentence Skills*

☑ Have I used a consistent point of view throughout my essay?

☑ Have I used specific rather than general words?

☑ Have I avoided wordiness and used concise wording?

☑ Are my sentences varied?

☑ Have I checked my writing for spelling and other sentence skills, as listed on the inside back cover of the book?

Writing | Assignment

3 Write a cause-and-effect essay in which you advance an idea about a poem, story, play, film, literary essay, or novel. The work you choose may be assigned by your instructor or may require your instructor's approval. To develop your idea, use a series of two or more reasons and specific supporting evidence for each reason. A student model follows.

Paul's Suicide

Paul, the main character in Willa Cather's short story "Paul's Case," is a   1
young man on a collision course with death. As Cather reveals Paul's story,
we learn about elements of Paul's personality that inevitably come together
and cause his suicide. Paul takes his own life as a result of his inability to
conform to his society, his passive nature, and his emotional isolation.

(continued)

First of all, Paul cannot conform to the standards of his own society.   2
At school, Paul advertises his desire to be part of another, more glamorous
world by wearing fancy clothes that set him apart from the other students.
At home on Cordelia Street, Paul despises everything about his middle-
class neighborhood. He hates the houses "permeated by kitchen odors," the
"ugliness and commonness of his own home," and the respectable neighbors
sitting on their front stoops every Sunday, "their stomachs comfortably
protruding." Paul's father hopes that Paul will settle down and become like
the young man next door, a nearsighted clerk who works for a corporate
steel magnate. Paul, however, is repelled by the young man and all he
represents. It seems inevitable, then, that Paul will not be able to cope with
the office job his father obtains for him at the firm of Denny & Carson; and
this inability to conform will, in turn, lead to Paul's theft of $1,000.

Paul's suicide is also due, in part, to his passive nature. Throughout his   3
life, Paul has been an observer and an onlooker. Paul's only escape from the
prison of his daily life comes from his job as an usher at Pittsburgh's Carnegie
Hall; he lives for the moments when he can watch the actors, singers, and
musicians. However, Paul has no desire to be an actor or musician. As Cather
says, "What he wanted was to see, to be in the atmosphere, float on the wave
of it, to be carried out . . . away from everything." Although Paul steals the
money and flees to New York, these uncharacteristic actions underscore the
desperation he feels. Once at the Waldorf in New York, Paul is again content
to observe the glamorous world he has craved for so long: "He had no
especial desire to meet or to know any of these people; all he demanded was
the right to look on and conjecture, to watch the pageant." During his brief
stay in the city, Paul enjoys simply sitting in his luxurious rooms, glimpsing
the show of city life through a magical curtain of snow. At the end, when
the forces of ordinary life begin to close in again, Paul kills himself. But it is
typical that he does not use the gun he has bought. Rather, more in keeping
with his passive nature, Paul lets himself fall under the wheels of a train.

Finally, Paul ends his life because he is emotionally isolated. Throughout   4
the story, not one person makes any real contact with Paul. His teachers do
not understand him and merely resent the attitude of false bravado that he
uses as a defense. Paul's mother is dead; he cannot even remember her. Paul
is completely alienated from his father, who obviously cares for him but
who cannot feel close to this withdrawn, unhappy son. To Paul, his father
is only the man waiting at the top of the stairs, "his hairy legs sticking out
of his nightshirt," who will greet him with "inquiries and reproaches." When
Paul meets a college boy in New York, they share a night on the town. But
the "champagne friendship" ends with a "singularly cool" parting. Paul is not
the kind of person who can let himself go or confide in one of his peers.

(continued)

For the most part, Paul's isolation is self-imposed. He has drifted so far into his fantasy life that people in the "real" world are treated like invaders. As he allows no one to enter his dream, there is no one Paul can turn to for understanding.

The combination of these personality factors—inability to conform, passivity, and emotional isolation—makes Paul's tragic suicide inevitable. Before he jumps in front of the train, Paul scoops a hole in the snow and buries the carnation that he has been wearing in his buttonhole. Like a hothouse flower in the winter, Paul has a fragile nature that cannot survive in its hostile environment.

5

Writing | Assignment

4 ## Writing for a Specific Purpose and Audience

In this cause-and-effect essay, you will write with a specific purpose and for a specific audience. Imagine that several friends of yours say they are having a hard time learning anything in a class taught by Professor X. You volunteer to attend the class and see for yourself. You also get information from your friends about the course requirements.

Afterward, you write a letter to Professor X, politely calling attention to what you see as causes of the learning problems that students are having in the class. To organize your essay, you might develop each of these causes in a separate supporting paragraph. In the second part of each supporting paragraph, you might suggest changes that Professor X could make to deal with each problem.

Comparison or Contrast

13

© vario images GmbH & Co.KG/Alamy

© Photodisc/SuperStock

This chapter will explain and illustrate how to

- develop an essay of comparison or contrast

- write an essay of comparison or contrast

- revise an essay of comparison or contrast

In addition, you will read and consider

- two student essays of comparison or contrast

- one professional essay of contrast

Looking at the two photographs above, write an essay in which you compare or contrast lecture classes with smaller classes.

Comparison and contrast are two thought processes we go through constantly in everyday life. When we *compare* two things, we show how they are similar; when we *contrast* two things, we show how they are different. We may compare or contrast two brand-name products (for example, Pepsi and Coca-Cola), two television shows, two cars, two teachers, two jobs, two friends, or two possible solutions to a problem we are facing. The purpose of comparing or contrasting is to understand each of the two things more clearly and, at times, to make judgments about them.

You will be asked in this chapter to write an essay of comparison or contrast. To prepare for this assignment, first read about the two methods of development you can use in writing your essay. Then read the student essays and the professional essay that follow and work through the questions that accompany the essays.

Methods of Development

A comparison or contrast essay calls for one of two types of development. Details can be presented *one side at a time* or *point by point*. Each format is illustrated below.

One Side at a Time

Look at the following supporting paragraph from "A Vote for McDonald's," one of the model essays that will follow.

> For one thing, going to the Chalet is more difficult than going to McDonald's. The Chalet has a jacket-and-tie rule, which means I have to dig a sport coat and tie out of the back of my closet, make sure they're semiclean, and try to steam out the wrinkles somehow. The Chalet also requires reservations. Since it is downtown, I have to leave an hour early to give myself time to find a parking space within six blocks of the restaurant. The Chalet cancels reservations if a party is more than ten minutes late. Going to McDonald's, on the other hand, is easy. I can feel comfortable wearing my jeans or warm-up suit. I don't have to do any advance planning. I can leave my house whenever I'm ready and pull into a doorside parking space within fifteen minutes.

The first half of this paragraph fully explains one side of the contrast (the difficulty of going to the Chalet). The second half of the paragraph deals entirely with the other side (the ease of going to McDonald's). When you use this method, be sure to follow the same order of points of contrast (or comparison) for each side. An outline of the paragraph shows how the points for each side are developed in a consistent sequence.

One Side at a Time   Outline

Thesis: Going to the Chalet is more difficult than going to McDonald's.

1. Chalet
   a. Dress code
   b. Advance reservations
   c. Leave an hour early
   d. Find parking space
2. McDonald's
   a. Casual dress
   b. No reservations
   c. Leave only fifteen minutes ahead of time
   d. Plenty of free parking

Point by Point

Now look at the supporting paragraph below, which is taken from another essay you will read, "Studying: Then and Now":

Ordinary studying during the term is another area where I've made changes. In high school, I let reading assignments go. I told myself that I'd have no trouble catching up on two hundred pages during a fifteen-minute ride to school. College courses have taught me to keep pace with the work. Otherwise, I feel as though I'm sinking into a quicksand of unread material. When I finally read the high school assignment, my eyes would run over the words but my brain would be plotting how to get the car for Saturday night. Now, I use several techniques that force me to really concentrate on my reading.

The paragraph contrasts two styles of studying point by point. The following outline illustrates the point-by-point method.

Outline   **Point by Point**

Thesis: *Studying is something I do differently in college than in high school.*

    1.   *Keeping up with reading assignments*

        a. *High school*

        b. *College*

    2.   *Concentration while reading*

        a. *High school*

        b. *College*

When you begin writing a comparison or contrast paper, you should decide right away which format you will use: one side at a time or point by point. Use that format as you create the outline for your paper. Remember that an outline is an essential step in planning and writing a clearly organized paper.

Student Essays to Consider

A Vote for McDonald's

    For my birthday this month, my wife has offered to treat me to dinner   1
at the restaurant of my choice. I think she expects me to ask for a meal at
the Chalet, the classiest, most expensive restaurant in town. However, I'm
going to eat my birthday dinner at McDonald's. When I compare the two
restaurants, the advantages of eating at McDonald's are clear.

    For one thing, going to the Chalet is more difficult than going to   2
McDonald's. The Chalet has a jacket-and-tie rule, which means I have to dig a
sport coat and tie out of the back of my closet, make sure they're semiclean,
and try to steam out the wrinkles somehow. The Chalet also requires
reservations. Since it is downtown, I have to leave an hour early to give

(continued)

myself time to find a parking space within six blocks of the restaurant. The Chalet cancels reservations if a party is more than ten minutes late. Going to McDonald's, on the other hand, is easy. I can feel comfortable wearing my jeans or warm-up suit. I don't have to do any advance planning. I can leave my house whenever I'm ready and pull into a doorside parking space within fifteen minutes.

The Chalet is a dimly lit, formal place. While I'm struggling to see 3 what's on my plate, I worry that I'll knock one of the fragile glasses off the table. The waiters at the Chalet can be uncomfortably formal, too. As I awkwardly pronounce the French words on the menu, I get the feeling that I don't quite live up to their standards. Even the other diners can make me feel uncomfortable. And though the food at the Chalet is gourmet, I prefer simpler meals. I don't like unfamiliar food swimming in a pasty white sauce. Eating at the Chalet is, to me, less enjoyable than eating at McDonald's. McDonald's is a pleasant place where I feel at ease. It is well lit, and the bright-colored decor is informal. The employees serve with a smile, and the food is easy to pronounce and identify. I know what I'm going to get when I order a certain type of sandwich.

The most important difference between the Chalet and McDonald's, 4 though, is price. Dinner for two at the Chalet, even without appetizers or desserts, would easily cost $100. And the $100 doesn't include the cost of parking the car and tipping the waiter, which can come to an additional $20. Once, I forgot to bring enough money. At McDonald's, a filling meal for two will cost around $10. With the extra $110, my wife and I can eat at McDonald's eleven more times, or go to the movies five times, or buy tickets to a football game.

So, for my birthday dinner, or any other time, I prefer to eat at 5 McDonald's. It is convenient, friendly, and cheap. And with the money my wife saves by taking me to McDonald's, she can buy me what I really want for my birthday—a new Sears power saw.

Studying: Then and Now

One June day, I staggered into a high school classroom to take my final 1 exam in United States History IV. I had made my usual desperate effort to cram the night before, with the usual dismal results—I had gotten only to page 75 of a four-hundred-page textbook. My study habits in high school,

(continued)

obviously, were a mess. But in college, I've made an attempt to reform my note-taking, studying, and test-taking skills.

As I took notes in high school classes, I often lost interest and began doodling, drawing Martians, or seeing what my signature would look like if I married the cute guy in the second row. Now, however, I try not to let my mind wander, and I pull my thoughts back into focus when they begin to go fuzzy. In high school, my notes often looked like something written in another language. In college, I've learned to use a semiprint writing style that makes my notes understandable. When I would look over my high school notes, I couldn't understand them. There would be a word like "Reconstruction," then a big blank, then the word "important." Weeks later, I had no idea what Reconstruction was or why it was important. I've since learned to write down connecting ideas, even if I have to take the time to do it after class. Taking notes is one thing I've really learned to do better since high school days.

Ordinary studying during the term is another area where I've made changes. In high school, I let reading assignments go. I told myself that I'd have no trouble catching up on two hundred pages during a fifteen-minute ride to school. College courses have taught me to keep pace with the work. Otherwise, I feel as though I'm sinking into a quicksand of unread material. When I finally read the high school assignment, my eyes would run over the words but my brain would be plotting how to get the car for Saturday night. Now, I use several techniques that force me to really concentrate on my reading.

In addition to learning how to cope with daily work, I've also learned to handle study sessions for big tests. My all-night study sessions in high school were experiments in self-torture. Around 2:00 a.m., my mind, like a soaked sponge, simply stopped absorbing things. Now, I space out exam study sessions over several days. That way, the night before can be devoted to an overall review rather than raw memorizing. Most important, though, I've changed my attitude toward tests. In high school, I thought tests were mysterious things with completely unpredictable questions. Now, I ask instructors about the kinds of questions that will be on the exam, and I try to "psych out" which areas or facts instructors are likely to ask about. These practices really work, and for me they've taken much of the fear and mystery out of tests.

Since I've reformed, note-taking and studying are not as tough as they once were. And I am beginning to reap the benefits. As time goes on, my college test sheets are going to look much different from the red-marked tests of my high school days.

About Unity

1. Which supporting paragraph in "A Vote for McDonald's" has its topic sentence within the paragraph, rather than at the beginning? *(Write the paragraph number and the opening words of the topic sentence.)*

2. Which sentence in paragraph 4 of "A Vote for McDonald's" should be omitted in the interest of paragraph unity? *(Write the opening words.)*

3. In which supporting paragraph in "Studying: Then and Now" is the topic sentence at the end rather than at the beginning, where it generally belongs in student essays?

About Support

4. In paragraph 3 of "A Vote for McDonald's," what three points does the writer make to support his statement that, for him, dining at McDonald's is a more pleasant experience than dining at the Chalet?

5. In paragraph 3 of "A Vote for McDonald's," what sentence should be followed up by supporting details? *(Write the opening words of that sentence.)*

6. Which sentence in paragraph 3 of "Studying: Then and Now" needs to be followed by more supporting details? *(Write the opening words.)*

About Coherence

7. In paragraph 2 of "A Vote for McDonald's," what "change of direction" signal does the author use to indicate that he has finished discussing the Chalet and is now going to discuss McDonald's?

8. Write the words in paragraph 4 of "A Vote for McDonald's" that indicate the writer has used emphatic order in organizing his supporting points.

About the Introduction and Conclusion

9. Which sentence best describes the opening paragraph of "Studying: Then and Now"?

   a. It begins with a broad statement that narrows down to the thesis.

   b. It explains the importance of the topic to the reader.

   c. It uses an incident or a brief story.

   d. It asks a question.

10. The conclusion of "Studying: Then and Now" falls into which category?

   a. Some observations and a prediction

   b. Summary and final thought

   c. Question or series of questions

Developing a Comparison or Contrast Essay

Considering Purpose and Audience

The purpose of a comparison or contrast essay is to make a point by showing readers that two distinct items are either similar or different. Whether you choose to compare or contrast two items depends on the specific point you want to convey to readers. Suppose, for instance, the main point of your essay is that home-cooked hamburgers are superior to fast-food burgers. To convince your audience of your claim, you might contrast the two items, pointing out those differences—price, taste, and nutrition—that make the homemade dish better. If, however, your main point is that tap water is just as good as store-bought bottled water, you could compare the two, pointing out the similarities that support your main point. Tap water and bottled water, for example, might be equally clean, fresh, and mineral-rich. In both examples above, comparing or contrasting is used to convince readers of a larger main point.

As you think about your own essay, ask yourself what two things you wish to discuss. Then determine whether you want to focus on the differences between the two items or their similarities. You may even decide that you want to do both. If, say, you choose as your topic Macintosh and PCs, you may write paragraphs on the similarities and differences between the two computer systems. But remember, no matter what topic you select, be sure that your comparison or contrast is connected to a main point that readers can see and understand.

Be sure to keep your audience in mind when planning your essay. If you were writing about Macs and PCs for computer majors, for example, you could assume your readers were familiar with the two systems. On the other hand, if your audience was made up of liberal arts majors, you could not make such an assumption, and it would be up to you to provide background information. Thinking about your audience will help you determine the tone of your essay as well. Once again, if you are writing for an audience of programmers, it is appropriate to write in an objective, technical tone. But if you are writing for a more general audience, you should assume a friendly, informal tone.

Development through Prewriting

When Jesse, one of the student writers featured earlier, had to choose two things to compare or contrast, the Chalet and McDonald's quickly came to mind: "My wife and I had been talking that morning about where I wanted to go for my birthday," he said. "I'd been thinking how I would explain to her that I'd really prefer McDonald's. So the comparisons and contrasts between the two restaurants were fresh in my mind."

To generate ideas for his paper, Jesse turned to the technique of freewriting. Without concerning himself with organization, finding the perfect word, or even spelling, he simply wrote whatever came into his mind as he asked himself, Why would I rather eat at McDonald's than at the Chalet? Here is what Jesse came up with:

> The Chalet is a beautiful restaurant and it's sweet of Lilly to want to take me there. But I honestly like McDonald's better. To me, food is food, and a meal at the Chalet is not eleven times better than a meal at McDonald's but that's what it costs. I like a plain cheeseburger better than something I can't pronounce or identify. The waiters at the Chalet are snooty and make me feel awkward—how can you enjoy eating when you're tensed up like that? Have to wear jacket and tie to the Chalet and I've gained weight; not sure jacket will even fit. Sweats or jeans are great at McDonald's. Desserts at Chalet are great, better than McCookies or whatever they're called. Parking is a hassle at the Chalet and easy at McD's. No tipping at McD's, either. I don't know why they keep it so dark at the Chalet—guess it's supposed to be relaxing, but seems creepy to me. McD's is bright and cheerful.

As Jesse looked over his freewriting, he saw that most of what he had written fell into three categories that he could use as the three supporting points of his essay. Using these three points, he prepared this first scratch outline for the essay:

I'd rather eat my special dinner at McDonald's than at the Chalet.
1. *Can wear anything I want to McD's.*
2. *Waiters, lighting, menu at Chalet make me feel awkward.*
3. *Chalet is <u>much</u> more expensive than McD's.*

Next, Jesse went back and inserted some supporting details that fit in with his three main points.

I'd rather eat my special dinner at McDonald's than at the Chalet.
1. *Going to the Chalet is a hassle.*
   a. *Have to wear jacket, tie to Chalet*
   b. *Have to make reservations*
   c. *Long drive; trouble parking*
2. *Waiters, lighting, menu at Chalet make me feel awkward.*
   a. *Waiters are snooty*
   b. *Lighting is dim*
   c. *French names on menu don't mean anything to me*
3. *Chalet is <u>much</u> more expensive than McD's.*
   a. *Meal costs eleven times as much*
   b. *Parking, tips on top of that*
   c. *Rather spend that money on other things*

Working from this scratch outline, Jesse wrote the following first draft of his essay.

First Draft

A Vote for McDonald's

Lilly has offered to take me anywhere I want for my birthday dinner. She thinks I'll choose the Chalet, but instead I want to eat at McDonald's.

The Chalet has a jacket-and-tie rule, and I hate wearing a jacket and tie, and the jacket's probably too tight for me anyway. I have to dig them out of the closet and get them cleaned. I can wear any old thing to McDonald's. We'd also have to leave the house early, since the Chalet requires

(continued)

reservations. Since it is downtown, I have to leave an hour early so I'm sure to have time to park. The Chalet cancels reservations if a party is more than ten minutes late. Going to McDonald's, on the other hand, is easy. I don't have to do any advance planning. I can leave my house whenever I'm ready.

McDonald's is a pleasant place where I feel at ease. It is bright and well lit. The employees serve with a smile, and the food is easy to pronounce and identify. I know what I'm going to get when I order a certain type of sandwich. I like simple meals more than gourmet ones. The Chalet is dimly lit. While I'm struggling to see what's on my plate, I worry that I'll knock one of the glasses off the table. The waiters at the Chalet can be uncomfortably formal, too. I get the feeling that I don't quite live up to their standards. Even the other diners can make me feel uncomfortable.

There's a big price difference between the Chalet and McDonald's. Dinner for two at the Chalet can easily cost $100, even without any "extras" like appetizers and dessert. And the $100 doesn't include the cost of parking the car and tipping the waiter. Once, I forgot to bring enough money. At McDonald's, a meal for two will cost around $10.

So, for my birthday dinner, or any other time, I prefer to eat at McDonald's. It is convenient, friendly, and cheap.

Development through Revising

Jesse put the first draft of his essay aside and took it to his writing class the next day. His instructor asked Jesse and the other students to work in small groups reading their drafts aloud and making suggestions for revision to one another. Here are the notes Jesse made on his group's comments:

- I need to explain that Lilly is my wife.
- I'm not consistent in developing my paragraphs. I forgot to do a "one side at a time" or "point by point" comparison. I think I'll try "one side at a time." I'll describe in each paragraph what the Chalet is like, then what McDonald's is like.
- I could use more support for some of my points, like when I say that the waiters at the Chalet make me uncomfortable. I should give some examples of what I mean by that.
- I want to say something about what I'd rather do with the money we save by going to McDonald's. For me that's important—we can "eat" that money at the Chalet, or do other things with it that we both enjoy.

After making these observations about his first draft, Jesse proceeded to write the version of his essay that appears on page 290.

A Professional Essay to Consider

Read the following professional essay. Then answer the questions and read the comments that follow.

Born to Be Different?

by Camille Lewis

www.mhhe.com/langan

Some years ago, when my children were very young, I cut a cartoon out of 1 a magazine and taped it to my refrigerator. It showed a young couple welcoming friends over for Christmas. The hosts rather proudly announce that instead of dolls, they have given their little daughter her own set of tools. And sure enough, the second panel shows their little girl playing in her room, a wrench in one hand and a hammer in the other. But she's making the wrench say, "Would you like to go to the prom, Barbie?" and the hammer answer, "Oh, Ken! I'd love to!"

Oh my, did that cartoon strike a chord. I grew up with *Ms.* magazine and the 2 National Organization of Women and a firm belief that gender differences were *learned,* not inborn. Other parents may have believed that pink and baby dolls and kindergarten teaching were for girls, and blue and trucks and engineering were for boys, but by golly, *my* kids were going to be different. They were going to be raised free of all that harmful gender indoctrination. They were just going to be *people.*

I don't remember exactly when I began to suspect I was wrong. Maybe it was 3 when my three-year-old son, raised in a "no weapons" household, bit his toast into a gun shape and tried to shoot the cat. Maybe it was when his younger brother nearly levitated out of his car seat, joyously crowing "backhoe!" upon spotting his first piece of earth-moving equipment. Maybe it was when my little daughter first lined up her stuffed animals and began teaching them their ABC's and bandaging their boo-boos.

It wasn't that my sons couldn't be sweet and sensitive, or that my daughter 4 wasn't sometimes rowdy and boisterous. But I had to rethink my earlier assumptions. Despite my best efforts not to impose gender-specific expectations on them, my boys and my girl were, well, different. *Really* different.

Slowly and hesitantly, medical and psychological researchers have begun 5 confirming my observations. The notion that the differences between the sexes (beyond the obvious anatomical ones) are biologically based is fraught[1] with controversy. Such beliefs can easily be misinterpreted and used as the basis for harm-

---

[1]*fraught:* filled.

ful, oppressive stereotypes. They can be overstated and exaggerated into blanket statements about what men and women "can" and "can't" do; about what the genders are "good" and "bad" at. And yet, the unavoidable fact is that studies are making it ever clearer that, as groups, men and women differ in almost every measurable aspect. Learning about those differences helps us understand why men and women are simultaneously so attracted and fascinated, and yet so frequently stymied and frustrated, by the opposite sex. To dig into what it really means to be masculine and feminine helps to depersonalize our responses to one another's behavior—to avoid the "*My* perceptions and behaviors are normal; *yours* don't make sense" trap. Our differences are deep-rooted, hard-wired, and present from the moment of conception.

To begin with, let's look at something as basic as the anatomy of the brain. 6 Typically, men have larger skulls and brains than women. But the sexes score equally well on intelligence tests. This apparent contradiction is explained by the fact that our brains are apportioned differently. Women have about 15 percent more "gray matter" than men. Gray matter, made up of nerve cells and the branches that connect them, allows the quick transference of thought from one part of the brain to another. This high concentration of gray matter helps explain women's ability to look at many sides of an argument at once, and to do several tasks (or hold several conversations) simultaneously.

Men's brains, on the other hand, have a more generous portion of "white mat- 7 ter." White matter, which is made up of neurons, actually inhibits the spread of information. It allows men to concentrate very narrowly on a specific task, without being distracted by thoughts that might conflict with the job at hand. In addition, men's larger skulls contain more cerebrospinal fluid, which cushions the brain. Scientists theorize that this reflects men's history of engaging in warfare and rough sports, activities which bring with them a high likelihood of having one's head banged about.

Our brains' very different makeup leads to our very different methods of in- 8 teracting with the world around us. Simon Baron-Cohen, author of *The Essential Difference: Men, Women and the Extreme Male Brain,* has labeled the classic female mental process as "empathizing." He defines empathizing as "the drive to identify another person's emotions and thoughts, and to respond to these with an appropriate emotion." Empathizers are constantly measuring and responding to the surrounding emotional temperature. They are concerned about showing sensitivity to the people around them. This empathetic quality can be observed in virtually all aspects of women's lives: from the choice of typically female-dominated careers (nursing, elementary school teaching, social work) to reading matter popular mainly with women (romantic fiction, articles about relationships, advice columns about how people can get along better) to women's interaction with one another (which typically involves intimate discussion of relationships with friends and family, and sympathy for each others' concerns). So powerful is the empathizing mindset that it even affects how the typical female memory works. Ask a woman when a particular event happened, and she often pinpoints it in terms of an occurrence that had emotional content: "That was the summer my sister broke her leg," or "That was around the time Gene and Mary got into such an awful argument." Likewise, she is likely to bring her empathetic mind to bear on geography. She'll remember a particular address not as 11th and Market Streets but being "near the restaurant where we went on our anniversary," or "around the corner from Liz's old apartment."

In contrast, Baron-Cohen calls the typical male mindset "systemizing," which 9 he defines as "the drive to analyze and explore a system, to extract underlying rules that govern the behavior of a system." A systemizer is less interested in how people feel than in how things work. Again, the systematic brain influences virtually all aspects of the typical man's life. Male-dominated professions (such as engineering, computer programming, auto repair, and mathematics) rely heavily on systems, formulas, and patterns, and very little on the ability to intuit another person's thoughts or emotions. Reading material most popular with men includes science fiction and history, as well as factual "how-to" magazines on such topics as computers, photography, home repair, and woodworking. When they get together with male friends, men are far less likely to engage in intimate conversation than they are to share an activity: watching or playing sports, working on a car, bowling, golfing, or fishing. Men's conversation is peppered with dates and addresses, illustrating their comfort with systems: "Back in 1996 when I was living in Boston . . ." or "The best way to the new stadium is to go all the way out Walnut Street to 33rd and then get on the bypass. . . ."

One final way that men and women differ is in their typical responses to 10 problem-solving. Ironically, it may be this very activity—intended on both sides to eliminate problems—that creates the most conflict between partners of the opposite sex. To a woman, the *process* of solving a problem is all-important. Talking about a problem is a means of deepening the intimacy between her and her partner. The very anatomy of her brain, as well as her accompanying empathetic mindset, makes her want to consider all sides of a question and to explore various possible solutions. To have a partner who is willing to explore a problem with her is deeply satisfying. She interprets that willingness as an expression of the other's love and concern.

But men have an almost completely opposite approach when it comes to deal- 11 ing with a problem. Everything in their mental makeup tells them to focus narrowly on the issue, solve it, and get it out of the way. The ability to fix a problem quickly and efficiently is, to them, a demonstration of their power and competence. When a man hears his female partner begin to describe a problem, his strongest impulse is to listen briefly and then tell her what to do about it. From his perspective, he has made a helpful and loving gesture; from hers, he's short-circuited a conversation that could have deepened and strengthened their relationship.

The challenge that confronts men and women is to put aside ideas of "better" 12 and "worse" when it comes to their many differences. Our diverse brain development, our ways of interacting with the world, and our modes of dealing with problems all have their strong points. In some circumstances, a typically feminine approach may be more effective; in others, a classically masculine mode may have the advantage. Our differences aren't going to disappear: my daughter, now a middle-schooler, regularly tells me she loves me, while her teenage brothers express their affection by grabbing me in a headlock. Learning to understand and appreciate one another's gender-specific qualities is the key to more rich and rewarding lives together.

About Unity

1. Which of the following statements best represents the implied thesis of "Born to Be Different"?

   a. Although the author believed that gender differences were learned rather than inborn, experience with her own children convinced her otherwise.

   b. Researchers have classified the typical female mental process as "empathizing" and the typical male process as "systemizing."

   c. Many of the differences in the ways men and women think and behave may be due to their biological makeup.

   d. In order to live together happily, men and women need to appreciate and understand their gender-based differences.

2. Which statement would best serve as a topic sentence for paragraphs 6 and 7?

   a. Because of their different construction, men's and women's brains function differently.

   b. Women are skilled at doing several tasks or holding several conversations simultaneously.

   c. Although men's brains are larger than women's, men and women score equally on tests of intelligence.

   d. Men's brains have a larger allocation of white matter, which contributes to the ability to focus narrowly on a particular task.

3. What statement below would best serve as the topic sentence of paragraph 11?

   a. Men solve problems quickly to demonstrate power and competence.

   b. Men's approach to solving problems usually involves giving instructions.

   c. Men's gestures of love are often unhelpful to women.

   d. Men's approach to problem solving is the opposite of women's.

About Support

4. Paragraph 8 states that the "empathizing" mindset "can be observed in virtually all aspects of women's lives." What evidence does Lewis provide to support that claim?

_____

_____

_____

Questions

2

5. According to the author, what are the three major differences between men and women?

   _____

   _____

   _____

About Coherence

6. Has the author presented her evidence one side at a time or point by point? Explain your answer.

   _____

   _____

   _____

7. As shown by the outline below, the organization of "Born to Be Different?" resembles the traditional one-three-one essay model. Fill in the missing paragraph numbers.

Introduction:	Paragraphs	_____
Supporting Point 1:	Paragraph(s)	_____
Supporting Point 2:	Paragraph(s)	_____
Supporting Point 3:	Paragraph(s)	_____
Conclusion:	Paragraph	_____

8. What are the three contrast signals used to introduce the main supporting paragraphs in the essay? Where do they occur? *(Write the paragraph number after the signal.)*

   _____   _____   _____

About the Introduction and Conclusion

9. What method best describes the introductory paragraph to the essay?

   a. Broad, general statement narrowing to a thesis

   b. Questions

   c. Idea that is the opposite of the one to be developed

   d. Anecdote

10. With which common method of conclusion does the essay end?

    a. A summary and final thought

    b. Questions that prompt the reader to think further about what's been written

    c. A prediction

Writing a Comparison or Contrast Essay

Write an essay of comparison or contrast on one of these topics:

Two teachers you've had

Two jobs you'd held

Two bosses you've worked for

Two restaurants you've eaten in

Two parenting styles you've observed

Two friends you've had

Two pets you've had or seen

Two sports you're acquainted with

Two singers or bands you've heard

Two dates you've been on

Two places you've lived

Prewriting

a. As you select your topic, keep in mind that you won't be merely *describing* the two things you're writing about—you will be emphasizing the ways they are alike or different.

b. Make two columns on a sheet of paper, one for each of the two things you'll write about. In the left-hand column, jot down words or phrases that describe the first of the two. Write anything that comes into your head about that half of your topic. Then go back and write a corresponding word or phrase about the item in the right-hand column. For example, here is one student's list of characteristics about two games. He began brainstorming for words and phrases to describe Scrabble.

Scrabble	Volleyball
quiet	
involves words	
played sitting down	
involves small group of people	

(continued)

can let mind wander when it's not your turn

mental concentration, not physical

part chance—don't know what letters you'll get

part strategy and skill

some see as boring, nerdy game

Then he wrote a corresponding list of characteristics for volleyball, which helped him modify and add to his first list:

Scrabble	Volleyball
quiet	noisy, talking and yelling
involves words	involves ball and a net
played sitting down	played standing up, jumping
involves as few as two players	involves twelve players
can let mind wander when it's not your turn	have to stay alert every minute
mental concentration, not physical	mental and physical concentration required
part chance (what letters you get), part strategy and skill	mostly skill, strategy; little chance
some see as boring, nerdy game	seen as glamorous—stars get advertising contracts
players' sizes don't matter	being tall helps

  c. Your list of characteristics will help you decide if the two things you are writing about are more alike (in which case you'll write an essay *comparing* them) or different (in which case you'll emphasize how they *contrast*).

  d. As you look over your lists, think how the characteristics you've written down (and others that occur to you) could fit into three categories that can serve as your supporting points. Prepare a scratch outline for your essay based on these three supporting points.

For instance, the student writing about Scrabble and volleyball came up with these three groupings of characteristics. Fill in the blanks in his outline to indicate the supporting points.

Thesis: Although they are two of my favorite activities, Scrabble and volleyball could hardly be more different.

Point _____

Scrabble requires a board and letter tiles.

Volleyball needs a ball and net.

Scrabble can be played by two people.

Twelve people are needed for a volleyball game.

Scrabble can be played anywhere there's room for two people to sit down.

Volleyball needs a large room and high ceilings or an outdoor playing area.

Point _____

You have to concentrate mentally to play Scrabble.

You need mental and physical concentration to play volleyball.

It doesn't matter what size you are to play Scrabble.

It helps to be tall to play volleyball.

There's some chance involved in playing Scrabble.

Chance is not a big part of volleyball.

Point _____

Scrabble players are seen as nerdy by the general public.

Star volleyball players are seen as glamorous by the public.

Volleyball players get contracts to endorse athletic shoes.

Scrabble players don't endorse anything, even dictionaries.

Volleyball players are admired for the power of their spike.

Scrabble players are admired for the number of unusual two-letter words they know.

e. Decide which method of development you will use to design your essay: one side at a time or point by point. Be consistent in your use of one method or the other in each of your paragraphs.

f. Write the first draft of your essay.

Revising

Reread your essay and then show it to a friend or classmate who will give you honest feedback. You should both review it with these questions in mind:

FOUR BASES Checklist for Comparison or Contrast

About *Unity*

☑ Have I made it clear in my opening paragraph what two things I am writing about, and whether I will compare or contrast them?

About *Support*

☑ Do my supporting points offer three areas in which I will compare or contrast my two subjects?

About *Coherence*

☑ Have I consistently used a single method of development—one side at a time or point by point—in each supporting paragraph?

☑ Have I used transition words to help readers follow my train of thought?

☑ If one area of comparison or contrast is stronger than the others, am I using emphatic order and saving that area for my final supporting paragraph?

☑ Have I rounded off my essay with an appropriate concluding paragraph?

About *Sentence Skills*

☑ Have I avoided wordiness and used concise wording?

☑ Are my sentences varied?

☑ Have I checked my writing for spelling and other sentence skills, as listed on the inside back cover of the book?

As you revise your essay through one or more additional drafts, continue to refer to this list until you and your reader can answer yes to each question.

Writing Assignment

2   Write an essay in which you contrast two attitudes on a controversial subject. You may want to contrast your views with those of someone else, or contrast the way you felt about the subject in the past with the way you feel now. You might consider writing about one of these subjects:

Legalization of narcotics

Abortion

Men and women serving together in military units

Prayer in public schools

Nuclear power plants

Homosexual couples adopting children

Fertility methods that allow older women to have children

Welfare reform

The death penalty

Euthanasia

Prostitution

The public's right to know about elected officials' private lives

The Iraq war

Prewriting

a. To gather information for the point of view that contrasts with your own, you will need to do some research. You'll find useful material if you go to the library and search through article indexes for recent newsmagazines. (If you need help, ask your instructor or the research librarian.) Or interview friends and acquaintances whose attitude on the subject is different from yours.

b. To generate ideas for your essay, try the following two-part exercise.

- Part 1: Pretend that a visitor from Mars who has never heard of the topic of your paper has asked you to explain it, as well as why you take the attitude you do toward it. Using the technique of freewriting—not worrying about sentence structure, organization, spelling, repetition, etc.—write an answer for the Martian. Throw in every reason you can think of for your attitude.

- Part 2: Now the Martian asks you to do the same, taking the opposing point of view. Remember that it's up to you to make this interplanetary visitor understand both sides of the issue, so really try to put yourself in the other person's shoes as you represent the contrasting attitude.

© Bob Daemmrich/PhotoEdit

© Peter M. Fisher/Corbis

c. As you look over the writing on both sides of the issue you've done for the Martian, note the strongest points on both sides. From them, select your three main supporting points. Are there other thoughts in your writing that can be used as supporting details for those points?

d. Write your three supporting paragraphs. Decide whether it is more effective to contrast your attitude and the opposing attitude point by point within each paragraph, or by devoting the first half of each paragraph to one side's attitude and then contrasting it with the other's.

e. In your concluding paragraph, summarize the contrast between your attitude and the other point of view. Consider closing with a final comment that makes it clear why you stand where you do.

Revising

Refer to the guidelines for rewriting provided on page 306.

Writing Assignment

3 Write an essay that contrasts two characters or two points of view in one or more poems, stories, plays, or novels. The work you choose may be assigned by your instructor, or it may require your instructor's approval. For this assignment, your essay may have two supporting paragraphs, with each paragraph representing one side of the contrast. A student model follows.

Warren and Mary

In "Death of the Hired Man," Robert Frost uses a brief incident—the   1
return of Silas, an aging farmhand—to dramatize the differences between a husband and wife. As Warren and Mary talk about Silas and reveal his story, the reader learns their story, too. By the end of the poem, Warren and Mary emerge as contrasting personalities; one is wary and reserved, while the other is open and giving.

Warren is a kindly man, but his basic decency is tempered by practicality   2
and emotional reserve. Warren is upset with Mary for sheltering Silas, who is barely useful and sometimes unreliable: "What use he is there's no depending on." Warren feels that he has already done his duty toward Silas by hiring him the previous summer and is under no obligation to care for him now. "Home," says Warren, "is the place where, when you have to go there / They have to

(continued)

take you in." Warren's home is not Silas's home, so Warren does not have a legal or moral duty to keep the shiftless old man. Warren's temperament, in turn, influences his attitude toward Silas's arrival. Warren hints to Mary—through a condescending smile—that Silas is somehow playing on her emotions or faking his illness. Warren considers Silas's supposed purpose in coming to the farm—to ditch the meadow—nothing but a flimsy excuse for a free meal. The best that Warren can find to say about Silas is that he does have one practical skill: the ability to build a good load of hay.

Mary, in contrast, is distinguished by her giving nature and her concentration on the workings of human emotion. In caring for Silas, Mary sees not his lack of ability or his laziness but the fact that he is "worn out" and needs help. To Mary, home represents not obligation ("They have to take you in") but unconditional love: "I should have called it/Something you somehow haven't to deserve." Mary is observant, not only of outer appearances but also of the inner person; this is why she thinks not that Silas is trying to trick them but that he is a desperate man trying to salvage a little self-respect. She realizes, too, that he will never ditch the meadow, and she knows that Silas's insecurity prompted his arguments with the college boy who helped with the haying. Mary is also perceptive enough to see that Silas could never humble himself before his estranged brother. Mary's attitude is more sympathetic than Warren's; whereas Warren wonders why Silas and his brother don't get along. Mary thinks about how Silas "hurt my heart the way he lay/And rolled his old head on that sharp-edged chairback."

In describing Silas, Warren and Mary describe themselves. We see a basically good man whose spirit has been toughened by a hard life. Warren, we learn, would have liked to pay Silas a fixed wage but simply couldn't afford to. Life has taught Warren to be practical and to rein in his emotions. In contrast, we see a nurturing woman, alert to human feelings, who could never refuse to care for a lonely, dying man. Warren and Mary are both decent people. This is the reason why, as Mary instinctively feels, Silas chooses their home for his final refuge.

Writing | Assignment

4 | Writing for a Specific Purpose and Audience

In this comparison or contrast essay, you will write with a specific purpose and for a specific audience.

Option 1 Your niece or nephew is finishing high school soon and is thinking about getting a job instead of going to college. You would prefer to see him or her give college a try. Write him or her a letter in which you compare and contrast the advantages and disadvantages of each course of action. Use the one-side-at-a-time method in making your analysis.

Option 2 Write a letter to your boss in which you compare your abilities with those of the ideal candidate for a position to which you'd like to be promoted. Use the point-by-point method, discussing each desired qualification and then describing how well you measure up to it. Use the requirements of a job you are familiar with, ideally a job you would really like to apply for someday.

www.mhhe.com/langan

Definition

14

© Digital Vision/Getty Images

This chapter will explain and illustrate how to

- develop a definition essay

- write a definition essay

- revise a definition essay

In addition, you will read and consider

- two student definition essays

- one professional definition essay

What does it mean to be a successful student? What qualities and attributes does a successful student possess? Looking at the photograph above and thinking about these questions, write an essay in which you define what it means to be a successful student.

In talking with other people, we sometimes offer informal definitions to explain just what we mean by a particular term. Suppose, for example, we say to a friend, "Larry is really an inconsiderate person." We might then explain what we mean by "inconsiderate" by saying, "He borrowed my accounting book 'overnight' but didn't return it for a week. And when I got it back, it was covered with coffee stains." In a written definition, we make clear in a more complete and formal way our own personal understanding of a term. Such a definition typically starts with one meaning of a term. The meaning is then illustrated with a series of details.

In this chapter, you will be asked to write an essay in which you define and illustrate a term. To prepare for this assignment, first read the student essays and the professional essay that follow and work through the questions that accompany the essays.

Student Essays to Consider

Definition of a Football Fan

What is a football fan? The word "fan" is an abbreviation of "fanatic," meaning "an insane or crazy person." In the case of football fans, the term is appropriate. They behave insanely, they are insane about the past, and they are insanely loyal.   1

Football fans wear their official team T-shirts and warm-up jackets to the mall, the supermarket, the classroom, and even—if they can get away with it—to work. If the team offers a giveaway item, the fans rush to the stadium to claim the hat or sports bag or water bottle that is being handed out that day. Baseball fans go similarly nuts when their favorite teams give away some attractive freebie. Football fans just plain behave insanely. Even the fact that fans spend the coldest months of the year huddling on icy metal benches in places like Chicago proves it. In addition, football fans decorate their houses with football-related items of every kind. To them, team bumper stickers belong not only on car bumpers, but also on fireplace mantels and front doors. When they go to a game, which they do as often as possible, they also decorate their bodies. True football fans not only put on their team jackets and grab their pennants but also paint their heads to look like helmets or wear glow-in-the-dark cheeseheads. At the game, these fans devote enormous energy to trying to get a "wave" going.   2

Football fans are insanely fascinated by the past. They talk about William "Refrigerator" Perry's 1985 Super Bowl touchdown as though it had happened last week. They describe the "Fog Bowl" as if dense fog had blanketed yesterday's game, not 1988's playoff match between the   3

(continued)

Philadelphia Eagles and the Chicago Bears. They excitedly discuss John Elway's final game before retiring—when he won the 1999 Super Bowl and received MVP honors—as if it were current news. And if you can't manage to get excited about such ancient history, they look at you as though <u>you</u> were the insane one.

Last of all, football fans are insanely loyal to the team of their choice, often dangerously so. Should their beloved team lose three in a row, fans may begin to react negatively as a way to hide their broken hearts. They still obsessively watch each game and spend the entire day afterward reading and listening to the postgame commentary in newspapers, on TV sports segments, and on sports radio. Further, this intense loyalty makes fans dangerous. To anyone who dares to say to a loyal fan that another team has better players or coaches or, God forbid, to anyone wandering near the home cheering section wearing the jacket of the opposing team, physical damage is a real possibility. Bloody noses, black eyes, and broken bones are just some of the injuries inflicted on people cheering the wrong team when fans are around. In 1997, one man suffered a concussion at a game in Philadelphia when Eagles fans beat him up for wearing a jacket with another team's insignia.

From February through August, football fans act like any other human beings. They pay their taxes, take out the garbage, and complain about the high cost of living. But when September rolls around, the colors and radios go on, the record books come off the shelves, and the devotion returns. For the true football fan, another season of insanity has begun.

Student Zombies

Schools divide people into categories. From first grade on up, students are labeled "advanced" or "deprived" or "remedial" or "antisocial." Students pigeonhole their fellow students, too. We've all known the "brain," the "jock," the "dummy," and the "teacher's pet." In most cases, these narrow labels are misleading and inaccurate. But there is one label for a certain type of college student that says it all: "zombie."

Zombies are the living dead. Most of us haven't known a lot of real zombies personally, but we do know how they act. We have horror movies to guide us. The special effects in horror movies are much better these days. Over the years, we've learned from the movies that zombies stalk around graveyards, their eyes glued open by Hollywood makeup artists, bumping like cheap toy robots into living people. Zombie students in college do

(continued)

just about the same thing. They stalk around campus, eyes glazed, staring off into space. When they do manage to wander into a classroom, they sit down mechanically and contemplate the ceiling. Zombie students rarely eat, dance, talk, laugh, or toss Frisbees on campus lawns. Instead, they vanish when class is dismissed and return only when some mysterious zombie signal summons them back into a classroom. The signal may not occur for weeks.

Zombies are controlled by some mysterious force. According to legend, real zombies are corpses that have been brought back to life to do the bidding of a voodoo master. Student zombies, too, seem directed by a strange power. They continue to attend school although they have no apparent desire to do so. They show no interest in college-related activities like tests, grades, papers, and projects. And yet some inner force compels them to wander through the halls of higher education.   3

An awful fate awaits all zombies unless something happens to break the spell they're under. In the movies, zombies are often shot, stabbed, drowned, electrocuted, and run over by large vehicles, all to no avail. Finally the hero or heroine realizes that a counterspell is needed. Once that spell is cast, with the appropriate props of chicken feet, human hair, and bats' eyeballs, the zombie-corpse can return peacefully to its coffin. The only hope for a student zombie to change is for him or her to undergo a similarly traumatic experience. Sometimes the evil spell can be broken by a grade transcript decorated with large red "F's." At other times a professor will succeed through a private, intensive exorcism session. But in other cases zombies blunder around for years until they are gently persuaded by the college administration to head for another institution. Then they enroll in a new college or get a job in the family business.   4

Every college student knows that it's not necessary to see Night of the Living Dead or The Dead Don't Die to see zombies in action—or nonaction. Forget the campus film series or the late-late show. Just sit in a classroom and wait. You know what you're looking for—the students who walk in without books or papers and sit in the very last row of seats. The ones with personal stereos plugged into their ears don't count as zombies—that's a whole different category of "student." Day of the Living Dead is showing every day at a college near you.   5

Questions

1

About Unity

1. Which supporting paragraph in "Definition of a Football Fan" has a topic sentence buried within the paragraph, rather than at the paragraph's beginning? *(Write the paragraph number and the opening words of the topic sentence.)*

2. What sentence in paragraph 2 of "Definition of a Football Fan" should be omitted in the interest of paragraph unity? *(Write the opening words.)*

_____

3. Which sentence in paragraph 2 of "Student Zombies" should be omitted in the interest of paragraph unity? *(Write the opening words.)*

_____

4. What sentence in the final paragraph of "Student Zombies" introduces a new topic and so should be eliminated? *(Write the opening words.)*

_____

About Support

5. Which essay develops its definitions through a series of comparisons?

_____

6. After which sentence in paragraph 4 of "Definition of a Football Fan" is more support needed? *(Write the opening words.)*

_____

7. In the second paragraph of "Definition of a Football Fan," how many examples are given of fans' "insane" behavior? *(Circle the letter of the answer.)*

    a. two

    b. four

    c. six

About Coherence

8. Which paragraph in "Definition of a Football Fan" begins with a transitional

    phrase? _____

9. Which sentence in paragraph 2 of "Student Zombies" begins with a change-of-direction transitional word? *(Write the opening words.)*

_____

About the Introduction and Conclusion

10. Which method of introduction is used in the opening paragraph of "Student Zombies"? *(Circle the letter of the answer.)*

    a. Anecdote

    b. Idea that is the opposite of the one to be developed

    c. Quotation

    d. Broad, general statement narrowing to a thesis

    e. Questions

Developing a Definition Essay

Considering Purpose and Audience

When you write a definition essay, your main purpose is to explain to readers your understanding of a key term or concept, while your secondary purpose is to persuade them that your definition is a legitimate one. Keep in mind that a definition essay does not simply repeat a word's dictionary meaning. Instead, it conveys what a particular term means *to you*. For example, if you were to write about the term *patriotism,* you might begin by presenting your definition of the word. You might say patriotism means turning out for Fourth of July parades, displaying the flag, or supporting the government. Or perhaps you think patriotism is about becoming politically active and questioning government policy. Whatever definition you choose, be sure to provide specific instances so that readers can fully understand your meaning of the term. For example, in writing an essay on patriotism, you might describe three people who you see as truly patriotic. Writing about each person will help ensure that readers see and understand the term as you do.

As with other essay forms, keep your audience in mind. If, for instance, you were proposing a new definition of patriotism, an audience of war veterans might require different examples than would an audience of college students.

Development through Prewriting

Brian, the author of "Definition of a Football Fan," spent a few minutes jotting down a number of possible essay topics, keeping in mind the question, What do I know a good deal about, or at least have an interest in exploring? Here is his list of topic ideas. Notice how they reflect Brian's interest in outdoor activities, sports, and history:

Definition of . . .

A person who fishes

A soccer goalie

A reenactor of Civil War battles

People who vacation at Gettysburg

A bodybuilder

A Green Bay Packers fan

A history buff

A Little League coach

After looking over his list, Brian selected "A Green Bay Packers fan" as the topic that interested him most. He thought it would lend itself well to a lighthearted essay that defined the sometimes nutty fans of the Wisconsin football team. After giving it further thought, however, Brian decided to broaden his topic to include all football fans. "I realized I just didn't know enough specifically about Green Bay fans to support an entire essay," he said.

A person who likes to think in visual terms, Brian decided to develop ideas and details about his topic by clustering his thoughts.

Football fans

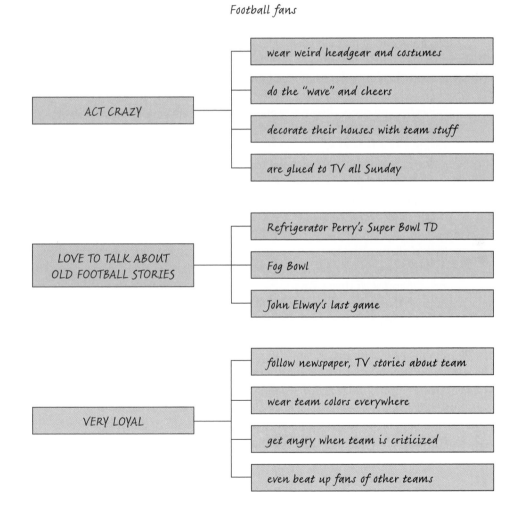

ACT CRAZY	wear weird headgear and costumes
	do the "wave" and cheers
	decorate their houses with team stuff
	are glued to TV all Sunday

LOVE TO TALK ABOUT OLD FOOTBALL STORIES	Refrigerator Perry's Super Bowl TD
	Fog Bowl
	John Elway's last game

VERY LOYAL	follow newspaper, TV stories about team
	wear team colors everywhere
	get angry when team is criticized
	even beat up fans of other teams

When he looked over his diagram, Brian realized that he could characterize each of his three main topics as a kind of "insanity." He decided on a thesis (he would define football fans as insane) that would indicate his essay's plan of development ("they behave insanely, they are insane about the past, and they are insanely loyal").

With that thesis and plan of development in mind, Brian wrote the first draft of his essay.

First Draft

Definition of a Football Fan

Football fans are by definition crazy. They behave insanely, they are insane about the past, and they are insanely loyal.

If their team gives away something free, the fans rush to the stadium to get the hat or whatever. Football fans just plain behave insanely. Baseball fans go similarly nuts when their favorite teams give away some attractive freebie. But football fans are even worse. Football fans freeze themselves in order to watch their favorite game. In addition, football fans decorate their houses with football-related items of every kind. When they go to a game, which they do as often as possible, the true football fans make themselves look ridiculous by decorating themselves in weird team-related ways. At the game, these fans do the "wave" more than they watch the game.

Football fans love to talk about the past. They talk about William "Refrigerator" Perry's 1985 Super Bowl touchdown as though it had happened last week. They still get all excited about 1988's "Fog Bowl." They talk about John Elway's final game as though it's today's news, though it happened in 1999. They think everyone should be as excited as they are about such old stories.

Last of all, football fans are insanely loyal to the team of their choice. Football fans wear their team T-shirts and warm-up jackets everywhere, even to work. Of course, if they have to dress up in business clothes, they can't do that. Should their beloved team lose three in a row, their fans may begin to criticize their team. But these reactions only hide their broken hearts. They still obsessively watch each game and read all the newspaper stories about it. This intense loyalty makes fans dangerous. To anyone who dares to say to a loyal fan that another team is better or, God forbid, to anyone wandering near the home cheering section wearing the jacket of the opposing team, physical damage is a real possibility. Incidents of violence in football stadiums have increased in recent years and are a matter of growing concern.

Football fans really act as if they're crazy. They behave insanely, they are crazy about the past, and they're too loyal.

Development through Revising

The next day, Brian showed his first draft to a study partner from his composition class. She returned it with comments noted in the margins.

Definition of a Football Fan

Football fans are by definition crazy. They behave insanely, they are insane about the past, and they are insanely loyal.

If their team gives away something free, the fans rush to the stadium to get the hat or whatever. Football fans just plain behave insanely. Baseball fans go similarly nuts when their favorite teams give away some attractive freebie. But football fans are even worse. Football fans freeze themselves in order to watch their favorite game. In addition, football fans decorate their houses with football-related items of every kind. When they go to a game, which they do as often as possible, the true football fans make themselves look ridiculous by decorating themselves in weird team-related ways. At the game, these fans do the "wave" more than they watch the game.

Football fans love to talk about the past. They talk about William "Refrigerator" Perry's 1985 Super Bowl touchdown as though it had happened last week. They still get all excited about 1988's "Fog Bowl." They talk about John Elway's final game as though it's today's news, though it happened in 1999. They think everyone should be as excited as they are about such old stories.

Last of all, football fans are insanely loyal to the team of their choice. Football fans wear their team T-shirts and warm-up jackets everywhere, even to work. Of course, if they have to dress up in business clothes, they can't do that. Should their beloved team lose three in a row, their fans may begin to criticize their team. But these reactions only hide their broken hearts. They still obsessively watch each game and read all the newspaper stories about it. This intense loyalty makes fans dangerous. To anyone who dares to say to a loyal fan that another team is better or, God forbid, to anyone wandering near the home cheering section wearing the jacket of the

(continued)

Reader's Comments

Huh? I guess this is about the weather—make it clearer.

Like what? Details here.

Details needed. How do they decorate themselves?

I'm not a football fan, so I don't understand these references. Can you briefly explain them?

Shouldn't this be in the second paragraph? It seems to belong to "they behave insanely," not "loyalty."

This doesn't support your topic statement, so take it out.

opposing team, physical damage is a real possibility. Incidents of violence in football stadiums have increased in recent years and are a matter of growing concern.

Football fans really act as if they're crazy. They behave insanely, they are crazy about the past, and they're too loyal.

Kind of a boring way to end it. You're just repeating your thesis.

After reading his classmate's comments, Brian went to work on his next draft. As he worked, he read his essay aloud several times and noticed places where his wording sounded awkward or too informal. (Example: "If their team gives away a freebie, the fans rush to the stadium to get the hat or whatever.") A few drafts later, he produced the version of "Definition of a Football Fan" that appears on page 312.

A Professional Essay to Consider

Read the following professional essay. Then answer the questions and read the comments that follow.

Television Addiction
by Marie Winn

www.mhhe.com/langan

The word "addiction" is often used loosely and wryly in conversation. People 1 will refer to themselves as "mystery book addicts" or "cookie addicts." E. B. White writes of his annual surge of interest in gardening, "We are hooked and are making an attempt to kick the habit." Yet nobody really believes that reading mysteries or ordering seeds by catalogue is serious enough to be compared to an addiction to heroin or alcohol. The word "addiction" is here used jokingly to denote a tendency to overindulge in some pleasurable activity.

People often refer to being "hooked on TV." Does this, too, fall into the light- 2 hearted category of eating cookies and other pleasures that people pursue with unusual intensity, or is there a kind of television viewing that falls into the more serious category of destructive addiction?

When we think about addiction to drugs or alcohol, we frequently focus on 3 negative aspects, ignoring the pleasures that accompany drinking or taking drugs. And yet the essence of any serious addiction is a pursuit of pleasure, a search for a "high" that normal life does not supply. It is only the inability to function without the addictive substance that is dismaying, the dependence of the organism upon a certain experience and an increasing inability to function without it. Thus a person will take two or three drinks at the end of the day not merely for the pleasure drinking provides, but also because he "doesn't feel normal" without them.

An addict does not merely pursue a pleasurable experience and need to experience it in order to function normally. He needs to repeat it again and again. Something about that particular experience makes life without it less than complete. Other potentially pleasurable experiences are no longer possible, for under the spell of the addictive experience, his life is peculiarly distorted. The addict craves an experience, and yet he is never really satisfied. The organism may be temporarily sated, but soon it begins to crave again. 4

Finally, a serious addiction is distinguished from a harmless pursuit of pleasure by its distinctly destructive elements. A heroin addict, for instance, leads a damaged life: his increasing need for heroin in increasing doses prevents him from working, from maintaining relationships, from developing in human ways. Similarly, an alcoholic's life is narrowed and dehumanized by his dependence on alcohol. 5

Let us consider television viewing in the light of the conditions that define serious addictions. 6

Not unlike drugs and alcohol, the television experience allows the participant to blot out the real world and enter into a pleasurable and passive mental state. The worries and anxieties of reality are as effectively deferred by becoming absorbed in a television program as by going on a "trip" induced by drugs or alcohol. And just as alcoholics are only vaguely aware of their addiction, feeling that they control their drinking more than they really do ("I can cut it out any time I want—I just like to have three or four drinks before dinner"), people similarly overestimate their control over watching television. Even as they put off other activities to spend hour after hour watching television, they feel they could easily resume living in a different, less passive style. But somehow or other while the television set is present in their homes, the click doesn't sound. With television pleasures available, those other experiences seem less attractive, more difficult somehow. 7

A heavy viewer (a college English instructor) observes: "I find television almost irresistible. When the set is on, I cannot ignore it. I can't turn it off. I feel sapped, will-less, enervated. As I reach out to turn off the set, the strength goes out of my arms. I sit there for hours and hours." 8

The self-confessed television addict often feels he "ought" to do other things—but the fact that he doesn't read and doesn't plant his garden or sew or crochet or play games or have conversations means that those activities are no longer as desirable as television. In a way the heavy viewer's life is as imbalanced by his television "habit" as a drug addict's or an alcoholic's. He is living in a holding pattern, as it were, passing up the activities that lead to growth or development or a sense of accomplishment. This is one reason people talk about their television viewing 9 so ruefully, so apologetically. They are aware that it is an unproductive experience, that almost any other endeavor is more worthwhile by any human measure.

Finally, it is the adverse effect of television viewing on the lives of so many 10 people that defines it as a serious addiction. The television habit distorts the sense of time. It renders other experiences vague and curiously unreal while taking on a greater reality for itself. It weakens relationships by reducing and sometimes eliminating normal opportunities for talking, for communicating.

And yet television does not satisfy, else why would the viewer continue to 11 watch hour after hour, day after day? "The measure of health," writes Lawrence Kubie, "is flexibility . . . and especially the freedom to cease when sated." But the television viewer can never be sated with his television experiences—they do not provide the true nourishment that satiation requires—and thus he finds that he cannot stop watching.

Questions
2

About Unity

1. Winn's thesis is not presented directly in the essay. See whether you can state it in your own words.

   _____

   _____

2. Which statement would best serve as a topic sentence for paragraph 4?
   a. Addicts enjoy pleasurable experiences more than nonaddicts.
   b. Addicts feel that their lives are not really complete.
   c. Addicts would give up their addiction if other pleasurable experiences were available.
   d. Addicts need to endlessly repeat the experience on which they are dependent.

3. Which statement would best serve as a topic sentence for paragraph 7?
   a. People become television addicts because they have more troubled lives than most other people.
   b. Television addicts develop a distorted perception of reality and lose self-control.
   c. Few experiences in life are as pleasurable as watching television.
   d. Alcoholics often believe they have more control over their drinking than they really do.

About Support

4. The author defines TV as an addiction by first defining
   a. being hooked on TV.
   b. serious addiction.

c. a heavy viewer.

d. the real world.

5. The topic sentence of paragraph 5 states, "Finally, a serious addiction is distinguished from a harmless pursuit of pleasure by its distinctly destructive elements." What details does the author use to support this point?

_____

_____

6. Paragraph 8

a. supports the idea in paragraph 7 that TV addicts overestimate their control over TV watching.

b. raises a point not dealt with elsewhere.

c. supports the idea in paragraph 9 that TV addicts are stuck in a living holding pattern.

About Coherence

7. Which paragraph fully signals the author's switch from discussing addiction in general terms to talking specifically about addiction to television? _____

8. What key transitional word is used twice in the essay? _____

About the Introduction and Conclusion

9. Which statement best describes the introductory paragraph of Winn's essay?

a. It explains the importance of the topic of television addiction.

b. It tells an anecdote that illustrates the nature of television addiction.

c. It presents a type of "addiction" very different from the one discussed in the essay.

10. Which statement best describes the conclusion of "Television Addiction"?

a. Winn recommends that the television addict try to "kick the habit."

b. Winn summarizes the points made in the body of the essay.

c. Winn comments on the damage television does to society at large.

Writing a Definition Essay

Writing | Assignment

1

Below are an introduction, a thesis, and supporting points for an essay that defines the word *maturity*. Using a separate sheet of paper, plan out and write the supporting paragraphs and a conclusion for the essay.

The Meaning of Maturity

Being a mature student does not mean being an old-timer. Maturity is not measured by the number of years a person has lived. Instead, the yardstick of maturity is marked by the qualities of self-denial, determination, and dependability.

Self-denial is an important quality in the mature student. . . .

Determination is another characteristic of a mature student. . . .

Although self-denial and determination are both vital, probably the most important measure of maturity is dependability. . . .

In conclusion, . . .

Prewriting

a. Prepare examples for the three qualities of maturity. For each quality, you should have either one extended example that takes up an entire paragraph or two or three shorter examples that together form enough material for a paragraph.

b. To generate these details, ask yourself questions like these, based on the topic sentence of the first supporting paragraph:

What could I do, or what have I done, that would be an example of self-denial?

What has someone I know ever done that could be described as self-denial?

What kind of behavior on the part of a student could be considered self-denial?

Write down quickly whatever answers occur to you. As when you freewrite, don't worry about grammar, punctuation, or spelling. Instead, concentrate on getting down as many details relating to self-denial as you can think of. Then repeat the questioning and writing process, substituting "determination" and "dependability" for "self-denial."

c. Now go through the material you have compiled. If you think of other details as you read, jot them down. Next, decide just what information you will use in each supporting paragraph. List the details in the order in which you will present them.

d. Now write the first draft of your essay.

Revising

After you have completed the first draft of the essay, set it aside for a while (if possible). When you reread what you have written, prepare for rewriting by asking yourself these questions:

FOUR BASES Checklist for Definition

About *Unity*

☑ Have I eliminated or rewritten any irrelevant material?

About *Support*

☑ Have I provided enough details to support each of the three characteristics of maturity?

About *Coherence*

☑ Have I used transition words to help readers follow my train of thought?

☑ Does my concluding paragraph provide a summary or a final thought or both?

About *Sentence Skills*

☑ Have I used a consistent point of view throughout my essay?

☑ Have I used specific rather than general words?

☑ Have I avoided wordiness and used concise wording?

☑ Are my sentences varied?

☑ Have I checked my writing for spelling and other sentence skills, as listed on the inside back cover of the book?

As you revise your essay through one or more additional drafts, continue to refer to this list until you can answer yes to each question.

Writing | Assignment

2   Choose one of the terms below as the subject of a definition essay. Each term refers to a certain kind of person.

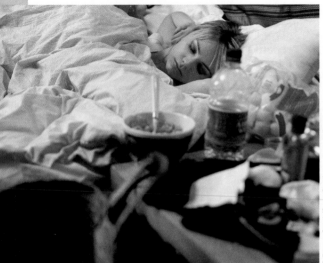

Slob

Cheapskate

Loser

Good neighbor

Busybody

Whiner

Con artist

Optimist

Pessimist

Team player

Bully

Scapegoat

Religious person

Hypocrite

Snob

Tease

Practical joker

Procrastinator

Loner

Pig

Type A

Prewriting

a. As you devise your opening paragraph, you may want to refer to the dictionary definition of the term. If so, be sure to use only one meaning of the term. (Dictionaries often provide several different meanings for a term.) *Don't* begin your paper with the overused phrase "According to Webster. . . ."

b. Remember that the thesis of a definition essay is a version of "What _____ means to me." The thesis presents what *your* experience has made *you* think the term actually means.

c. As you plan your supporting paragraphs, think of different parts or qualities of your term. Here, for example, are the three-part divisions of the student essays considered in this chapter:

> Football fans are crazy in terms of their behavior, their fascination with the past, and their loyalty.
>
> Student zombies are the "living dead," are controlled by a "mysterious force," and are likely to suffer an "awful fate."

d. Support each part of your division with either a series of examples or a single extended example.

e. You may find outlining to be the most helpful prewriting strategy for your definition essay. As a guide, write your thesis and three supporting points in the spaces below.

Thesis: _____

Support: 1. _____

              2. _____

              3. _____

Revising

Once you have the first draft of your essay completed, read it aloud to a friend or classmate. The two of you should review it with these questions in mind:

FOUR BASES Checklist for Definition

About *Unity*

- [x] Does my thesis statement indicate how I define the term, and does it indicate my plan of development for the essay?

- [x] Does each of my supporting paragraphs have a clear topic sentence?

About *Support*

- [x] Have I supported each of my three topic sentences with one extended example or a series of examples?

About *Coherence*

- [x] Have I rounded off my essay with an appropriate concluding paragraph?

About *Sentence Skills*

- [x] Have I used a consistent point of view throughout my essay?

- [x] Have I used specific rather than general words?

- [x] Have I avoided wordiness and used concise wording?

- [x] Are my sentences varied?

- [x] Have I proofread my essay for spelling and other sentence skills, as listed on the inside back cover of the book?

Writing | Assignment

3

Write an essay that defines one of these terms:

Persistence	Responsibility	Fear
Rebellion	Insecurity	Arrogance
Sense of humor	Assertiveness	Conscience
Escape	Jealousy	Class
Laziness	Practicality	Innocence
Danger	Nostalgia	Freedom
Curiosity	Gentleness	Violence
Common sense	Depression	Shyness
Soul	Obsession	Idealism
Family	Christianity	Spirituality

Writing | Assignment

4

Writing for a Specific Purpose and Audience

In this definition essay, you will write with a specific purpose and for a specific audience.

You work in a doctor's office and have been asked to write a brochure that will be placed in the waiting room. The brochure is intended to tell patients what a healthy lifestyle is. Write a definition of *healthy lifestyle* for your readers, using examples wherever appropriate. Your definition might focus on both mental and physical health and might include eating, sleeping, exercise, and recreational habits.

Alternatively, you might decide to take a playful point of view and write a brochure defining an *unhealthy lifestyle*.

www.mhhe.com/langan

Division-Classification

This chapter will explain and illustrate how to

- develop a division-classification essay

- write a division-classification essay

- revise a division-classification essay

In addition, you will read and consider

- two student division-classification essays

- one professional division-classification essay

Amazon.com. Used with permission.

Amazon.com: Styles: Music: Pop, Classical, Rock, International, Jazz, Alternative Rock, Latin Music, Dance & DJ & More

http://www.amazon.com/exec/obidos/tg/browse/-/301668/ref=sv_m_1/102-7013071-78665

Apple (113) ▾ Amazon eBay Yahoo! News (1061) ▾

amazon.com | Amanda's Amazon.com | Music | See All 40 Product Categories | Your Account | Cart | Your Lists | History | Help | NEW

Advanced Search | Browse Styles | Classical | Top Sellers | New & Future Releases | Music You Should Hear | Blowout Music | Classical Blowout

Search Music ▾   GO   Find Gifts   Web Search   GO

ANONYMOUS 4 TRACY BONHAM PETER CINCOTTI ELVIS COSTELLO RENÉE FLEMING BEN FOLDS SARAH LEE GUTHRIE & JOHNNY IRION PAAVO JÄRVI KAISER CHIEFS KEANE BEN LEE LYRICS BORN STEPHEN MALKMUS AIMEE MANN ROGER McGUINN MOBY MORCHEEBA MOTÖRHEAD MOUNTAIN GOATS DONNY OSMOND AMY RAY KIMBERLEY REW JAKE SLICHTER VISQUEEN TEGAN & SARA TOM WAITS WEDDING PRESENT
All these artists have picked Music You Should Hear See their lists

Browse Genres

Free Downloads • Blowout Music • Best of the Decade... So Far • Best of 2006 • Music You Should Hear: Artists' Picks • Label Stores • Blog • Podcast • Newsletters

Alternative Rock
· Britpop, Hardcore & Punk, Indie & Lo-Fi...

Blowout Music
· Great deals in all genres

Broadway & Vocalists
· Musicals, Classic Vocalists, Cabaret...

Christian & Gospel
· CCM, Praise & Worship, Christian Rock, Rap & Alternative...

Classical: Instrumental
· Composers, Historical Periods, Forms, Performers...

Country
· Traditional, Contemporary, Alt-Country, Honky-Tonk, Bluegrass...

Folk
· Contemporary, Traditional, British Isles, Folk-Rock...

Imports
· Hard-to-find Dance & DJ, Pop, Rock, Classical...

International
· European, Latin, Reggae, Asian, Celtic...

Latin
· Latin Pop, Salsa, Brazilian Jazz, Rock en Español, Cuban Music...

Musical Instruments
· Guitars, Keyboards, Band & Orchestra, Recording Equipment...

Opera & Vocal Music
· Composers, Historical Periods, Languages, Singers...

R&B & Soul
· Contemporary, Classic, Funk, Motown...

Rock
· Blues-Rock, Folk-Rock, Jam Bands, Progressive...

Blues
· Regional, Blues Rock, Modern, Traditional...

Box Sets
· New Releases, Browse by Genre, Editors' Picks...

Children's
· Disney, Sesame Street, Music for Little People...

Classical
· Instrumental, Opera, Vocals...

Classic Rock
· Reissues and the best of the '50s, '60s, '70s, and '80s

Dance & DJ
· Techno-House, Dance-Pop, Trance, Drum & Bass...

Hard Rock & Metal
· Funk Rock, Grunge, Industrial, Pop Metal...

Indie Music
· Independent releases in all genres

Jazz
· Vocal, Cool, Bebop, Fusion, Swing, Acid, by Instrument...

Miscellaneous
· Comedy, Karaoke, Interviews, Wedding Music, Holiday Music...

New Age
· Meditation, Celtic, Environmental, Ambient...

Pop
· Teen Pop, Adult Contemporary, Oldies...

Rap & Hip-Hop
· Gangsta, West Coast, East Coast, Underground, Old School...

Soundtracks
· Movie Soundtracks, Movie Scores, TV Soundtracks...

Where's My Stuff?   Shipping & Returns   Need Help?

Visit an online bookstore like Powell's at http://www.powells.com.psection/psection.html and browse through the categories of books. Or visit Amazon at http://www.amazon.com and browse through the categories of music. Then design your own site selling something similar (you can be as creative as you like). Provide at least five different categories for your "product" and explain what distinguishes each one.

When you return home from your weekly trip to the supermarket with five bags packed with your purchases, how do you sort them out? You might separate food items from nonfood items (like toothpaste, paper towels, and detergent). Or you might divide and classify the items into groups intended for the freezer compartment, the refrigerator, and the kitchen cupboards. You might even put the items into groups like "to be used tonight," "to be used soon," and "to be used last." Sorting supermarket items in such ways is just one simple example of how we spend a great deal of our time organizing our environment in one manner or another.

In this chapter, you will be asked to write an essay in which you divide or classify a subject according to a single principle. To prepare for this assignment, first read the student essays and the professional essay that follow and work through the questions that accompany the essays.

Student Essays to Consider

Mall People

Just what goes into "having fun"? For many people, "fun" involves getting out of the house, seeing other people, having something interesting to look at, and enjoying a choice of activities, all at a reasonable price. Going out to dinner or to the movies may satisfy some of those desires, but often not all. But an attractive alternative does exist in the form of the free-admission shopping mall. Teenagers, couples on dates, and the nuclear family can all be observed having a good time at the mall.

1

Teenagers are drawn to the mall to pass time with pals and to see and be seen by other teens. The guys saunter by in sneakers, T-shirts, and blue jeans, complete with a package of cigarettes sticking out of a pocket. The girls stumble along in midriff-baring tank tops, with a cell phone tucked snugly in the rear pocket of their low-waisted jeans. Traveling in a gang that resembles a wolf pack, the teenagers make the shopping mall their hunting ground. Mall managers have obviously made a decision to attract all this teenage activity. The kids' raised voices, loud

2

© BananaStock/SuperStock

(continued)

laughter, and occasional shouted obscenities can be heard from as far as half a mall away. They come to "pick up girls," to "meet guys," and just to "hang out."

Couples find fun of another sort at shopping malls. The young lovers are 3 easy to spot because they walk hand in hand, stopping to sneak a quick kiss after every few steps. They first pause at a jewelry store window so that they can gaze at diamond engagement rings and platinum wedding bands. Then, they wander into furniture departments in the large mall stores. Finally, they drift away, their arms wrapped around each other's waist.

Mom, Dad, little Jenny, and Fred Jr., visit the mall on Friday and Saturday 4 evenings for inexpensive recreation. Hearing the music of the antique carousel housed there, Jenny begs to ride her favorite pony with its shining golden mane. Shouting, "I'm starving!" Fred Jr., drags the family toward the food court, where he detects the seductive odor of pizza. Mom walks through a fabric store, running her hand over the soft velvets and slippery silks. Meanwhile, Dad has wandered into an electronics store and is admiring the sound system he'd love to buy someday. The mall provides something special for every member of the family.

Sure, some people visit the mall in a brief, businesslike way, just to pick 5 up a specific purchase or two. But many more are shopping for inexpensive recreation. The teenagers, the dating couples, and the nuclear families all find cheap entertainment at the mall.

Genuine Draft

The other night, my six-year-old son turned to me and asked for a light   1
beer. My husband and I sat there for a moment, stunned, and then explained
to him that beer was only for grown-ups. I suddenly realized how many beer
ads appear on television and how often they appear. To my little boy, it must
seem that every American drinks beer after work, or after playing softball,
or while watching a football game. Brewers have pounded audiences with
all kinds of campaigns to sell beer. There seems to be an ad to appeal to the
self-image of every beer drinker.

One type of ad attracts people who think of themselves as grown-up   2
kids. Budweiser's animated frogs, squatting on lily pads and croaking, "Bud,"
"Weis," "Er," are a perfect example of this type. The frogs are an example of
the wonders of computer animation, which is being increasingly mixed in
with real-life action in advertisements. The campaign was an immediate hit
with the underage set as well as with adult beer-drinkers. Within weeks, the
frogs were as recognizable to children as Tony the Tiger or Big Bird. They
became so popular that the new Bud ads were a feverishly anticipated part
of the Super Bowl—as much a part of the entertainment as the game itself
or the halftime show. These humorous ads suggest that beer is part of a
lighthearted approach to life.

A second kind of ad is aimed not at wanna-be kids but at macho men,   3
guys who think of themselves as "men's men," doing "guy things" together.
One campaign features men who see themselves as victims of their nagging
wives. Ads in this series show men howling with laughter about how they've
fooled their wives into thinking they're home doing chores (by leaving
dummy-stuffed pants lying under leaky sinks or broken furnaces) while

(continued)

they're really out drinking. Beer is a man's drink, the ads seem to say, and
women are a nuisance to be gotten around.

European and European-sounding beers such as Löwenbräu and   4
Heineken like to show handsome, wealthy-looking adults enjoying their
money and leisure time. A typical scene shows such people enjoying an
expensive hobby in a luxurious location. Beer, these ads tell us, is an essential
part of the "good life." This type of ad appeals to people who want to see
themselves as successful and upper class.

To a little boy, it may well seem that beer is necessary to every adult's   5
life. After all, we need it to make us laugh, to bond with our friends, and to
celebrate our financial success. At least, that's what advertisers tell him—
and us.

Questions

1

About Unity

1. In which supporting paragraph in "Genuine Draft" is the topic sentence at the
   end rather than, as is more appropriate for student essays, at the beginning?

   _____

2. Which sentence in paragraph 2 of "Mall People" should be omitted in the interest of paragraph unity? *(Write the opening words.)*

   _____

3. What sentence in paragraph 2 of "Genuine Draft" should be omitted in the
   interest of paragraph unity? *(Write the opening words.)*

   _____

About Support

4. After which sentence in paragraph 3 of "Mall People" are more supporting
   details needed? *(Write the opening words.)*

   _____

5. Which paragraph in "Genuine Draft" lacks sufficient specific details? _____

6. Label as *sight, touch, hearing,* or *smell* all the sensory details in the following
   sentences taken from "Mall People."

   a. "Hearing the music of the antique carousel housed there, Jenny begs to
      ride her favorite pony with its shining golden mane."

   b. "Shouting, 'I'm starving!' Fred Jr., drags the family toward the food court,
      where he detects the seductive odor of pizza."

   c. "Mom walks through a fabric store, running her hand over the soft velvets and slippery silks."

About Coherence

7. What are the time transition words used in paragraph 3 of "Mall People"?

_____ _____ _____

8. Which topic sentence in "Genuine Draft" functions as a linking sentence between paragraphs? *(Write the opening words.)*

_____

About the Introduction and Conclusion

9. What kind of introduction is used in "Genuine Draft"? *(Circle the appropriate letter.)*

   a. Broad, general statement narrowing to a thesis

   b. Idea that is the opposite of the one to be developed

   c. Quotation

   d. Anecdote

   e. Questions

10. What conclusion technique is used in "Mall People"? *(Circle the appropriate letter.)*

   a. Summary

   b. Prediction or recommendation

   c. Question

Developing a Division-Classification Essay

Considering Purpose and Audience

When writing a division-classification essay, your purpose is to present your audience with your own unique way of dividing and classifying a particular topic. To write a successful essay, you will need to first choose a topic that interests readers and lends itself to being divided and classified. Once you pick your topic, you will then have to come up with your own unique sorting system—one that readers will be able to understand.

    For example, if you choose clothing, there are a number of ways to sort this topic into categories. You could divide clothing by the function it serves: shirts and jackets (to cover the upper body), pants and skirts (for the lower body), and shoes and socks (for the feet). Or you could divide clothes according to the materials they are made from: animal products, plant products, and synthetic materials.

A more interesting, and potentially humorous, way to divide clothes is by fashion: clothes that are stylish, clothes that are going out of style, and clothes that are so unattractive that they never were in style. Notice that in all three of these cases, the broad topic of clothing has been divided into categories according to a particular principle (function, materials, and fashion). When you divide your topic for your essay, be sure to come up with your own division principle and make it clear to your readers.

Once you've selected your topic and figured out how to divide it, you will need to provide specific details so that readers fully understand the categories you made. For the example about fashion above, you might classify plaid bell-bottom pants as part of the "going out of style" category, while blue jeans might belong in the "clothes that are stylish" group and a mustard-yellow velour jacket might fit in the "never stylish" group. Whatever divisions you make, be sure to include enough details to make your division-classification method—your main point—clear to your readers. Equally important, keep your audience in mind. An audience of fashion-conscious young people, for instance, would probably have very different opinions about what is and isn't stylish than an audience of middle-aged bankers. Or an audience made up of the parents of middle-school students who are clamoring for "cool" clothes would have much more interest in clothing styles than the parents of students about to enter college.

Development through Prewriting

Julia, the writer of "Mall People," believed from her observations that "people at malls" would make a good topic for a division-classification essay. But she did not immediately know how she wanted to group those people or what she wanted to say about them. She decided to begin her prewriting by making a list of observations about mall shoppers. Here is what she came up with:

Families with kids

Lots of snacking

Crowds around special displays—automobiles, kiddie rides

Older people walking in mall for exercise

Groups of teenagers

Women getting made over at makeup counter

Dating couples

Blind woman with Seeing Eye dog

(continued)

Lots of people talking and laughing rather than shopping
Interviewers stopping shoppers to fill out questionnaires
Kids hanging out, meeting each other

As Julia reviewed her list, she concluded that the three largest groups of "mall people" were families with children, groups of teens, and dating couples. She decided to organize her essay around those three groups. To further flesh out her idea, she created a scratch outline that her essay would follow. Here is the scratch outline Julia prepared:

Thesis statement: Mall offers inexpensive fun for several groups.

1. *Teens*
    a. *Roam in packs*
    b. *Dress alike*
    c. *Meet new people*
2. *Dating couples*
    a. *Act romantic*
    b. *Window-shop for future home*
    c. *Have lovers' quarrels*
3. *Families*
    a. *Kids' activities*
    b. *Cheap food*
    c. *Adults shop*

Julia's list and outline prepared her to write the first draft of her essay.

Mall People

First Draft

Malls aren't only places to go shopping. They also offer free or at least cheap fun and activities for lots of people. Teenagers, dating couples, and families all like to visit the mall.

(continued)

Teenagers love to roam the mall in packs, like wolves. They often dress alike, depending on the latest fashion. They're noisy and sometimes rude, and mall security officers sometimes kick them out of the building. Then they find somewhere else to go, maybe one of the warehouse-sized amusement and video-game arcades that are springing up everywhere. Those places are fun, but they tend to be more expensive than just "hanging out" at the mall. Teens are usually not as interested in shopping at the mall as they are in picking up members of the opposite sex and seeing their friends.

Dating couples also enjoy wandering around the mall. They are easy to spot because they walk along holding hands and sometimes kissing. They stare at diamond rings and wedding bands and shop for furniture together. Sometimes they have spats and one of them stomps off to sulk on a bench for a while.

Little kids and their parents make up a big group of mall-goers. There is something for every member of the family there. There are usually some special displays that interest the kids, and Mom and Dad can always find things they like to window-shop for. Another plus for the family is that there is inexpensive food, like burgers and pizza, available at the mall's food court.

Development through Revising

After Julia completed her first draft, she put it aside. She knew from previous experience that she was a better critic of her own writing after she took a break from it. The following morning, when Julia read over her first draft, she noticed several places where it could be improved. Here are the observations she put in her writing journal:

- *My first paragraph does present a thesis (malls offer inexpensive entertainment), and it tells how I'm going to develop that thesis (by discussing three groups of people). But it isn't very interesting. I think I could do a better job of drawing readers in by describing what is fun about malls.*

- *Some of the details in the essay aren't necessary; they don't support my main idea. For instance, the stuff about teens being kicked out of the mall and about dating couples having fights doesn't have anything to do with the entertainment malls provide. I'll eliminate this.*

- *Some of my statements that do support the main idea need more support. For example, when I say there are "special displays that*

(continued)

interest the kids" in paragraph 4, I should give an example of such a display. I should also back up the idea that many teens dress alike.

With these observations in mind, Julia returned to her essay and revised it, producing the version that appears on page 331.

A Professional Essay to Consider

Now read the following professional essay. Then answer the questions and read the comments that follow.

Wait Divisions
by Tom Bodett

www.mhhe.com/langan

I read somewhere that we spend a full third of our lives waiting. I've also read   1
that we spend a third of our lives sleeping, a third working, and a third at our leisure. Now either somebody's lying, or we're spending all our leisure time waiting
to go to work or sleep. That can't be true or league softball and Winnebagos never
would have caught on.

So where are we doing all of this waiting, and what does it mean to an impa-   2
tient society like ours? Could this unseen waiting be the source of all our problems? A shrinking economy? The staggering deficit? Declining mental health
and moral apathy? Probably not, but let's take a look at some of the more classic
"waits" anyway.

The very purest form of waiting is what we'll call the *Watched-Pot Wait*. This   3
type of wait is without a doubt the most annoying of all. Take filling up the kitchen
sink. There is absolutely nothing you can do while this is going on but keep both
eyes glued to the sink until it's full. If you try to cram in some extracurricular activity, you're asking for it. So you stand there, your hands on the faucets, and wait.
A temporary suspension of duties. During these waits it's common for your eyes
to lapse out of focus. The brain disengages from the body and wanders around
the imagination in search of distraction. It finds none and springs back into action
only when the water runs over the edge of the counter and onto your socks.

The phrase "a watched pot never boils" comes of this experience. Pots don't   4
care whether they are watched or not; the problem is that nobody has ever seen a
pot actually come to a boil. While people are waiting, their brains turn off.

Other forms of the Watched-Pot Wait would include waiting for your dryer to   5
quit at the Laundromat, waiting for your toast to pop out of the toaster, or waiting
for a decent idea to come to mind at a typewriter. What they all have in common is
that they render the waiter helpless and mindless.

A cousin to the Watched-Pot Wait is the *Forced Wait*. Not for the weak of 6
will, this one requires a bit of discipline. The classic Forced Wait is starting your
car in the winter and letting it slowly idle up to temperature before engaging the
clutch. This is every bit as uninteresting as watching a pot, but with one big difference. You have a choice. There is nothing keeping you from racing to work behind
a stone-cold engine save[1] the thought of the early demise of several thousand dollars' worth of equipment you haven't paid for yet. Thoughts like that will help you
get through a Forced Wait.

Properly preparing packaged soup mixes also requires a Forced Wait. Direc- 7
tions are very specific on these mixes. "Bring three cups of water to boil, add mix,
simmer three minutes, remove from heat, let stand five minutes." I have my doubts
that anyone has actually done this. I'm fairly spineless when it comes to instant soups and usually just boil the bejeezus out of them until the noodles sink. Some things just aren't worth a Forced Wait.

All in all Forced Waiting re- 8
quires a lot of a thing called patience, which is a virtue. Once we get into virtues I'm out of my element and can't expound on the virtues of virtue, or even lie about them. So let's move on to some of the more far-reaching varieties of waiting.

The *Payday Wait* is certainly a 9
leader in the long-term anticipation field. The problem with waits that last more than a few minutes is that you have to actually do other things in the meantime. Like go to work. By far the most aggravating feature of the Payday Wait is that even though you must keep functioning in the in-terludes,[2] there is less and less you are able to do as the big day draws near. For some of us the last few days are best spent alone in a dark

What, in your opinion, is worth waiting for? Think about this question and create a scratch outline for a division-classification essay on things you feel are worth waiting for.

© John Gress/Reuters/Corbis

room for fear we'll accidentally do something that costs money. With the Payday
Wait comes a certain amount of hope that we'll make it, and faith that everything
will be all right once we do.

---

[1] *save:* except.
[2] *interludes:* times in between.

With the introduction of faith and hope, I've ushered in the most potent wait 10 class of all, the *Lucky-Break Wait,* or the *Wait for One's Ship to Come In.* This type of wait is unusual in that it is for the most part voluntary. Unlike the Forced Wait, which is also voluntary, waiting for your lucky break does not necessarily mean that it will happen.

Turning one's life into a waiting game of these proportions requires gobs of 11 the aforementioned faith and hope, and is strictly for the optimists among us. For these people life is the thing that happens to them while they're waiting for something to happen to them. On the surface it seems as ridiculous as following the directions on soup mixes, but the Lucky-Break Wait performs an outstanding service to those who take it upon themselves to do it. As long as one doesn't come to rely on it, wishing for a few good things to happen never hurt anybody.

In the end it is obvious that we certainly do spend a good deal of our time wait- 12 ing. The person who said we do it a third of the time may have been going easy on us. It makes a guy wonder how anything at all gets done around here. But things do get done, people grow old, and time boils on whether you watch it or not.

The next time you're standing at the sink waiting for it to fill while cooking 13 soup mix that you'll have to eat until payday or until a large bag of cash falls out of the sky, don't despair. You're probably just as busy as the next guy.

About Unity

1. The thesis of Bodett's essay is not presented directly. See if you can state it in your own words.

   _____

2. In paragraph 2, Bodett introduces several possible effects of waiting, then dismisses them with a "probably not." Is it a sign of careless writing that Bodett mentions irrelevant topics and then dismisses them? Or does he intend a particular effect by introducing unnecessary topics? If he does intend an effect, how would you describe it?

   _____

   _____

About Support

3. Bodett writes of four "classic waits": the Watched-Pot Wait, the Forced Wait, the Payday Wait, and the Lucky-Break Wait. For which two "waits" does he provide several examples?

   _____   _____

4. Bodett refers to the first two waits as cousins. How does he differentiate between them?

   _____

   _____

Questions

2

5. How does Bodett support his claim that the Forced Wait "requires a bit of discipline"?

_____

_____

About Coherence

6. Bodett's essay does not follow the strict one-three-one model (introduction, three supporting paragraphs, conclusion) often used in student essays. Instead, its form is a looser one that includes an introduction, four topics for development (the four "waits"), and a conclusion. Indicate in the following outline how the paragraphs of Bodett's essay are broken up:

Introduction: Paragraph(s)   _____

Topic 1:   Paragraph(s)   _____

Topic 2:   Paragraph(s)   _____

Topic 3:   Paragraph(s)   _____

Topic 4:   Paragraph(s)   _____

Conclusion: Paragraph(s)   _____

7. Which words in the first sentence of paragraph 6 link that sentence to the preceding three paragraphs?

_____

8. Bodett organizes the waits
   a. from the most harmful to the least harmful.
   b. from the shortest waits to the longest.
   c. from the most difficult wait to the easiest one.
   d. in no particular order.

About the Introduction and Conclusion

9. Which method best describes the introduction to "Wait Divisions"?
   a. Quotation
   b. Idea that is the opposite of the one to be developed
   c. Anecdote
   d. Broad, general statement narrowing to thesis

10. In what way does the first sentence in paragraph 13 serve as a summary of Bodett's main points?

_____

_____

Writing a Division-Classification Essay

Writing **Assignment**

1

Shown below are an introduction, a thesis, and supporting details for a classification essay on stress in college. Using separate paper, plan out and write the supporting paragraphs and a conclusion for the essay.

College Stress

Jack's heart pounds as he casts panicky looks around the classroom. He doesn't recognize the professor, he doesn't know any of the students, and he can't even figure out what the subject is. In front of him is a test. At the last minute his roommate awakens him. It's only another anxiety dream. The very fact that dreams like Jack's are common suggests that college is a stressful situation for young people. The causes of this stress can be academic, financial, and personal.

© Myrleen Ferguson Cate/PhotoEdit

Academic stress is common. . . .

In addition to academic stress, the student often feels financial pressure. . . .

Along with academic and financial worries, the student faces personal pressures. . . .

In conclusion . . .

Prewriting

a. To develop some ideas for the division-classification essay in Writing Assignment 1, freewrite for five minutes apiece on (1) *academic,* (2) *financial,* and (3) *personal* problems of college students.

b. Then add to the material you have written by asking yourself these questions:

> What are some examples of academic problems that are stressful for students?
>
> What are some examples of financial problems that students must contend with?
>
> What are some examples of personal problems that create stress in students?

Write down quickly whatever answers occur to you. As with freewriting, do not worry at this stage about writing correct sentences. Instead, concentrate on getting down as much information as you can think of that supports each of the three points.

c. Now go through all the material you have accumulated. Perhaps some of the details you have written down may help you think of even better details that would fit. If so, write down these additional details. Then make decisions about the exact information that you will use in each supporting paragraph. List the details in the order in which you will present them (1, 2, 3, and so on).

d. Now write the first draft of your essay.

Revising

After you have completed the first draft of the essay (and ideally have set it aside for a while), you should prepare yourself to rewrite by asking the following questions:

FOUR BASES Checklist for Division-Classification

About *Unity*

☑ Have I introduced my essay with a clearly stated thesis?

☑ Have I eliminated or rewritten any irrelevant material?

About *Support*

☑ Have I provided relevant examples for each of the three kinds of stress?

☑ Have I provided enough details to support each of the three kinds of stress?

(continued)

About *Coherence*

Have I used transition words to help readers follow my train of thought?

Have I added a concluding paragraph that rounds out and completes the essay?

About *Sentence Skills*

Have I used a consistent point of view throughout my essay?

Have I used specific rather than general words?

Have I avoided wordiness and used concise wording?

Are my sentences varied?

Have I checked my essay carefully for spelling and other sentence skills, as listed on the inside back cover of the book?

As you revise your essay, continue to refer to this list until you can answer yes to each question.

Writing Assignment

2

Choose one of the following subjects as the basis for a division-classification essay:

Music	Pet owners
Videos	Junk food
TV shows	College courses
Fiction	Dating couples
Comic strips	Shoppers
Vacations	Bosses
Answering-machine messages	Parties
Breakfast foods	Advertisements
Pets	Catalogs
Attitudes toward exercise	Technology

Prewriting

a. For a division-classification essay, the prewriting strategy that may be especially helpful is outlining. The success of your essay will depend on your division of your topic into three well-balanced parts. To create those three parts, you must use the same rule, or principle, of division for each. Most topics can be divided in several ways according to several principles. For example, the topic "Hit movies" could be divided in the following ways:

> By *film categories:* Action, comedy, romance
>
> By *intended audience:* Families, dating couples, teens

The topic "My favorite books" could be divided like this:

> By *book categories:* Novels, how-to books, biographies
>
> By *purpose they serve for me:* Escape, self-improvement, amusement

The topic "Places to eat" could be divided in these ways:

> By *cost:* Cheap, moderate, expensive
>
> By *type of food:* American, Italian, Chinese

If you look back at the essays that appear earlier in this chapter, you'll see that the topics are divided according to the following principles:

> "Mall People" is divided by *groups of shoppers:* Teens, dating couples, families
>
> "Genuine Draft" is divided by *beer-drinkers' self-images:* Grown-up kids, men's men, upper class
>
> "Wait Divisions" is divided by *types of waits:* Watched-Pot Wait, Forced Wait, Payday Wait, Lucky-Break Wait

The important point to remember is to divide your topic consistently, according to a single principle. It would be illogical, for example, to divide the topic "Places to eat" into "American" (type of food served), "Italian" (type of food served), and "Expensive" (cost). For the essay to be balanced and consistent, choose one principle of division and stick to it.

b. As you consider a topic for your own paper, think of principles of division you might use. Test them by filling out this outline and answering the question.

Topic: _____

Principle of division: _____

Three-part division of topic: _____

    1. _____

2. _____

3. _____

Have I used the same principle of division for each of the three parts?

When you are confident that you have chosen a topic of interest to you that you can divide into three parts according to one principle, you are ready to begin writing.

c. Before writing your first draft, you may want to freewrite on each of the three parts, make lists, or ask and answer questions to generate the supporting details you will need to develop your ideas.

Revising

Once you have completed a first draft of your essay, share it with a friend or class-mate. You should both review it with these questions in mind:

FOUR BASES Checklist for Division-Classification

About *Unity*

☑ Have I included the essay's thesis in my introductory paragraph?

☑ Does my thesis state my topic and the principle of division I have chosen?

☑ Have I eliminated irrelevant material that does not support my thesis?

About *Support*

☑ Have I backed up statements in my essay with relevant examples or illustrations?

☑ Have I provided enough details to support each of the three kinds of stress?

About *Coherence*

☑ Is each of the paragraphs in the body of my essay based on one division of my topic?

☑ Have I used transition words to help readers follow my train of thought?

☑ Have I included a concluding paragraph that provides a sense of completion to the essay?

(continued)

> ☑ Have I used linking sentences between paragraphs to help tie those paragraphs together?
>
> **About *Sentence Skills***
>
> ☑ Have I used a consistent point of view throughout my essay?
>
> ☑ Have I used specific rather than general words?
>
> ☑ Have I avoided wordiness and used concise wording?
>
> ☑ Are my sentences varied?
>
> ☑ Have I proofread my essay for spelling and other sentence skills, as listed on the inside back cover of the book?

As you revise your essay, continue to refer to this list until you and your reader can answer yes to each question.

Writing | Assignment

3 Writing for a Specific Purpose and Audience

In this division-classification essay, you will write with a specific purpose and for a specific audience.

Option 1 Your younger sister or brother has moved to another city and is about to choose a roommate. Write her or him a letter about what to expect from different types of roommates. Label each type of roommate ("The Messy Type," "The Neatnik," "The Loud-Music Lover," etc.), and explain what it would be like to live with each.

Option 2 Unsure about your career direction, you have gone to a vocational counseling service. To help you select the type of work you are best suited for, a counselor has asked you to write a detailed description of your ideal job. You will present this description to three other people who are also seeking to choose a career.

To describe your ideal job, divide work life into three or more elements, such as

Activities done on the job

Skills used on the job

Physical environment

People you work with and under

How the job affects society

In your essay, explain your ideals for each element. Use specific examples where possible to illustrate your points.

Argument

16

Should cell phones be permitted in class? Look at the photograph above and write an essay in which you argue for or against the use of cell phones in the classroom. Include at least three separate reasons that support your point of view.

This chapter will explain and illustrate how to

- develop an argument essay
- write an argument essay
- revise an argument essay

In addition, you will read and consider

- two student argument essays
- one professional argument essay

© Bill Aron/PhotoEdit

Do you know someone who enjoys a good argument? Such a person likes to challenge any sweeping statement we might make. For example, when we say something like "Ms. Lucci doesn't grade fairly," he or she comes back with "Why do you say that? What are your reasons?"

Our questioner then listens carefully as we state our case, judging if we really do have solid evidence to support our point of view. We realize that saying, "Ms. Lucci just doesn't, that's all," sounds weak and unconvincing, so we try to come up with stronger evidence to back up our statement. Such a questioner may make us feel uncomfortable, but we may also feel grateful to him or her for helping us clarify our opinions.

The ability to put forth sound and compelling arguments is an important skill in everyday life. You can use argument to make a point in a class discussion, persuade a friend to lend you money, or talk an employer into giving you a day off. Becoming skilled in clear, logical reasoning can also help you see through faulty arguments that others may make. You'll become a better critic of advertisements, newspaper articles, political speeches, and the other persuasive appeals you see and hear every day.

In this chapter, you will be asked to write an essay in which you defend a position with a series of solid reasons. In a general way, you have done the same thing—making a point and then supporting it—with all the essays in this book. The difference here is that argument advances a *controversial* point, a point that at least some of your readers will not be inclined to accept. To prepare for this assignment, first read about five strategies you can use in advancing an argument. Then read the student essays and the professional essay that follow and work through the questions that accompany the essays.

Strategies for Argument

Because argument assumes controversy, you have to work especially hard to convince readers of the validity of your position. Here are five strategies you can use to help win over readers whose viewpoint may differ from yours.

1 Use Tactful, Courteous Language

In an argument essay, you are attempting to persuade readers to accept your viewpoint. It is important, therefore, not to anger them by referring to them or their opinions in rude or belittling terms. Stay away from sweeping statements like "Everybody knows that . . ." or "People with any intelligence agree that. . . ." Also, keep the focus on the issue you are discussing, not on the people involved in the debate. Don't write, "*My opponents* say that orphanages cost less than foster care." Instead, write, "*Supporters of orphanages* say that orphanages cost less than foster care." Terms like *my opponents* imply that the argument is between you and anyone who disagrees with you. By contrast, a term such as *supporters of orphanages* suggests that those who don't agree with you are nevertheless reasonable people who are willing to consider differing opinions.

2   Point Out Common Ground

Another way to persuade readers to consider your opinion is to point out common ground—opinions that you share. Find points on which people on all sides of the argument can agree. Perhaps you are arguing that there should be an 11 p.m. curfew for juveniles in your town. Before going into detail about your proposal, remind readers who oppose such a curfew that you and they share certain goals: a safer city, a lower crime rate, and fewer gang-related tragedies. Readers will be more receptive to your idea once they have considered how you and they think alike.

3   Acknowledge Differing Viewpoints

It is a mistake to simply ignore points of view that conflict with yours. Acknowledging other viewpoints strengthens your position in several ways. First, it helps you spot flaws in the opposing position—as well as in your own argument. Second, and equally important, it gives the impression that you are a reasonable person, willing to look at an issue from all sides. Readers will be more likely to consider your point of view if you indicate a willingness to consider theirs.

At what point in your essay should you acknowledge opposing arguments? The earlier the better—ideally, in the introduction. By quickly establishing that you recognize the other side's position, you get your readers on board with you, ready to hear what else you have to say.

One effective technique is to *cite the opposing viewpoint in your thesis statement.* You do this by dividing your thesis into two parts. In the first part, you acknowledge the other side's point of view; in the second, you state your opinion, suggesting that yours is the stronger viewpoint. In the following example, the opposing viewpoint is underlined once; the writer's own position is underlined twice:

> Although some students believe that studying a foreign language is a waste of time, two years of foreign-language study should be required of all college graduates.

For another example of a thesis that acknowledges an opposing viewpoint, look at this thesis statement, taken from the essay titled "Once Over Lightly: Local TV News" (page 355):

> While local TV newscasts can provide a valuable community resource, too often such programs provide mere entertainment at the expense of solid news.

Another effective technique is to use one or two sentences (separate from the thesis) in the introduction to acknowledge the alternative position. Such sentences briefly state the "other side's" argument. To see this technique at work, look at the introduction to the essay "Teenagers and Jobs" (page 354), noting the sentence "Many people argue that working can be a valuable experience for the young."

© Mary Kate Denny/PhotoEdit

Arguments can be made through visual images as well. What visual argument is suggested by this photograph? Is it effective? Why or why not?

A third technique is to *use a paragraph within the body of your essay to summarize opposing opinions in greater detail.* To do this successfully, you must spend some time researching those opposing arguments. A fair, even-handed summary of the other side's ideas will help convince readers that you have looked at the issue from all angles before deciding where you stand. Imagine, for instance, that you are writing an essay arguing that the manufacture and sale of handguns should be outlawed. You would begin by doing some library research to find information on both sides of the issue, making sure to pay attention to material that argues against your viewpoint. You might also talk with local representatives of the National Rifle Association or other organizations that support gun ownership. Having done your research, you would be in a good position to write a paragraph summarizing the opposing viewpoints. In this paragraph, you might mention that many citizens believe that gun ownership is a right guaranteed by the Constitution and that gun owners fear that outlawing handguns would deprive law-abiding people of protection against gun-toting criminals. Once you had demonstrated that you understood opposing views, you would be in a stronger position to present your own point of view.

4 When Appropriate, Grant the Merits of Differing Viewpoints

Sometimes an opposing argument contains a point whose validity you cannot deny. What should you do then? The strongest strategy is to admit that the point is a good one. You will lose credibility if you argue against something that clearly makes sense. Admit the merit of one aspect of the other argument while making it clear that you still believe your argument to be stronger overall. Suppose that you were arguing against the use of computers in writing classrooms. You might say, "Granted, students who are already accustomed to computers can use them to write papers more quickly and efficiently"—admitting that the other side has a valid point. But you could quickly follow this admission with a statement making your own viewpoint clear: "But for students like me who write and think in longhand, a computer in the classroom is more a hindrance than a help; it would require too long a learning curve to be of any value to me."

5 Rebut Differing Viewpoints

Sometimes it may not be enough simply to acknowledge other points of view and present your own argument. When you are dealing with an issue that your readers feel strongly about, you may need to *rebut* the opposing arguments. To *rebut* means to point out problems with an opposing view, to show where an opponent's argument breaks down.

Imagine that you are writing an essay arguing that your college should use money intended to build a campus health and fitness center to upgrade the library instead. From reading the school paper, you know that supporters of the center say it will help attract new students to the college. You rebut that point by citing a study conducted by the admissions office that shows that most students choose a college because they can afford it and because they like its academic programs and facilities. You also emphasize that many students, already financially strapped, would have trouble paying the proposed fee for using the center.

A rebuttal can take two forms: (1) You can first mention all the points raised by the other side and then present your counterargument to each of those points. (2) You can present the first point raised by the opposition and rebut that point, then move on to the second opposing point and rebut that, and so on.

Student Essays to Consider

Teenagers and Jobs

"The pressure for teenagers to work is great, and not just because of the economic plight in the world today. Much of it is peer pressure to have a little bit of freedom and independence, and to have their own spending money. The concern we have is when the part-time work becomes the primary focus." These are the words of Roxanne Bradshaw, educator and officer of the National Education Association. Many people argue that working can be a valuable experience for the young. However, working more than about fifteen hours a week is harmful to adolescents because it reduces their involvement with school, encourages a materialistic and expensive lifestyle, and increases the chance of having problems with drugs and alcohol.

Schoolwork and the benefits of extracurricular activities tend to go by the wayside when adolescents work long hours. As more and more teens have filled the numerous part-time jobs offered by fast-food restaurants and malls, teachers have faced increasing difficulties. They must both keep the attention of tired pupils and give homework to students who simply don't have time to do it. In addition, educators have noticed less involvement in the extracurricular activities that many consider a healthy influence on young people. School bands and athletic teams are losing players to work, and sports events are poorly attended by working students. Those teens who try to do it all—homework, extracurricular activities, and work—may find themselves exhausted and prone to illness. A recent newspaper story, for example, described a girl in Pennsylvania who came down with mononucleosis as a result of aiming for good grades, playing on two school athletic teams, and working thirty hours a week.

Another drawback of too much work is that it may promote materialism and an unrealistic lifestyle. Some parents claim that working helps teach adolescents the value of a dollar. Undoubtedly that can be true. It's also true that some teens work to help out with the family budget or to save for college. However, surveys have shown that the majority of working teens use their earnings to buy luxuries—computers, video-game systems, clothing, even cars. These young people, some of whom earn $500 or more a month, don't worry about spending wisely—they can just about have it all. In many cases, experts point out, they are becoming accustomed to a lifestyle they won't be able to afford several years down the road, when they no longer

(continued)

have parents paying for car insurance, food, lodging, and so on. At that point, they'll be hard-pressed to pay for necessities as well as luxuries.

Finally, teenagers who work a lot are more likely than others to get involved with alcohol and drugs. Teens who put in long hours may seek a quick release from stress, just like the adults who need to drink a couple of martinis after a hard day at work. Stress is probably greater in our society today than it has been at any time in the past. Also, teens who have money are more likely to get involved with drugs. **4**

Teenagers can enjoy the benefits of work while avoiding its drawbacks, simply by limiting their work hours during the school year. As is often the case, a moderate approach will be the most healthy and rewarding. **5**

Once Over Lightly: Local TV News

Are local television newscasts a reliable source of news? Do they provide in-depth coverage and analysis of important local issues? Unfortunately, all too often they do not. While local TV newscasts can provide a valuable community resource, too often such programs provide mere entertainment at the expense of solid news. In their battle for high ratings, local programs emphasize news personalities at the expense of stories. Visual appeal has a higher priority than actual news. And stories and reports are too brief and shallow. **1**

Local TV newscasters are as much the subject of the news as are the stories they present. Nowhere is this more obvious than in weather reports. Weatherpersons spend valuable news time joking, drawing cartoons, chatting about weather fronts as "good guys" and "bad guys," and dispensing weather trivia such as statistics about relative humidity and record highs and lows for the date. Reporters, too, draw attention to themselves. Rather than just getting the story, the reporters are shown jumping into or getting out of helicopters to get the story. When reporters interview crime victims or the residents of poor neighborhoods, the camera angle typically includes them and their reaction as well as their subjects. When they report on a storm, they stand outside in the storm, their styled hair blowing, so we can admire how they "brave the elements." Then there are the anchorpersons, who are chosen as much for their looks as their skills. They, too, dilute the news by putting their personalities at center stage. **2**

(continued)

Often the selection of stories and the way they are presented are based   3
on visual impact rather than news value. If a story is not accompanied by
an interesting film clip, it is not likely to be shown on the local news. The
result is an overemphasis on fires and car crashes and little attention to
such important issues as the economy. A tractor-trailer spill on the highway
slightly injures one person and inconveniences motorists for only an hour.
But because it provides dramatic pictures—the big truck on its side, its load
spilled, emergency personnel running around, lots of flashing lights—it
is given greater emphasis in the local newscast than a rise in local taxes,
which has far more lasting effect on the viewer. "If it bleeds, it leads" is the
unofficial motto of many local news programs. A story that includes pictures
of death and destruction, no matter how meaningless, is preferable on the
local news to a solid, important story without flashy visuals. The mania
for visuals is so strong that local news programs will even slap irrelevant
visuals onto an otherwise strong story. A recent story on falling oil prices,
for example, was accompanied by footage of a working oil well that drew
attention away from the important economic information in the report.

On the average, about half a minute is devoted to a story. Clearly, stories   4
that take less than half a minute are superficial. Even the longest stories,
which can take up to several minutes, are not accompanied by meaningful
analysis. Instead, the camera jumps from one location to another, and the
newscaster simplifies and trivializes the issues. For instance, one recent
"in-depth" story about the homeless consisted of a glamorous reporter
talking to a homeless person and asking him what should be done about
the problem. The poor man was in no condition to respond thoughtfully.
The story then cut to an interview with a city bureaucrat who mechanically
rambled on about the need for more government funding. Is raising taxes the
answer to every social problem? There were also shots of homeless people
sleeping in doorways and on top of heating vents, and there were interviews
with people in the street, all of whom said that something should be done
about the terrible problem of homelessness. There was, in all of this, no real
exploration of the issue and no proposed solution. It was also apparent that
the homeless were just the issue of the week. After the week's coverage was
over, the topic was not mentioned again.

Because of the emphasis on newscasters' personalities and on the visual   5
impact of stories and the short time span for stories, local news shows
provide little more than diversion. What viewers need instead is news that
has real significance. Rather than being amused and entertained, we need to
deal with complex issues and learn uncomfortable truths that will help us
become more responsible consumers and citizens.

About Unity

1. Which paragraph in "Once Over Lightly" lacks a topic sentence? _____
Write a topic sentence for the paragraph:

_____

2. What sentence in paragraph 4 of "Once Over Lightly" should be omitted in the interest of paragraph unity? *(Write the opening words.)*

_____

3. Which sentence in paragraph 4 of "Teenagers and Jobs" should be omitted in the interest of paragraph unity? *(Write the opening words.)*

_____

About Support

4. Which sentence in paragraph 4 of "Teenagers and Jobs" needs to be followed by more supporting details? Which sentence in paragraph 2 of "Once Over Lightly" needs to be followed by supporting details? *(Write the opening words of each sentence.)*

_____

_____

5. In "Teenagers and Jobs," which supporting paragraph raises an opposing idea and then argues against that idea? _____ What transition word is used to signal the author's change of direction? _____

6. In paragraph 2 of "Once Over Lightly," the topic sentence is supported by details about three types of newscasters. What are those three types?

_____   _____   _____

About Coherence

7. Which two paragraphs of "Teenagers and Jobs" begin with an addition transition, and what are those words?

_____   _____

8. Write the change-of-direction transition and the illustration transition in paragraph 3 of "Once Over Lightly."

Change of direction: _____   *Illustration:* _____

About the Introduction and Conclusion

9. Two methods of introduction are used in "Teenagers and Jobs." Circle the letters of these two methods.

   a. Broad, general statement narrowing to thesis

   b. Idea that is the opposite of the one to be developed

   c. Quotation

   d. Anecdote

   e. Questions

10. Both essays end with the same type of conclusion. What method do they use?

   a. Summary only

   b. Summary and recommendation

   c. Prediction

Developing an Argument Essay

Considering Purpose and Audience

When you write an argument essay, your main purpose is to convince readers that your particular view or opinion on a *controversial* issue is correct. In addition, at times, you may have a second purpose for your argument essay: to persuade your audience to take some sort of action.

To convince readers in an argument essay, it is important to provide them with a clear main point and plenty of logical evidence to back it up. Say, for example, you want to argue that public schools should require students to wear uniforms. In this case, you might do research to gather as much evidence as possible to support your point. You may check to see, for instance, if uniforms are cheaper than the alternative. Perhaps you could find out if schools with uniforms have a lower rate of violence than those without them. You may even look for studies to see if students' academic performance improves when school uniforms are adopted. As you search for evidence, be sure that it clearly links to your topic and supports the main point you are trying to get across to your audience,

While consideration of your audience is important for all essay forms, it is absolutely critical to the success of your argument essay. Depending on the main point you choose, your audience may be firmly opposed to your view or somewhat supportive of it. As you begin planning your own argument essay, then, consider what your audience already knows, and how it feels, about the main point of your argument. Using the example above, for instance, ask yourself what opinion your audience holds about school uniforms. What are likely to be their objections to your argument? Why would people *not* support your main point? What, if anything, are the merits of the opposing point of view? To "get inside the head" of your opposition, you might even want to interview a few people you're sure will disagree with you: say, for instance, a student with a very funky personal style who you know would dislike wearing a uniform. By becoming aware of the points of view your audience might have, you will know how to proceed in researching your rebuttal to their arguments.

> **TIP** For more information on how to deal with opposing views in your essay, see pages 351–352. By directly addressing your opposition, you add credibility to your argument and increase the chances that others will be convinced that your main point is valid.

Development through Prewriting

Before choosing a topic for her essay, Anna, the writer of "Teenagers and Jobs," asked herself what controversial subject she was particularly well qualified to argue. She wanted to select something she cared about, something she could sink her teeth into. As a person who had been an active member of her high school community—she had worked on the newspaper, played basketball, and sung in a chorus—Anna first thought of writing about student apathy. It had always bothered her to see few students taking advantage of the opportunities available to them in school. But as she thought more about individual students she knew and their reasons for not getting more involved in school and extracurricular activities, she changed her opinion. "I realized that 'apathy' was not really the problem," she explained. "Many of them worked so much that they literally didn't have time for school life."

After narrowing her thesis to the idea of "teenagers and work," Anna made a list of what she perceived as the bad points of students' working too much:

No time for real involvement in school and school activities

Students leave right after school—can't stay for clubs, practices

Don't have time to attend games, other school functions

Students sleep in class and skip homework

Stress, extra money contribute to drug and alcohol use

Teachers frustrated trying to teach tired students

Having extra money makes teens materialistic

(continued)

> *Some get so greedy they drop out of school to work full time*
>
> *Students miss the fun of being young, developing talents and social abilities*
>
> *Students burn out, even get sick*
>
> *Hanging around older coworkers can contribute to drug, alcohol use*
>
> *Buying luxuries gives teens unrealistic idea of standard of living*

As she reviewed and revised her list of points, Anna identified three main points to develop in her essay. Those she identified as points 1, 2, and 3. She realized that some of the other items she had jotted down were related ideas that might be used to support her main topics. She marked those with the number of the main idea they supported, in parentheses, like this: (1). She also crossed out points that did not fit.

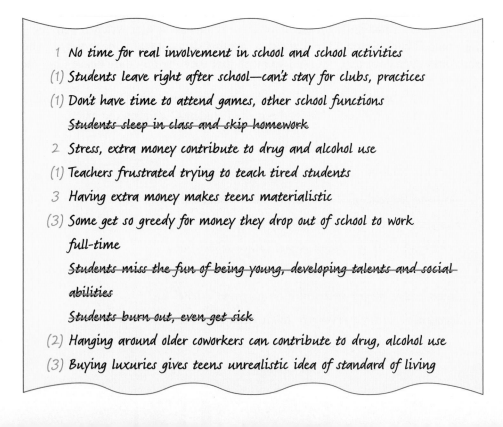

> *1 No time for real involvement in school and school activities*
>
> *(1) Students leave right after school—can't stay for clubs, practices*
>
> *(1) Don't have time to attend games, other school functions*
>
> ~~*Students sleep in class and skip homework*~~
>
> *2 Stress, extra money contribute to drug and alcohol use*
>
> *(1) Teachers frustrated trying to teach tired students*
>
> *3 Having extra money makes teens materialistic*
>
> *(3) Some get so greedy for money they drop out of school to work full-time*
>
> ~~*Students miss the fun of being young, developing talents and social abilities*~~
>
> ~~*Students burn out, even get sick*~~
>
> *(2) Hanging around older coworkers can contribute to drug, alcohol use*
>
> *(3) Buying luxuries gives teens unrealistic idea of standard of living*

Referring to this list, Anna wrote the following first draft of her essay.

First Draft

Teenagers and Jobs

Many people think that working is a valuable experience for young people. But when teenagers have jobs, they are too likely to neglect their schoolwork, become overly materialistic, and get into trouble with drugs and alcohol.

Schoolwork and the benefits of extracurricular activities tend to go by the wayside when adolescents work long hours. As more and more teens have taken jobs, teachers have faced increasing difficulties. They must both keep the attention of tired pupils and give homework to students who simply don't have time to do it. In addition, educators have noticed less involvement in extracurricular activities. School bands and athletic teams are losing players to work, and sports events are poorly attended by working students. Those teens who try to do it all—homework, extracurricular activities, and work—may find themselves exhausted and burned out.

Another drawback of too much work is that it may promote materialism and an unrealistic lifestyle. Most working teens use their earnings to buy luxuries. These young people don't worry about spending wisely—they can just about have it all. They are becoming accustomed to a lifestyle they won't be able to afford several years down the road, when they have to support themselves.

Finally, teenagers who work are more likely than others to get involved with alcohol and drugs. Teens who put in long hours may seek a quick release from stress, just like the adults who need to drink a couple of martinis after a hard day at work. Also, teens who have money are more likely to get involved with drugs.

In short, teens and work just don't mix.

Development through Revising

Anna's instructor had offered to look over students' first drafts and suggest improvements for revision. Here is the note she wrote at the end of Anna's work:

Anna—Good beginning. While I think your thesis is overstated, it and each of your main topics are on the right track. Here are some points to consider as you write your next draft:

- Many teenagers find working a limited number of hours a week to be a good experience. I think it's a mistake to state flatly that it's always a

(continued)

negative thing for teenagers to have jobs. Think about acknowledging that there can be good points to students' working part-time.

- You do a pretty good job of supporting your first main point ("Schoolwork and the benefits of extracurricular activities tend to go by the wayside when adolescents work long hours") by noting the effect of too much work on scholastic achievement and extracurricular activities. You less effectively support points 2 and 3 ("Another drawback of too much work is that it may promote materialism and an unrealistic lifestyle" and "Finally, teenagers who work are more likely than others to get involved with alcohol and drugs"). Show how teens become too materialistic; don't just state that they do. And what evidence do you have that working teens use drugs and alcohol more than others?

- Throughout the essay, can you come up with evidence beyond your own observations to support the idea that too much working is detrimental to teens? Look in the magazine indexes in the library and on the Internet for studies or stories that might support your thesis.

I'll look forward to seeing your final draft.

After considering her instructor's comments, Anna wrote the version of "Teenagers and Jobs" that appears on page 354.

A Professional Essay to Consider

Read the following professional essay. Then answer the questions and read the comments that follow.

Ban the Things. Ban Them All.
by Molly Ivins

Guns. Everywhere guns.   1

Let me start this discussion by pointing out that I am not anti-gun. I'm pro- 2
knife. Consider the merits of the knife.

In the first place, you have to catch up with someone to stab him. A general 3
substitution of knives for guns would promote physical fitness. We'd turn into a
whole nation of great runners. Plus, knives don't ricochet. And people are seldom
killed while cleaning their knives.

As a civil libertarian,[1] I of course support the Second Amendment. And I believe it means exactly what it says: "A well-regulated militia being necessary to the security of a free state, the right of the people to keep and bear arms shall not be infringed[2]." Fourteen-year-old boys are not part of a well-regulated militia. Members of wacky religious cults are not part of a well-regulated militia. Permitting unregulated citizens to have guns is destroying the security of this free state.

I am intrigued by the arguments of those who claim to follow the judicial doctrine of original intent. How do they know it was the dearest wish of Thomas Jefferson's heart that teenage drug dealers should cruise the cities of this nation perforating their fellow citizens with assault rifles? Channeling[3]?

There is more hooey spread about the Second Amendment. It says quite clearly that guns are for those who form part of a well-regulated militia, i.e., the armed forces including the National Guard. The reasons for keeping them away from everyone else get clearer by the day.

The comparison most often used is that of the automobile, another lethal object that is regularly used to wreak great carnage. Obviously, this society is full of people who haven't got enough common sense to use an automobile properly. But we haven't outlawed cars yet.

We do, however, license them and their owners, restrict their use to presumably sane and sober adults and keep track of who sells them to whom. At a minimum, we should do the same with guns.

In truth, there is no rational argument for guns in this society. This is no longer a frontier nation in which people hunt their own food. It is a crowded, overwhelmingly urban country in which letting people have access to guns is a continuing disaster. Those who want guns—whether for target shooting, hunting or potting[4] rattlesnakes (get a hoe)—should be subjected to the same restrictions placed on gun owners in England, a nation in which liberty has survived nicely without an armed populace.

The argument that "guns don't kill people" is patent nonsense. Anyone who has ever worked in a cop shop knows how many family arguments end in murder because there was a gun in the house. Did the gun kill someone? No. But if there had been no gun, no one would have died. At least not without a good footrace first. Guns do kill. Unlike cars, that is all they do.

Michael Crichton makes an interesting argument about technology in his thriller *Jurassic Park*. He points out that power without discipline is making this society into wreckage. By the time someone who studies the martial arts becomes a master—literally able to kill with bare hands—that person has also undergone years of training and discipline. But any fool can pick up a gun and kill with it.

---

[1]*civil liberation:* someone actively concerned with protecting rights guaranteed to the individual by law.
[2]*infringed:* violated.
[3]*channeling:* serving as a medium in order to communicate with spirits.
[4]*potting:* shooting with a potshot (an easy shot).

"A well-regulated militia" surely implies both long training and long disci- 12
pline. That is the least, the very least, that should be required of those who are permitted to have guns, because a gun is literally the power to kill. For years, I used to
enjoy taunting my gun-nut friends about their psychosexual hangups—always in a
spirit of good cheer, you understand. But letting the noisy minority in the National
Rifle Association force us to allow this carnage to continue is just plain insane.

I do think gun nuts have a power hangup. I don't know what is missing in 13
their psyches that they need to feel they have the power to kill. But no sane society
would allow this to continue.

Ban the damn things. Ban them all.   14

You want protection? Get a dog.   15

Questions

2

About Unity

1. Which of the following statements best represents the implied thesis of the essay?

    a. The author is pro-knife.

    b. The Second Amendment is poorly understood.

    c. Despite arguments to the contrary, people without long training and discipline should not be allowed to have guns.

    d. In his novel *Jurassic Park,* Michael Crichton argues that power without discipline is wrecking society.

2. Which statement would best serve as a topic sentence for paragraphs 5 and 6?

    a. Drug dealers should not be allowed to purchase assault rifles.

    b. Ivins is interested in other people's points of view concerning gun ownership.

    c. Thomas Jefferson was opposed to the idea of a "well-regulated militia."

    d. Applying the original intent of the Second Amendment to modern circum-stances is not clear-cut and must be done with common sense.

3. Which is the topic sentence of paragraph 9?

    a. "In truth, there is no rational argument for guns in this society."

    b. "This is no longer a frontier nation in which people hunt their own food."

    c. "It is a crowded, overwhelmingly urban country in which letting people have access to guns is a continuing disaster."

    d. "Those who want guns . . . should be subjected to the same restrictions placed on gun owners in England. . . ."

About Support

4. Why does Ivins contrast the use of martial arts with the use of guns?

   a. To support the idea that gun owners should be required to study the martial arts

   b. To support the idea that a martial arts master can kill with his bare hands

   c. To support the idea that power without discipline is dangerous

   d. To support the idea that guns are more practical than the martial arts

5. Which statement best expresses the implied point of paragraph 10?

   a. Guns kill people.

   b. Many family arguments are surprisingly violent.

   c. Many arguments end in death only because a gun was handy.

   d. Guns and cars are similar.

6. In what ways, according to Ivins, is the knife preferable to the gun? Is Ivins really "pro-knife," or is she making some other point in her discussion of knives versus guns?

   _____

   _____

   _____

About Coherence

7. In paragraph 3, Ivins uses three addition signals—one to introduce each of her three reasons for being pro-knife. What are those three signals? (Two are *not* in the list of addition signals on page 83.)

   _____   _____   _____

8. In paragraph 7, Ivins acknowledges an opposing point of view when she mentions that automobiles, like guns, "wreak great carnage." In paragraph 8, what sentence includes a "change of direction" signal indicating that Ivins will present her argument against that point of view? *(Write the first few words of that sentence.)*

   _____

About the Introduction and Conclusion

9. Ivins's introduction consists of three very brief paragraphs. Which statement best describes the style of her introduction?

   a. It presents an anecdote that is related to the topic of unregulated gun ownership.

   b. It presents a provocative question that grabs the reader's attention.

   c. It makes a startling point that at first seems unrelated to the topic.

   d. It presents a quotation that puts the topic in some sort of historical context.

10. Which of these best describes the conclusion of "Ban the Things"?

    a. It makes a blunt recommendation.

    b. It asks a thought-provoking question.

    c. It narrates an anecdote about guns.

    d. It predicts what will happen if guns are not banned.

Writing an Argument Essay

Writing **Assignment**

1 Write an essay in which you argue *for* or *against* any one of the three comments below (options 1–3). Support and defend your argument by drawing on your reasoning ability and general experience.

Option 1 In many ways, television has proved to be one of the worst inventions of modern times. All too often, television is harmful because of the shows it broadcasts and the way it is used in the home.

Option 2 Many of society's worst problems with drugs result from the fact that they are illegal. During Prohibition, Americans discovered that making popular substances unlawful causes more problems than it solves. Like alcohol and tobacco, drugs should be legal in this country.

Option 3 Statistics show that newly licensed teenage boys cause a higher number of serious automobile accidents than any other group. It is evident that many young men are too reckless and impulsive to be good drivers. To protect the larger society, the age at which a boy can earn his license should be raised to eighteen.

© Tony Freeman/PhotoEdit

Writing Assignment

2

Write an essay in which you argue *for* or *against* any one of the three comments below. Support and defend your argument by drawing on your reasoning ability and general experience.

Option 1 Giving students grades does more harm than good. Schools should replace grades with written evaluations of the student's strengths and weaknesses. These would benefit both students and parents.

Option 2 Jails are overcrowded. Furthermore, jails often function as "schools for crime" in which petty lawbreakers learn to become hardened criminals. Of course, it is necessary to put violent criminals in jail to protect others. But society would benefit if nonviolent criminals received punishments other than jail sentences.

Option 3 Physical punishment "works" in the sense that it may stop a child from misbehaving, but adults who frequently spank and hit are also teaching children that violence is a good method of accomplishing a goal. Nonviolent methods are a more effective way of training children.

Prewriting

a. As you write your opening paragraph, acknowledge the opposing point of view before stating your thesis. If you have trouble figuring out what the "other side" would argue, completing this exercise will give you practice in acknowledging another way of looking at the question.

In each item, you will see a statement and then a question related to that statement. Write *two* answers to each question. Your first will answer yes to the question and briefly explain why. The other will answer no to the question, and also state why. The first item is done for you as an example:

1. Smoking has been proved to be bad for health. Should it therefore be made illegal?

   Yes: *Because smoking has been shown to have so many negative effects on health, the sale of tobacco should be made illegal.*

   No: *Although smoking has been linked to various health problems, adults should have the right to make their own decision about whether or not to smoke. Smoking should not be made illegal.*

2. Animals feel pain when they are killed for food. Is eating animals therefore immoral?

Yes: _____

_____

No: _____

_____

3. Professional boxing often leads to serious injury. Should it be outlawed?

Yes: _____

_____

No: _____

_____

4. Some high school students are sexually active. Should birth control devices and information be given out by high schools to their students?

Yes: _____

_____

No: _____

_____

b. Make a list of the thoughts that support your argument. Don't worry about repetition, spelling, or grammar at this point. Just write down everything that occurs to you.

c. Once you have written down all the thoughts that occur to you, identify what you see as your strongest points. Select your three main supporting points. Are there other thoughts in your list that you can use as supporting details for those points?

d. Write your three supporting paragraphs. Keep in mind that you are writing for an audience of people who, initially, will not all agree with you. It isn't enough to state your opinion. You must show *why* you feel as you do, persuading your reader that your point of view is valid.

e. Your concluding paragraph is your final chance to persuade your readers to accept your argument. Consider ending with a prediction of what will happen if your point of view does not prevail. Will an existing situation grow worse? Will a new problem arise?

Revising

Follow the suggestions for revising provided on pages 367–368.

Writing Assignment

3

Write an essay in which you argue *for* or *against* any one of the three comments below. Support and defend your argument by drawing on your reasoning ability and general experience.

Option 1 Junk food is available in school cafeterias and school vending machines, and the cafeteria menus do not encourage the best eating habits. But good education should include good examples as well as classwork. Schools should practice what they preach about a healthy diet and stop providing junk food.

© BananaStock/Imagestate

Option 2 By the time many students reach high school, they have learned the basics in most subjects. Some still have much to gain from the education that high schools offer, but others might be better off spending the next four years in other ways. For their benefit, high school attendance should be voluntary.

Option 3 Many of today's young people are mainly concerned with prestigious careers, making money, and owning things. It seems we no longer teach the benefits of spending time and money to help the community, the country, or the world. Our country can strengthen these human values and improve the world by requiring young people to spend a year working in some type of community service.

Writing | Assignment

4 | Writing for a Specific Purpose and Audience

In this argument essay, you will write with a specific purpose and for a specific audience.

Option 1 You'd like to live in a big city, but your parent or spouse refuses to budge from the suburbs. Write him or her a letter in which you argue the advantages of city life. Since the success of your argument will depend to some degree on how well you overcome the other person's objections to city life, be sure to address those as well. Use specific, colorful examples wherever possible.

Option 2 Find an editorial in your local newspaper that you either strongly agree with or strongly disagree with. Write a letter to the editor responding to that editorial. State why you agree or disagree with the position taken by the paper. Provide several short paragraphs of supporting evidence for your position. Actually send your letter to the newspaper. When you turn in a copy of your letter to your instructor, also turn in the editorial that you are responding to.

www.mhhe.com/langan

PART 3

Special Skills

Write an essay about a skill you have learned outside of the classroom, which has helped you succeed in college. Maybe it is teamwork, persistence, time management, or something else. Be sure to provide specific examples of how this skill has been beneficial to you.

17

Taking Essay Exams

This chapter will explain and illustrate

- *five steps in writing an effective exam essay*

© Comstock/Imagestate

Visit AltaVista at http://www.altavista.com and enter the phrase "taking an essay exam" into the search box. Then visit a handful of the sites that AltaVista finds and choose one to recommend to your classmates. Write a one-paragraph review of the site to hand in to your instructor. Was it helpful? What advice did it offer?

Essay exams are perhaps the most common type of writing you will do in school. They include one or more questions to which you must respond in detail, writing your answers in a clear, well-organized manner. Many students have trouble with essay exams because they do not realize there is a sequence to follow that will help them do well on such tests. This section describes five basic steps needed to prepare adequately for an essay test and to take the test. It is assumed, however, that you are already doing two essential things: first, attending class regularly and taking notes on what happens in class; second, reading your textbook and other assignments and taking notes on them. If you are *not* consistently going to class, reading your text, and taking notes in both cases, you are likely to have trouble with essay exams and other tests as well.

To write an effective exam essay, follow these five steps:

Step 1: Anticipate ten probable questions.

Step 2: Prepare and memorize an informal outline answer for each question.

Step 3: Look at the exam carefully and do several things.

Step 4: Prepare a brief, informal outline before writing your essay answer.

Step 5: Write a clear, well-organized essay.

The following pages explain and illustrate these steps.

Step 1: Anticipate Ten Probable Questions

Because exam time is limited, the instructor can give you only several questions to answer. He or she will focus on questions dealing with the most important areas of the subject. You can probably guess most of them.

Go through your class notes with a colored pen and mark off those areas where your instructor has spent a good deal of time. The more time spent on any one area, the better the chance you will get an essay question on it. If the instructor spent a week talking about present-day changes in the traditional family structure, or the importance of the carbon molecule, or the advantages of capitalism, or key early figures in the development of psychology as a science, you can reasonably expect that you will get a question about the emphasized area.

In both your class notes and your textbooks, pay special attention to definitions and examples and to basic lists of items (enumerations). Enumerations in particular are often a key to essay questions. For instance, if your instructor spoke at length about causes of the Great Depression, effects of water pollution, or advantages of capitalism, you should probably expect a question such as What were the causes of the Great Depression? or What are the effects of water pollution? or What are the advantages of capitalism?

If your instructor has given you a study guide, look there for probable essay questions. (Some instructors choose essay questions from those listed in study guides.) Look for clues to essay questions on any short quizzes that you might have been given. Finally, consider very carefully any review that the instructor provides. Always write down such reviews—your instructor has often made up the test or is making it up at the time of the review and is likely to give you valuable hints about it. Take advantage of them! Note also that if the instructor does not offer to provide a review, do not hesitate to *ask* for one in a friendly way. Essay questions are likely to come from areas the instructor may mention.

An Illustration of Step 1

A psychology class was given one day to prepare for an essay exam on stress—a subject that had been covered in class and by a chapter in the textbook for the course. One student, Mark, read carefully through his class notes and the textbook chapter. On the basis of the headings, major enumerations, and definitions he noted, he decided that there were five likely essay questions:

1. What are the common sources of stress?
2. What are the types of conflict?
3. What are the defense mechanisms that people use to cope with stress?
4. What effects can stress have on people?
5. What are the characteristics of a well-adjusted person?

Step 2: Prepare and Memorize an Informal Outline Answer for Each Question

Write out each question you have made up and, under it, list the main points that need to be discussed. Put important supporting information in parentheses after each main point. You now have an informal outline that you can memorize.

Pick out a *key word* in each part, and then create a *catchphrase* to help you remember the key words.

TIP If you have spelling problems, make up a list of words you might have to spell in writing your answers. For example, if you are having a psychology test on the principles of learning, you might want to study such terms as *conditioning, reinforcement, Pavlov, reflex, stimulus,* and so on.

An Illustration of Step 2

After identifying the likely questions on the exam, Mark made up an outline answer for each of the questions. For example, here is the outline answer that he made up for the first question:

Common sources of stress:

1. (Pressure)(internal and external)
2. (Anxiety)(sign of internal conflict)
3. (Frustration)(can't reach desired goal)
4. (Conflict)(three types of approach-avoidance)

   P A F C (People are funny creatures.)

See whether you can complete the following explanation of what Mark has done in preparing for the essay question.

Activity

1

     First, Mark wrote down the heading and then numbered the sources of stress under it. Also, in parentheses beside each point he added _____. Then he circled the four key words, and he wrote down the first _____ of each word underneath his outline. Mark then used the first letter in each key word to make up a catchphrase that he could easily remember. Finally, he _____ himself over and over until he could recall all four of the sources of stress that the first letters stood for. He also made sure that he recalled the supporting material that went with each idea.

Step 3: Look at the Exam Carefully and Do Several Things

1. Get an overview of the exam by reading *all* the questions on the test.

2. Note *direction words* (*compare, illustrate, list,* and so on) for each question. Be sure to write the kind of answer that each question requires. For example, if a question says "illustrate," do not "compare." The list on the next page will help clarify the distinctions among various direction words.

3. Budget your time. Write in the margin the number of minutes you should spend for each essay. For example, if you have three essays worth an equal number of points and a one-hour time limit, figure twenty minutes for each essay. Make sure you are not left with only a couple of minutes to do a high-point essay.

4. Start with the easiest question. Getting a good answer down on paper will help build up your confidence and momentum. Number your answers plainly so that your instructor knows what question you are answering first.

An Illustration of Step 3

When Mark received the exam, the question was "Describe the four common sources of stress in our lives." Mark circled the direction word *describe,* which meant he should explain in detail each of the four causes of stress. He also jotted a "30" in the margin when the instructor said that students would have a half hour to write the answer.

Activity **2**	Complete the short matching quiz below. It will help you review the meanings of some of the direction words listed in the box below.

1. List ＿＿＿
2. Contrast ＿＿＿
3. Define ＿＿＿
4. Summarize ＿＿＿
5. Describe ＿＿＿

   a. Tell in detail about something.
   b. Give a series of points and number them 1, 2, 3, etc.
   c. Give a condensed account of the main points.
   d. Show differences between two things.
   e. Give the normal meaning of a term.

www.mhhe.com/langan

Direction Words

Term	Meaning
Compare	Show similarities between things.
Contrast	Show differences between things.
Criticize	Give the positive and negative points of a subject as well as evidence for those positions.
Define	Give the formal meaning of a term.
Describe	Tell in detail about something.
Diagram	Make a drawing and label it.
Discuss	Give details and, if relevant, the positive and negative points of a subject as well as evidence for those positions.
Enumerate	List points and number them 1, 2, 3, and so on.
Evaluate	Give the positive and negative points of a subject as well as your judgment about which outweighs the other and why.
Illustrate	Explain by giving examples.
Interpret	Explain the meaning of something.

Justify	Give reasons for something.
List	Give a series of points and number them 1, 2, 3, and so on.
Outline	Give the main points and important secondary points. Put main points at the margin and indent secondary points under the main points. Relationships may also be described with logical symbols, as follows:

1. _____
    a. _____
    b. _____
2. _____

Prove	Show to be true by giving facts or reasons.
Relate	Show connections among things.
State	Give the main points.
Summarize	Give a condensed account of the main points.
Trace	Describe the development or history of a subject.

Step 4: Prepare a Brief, Informal Outline before Writing Your Essay Answer

Use the margin of the exam or a separate piece of scratch paper to jot down quickly, as they occur to you, the main points you want to discuss in each answer. Then decide in what order you want to present these points in your response. Write 1 in front of the first item, 2 beside the second, and so on. You now have an informal outline to guide you as you answer your essay question.

If a question on the exam is similar to the questions you anticipated and outlined at home, quickly write down the catchphrase that calls back the content of the outline. Below the catchphrase, write the key words represented by each letter in the catchphrase. The key words, in turn, will remind you of the concepts they represent. If you have prepared properly, this step will take only a minute or so, and you will have before you the guide you need to write a focused, supported, organized answer.

An Illustration of Step 4

Mark immediately wrote down his catchphrase, "People are funny creatures." He next jotted down the first letters in his catchphrase and then the key words that went with each letter. He then filled in several key details and was ready to write his essay answer. Here is what his brief outline looked like:

People are funny creatures.

P   *Pressure (internal and external)*

A   *Anxiety (internal conflict)*

F   *Frustration (prevented from reaching goal)*

C   *Conflict (approach-avoidance)*

Step 5: Write a Clear, Well-Organized Essay

If you have followed steps 1 through 4, you have done all the preliminary work needed to write an effective essay. Now, be sure not to ruin your chance of getting a good grade by writing carelessly. Keep in mind the principles of good writing: unity, support, coherence, and clear, error-free sentences.

First, start your essay with a sentence that clearly states what your answer will be about. Then make sure that everything in your paper relates to your opening statement.

Second, though you must obviously take time limitations into account, provide as much support as possible for each of your main points.

Third, use transitions to guide your reader through your answer. Words such as *first, next, then, however,* and *finally* make it easy to follow your thought.

Last, leave time to proofread your essay for sentence-skills mistakes you might have made while you concentrated on writing your answer. Look for words omitted, miswritten, or misspelled (if it is allowed, bring a dictionary with you); look for awkward phrasings or misplaced punctuation marks; and look for whatever else may prevent the reader from understanding your thought. Cross out any mistakes and make your corrections neatly above the errors. If you want to change or add to some point, insert an asterisk at the appropriate spot, put another asterisk at the bottom of the page, and add the corrected material there.

An Illustration of Step 5

Read Mark's answer, reproduced below, and then do the activity that follows.

There are four common sources of stress in our lives. The first one is pressure, which can be internal or external. Internal pressure occurs when a person tries to live up to his or her own goals and standards.

This kind of pressure can help (when a person strives to be a better musician, for instance) or hurt (as when someone tries to reach impossible standards of beauty). External pressure occurs when people must compete, deal with rapid change, or cope with outside demands. Another source of stress is anxiety. People who are ~~anxous~~ *anxious* often don't know why they feel this way. Some psychologists think anxiety comes from some internal conflict, like feeling angry and trying hard to repress this ~~angry feeling~~ anger. A third source of stress is frustration, which occurs when people are prevented from reaching goals or obtaining certain needs. For example, a woman may do poorly on an *important* exam because she has a bad cold. She feels angry and frustrated because she could not reach her goal of an A or B grade. The most common source of stress is conflict. Conflict results when a person is faced with two incompatible ~~goals.~~ *desires* The person may want both goals (a demanding career and motherhood, for instance). This is called approach-approach. Or a person may want to avoid both choices (avoidance-avoidance). Or a person may be both attracted to and repelled by a desire (as a woman *who* wants to marry a gambler). This is approach-avoidance.

The following sentences comment on Mark's essay. Fill in the missing word or words in each case.

1. Mark begins with a sentence that clearly states what his essay _____. Always begin with such a clear statement!

2. Notice the _____ that Mark made when writing and proofreading his paper. He neatly crossed out miswritten or unwanted words, and he used insertion signs (^) to add omitted words.

3. The four signal words that Mark used to guide his readers, and himself, through the main points of his answer are _____, _____, _____, and _____.

Activity 3

1. Make up five questions you might be expected to answer on an essay exam for a course in a social or physical science (such as sociology, psychology, or biology).

Activity 4

2. For each of the five questions, make up an outline answer comparable to the one on anxiety.

3. Finally, write a full essay answer, in complete sentences, to one of the questions. Your outline will serve as your guide.

Be sure to begin your essay with a statement that makes clear the direction of your answer. An example might be "The six major defense mechanisms are defined and illustrated below." If you are explaining in detail the different causes of, reasons for, or characteristics of something, you may want to develop each point in a separate paragraph. For example, if you were answering a question in sociology about the primary functions of the family unit, you could start with the statement "The family unit has three primary functions" and go on to develop and describe each function in a separate paragraph.

You will submit the essay answer to your English instructor, who will evaluate it using the standards for effective writing applied to your other written assignments.

Writing a Summary

This chapter will explain and illustrate how to

- summarize an article
- summarize a book

© Bill Aron/PhotoEdit

Find an article in your school or local newspaper about which you can write an essay-length summary. Include an introductory paragraph in which you state the article's thesis.

At some point in a course, your instructor may ask you to write a summary of a book, an article, a TV show, or the like. In a *summary* (also referred to as a *précis* or an *abstract*), you reduce material in an original work to its main points and key supporting details. Unlike an outline, however, a summary does not use symbols such as I, A, 1, 2, etc., to indicate the relations among parts of the original material.

A summary may consist of a single word, a phrase, several sentences, or one or more paragraphs. The length of any summary you prepare will depend on your instructor's expectations and the length of the original work. Most often, you will be asked to write a summary consisting of one or more paragraphs.

Writing a summary brings together a number of important reading, study, and writing skills. To condense the original assigned material, you must preview, read, evaluate, organize, and perhaps outline it. Summarizing, then, can be a real aid to understanding; you must "get inside" the material and realize fully what is being said before you can reduce its meaning to a few words.

How to Summarize an Article

www.mhhe.com/langan

To write a summary of an article, follow the steps described below. If the assigned material is a TV show or film, adapt the suggestions accordingly.

1. Take a few minutes to preview the work. You can preview an article in a magazine by taking a quick look at the following:

   a. *Title.* A title often summarizes what an article is about. Think about the title for a minute and about how it may condense the meaning of the article.

   b. *Subtitle.* A subtitle, if given, is a short summary appearing under or next to the title. For example, in a *Newsweek* article titled "Growing Old, Feeling Young," the following caption appeared: "Not only are Americans living longer, they are staying active longer—and their worst enemy is not nature, but the myths and prejudices about growing old." In short, the subtitle, the caption, or any other words in large print under or next to the title often provide a quick insight into the meaning of an article.

   c. *First and last several paragraphs.* In the first several paragraphs, the author may introduce you to the subject and state the purpose of the article. In the last several paragraphs, the writer may present conclusions or a summary. The previews or summaries can give you a quick overview of what the entire article is about.

   d. *Other items.* Note any heads or subheads that appear in the article. They often provide clues to the article's main points and give an immediate sense of what each section is about. Look carefully at any pictures, charts, or diagrams that accompany the article. Page space in a magazine or journal is limited, and such visual aids are generally used only to illustrate important points in the article. Note any words or phrases set off in *italic type* or **boldface type;** such words have probably been emphasized because they deal with important points in the article.

2. Read the article for all you can understand the first time through. Do not slow down or turn back. Check or otherwise mark main points and key supporting details. Pay special attention to all the items noted in the preview. Also, look for definitions, examples, and enumerations (lists of items), which often indicate key ideas. You can also identify important points by turning any headings into questions and reading to find the answers to the questions.

3. Go back and reread more carefully the areas you have identified as most important. Also, focus on other key points you may have missed in your first reading.

4. Take notes on the material. Concentrate on getting down the main ideas and the key supporting points.

5. Prepare the first draft of your summary, keeping these points in mind:

    a. Identify at the start of the summary the title and author of the work. Include in parentheses the date of publication. For example, "In 'Leaking with a Vengeance' (*Time,* October 13, 2003), Michael Duffy states . . ."

    b. Do not write an overly detailed summary. Remember that the purpose of a summary is to reduce the original work to its main points and essential supporting details.

    c. Express the main points and key supporting details in your own words. Do not imitate the style of the original work.

    d. Quote from the material only to illustrate key points. Also, limit your quotations. A one-paragraph summary should not contain more than one or two quoted sentences or phrases.

    e. Preserve the balance and proportion of the original work. If the original devoted 70 percent of its space to one idea and only 30 percent to another, your summary should reflect that emphasis.

    f. Revise your first draft, paying attention to the four bases of effective writing (*unity, support, coherence,* and *sentences skills*) explained in Part One.

    g. Write the final draft of the paper.

www.mhhe.com/langan

A Model Summary of an Article

Here is a model summary of a magazine article:

In "How to Heal a Hypochondriac" (*Time*, October 6, 2003), Michael Lemonick reports on research into ways of dealing with hypochondria, a thinking disorder that makes healthy people believe that they are suffering from one or more serious diseases. Not only do hypochondriacs genuinely suffer from their disorder but they create a significant burden on the health care system. Research suggests that hypochondriacs fall into three categories: those who have a variant of obsessive-compulsive disorder, those who had a stressful life event that triggered the hypochondria, and those who are hypersensitive to any physical symptoms. Cognitive therapy, in which patients are trained to direct their attention away from their symptoms, and antidepressant medication both seem helpful in treating hypochondria. The most difficult part of treatment is suggesting that a patient suffers from hypochondria without angering or embarrassing him or her.

Activity

1

Write an essay-length summary of the following article. Include a short introductory paragraph that states the thesis of the article. Then summarize in your three supporting paragraphs the three important areas in which study skills can be useful. Your conclusion might be a single sentence restating the thesis.

Power Learning

Jill had not done as well in high school as she had hoped. Since college   1
involved even more work, it was no surprise that she didn't do better there.

The reason for her so-so performance was not a lack of effort. She   2
attended most of her classes and read her textbooks. And she never missed
handing in any assignment, even though it often meant staying up late the
night before homework was due. Still, she just got by in her classes. Before
long, she came to the conclusion that she simply couldn't do any better.

Then one day, one of her instructors said something to make her think   3
otherwise. "You can probably build some sort of house by banging a few
boards together," he said. "But if you want a sturdy home, you'll have to
use the right techniques and tools. Building carefully takes work, but it
gets better results. The same can be said of your education. There are no

(continued)

shortcuts, but there are some proven study skills that can really help. If you don't use them, you may end up with a pretty flimsy education."

Jill signed up for a study-skills course and found out a crucial fact—that 4 learning how to learn is the key to success in school. Certain dependable skills have made the difference between disappointment and success for generations of students. These techniques won't free you from work, but they will make your work far more productive. They include three important areas: time control, classroom note-taking, and textbook study.

Time Control

Success in college depends on time control. *Time control* means that 5 you deliberately organize and plan your time, instead of letting it drift by. Planning means that you should never be faced with an overdue term paper or a cram session the night before a test.

Three steps are involved in time control. *First*, you should prepare a 6 large monthly calendar. Buy a calendar with a large white block around each date, or make one yourself. At the beginning of the college semester, circle important dates on this calendar. Circle the days on which tests are scheduled; circle the days when papers are due. This calendar can also be used to schedule study plans. At the beginning of the week, you can jot down your plans for each day. An alternative method would be to make plans for each day the night before. On Tuesday night, for example, you might write down "Read Chapter 5 in psychology" in the Wednesday block. Hang this calendar where you will see it every day—your kitchen, bedroom, even your bathroom!

The *second step* in time control is to have a weekly study schedule for 7 the semester—a chart that covers all the days of the week and all the waking hours in each day. Below is part of one student's schedule:

Time	Mon.	Tue.	Wed.	Thurs.	Fri.	Sat.	
6:00 a.m.							
7:00	Breakfast	Breakfast	Breakfast	Breakfast	Breakfast		
8:00	Math	STUDY	Math	STUDY	Math	Breakfast	
9:00	STUDY	Biology	STUDY	Biology	STUDY	Job	
10:00	Psychology	↓	Psychology	↓	Psychology		
11:00		English		English			
12:00	Lunch		Lunch		Lunch	↓	

On your own schedule, fill in all the fixed hours in each day—hours for meals, classes, job (if any), and travel time. Next, mark time blocks that you

(continued)

can *realistically* use for study each day. Depending on the number of courses you are taking and the demands of these courses, you may want to block off five, ten, or even twenty or more hours of study time a week. Keep in mind that you should not block off time that you do not truly intend to use for study. Otherwise, your schedule will be a meaningless gimmick. Also, remember that you should allow time for rest and relaxation. You will be happiest, and able to accomplish the most, when you have time for both work and play.

The *third step* in time control is to make a daily or weekly to-do list. **8**
This may be the most valuable time-control method you ever use. On this list, write down the things you need to do for the following day or the following week. If you choose to write a weekly list, do it on Sunday night. If you choose to write a daily list, do it the night before. Here is part of one student's daily list:

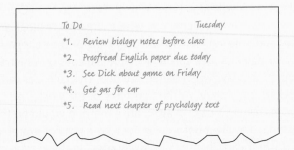

You may use a three-by-five-inch notepad or a small spiral-bound notebook for this list. Carry the list around with you during the day. Always concentrate on doing the most important items first. To make the best use of your time, mark high-priority items with an asterisk and give them precedence over low-priority items. For instance, you may find yourself wondering what to do after dinner on Thursday evening. Among the items on your list are "Clean inside of car" and "Review chapter for math quiz." It is obviously more important for you to review your notes at this point; you can clean out the car some other time. As you complete items on your to-do list, cross them out. Do not worry about unfinished items. They can be rescheduled. You will still be accomplishing a great deal and making more effective use of your time.

Classroom Note-Taking

One of the most important single things you can do to perform well in **9**
a college course is to take effective class notes. The following hints should help you become a better note-taker.

(continued)

First, attend class faithfully. Your alternatives—reading the text, reading   **10**
someone else's notes, or both—cannot substitute for the class experience
of hearing ideas in person as someone presents them to you. Also, in class
lectures and discussions, your instructor typically presents and develops the
main ideas and facts of the course—the ones you will be expected to know
on exams.

Another valuable hint is to make use of abbreviations while taking notes.   **11**
Using abbreviations saves time when you are trying to get down a great deal
of information. Abbreviate terms that recur frequently in a lecture and put a
key to your abbreviations at the top of your notes. For example, in sociology
class, *eth* could stand for *ethnocentrism;* in a psychology class, *STM* could
stand for *short-term memory.* (When a lecture is over, you may want to go
back and write out the terms you have abbreviated.) Also, use *e* for *example;*
def for *definition; info* for *information;* + for *and;* and so on. If you use the
same abbreviations all the time, you will soon develop a kind of personal
shorthand that makes taking notes much easier.

A third hint for taking notes is to be on the lookout for signals of   **12**
importance. Write down whatever your instructor puts on the board. If he
or she takes the time to put material on the board, it is probably important,
and the chances are good that it will come up later on exams. Always write
down definitions and enumerations. Enumerations are lists of items. They are
signaled in such ways as "The four steps in the process are . . ."; "There were
three reasons for . . ."; "The two effects were . . ."; "Five characteristics of . . .";
and so on. In your notes, always number such enumerations (1, 2, 3, etc.).
They will help you understand relationships among ideas and organize the
material of the lecture. Watch for emphasis words—words your instructor
may use to indicate that something is important. Examples of such words are
"This is an important reason . . ."; "A point that will keep coming up later . . .";
"The chief cause was . . ."; "The basic idea here is . . ."; and so on. Always write
down the important statements announced by these and other emphasis
words. Finally, if your instructor repeats a point, you can assume that it is
important. You might put an *R* for *repeated* in the margin so that later you
will know that your instructor stressed it.

Next, be sure to write down the instructor's examples and mark them   **13**
with an *e.* The examples help you understand abstract points. If you do not
write them down, you are likely to forget them later, when they are needed
to help make sense of an idea.

Also, be sure to write down the connections between ideas. Too many   **14**
students merely copy terms the instructor puts on the board. They forget
that, as time passes, the details that serve as connecting bridges between
(continued)

ideas quickly fade. You should, then, write down the relationships and connections in class. That way you'll have them to help tie together your notes later on.

Review your notes as soon as possible after class. You must make them **15** as clear as possible while they are fresh in your mind. A day later may be too late, because forgetting sets in very quickly. Make sure that punctuation is clear, that all words are readable and correctly spelled, and that unfinished sentences are completed (or at least marked off so that you can check your notes with another student's). Add clarifying or connecting comments wherever necessary. Make sure that important ideas are clearly marked. Improve the organization if necessary so that you can see at a glance main points and relationships among them.

Finally, try in general to get down a written record of each class. You **16** must do this because forgetting begins almost immediately. Studies have shown that within two weeks you are likely to have forgotten 80 percent or more of what you have heard. And in four weeks you are lucky if 5 percent remains! This is so crucial that it bears repeating: To guard against the relentlessness of forgetting, it is absolutely essential that you write down what you hear in class. Later you can concentrate on working to understand fully and to remember the ideas that have been presented in class. And then, the more complete your notes are, the more you are likely to learn.

Textbook Study

In many college courses, success means being able to read and study a **17** textbook skillfully. For many students, unfortunately, textbooks are heavy going. After an hour or two of study, the textbook material is as formless and as hard to understand as ever. But there is a way to attack even the most difficult textbook and make sense of it. Use a sequence in which you preview a chapter, mark it, take notes on it, and then study the notes.

Previewing

Previewing a selection is an important first step to understanding. Taking **18** the time to preview a section or chapter can give you a bird's-eye view of the way the material is organized. You will have a sense of where you are beginning, what you will cover, and where you will end.

There are several steps in previewing a selection. First, study the title. **19** The title is the shortest possible summary of a selection and will often tell you the limits of the material you will cover. For example, the title "FDR and the Supreme Court" tells you to expect a discussion of President Roosevelt's dealings with the Court. You know that you will probably not encounter

(continued)

any material dealing with FDR's foreign policies or personal life. Next, quickly read over the first and last paragraphs of the selection; these may contain important introductions to, and summaries of, the main ideas. Then briefly examine the headings and subheadings in the selection. Together, the headings and subheadings are a mini-outline of what you are reading. Headings are often main ideas or important concepts in capsule form; subheadings are breakdowns of ideas within main areas. Finally, read the first sentence of some paragraphs, look for words set off in **boldface** or *italics*, and look at pictures or diagrams. After you have previewed a selection in this way, you should have a good general sense of the material to be read.

Marking

You should mark a textbook selection at the same time that you read it through carefully. Use a felt-tip highlighter to shade material that seems important, or use a ballpoint pen and put symbols in the margin next to the material: stars, checks, or NB (*nota bene,* Latin for "note well"). What to mark is not as mysterious as some students believe. You should try to find main ideas by looking for clues: definitions and examples, enumerations, and emphasis words.   20

1. *Definitions and examples:* Definitions are often among the most impor-   21
   tant ideas in a selection. They are particularly significant in introductory courses in almost any subject area, where much of your learning involves mastering the specialized vocabulary of that subject. In a sense, you are learning the "language" of psychology or business or whatever the subject might be.

   Most definitions are abstract, and so they usually are followed by   22
   one or more examples to help clarify their meaning. Always mark off definitions and at least one example that makes a definition clear to you. In a psychology text, for example, we are told that "rationalization is an attempt to reduce anxiety by deciding that you have not really been frustrated." Several examples follow, among them: "A young man, frustrated because he was rejected when he asked for a date, convinces himself that the girl is not very attractive or interesting."

2. *Enumerations:* Enumerations are lists of items (causes, reasons, types,   23
   and so on) that are numbered 1, 2, 3, . . . or that could easily be numbered. They are often signaled by addition words. Many of the paragraphs in this book, for instance, use words like *First of all, Another, In addition,* and *Finally* to signal items in a series. Other textbooks also use this very common and effective organizational method.

(continued)

3. *Emphasis words:* Emphasis words tell you that an idea is important. Common emphasis words include phrases such as *a major event, a key feature, the chief factor, important to note, above all,* and *most of all.* Here is an example: "The most significant contemporary use of marketing is its application to nonbusiness areas, such as political parties."   24

Note-Taking

Next, you should take notes. Go through the chapter a second time, rereading the most important parts. Try to write down the main ideas in a simple outline form. For example, in taking notes on a psychology selection, you might write down the heading "Defense Mechanisms." Below the heading you would define them, number and describe each kind, and give an example of each.   25

Defense Mechanisms

a. Definition: unconscious attempts to reduce anxiety

b. Kinds:

(1) Rationalization: An attempt to reduce anxiety by deciding that you have not really been frustrated.

Example: A man turned down for a date decides that the woman was not worth going out with anyway.

(2) Projection: Projecting onto other people motives or thoughts of one's own.

Example: A wife who wants to have an affair accuses her husband of having one.

Studying Notes

To study your notes, use repeated self-testing. For example, look at the heading "Defense Mechanisms" and say to yourself, "What are the kinds of defense mechanisms?" When you can recite them, then say to yourself, "What is rationalization?" "What is an example of rationalization?" Then ask yourself, "What is projection?" "What is an example of projection?" After you learn each section, review it, and then go on to the next section.   26

Do not simply read your notes; keep looking away and seeing if you can recite them to yourself. This self-testing is the key to effective learning.   27

(continued)

Summary: Textbook Study

In summary, remember this sequence for dealing with a textbook: preview, mark, take notes, study the notes. Approaching a textbook in this methodical way will give you very positive results. You will no longer feel bogged down in a swamp of words, unable to figure out what you are supposed to know. Instead, you will understand exactly what you have to do and how to go about doing it.

Take a minute now to evaluate your own study habits. Do you practice many of the above skills to take effective classroom notes, control your time, and learn from your textbooks? If not, perhaps you should. The skills are not magic, but they are too valuable to ignore. Use them carefully and consistently, and they will make academic success possible for you. Try them, and you won't need convincing.

28

29

Write an essay-length summary of a broadcast of the CBS television show *60 Minutes*. In your first sentence, include the date of the show. For example, "The September 6, 2007, broadcast of CBS's *60 Minutes* dealt with three subjects most people would find of interest. The first segment of the show centered on . . . ; the second segment examined . . . ; the final segment discussed . . ." Be sure to use parallel form in describing the three segments of the show. Then summarize each segment in the three supporting paragraphs that follow.

Activity

2

Write an essay-length summary of a cover story of interest to you in a recent issue of *Time*, *Newsweek*, or *U.S. News & World Report*.

Activity

3

www.mhhe.com/langan

How to Summarize a Book

To write a summary of a book, first preview the book by briefly looking at the following:

1. *Title.* A title is often the shortest possible summary of what a book is about. Think about the title and how it may summarize the whole book.

2. *Table of contents.* The contents will tell you the number of chapters in the book and the subject of each chapter. Use the contents to get a general sense of how the book is organized. You should also note the number of pages in each chapter. If thirty pages are devoted to one episode or idea and an average of fifteen pages to other episodes or ideas, you should

probably give more space in your summary to the contents of the longer chapter.

3. *Preface.* Here you will probably find out why the author wrote the book. Also, the preface may summarize the main ideas developed in the book and may describe briefly how the book is organized.

4. *First and last chapters.* In these chapters, the author may preview or review important ideas and themes developed in the book.

5. *Other items.* Note how the author has used headings and subheadings to organize information in the book. Check the opening and closing paragraphs of each chapter to see if these paragraphs contain introductions or summaries. Look quickly at charts, diagrams, and pictures in the book, since they are probably there to illustrate key points. Note any special features (index, glossary, appendixes) that may appear at the end of the book.

Next, adapt steps 2 through 5 for summarizing an article on page 387.

Activity

4

Write an essay-length summary of a book you have read.

Writing a Report

19

This chapter will explain and illustrate

- the two parts of a report

  PART 1: A summary of the work

  PART 2: Your reaction to the work

This chapter also includes

- points to keep in mind when writing a report

- a model report

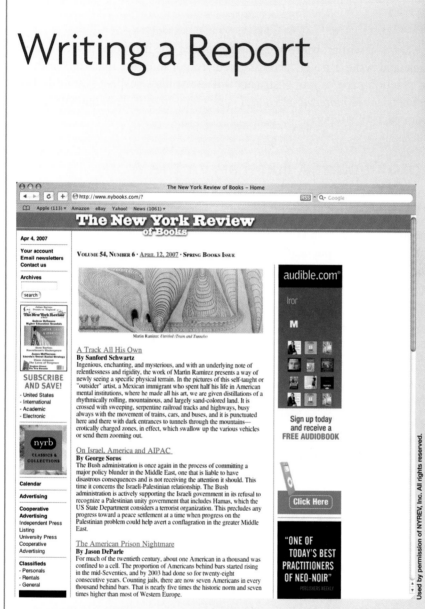

To gain a sense of how to review a text, visit the New York Review of Books Web site at http://www.nybooks.com and choose a review to read. Write a short paragraph explaining why you chose that review and what you've learned from it.

Each semester, you will probably be asked by at least one instructor to read a book or an article and write a paper recording your response to the material. In these reports or reaction papers, your instructor will most likely expect you to do two things: *summarize the material* and *detail your reaction to it*. The following pages explain both parts of a report.

Part 1 of a Report: A Summary of the Work

To develop the first part of a report, do the following. (An example follows, on page 399.)

www.mhhe.com/langan

1. Identify the author and title of the work, and include in parentheses the publisher and publication date. With magazines, give the date of publication.

2. Write an informative summary of the material. Condense the content of the work by highlighting its main points and key supporting points. (See pages 385–396 for a complete discussion of summarizing techniques.) Use direct quotations from the work to illustrate important ideas.

Do *not* discuss in great detail any single aspect of the work while neglecting to mention other equally important points. Summarize the material so that the reader gets a general sense of *all* key aspects of the original work. Also, keep the summary objective and factual. Do not include in the first part of the paper your personal reaction to the work; your subjective impression will form the basis of the second part of the paper.

Part 2 of a Report: Your Reaction to the Work

To develop the second part of a report, do the following:

www.mhhe.com/langan

1. Focus on any or all of the questions below. (Check with your instructor to see whether you should emphasize specific points.)

    a. How is the assigned work related to ideas and concerns discussed in the course? For example, what points made in the course textbook, class discussions, or lectures are treated more fully in the work?

    b. How is the work related to problems in our present-day world?

    c. How is the work related to your life, experiences, feelings, and ideas? For instance, what emotions did it arouse in you? Did it increase your understanding of an issue or change your perspective?

2. Evaluate the merit of the work: the importance of its points; its accuracy, completeness, and organization; and so on. You should also indicate here whether you would recommend the work to others, and why.

Points to Keep in Mind When Writing a Report

Here are some important matters to consider as you prepare a report:

1. Apply the four basic standards of effective writing (unity, support, coherence, and clear, error-free sentences).

   a. Make sure each major paragraph presents and then develops a single main point. For example, in the model report that follows, a paragraph summarizes the book, and the three paragraphs that follow detail three separate reactions that the student writer had. The student then closes the report with a short concluding paragraph.

   b. Support with specific reasons and details any general points or attitudes you express. Statements such as "I agreed with many ideas in this article" and "I found the book very interesting" are meaningless without specific evidence that shows why you feel as you do. Look at the model report to see how the main point or topic sentence of each paragraph is developed by specific supporting evidence.

   c. Organize the material in the paper. Follow the basic *plan of organization* already described: an introduction, a summary consisting of one or more paragraphs, a reaction consisting of two or more paragraphs, and a conclusion. Use *transitions* to connect the parts of the paper.

   d. Proofread the paper for grammar, mechanics, punctuation, and word use.

2. Document quotations from all works by giving the page number in parentheses after the quoted material (see the model report). You may use quotations in the summary and reaction parts of the paper, but do not rely too much on them. Use them only to emphasize key ideas.

A Model Report

Here is a report written by a student in an introductory sociology course. Look at the paper closely to see how it follows the guidelines for report writing described in this chapter.

A Report on I Know Why the Caged Bird Sings

In I Know Why the Caged Bird Sings (New York: Bantam Books, 1971),   1   Introductory
Maya Angelou tells the story of her earliest years. Angelou, a dancer, poet,   paragraph
and television producer as well as a writer, has continued her life story in
(continued)

three more volumes of autobiography. I Know Why the Caged Bird Sings is the start of Maya Angelou's story; in this book, she writes with crystal clarity about the pains and joys of being black in America.

I Know Why the Caged Bird Sings covers Maya Angelou's life from age three to age sixteen. We first meet her as a gawky little girl in a white woman's cut-down lavender silk dress. She has forgotten the poem she had memorized for the Easter service, and all she can do is rush out of the church. At this point, Angelou is living in Stamps, Arkansas, with her grandmother and uncle. The town is rigidly segregated: "People in Stamps used to say that the whites in our town were so prejudiced that a Negro couldn't buy vanilla ice cream" (40). Yet Angelou has some good things in her life: her adored older brother Bailey, her success in school, and her pride in her grandmother's quiet strength and importance in the black community. There is laughter, too, as when a preacher is interrupted in midsermon by an overly enthusiastic woman shouting, "Preach it, I say preach it!" The woman, in a frenzied rush of excitement, hits the preacher with her purse; his false teeth fly out of his mouth and land at Angelou's feet. Shortly after this incident, Angelou and her brother are taken by her father to live in California with their mother. Here, at age eight, she is raped by her mother's boyfriend, who is mysteriously murdered after receiving only a suspended sentence for his crime. She returns, silent and withdrawn, to Stamps, where the gloom is broken when a friend of her mother introduces her to the magic of great books. Later, at age thirteen, Angelou returns to California. She learns how to dance. She runs away after a violent family fight and lives for a month in a junkyard. She becomes the first black female to get a job on the San Francisco streetcars. She graduates from high school eight months pregnant. And she survives.

2

I was impressed with the vividness of Maya Angelou's writing style. For example, she describes the lazy dullness of her life in Stamps: "Weekdays revolved in a sameness wheel. They turned into themselves so steadily and inevitably that each seemed to be the original of yesterday's rough draft" (93). She also knows how to bring a scene to life, as when she describes her eighth-grade graduation. For months, she has been looking forward to this event, knowing she will be honored for her academic successes. She is even happy with her appearance: her hair has become pretty, and her yellow dress is a miracle of hand-sewing. But the ceremony is spoiled when the speaker—a white man—implies that the only success available to blacks is in athletics. Angelou remembers: "The man's dead words fell like bricks around the auditorium and too many settled in my belly. . . . The proud graduating class of 1940 had dropped their heads" (152). Later, Angelou uses a crystal-clear image to describe her father's mistress sewing: "She worked the thread

3

(continued)

through the flowered cloth as if she were sewing the torn ends of her life together" (208). With such vivid details and figures of speech, Maya Angelou re-creates her life for her readers.

I also reacted strongly to the descriptions of injustices suffered by blacks two generations ago. I was as horrified as the seven-year-old Maya when some "powhitetrash" girls torment her dignified grandmother, calling her "Annie" and mimicking her mannerisms. In another incident, Mrs. Cullinan, Angelou's white employer, decides that Marguerite (Angelou's given name) is too difficult to pronounce and so renames her Mary. This loss of her name—a "hellish horror" (91)—is another humiliation suffered at white hands, and Angelou leaves Mrs. Cullinan's employ soon afterward. Later, Angelou encounters overt discrimination when a white dentist tells her grandmother, "Annie, my policy is I'd rather stick my hand in a dog's mouth than in a nigger's" (160)—and only slightly less obvious prejudice when the streetcar company refuses to accept her application for a conductor's job. We see Angelou over and over as the victim of a white society.

4 — Topic sentence for second reaction paragraph

Although I was saddened to read about the injustices, I rejoiced in Angelou's triumphs. Angelou is thrilled when she hears the radio broadcast of Joe Louis's victory over Primo Carnera: "A Black boy. Some Black mother's son. He was the strongest man in the world" (114). She weeps with pride when the class valedictorian leads her and her fellow eighth-graders in singing the Negro National Anthem. And there are personal victories, too. One of these comes after her father has gotten drunk in a small Mexican town. Though she has never driven before, she manages to get her father into the car and drives fifty miles through the night as he lies intoxicated in the backseat. Finally, she rejoices in the birth of her son: "He was beautiful and mine. Totally mine. No one had bought him for me" (245). Angelou shows us, through these examples, that she is proud of her race—and of herself.

5 — Topic sentence for third reaction paragraph

I Know Why the Caged Bird Sings is a remarkable book. Angelou could have been just another casualty of race prejudice. Yet by using her intelligence, sensitivity, and determination, she succeeds in spite of the odds against her. And by writing with such power, she lets us share her defeats and joys. She also teaches us a vital lesson: With strength and persistence, we can all escape our cages—and sing our songs.

6 — Concluding paragraph

20 Writing a Résumé and Cover Letter

This chapter will provide

- a sample résumé and cover letter

- points to note when writing a résumé and cover letter

© Kayte M. Deioma/PhotoEdit

Write an essay about your first job interview. What was the job for? Did the interview go well? How did you feel before, during, and after the interview? Is there anything you would have done differently?

When applying for a job through the mail, you should ordinarily send (1) a résumé and (2) a cover letter.

Résumé

A résumé is a summary of your personal background and your qualifications for a job. It helps your potential employer see at a glance whether you are suited for a job opening. A sample job résumé follows.

ERIC KURLAND
27 Hawkins Road
Clarksboro, New Jersey 08020
609-723-2166

Professional objective	A challenging position in the computer technology field.
Education	2004 to present: Rowan University, Glassboro, New Jersey 08028
	Degree: BS (in June)
Major courses:	Introduction to Computer Science I and II Data Structures and Algorithms I and II Programming Languages Programming in Pascal Assembly Language Operating Systems I and II
Related courses:	Introduction to Discrete Mathematics I and II Calculus I and II Logic Entrepreneurship and Small Business Management Business Law Organizational Behavior
Special school project	As part of a class project, I chaired a study group that advised a local business about the advantages of installing a computerized payroll system. We projected comparative cost figures, developed a time-sharing purchase plan, and

(continued)

---

prepared a budget. The fifteen-page report received the highest grade in the class.

Work experience	2006 to present: As a salesperson at Radio Shack, I am involved in sales, inventory control, repairs, and customer relations. I have designed a computer program that our store uses to demonstrate the multimedia aspects of a personal computer. This program, written in Visual Basic, demonstrates ways the Compaq Presario 5062 can be used in homes and small businesses.
	2003–2006: My temporary jobs included word-processing secretary, theater usher, and child-care aide.
Skills	I am experienced in the following computer languages: C++, Visual Basic, Pascal, and COBOL. I have sales experience, am good with figures, am detail-oriented, relate easily to people, have initiative, and am dependable.
References	My references are available on request from Rowan University Placement Office, Glassboro, New Jersey 08028.

Points to Note about the Résumé

www.mhhe.com/langan

1. Your résumé, along with your cover letter, is your introduction to a potential employer. First impressions count, so *make the résumé neat!*

   a. Be sure to print the résumé on good-quality letter paper (8½ by 11 inches). If possible, prepare your résumé on a computer; if you don't have access to a computer, you can use a résumé service listed in the yellow pages of the telephone directory.

   b. Proofread *very carefully* for sentence-skills and spelling mistakes. A potential employer may regard such mistakes as signs of carelessness in your character. You might even want to get someone else to proofread the résumé for you. If you are using word-processing software, see if it has a spell-checker.

   c. Be brief and to the point: use only one page if possible.

   d. Use a format like that of the model résumé (consider also the variations described below). Balance your résumé on the page so that you have roughly the same margin on all sides.

   e. Note that you should start with your most recent education or employment and work backward in time.

2. Your résumé should point up strengths, not weaknesses. Don't include "Special Training" if you have had none. Don't refer to your grade-point average if it's a low C.

   On the other hand, include a main heading like "Extracurricular Activities" if the activities or awards seem relevant. For example, if Eric Kurland had been a member of the Management Club or vice president of the Computer Club in high school or college, he should have mentioned those facts.

   If you have no work experience related to the job for which you're applying, then list the jobs you have had. Any job that shows a period of responsible employment may favorably impress a potential employer.

3. You can list the names of your references directly on the résumé. Be sure to get the permission of people you cite before listing their names.

   You can also give the address of a placement office file that holds references, as shown on the model résumé.

   Or you can simply say that you will provide references on request.

Cover Letter

The purpose of the cover letter that goes with your résumé is to introduce yourself briefly and to try to make an employer interested in you. You should include only the high points of the information in your résumé.

Following is the letter cover letter that Eric Kurland sent with his résumé.

---

27 Hawkins Road
Clarksboro, New Jersey 08020
May 13, 2004

Mr. George C. Arline
Personnel Manager, Indesco Associates
301 Sharptown Road
White Plains, New York 10019

Dear Mr. Arline:

   I would like to be considered as a candidate for the assistant computer programmer position advertised in the *Philadelphia Inquirer* on April 28, 2007.

   I am currently finishing my degree in Computer Science at Rowan University. I have taken every required computer course offered at Rowan and have a solid background in the following computer languages: C++, Visual Basic, Pascal, and COBOL. In addition to my computer background, I have supplemented my education with business and mathematics courses.

(continued)

My knowledge of computers and the business field goes beyond my formal classroom education. For the past three years I have worked part-time at Radio Shack, where I have gained experience in sales and inventory control. Also, on my own initiative, I designed a demonstration program for the Compaq Presario 5062 and developed promotional fliers about the program.

In short, I believe I have the up-to-date computer background and professional drive needed to contribute to your organization. I have enclosed a copy of my résumé to give you further details about my experience. Sometime next week, I'll give you a call to see whether I can come in for an interview at your convenience. I look forward to speaking with you then.

Sincerely,

Eric Kurland
Eric Kurland

Points to Note about the Cover Letter

1. Your letter should do the following:

   a. In the first paragraph, state that you are an applicant for a job and identify the source through which you learned about the job.

   Here is how Eric Kurland's letter might have opened if his source had been the college placement office. "I learned through the placement office at Rowan University of the assistant computer programmer position at your company. I would like to be considered as a candidate for the job."

   Sometimes an ad will list only a box number (such as Y 172) to reply to. Your inside address should then be:

   Y 172
   Philadelphia Inquirer
   Philadelphia, Pennsylvania 19101

   Dear Sir or Madam:

   b. In the second paragraph, briefly state your qualifications for the job and refer the reader to your résumé.

   c. In the last paragraph, state your willingness to come for an interview. If you can be available for an interview only at certain times, indicate this.

2. As with your résumé, neatness is crucial. Follow the same hints for the letter that you did for the résumé.

   a. Print the letter on good paper.

   b. Proofread *very carefully* for sentence-skills mistakes and spelling mistakes. Use the checklist of sentence skills on the inside back cover.

   c. Be brief and to the point: use no more than one page.

   d. Use a format like the model letter. Keep roughly the same margin on all sides.

   e. Use punctuation and spelling in the model letter as a guide. For example:

      (1) Skip two spaces between the inside address and the salutation ("Dear Mr. Arline").

      (2) Use a colon after the salutation.

      (3) Sign your name at the bottom, in addition to typing it.

Clip a job listing from a newspaper or copy a job description posted in your school placement office. The job should be one that you feel you are qualified for or that you would one day like to have.

Write a résumé and a cover letter for the job. Use the models already considered as guides.

Use the checklist on the inside back cover as a guide in your writing.

Activity

1

www.mhhe.com/langan

21 Using the Library and the Internet

This chapter will explain and illustrate how to

- research topics using the library
- research topics using the Internet
- evaluate Internet sources

© Mika/zefa/Corbis

Write a letter to a new student on campus in which you describe the various uses of the college library.

This chapter provides the basic information you need to use your college library and the Internet with confidence. You will learn that for most research topics there are two basic steps you should take:

1. Find books on your topic.
2. Find articles on your topic.

You will learn, too, that while the library is the traditional place for doing such research, a home computer with Internet access now enables you to thoroughly investigate any topic.

Using the Library

Most students know that libraries provide study space, computer workstations, and copying machines. They are also aware of a library's reading area, which contains recent copies of magazines and newspapers. But the true heart of a library consists of a *main desk, the library's catalog(s) of holdings, book stacks,* and *the periodicals storage area.* Each of these will be discussed in the pages that follow.

www.mhhe.com/langan

Main Desk

The main desk is usually located in a central spot. Check with the main desk to see whether a brochure describes the layout and services of the library. You might also ask whether the library staff provides tours. If not, explore your library to find each of the areas in the activity below.

Make up a floor plan of your college library. Label the main desk, catalogs (in print or computerized), book stacks, and periodicals storage area.

Activity

1

Library Catalog

The library catalog will be your starting point for almost any research project. The catalog is a list of all the holdings of the library. It may be an actual card catalog: a file of cards alphabetically arranged in drawers. More likely, the catalog is computerized and can be accessed on computer terminals located at different spots in the library. And increasingly, local and college library catalogs can be accessed online, so you may be able to check their book holdings on your computer.

Finding a Book: Author, Title, and Subject

Whether you use an actual file of cards or a computer terminal or visit your library's holdings online, it is important for you to know that there are three ways to look up a book: according to *author, title,* or *subject.* For example, suppose you wanted to see if the library had the book *A Tribe Apart,* by Patricia Hersch. You could check for the book in any of three ways:

1. You could do an *author* search and look it up under *Hersch, Patricia.* An author is always listed under his or her last name.

2. You could do a *title* search and look it up under *Tribe Apart, A.* Note that you always look up a book under the first word in the title, excluding the words *A, An,* or *The.*

3. If you know the subject that the book deals with—in this case the subject is "teenagers"—you could do a *subject* search and look it up under *Teenagers.*

Here is the author entry in a computerized card catalog for Hersch's book *A Tribe Apart:*

Author:	Hersch, Patricia
Title:	A tribe apart: a journey into the heart of American adolescence
Publisher:	New York: Ballantine, 1998
LC Subjects:	Teenagers—United States
Call Number:	HQ796/H43
Location:	Gibbsboro
Status:	Available

Note that in addition to giving you the publisher (Ballantine) and year of publication (1998), the entry also tells you the *call number*—where to find the book in the library. If the computerized catalog is part of a network of libraries, you may also learn at what branch or location the book is available. If the book is not at your library, you can probably arrange for an interlibrary loan.

Using Subject Headings to Research a Topic

Generally, if you are looking for a particular book, it is easier to search by *author* or *title.* On the other hand, if you are researching a topic, then you should search by *subject.*

The subject section performs three valuable functions:

- It will give you a list of books on a given topic.
- It will often provide related topics that might have information on your subject.
- It will suggest more-limited topics, helping you narrow your general topic.

Chances are you will be asked to do a research paper of about five to fifteen pages. You do not want to choose a topic so broad that it could be covered only by an entire book or more. Instead, you want to come up with a limited topic that can be adequately supported in a relatively short paper. As you search the subject section, take advantage of ideas that it might offer on how you can narrow your topic.

Activity

2

Part A. Team up with a partner in class and answer the following questions about your library's catalog.

1. Is your library's catalog an actual file of cards in drawers, or is it computerized? _____

2. Which type of catalog search will help you research and limit a topic?

   _____

Part B. Use your library's catalog to answer the following questions.

1. What is the title of one book by Anna Quindlen? _____

   _____

2. What is the title of one book by Bill Geist?

   _____

3. Who is the author of *A Tree Grows in Brooklyn?* (Remember to look up the title under *Tree,* not *A.*)

   _____

4. Who is the author of *Seven Habits of Highly Effective People?*

   _____

5. List two books and their authors dealing with the subject of adoption.

   a. _____

   b. _____

6. Look up a book titled *When Bad Things Happen to Good People* or *Silent Spring* and give the following information:

   a. Author _____

   b. Publisher _____

   c. Date of publication _____

   d. Call number _____

   e. One subject heading _____

7. Look up a book written by Deborah Tannen or Garrison Keillor and give the following information:

   a. Title _____

   b. Publisher _____

   c. Date of publication _____

   d. Call number _____

   e. One subject heading _____

Book Stacks

The book stacks are the library shelves where books are arranged according to their call numbers. The call number, as distinctive as a social security number, always appears on the catalog entry for any book. It is also printed on the spine of every book in the library.

If your library has open stacks (ones that you are permitted to enter), here is how to find a book. Suppose you are looking for *A Tribe Apart,* which has the call number HQ796/H43 in the Library of Congress system. (Libraries using the Dewey decimal system have call letters made up entirely of numbers rather than letters and numbers. However, you use the same basic method to locate a book.) First, you go to the section of the stacks that holds the *H*'s. When you locate the *H*'s, you look for the *HQ*'s. After that, you look for *HQ796*. Finally, you look for *HQ796/H43,* and you have the book.

If your library has closed stacks (ones you are not permitted to enter), you will have to write down the title, author, and call number on a request form. (Such forms will be available near the card catalog or computer terminals.) You'll then give the form to a library staff person, who will locate the book and bring it to you.

Activity

3

Use the book stacks to answer one of the following sets of questions. Choose the questions that relate to the system of classifying books used by your library.

Option 1: Library of Congress system (letters and numbers)

1. Books in the E184.6–E185.9 area deal with
   a. Benjamin Franklin.   c. American presidents.
   b. American Indians.   d. African Americans.

2. Books in the HM–HN65 area deal with
   a. sociology.   c. economics.
   b. history.   d. psychology.

3. Books in the M1–M220 area deal with
   a. painting.   c. music.
   b. sculpture.   d. architecture.

Option 2: Dewey decimal system (numbers)

1. Books in the 200–299 area deal with

    a. language.   c. religion.
    b. philosophy.   d. sports.

2. Books in the 370–372 area deal with

    a. education.   c. the military.
    b. death.   d. waste disposal.

3. Books in the 613 area deal with

    a. wildflowers.   c. drugs.
    b. health.   d. the solar system.

Periodicals

The first step in researching a topic is to check for relevant books; the second step is to locate relevant periodicals. *Periodicals* (from the word *periodic,* which means "at regular periods") are magazines, journals, and newspapers. Periodicals often contain recent or very specialized information about a subject, which may not be available in a book.

The library's catalog lists the periodicals that it holds, just as it lists its book holdings. To find articles in these periodicals, however, you will need to consult a periodicals index. Following are three indexes that are widely used in libraries.

Readers' Guide to Periodical Literature

The old-fashioned way to do research is to use the familiar green volumes of the *Readers' Guide,* found in just about every library. They list articles published in more than one hundred popular magazines, such as *Newsweek, Health, People, Ebony, Redbook,* and *Popular Science.* Articles appear alphabetically under both subject and author. For example, if you wanted to learn the titles of articles published on the subject of child abuse within a certain time span, you would look under the heading "Child abuse."

Following is a typical entry from the *Guide.*

Subject heading   Title of article   Author of article   "Illustrated"

Parenting
The Case for Staying Home C. Wallis il
    Time p51–9 Mr 22 '04

Name of magazine   Page numbers   Date

Note the sequence in which information is given about the article:

1. Subject heading.

2. Title of the article. In some cases, bracketed words ([ ]) after the title help make clear just what the article is about.

3. Author (if it is a signed article). The author's first name is always abbreviated.

4. Whether the article has a bibliography (*bibl*) or is illustrated with pictures (*il*). Other abbreviations sometimes used are shown in the front of the *Readers' Guide*.

5. Name of the magazine. Before 1988, the *Readers Guide* used abbreviations for most of the magazines indexed. For example, the magazine *Popular Science* is abbreviated *Pop Sci*. If necessary, refer to the list of magazines in the front of the index to identify abbreviations.

6. Page numbers on which the article appears.

7. Date when the article appeared. Dates are abbreviated: for example, *Mr* stands for March, *Ag* for August, *O* for October. Other abbreviations are shown in the front of the *Guide*.

The *Readers' Guide* is published in monthly supplements. At the end of a year, a volume is published covering the entire year. You will see in your library large green volumes titled, for instance, *Readers' Guide 2000* or *Readers' Guide 2007*. You will also see the small monthly supplements for the current year.

The drawback of the *Readers' Guide* is that it gives you only a list of articles; you must then go to your library's catalog to see if the library actually has copies of the magazines that contain those articles. If you're lucky and it does, you must take the time to locate the relevant issue and then to read and take notes on the articles or to make copies of them.

The *Readers' Guide* may also be available at your library online. If so, you can quickly search for articles on a given subject simply by typing in a key word or key phrase.

EBSCOhost

Many libraries now provide an online computer search service such as InfoTrac or EBSCOhost. Sitting at a terminal and using EBSCOhost, for instance, you will be able to use key words to quickly search many hundreds of periodicals for full-text articles on your subject. When you find relevant articles, you can either print them out using a library printer (libraries may charge you about ten cents a page) or e-mail them to yourself to print elsewhere. Obviously, if an online resource is available, that is the way you should conduct your research.

At this point in the chapter, you now know the two basic steps in researching a topic in the library. What are the steps?

Activity

4

1. _____

2. _____

Activity

5

1. Look up a recent article on nursing home costs using one of your library's periodicals indexes, and fill in the following information:

    a. Name of the index you used _____

    b. Article title _____

    c. Author (if given) _____

    d. Name of magazine _____

    e. Pages _____ f. Date _____

2. Look up a recent article on organ donation using one of your library's periodicals indexes, and fill in the following information:

    a. Name of the index you used _____

    b. Article title _____

    c. Author (if given) _____

    d. Name of magazine _____

    e. Pages _____ f. Date _____

Using the Internet

www.mhhe.com/langan

The Internet is dramatic proof of the computer revolution that has occurred in our lives. It is a giant network that connects computers at tens of thousands of educational, scientific, government, and commercial agencies around the world. Within the Internet is the World Wide Web, a global information system that got its name because countless individual Web sites contain *links* to other sites, forming a kind of web.

To use the Internet, you need a personal computer with a *modem*—a device that sends and receives electronic data over a telephone or cable line. You also need an Internet service provider such as America Online. If you also have a printer, you can do a good deal of your research for a paper at home. As you would in a library, you should proceed by searching for books and articles on your topic.

Before you begin searching the Internet on your own, though, take the time to learn whether your local or school library is online. If it is, visit its Web site to find out exactly what sources and databases it has available. You may be able to do all your research using the online resources available through your library. On the other hand, if your library's resources are limited, you can turn on your own to the Internet to search for material on any topic, as explained below.

Finding Books on Your Topic

To find current books on your topic, go online and type in the address of one of the large commercial online booksellers:

Amazon at www.amazon.com

Barnes and Noble at www.barnesandnoble.com

The easy-to-use search facilities of both Amazon and Barnes and Noble are free, and you are under no obligation to buy books from them.

The "Browse" Tab

After you arrive at the Amazon or Barnes and Noble Web site (or the online library site of your choice), go to the "Browse" tab. You'll then get a list of categories of books where you might locate books on your general subject. For example, if your assignment was to report on personal obstacles faced by an American president, you would notice that one of the listings is "Biography." Upon choosing "Biography," you would get several subcategories, one of which is "Presidents." When you click on that, you would get a list of recent books on American presidents. You could then click on each title for information about each book. All this browsing and searching could be done very quickly and would help you decide on a specific president as your topic.

The "Search" Box

If your assignment is, for instance, to prepare a paper on some aspect of adoption, type the word *adoption* in the search box provided. You'll then get a list of books on that subject. Just looking at the list may help you narrow your subject and decide on a specific topic you might want to develop. For instance, one student typed "adoption" in the search box on Barnes and Noble's site and got back a list of three thousand books. Considering just part of that list helped her realize that she wanted to write on some aspect of international adoption. She typed "international adoption" and got back a list of three hundred titles. After looking at information about those books, she was able to decide on a limited topic for her paper.

A Note on the Library of Congress

The commercial bookstore sites described are especially quick and easy to use. But you should know that to find additional books on your topic, you can also visit the Library of Congress Web site (www.loc.gov). The Library of Congress, in Washington, D.C., has copies of all books published in the United States. Its online catalog contains about twelve million entries. You can browse this catalog by subject or search by key words. The search form permits you to check just those books that interest you. After you find a given book, click on the "Full Record" option to view publication information and call number. You can then try to obtain the book from your college library or through an interlibrary loan.

Other Points to Note

Remember that at any time you can use your printer to quickly print out information presented on the screen. (For example, the student planning a paper on adoption could print out a list of the three hundred books on international adoption, along with sheets of information about individual books.) You could then go to your library knowing just what books you want to borrow. Indeed, if your own local or school library is accessible online, you can visit in advance to find out whether it has the books you want. Also, you may want to make a trip to your local bookstore to buy the book. If you have time and money, you may want to purchase them from an online bookstore such as Amazon. Used books are often available at greatly reduced prices, and they often ship out in just a couple of days.

Finding Articles on Your Topic

Online Magazines and Newspaper Articles

As already mentioned, your library may have an online search service such as EBSCOhost or InfoTrac that you can use to find and access relevant articles on your subject. Another online research service, one that you can subscribe to individually on a home computer, is eLibrary. You may be able to get a free seven-day trial subscription or pay for a monthly subscription at a limited cost. The service provides millions of newspaper and magazine articles as well as many thousands of book chapters and television and radio transcripts. After typing in one or more key words on the eLibrary Web site, you'll get long lists of articles that may relate to your subject. Click on a title to see the full text of the article. If it fits your needs, you can print it out right away. Very easily, then, you can research a full range of magazine and newspaper articles.

Search Engines

An Internet search engine will help you quickly go through a vast amount of information on the Web to find articles about almost any topic. One extremely helpful search engine is Google; you can access it by typing www.google.com. A screen will then appear with a box in which you can type one or more key words. For example, if you are thinking of doing a paper on road rage, type "road rage." Within a second or so, you will get a list of over three million articles and sites on the Web about road rage!

You should then try to narrow your topic by adding other key words. For instance, if you typed "preventing road rage," you would get a list of over one million articles and sites. If you narrowed your potential topic further by typing

www.mhhe.com/langan

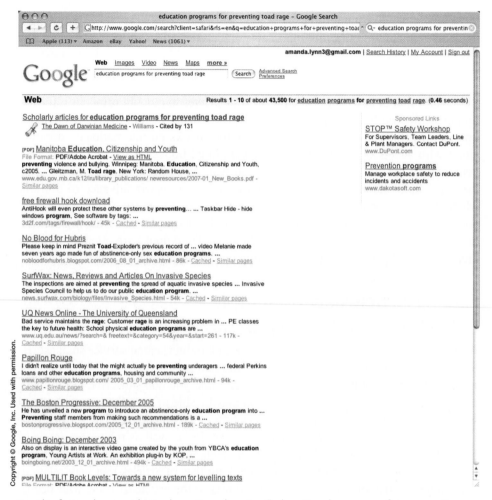

Results from a key word search on Google using "educational programs for preventing road rage" in the search box.

"educational programs for preventing road rage," you would get a list of almost a half million items. Google does a superior job of returning hits that are genuinely relevant to your search, so just scanning the early part of a list may be enough to provide you with the information you need.

Very often your challenge with searches will be getting too much information rather than too little. Try making your key words more specific, or use different combinations of key words. You might also try another search engine, such as www.yahoo.com. In addition, consult the search engine's Advanced Search feature for tips on successful searching.

Finally, remember while you search to save the addresses of relevant Web sites that you may want to visit again. The browser that you are using (for example,

Internet Explorer) will probably have a Bookmark or Favorite Places option. With the click of a mouse, you can "bookmark" a site. You will then be able to return to it simply by clicking on its name in a list, rather than having to remember and type its address.

Evaluating Internet Sources

Keep in mind that the quality and reliability of information you find on the Internet may vary widely. Anyone with a bit of computer know-how can create a Web site and post information there. That person may be a Nobel Prize winner, a leading authority in a specialized field, a high school student, or a crackpot. Be careful, then, to look closely at the source in the following ways:

www.mhhe.com/langan

1. **Internet address**   In a Web address, the three letters following the "dot" are the domain. The most common domains are .com, .edu, .gov, .net, and .org. A common misconception is that a Web site's reliability can be determined by its domain. This is not the case, as almost anyone can get a Web address ending in .com, .edu, .org or any of the other domains. Therefore, it is important that you examine every Web site carefully, considering the three points that follow.

2. **Author**   What credentials does the author have (if any)? Has the author published other material on the topic?

3. **Internal evidence**   Does the author seem to proceed objectively—presenting all sides of a topic fairly before arguing his or her own views? Does the author produce solid, adequate support for his or her views?

4. **Date**   Is the information up to date? Check at the top or bottom of the document for copyright, publication, or revision dates. Knowing such dates will help you decide whether the material is current enough for your purposes.

Part A Go to www.google.com and search for "education." Then complete the items below.

1. How many items did your search yield? _____

2. In the early listings, you will probably find each of the following domains: edu, gov, org, and com. Pick one site with each domain and write its full address.

   a.   Address of one .com site you found: _____

   b.   Address of one .gov site: _____

   c.   Address of one .org site: _____

   d.   Address of one .edu site: _____

Activity

6

Part B Circle *one* of the sites you identified above and use it to complete the following evaluation. Answers will vary.

3. Name of site's author or authoring institution: _____

4. Is site's information current (within two years)? _____

5. Does the site serve obvious business purposes (with advertising or attempts to sell products)? _____

6. Does the site have an obvious connection to a governmental, commercial, business, or religious organization? If so, which one?

   _____

7. Does the site's information seem fair and objective?

   _____

   _____

8. Based on the information above, would you say the site appears reliable?

   _____

Practice in Using the Library and the Internet

Activity

7

Use your library or the Internet to research a subject that interests you. Select one of the following areas or (with your instructor's permission) an area of your own choice:

Assisted suicide	Prenatal care
Interracial adoption	Acid rain
Ritalin and children	New aid for people with disabilities
Sexual harassment	New remedies for allergies
Gay marriage	Censorship on the Internet
Greenhouse effect	Prison reform
Nursing home costs	Drug treatment programs
Pro-choice movement today	Sudden infant death syndrome
Pro-life movement today	New treatments for insomnia
Health insurance reform	Organ donation
Pollution of drinking water	Child abuse
Problems of retirement	Voucher system in schools
Cremation	Food poisoning (salmonella)
Capital punishment	Alzheimer's disease

Holistic healing	Airbags
Best job prospects today	Gambling and youth
Heroes for today	Nongraded schools
Computer use and carpal tunnel syndrome	Forecasting earthquakes
	Ethical aspects of hunting
Noise control	Ethics of cloning
Animals nearing extinction	Recent consumer frauds
Animal rights movement	Stress reduction in the workplace
Antigay violence	Sex on television
Drug treatment programs for adolescents	Everyday addictions
	Toxic waste disposal
Fertility drugs	Self-help groups
Witchcraft today	Telephone crimes
New treatments for AIDS	Date rape
Mind-body medicine	Steroids
Origins of Kwanzaa	Surrogate mothers
Hazardous substances in the home	Vegetarianism

Research the topic first through a subject search in your library's catalog or that of an online bookstore. Then research the topic through a periodicals index (print or online). On a separate sheet of paper, provide the following information:

1. Topic

2. Three books that either cover the topic directly or at least touch on the topic in some way. Include the following:

   Author
   Title
   Place of publication
   Publisher
   Date of publication

3. Three articles on the topic published in 2003 or later. Include the following:

   Title of article
   Author (if given)
   Title of magazine
   Date
   Pages (if given)

4. Finally, write a paragraph describing just how you went about researching your topic. In addition, include a photocopy or printout of one of the three articles.

22

Writing a Research Paper

This chapter will explain and illustrate

- the six steps in writing a research paper:

  STEP 1: Select a topic that you can readily research.

  STEP 2: Limit your topic and make the purpose of your paper clear.

  STEP 3: Gather information on your limited topic.

  STEP 4: Plan your paper and take notes on your limited topic.

  STEP 5: Write the paper.

  STEP 6: Use an acceptable format and method of documentation.

This chapter also provides

- a model research paper

© Alan D. Monyelle/U.S.Navy/Handout/Reuters/Corbis

If you were to write a research paper on war, what would you focus on? War itself is too broad a topic to cover in one research paper. You would need to select a more limited topic to write about, for example, the effect of war on the economy. Looking at the above photograph of American soldiers in Iraq, can you think of some other limited topics of war you might cover in a research paper?

Step 1: Select a Topic That You Can Readily Research

Researching at a Local Library

First of all, do a subject search of your library's catalog and see whether there are several books on your general topic. For example, if you initially choose the broad topic "parenting," try to find at least three books on being a parent. Make sure that the books are actually available on the library shelves.

Next, go to a periodicals index in your library to see if there are a fair number of magazine, newspaper, or journal articles on your subject. You can use the *Readers' Guide to Periodical Literature* (found in just about every library) to find articles that appear in the back issues of periodicals that your library may keep. But you may find that your library subscribes to a provider of electronic databases such as EBSCOhost, which will allow you access to articles published in a far greater range of publications. For instance, when Sonya Philips, author of the model research paper "Successful Families," visited her local library, she connected to EBSCOhost and typed "parenting" in the search box. In seconds, EBSCOhost came back with hundreds of hits—titles, publication information, and the complete text of articles about parenting.

Researching on the Internet

If you have access to the Internet on a home or library computer, you can use it to determine whether resources are available for your topic.

The first step is to go to the subjects section of a library catalog or large online bookseller to find relevant books. (Don't worry—you don't have to buy any books; you're just browsing for information.) Two of the largest online booksellers are Barnes and Noble and Amazon.

"I checked out both Barnes and Noble and Amazon as I began my research," said Sonya Philips. "When I went to their Web sites, I saw that I could search for books by subject, and I knew that I was in business.

"Barnes and Noble has a category called 'Parenting and Family,' and

when I clicked on that, I got a bunch of subcategories, including one for 'Teenagers.' I clicked on 'Teenagers,' and that brought up a list of hundreds of books! I went through the list, and when I got to a book that sounded promising, I just clicked on that title and up like magic came reviews of the book—and sometimes a table of contents and a summary as well! All of this information helped me decide on the dozen or so books I eventually picked out that seemed relevant to my paper. I then went to my local library and found five of those titles on the shelves. Another title was a recent paperback, so I went to a nearby bookstore and bought it." (If you find relevant books in your online search that your local library does not own, ask your research librarian if he or she can obtain them from another library through an interlibrary loan program.)

Next, determine whether magazine or newspaper articles on your topic are available online. The simplest way is to use the Internet search engine Google (google.com), which allows you to search the Internet for information on any topic you like. Sonya relates her experience using Google in this way:

"First I typed in the word 'parenting' in the keyword box," she said. "I got more than eight million hits! So I tried more specific search terms. I tried 'parenting and teenagers' first, but that was still too general. I got several hundred thousand hits, and I didn't know where to start reading. So I narrowed my topics even more: 'parenting and teenagers and television' and 'parenting and teenagers and homeschooling.' Those reduced the number of hits a lot. I was still getting thousands, but I could see that some of the very first ones looked really promising. Better yet, I found some useful sites, like 'The Television Project,' which is an online resource that doesn't exist anywhere else.

"To look just for magazine and newspaper articles, I went directly to the site of some popular publications, such as *Time* (time.com), *Newsweek* (newsweek.com), and *USA Today* (usatoday.com). I was able to search each one for recent articles about parenting. I saw that I would have to use a credit card and pay a fee of about two dollars to read each article online. So I noted the date and page number of the articles I was interested in and looked up the ones that were available in the back-issue section of my library's reading room. Between doing that and using EBSCO-host, I found plenty of recent material related to my subject."

In summary, then, the first step in doing a research paper is to find out if both books and articles are available on the topic in which you are interested. If they are, pursue your topic. Otherwise, you may have to explore another topic. You cannot write a paper on a topic for which research materials are not available.

Step 2: Limit Your Topic and Make the Purpose of Your Paper Clear

A research paper should *thoroughly* develop a *limited* topic. The paper should be narrow and deep rather than broad and shallow. Therefore, as you read through books and articles, look for ways to limit your general topic.

For instance, as Sonya read through materials on the general topic "parenting," she chose to limit her topic to the particular problems of parents raising children in today's culture. Furthermore, she decided to limit it even more by focusing on what successful parents do to deal with those challenges. To take some other examples, the general topic "drug abuse" might be narrowed to successful drug treatment programs for adolescents. After doing some reading on the worldwide problem of overpopulation, you might decide to limit your paper to the birth-control policies enforced by the Chinese government. The broad subject "death" could be reduced to euthanasia or the unfair pricing practices in some funeral homes. "Divorce" might be limited to its most damaging effects on the children of divorced parents; "stress in everyday life" could be narrowed to methods of reducing stress in the workplace.

The subject headings in your library's catalog and periodicals indexes will give you helpful ideas about how to limit your subject. For example, under the subject heading "Parenting" in the book file were several related headings, such as "moral and ethical considerations of parenting" and "stepparenting." In addition, there was a list of seventy-eight books, including several titles that suggested limited directions for research: parents and discipline, parenting and adolescent girls, how parents can protect their kids from violence, and parents' questions about teenagers' development. Under the subject heading "Parenting" in the library's periodicals index were subheadings and titles of many articles that suggested additional limited topics that a research paper might explore: how parents can limit the impact of TV on kids, keeping the lines of communication open between parents and teenagers, how much influence parents can have on kids, and secrets to raising a successful teen. The point is that *subject headings and related headings, as well as book and article titles, may be of great help to you in narrowing your topic.* Take advantage of them.

Do not expect to limit your topic and make your purpose clear all at once. You may have to do quite a bit of reading as you work out the limited focus of your paper. Note that many research papers have one of two general purposes. Your purpose might be to make and defend a point of some kind. (For example, your purpose in a paper might be to provide evidence that elected officials should be limited to serving a single term in office.) Or, depending on the course and the instructor, your purpose might simply be to present information about a particular subject. (For instance, you might be asked to write a paper describing the most recent scientific findings about the effect of diet on heart disease.)

Step 3: Gather Information on Your Limited Topic

After you have a good sense of your limited topic, you can begin gathering relevant information. A helpful way to proceed is to sign out the books that you need from your library. In addition, make copies of all relevant articles from magazines, newspapers, or journals. If your library has an online periodicals database, you may be able to print those articles from there.

In other words, take the steps needed to get all your key source materials together in one place. You can then sit and work on these materials in a quiet, unhurried way in your home or some other place of study.

Step 4: Plan Your Paper and Take Notes on Your Limited Topic

Preparing a Scratch Outline

As you carefully read through the material you have gathered, think constantly about the specific content and organization of your paper. Begin making decisions about exactly what information you will present and how you will arrange it. Prepare a scratch outline for your paper that shows both its thesis and the areas of support for the thesis. Try to plan at least three areas of support.

Thesis: _____

Support: (1) _____

         (2) _____

         (3) _____

Following, for example, is the brief outline that Sonya Philips prepared for her paper on successful parenting.

Thesis: There are things parents can do to overcome the negative influences hurting their families.

Support: (1) Create quality time with families

         (2) Increase families' sense of community

         (3) Minimize the impact of media and technology

Note-Taking

With a tentative outline in mind, you can begin taking notes on the information that you expect to include in your paper. Write your notes on four-by-six-inch or five-by-eight-inch cards, on sheets of loose-leaf paper, or in a computer file. The notes you take should be in the form of *direct quotations, summaries in your own words,* or both. At times, you may also *paraphrase*—use your own words in place of someone else's words. Since most research involves condensing information, you will summarize much more than you will paraphrase. (For more information on summarizing, see pages 385–396.)

A *direct quotation* must be written *exactly* as it appears in the original work. But as long as you don't change the meaning, you may omit words from a quotation if they are not relevant to your point. To show such an omission, or ellipsis, use three spaced periods (known as *ellipsis points*) in place of the deleted words:

> We cannot guarantee that bad things will happen, but we can argue that good things are not happening. It is the contention of this report that increasing numbers of young people are left to their own devices at a critical time in their development.

Original passage

> "We cannot guarantee that bad things will happen, but we can argue that good things are not happening. . . . [I]ncreasing numbers of young people are left to their own devices at a critical time in their development."

Direct quotation with an ellipsis

(Note the four dots in the above example; the first dot is the period at the end of the sentence. The capital letter in brackets shows that the word was capitalized by the student and was not capitalized in the original source.)

In a *summary,* you condense the original material by expressing it in your own words. Summaries may be written as lists, as brief paragraphs, or both. Below is one of Sonya Philips's summary note cards.

> *Movie content*
>
> *Study conducted in 2006 showed that of PG-13 movies, 91 percent had crude language, 89 percent had obscene language, 45 percent had actual or suggested sex. Worrisome because most parents assume PG-13 movies are OK for their kids.*
>
> *Medved and Medved, 62*

Keep in mind the following points about your research notes:

- Write on only one side of each card or sheet of paper.

- Write only one kind of information, from one source, on any one card or sheet. For example, the sample card on the previous page has information on only one idea (movie content) from one source (Medved and Medved).

- At the top of each card or sheet, write a heading that summarizes its content. This will help you organize the different kinds of information that you gather.

- Identify the source and page number at the bottom.

Whether you quote or summarize, be sure to record the exact source and page from which you take each piece of information. In a research paper, you must document all information that is not common knowledge or not a matter of historical record. For example, the birth and death dates of Dr. Martin Luther King Jr. are established facts and do not need documenting. On the other hand, the average number of hours worked annually today compared with the 1980s is a specialized fact that should be documented. As you read several sources on a subject, you will develop a sense of what authors regard as generally shared, or common, information and what is more specialized information that must be documented.

A Caution about Plagiarism

www.mhhe.com/langan

If you fail to document information that is not your own, you will be stealing. The formal term is *plagiarizing*—using someone else's work as your own, whether you borrow a single idea, a sentence, or an entire essay.

One example of plagiarism is turning in a friend's paper as if it is your own. Another example is copying an article found in a magazine, newspaper, journal, or on the Internet and turning it in as your own. By copying someone else's work, you risk being failed or even expelled. Equally, plagiarism deprives you of what can be a most helpful learning and organization experience—researching and writing about a selected topic in detail.

Keep in mind, too, that while the Internet has made it easier for students to plagiarize, it has also made it riskier. Teachers can easily discover that a student has taken material from an Internet source by typing a sentence or two from the student's paper into a powerful search engine like Google; that source is then often quickly identified.

With the possibility of plagiarism in mind, then, be sure to take careful, documented notes during your research. Remember that if you use another person's material, *you must acknowledge your source.* When you cite a source properly, you give credit where it is due, you provide your readers with a way to locate the original material on their own, and you demonstrate that your work has been carefully researched.

Here are three sets of passages. Each set begins with an original passage followed by notes on the passage. Both notes include a parenthetical citation, "(24)," crediting the original source. But while one note is an acceptable paraphrase or summary, the other is an unacceptable paraphrase or summary in which the sentences and ideas too closely follow the original, using some of the same structure and the same words as the original. Identify the acceptable note with an A and the unacceptable note with a U.

Set 1: Original Passage

The self-confessed television addict often feels he "ought" to do other things— but the fact that he doesn't read and doesn't plant his garden or sew or crochet or play games or have conversations means that those activities are no longer as desirable as television. In a way the heavy viewer's life is as imbalanced by his television "habit" as a drug addict's or an alcoholic's. He is living in a holding pattern, as it were, passing up the activities that lead to growth or development or a sense of accomplishment. This is one reason people talk about their television viewing so ruefully, so apologetically. They are aware that it is an unproductive experience, that almost any other endeavor is more worthwhile by any human measure.

—Marie Winn, from "Television Addiction,"
in *The Plug-In Drug* (Viking Penguin, 2002)

_____ a. Television addicts may feel they should do other things like play games or have conversations. But they pass up activities that might lead to a sense of accomplishment. Their lives are as imbalanced by their television watching as a drug addict's or alcoholic's. Aware of how unproductive television viewing is, they talk about it apologetically (24).

_____ b. TV addicts feel that they ought to spend their time doing more worthwhile activities. But like alcohol or drugs, TV has taken over their lives. The addicts' apologetic tone when they talk about their TV watching indicates that they know they're wasting time on a completely unproductive activity (24).

Set 2: Original Passage

Now, however, there is growing evidence that restorative naps are making a comeback. Recognizing that most of their employees are chronically sleep-deprived, some companies have set up nap rooms with reclining chairs, blankets and alarm clocks. If unions are truly interested in worker welfare, they should make such accommodations a standard item in contract negotiations. Workers who take advantage of the opportunity to sleep for twenty minutes or so during the workday report that they can go back to work with renewed enthusiasm and energy. My college roommate, Dr. Linda Himot, a psychiatrist in Pittsburgh, who has a talent for ten-minute catnaps between patients, says these respites help her focus better on each patient's problems, which are not always scintillating. And companies that encourage napping report that it reduces accidents and errors and increases productivity, even if it shortens the workday a bit. Studies have shown that sleepy workers make more mistakes and cause more accidents, and are more susceptible to heart attacks and gastrointestinal disorders.

—Jane Brody, from "New Respect for the Nap"
(*New York Times,* 2001)

_____ a. As employers realize that many workers are short on sleep, they are becoming more open to the idea of napping on the job. Some even provide places for workers to stretch out and nap briefly. Companies that allow napping find their employees are more alert and productive, and even suffer fewer physical ailments (24).

_____ b. Naps are becoming more acceptable. Some companies have done such things as set up nap rooms with reclining chairs and blankets. Naps provide workers with renewed enthusiasm and energy. Although naps shorten the workday a bit, they reduce accidents and increase productivity. Sleep-deprived workers are prone to heart attacks and gastrointestinal disorders.

Set 3: Original Passage

Chances are, you are going to go to work after you complete college. How would you like to earn an extra $950,000 on your job? If this sounds appealing, read on. I'm going to reveal how you can make an extra $2,000 a month between the ages of 25 and 65. Is this hard to do? Actually, it is simple for some, but impossible for others. All you have to do is be born a male and graduate from college. If we compare full-time workers, this is how much more the average male college graduate earns over the course of his career. Hardly any single factor pinpoints gender discrimination better than this total. The pay gap, which shows up at all levels of education, is so great that women who work full-time average only two-thirds (67 percent) of what men are paid. This gap does not occur only in the United States. All industrialized nations have it, although only in Japan is the gap larger than in the United States.

—James Henslin, from *Essentials of Sociology,*
fourth edition (Allyn and Bacon, 2002)

_____ a. To make an extra $2,000 a month between the ages of 25 and 65, you need to be born male and graduate from college. This adds up to an additional $950,000. The pay gap between genders shows up at all levels of education. It is so great that women who work full time make only two-thirds what men make. The gender gap occurs in all industrialized nations, although only in Japan is it greater than in the U.S. (24).

_____ b. The effect of gender on salary is significant. At all levels of education, a woman who works full time earns about two-thirds as much as a man who works full time. For college graduates, this adds up to a difference of $950,000 over the course of a 40-year working life. The gender gap exists in all industrialized nations, but it is greatest in Japan and the U.S. (24).

Step 5: Write the Paper

After you have finished your reading and note-taking, you should have a fairly clear idea of the plan of your paper. Make a *final outline* and use it as a guide to write your first full draft. If your instructor requires an outline as part of your paper, you should prepare either a *topic outline,* which contains your thesis plus supporting words and phrases; or a *sentence outline,* which consists of complete sentences. In the model paper shown on pages 436–444, a topic outline appears on page 437. You will note that roman numerals are used for first-level headings, capital letters for second-level headings, and arabic numbers for third-level headings.

www.mhhe.com/langan

In an *introduction,* include a thesis statement expressing the purpose of your paper and indicate the plan of development that you will follow. The section on writing introductions for an essay (pages 90–93) is also appropriate for the introductory section of the research paper. Notice that the model research paper uses a two-paragraph introduction (page 438).

As you move from *introduction* to *main body* to *conclusion,* strive for unity, support, and coherence so that your paper will be clear and effective. Repeatedly ask, Does each of my supporting paragraphs develop the thesis of my paper? Use the checklist on the inside back cover of this book to make sure that your paper follows all four bases of effective writing.

Step 6: Use an Acceptable Format and Method of Documentation

Format

The model paper included in this chapter (pages 436–444) shows acceptable formats for a research paper, including the style recommended by the Modern Language Association (MLA). Be sure to note carefully the comments and directions that are set in small print in the margins of each page.

Documentation of Sources

You must tell the reader the sources (books, articles, and so on) of borrowed material in your paper. Whether you quote directly or summarize ideas in your own words, you must acknowledge your sources. In the past, you may have used footnotes and a bibliography to cite your sources. Here you will learn a simplified and widely accepted documentation style used by the MLA.

Citations within a Paper

When citing a source, you must mention the author's name and the relevant page number. The author's name may be given either in the sentence you are writing or in parentheses following the sentence. Here are two examples:

> In The Way We Really Are, Stephanie Coontz writes, "Right up through the 1940s, ties of work, friendship, neighborhood, ethnicity, extended kin, and voluntary organizations were as important a source of identity for most Americans, and sometimes a more important source of obligation, than marriage and the nuclear family" (37).

> "Some . . . are looking for a way to reclaim family closeness in an increasingly fast-paced society. . . . Still others worry about unsavory influences in school—drugs, alcohol, sex, violence" (Kantrowitz and Wingert 66).

There are several points to note about citations within the paper:

- When the author's name is provided in parentheses, only the last name is given.

- There is no punctuation between the author's name and the page number.

- The parenthetical citation is placed after the borrowed material but before the period at the end of the sentence.

- If you are using more than one work by the same author, include a shortened version of the title within the parenthetical citation. For example, suppose you were using two books by Stephanie Coontz, and you included a second quotation from her book *The Way We Really Are.* Your citation within the text would be

> (Coontz, Really Are 39).

Note that a comma separates the author's last name from the abbreviated title and page number.

Citations at the End of a Paper

Your paper should end with a list of works cited that includes all the sources actually used in the paper. (Don't list any other sources, no matter how many you have read.) Look at the "Works Cited" page in the model research paper (page 444) and note the following points:

- The list is organized alphabetically according to the authors' last names. Entries are not numbered.

- Entries are double-spaced, with no extra space between entries.

- After the first line of each entry, a half-inch indentation separates each additional line in the entry.

- Use the abbreviation *qtd. in* when citing a quotation from another source. For example, a quotation from Edward Wolff on page 2 of the paper is from a book not by Wolff but by Sylvia Ann Hewlett and Cornel West. The citation is therefore handled as follows:

The economist Edward Wolff explains the loss of time:

> Over a thirty-year time span, parental time has declined 13 percent. The time parents have available for their children has been squeezed by the rapid shift of mothers into the paid labor force, by escalating divorce rates and the subsequent abandonment of children by their fathers, and by an increase in the number of hours required on the job. The average worker is now at work 163 hours a year more than in 1969, which adds up to an extra month of work annually (qtd. in Hewlett and West 48).

Model Entries for a List of Works Cited

Model entries of works cited are given below. Use these entries as a guide when you prepare your own list.

Bryson, Bill. A Short History of Nearly Everything. New York: Broadway Books, 2003.

Book by One Author

Note that the author's last name is written first.

---. I'm a Stranger Here Myself. New York: Broadway Books, 1999.

Two or More Entries by the Same Author

If you cite two or more entries by the same author (in the example above, a second book by Bill Bryson is cited), do not repeat the author's name. Instead, begin the line with three hyphens followed by a period. Then give the remaining information as usual. Arrange works by the same author alphabetically by title. The words *A, An,* and *The* are ignored in alphabetizing by title.

Simon, David, and Edward Burns. The Corner. New York: Broadway Books, 1997.

Book by Two or More Authors

For a book with two or more authors, give all the authors' names but reverse only the first author's name.

Kalb, Claudia. "Brave New Babies." Newsweek 26 Jan. 2004: 45–52.

Magazine Article

Farrell, Greg. "Online Time Soars at Office." USA Today 18 Feb. 2000: A1–2.

Newspaper Article

The final letter and numbers refer to pages 1 and 2 of section A.

If the article is not printed on consecutive pages, simply list the first page followed by a plus sign (+; in that case, the above example would read "A1+").

Editorial

"Fouling the Air." Editorial. New York Times 23 Aug. 2003: A12.

List an editorial as you would any signed or unsigned article, but indicate the nature of the piece by adding *Editorial* after the article's title.

Selection in an Edited Collection

Paige, Satchel. "Rules for Staying Young." Baseball: A Literary Anthology. Ed. Nicholas Dawidoff. New York: Library of America, 2002. 318.

Revised or Later Edition

Henslin, James M. Essentials of Sociology. 5th ed. Boston: Allyn and Bacon, 2004.

The abbreviations *Rev. ed., 2nd ed., 3rd ed.,* and so on, are placed right after the title.

Chapter or Section in a Book by One Author

Krugman, Paul. "The Angry People." The Great Unraveling. New York: Norton, 2003. 272–74.

Pamphlet

Funding Your Education, 2003–2004. Washington: Dept. of Education Office of Federal Student Aid, 2003.

Television Program

"Musically Speaking." 60 Minutes. Report. Lesley Stahl. CBS. 28 Sept. 2003.

Film

The Lord of the Rings: The Return of the King. Dir. Peter Jackson. New Line Cinema, 2003.

Sound Recording

Springsteen, Bruce. "Empty Sky." The Rising. Sony Music, 2002.

Videocassette

"Cedric's Journey." Nightline. Narr. Ted Koppel, ABC, WABC, New York. 24 June 1998. Videocassette. ABC/FDCH, 1998.

Personal Interview

McClintock, Ann. Personal interview. 23 June 2004.

Article in an Online Magazine

Hobson, Katherine. "Cancer: The Best Tests to Find a Killer." USnews.com 1 Sept. 2003. 9 Oct. 2004 ‹http://www.usnews.com/usnews/issue/archive/030901/20030901041310.php›.

The first date (1 Sept. 2003) refers to the issue of the publication in which the article appeared; the second date (9 Oct. 2004) refers to the day when the student researcher accessed the source.

Article in an Online Web site

"Being Chased." Dreams and Nightmares. Internet Resources. 2003. 17 Mar. 2004 ‹http://www.dreamnightmares.com/chasedindreams.html›.

No author is given, so the article is cited first, followed by the title of the Web site (*Dreams and Nightmares*) and the sponsor of the Web site (Internet Resources).

The first date (2003) refers to when the material was electronically published, updated, or posted; the second date (17 Mar. 2004) refers to when the student researcher accessed the source.

> "Dreams." <u>Encyclopaedia Britannica</u>. 2003. Encyclopaedia Britannica Premium Service. 8 Oct. 2004 ‹http://www.britannica.com/eb/article?eu=117531›.

Article in a Reference Database

The first date (2003) refers to when the material was electronically published, updated, or posted; the second date (8 Oct. 2004) refers to when the student researcher accessed the source.

> Graham, Vanessa. "Teenager Problems." E-mail to Sonya Philips. 12 Apr. 2004.

Electronic Mail (E-mail) Posting

On a separate sheet of paper, convert the information in each of the following references into the correct form for a list of works cited. Use the appropriate model above as a guide.

Activity

2

www.mhhe.com/langan

1. A book by David Anderegg called *Worried All the Time* and published in New York by Free Press in 2003.

2. An article by Susan Page titled "No Experience Necessary" on pages 1A–2A of the October 8, 2003, issue of *USA Today.*

3. A book by Michael W. Passner and Ronald E. Smith titled *Psychology: The Science of Mind and Behavior* and published in a second edition by McGraw-Hill in New York in 2006.

4. An article by Mark Miller titled "Parting with a Pet" found on May 16, 2007, at <http://www.msnbc.com/news/977726.asp?Ocv-KB20> in the October 8, 2006, issue of *Newsweek Online.*

5. An article titled "Depression in Teenagers" found on April 24, 2007, on the Web site titled *Troubled Teens* at <http://www.4troubledteens.com> and sponsored by the Aspen Education Group.

Model Paper

While the *MLA Handbook* does not require a title page or an outline for a paper, your instructor may ask you to include one or both. Here is a model title page.

Model Title Page

The title should begin about one-third of the way down the page. Center the title. Double-space the lines of the title and your name. Also center and double-space the instructor's name and the date.

> Successful Families:
>
> Fighting for Their Kids
>
> by
>
> Sonya Philips
>
> English 101
>
> Professor Lessing
>
> 5 May 2007

Papers written in MLA style use the simple format shown below. There is no title page or outline.

Model First Page of MLA-Style Paper

1 inch

1/2 inch

Philips 1

Sonya Philips
Professor Lessing
English 101
5 May 2007

Successful Families: Fighting for Their Kids

Double-space lines. Leave a one-inch margin on all sides.

It's a terrible time to be a teenager, or even a teenager's parent. That message is everywhere. Television, magazines, and newspapers are all full of frightening stories about teenagers and families. They say that America's families are falling apart, that kids don't care about anything, and that parents have trouble doing anything. . . .

Use this format if your instructor asks you to submit an outline of your paper.

Philips i

Model Outline Page

After the title page, number all pages in the upper-right corner, a half inch from the top. Place your name before the page number. Use small roman numerals on outline pages. Use arabic numerals on pages following the outline.

The word *Outline* (without underlining or quotation marks) is centered one inch from the top. Double-space lines. Leave a one-inch margin on all sides.

Outline

Thesis: Although these are difficult times to be raising teenagers, successful families are finding ways to cope with the challenges.

I.   Meeting the challenge of spending quality time together

   A.   Barriers to spending quality time

      1.   Increased working hours

      2.   Rising divorce rates

      3.   Women in workforce

   B.   Danger of lack of quality time

   C.   Ways found to spend time together

      1.   Working less and scaling back lifestyle

      2.   Homeschooling

II.   Meeting the challenge of creating sense of community

   A.   Lack of traditional community ties

   B.   Ways found to create sense of community

      1.   Intentional communities

      2.   Religious ties

III.   Meeting the challenge of limiting the negative impact of media and technology

   A.   Negative impact of media and technology

      1.   Creation of environment without protection

      2.   Flood of uncontrolled, inappropriate information

   B.   Ways of controlling media and technology

      1.   Banning TV

      2.   Using technology in beneficial ways

Here is a full model paper. It assumes the writer has included a title page.

Philips 1

Successful Families: Fighting for Their Kids

It's a terrible time to be a teenager, or even a teenager's parent. That message is everywhere. Television, magazines, and newspapers are all full of frightening stories about teenagers and families. They say that America's families are falling apart, that kids don't care about anything, and that parents have trouble doing anything about it. Bookstores are full of disturbing titles like these: <u>Parenting Your Out-of-Control Teenager</u>, <u>Teenage Wasteland</u>, <u>Unhappy Teenagers</u>, and <u>Teen Torment</u>. These books describe teenage problems that include apathy, violence, suicide, sexual abuse, depression, loss of values, poor mental health, crime, gang involvement, and drug and alcohol addiction.

Naturally, caring parents are worried by all this. Their worry showed in a 2005 national poll in which 76% of parents said that raising children was "a lot harder" than it was when they were growing up ("A Lot Easier Said"). But just as most popular TV shows don't give a realistic view of American teens, these frightening books and statistics do not provide a complete picture of what's going on in families today. The fact is that not all teens and families are lost and without values. While they struggle with problems in our culture like everyone else, successful families are doing what they've always done: finding ways to protect and nurture their children. They are fighting the battle for their families in three ways: by fighting against the loss of quality family time, by fighting against the loss of community, and by fighting against the influence of the media.

It's true that these days parents face more challenges than ever before when it comes to finding quality time to spend with their children. The economist Edward Wolff explains the loss of time:

Over a thirty-year time span, parental time has declined 13%. The time parents have available for their children has been squeezed by

---

Margin annotations:

Double- space lines of the text. Leave a one-inch margin all the way around the page. Your name and the page number should be typed one-half inch from the top of the page.

Common knowledge is not documented.

This typical citation shows the source by giving the author's last name or (as here, if no author is provided) the title of the article (and if relevant, a page number). "Works Cited" then provides full information about the source.

Thesis, followed by plan of development.

Source is identified by name and area of expertise.

the rapid shift of mothers into the paid labor force, by escalating

divorce rates and the subsequent abandonment of children by their

fathers, and by an increase in the number of hours required on the

job. The average worker is now at work 163 hours a year more than

in 1969, which adds up to an extra month of work annually (qtd. in

Hewlett and West 48).

As a result, more children are at home alone than ever before. And
this situation does leave children vulnerable to getting into trouble.
Richardson and others, in their study of five thousand eighth graders in
California, found that children who were home alone after school were
twice as likely to experiment with drugs and alcohol as children who had
a parent (or another adult) home in the after-school hours.

But creative parents still come up with ways to be there for their
kids. For some, it's been a matter of cutting back on working hours
and living more simply. For example, in her book <u>The Shelter of Each
Other</u>, Mary Pipher tells the story of a couple with three-year-old twin
boys. Eduardo worked sixty-hour weeks at a factory. Sabrina supervised
checkers at a Kmart, cared for the boys, and tried to watch over her
mother, who had cancer. Money was tight, especially, since day care
was expensive and the parents felt they had to keep the twins stylishly
dressed and supplied with new toys. The parents were stressed over
money problems, their lack of time together, and especially, having so
little time with their boys. It bothered them that the twins had begun to
cry when their parents picked them up at day care, as if they'd rather stay
with the day care workers. Finally, Sabrina and Eduardo made a difficult
decision. Sabrina quit her job, and the couple invited her mother (whose
illness was in remission) to live with them. With three adults pooling their
resources, Sabrina and Eduardo found that they could manage without
Sabrina's salary. The family no longer ate out, and they gave up their cable
TV. Their sons loved having their grandmother in the house. Sabrina was

Direct quotations of five typed lines or more are indented ten spaces (or one inch) from the left margin. Quotation marks are not used.

The abbreviation *qtd.* means *quoted*. No comma is used between the author name and the page number.

When citing a work in general, not part of a work, it is best to include the author's name in the text instead of using a parenthetical citation. No page number is needed, as the citation refers to the overall findings of the study.

able to begin doing relaxed, fun projects with the boys. They planted a garden and built a sandbox together. Sabrina observed, "I learned I could get off the merry-go-round" (195). Other parents have gotten off the merry-go-round by working at home, even if it means earning less money than they had previously.

Only the page number is needed, as the author has already been named in the text.

Some parents even homeschool their children as a way to be sure they have plenty of time together. Homeschooling used to be thought of as a choice made only by very religious people or back-to-nature radicals. Now, teaching children at home is much less unusual. It's estimated that as many as two million American children are being homeschooled. Harvard even has an admissions officer whose job it is to review applications from homeschooled kids. Parents who homeschool have different reasons, but according to a cover story in <u>Newsweek</u>, "some . . . are looking for a way to reclaim family closeness in an increasingly fast-paced society. . . . Still others worry about unsavory influences in school—drugs, alcohol, sex, violence" (Kantrowitz and Wingert 66). Homeschooling is no guarantee that a child will resist those temptations, but some families do believe it's a great way to promote family closeness. One fifteen-year-old, homeschooled since kindergarten, explained why he liked the way he'd been raised and educated. He ended by saying, "Another way I'm different is that I love my family. One guy asked me if I'd been brainwashed. I think it's spooky that liking my family is considered crazy" (Pipher 103).

Many parents can't quit their jobs or teach their children at home. But some parents find a second way to nurture their children, through building community ties. They help their children develop a healthy sense of belonging by creating links with positive, constructive people and activities. In the past, community wasn't so hard to find. In <u>The Way We Really Are</u>, Stephanie Coontz writes, "Right up through the 1940s, ties of work, friendship, neighborhood, ethnicity, extended kin, and voluntary organizations were as important a source of identity for most Americans, and sometimes a <u>more</u> important source of obligation, than marriage and the nuclear family" (37). Even when today's parents were teenagers, neighborhoods were places where kids felt a sense of belonging and responsibility. But today "parents . . . mourn the disappearance of neighborhoods where a web of relatives and friends kept a close eye on everyone's kids. And they worry their own children grow up isolated, knowing more about the cast of <u>Friends</u> than the people in surrounding homes" (Donahue D1).

One way that some families are trying to build old-fashioned community is through "intentional community," or "cohousing." Begun in Denmark in 1972, the cohousing movement is modeled after the traditional village. It brings together a number of families who live in separate houses but share some common space. For instance, families might share central meeting rooms, dining areas, gardens, day care, workshops, or office space. They might own tools and lawn mowers together, rather than each household having its own. The point is that they treat their neighbors as extended family, not as strangers. As described by the online site <u>Cohousing.org</u>, cohousing is "a type of collaborative housing that attempts to overcome the alienation of modern subdivisions in which no one knows their neighbors, and there is no sense of community." In its 2007 database, the Intentional Communities Web site estimates that over one thousand such communities exist in North America.

Other families turn to religion as a source of community. Michael Medved and Diane Medved, authors of <u>Saving Childhood</u>, are raising their family in a religious Jewish home. Their children attend Jewish schools, go to synagogue, and follow religious customs. They frequently visit, eat, play with, and are cared for by neighboring Jewish families. The Medveds

Ellipsis points show where the student has omitted material from the original source. The quoted material is not capitalized because the student has blended it into a sentence with an introductory phrase.

believe their family is stronger because of their belief "in planting roots—in your home, in your family, in your community. That involves making a commitment, making an investment both physically and emotionally, in your surroundings" (200). Other religious traditions offer families a similar sense of community, purpose, and belonging. Marcus and Tracy Glover are members of the Nation of Islam. They credit the Nation with making their marriage and family strong and breaking a three-generation cycle of single motherhood (Hewlett and West 201–02).

A third way that families are fighting to protect their children is by controlling the impact of the media and technology. Hewlett and West and Pipher use similar words to describe this impact. As they describe growing up today, Hewlett and West write about children living "without a skin" (xiii), and Pipher writes about "houses without walls" (12). These authors mean that today—unlike in the old days, when children were protected from the outside world while they were in their homes—the home offers little protection. Even in their own living rooms, all children have to do is to turn on a TV, radio, or computer to be hit with a flood of violence, sick humor, and often weird sexuality. Children are growing up watching shows like The Osbournes, a program that celebrated two spoiled, foul-mouthed children and their father—a burned-out rock star slowed by years of carefree drug abuse. A recent article in Science magazine offered the most damning link yet between TV watching and antisocial behavior. Reporting on the results of its seventeen-year study that followed viewers from youth to adulthood, Science found that the more television a teen watched, the higher the chances he or she would commit violent acts later in life. Of kids who watched an hour or less of TV a day, fewer than 6% of teens went on to commit assaults, robberies, or other violent acts as adults. But nearly 28% of teens who watched TV three or more hours a day did commit crimes of violence. Sadly, many parents seem to have given up even trying to protect their growing kids

Cited material extends from one page to another, so both page numbers are given.

against the flood of televised garbage. They are like the mother quoted in <u>USA Today</u> as saying, "How can I fight five hundred channels on TV?" (Donahue D1).

Fortunately, some parents are still insisting on control over the information and entertainment that comes into their homes. Some subscribe to "The Television Project," an online educational organization that helps parents "understand how television affects their families and community and proposes alternatives that foster positive emotional, cognitive and spiritual development within families and communities." Others ban TV entirely from their homes. More try to find a way to use TV and other electronics as helpful tools but not allow them to dominate their homes. One family in Nebraska, the Millers, who homeschool their children, described to Mary Pipher their attitude toward TV. They hadn't owned a TV for years, but they bought one so that they could watch the Olympics. The set is now stored in a closet unless a program is on that the family agrees is worthwhile. Some programs the Millers have enjoyed together include the World Cup soccer games, the TV drama <u>Sarah Plain and Tall</u>, and an educational TV course in sign language. Pipher was impressed by the Miller children, and she thought their limited exposure to TV was one reason why. In her words,

> Calm, happy children and relaxed, confident parents are so rare today. Probably most notable were the long attention spans of the children and their willingness to sit and listen to the grown-ups talk. The family had a manageable amount of information to deal with. They weren't stressed by more information than they could assimilate. The kids weren't overstimulated and edgy. Nor were they sexualized in the way most kids now are. (107)

Pipher's words describe children raised by parents who won't give in to the idea that their children are lost. Such parents structure ways to be present in the home, build family ties to a community, and control the

The conclusion provides a summary and restates the thesis.

impact of the media in their homes. Through their efforts, they succeed in raising nurtured, grounded, successful children. Such parents acknowledge the challenges of raising kids in today's America, but they are up to the job.

Works cited should be double-spaced. Titles of books, magazines, and the like should be underlined.

Include the date you accessed a Web source—in the first case, 4 October 2007.

Several of these sources—*Public Agenda, Intentional Communities,* and the *Television Project*—are online. By going online and typing the letters after "www." in each citation, you can access any of the sources.

Works Cited

"A Lot Easier Said Than Done: Parents Talk about Raising Children in Today's America." Public Agenda. Oct. 2005. 4 Oct. 2007 <http://www.publicagenda.org/specials/parents/parents1.htm>.

Anderson, Craig A., and Brad J. Bushman. "The Effects of Media Violence on Society." Science 29 Mar. 2002: 2377–79.

Coontz, Stephanie. The Way We Really Are. New York: Basic Books, 1997.

Donahue, Deirdre. "Struggling to Raise Good Kids in Toxic Times." USA Today 1 Oct. 1998: D1+.

Hewlett, Sylvia Ann, and Cornel West. The War Against Parents. Boston: Houghton Mifflin, 1998.

The Intentional Communities Home Page. Fellowship of Intentional Communities. 2 Sept. 2007 <http://www.ic.org/>.

Kantrowitz, Barbara, and Pat Wingert. "Learning at Home: Does It Pass the Test?" Newsweek 5 Oct. 1998: 64–70.

Medved, Michael, and Diane Medved. Saving Childhood. New York: HarperCollins, 1998.

Pipher, Mary. The Shelter of Each Other. New York: Putnam, 1996.

The Television Project Home Page. The Television Project. 2 Feb. 2007 <http://www.tvp.org>.

"What Is Cohousing?" Cohousing. The Cohousing Association of the United States. 10 Sept. 2006: 10 pars. 2 Feb. 2007 <http://www.cohousing.org/resources/whatis.html>.

© Zave Smith/Corbis

Although the student writer of the research paper emphasized the impact of TV on children, she referred to the computer as another source of "violence, sick humor, and often weird sexuality." In your opinion, which do you feel is more dangerous for children when unsupervised, the computer or the TV? Why?

Handbook of Sentence Skills

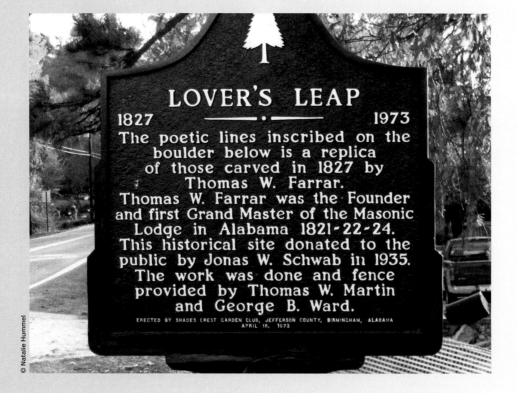

How could you change this sign's wording to make it grammatically correct? What specific errors have been made?

Grammar

© Bill Aron/PhotoEdit

Can you find any sentence-skills errors in the sign pictured above? What are they?

Subjects and Verbs

23

This chapter will explain two of the basic building blocks of English sentences: subjects and verbs.

KEY TERMS

auxiliary verbs: verbs that work with the main verb to make up the complete verb in a sentence; also called helping verbs. Example: *The woman is working.* (Auxiliary verb: working)

linking verbs: verbs that help describe a subject by connecting it to another word. Example: *The man is handsome.* (Linking verb: is)

preposition: one of a group of words that precede a noun or pronoun and indicate direction, position, placement, duration, or another kind of connection to the other words in the sentence. Examples: *about, above, through, under, with.*

subject: who or what a sentence speaks about; usually a noun or pronoun that acts, is acted upon, or is described. Example: *The boy cries.* (Subject: boy)

verb: what the sentence says about the subject; a word that shows what a subject does or that helps describe the subject by linking it to an adjective. Example: *The boy cries.* (Verb: cries)

The basic building blocks of English sentences are subjects and verbs. Understanding them is an important first step toward mastering a number of sentence skills.

Every sentence has a subject and a verb. Who or what the sentence speaks about is called the *subject;* what the sentence says about the subject is called the *verb.* In the following sentences, the subject is underlined once and the verb twice.

The boy cried.

That fish smells.

Many people applied for the job.

The show is a documentary.

A Simple Way to Find a Subject

To find a subject, ask *who* or *what* the sentence is about. As shown below, your answer is the subject.

Who is the first sentence about? The boy

What is the second sentence about? That fish

Who is the third sentence about? Many people

What is the fourth sentence about? The show

A Simple Way to Find a Verb

To find a verb, ask what the sentence *says about* the subject. As shown below, your answer is the verb.

What does the first sentence *say about* the boy? He cried.

What does the second sentence *say about* the fish? It smells.

What does the third sentence *say about* the people? They applied.

What does the fourth sentence *say about* the show? It is a documentary.

A second way to find the verb is to put *I, you, we, he, she, it,* or *they* in front of the word you think is a verb. If the result makes sense, you have a verb. For example, you could put *he* in front of *cried* in the first sentence, with the result, *he cried,* making sense. Therefore, you know that *cried* is a verb. You could use the same test with the other three verbs as well.

Finally, it helps to remember that most verbs show action. In the sentences already considered, the three action verbs are *cried, smells,* and *applied.* Certain other verbs, known as *linking verbs,* do not show action. They do, however, give information about the subject. In "The show is a documentary," the linking verb *is* joins the subject (*show*) with a word that identifies or describes it (*documentary*). Other common linking verbs include *am, are, was, were, feel, appear, look, become,* and *seem.*

In each of the following sentences, draw one line under the subject and two lines under the verb.

1. The ripening tomatoes glistened on the sunny windowsill.

2. Acupuncture reduces the pain of my headaches.

3. Elena twisted a strand of hair around her fingers.

4. My brother built his bookshelves from cinder blocks and wood planks.

5. A jackrabbit bounds up to fifteen feet in one leap.

6. The singer's diamond earrings sparkled in the spotlight.

7. My roommate crashed his car on the icy highway.

8. On St. Patrick's Day, our neighborhood tavern serves green beer.

9. My six-year-old brother survives on a diet of peanut butter and jelly.

10. During my parents' divorce, I felt like a rag doll being torn between two people.

More about Subjects and Verbs

1. A sentence may have more than one verb, more than one subject, or several subjects and verbs.

   The <u>engine</u> <u><u>coughed</u></u> and <u><u>sputtered</u></u>.

   Broken <u>glass</u> and empty <u>cans</u> <u><u>littered</u></u> the parking lot.

   <u>Marta</u>, <u>Nilsa</u>, and <u>Robert</u> <u><u>met</u></u> after class and <u><u>headed</u></u> downtown.

2. The subject of the sentence never appears within a prepositional phrase. A *prepositional phrase* is simply a group of words that begins with a preposition. Following is a list of common prepositions.

www.mhhe.com/langan

Prepositions

about	before	by	inside	over
above	behind	during	into	through
across	below	except	like	to
among	beneath	for	of	toward
around	beside	from	off	under
at	between	in	on, onto	with

Crossing out prepositional phrases will help you find the subject or subjects of a sentence.

A stream ~~of cold air~~ seeps in ~~through the space below the door~~.

Specks ~~of dust~~ dance gently ~~in a ray of sunlight~~.

The people ~~in the apartment above ours~~ fight loudly.

The murky waters ~~of the polluted lake~~ spilled ~~over the dam~~.

The amber lights ~~on its sides~~ outlined the tractor-trailer ~~in the hazy dusk~~.

3. Many verbs consist of more than one word. (The extra verbs are called *auxiliary*, or *helping*, verbs.) Here, for example, are some of the many forms of the verb *work*.

Forms of *work*		
work	worked	should work
works	were working	will be working
does work	have worked	can work
is working	had worked	could be working
are working	had been working	must have worked

4. Words like *not, just, never, only,* and *always* are not part of the verb, although they may appear within the verb.

Ruby has never liked cold weather.

Our boss will not be singing with the choir this year.

The intersection has not always been this dangerous.

5. A verb preceded by *to* is never the verb of a sentence.

At night, my son likes to read under the covers.

Evelyn decided to separate from her husband.

6. An *-ing* word by itself is never the verb of a sentence. (It may be part of the verb, but it must have a helping verb in front of it.) The following is *not* a sentence, because the verb is not complete:

They going on a trip this weekend.

This *is* a sentence:

They are going on a trip this weekend.

Draw a single line under subjects and a double line under verbs. Cross out prepositional phrases as necessary to find the subjects.

Activity

2

1. A thick layer of dust covers the top of our refrigerator.

2. In June, sagging Christmas decorations were still hanging in the windows of the abandoned house.

3. The people in the all-night coffee shop seemed weary and lost.

4. Every plant in the dim room bent toward the small window.

5. A glaring headline about the conviction of a local congressman attracted my attention.

6. Two of the biggest stores in the mall are going out of business.

7. The battery tester's tiny red lights suddenly started to flicker.

8. A neighbor of mine does all her work at home and e-mails it to her office.

9. The jar of peppercorns tumbled from the spice shelf and shattered on the floor.

10. The scar in the hollow of Brian's throat is the result of an emergency operation to clear his windpipe.

Review Test 1

Draw a single line under subjects and a double line under verbs. Cross out prepositional phrases as necessary to find the subjects.

1. With one graceful motion, the shortstop fielded the grounder and threw to first base.

2. Like human mothers, sheep and goat mothers develop close bonds with their babies.

3. Before class, Antonietta and Jorge rushed to the coffee machine in the hall.

4. I shifted uncomfortably on the lumpy mattress before falling into a restless sleep.

5. Waiting in the long ticket line, Matt shifted his weight from one foot to the other.

6. Ancient Egyptians were branding cattle more than four thousand years ago.

7. Dogs and cats crowded the veterinarian's office on Monday morning.

8. The driver abruptly halted her Jeep and backed up toward a narrow parking place.

9. During the American Revolution, some brides rejected white wedding gowns and wore red as a symbol of rebellion.

10. The little girl's frantic family called a psychic to locate the child.

Fragments

This chapter will explain how to avoid the most common types of fragments. A fragment is a word group that lacks a subject or a verb and/or one that does not express a complete thought.

FRAGMENT:

Whenever I go to school.

"Whenever," a dependent word, cannot introduce a complete thought, so it cannot stand alone.

CORRECT SENTENCE:

Whenever I go to school, I take the bus.

The fragment introduces a complete thought.

Every sentence must have a subject and a verb and must express a complete thought. A word group that lacks a subject or a verb and does not express a complete thought is a *fragment.* Following are the most common types of fragments that people write:

1. Dependent-word fragments
2. *-ing* and *to* fragments
3. Added-detail fragments
4. Missing-subject fragments

Once you understand what specific kinds of fragments you might write, you should be able to eliminate them from your writing. The following pages explain all four types.

Dependent-Word Fragments

www.mhhe.com/langan

Some word groups that begin with a dependent word are fragments. Following is a list of common dependent words. Whenever you start a sentence with one of these words, you must be careful that a fragment does not result.

Dependent Words		
after	if, even if	when, whenever
although, though	in order that	where, wherever
as	since	whether
because	that, so that	which, whichever
before	unless	while
even though	until	who
how	what, whatever	whose

In the example below, the word group beginning with the dependent word *After* is a fragment:

After I cashed my paycheck. I treated myself to dinner.

A *dependent statement*—one starting with a dependent word like *after*—cannot stand alone. It depends on another statement to complete the thought. *After I cashed my paycheck* is a dependent statement. It leaves us hanging. We expect to find out, in the same sentence, *what happened after* the writer cashed the check. When a writer does not follow through and complete a thought, a fragment results.

To correct the fragment, simply follow through and complete the thought:

After I cashed my paycheck, I treated myself to dinner.

Remember, then, that *dependent statements by themselves are fragments.* They must be attached to a statement that makes sense standing alone.

Here are two other examples of dependent-word fragments:

I won't leave the house. Until I hear from you.

Rick finally picked up the socks. That he had thrown on the floor days ago.

Until I hear from you is a fragment; it does not make sense standing by itself. We want to know in the same statement *what cannot happen* until I hear from you. The writer must complete the thought. Likewise, *That he had thrown on the floor days ago* is not in itself a complete thought. We want to know in the same statement what *that* refers to.

How to Correct a Dependent-Word Fragment

In most cases you can correct a dependent-word fragment by attaching it to the sentence that comes after it or to the sentence that comes before it. Look at how the fragments above have been converted:

After I cashed my paycheck, I treated myself to dinner.

(The fragment has been attached to the sentence that comes after it.)

I won't leave the house until I hear from you.

(The fragment has been attached to the sentence that comes before it.)

Rick finally picked up the socks that he had thrown on the floor days ago.

(The fragment has been attached to the sentence that comes before it.)

Another way of connecting a dependent-word fragment is simply to eliminate the dependent word by rewriting the sentence:

I cashed my paycheck and then treated myself to dinner.

I will wait to hear from you.

He had thrown them on the floor days ago.

TIPS

a. Use a comma if a dependent-word group comes at the *beginning* of a sentence (see also page 567):

After I cashed my paycheck, I treated myself to dinner.

However, do not generally use a comma if the dependent word group comes at the *end* of a sentence.

I won't leave the house until I hear from you.

Rick finally picked up the socks that he had thrown on the floor days ago.

(continued)

b. Sometimes the dependent words *who, that, which,* or *where* appear not at the very start but *near* the start of a word group. A fragment often results:

I drove slowly past the old brick house. The place where I grew up.

The place where I grew up is not in itself a complete thought. We want to know in the same statement *where was the place* the writer grew up. The fragment can be corrected by attaching it to the sentence that comes before it:

I drove slowly past the old brick house, the place where I grew up.

Activity 1

Turn each of the following dependent-word groups into a sentence by adding a complete thought. Use a comma after the dependent-word group if a dependent word starts the sentence. Note the examples.

EXAMPLES

Although I felt miserable

Although I felt miserable, I tried to smile for the photographer.

The man who found my wallet

The man who found my wallet returned it the next day.

1. If I don't get a raise soon

2. Because it was raining

3. When I heard the news

4. Because I couldn't find the car keys

5. The restaurant that we tried

_____

_____

Underline the dependent-word fragment in each item. Then rewrite the items, correcting each fragment by attaching it to the sentence that comes before or the sentence that comes after it—whichever sounds more natural. Use a comma after the dependent-word group if it starts the sentence.

1. Whenever I spray deodorant. My cat arches her back. She thinks she is hearing a hissing enemy.

_____

_____

2. My father, a salesman, was on the road all week. We had a great time playing football in the house. Until he came home for the weekend.

_____

_____

3. If Kim takes too long saying good-bye to her boyfriend. Her father will start flicking the porch light. Then he will come out with a flashlight.

_____

_____

4. Scientists are studying mummified remains. That are thousands of years old. Most of the people were killed by parasites.

_____

_____

5. After I got to class. I realized my report was still on the kitchen table. I had been working there the night before.

_____

_____

-*ing* and *to* Fragments

When an -*ing* word appears at or near the start of a word group, a fragment may result. Such fragments often lack a subject and part of the verb. In the items on the following page, underline the word groups that contain -*ing* words. Each is a fragment.

www.mhhe.com/langan

1. Ellen walked all over the neighborhood yesterday. Trying to find her dog Bo. Several people claimed they had seen him only hours before.

2. We sat back to watch the movie. Not expecting anything special. To our surprise, we clapped, cheered, and cried for the next two hours.

3. I telephoned the balloon store. It being the day before our wedding anniversary. I knew my wife would be surprised to receive a dozen heart-shaped balloons.

People sometimes write *-ing* fragments because they think that the subject of one sentence will work for the next word group as well. Thus, in item 1 the writer thinks that the subject *Ellen* in the opening sentence will also serve as the subject for *Trying to find her dog Bo*. But the subject must be in the same sentence.

How to Correct -ing Fragments

1. Attach the fragment to the sentence that comes before it or the sentence that comes after it, whichever makes sense. Item 1 could read "Ellen walked all over the neighborhood yesterday trying to find her dog Bo."

2. Add a subject and change the *-ing* verb part to the correct form of the verb. Item 2 could read "We didn't expect anything special."

3. Change *being* to the correct form of the verb be *(am, are, is, was, were)*. Item 3 could read "It was the day before our wedding anniversary."

How to Correct to Fragments

When *to* appears at or near the start of a word group, a fragment sometimes results:

At the Chinese restaurant, Tim used chopsticks. To impress his date. He spent one hour eating a small bowl of rice.

The second word group is a fragment and can be corrected by adding it to the preceding sentence:

At the Chinese restaurant, Tim used chopsticks to impress his date.

Activity 3

Underline the *-ing* fragment in each of the following items. Then correct the item by using the method described in parentheses.

EXAMPLE

Stepping hard on the accelerator. Armon tried to beat the truck to the intersection. He lost by a hood.
(Add the fragment to the sentence that comes after it.)

Stepping hard on the accelerator, Armon tried to beat the truck to the

intersection.

1. Marble-sized hailstones fell from the sky. Flattening the young plants in the cornfield. A year's work was lost in an hour.
   (Add the fragment to the preceding sentence.)

   _____

   _____

2. A noisy fire truck suddenly raced down the street. Coming to a stop at my house. My home security system had sent a false alarm.
   (Correct the fragment by adding the subject *it* and changing *coming* to the proper form of the verb, *came*.)

   _____

   _____

3. My phone doesn't ring. Instead, a light on it blinks. The reason for this being that I am partially deaf.
   (Correct the fragment by changing *being* to the proper form of the verb, *is*.)

   _____

   _____

Underline the *-ing* or *to* fragment in each item. Then rewrite each item, correcting the fragment by using one of the three methods described above.

1. Looking at the worm on the table. Shelby groaned. She knew she wouldn't like what the biology teacher said next.

   _____

   _____

2. I put a box of baking soda in the freezer. To get rid of the musty smell. However, my ice cubes still taste like old socks.

   _____

   _____

3. Staring at the clock on the far wall. I nervously began my speech. I was afraid to look at any of the people in the room.

   _____

   _____

4. Jerome sat quietly at his desk. Fantasizing about the upcoming weekend. He might meet the girl of his dreams at Saturday night's party.

_____

_____

5. To get to the bus station from here. You have to walk two blocks out of your way. The sidewalk is torn up because of construction work.

_____

_____

Added-Detail Fragments

Added-detail fragments lack a subject and a verb. They often begin with one of the following words:

also	especially	except	for example
like	including	such as	

Underline the one added-detail fragment in each of the following items:

1. Before a race, I eat starchy foods. Such as bread and spaghetti. The carbohydrates provide quick energy.
2. Bob is taking a night course in auto mechanics. Also, one in plumbing. He wants to save money on household repairs.
3. My son keeps several pets in his room. Including hamsters and mice.

People often write added-detail fragments for much the same reason they write *-ing* fragments. They think the subject and verb in one sentence will serve for the next word group. But the subject and verb must be in *each* word group.

How to Correct Added-Detail Fragments

1. Attach the fragment to the complete thought that precedes it. Item 1 could read "Before a race, I eat starchy foods such as bread and spaghetti."
2. Add a subject and a verb to the fragment to make it a complete sentence. Item 2 could read "Bob is taking a night course in auto mechanics. Also, he is taking one in plumbing."
3. Insert the fragment within the preceding sentence. Item 3 could read "My son keeps several pets, including hamsters and mice, in his room."

Underline the fragment in each of the following items. Then make it a sentence by rewriting it, using the method described in parentheses.

EXAMPLE

My mother likes watching daytime television shows. <u>Especially old movies and soap operas.</u> She says that daytime television is less violent.
(Add the fragment to the preceding sentence.)

My mother likes watching daytime television shows, especially old movies

and soap operas.

1. Luis works evenings in a video store. He enjoys the fringe benefits. For example, seeing the new movies first.
   (Correct the fragment by adding the subject and verb *he sees*.)

   _____

   _____

2. Bob's fingernails are ragged from years of working as a mechanic. And his fingertips are always black. Like ink pads.
   (Attach the fragment to the preceding sentence.)

   _____

   _____

3. Electronic devices keep getting smaller. Such as video cameras and cell phones. Some are so tiny they look like toys.
   (Correct the fragment by inserting it in the preceding sentence.)

   _____

   _____

Underline the added-detail fragment in each item. Then rewrite to correct the fragment. Use one of the three methods described on the previous page.

1. Left-handed students face problems. For example, right-handed desks. Spiral notebooks can also be uncomfortable to use.

   _____

   _____

2. Mrs. Fields always wears her lucky clothes to bingo. Such as a sweater printed with four-leaf clovers. She also carries a rhinestone horseshoe.

   _____

   _____

3. Hundreds of moths were swarming around the stadium lights. Like large flecks of snow. However, I knew they couldn't be snow—it was eighty degrees outside.

_____

_____

4. Trevor buys and sells paper collectors' items. For instance, comic books and movie posters. He sets up a display at local flea markets and carnivals.

_____

_____

5. I wonder now why I had to learn certain subjects. Such as geometry. No one has ever asked me about the hypotenuse of a triangle.

_____

_____

www.mhhe.com/langan

Missing-Subject Fragments

In each item below, underline the word group in which the subject is missing:

1. Alicia loved getting wedding presents. But hated writing thank-you notes.
2. Mickey has orange soda and potato chips for breakfast. Then eats more junk food, like root beer and cookies, for lunch.

How to Correct Missing-Subject Fragments

1. Attach the fragment to the preceding sentence. Item 1 could read "Alicia loved getting wedding presents but hated writing thank-you notes."
2. Add a subject (which can often be a pronoun standing for the subject in the preceding sentence). Item 2 could read "Then he eats more junk food, like root beer and cookies, for lunch."

Activity

7

Underline the missing-subject fragment in each item. Then rewrite that part of the item needed to correct the fragment. Use one of the two methods of correction described above.

1. Every other day, Kara runs two miles. Then does fifty sit-ups. She hasn't lost weight, but she looks trimmer and more muscular.

_____

_____

2. I like all kinds of fresh pizza. But refuse to eat frozen pizza. The sauce is always dried out, and the crust tastes like leather.

_____

_____

3. Many people are allergic to seafood. They break out in hives when they eat it. And can even have trouble breathing.

_____

_____

4. To distract me, the dentist tugged at a corner of my mouth. Then jabbed a needle into my gums and injected a painkiller. I hardly felt it.

_____

_____

5. Last semester, I took six courses. And worked part-time in a discount drugstore. Now that the term is all over, I don't know how I did it.

_____

_____

www.mhhe.com/langan

A Review: How to Check for Sentence Fragments

1. Read your paper aloud from the *last* sentence to the *first*. You will be better able to see and hear whether each word group you read is a complete thought.

2. If you think a word group may be a fragment, ask yourself, Does this contain a subject and a verb and express a complete thought?

3. More specifically, be on the lookout for the most common fragments:
   • Dependent-word fragments (starting with words like *after, because, since, when,* and *before*)
   • *-ing* and *to* fragments (*-ing* and *to* at or near the start of a word group)
   • Added-detail fragments (starting with words like *for example, such as, also,* and *especially*)
   • Missing-subject fragments (a verb is present but not the subject)

Review Test 1

Each word group in the following student paragraph is numbered. In the space provided, write C if a word group is a complete sentence; write F if it is a fragment. You will find eight fragments in the paragraph.

_____ 1. [1]I'm starting to think that there is no safe place left. [2]To ride

_____ 2. a bicycle. [3]When I try to ride on the highway, to

_____ 3. go school. [4]I feel like a rabbit being pursued by predators.

_____ 4. [5]Drivers whip past me at high speeds. [6]And try to see how

_____ 5. close they can get to my bike without actually killing me.

_____ 6. [7]When they pull onto the shoulder of the road or make a

_____ 7. right turn. [8]Drivers completely ignore my vehicle. [9]On city

_____ 8. streets, I feel more like a cockroach than a rabbit. [10]Drivers

_____ 9. in the city despise bicycles. [11]Regardless of an approaching

_____ 10. bike rider. [12]Street-side car doors will unexpectedly open.

_____ 11. [13]Frustrated drivers who are stuck in traffic will make nasty

_____ 12. comments. [14]Or shout out obscene propositions. [15]Even

_____ 13. pedestrians in the city show their disregard for me. [16]While

_____ 14. jaywalking across the street. [17]The pedestrian will treat

_____ 15. me, a law-abiding bicyclist, to a withering look of disdain.

_____ 16. [18]Pedestrians may even cross my path deliberately. [19]As if to

_____ 17. prove their higher position in the pecking order of the city

_____ 18. streets. [20]Today, bicycling can be hazardous to the rider's

_____ 19. health.

_____ 20.

Now (on separate paper) correct the fragments you have found. Attach the fragments to sentences that come before or after them or make whatever other change is needed to turn each fragment into a sentence.

Review Test   2

Underline the two fragments in each item below. Then make whatever changes are needed to turn the fragments into sentences.

EXAMPLE

Sharon was going to charge her new suit_x <u>*b*But then decided to pay cash instead.</u> She remembered her New Year's resolution_x <u>*t*To cut down on her use of credit cards.</u>

1. We both began to tire. As we passed the halfway mark in the race. But whenever I'd hear Reggie's footsteps behind me. I would pump my legs faster.

2. I have a few phobias. Such as fear of heights and fear of dogs. My nightmare is to be trapped in a hot-air balloon. With three German shepherds.

3. Punching all the buttons on his radio in sequence. Phil kept looking for a good song. He was in the mood to cruise down the highway. And sing at the top of his voice.

4. My children joke that we celebrate "Hanumas." With our Jewish neighbors. We share Hanukkah and Christmas activities. Including making potato pancakes at their house and decorating our tree.

5. I noticed two cartons of cigarettes. Sticking up out of my neighbor's trash bag. I realized he had made up his mind. To give up smoking for the fifth time this year.

6. I've decided to leave home. And rent an apartment. By being away from home and on my own. I will get along better with my parents.

7. The alley behind our house was flat. Except for a wide groove in the center. We used to sail paper boats down the groove. Whenever it rained hard enough to create a "river" there.

8. Don passed the computer school's aptitude test. Which qualifies him for nine months of training. Don kidded that anyone could be accepted. If he or she had $4,000.

Review Test 3

Turn each of the following word groups into a complete sentence.

EXAMPLES

With trembling hands

With trembling hands, I headed for the front of the classroom.

As the race wore on

Some runners dropped out as the race wore on.

1. After the storm passed

   _____

2. Such as fresh fruits and vegetables

   _____

3. During the mystery movie

   _____

4. Unless I study harder

   _____

5. Enrique, who works at his uncle's restaurant

   _____

6. Knocking over the table

   _____

7. To get to class on time

   _____

8. Hurrying to get dressed

   _____

9. Up in the attic

   _____

10. Losing my temper

    _____

Run-Ons

Run-ons are two complete thoughts that are run together with no adequate sign given to mark the break between them. In this text, the term "run-on" refers to both comma splices and fused sentences.

KEY TERMS

clause: a group of words having a subject and a verb.

comma splice: a comma incorrectly used to connect ("splice" together) two complete thoughts. Example:

> Comma splice: *I go to school, my brother stays home.*

> Correct sentences: *I go to school. My brother stays home.*

dependent clause: a group of words having a subject and a verb that does not express a complete thought and is not able to stand alone; also called a subordinate clause.

fused sentence: a run-on with no punctuation to mark the break between thoughts. Example:

> Fused sentence: *I go to school my brother stays home.*

> Correct sentences: *I go to school. My brother stays home.*

independent clause: a group of words having a subject and a verb that expresses a complete thought and is able to stand alone.

What Are Run-Ons?

A *run-on* is two complete thoughts that are run together with no adequate sign given to mark the break between them.*

Some run-ons have no punctuation at all to mark the break between the thoughts. Such run-ons are known as *fused sentences:* they are fused, or joined together, as if they were only one thought.

Fused Sentences

The bus stopped suddenly, I spilled coffee all over my shirt.

Mario told everyone in the room to be quiet his favorite show was on.

In other run-ons, known as *comma splices,* a comma is used to connect, or "splice" together, the two complete thoughts. However, a comma alone is *not enough* to connect two complete thoughts. Some stronger connection than a comma alone is needed.

Comma Splices

The bus stopped suddenly, I spilled coffee all over my shirt.

Mario told everyone in the room to be quiet, his favorite show was on.

Comma splices are the most common kind of run-on. Students sense that some kind of connection is needed between two thoughts, and so they often put a comma at the dividing point. But the comma alone is *not sufficient.* A stronger, clearer mark is needed between the two complete thoughts.

A Warning—Words That Can Lead to Run-Ons People often write run-ons when the second complete thought begins with one of the following words:

I	we	there	now
you	they	this	then
he, she, it	that	next	

Whenever you use one of these words in writing a paper, remember to be on the alert for run-ons.

---

* Some instructors regard all run-ons as fused sentences. But for many other instructors, and for our purposes in this book, the term *run-on* applies equally to fused sentences and comma splices. The bottom line is that you do not want either fused sentences or comma splices in your writing.

   Some instructors refer to each complete thought in a run-on as an *independent clause.* A *clause* is simply a group of words having a subject and a verb. A clause may be *independent* (expressing a complete thought and able to stand alone) or *dependent* (not expressing a complete thought and not able to stand alone). Using this terminology, we'd say that a run-on is two independent clauses run together with no adequate sign given to mark the break between them.

How to Correct Run-Ons

Here are three common methods of correcting a run-on:

1. Use a period and a capital letter to break the two complete thoughts into separate sentences:

   The bus stopped suddenly. I spilled coffee all over my shirt.

   Mario told everyone in the room to be quiet. His favorite show was on.

2. Use a comma and a joining word (*and, but, for, or, nor, so, yet*) to connect the two complete thoughts:

   The bus stopped suddenly, and I spilled coffee all over my shirt.

   Mario told everyone in the room to be quiet, for his favorite show was on.

3. Use a semicolon to connect the two complete thoughts:

   The bus stopped suddenly; I spilled coffee all over my shirt.

   Mario told everyone in the room to be quiet; his favorite show was on.

A fourth method of correcting a run-on is to use *subordination*. The following activities will give you practice in the first three methods. Subordination is described fully on pages 119–120, in the section of the book that deals with sentence variety.

Method 1: Period and a Capital Letter

One way of correcting a run-on is to use a period and a capital letter between the two complete thoughts. Use this method especially if the thoughts are not closely related or if another method would make the sentence too long.

In each of the following run-ons, locate the point at which one complete thought ends and another begins. Each is a *fused sentence*—that is, each consists of two sentences fused, or joined together, with no punctuation at all between them. Reading each sentence aloud will help you hear where a major break or split between the thoughts occurs. At such a point, your voice will probably drop and pause.

Correct the run-on by putting a period at the end of the first thought and a capital letter at the start of the next thought.

Activity

1

EXAMPLE

Bev's clock radio doesn't work anymore. She spilled a glass of soda on it.

1. The men at the door claimed to have paving material left over from another job they wanted to pave our driveway for a "bargain price."

2. Linh, a paralegal who speaks Vietnamese, helps other people from her country write wills she assists others by going with them when they have to appear in court.

3. Vicky has a unique style of dressing she wore a man's tuxedo with a red bow tie to her cousin's wedding.

4. In the summer, ants are attracted to water they will often enter a house through the dishwasher.

5. Humans have managed to adapt to any environment they can survive in Arctic wastes, tropical jungles, and barren deserts.

6. A five-year-old child knows over six thousand words he or she has also learned more than one thousand rules of grammar.

7. I rummaged around the crowded drawer looking for a pair of scissors then it suddenly stabbed me in the finger.

8. Squirrels like to jump from trees onto our roof their footsteps sound like ghosts running around our attic.

9. Today I didn't make good time driving to work every traffic light along the way was red.

10. Since I started using the Internet, I've sent hundreds of e-mails to my friends I never write letters by hand anymore.

Method 2: Comma and a Joining Word

Another way of correcting a run-on is to use a comma and a joining word to connect the two complete thoughts. Joining words (also called *conjunctions*) include *and, but, for, or, nor, so,* and *yet*. Here are what the four most common joining words mean:

and   in addition

Teresa works full time for an accounting firm, and she takes evening classes.

(*And* means *in addition:* Teresa works full time for an accounting firm; *in addition,* she takes evening classes.)

but   however, on the other hand

I turned to the want ads, but I knew my dream job wouldn't be listed.

(*But* means *however:* I turned to the want ads; *however,* I knew my dream job wouldn't be listed.)

for   because

Lizards become sluggish at night, for they need the sun's warmth to maintain an active body temperature.

(*For* means *because:* Lizards become sluggish at night *because* they need the sun's warmth to maintain an active body temperature.)

so   as a result, therefore

The canoe touched bottom, so Dave pushed it toward deeper water.

(*So* means *as a result:* The canoe touched bottom; *as a result,* Dave pushed it toward deeper water.)

Insert the joining word (*and, but, for, so*) that logically connects the two thoughts in each sentence.

1. Napoleon may have been a brave general, _____ he was afraid of cats.

2. The large dog was growling at me, _____ there were white bubbles of foam around its mouth.

3. The library had just closed, _____ I couldn't get any of the reserved books.

4. He checked on the new baby every five minutes, _____ he was afraid that something would happen to her.

5. Kate thought the milk was fresh, _____ it broke up into little sour flakes in her coffee.

6. Elephants have no thumbs, _____ baby elephants suck their trunks.

7. Lonnie heard a noise and looked out the window, _____ the only thing there was his reflection.

8. Although I like most creatures, I am not fond of snakes, _____ I like spiders even less.

9. My sister wants to exercise more and use her car less, _____ she walks to the grocery store.

10. Barry spends hours every day on his computer, _____ he often has the television on at the same time.

Activity **3**	Add a complete and closely related thought to go with each of the following statements. Use a comma and the indicated joining word when you write the second thought.

EXAMPLE

for I decided to leave school an hour early, _____

  for I had a pounding headache.

but 1. The corner store is convenient _____

_____

for 2. Leo attended night class _____

_____

and 3. Aisha studied for an hour before dinner _____

_____

so 4. Paul can't retrieve his e-mail _____

_____

but 5. I needed a haircut _____

_____

Activity **4**	Correct each run-on with either (1) a period and a capital letter or (2) a comma and a logical joining word. Do not use the same method of correction for every sentence.

Some of the run-ons are fused sentences (there is no punctuation between the two complete thoughts), and some are comma splices (there is only a comma between the two complete thoughts). One sentence is correct.

EXAMPLE

  There was a strange odor in the house, �ᵒBurt called the gas company immediately.

1. Antonio got a can of soda from the refrigerator, then he walked outside to sit on the porch steps.

2. Cockroaches adapt to any environment they have even been found living inside nuclear reactors.

3. My dog was panting from the heat I decided to wet him down with the garden hose.

4. Our science class is working on a weather project with students from Russia we communicate by computer almost every day.

5. The best-selling items in the zoo gift shop are the stuffed pandas and the polar-bear T-shirts the profits from these items help support the real animals in the zoo.

6. The bristles of the paintbrushes were very stiff, soaking them in turpentine made them soft again.

7. Chen borrows cassettes from the library to listen to on the way to work, some are music, and some are recordings of best-selling books.

8. Last week, Rita's two boys chased the babysitter out of the house, now the sitter won't come back.

9. We knew a power failure had occurred, for all the clocks in the building were forty-seven minutes slow.

10. I volunteered to run the Meals on Wheels service in our city we deliver hot meals to sick or housebound people.

Method 3: Semicolon

A third method of correcting a run-on is to use a semicolon to mark the break between two thoughts. A *semicolon* (;) looks like a period above a comma and is sometimes called a *strong comma*. A semicolon signals more of a pause than a comma alone but not quite the full pause of a period. When it is used to correct run-ons, the semicolon can be used alone or with a transitional word.

Semicolon Alone Here are some earlier sentences that were connected with a comma and a joining word. Now they are connected by a semicolon alone. Notice that the semicolon alone—unlike the comma alone—can be used to connect the two complete thoughts in each sentence:

Lonnie heard a noise and looked out the window; the only thing there was his reflection.

He checked on the new baby every five minutes; he was afraid something would happen to her.

Lizards become sluggish at night; they need the sun's warmth to maintain an active body temperature.

The large dog was growling at me; there were white bubbles of foam around its mouth.

We knew a power failure had occurred; all the clocks in the building were forty-seven minutes slow.

Using semicolons can add to sentence variety. For some people, however, the semicolon is a confusing punctuation mark. Keep in mind that if you are not comfortable using it, you can and should use one of the the first two methods of correcting run-ons.

Activity

5

Insert a semicolon where the break occurs between the two complete thoughts in each of the following sentences.

EXAMPLE

The plumber gave me an estimate of $260; I decided to repair the faucet myself.

1. The children stared at the artichokes on their plates they didn't know how to eat the strange vegetable.
2. I changed that lightbulb just last week now it's blown again.
3. The Great Wall of China is immense it's the only human construction visible from the Moon.
4. Elaine woke up at 3 a.m. to the smell of sizzling bacon her husband was having another insomnia attack.
5. Maya curled up under the covers she tried to get warm by grasping her icy feet with her chilly hands.
6. Three single mothers rent one house they share bills and help each other out.
7. Ice had formed on the inside edge of our window Joey scratched a *J* in it with his finger.
8. Charles peered into the microscope he saw only his own eyelashes.
9. A man in a bear suit walked slowly down the street the children stopped their play to stare at him.
10. I angrily punched a hole in the wall with my fist later I covered the hole with a picture.

Semicolon with a Transitional Word A semicolon can be used with a transitional word and a comma to join two complete thoughts. Here are some examples:

Larry believes in being prepared for emergencies; therefore, he stockpiles canned goods in his basement.

I tried to cash my paycheck; however, I had forgotten to bring identification.

Athletic shoes must fit perfectly; otherwise, wearers may injure their feet or ankles.

A short nap at the end of the day relaxes me; in addition, it gives me the energy to spend the evening on my homework.

Some zoo animals have not learned how to be good parents; as a result, baby animals are sometimes brought up in zoo nurseries and even in private homes.

People use seventeen muscles when they smile; on the other hand, they use forty-three muscles when they frown.

Following is a list of common transitional words (also known as *adverbial conjunctions*), with brief meanings.

Transitional Word	Meaning
however	but
nevertheless	however
on the other hand	however
instead	as a substitute
meanwhile	in the intervening time
otherwise	under other conditions
indeed	in fact
in addition	also, and
also	in addition
moreover	in addition
furthermore	in addition
as a result	thus, therefore
thus	as a result
consequently	as a result
therefore	as a result

For each sentence, choose a logical transitional word from the box above, and write it in the space provided. Use a semicolon *before* the connector and a comma *after* it.

Activity

6

EXAMPLE

I dread going to parties; _*however,*_ my husband loves meeting new people.

1. Jackie suffers from migraine headaches _____ her doctor has advised her to avoid caffeine and alcohol.

2. Ray's apartment is always neat and clean _____ the interior of his car looks like the aftermath of a tornado.

3. I try to attend all my math classes _____ I'll get too far behind to pass the weekly quizzes.

4. B.J. was singing Aretha Franklin tunes in the shower _____ his toast was burning in the kitchen.

5. The reporter was tough and experienced _____ even he was stunned by the tragic events.

A Note on Subordination

A fourth method of joining related thoughts is to use subordination. *Subordination* is a way of showing that one thought in a sentence is not as important as another thought. (Subordination is explained in full on pages 119–120.) Below are three earlier sentences, recast so that one idea is subordinated to (made less important than) the other idea. In each case, the subordinate (or less important) thought is underlined. Note that each subordinate clause begins with a dependent word.

<u>Because the library had just closed</u>, I couldn't get any of the reserved books.

<u>When the canoe touched bottom</u>, Dave pushed the craft toward deeper water.

I didn't make good time driving to work today <u>because every traffic light along the way was red.</u>

www.mhhe.com/langan

A Review: How to Check for Run-Ons

1. To see if a sentence is a run-on, read it aloud and listen for a break marking two complete thoughts. Your voice will probably drop and pause at the break.

2. To check an entire paper, read it aloud from the *last* sentence to the *first*. Doing so will help you hear and see each complete thought.

3. Be on the lookout for words that can lead to run-on sentences:

I	he, she, it	they	this	then	now
you	we	there	that	next	

(continued)

4. Correct run-ons by using one of the following methods:

Period and a capital letter

Comma and a joining word (*and, but, for, or, nor, so, yet*)

Semicolon, alone or with a transitional word

Subordination

Review Test 1

Correct each run-on with either (1) a period and a capital letter or (2) a comma (if needed) and the joining word *and, but, for,* or *so.* Do not use the same method of correction for every sentence.

Some of the run-ons are fused sentences (there is no punctuation between the two complete thoughts), and some are comma splices (there is only a comma between the two complete thoughts). One sentence is correct.

1. Our boss expects us to work four hours without a break, he wanders off to a vending machine at least once an hour.

2. The children in the next car were making faces at other drivers. when I made a face back, they giggled and sank out of sight.

3. Chuck bent over and lifted the heavy tray then he heard an ominous crack in his back.

4. The branches of the tree were bare they made a dark feathery pattern against the orange-pink sunset.

5. In the dark alley, the air smelled like rotten garbage a large rat crept in the shadows.

6. Our class wanted to do something for the earthquake victims, we sent a donation to the Red Cross.

7. My ex-husband hit me just once in our marriage. five minutes later I was packed and walking out the door.

8. Aunt Jeanne thought a warm dry climate would improve her health she moved to Arizona.

9. The average American teenager spends thirty-eight hours a week on school-work. the average Japanese teenager spends about sixty.

10. We stocked our backpacks with high-calorie candy bars, and we also brought bags of dried apricots and peaches.

Review Test 2

Correct each run-on by using (1) a period and a capital letter, (2) a comma and a joining word, or (3) a semicolon. Do not use one method exclusively.

1. The magazine had lain in the damp mailbox for two days its pages were blurry and swollen.

2. With a groan, Margo pried off her high heels, then she plunged her swollen feet into a bucket of baking soda and hot water.

3. At 2 a.m. the last customer left the diner, a busboy began stacking chairs on the tables for the night.

4. Hypnosis has nothing to do with the occult. it is merely a state of deep relaxation.

5. Many young adults today live at home with their parents this allows them to save money.

6. I waited for the clanking train to clear the intersection rusty boxcars just kept rolling slowly along the rails.

7. Early in life, Thomas Edison suffered with deafness, he taught his wife-to-be Morse code while he was courting her.

8. Originally, horses were too small to carry riders very far larger horses had to be bred for use in warfare.

9. The words *month, silver, purple,* and *orange* have something in common, no other English words rhyme with them.

10. The broken soda machine dispensed a cup or soda, it would not provide both at the same time.

Review Test 3

Locate and correct the five run-ons in the passage that follows.

My worst experience of the week was going home for lunch, rather than eating at work. My children didn't know I was coming, they had used most of the bread. All I had to make a sandwich with were two thin, crumpled pieces of crust. I sat there eating my tattered sandwich and trying to relax, then the telephone rang. It was for my daughter, who was in the bathroom, she called down to me that I should get the person's name and number. As soon as I sat down again, someone knocked on the door, it was a neatly dressed couple with bright eyes who wanted to talk with me about a higher power in life. I politely got rid of them and went back to finish lunch. I thought I would relax over my coffee, I had to break up a fight between my two young sons about which television channel to watch. As a last bit of frustration, my daughter came downstairs and asked me to drive her over to a friend's house before I went back to work.

Review Test 4

On separate paper, write quickly for five minutes about what you did this past weekend. Don't worry about spelling, punctuation, finding exact words, or organizing your thoughts. Just focus on writing as many words as you can without stopping.

After you have finished, go back and correct any run-ons in your writing.

26 Regular and Irregular Verbs

This chapter will review the principal characteristics of regular and irregular verbs.

KEY TERMS

irregular verb: a verb that has an irregular form in the past tense and past participle. For example, *choose* becomes *chose* or *chosen*.

past participle: one of the principal parts of every verb; formed by adding -d or -ed to the present; used with the helping verbs *have, has,* or *had,* or with a form of *be* (with passive verbs).

present participle: one of the principal parts of every verb; formed by adding -ing to the present.

principal parts of verbs: the four parts of every verb: present, past, past participle, and present participle.

verb tense: the times shown by verbs: present, past, and future.

Regular Verbs

A Brief Review of Regular Verbs

Every verb has four principal parts: *present, past, past participle,* and *present participle.* These parts can be used to build all the verb *tenses*—the times shown by verbs.

Most verbs in English are regular. The past and past participle of a regular verb are formed by adding *-d* or *-ed* to the present. The *past participle* is the form of the verb used with the helping verbs *have, has,* or *had* (or some form of *be* with passive verbs). The *present participle* is formed by adding *-ing* to the present.

Here are the principal parts of some regular verbs:

Present	Past	Past Participle	Present Participle
shout	shouted	shouted	shouting
prepare	prepared	prepared	preparing
surprise	surprised	surprised	surprising
tease	teased	teased	teasing
frighten	frightened	frightened	frightening

Nonstandard Forms of Regular Verbs

Many people have grown up in communities where nonstandard forms of regular verbs are used in everyday speech. Instead of saying, for example, "That girl *looks* tired," a person using a community dialect might say, "That girl *look* tired." Instead of saying, "Yesterday I *fixed* the car," a person using a community dialect might say, "Yesterday I *fix* the car." Community dialects have richness and power but are a drawback in college and in the world of work, where regular English verb forms must be used.

The following chart compares the nonstandard and the regular verb forms of the verb *work.*

Nonstandard Verb Form		Regular Verb Form	
(Do *not* use in your writing)		(Use for clear communication)	
Present tense			
I works	we works	I work	we work
you works	you works	you work	you work
he, she, it work	they works	he, she, it works	they work

(continued)

	Past tense		
I work	we work	I worked	we worked
you work	you work	you worked	you worked
he, she, it work	they work	he, she, it worked	they worked

To avoid nonstandard usage, memorize the forms shown above for the regular verb *work*. Then use the activities that follow to help make the inclusion of verb endings a writing habit.

Present Tense Endings The verb ending -*s* or -*es* is needed with a regular verb in the present tense when the subject is *he, she, it*, or any *one person or thing*.

He reads every night.

She watches television every night.

It appears they have little in common.

Activity

1

Some verbs in the sentences that follow need -*s* or -*es* endings. Cross out each nonstandard verb form and write the standard form in the space provided.

_____ 1. My radio wake me up every morning with soft music.

_____ 2. Felix always clown around at the start of the class.

_____ 3. My wife watch our baby in the morning, and I take over afternoons.

_____ 4. Brenda want to go to nursing school next year.

_____ 5. My brain work much better at night than it does in early morning.

Past Tense Endings The verb ending -*d* or -*ed* is needed with a regular verb in the past tense.

This morning I completed my research paper.

The recovering hospital patient walked slowly down the corridor.

Some students hissed when the new assignment was given out.

Some verbs in the sentences that follow need *-d* or *-ed* endings. Cross out each nonstandard verb form and write the standard form in the space provided.

Activity

2

_____ 1. One of my teeth crack when I bit on the hard pretzel.

_____ 2. The accident victim complain of dizziness right before passing out.

_____ 3. We realize a package was missing when we got back from shopping.

_____ 4. I burn a hole in my shirt while ironing it.

_____ 5. The driver edge her car into the intersection while the light was still red.

Irregular Verbs

Irregular verbs have irregular forms in past tense and past participle. For example, the past tense of the irregular verb *choose* is *chose;* its past participle is *chosen.*

Almost everyone has some degree of trouble with irregular verbs. When you are unsure about the form of a verb, you can check the following list of irregular verbs. (The present participle is not shown on this list because it is formed simply by adding *-ing* to the base form of the verb.) Or you can check a dictionary, which gives the principal parts of irregular verbs.

A List of Irregular Verbs

Present	Past	Past Participle
arise	arose	arisen
awake	awoke *or* awaked	awoken *or* awaked
be (am, are, is)	was (were)	been
become	became	become
begin	began	begun
bend	bent	bent
bite	bit	bitten
blow	blew	blown
break	broke	broken
bring	brought	brought
build	built	built
burst	burst	burst
buy	bought	bought
catch	caught	caught

Present	Past	Past Participle
choose	chose	chosen
come	came	come
cost	cost	cost
cut	cut	cut
do (does)	did	done
draw	drew	drawn
drink	drank	drunk
drive	drove	driven
eat	ate	eaten
fall	fell	fallen
feed	fed	fed
feel	felt	felt
fight	fought	fought
find	found	found
fly	flew	flown
freeze	froze	frozen
get	got	got *or* gotten
give	gave	given
go (goes)	went	gone
grow	grew	grown
have (has)	had	had
hear	heard	heard
hide	hid	hidden
hold	held	held
hurt	hurt	hurt
keep	kept	kept
know	knew	known
lay	laid	laid
lead	led	led
leave	left	left
lend	lent	lent
let	let	let
lie	lay	lain
light	lit	lit

Present	Past	Past Participle
lose	lost	lost
make	made	made
meet	met	met
pay	paid	paid
ride	rode	ridden
ring	rang	rung
run	ran	run
say	said	said
see	saw	seen
sell	sold	sold
send	sent	sent
shake	shook	shaken
shrink	shrank	shrunk
shut	shut	shut
sing	sang	sung
sit	sat	sat
sleep	slept	slept
speak	spoke	spoken
spend	spent	spent
stand	stood	stood
steal	stole	stolen
stick	stuck	stuck
sting	stung	stung
swear	swore	sworn
swim	swam	swum
take	took	taken
teach	taught	taught
tear	tore	torn
tell	told	told
think	thought	thought
wake	woke *or* waked	woke *or* waked
wear	wore	worn
win	won	won
write	wrote	written

Activity

3

Cross out the incorrect verb form in each of the following sentences. Then write the correct form of the verb in the space provided.

EXAMPLE

flown After it had ~~flew~~ into the picture window, the dazed bird huddled on the ground.

_____ 1. As graduation neared, Michelle worried about the practicality of the major she'd chose.

_____ 2. Before we could find seats, the theater darkened and the opening credits begun to roll.

_____ 3. To be polite, I drunk the slightly sour wine that my grandfather poured from his carefully hoarded supply.

_____ 4. With a thunderous crack, the telephone pole breaked in half from the impact of the speeding car.

_____ 5. The inexperienced nurse shrunk from touching the patient's raw, burned skin.

_____ 6. After a day on the noisy construction site, Sam's ears rung for hours with a steady hum.

_____ 7. Sheila had forgot to write her social security number on the test form, so the computer rejected her answer sheet.

_____ 8. If I had went to work ten minutes earlier, I would have avoided being caught in the gigantic traffic snarl.

_____ 9. After the bicycle hit a patch of soft sand, the rider was throwed into the thorny bushes along the roadside.

_____ 10. Prehistoric people blowed paint over their outstretched hands to stencil their handprints on cave walls.

Nonstandard Forms of Three Common Irregular Verbs

People who use nonstandard forms of regular verbs also tend to use nonstandard forms of three common irregular verbs: *be, have,* and *do.* Instead of saying, for example, "My neighbors *are* nice people," a person using a nonstandard form might say, "My neighbors *be* nice people." Instead of saying, "She doesn't agree," they might say, "She *don't* agree." Instead of saying, "We have tickets," they might say, "We *has* tickets."

The following charts compare the nonstandard and the standard forms of *be, have,* and *do.*

Be

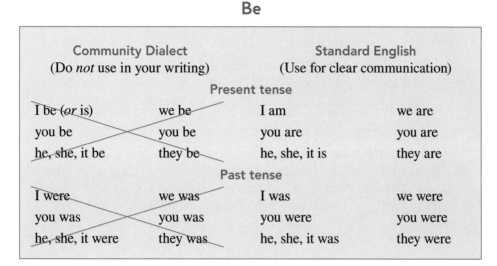

Community Dialect (Do *not* use in your writing)		Standard English (Use for clear communication)	
Present tense			
I be (*or* is)	we be	I am	we are
you be	you be	you are	you are
he, she, it be	they be	he, she, it is	they are
Past tense			
I were	we was	I was	we were
you was	you was	you were	you were
he, she, it were	they was	he, she, it was	they were

Have

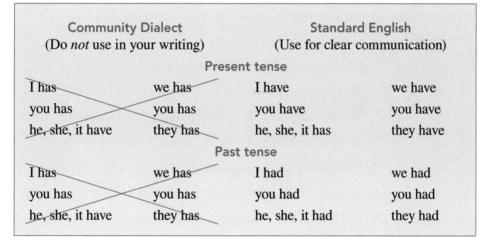

Community Dialect (Do *not* use in your writing)		Standard English (Use for clear communication)	
Present tense			
I has	we has	I have	we have
you has	you has	you have	you have
he, she, it have	they has	he, she, it has	they have
Past tense			
I has	we has	I had	we had
you has	you has	you had	you had
he, she, it have	they has	he, she, it had	they had

Do

Community Dialect (Do *not* use in your writing)		Standard English (Use for clear communication)	
Present tense			
I does	we do	I do	we do
you does	you does	you do	you do
he, she, it do	they does	he, she, it does	they do

(continued)

	Past tense		
I ~~done~~	we ~~done~~	I did	we did
you done	you done	you did	you did
~~he, she~~, it done	they ~~done~~	he, she, it did	they did

www.mhhe.com/langan

> **TIP** Many people have trouble with one negative form of *do.* They will say, for example, "He don't agree," instead of, "He doesn't agree," or they will say, "The door don't work," instead of, "The door doesn't work." Be careful to avoid the common mistake of using *don't* instead of *doesn't.*

Activity

4

Cross out the nonstandard verb form in each sentence. Then write the standard form of *be, have,* or *do* in the space provided.

_____ 1. My cat, Tugger, be the toughest animal I know.

_____ 2. He have survived many close calls.

_____ 3. Three years ago, he were caught inside a car's engine.

_____ 4. He have one ear torn off and lost the sight in one eye.

_____ 5. We was surprised that he lived through the accident.

_____ 6. Within weeks, though, he were back to normal.

_____ 7. Then, last year, we was worried that we would lose Tugger.

_____ 8. Lumps that was growing on his back turned out to be cancer.

_____ 9. But the vet done an operation that saved Tugger's life.

_____ 10. By now, we know that Tugger really do have nine lives.

Review Test   1

Cross out the incorrect verb form in each sentence. Then write the correct form in the space provided.

_____ 1. The health inspectors walk into the kitchen as the cook was picking up a hamburger off the floor.

_____ 2. The thieves would have stole my stereo, but I had had it engraved with a special identification number.

_____ 3. At the Chinese restaurant, Hollis choose his food by the number.

_____ 4. He had tore his girlfriend's picture into little pieces and tossed them out the window.

_____ 5. Because I has asthma, I carry an inhaler to use when I have trouble breathing.

_____ 6. Baked potatoes doesn't have as many calories as I thought.

_____ 7. The grizzly bear, with the dart dangling from its side, begun to feel the effects of the powerful tranquilizer.

_____ 8. Yesterday I check my bank balance and saw that the amount was getting low.

_____ 9. Many childhood diseases has almost vanished in the United States.

_____ 10. Nancy sticked notes on the refrigerator with fruit-shaped magnets.

Review Test 2

Write short sentences that use the form requested for the following verbs.

EXAMPLE

Past of *grow* _I grew my own tomatoes last year._

1. Past of *know* _____

2. Present of *take* _____

3. Past participle of *give* _____

4. Past participle of *write* _____

5. Past of *do* _____

6. Past of *talk* _____

7. Present of *begin* _____

8. Past of *go* _____

9. Past participle of *see* _____

10. Present of *drive* _____

27 Subject-Verb Agreement

Subject-verb agreement is the correspondence in number between the subject and the verb of a sentence; plural subjects take plural verbs, and singular subjects take singular verbs. This chapter will review the necessity for subject-verb agreement.

INCORRECT:

The crinkly lines around Joan's mouth gives her a friendly look.

The subject of "crinkly lines" is a plural, so the verb should be "give," not "gives."

CORRECT:

The crinkly lines around Joan's mouth give her a friendly look.

The verb "give" agrees with the plural "crinkly lines."

KEY TERMS

compound subject: two subjects separated by a joining word such as *and*. Compound subjects generally take a plural verb.

indefinite pronoun: a word that refers to people and things that are not named or are not specific. Many indefinite pronouns (such as *one, nobody, nothing,* and *each*) take a singular verb; others, such as *both* or *few,* take plural verbs.

A verb must agree with its subject in number. A *singular subject* (one person or thing) takes a singular verb. A *plural subject* (more than one person or thing) takes a plural verb. Mistakes in subject-verb agreement are sometimes made in the following situations:

1. When words come between the subject and the verb
2. When a verb comes before the subject
3. With compound subjects
4. With indefinite pronouns

Each of these situations is explained in this chapter.

Words between Subject and Verb

Words that come between the subject and the verb do not change subject-verb agreement. In the sentence

The sharp <u>fangs</u> in the dog's mouth <u>look</u> scary.

the subject (*fangs*) is plural, and so the verb (*look*) is plural. The words that come between the subject and the verb are a prepositional phrase: *in the dog's mouth.* They do not affect subject-verb agreement. (A list of prepositions can be found on page 451.)

To help find the subject of certain sentences, you should cross out prepositional phrases.

The lumpy <u>salt</u> ~~in the shakers~~ <u>needs</u> to be changed.

An old <u>chair</u> ~~with broken legs~~ <u>has</u> sat in our basement for years.

www.mhhe.com/langan

Underline the subject and lightly cross out any words that come between the subject and the verb. Then double-underline the verb in parentheses that you believe is correct.

Activity

1

1. Some members of the parents' association (want, wants) to ban certain books from the school library.

2. Chung's trench coat, with its big lapels and shoulder flaps, (make, makes) him feel like a tough private eye.

3. Misconceptions about apes like the gorilla (has, have) turned a relatively peaceful animal into a terrifying monster.

4. The rising cost of necessities like food and shelter (force, forces) many elderly people to live in poverty.

5. In my opinion, a few slices of pepperoni pizza (make, makes) a great evening.

Verb before Subject

A verb agrees with its subject even when the verb comes *before* the subject. Words that may precede the subject include *there, here,* and, in questions, *who, which, what,* and *where.*

Here are some examples of sentences in which the verb appears before the subject:

There are wild dogs in our neighborhood.

In the distance was a billow of black smoke.

Here is the newspaper.

Where are the children's coats?

If you are unsure about the subject, ask *who* or *what* of the verb. With the first example above, you might ask, "*What* are in our neighborhood?" The answer, *wild dogs,* is the subject.

Activity

Activity 2

(is, are)

(is, are)

(do, does)

(was, were)

(was, were)

Write the correct form of each verb in the space provided.

1. There _____ dozens of frenzied shoppers waiting for the store to open.

2. Here _____ the notes from yesterday's anthropology lecture.

3. When _____ we take our break?

4. There _____ scraps of yellowing paper stuck between the pages of the cookbook.

5. At the very bottom of the grocery list _____ an item that meant a trip all the way back to aisle one.

Compound Subjects

A *compound subject* is two subjects separated by a joining word, such as *and.* Subjects joined by *and* generally take a plural verb.

A patchwork quilt and a sleeping bag cover my bed in the winter.

Clark and Lois are a contented couple.

When subjects are joined by *either . . . or, neither . . . nor, not only . . . but also,* the verb agrees with the subject closer to the verb.

Neither the negotiator nor the union leaders want the strike to continue.

The nearer subject, *leaders,* is plural, and so the verb is plural.

Neither the union <u>leaders</u> nor the <u>negotiator</u> <u>wants</u> the strike to continue.

In this version, the nearer subject, *negotiator,* is singular, so the verb is singular.

Write the correct form of the verb in the space provided.

1. A crusty baking pan and a greasy plate _____ on the countertop. (sit, sits)

2. Spidery cracks and a layer of dust _____ the ivory keys on the old piano. (cover, covers)

3. Not only the assistant managers but also the secretary _____ that the company is folding. (know, knows)

4. In eighteenth-century France, makeup and high heels _____ worn by men. (was, were)

5. Either the trash can or those socks _____ horrible. (smell, smells)

Activity 3

Indefinite Pronouns

The following words, known as *indefinite pronouns,* always take singular verbs:

(-*one* words)	(-*body* words)	(-*thing* words)	
one	nobody	nothing	each
anyone	anybody	anything	either
everyone	everybody	everything	neither
someone	somebody	something	

> **TIP** *Both* always takes a plural verb.

www.mhhe.com/langan

Write the correct form of the verb in the space provided.

1. Neither of those hairstyles _____ the shape of your face. (suit, suits)

2. Somebody without much sensitivity always _____ my birthmark. (mention, mentions)

3. Both of the puppies _____ cute in their own ways. (is, are)

Activity 4

(enter,
enters)

(fall, falls)

4. Everyone _____ the college kite-flying contest in the spring.

5. One of these earrings constantly _____ off my ear.

Review Test   1

In the space provided, write the correct form of the verb shown in the margin.

(is, are)

1. Some wheelchair-bound patients, as a result of a successful experiment, _____ using trained monkeys as helpers.

(was, were)

2. Each of their children _____ given a name picked at random from a page of the Bible.

(seem,
seems)

3. Many of the headlines in the *National Enquirer* _____ hard to believe.

(is, are)

(contains,
contain)

4. Envelopes, file folders, and a telephone book _____ jammed into Lupe's kitchen drawers.

5. Neither of the main dishes at tonight's dinner _____ any meat.

(damage,
damages)

6. The use of metal chains and studded tires _____ roadways because metal and studs chip away at the paved surface.

(was, were)

7. Next to the cash register _____ a can for donations to the animal protection society.

(makes,
make)

8. A metal grab bar bolted onto the tiles _____ it easier for elderly people to get into and out of the bathtub.

(cleans,
clean)

9. In exchange for reduced rent, Karla and James _____ the dentist's office beneath their second-floor apartment.

(is, are)

10. One of the hospital's delivery rooms _____ furnished with bright carpets and curtains to resemble a room at home.

Review Test   2

Cross out the incorrect verb form in each sentence. In addition, underline the subject or subjects that go with the verb. Then write the correct form of the verb in the space provided.

_____   1. Why is Martha and her mother digging a hole in their garden so late at night?

_____ 2. Neither of my children look like me.

_____ 3. Three goats, a potbellied pig, and a duck was among the entrants in the pet parade.

_____ 4. The little balls all over my pink sweater looks like woolen goose bumps.

_____ 5. Here is the low-calorie cola and the double-chocolate cake you ordered.

_____ 6. The odor of those perfumed ads interfere with my enjoyment of a magazine.

_____ 7. One of my roommates are always leaving wet towels on the bathroom floor.

_____ 8. A tiny piece of gum and some tape is holding my old glasses together.

_____ 9. A person in his or her forties often begin to think about making a contribution to the world and not just about himself or herself.

_____ 10. Each of the child's thirty-four stuffed animals have a name and an entire life history.

Review Test 3

Complete each of the following sentences using *is*, *are*, *was*, *were*, *have*, or *has*. Then underline the subject.

EXAMPLE

For me, popcorn at the movies _is like coffee at breakfast._

1. The magazines under my roommate's bed _____

2. The car with the purple fenders _____

3. My boss and her secretary _____

4. Neither of the football players _____

5. Here _____

28 Additional Information about Verbs

This chapter will provide additional information about verbs, specifically:

- verb tense
- helping verbs
- verbals

KEY TERMS

gerund: a verbal; the -ing form of the verb used as a noun. Example: I love *dancing*.

infinitive: a verbal; to plus the base form of the verb. Example: I love *to dance*.

participle: a verbal; the -ing or -ed form of the verb used as an adjective. Example: I love *dancing* bears.

verbals: words formed from verbs that often express action; these include gerunds, infinitives, and participles.

This chapter provides additional information about verbs. Some people will find the grammatical terms here a helpful reminder of what they've learned earlier, in school, about verbs. For them, the terms will increase their understanding of how verbs function in English. Other people may welcome more detailed information about terms used elsewhere in the text. In either case, remember that the most common mistakes people make with verbs have been treated in previous chapters of this book.

Verb Tense

Verbs tell us the time of an action. The time that a verb shows is usually called *tense*. The most common tenses are the simple present, past, and future. In addition, nine tenses enable us to express more specific ideas about time than we could with the simple tenses alone. Following are the twelve verb tenses and examples of each tense. Read them over to increase your sense of the many different ways of expressing time in English.

www.mhhe.com/langan

Tenses	Examples
Present	I *work*. Tony *works*.
Past	Ellen *worked* on her car.
Future	You *will work* on a new project next week.
Present perfect	He *has worked* on his term paper for a month. They *have worked* out a compromise.
Past perfect	The nurse *had worked* two straight shifts.
Future perfect	Next Monday, I *will have worked* here exactly two years.
Present progressive	I *am working* on my speech for the debate. You *are working* too hard. The tape recorder *is* not *working* properly.
Past progressive	He *was working* in the basement. The contestants *were working* on their talent routines.
Future progressive	My son *will be working* in our store this summer.
Present perfect progressive	Sarah *has been working* late this week.

(continued)

Tenses	Examples
Past perfect progressive	Until recently, I *had been working* nights.
Future perfect progressive	My mother *will have been working* as a nurse for forty-five years by the time she retires.

Activity

1

On a separate sheet of paper, write twelve sentences using the twelve verb tenses.

Helping Verbs

Three common verbs can either stand alone or combine with (and "help") other verbs. Here are the verbs and their forms:

> be (am, are, is, was, were, being, been)
> have (has, having, had)
> do (does, did)

Here are examples of the helping verbs:

Used Alone	Used as Helping Verbs
I *was* angry.	I *was growing* angry.
Sue *has* the key.	Sue *has forgotten* the key.
He *did* well in the test.	He *did fail* the previous test.

Nine helping verbs (traditionally known as *modals,* or *modal auxiliaries*) are always used in combination with other verbs. Here are the nine verbs and a sentence example of each:

can	I *can see* the rainbow.
could	I *could* not *find* a seat.
may	The game *may be postponed.*
might	Cindy *might resent* your advice.

(continued)

shall	I *shall see* you tomorrow.
should	He *should get* his car serviced.
will	Tony *will want* to see you.
would	They *would* not *understand*.
must	You *must visit* us again.

Note from the examples that these verbs have only one form. They do not, for instance, add an *-s* when used with *he, she, it,* or any one person or thing.

On a separate sheet of paper, write nine sentences using the nine helping verbs.

Activity

2

Verbals

Verbals are words formed from verbs. Verbals, like verbs, often express action. They can add variety to your sentences and vigor to your writing style. The three kinds of verbals are *infinitives, participles,* and *gerunds.*

Infinitive

An infinitive is *to* and the base form of the verb.

I love *to dance.*

Lina hopes *to write* for a newspaper.

I asked the children *to clean* the kitchen.

Participle

A participle is a verb form used as an adjective (a descriptive word). The present participle ends in *-ing.* The past participle ends in *-ed* or has an irregular ending.

Peering into the cracked mirror, the *crying* woman wiped her eyes.

The *astounded* man stared at his *winning* lottery ticket.

Swinging a sharp ax, Omar split the *rotted* beam.

www.mhhe.com/langan

Gerund

A gerund is the *-ing* form of a verb used as a noun.

Swimming is the perfect exercise.

Eating junk food is my diet downfall.

Through *doodling,* people express their inner feelings.

Activity

3

On a separate sheet of paper, write three sentences using infinitives, three sentences using participles, and three sentences using gerunds.

Pronoun Agreement and Reference

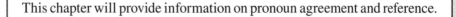

29

This chapter will provide information on pronoun agreement and reference.

INCORRECT:

Miriam was annoyed when they failed her car for a faulty turn signal.

In this case, "they" should be replaced by a specific noun, such as "the inspectors," so the reader knows who the word "they" refers to.

CORRECT:

Miriam was annoyed when the inspectors failed her car for a faulty turn signal.

Now it is made clear that it was the inspectors who failed the car.

KEY TERMS

indefinite pronouns: a word that refers to people and things that are not named or are not specific. Many indefinite pronouns (such as *one, nobody, nothing,* and *each*) take a singular verb; others, such as *both* or *few,* take plural verbs.

nouns: words that name persons, places, or things.

pronoun: words that take the place of nouns. Pronouns are shortcuts that keep you from unnecessarily repeating words in writing.

pronoun agreement: correspondence in number between the pronoun and the noun it replaces. Example: *Students enrolled in the art class must prove that they can paint.*

pronoun reference: the relationship between the pronoun and the noun in the sentence to which it refers. A sentence may be confusing if a pronoun appears to refer to more than one noun or does not appear to refer to any specific noun.

Nouns name persons, places, or things. *Pronouns* are words that take the place of nouns. In fact, the word *pronoun* means "for a noun." Pronouns are shortcuts that keep you from unnecessarily repeating words in writing. Here are some examples of pronouns:

Eddie left *his* camera on the bus.
(*His* is a pronoun that takes the place of *Eddie's*.)

Elena drank the coffee even though *it* was cold.
(*It* replaces *coffee*.)

As I turned the newspaper's damp pages, *they* disintegrated in my hands.
(*They* is a pronoun that takes the place of *pages*.)

This chapter presents rules that will help you avoid two common mistakes people make with pronouns. The rules are the following:

1. A pronoun must agree in number with the word or words it replaces.
2. A pronoun must refer clearly to the word it replaces.

Pronoun Agreement

A pronoun must agree in number with the word or words it replaces. If the word a pronoun refers to is singular, the pronoun must be singular; if that word is plural, the pronoun must be plural. (Note that the word a pronoun refers to is known as the *antecedent*.)

Marie showed me her antique wedding band.

Students enrolled in the art class must provide their own supplies.

In the first example, the pronoun *her* refers to the singular word *Marie;* in the second example, the pronoun *their* refers to the plural word *Students*.

Activity 1

Write the appropriate pronoun (*their, they, them, it*) in the blank space in each of the following sentences.

EXAMPLE

I opened the wet umbrella and put _____*it*_____ in the bathtub to dry.

1. Kate and Omar left for the movies earlier than usual, because _____ knew the theater would be packed.

2. The clothes were still damp, but I decided to fold _____ anyway.

3. Young adults often face a difficult transition period when _____ leave home for the first time.

4. Paul's grandparents renewed _____ marriage vows at a huge fifti-eth wedding anniversary celebration.

5. The car's steering wheel began to pull to one side, and then _____ started to shimmy.

Indefinite Pronouns

The following words, known as *indefinite pronouns,* are always singular.

(-*one* words)	(-*body* words)	
one	nobody	each
anyone	anybody	either
everyone	everybody	neither
someone	somebody	

If a pronoun in a sentence refers to one of these singular words, the pronoun should be singular.

Somebody left (her) shoulder bag on the back of a chair.

One of the busboys just called and said (he) would be an hour late.

Everyone in the club must pay (his) dues next week.

Each circled pronoun is singular because it refers to an indefinite pronoun.

There are two important points to remember about indefinite pronouns:

1. In the last example, if everyone in the club was a woman, the pronoun would be *her.* If the club had women and men, the pronoun would be *his or her:*

    Everyone in the club must pay his or her dues next week.

    Some writers follow the traditional practice of using *his* to refer to both women and men. Some now use *his or her* to avoid an implied sexual bias. To avoid using *his* or the somewhat awkward *his or her,* a sentence can often be rewritten in the plural:

    Club members must pay their dues next week.

2. In informal spoken English, *plural* pronouns are often used with the indefinite pronouns. Many people would probably not say,

    Everybody has his or her own opinion about the election.

Instead, they would be likely to say,

> Everybody has their own opinion about the election.

Here are other examples:

> Everyone in the choir must buy their robes.
>
> Everybody in the line has their ticket ready.
>
> No one in the class remembered to bring their books.

In such cases, the indefinite pronouns are clearly plural in meaning, and using them helps people avoid the awkward *his or her.* In time, the plural pronoun may be accepted in formal speech or writing. Until then, however, you should use the grammatically correct singular form in your writing.

Activity

2

Underline the correct pronoun.

1. Neither of the potential buyers had really made up (her, their) mind.
2. Not one of the new cashiers knows what (he, they) should be doing.
3. Each of these computers has (its, their) drawbacks.
4. Anyone trying to reduce (his or her, their) salt intake should avoid canned and processed foods.
5. If anybody calls when I'm out, tell (him, them) I'll return in an hour.

www.mhhe.com/langan

Pronoun Reference

A sentence may be confusing and unclear if a pronoun appears to refer to more than one word or does not refer to any specific word. Look at this sentence:

> Miriam was annoyed when they failed her car for a faulty turn signal.

Who failed her car? There is no specific word that *they* refers to. Be clear:

> Miriam was annoyed when the inspectors failed her car for a faulty turn signal.

Here are sentences with other faulty pronoun references. Read the explanations of why they are faulty and look carefully at how they are corrected.

Faulty	Clear
Peter told Alan that his wife was unhappy. (Whose wife is unhappy: Peter's or Alan's? Be clear.)	Peter told Alan, "My wife is unhappy."

Faulty

Kia is really a shy person, but she keeps it hidden.
(There is no specific word that *it* refers to. It would not make sense to say, "Kia keeps shy hidden.")

Marsha attributed her success to her husband's support, which was generous.
(Does *which* mean that Marsha's action was generous or that her husband's support was generous?)

Clear

Kia is really a shy person, but she keeps her shyness hidden.

Generously, Marsha attributed her success to her husband's support. *Or:* Marsha attributed her success to her husband's generous support.

Working with a fellow classmate, rewrite each of the following sentences to make clear the vague pronoun reference. Add, change, or omit words as necessary.

Activity

3

EXAMPLE

Susan's mother wondered if she was tall enough to be a model.
Susan's mother wondered if Susan was tall enough to be a model.

1. Dad spent all day fishing but didn't catch a single one.

   _____

2. At that fast-food restaurant, they give you free glasses with your soft drinks.

   _____

3. Ruth told Denise that her bouts of depression were becoming serious.

   _____

4. Dipping her spoon into the pot of simmering spaghetti sauce, Helen felt it slip out of her hand. . . .

   _____

5. Pete visited the tutoring center because they can help him with his economics course.

   _____

Review Test 1

Underline the correct word in parentheses.

1. Each of the little girls may choose one prize for (her, their) own.

2. I asked at the body shop how quickly (they, the shop employees) could fix my car.

3. The coaches told each member of the football team that (his, their) position was the most important in the game.

4. Darlene tried to take notes during the class, but she didn't really understand (it, the subject).

5. When someone has a cold, (they, he or she) should take extra vitamin C and drink a lot of fluids.

Review Test 2

Cross out the pronoun error in each of the following sentences, and write the correction in the space provided at the left. Then circle the letter that correctly describes the type of error that was made.

EXAMPLES

his (or her)   Anyone without a ticket will lose ~~their~~ place in the line.

Mistake in   a. pronoun reference   (b.) pronoun agreement

Ellen (or Kim)   When Ellen takes her daughter Kim to the park, ~~she~~ enjoys herself.

Mistake in   (a.) pronoun reference   b. pronoun agreement

_____ 1. Could someone volunteer their services to clean up after the party?

Mistake in   a. pronoun reference   b. pronoun agreement

_____ 2. The referee watched the basketball game closely to make sure they didn't commit any fouls.

Mistake in   a. pronoun reference   b. pronoun agreement

_____ 3. If job-hunters want to make a good impression at an interview, he should be sure to arrive on time.

Mistake in   a. pronoun reference   b. pronoun agreement

_____ 4. Neither of those girls appreciates their parents' sacrifices.

Mistake in   a. pronoun reference   b. pronoun agreement

_____ 5. There wasn't much to do on Friday nights after they closed the only movie theater in town.

Mistake in   a. pronoun reference   b. pronoun agreement

Pronoun Types

This chapter will describe some common types of pronouns:

- subject pronouns
- object pronouns
- possessive pronouns
- demonstrative pronouns

KEY TERMS

demonstrative pronouns: pronouns that point to or single out a person or thing. The four demonstrative pronouns are *this, that, these,* and *those.*

object pronouns: pronouns that function as the objects of verbs or prepositions. Example: *Tony helped me.*

possessive pronouns: pronouns that show ownership or possession. Example: *The keys are mine.*

subject pronouns: pronouns that function as the subjects of verbs. Example: *He is wearing an artificial arm.*

Subject and Object Pronouns

Most pronouns change their form depending on what place they occupy in a sentence. In the box that follows is a list of subject and object pronouns.

Subject Pronouns	Object Pronouns
I	me
you	you (no change)
he	him
she	her
it	it (no change)
we	us
they	them

Subject Pronouns

Subject pronouns are subjects of verbs.

> *He* served as a soldier during the war in Iraq. (*He* is the subject of the verb *served.*)
>
> *They* are moving into our old apartment. (*They* is the subject of the verb *are moving.*)
>
> *We* students should have a say in the decision. (*We* is the subject of the verb *should have.*)

Following are several rules for using subject pronouns—and several kinds of mistakes people sometimes make with subject pronouns.

Rule 1

Use a subject pronoun when you have a compound subject (more than one subject).

Incorrect	Correct
My brother and *me* are Bruce Springsteen fanatics.	My brother and *I* are Bruce Springsteen fanatics.
Him and *me* know the lyrics to all of Bruce's songs.	*He* and *I* know the lyrics to all of Bruce's songs.

> **TIP** *Rule 1*
>
> If you are not sure what pronoun to use, try each pronoun by itself in the sentence. The correct pronoun will be the one that sounds right. For example, "Him knows the lyrics to all of Bruce's songs" does not sound right; "He knows the lyrics to all of Bruce's songs" does.

Rule 2

Use a subject pronoun after forms of the verb *be*. Forms of *be* include *am, are, is, was, were, has been, have been,* and others.

> It was *I* who left the light on.
>
> It may be *they* in that car.
>
> It is *he.*

The sentences above may sound strange and stilted to you because they are seldom used in conversation. When we speak with one another, forms such as "It was me," "It may be them," and "It is him" are widely accepted. In formal writing, however, the grammatically correct forms are still preferred.

> **TIP** *Rule 2*
>
> You can avoid having to use a subject pronoun after *be* by simply rewording a sentence. Here is how the preceding examples could be reworded:
>
> > I was the one who left the light on.
> >
> > They may be in that car.
> >
> > He is here.

Rule 3

Use subject pronouns after *than* or *as.* The subject pronoun is used because a verb is understood after the pronoun.

> You play better than I (play). (The verb *play* is understood after *I.*)
>
> Jenny is as bored as I (am). (The verb *am* is understood after *I.*)
>
> We don't need the money as much as they (do). (The verb *do* is understood after *they.*)

> **TIP** *Rule 3*
> Avoid mistakes by mentally adding the "missing" verb at the end of the sentence.

Object Pronouns

Object pronouns (me, him, her, us, them) are the objects of verbs or prepositions. (*Prepositions* are connecting words like *for, at, about, to, before, by, with,* and *of.* See also page 451.)

Tony helped me. (*Me* is the object of the verb *helped.*)

We took *them* to the college. (*Them* is the object of the verb *took.*)

Leave the children with *us.* (*Us* is the object of the preposition *with.*)

I got in line behind *him.* (*Him* is the object of the preposition *behind.*)

People are sometimes uncertain about what pronoun to use when two objects follow a verb.

Incorrect	Correct
I gave a gift to Ray and *she.*	I gave a gift to Ray and *her.*
She came to the movie with Bobbie and *I.*	She came to the movie with Bobbie and *me.*

> **TIP** If you are not sure what pronoun to use, try each pronoun by itself in the sentence. The correct pronoun will be the one that sounds right. For example, "I gave a gift to she" does not sound right; "I gave a gift to her" does.

Activity

1

Underline the correct subject or object pronoun in each of the following sentences. Then show whether your answer is a subject or object pronoun by circling the S or O in the margin. The first one is done for you as an example.

S   O   1. The sweaters Mom knitted for Victor and (I, me) are too small.

S   O   2. The umpire and (he, him) started to argue.

S   O   3. No one has a quicker temper than (she, her).

S   O   4. Your grades prove that you worked harder than (they, them).

S   O   5. (We, Us) runners train indoors when the weather turns cold.

S   O   6. (She, Her) and Betty never put the cap back on the toothpaste.

S   O   7. Chris and (he, him) are the most energetic kids in the first grade.

S   O   8. Arguing over clothes is a favorite pastime for my sister and (I, me).

S   O   9. The rest of (they, them) will be arriving in about ten minutes.

S   O   10. The head of the ticket committee asked Melba and (I, me) to help with sales.

Possessive Pronouns

Here is a list of possessive pronouns:

my, mine	our, ours
your, yours	your, yours
his	their, theirs
her, hers	
its	

Possessive pronouns show ownership or possession.

> Adam revved up *his* motorcycle and blasted off.
>
> The keys are *mine.*

> **TIP** A possessive pronoun *never* uses an apostrophe. (See also page 553.)

www.mhhe.com/langan

Incorrect	**Correct**
That coat is *hers'*.	That coat is *hers.*
The card table is *theirs'*.	The card table is *theirs.*

Cross out the incorrect pronoun form in each of the sentences below. Write the correct form in the space at the left.

Activity

2

EXAMPLE

___*hers*___   Those gloves are ~~hers'~~.

_____ 1. I discovered that my car had somehow lost its' rear license plate.

_____ 2. Are those seats theirs'?

_____ 3. I knew that sweater was hers' when I saw the monogram.

_____ 4. The dog in that cage is our's.

_____ 5. These books are yours' if you want them.

Demonstrative Pronouns

Demonstrative pronouns point to or single out a person or thing. There are four demonstrative pronouns:

this	these
that	those

Generally speaking, *this* and *these* refer to things close at hand; *that* and *those* refer to things farther away. The four demonstrative pronouns are also commonly used as demonstrative adjectives.

Is anyone using *this* spoon?

I am going to throw away *these* magazines.

I just bought *that* black pickup truck at the curb.

Pick up *those* toys in the corner.

> **TIP** Do not use *them, this here, that there, these here,* or *those there* to point out. Use only *this, that, these,* or *those.*

Activity 3

Cross out the incorrect form of the demonstrative pronoun, and write the correct form in the space provided.

EXAMPLE

_____*Those*_____ ~~Them~~ tires look worn.

_____ 1. This here map is out of date.

_____ 2. Leave them keys out on the coffee table.

_____ 3. I've seen them girls somewhere before.

_____ 4. Jack entered that there dog in an obedience contest.

_____ 5. Where are them new knives?

Review Test   1

Underline the correct word in the parentheses.

1. If the contract negotiations are left up to (they, them), we'll have to accept the results.

2. (Them, Those) student crafts projects have won several awards.

3. Our grandmother told David and (I, me) to leave our muddy shoes outside on the porch.

4. The judge decided that the fault was (theirs', theirs) and ordered them to pay the damages.

5. I gave the money to (she, her) and asked her to put it in the bank's night deposit slot.

6. The black-masked raccoon stared at Rudy and (I, me) for an instant and then ran away.

7. When we saw the smashed window, Lynn and (I, me) didn't know whether to enter the house.

8. (This here, This) is my cousin Manuel.

9. This coat can't be (hers, her's); it's too small.

10. Because we weren't wearing shoes, Tara and (I, me) had a hard time walking on the sharp gravel.

31

Adjectives and Adverbs

This chapter will describe the principal characteristics of adjectives and adverbs.

KEY TERMS

adjectives: words that describe nouns or pronouns. Example: Yoko is a *wise* woman.

adverbs: words that describe verbs, adjectives, or other adverbs. Example: I walked *quickly* to the store.

Adjectives

What Are Adjectives?

Adjectives describe nouns (names of persons, places, or things) or pronouns.

> Yoko is a *wise* woman. (The adjective *wise* describes the noun *woman*.)
>
> She is also *funny*. (The adjective *funny* describes the pronoun *she*.)
>
> I'll carry the *heavy* bag of groceries. (The adjective *heavy* describes the noun *bag*.)
>
> It is *torn*. (The adjective *torn* describes the pronoun *it*.)

Adjectives usually come before the word they describe (as in *wise* woman and *heavy* bag). But they also come after forms of the verb *be* (*is, are, was, were,* and so on). They also follow verbs such as *look, appear, seem, become, sound, taste,* and *smell*.

> That road is *slippery*. (The adjective *slippery* describes the road.)
>
> The dogs are *noisy*. (The adjective *noisy* describes the dogs.)
>
> Those customers were *impatient*. (The adjective *impatient* describes the customers.)
>
> Your room looks *neat*. (The adjective *neat* describes the room.)

Using Adjectives to Compare

For all one-syllable adjectives and some two-syllable adjectives, add *-er* when comparing two things and *-est* when comparing three or more things.

> Phil's beard is *longer* than mine, but Lee's is the *longest*.
>
> Meg may be the *quieter* of the two sisters; but that's not saying much, since they're the *loudest* girls in school.

For some two-syllable adjectives and all longer adjectives, use *more* when comparing two things and *most* when comparing three or more things.

> Liza Minnelli is *more famous* than her sister; but their mother, Judy Garland, is still the *most famous* member of the family.
>
> The red letters on the sign are *more noticeable* than the black ones, but the Day-Glo letters are the *most noticeable*.

You can usually tell when to use *more* and *most* by the sound of a word. For example, you can probably tell by its sound that "carefuller" would be too awkward to say and that *more careful* is thus correct. But there are many words for which both *-er* or *-est* and *more* or *most* are equally correct. For instance, either "a more fair rule" or "a fairer rule" is correct.

To form negative comparisons, use *less* and *least*.

During my first dance class, I felt *less graceful* than an injured elephant.

When the teacher came to our house to complain to my parents, I offered her the *least* comfortable chair in the room.

Points to Remember about Comparing

Point 1

Use only one form of comparison at a time. That is, do not use both an *-er* ending and *more* or both an *-est* ending and *most:*

Incorrect	Correct
My mother's suitcase is always *more heavier* than my father's.	My mother's suitcase is always *heavier* than my father's.
Psycho is still the *most frighteningest* movie I've ever seen.	*Psycho* is still the *most frightening* movie I've ever seen.

Point 2

Learn the irregular forms of the words shown below.

	Comparative (for comparing two things)	Superlative (for comparing three or more things)
bad	worse	worst
good, well	better	best
little (in amount)	less	least
much, many	more	most

Do not use both *more* and an irregular comparative or *most* and an irregular superlative.

Incorrect	Correct
It is *more better* to give than to receive.	It is *better* to give than to receive.
Last night I got the *most worst* snack attack I ever had.	Last night I got the *worst* snack attack I have ever had.

Add to each sentence the correct form of the word in the margin.

EXAMPLES

The _____*worst*_____ job I ever had was babysitting for spoiled four-year-old twins.

The ___*most wonderful*___ day of my life was when my child was born.

1. The _____ chocolate cake I have ever eaten had bananas in it.

2. Aunt Sonja is the _____ of the three sisters.

3. A rain that freezes is _____ than a snowstorm.

4. That's the _____ home I've ever seen—it's shaped like a teapot.

5. Being painfully shy has made Leon the _____ friendly person I know.

Activity

1

bad

wonderful

good

young

bad

unusual

little

Adverbs

What Are Adverbs?

Adverbs describe verbs, adjectives, or other adverbs. They usually end in *-ly*.

The father *gently* hugged the sick child. (The adverb *gently* describes the verb *hugged.*)

Newborns are *totally* innocent. (The adverb *totally* describes the adjective *innocent.*)

The lecturer spoke so *terribly* fast that I had trouble taking notes. (The adverb *terribly* describes the adverb *fast.*)

A Common Mistake with Adverbs and Adjectives

People often mistakenly use an adjective instead of an adverb after a verb.

Incorrect	Correct
Sam needs a haircut *bad.*	Sam needs a haircut *badly.*
She gets along *easy* with others.	She gets along *easily* with others.
You might have lost the race if you hadn't run so *quick* at the beginning.	You might have lost the race if you hadn't run so *quickly* at the beginning.

Underline the adjective or adverb needed.

> **HINT** Remember that adjectives describe nouns, and adverbs describe verbs and other adverbs.

1. As Mac danced, his earring bounced (rapid, rapidly).
2. A drop of (thick, thickly) pea soup dripped down his chin.
3. I hiccuped (continuous, continuously) for fifteen minutes.
4. The detective opened the door (careful, carefully).
5. All she heard when she answered the phone was (heavy, heavily) breathing.

Well and *Good*

Two words that are often confused are *well* and *good*. *Good* is an adjective; it describes nouns. *Well* is usually an adverb; it describes verbs. But *well* (rather than *good*) is used as an adjective when referring to health.

Team up with a fellow classmate and write *well* or *good* in each of the sentences that follow.

1. If you kids do a _____ job of cleaning the garage, I'll take you out for some ice cream.

2. If I organize the office records too _____, my bosses may not need me anymore.

3. After eating a pound of peanuts, I didn't feel too _____.

4. When Ernie got AIDS, he discovered who his _____ friends really were.

5. Just because brothers and sisters fight when they're young doesn't mean they won't get along _____ as adults.

Review Test   1

Underline the correct word in parentheses.

1. The waitress poured (littler, less) coffee into my cup than yours.
2. Humid air seems to make Sid's asthma (more worse, worse).

3. The movie is so interesting that the three hours pass (quick, quickly).

4. The talented boy sang as (confident, confidently) as a seasoned performer.

5. Our band played so (good, well) that a local firm hired us for its annual dinner.

6. Tamika is always (truthful, truthfully), even when it might be better to tell a white lie.

7. The driver stopped the bus (sudden, suddenly) and yelled, "Everybody out!"

8. Shirt and pants in the same color make you look (more thin, thinner) than ones in contrasting colors.

9. Your intentions may have been (good, well), but I'd prefer that you ask before arranging a blind date for me.

10. Our cat likes to sit in the (warmest, most warm) spot in any room—by a fireplace, on a windowsill in the sunshine, or on my lap.

Review Test 2

Write a sentence that uses each of the following adjectives and adverbs correctly.

1. careless _____

2. angrily _____

3. well _____

4. most relaxing _____

5. best _____

32 Misplaced Modifiers

This chapter will describe misplaced modifiers, which are words that, because of awkward placement, do not describe what the author intended them to describe.

INCORRECT:

George couldn't drive to work in his sports car with a broken leg.

The sentence makes it sound as if the car has the broken leg, not George.

CORRECT:

With his broken leg, George couldn't drive to work in his sports car.

The phrase "with a broken leg" has been moved so that it is closer to "George"; now it is more clear whose leg is broken.

Misplaced modifiers are words that, because of awkward placement, do not describe what the writer intended them to describe. A misplaced modifier can make a sentence confusing or unintentionally funny. To avoid this, place words as close as possible to what they describe.

www.mhhe.com/langan

Misplaced Words	Correctly Placed Words
George couldn't drive to work in his small sports car *with a broken leg.* (The sports car had a broken leg?)	With a broken leg, George couldn't drive to work in his small sports car. (The words describing George are now placed next to *George.*)
The toaster was sold to us by a charming salesman *with a money-back guarantee.* (The salesman had a money-back guarantee?)	The toaster with a money-back guarantee was sold to us by a charming salesman. (The words describing the toaster are now placed next to it.)
He *nearly* brushed his teeth for twenty minutes every night. (He came close to brushing his teeth but in fact did not brush them at all?)	He brushed his teeth for nearly twenty minutes every night. (The meaning—that he brushed his teeth for a long time—is now clear.)

Underline the misplaced word or words in each sentence. Then rewrite the sentence, placing related words together and thereby making the meaning clear.

Activity

1

EXAMPLES

Frozen shrimp lay in the steel pans <u>that were thawing rapidly</u>.
Frozen shrimp that were thawing rapidly lay in the steel pans.

The speaker discussed the problem of crowded prisons <u>at the college</u>.
At the college, the speaker discussed the problem of crowded prisons.

1. The patient talked about his childhood on the psychiatrist's couch.

2. The crowd watched the tennis players with swiveling heads.

3. Vonnie put four hamburger patties on the counter which she was cooking for dinner.

4. Steve carefully hung the new suit that he would wear to his first job interview in the bedroom closet.

_____

5. Anne ripped the shirt on a car door that she made in sewing class.

_____

6. The latest Denzel Washington movie has almost opened in 2,200 theaters across the country.

_____

7. The newscaster spoke softly into a microphone wearing a bulletproof vest.

_____

8. The tenants left town in a dilapidated old car owing two months' rent.

_____

9. The woman picked up a heavy frying pan with arthritis.

_____

10. I discovered an unusual plant in the greenhouse that oozed a milky juice.

_____

Review Test   1

Write MM for _misplaced modifier_ or C for _correct_ in the space provided for each sentence.

_____   1. I nearly napped for twenty minutes during the biology lecture.

_____   2. I napped for nearly twenty minutes during the biology lecture.

_____   3. Ron paused as the girl he had been following stopped at a shop window.

_____   4. Ron paused as the girl stopped at a shop window he had been following.

_____   5. Marta dropped out of school after taking ten courses on Friday.

_____   6. On Friday, Marta dropped out of school after taking ten courses.

_____ 7. Under his shirt, the player wore a good luck charm that re-sembled a tiny elephant.

_____ 8. The player wore a good luck charm under his shirt that re-sembled a tiny elephant.

_____ 9. I ordered a new telephone from the mail-order catalog shaped like a cartoon character.

_____ 10. I ordered from the mail-order catalog a new telephone shaped like a cartoon character.

Review Test 2

Make the changes needed to correct the misplaced modifier in each sentence.

1. Henry Wadsworth Longfellow wrote that rainbows are flowers that have died and gone to heaven in a poem.

   _____

   _____

2. Because of the storm, I almost arrived two hours late for my first day on the job.

   _____

   _____

3. The apprentice watched the carpenter expertly fit the door with envious eyes.

   _____

   _____

4. The photographer pointed the camera at the shy deer equipped with a special night-vision scope.

   _____

   _____

5. The people on the bus stared at the ceiling or read newspapers with tired faces.

   _____

   _____

33 Dangling Modifiers

This chapter will describe dangling modifiers—descriptive words that open a sentence but do not describe what the author intended them to describe.

INCORRECT:

While reading the newspaper, my dog sat with me on the steps.

The sentence misleadingly states that the dog was reading the newspaper.

CORRECT:

While I was reading the newspaper, my dog sat with me on the steps.

The sentence makes it clear that the subject "I" was reading the newspaper.

A modifier that opens a sentence must be followed immediately by the word it is meant to describe. Otherwise, the modifier is said to be *dangling*, and the sentence takes on an unintended meaning. For example, in the sentence

> While reading the newspaper, my dog sat with me on the front steps.

the unintended meaning is that the *dog* was reading the paper. What the writer meant, of course, was that *he* (or *she*), the writer, was reading the paper. The writer should have said,

> While reading the newspaper, *I* sat with my dog on the front steps.

The dangling modifier could also be corrected by placing the subject within the opening word group:

> While *I* was reading the newspaper, my dog sat with me on the front steps.

Here are other sentences with dangling modifiers. Read the explanations of why they are dangling, and look carefully at how they are corrected.

Dangling	Correct
Shaving in front of the steamy mirror, the razor nicked Ed's chin. (*Who* was shaving in front of the mirror? The answer is not *razor* but *Ed*. The subject *Ed* must be added.)	Shaving in front of the steamy mirror, *Ed* nicked his chin with the razor. *Or* When *Ed* was shaving in front of the steamy mirror, he nicked his chin with the razor.
While turning over the bacon, hot grease splashed my arm. (*Who* is turning over the bacon? The answer is not *hot grease,* as it unintentionally seems to be, but *I*. The subject *I* must be added.)	While *I* was turning over the bacon, hot grease splashed my arm. *Or* While turning over the bacon, *I* was splashed by hot grease.
Taking the exam, the room was so stuffy that Keisha almost fainted. (*Who* took the exam? The answer is not *the room* but *Keisha*. The subject *Keisha* must follow the modifier.)	Taking the exam, *Keisha* found the room so stuffy that she almost fainted. *Or* When *Keisha* took the exam, the room was so stuffy that she almost fainted.

| To impress the interviewer, punctuality is essential. (*Who* is to impress the interviewer? The answer is not *punctuality* but *you.* The subject *you* must be added.) | To impress the interviewer, *you* must be punctual. *Or* For *you* to impress the interviewer, punctuality is essential. |

The examples above show two ways of correcting a dangling modifier. Decide on a logical subject and do one of the following:

1. Place the subject *within* the opening word group:

    When *Ed* was shaving in front of the steamy mirror, he nicked his chin.

> **TIP** In some cases, an appropriate subordinating word such as *when* must be added and the verb may have to be changed slightly as well.

---

2. Place the subject right *after* the opening word group:

    Shaving in front of the steamy mirror, *Ed* nicked his chin.

Activity

1

Look at the opening words in each sentence and ask *who*. The subject that answers the question should be nearby in the sentence. If it is not, provide the logical subject by using either method of correction described above.

EXAMPLE

While pitching his tent, a snake bit Tony on the ankle.

While Tony was pitching his tent, a snake bit him on the ankle.

Or

While pitching his tent, Tony was bitten on the ankle by a snake.

1. Dancing on their hind legs, the audience cheered wildly as the elephants paraded by.

    _____

    _____

2. Last seen wearing dark glasses and a blond wig, the police spokesperson said the suspect was still being sought.

    _____

    _____

3. Pouring out the cereal, a coupon fell into my bowl of milk.

_____

_____

4. Escorted by dozens of police motorcycles, I knew the limousine carried someone important.

_____

_____

5. Tired and exasperated, the fight we had was inevitable.

_____

_____

6. Packed tightly in a tiny can, Fran had difficulty removing the anchovies.

_____

_____

7. Kicked carelessly under the bed, Raquel finally found her sneakers.

_____

_____

8. Working at the Xerox machine, the morning dragged on.

_____

_____

9. Sitting at a sidewalk café, all sorts of interesting people passed by.

_____

_____

10. Though somewhat warped, Uncle Zeke played his records from the forties.

_____

_____

Review Test   1

Write DM for *dangling modifier* or C for *correct* in the space provided for each sentence.

_____   1. While riding the bicycle, a vicious-looking German shepherd snapped at Tim's ankles.

_____ 2. While Tim was riding the bicycle, a vicious-looking German shepherd snapped at his ankles.

_____ 3. Afraid to look his father in the eye, Howard kept his head bowed.

_____ 4. Afraid to look his father in the eye, Howard's head remained bowed.

_____ 5. Boring and silly, I turned the TV show off.

_____ 6. I turned off the boring and silly TV show.

_____ 7. Munching leaves from a tall tree, the giraffe fascinated the children.

_____ 8. Munching leaves from a tall tree, the children were fascinated by the giraffe.

_____ 9. At the age of twelve, several colleges had already accepted the boy genius.

_____ 10. At the age of twelve, the boy genius had already been accepted by several colleges.

Review Test 2

Make the changes needed to correct the dangling modifier in each sentence.

1. Not having had much sleep, my concentration during class was weak.

    _____

    _____

2. Joined at the hip, a team of surgeons successfully separated the Siamese twins.

    _____

    _____

3. Wading in the shallow surf, a baby shark brushed past my leg.

    _____

    _____

4. While being restrained by federal marshals, the judge sentenced the kidnapper.

_____

_____

5. In a sentimental frame of mind, the music brought tears to Beth's eyes.

_____

_____

Review Test 3

Complete the following sentences. In each case, a logical subject should follow the opening words.

EXAMPLE

Looking through the door's peephole, *I couldn't see who rang the doorbell.*

_____

1. Noticing the light turn yellow, _____

2. Being fragile, _____

3. While washing the car, _____

4. Although very expensive, _____

5. Driving past the cemetery, _____

Mechanics

---

re: texas alignment files — Inbox

| Delete | Junk | | Reply | Reply All | Forward | | Print |

From: Shirley Michels
Subject: **re: texas alignment files**
Date: April 4, 2007 11:26:06 AM CDT
To: Amanda Crawford

Good morning, Amanda,

I have found the reports you were asking about for the texas project. our finance Department will get back to you as soon as they finalize the budget spreadsheets.

thanks,
shirley

People often forget to apply sentence skills to their writing when composing e-mails. What can be done to correct the sentence-skills mistakes in the e-mail pictured here? Do you think such mistakes should be excusable in e-mails?

Manuscript Form

34

This chapter will describe manuscript form: the required format for any paper you hand in.

KEY TERMS

format: the formal characteristics of a manuscript, comprising such things as paper size, margins, spacing, and font.

manuscript: literally, a paper written by hand; in this text, any paper handed in for a grade.

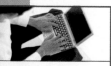

When you hand in a paper for any course, it will probably be judged first by its format. It is important, then, to make the paper look attractive, neat, and easy to read. Here is a checklist you should use when preparing a paper for an instructor:

———— • Is the paper full-size, 8½ by 11 inches?

———— • Are there wide margins (1 to 1½ inches) all around the paper? In particular, have you been careful not to crowd the right-hand or bottom margin?

———— • If the paper is handwritten, have you

> Used a blue or black pen?
>
> Been careful not to overlap letters or to make decorative loops on letters?
>
> Made all your letters distinct, with special attention to *a, e, i, o,* and *u*—five letters that people sometimes write illegibly?
>
> Kept all your capital letters clearly distinct from small letters?

———— • Have you centered the title of your paper on the first line of page 1? Have you been careful *not* to put quotation marks around the title and *not* to underline it? Have you capitalized all the words in the title except short connecting words like *of, for, the, and, in,* and *to?*

———— • Have you skipped a line between the title and the first line of your paper?

———— • Have you indented the first line of each paragraph about five spaces (half an inch) from the left-hand margin?

———— • Have you made commas, periods, and other punctuation marks firm and clear? If you are typing, have you left a double space after a period?

———— • If you have broken any words at the end of a line, have you been careful to break only between syllables?

———— • Have you put your name, the date, and other information at the end of the paper (or wherever your instructor has specified)?

Also ask yourself these important questions about the title and the first sentence of your paper:

———— • Is your title made up of several words that tell what the paper is about? (The title should be just several words, not a complete sentence.)

———— • Does the first sentence of your paper stand independent of the title? (The reader should *not* have to use the words in the title to make sense of the opening sentence.)

Use the checklist to locate the seven mistakes in format in the following lines from a student paper. Explain the mistakes in the spaces provided. One mistake is described for you as an example.

	"Being alone"
	This is something that I simply cannot tolerate, and I will predictably
	go to great lengths to prevent it. For example, if I know that

1. *Hyphenate only between syllables (predict-ably, not predi-ctably).*
2. _____
3. _____
4. _____
5. _____
6. _____
7. _____
   _____

35 Capital Letters

This chapter will describe

- the main uses of capital letters
- secondary uses of capital letters
- unnecessary use of capital letters

INCORRECT:

The Bank is located on the corner.

"The" is capitalized correctly because it appears at the beginning of the sentence, but "bank" is not the building's official, specific name.

CORRECT:

The bank is located on the corner.

"The" is capitalized to start the sentence, but "bank" is left lowercase.

Main Uses of Capital Letters

Capital letters are used with

1. First word in a sentence or direct quotation
2. Names of persons and the word *I*
3. Names of particular places
4. Names of days of the week, months, and holidays
5. Names of commercial products
6. Titles of books, magazines, newspapers, articles, stories, poems, films, television shows, songs, papers that you write, and the like
7. Names of companies, associations, unions, clubs, religious and political groups, and other organizations

Each use is illustrated in this chapter.

First Word in a Sentence or Direct Quotation

The corner grocery was robbed last night.

The alien said, "Take me to your leader."

"If you need help," said Teri, "call me. I'll be over in no time."

In the third example above, *If* and *I'll* are capitalized because they start new sentences. But *call* is not capitalized, because it is part of the first sentence.

Names of Persons and the Word *I*

Last night, I saw a hilarious movie starring Stan Laurel and Oliver Hardy.

Names of Particular Places and Institutions

Although Bill dropped out of Port Charles High School, he eventually earned his degree and got a job with Atlas Realty Company.

But   Use small letters if the specific name is not given.

Although Bill dropped out of high school, he eventually earned his degree and got a job with a real estate company.

Names of Days of the Week, Months, and Holidays

On the last Friday afternoon in May, the day before Memorial Day, my boss is having a barbecue for all the employees.

But   Use small letters for the seasons—summer, fall, winter, spring.

Most people feel more energetic in the spring and fall.

Names of Commercial Products

Keith installed a new Sony stereo and a Motorola cell phone into his old Ford Ranger pickup.

But   Use small letters for the *type* of product (stereo, cell phone, pickup, and so on).

Titles of Books, Magazines, Newspapers, Articles, Stories, Poems, Films, Television Shows, Songs, Papers That You Write, and the Like

We read the book *Hiroshima,* by John Hersey, for our history class.

In the doctor's waiting room, I watched *All My Children,* read an article in *Reader's Digest,* and leafed through the *Miami Herald.*

Names of Companies, Associations, Unions, Clubs, Religious and Political Groups, and Other Organizations

Joe Naples is a Roman Catholic, but his wife is a Methodist.

The Hilldale Square Dancers' Club has won many competitions.

Brian, a member of Bricklayers Local 431 and the Knights of Columbus, works for Ace Construction.

Activity

1

Underline the words that need capitals in the following sentences. Then write the capitalized form of each word in the space provided. The number of spaces tells you how many corrections to make in each case.

EXAMPLE

In our biology class, each student must do a report on an article in the magazine *scientific american.*   <u>*Scientific*</u>   <u>*American*</u>

1. Leon's collection of beatles souvenirs includes a pair of tickets from their last concert in candlestick park in San Francisco.

    _____   _____   _____

2. Yumi read in *natural health* magazine that abraham lincoln suffered from severe depression.

    _____   _____   _____   _____

3. When i have a cold, I use vicks ointment and chew listerine lozenges.

   _____   _____   _____

4. Since no man volunteered for the job, the boy scouts in springfield, illinois, have a woman troop leader.

   _____   _____   _____   _____

5. A nature trail for the blind in cape cod, massachusetts, has signs written in Braille that encourage visitors to smell and touch the plants.

   _____   _____   _____

6. Some of the most popular items at a restaurant called big river are chilean sea bass and atlantic clam chowder.

   _____   _____   _____   _____

7. My father is a confirmed Dallas cowboys fan, though he lives in boston.

   _____   _____

8. Martha bought a diet pepsi to wash down her hostess twinkie.

   _____   _____   _____   _____

9. Vince listened to a U2 album called *The Joshua Tree* while Donna read an article in *glamour* titled "What Do men Really want?"

   _____   _____   _____

10. After having her baby, joan received a card from one of her friends that read, "congratulations, we all knew you had it in you."

   _____   _____

Other Uses of Capital Letters

Capital letters are also used with

www.mhhe.com/langan

1. Names that show family relationships
2. Titles of persons when used with their names
3. Specific school courses
4. Languages
5. Geographic locations
6. Historical periods and events

7. Races, nations, and nationalities
8. Opening and closing of a letter

Each use is illustrated on the following pages.

Names That Show Family Relationships

All his life, Father has been addicted to gadgets.

I browsed through Grandmother's collection of old photographs.

Aunt Florence and Uncle Bill bought a mobile home.

But Do not capitalize words like *mother, father, grandmother, grandfather, uncle, aunt,* and so on when they are preceded by a possessive word (such as *my, your, his, her, our, their*).

All his life, my father has been addicted to gadgets.

I browsed through my grandmother's collection of old photographs.

My aunt and uncle bought a mobile home.

Titles of Persons When Used with Their Names

I contributed to Senator McGrath's campaign fund.

Is Dr. Gomez on vacation?

Professor Adams announced that there would be no tests in the course.

But   Use lowercase letters when titles appear by themselves, without specific names.

I contributed to my senator's campaign fund.

Is the doctor on vacation?

The professor announced that there would be no tests in the course.

Specific School Courses

The college offers evening sections of Introductory Psychology I, Abnormal Psychology, Psychology and Statistics, and Educational Psychology.

But   Use lowercase letters for general subject areas.

The college offers evening sections of many psychology courses.

Languages

My grandfather's Polish accent makes his English difficult to understand.

Geographic Locations

He grew up in the Midwest but moved to the South to look for a better job.

But Use lowercase letters in directions.

Head west for five blocks and then turn south on State Street.

Historical Periods and Events

During the Middle Ages, the Black Death killed over one-quarter of Europe's population.

Races, Nations, and Nationalities

The questionnaire asked whether the head of our household was Caucasian, African American, Asian, Latino, or Native American.

Tanya has lived on army bases in Germany, Italy, and Spain.

Denise's beautiful features reflect her Chinese and Mexican parentage.

Opening and Closing of a Letter

Dear Sir: Sincerely yours,

Dear Ms. Henderson: Truly yours,

Capitalize only the first word in a closing.

Underline the words that need capitals in the following sentences. Then write the capitalized forms of the words in the spaces provided. The number of spaces tells you how many corrections to make in each case.

1. During world war II, many americans were afraid that the japanese would invade California.

    _____ _____ _____ _____

2. On their job site in korea, the french, swiss, and chinese coworkers used English to communicate.

    _____ _____ _____ _____

3. When uncle harvey got the bill from his doctor, he called the American Medical Association to complain.

    _____ _____

4. Dr. Freeling of the business department is offering a new course called intro-duction to web design.

_____   _____   _____

5. A new restaurant featuring vietnamese cuisine has just opened on the south side of the city.

_____

Unnecessary Use of Capitals

Activity

3

Many errors occur when capitalization is used when it is not needed. Working with a fellow classmate, underline the incorrectly capitalized words in the following sentences, and write the correct forms in the spaces provided. The number of spaces tells you how many corrections to make in each sentence.

1. George Washington's Forces starved at Valley Forge because Pennsylvania Farmers preferred to sell food to the British for cash.

_____   _____

2. The virus damaged the files on my Brother's Dell Computer.

_____   _____

3. The country cheered in the summer of 1998 when Mark McGwire of the St. Louis Cardinals Baseball Team broke the single-season Home Run record set by Roger Maris.

_____   _____   _____   _____

4. In his Book titled *Offbeat Museums,* Saul Rubin tells about various Unusual Museums, such as the Kansas Barbed Wire museum.

_____   _____   _____   _____

5. Einstein's theory of relativity, which he developed when he was only twenty-six, led to the invention of the Electron Microscope, Television, and the Atomic bomb.

_____   _____   _____   _____

Review Test 1

Add capitals where needed in the following sentences.

EXAMPLE

    In an injured tone, Mary demanded, "~~w~~hy wasn't ~~u~~ncle Lou invited to the party?"

1. To keep warm, a homeless old man sits on a steam vent near hampton park on tenth street.

2. Silent movie stars of the twenties, like charlie chaplin and gloria swanson, earned more than a million tax-free dollars a year.

3. Insects living in mammoth cave in kentucky include blind crickets, spiders, and flies.

4. When former president Bill Clinton was a boy in arkansas, he traveled to Washington, D.C., where he was photographed shaking hands with president John F. Kennedy.

5. In an old movie, an attractive young lady invites groucho marx to join her.

6. "why?" asks groucho. "are you coming apart?"

7. I was halfway to the wash & dry Laundromat on elm street when i realized that my box of tide was still home on the kitchen counter.

8. Although I know that mother loves holidays, even I was surprised when she announced a party in february to celebrate groundhog day.

9. *Rolling stone* magazine features an article about plans to remake the Alfred Hitchcock classic *the birds* and a review of a new biography about elvis presley.

10. Celebrities have earned big money by endorsing products, including nike shoes, trident gum, and jell-O pudding.

Review Test 2

On separate paper, write

1. Seven sentences demonstrating the seven main uses of capital letters.

2. Eight sentences demonstrating the eight other uses of capital letters.

36 Numbers and Abbreviations

This chapter will describe the proper use of numbers and abbreviations.

INCORRECT:

It took us 5 weeks to find an apt. we both liked.

"5" can be written as one word ("five") so it should be spelled out. "Apartment" can be abbreviated on an envelope, but should be written out in a sentence.

CORRECT:

It took us five weeks to find an apartment we both liked.

Spelling out "five" and "apartment" is correct in this format.

INCORRECT:

We'll have the report for you in 72 hours.

"72" can be written out as "seventy-two," which is fewer than three words.

CORRECT:

We'll have the report for you in seventy-two hours.

Because the number can be expressed in fewer than three words, it is spelled out.

KEY TERM

abbreviations: shortened forms of words, often used for convenience in writing. Certain abbreviations (such as *Mr., a.m.,* and *e.g.*) are acceptable in formal writing; in general, however, the complete form of words is preferred.

Numbers

Here are three helpful rules for using numbers.

Rule 1

Spell out numbers that take no more than two words. Otherwise, use the numbers themselves.

> In Jody's kitchen is her collection of seventy-two cookbooks.
>
> Jody has a file of 350 recipes.
>
> It will take about two weeks to fix the computer database.
>
> Since a number of people use the database, the company will lose over 150 workdays.
>
> Only twelve students have signed up for the field trip.
>
> Nearly 250 students came to the lecture.

Rule 2

Be consistent when you use a series of numbers. If some numbers in a sentence or paragraph require more than two words, then use numbers for the others, too.

> After the storm, maintenance workers unclogged 46 drains, removed 123 broken tree limbs, and rescued 3 kittens who were stuck in a drainpipe.

Rule 3

Use numbers to show dates, times, addresses, percentages, and chapters of a book.

> The burglary was committed on October 30, 2006, but was not discovered until January 2, 2007.
>
> Before I went to bed, I set my alarm for 6:45 a.m. (But spell out numbers before *o'clock*. For example: I didn't get out of bed until seven o'clock.)
>
> The library is located at 45 West 52nd Street.
>
> When you take the skin off a piece of chicken, you remove about 40 percent of the fat.
>
> The name of the murderer is revealed in Chapter 8 on page 236.

Activity	Cross out the mistakes in numbers and write the corrections in the spaces provided.
1	

1. The Puerto Rican Pride Parade will begin at three-thirty in front of the newspaper office at one-oh-six South Forty-Second Street.

   _____   _____   _____

2. It took 4 hours to proofread all 75 pages of the manuscript.

   _____   _____

3. We expect to have fifty percent of the work completed by March tenth.

   _____   _____

Abbreviations

www.mhhe.com/langan

Using abbreviations can save you time when you take notes. In formal writing, however, you should avoid most abbreviations. Listed below are some of the few abbreviations that are considered acceptable in compositions. Note that a period is used after most abbreviations.

1. Mr., Mrs., Ms., Jr., Sr., Dr. when used with names:

   Mrs. Johnson   Dr. Garcia   Howard Kelley Jr.

2. Time references:

   a.m.   p.m.   BC, AD

3. Initials in a person's name:

   J. Edgar Hoover   John F. Kennedy   Michael J. Fox

4. Organizations, technical words, and company names known primarily by their initials:

   IBM   UNICEF   ABC   IRS   NBA   AIDS

Activity	Cross out the words that should not be abbreviated, and correct them in the spaces provided.
2	

1. Between mid-Nov. and the beginning of Jan., I typically gain about five lbs.

   _____   _____   _____

2. I had such a bad headache this aftern. that I called my doc. for an appt.

   _____   _____   _____

3. I stopped at the p.o. at about twenty min. past ten and bought five dol. worth of stamps.

    _____   _____   _____   _____

Review Test 1

Cross out the mistakes in numbers and abbreviations, and correct them in the spaces provided.

1. Sanjay was shocked when he transferred from a small h.s. to one with over 5,000 students.

    _____   _____   _____   _____

2. Grandpa lived to be ninety-nine despite smoking 3 packs of cigs. every day.

    _____   _____

3. Although the 2 girls are twins, they have different birthdays: one was born just before midnight on Feb. twenty-fifth and the other a few minutes later, after midnight.

    _____   _____   _____

4. In their first week of Span. class, students learned to count from 1 to twenty-one and studied Chapter One in their textbook.

    _____   _____   _____

5. When I cleaned out the junk drawer in the kitch., I found twelve rubber bands, thirty-seven paper clips, and 3 used-up batteries.

    _____   _____

Punctuation

Is there a punctuation error in the sign pictured here?
If so, how would you correct it?

Apostrophe

This chapter will describe the two main uses of the apostrophe. The sentences below will introduce you to one of these uses—to show ownership or possession. See if you can guess the other main use of the apostrophe before turning the page.

INCORRECT:

Because of the dogs constant barking, I could not sleep all night.

An apostrophe is needed before the *s* in dogs to show possession of the constant barking.

CORRECT:

Because of the dog's constant barking, I could not sleep all night.

With the apostrophe included it is clear that the dog is the possessor of the constant barking.

KEY TERMS

apostrophe: a punctuation mark generally used in order to (1) show the omission of one or more letters in a contraction, and to (2) show ownership or possession.

contraction: the combination of two words through omission of one or more letters and use of an apostrophe. Example: *hasn't* (for *has not*)

The two main uses of the apostrophe are

1. To show the omission of one or more letters in a contraction
2. To show ownership or possession

Each use is explained in this chapter.

www.mhhe.com/langan

Apostrophe in Contractions

A *contraction* is formed when two words are combined to make one word. An apostrophe is used to show where letters are omitted in forming the contraction. Here are two contractions:

have + not = haven't (the *o* in *not* has been omitted)

I + will = I'll (the *wi* in *will* has been omitted)

Following are some other common contractions:

I + am = I'm	it + is = it's
I + have = I've	it + has = it's
I + had = I'd	is + not = isn't
who + is = who's	could + not = couldn't
do + not = don't	I + would = I'd
did + not = didn't	they + are = they're

Will + not has an unusual contraction: won't.

Activity

1

Write the contractions for the words in parentheses. One is done for you.

1. (Are not) _____*Aren't*_____ the reserve books in the library kept at the circulation desk?

2. If (they are) _____ coming over, (I had) _____ better cook more hot dogs.

3. (I am) _____ the kind of student (who is) _____ extremely nervous before tests.

4. (We are) _____ hoping to find out (who is) _____ responsible for this error; (it is) _____ important to us to keep our customers happy.

5. I (cannot) _____ remember if (there is) _____ gas in the car or not.

> **TIP** Even though contractions are common in everyday speech and in written dialogue, it is often best to avoid them in formal writing.

Apostrophe to Show Ownership or Possession

To show ownership or possession, we can use such words as *belongs to, possessed by, owned by,* or (most commonly) *of.*

> the umbrella *that belongs to* Mark
>
> the toys *possessed by* children
>
> the tape recorder *owned by* the school
>
> the gentleness *of* my father

But the apostrophe and *s* (if the word does not end in *s*) is often the quickest and easiest way to show possession. Thus we can say

> Mark's umbrella
>
> children's toys
>
> the school's tape recorder
>
> my father's gentleness

Points to Remember

1. The *'s* goes with the owner or possessor (in the examples given, *Mark, children, the school, my father*). What follows is the person or thing possessed (in the examples given, *the umbrella, the toys, the tape recorder, gentleness*).

2. There should always be a break between the word and *'s*.

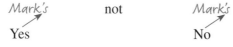

   Mark's   not   Mark's

   Yes   No

3. An apostrophe and *s* are used to show possession with a singular word even if the word already ends in *s*: for example, Doris's purse (the purse belonging to Doris).

www.mhhe.com/langan

Activity

2

Working in groups of two or three, rewrite the *italicized* part of each of the sentences below, using *'s* to show possession. Remember that the *'s* goes with the owner or possessor.

EXAMPLE

The wing of the bluejay was broken.

The bluejay's wing was broken.

1. *The annoying voice of the comedian* irritated me, so I changed the TV channel.

2. *The performance of the quarterback* is inconsistent.

3. *The thin hand belonging to the old woman* felt as dry as parchment.

4. *In the window of the jewelry store* is a sign reading "Ears Pierced While You Wait."

5. A fly flew into *the mouth of the TV weatherperson.*

6. *The new denim shirt belonging to Lamont* was as scratchy as sandpaper.

7. *The hair belonging to Rachel* is usually not green—she colored it for Halloween.

8. *The bowl of cereal belonging to Dennis* refused to snap, crackle, or pop.

9. *The Honda owned by Donna* was crammed with boxes and furniture.

10. *The previous tenant of the apartment* had painted all the walls bright green.

Add *'s* to each of the following words to make it the possessor or owner of something. Then write sentences using the words. The first one is done for you.

Activity

3

1. rock star *rock star's*

    The rock star's limousine pulled up to the curb.

2. Felipe _____

    _____

3. pilot _____

    _____

4. neighbor _____

    _____

5. school _____

    _____

6. gunslinger _____

    _____

Apostrophe versus Possessive Pronouns

Do not use an apostrophe with possessive pronouns. They already show ownership. Possessive pronouns include *his, hers, its, yours, ours,* and *theirs*.

Incorrect	Correct
The sun warped his' albums.	The sun warped his albums.
The restored Model T is theirs'.	The restored Model T is theirs.
The decision is yours'.	The decision is yours.
The plaid suitcase is ours'.	The plaid suitcase is ours.
The lion charged its' prey.	The lion charged its prey.

Apostrophe versus Simple Plurals

When you want to make a word plural, just add an *s* at the end of the word. Do not add an apostrophe. For example, the plural of the word *movie* is *movies,* not *movie's* or *movies'*.

Look at this sentence:

Tim coveted his roommate's collection of cassette tapes and compact discs.

The words *tapes* and *discs* are simple plurals, meaning more than one tape, more than one disc. The plural is shown by adding *s* only. On the other hand, the *'s* after *roommate* shows possession—that the roommate owns the tapes and discs.

Activity

4

Insert an apostrophe where needed to show possession in the following sentences. Write *plural* above words where the *s* ending simply means more than one thing. Once you have completed the activity, compare your answers with a fellow classmate.

EXAMPLE

Arlene's tinted contact lenses protect her eyes from glare.

(*plural* above "lenses"; *plural* above "eyes")

1. Harry grasped his wifes arm as she stood on in-line skates for the first time.

2. Vonettes decision to study computer science is based on predictions of good opportunities for women in that field.

3. The fires extreme heat had melted the telephones in the office and welded the metal chairs into a twisted heap.

4. At the doctors request, Lyndon pulled up his shirt and revealed the zipperlike scars from his operation.

5. Of all the peoples names in all the worlds countries, the most common is Muhammad.

6. At the end of the day, Hals shirt and pants smelled like gasoline, and his fingernails were rimmed with grease.

7. The childrens shouts of delight grew louder as the clown added eggs, lightbulbs, and a bowling ball to the items he was juggling.

8. Tinas camping handbook suggests that we bring water purification tablets and nylon ropes.

9. Carmens leaky pen had stained her fingers a deep blue.

10. The rattlesnakes head has a sensitive pit below the eyes, capable of detecting the body heat of warm-blooded prey.

Apostrophe with Plurals Ending in -*s*

Plurals that end in -*s* show possession simply by adding the apostrophe, rather than an apostrophe and *s*.

the Thompsons' porch
the players' victory
her parents' motor home
the Rolling Stones' last CD
the soldiers' hats

Add an apostrophe where needed.

Activity

5

1. Several campers tents collapsed during the storm.

2. The Murrays phone bills are often over two hundred dollars a month.

3. Many buildings steep steps make it difficult for wheelchair users to gain access.

4. The twins habit of dressing alike was started by their mother when they were children.

5. At the crowded intersection, several young men rushed out to wash the cars windshields.

Review Test   1

In each sentence, underline the two words that need apostrophes. Then write the words correctly in the spaces provided.

_____ 1. The sagging sofas stuffing was coming out in several places,

_____   and one of the chairs legs was broken.

_____ 2. A shaky rope ladder led from the barns wooden floor to the

_____   haylofts dusty shadows.

_____ 3. The paperback books glaring purple and orange cover was

_____   designed to attract a hurrying customers eye.

_____ 4. Sofias essay was due in a matter of hours, but she suffered

_____   writers block that emptied her brain.

_____ 5. While he waited in his bosss office, Charlies nervous fingers

_____   shredded a Styrofoam coffee cup into a pile of jagged white flakes.

_____ 6. Gregory couldnt remember whether he had left his wallet in

_____   his mothers car or at home.

_____ 7. Members of the parents association constructed a maze made

_____   of old tires for the childrens playground.

_____   8. The cats great green eyes grew even wider as the curious dogs
_____   sniffing nose came too close to her.
_____   9. The suns rays beat down until the streets blacktopped surface
_____   softened with the heat.
_____   10. The rivers swirling floodwaters lapped against the Hender-
_____   sons porch.

Quotation Marks

Quotation marks are punctuation marks that indicate exact words or the titles of short works. This chapter will describe the two main uses of quotation marks. The sentences below will introduce you to one of these uses—to set off the exact words of a speaker or writer. See if you can guess the other main use of quotation marks before turning the page.

INCORRECT:

I'm giving up smoking tomorrow said Jason.

Because it is a direct quote, what Jason said should be in quotation marks.

CORRECT:

"I'm giving up smoking tomorrow," said Jason.

Jason's words are directly attributed by the quotation marks.

The two main uses of quotation marks are

1. To set off the exact words of a speaker or writer
2. To set off the titles of short works

Each use is explained here.

Quotation Marks to Set Off the Words of a Speaker or Writer

www.mhhe.com/langan

Use quotation marks to show the exact words of a speaker or writer.

> "I feel as though I've been here before," Angie murmured to her husband.
> (Quotation marks set off the exact words that Angie spoke to her husband.)

> Ben Franklin once wrote, "To lengthen thy life, lessen thy meals."
> (Quotation marks set off the exact words that Ben Franklin wrote.)

> "Did you know," said the nutrition expert, "that it's healthier to be ten pounds overweight?"
> (Two pairs of quotation marks are used to enclose the nutrition expert's exact words.)

> The biology professor said, "Ants are a lot like human beings. They farm their own food and raise smaller insects as livestock. And like humans, ants send armies to war."
> (Note that the end quotation marks do not come until the end of the biology professor's speech. Place quotation marks before the first quoted word and after the last quoted word. As long as no interruption occurs in the speech, do not use quotation marks for each new sentence.)

TIP In the four examples above, notice that a comma sets the quoted part off from the rest of the sentence. Also, observe that commas and periods at the end of a quotation always go *inside* quotation marks.

Complete the following statements, which explain how capital letters, commas, and periods are used in quotations. Refer to the four examples above as guides.

1. Every quotation begins with a _____ letter.
2. When a quotation is split (as in the sentence about the nutrition expert), the second part does not begin with a capital letter unless it is a

    _____ sentence.

3. _____ are used to separate the quoted part of a sentence from the rest of the sentence.

4. Commas and periods that come at the end of a quotation go

_____ the quotation marks.

The answers are *capital, new, Commas,* and *inside.*

Place quotation marks around the exact words of a speaker or writer in the sentences that follow.

Activity 1

1. Several people have been credited with saying, The more I see of people, the more I like dogs.

2. Beatrice asked, Do you give a discount to senior citizens?

3. This hamburger is raw! cried Leon.

4. The bumper sticker on the rear of the battered old car read, Don't laugh—it's paid for.

5. I know why Robin Hood robbed only the rich, said the comedian. The poor don't have any money.

6. These CDs, proclaimed the television announcer, are not sold in any store.

7. When chefs go to great lengths, the woman at the diet center said, I go to great widths.

8. If I go with you to the dinner party, my friend said, you must promise not to discuss politics.

9. On a tombstone in a Maryland cemetery are the words Here lies an atheist, all dressed up and no place to go.

10. The columnist advised, Be nice to people on your way up because you'll meet them on your way down.

Activity 2

1. Write a sentence in which you quote a favorite expression of someone you know. In the same sentence, identify the person's relationship to you.

EXAMPLE

My grandfather loves to say, "It can't be as bad as all that."

_____

_____

_____

2. Write a quotation that contains the words *Pablo asked Teresa*. Write a second quotation that includes the words *Teresa replied*.

_____

_____

_____

_____

_____

3. Quote an interesting sentence or two from a book or magazine. In the same sentence, identify the title and author of the work.

EXAMPLE   *In The Dilbert Desk Calendar, by Scott Adams, the cartoon*
character Dilbert says, "I can please only one person per day. Today isn't
your day, and tomorrow isn't looking good either."

_____

_____

_____

_____

_____

_____

_____

Indirect Quotations

An indirect quotation is a rewording of someone else's comments rather than a word-for-word direct quotation. The word *that* often signals an indirect quotation.

Direct Quotation	Indirect Quotation
The nurse said, "Some babies cannot tolerate cows' milk." (The nurse's exact spoken words are given, so quotation marks are used.)	The nurse said that some babies cannot tolerate cows' milk. (We learn the nurse's words indirectly, so no quotation marks are used.)
Vicky's note to Dan read, "I'll be home by 7:30." (The exact words that Vicky wrote in the note are given, so quotation marks are used.)	Vicky left a note for Dan saying that she would be home by 7:30. (We learn Vicky's words indirectly, so no quotation marks are used.)

Rewrite the following sentences, changing words as necessary to convert the sentences into direct quotations. The first one has been done for you as an example.

1. Teddy asked Margie whether she wanted to see his spider collection.
   Teddy asked Margie, "Do you want to see my spider collection?"

2. Sonya said that her uncle looks just like a large basset hound.

3. Angelo said that he wanted a box of the extra-crispy chicken.

4. My boss told me that I could make mistakes as long as I didn't repeat them.

5. The instructor announced that Thursday's test had been canceled.

Quotation Marks to Set Off Titles of Short Works

Titles of short works are usually set off by quotation marks, while titles of long works are underlined (if writing longhand) or italicized (if writing on a computer). Use quotation marks to set off titles of such short works as articles in books, newspapers, or magazines; chapters in a book; short stories; poems; and songs. But you should underline or italicize titles of books, newspapers, magazines, plays, movies, CDs, and television shows. Following are some examples.

www.mhhe.com/langan

Quotation Marks	Underlines
the essay "On Self-Respect"	in the book Slouching Towards Bethlehem
the article "The Problem of Acid Rain"	in the newspaper the New York Times
the article "Living with Inflation"	in the magazine Newsweek
the chapter "Chinese Religion"	in the book Paths of Faith
the story "Hands"	in the book Winesburg, Ohio

the poem "When I Have Fears"   in the book Complete Poems of John
                                   Keats

the song "Ziggy Stardust"   in the CD Changes
                                   the television show 60 Minutes
                                   the movie High Noon

Activity

4

Use quotation marks or underlines as needed. Review your answers with a partner.

1. In her short story A Sea Worry, Maxine Hong Kingston describes a group of teenage surfers and a mother who tries to understand them.

2. I bought an issue of Glamour to read an article titled Painful Beauty Secrets of the Stars.

3. We read the chapter Pulling Up Roots in Gail Sheehy's book Passages.

4. Jamila used an article titled Winter Blues from Time magazine in her research paper about seasonal depression.

5. The movie Casablanca, which starred Humphrey Bogart, was originally cast with Ronald Reagan in the leading role.

6. One of my grandfather's favorite old TV shows was Thriller, a horror series hosted by Boris Karloff, the man who starred in the 1931 movie Frankenstein.

7. When the Beatles' movie A Hard Day's Night was first shown, fans screamed so much that no one could hear the songs or the dialogue.

8. On my father's wall is a framed front page of the New York Times of February 25, 1940—the day he was born.

9. The sociology test will cover the first two chapters: Culture and Diversity and Social Stratification.

10. An article in Consumer Reports called Which Cereal for Breakfast? claims that children can learn to like low-sugar cereals like Cheerios and Wheaties.

www.mhhe.com/langan

Other Uses of Quotation Marks

Quotation marks are also used as follows:

1. To set off special words or phrases from the rest of a sentence:

   In grade school, we were taught a little jingle about the spelling rule "*i* before *e*."

   What is the difference between "it's" and "its"?
   (In this and other books, *italics* are often used instead of quotation marks to set off words.)

2. To mark off a quotation within a quotation:

> The physics professor said, "For class on Friday, do the problems at the end of the chapter titled 'Work and Energy.'"

> Brendan remarked, "Did you know that Humphrey Bogart never actually said, 'Play it again, Sam,' in the movie *Casablanca*?"

TIP A quotation within a quotation is indicated by *single* quotation marks, as shown above.

Review Test   1

Insert quotation marks where needed in the sentences that follow.

1. The psychology class read a short story called Silent Snow, Secret Snow, about a young boy who creates his own fantasy world.

2. While filming the movie *Vertigo,* the actress Kim Novak was agonizing over how to play a particular scene until the director, Alfred Hitchcock, reminded her, Kim, it's only a movie!

3. I'm against grade school students' using pocket calculators, said Fred. I spent three years learning long division, and so should they.

4. The composer George Gershwin wrote many hundreds of hit songs, including classics like Summertime and Somebody Loves Me.

5. When I gagged while taking a foul-tasting medicine, my wife said, Put an ice cube on your tongue first, and then you won't taste it.

6. I looked twice at the newspaper headline that read, Man in River Had Drinking Problem.

7. To learn more about the stock market for his business class, Jared began reading the column by Pablo Galarza in *Money* magazine called MarketRap.

8. When a guest at the wedding was asked what he was giving the couple, he replied, About six months.

9. Theodore Roosevelt, a pioneer in conservation, once said, When I hear of the destruction of a species, I feel as if all the works of some great writer had perished.

10. If you're ever in trouble, said the police officer, you'll have a better chance of attracting aid if you shout Fire instead of Help.

Review Test 2

Go through the comics section of a newspaper to find a comic strip that amuses you. Be sure to choose a strip where two or more characters are speaking to each other. Write a full description that will enable people who have not read the comic strip to visualize it clearly and appreciate its humor. Describe the setting and action in each panel, and enclose the words of the speakers in quotation marks.

Comma

This chapter will describe the six main uses of the comma. The sentences below will introduce you to one of these uses—to set a direct quotation off from the rest of the sentence. See if you can guess the other five main uses of the comma before turning the page.

INCORRECT:

The journalist pleaded "Just one more question."

A comma is needed to set the direct quotation off from the rest of the sentence.

CORRECT:

The journalist pleaded, "Just one more question."

With the comma included, the direct quotation is properly set off from the rest of the sentence.

Six Main Uses of the Comma

Commas are used mainly as follows:

1. To separate items in a series
2. To set off introductory material
3. On both sides of words that interrupt the flow of thought in a sentence
4. Between two complete thoughts connected by *and, but, for, or, nor, so, yet*
5. To set off a direct quotation from the rest of a sentence
6. For certain everyday material

You may find it helpful to remember that the comma often marks a slight pause or break in a sentence. Read aloud the sentence examples given for each rule, and listen for the minor pauses or breaks that are signaled by commas.

1 Comma between Items in a Series

Use commas to separate items in a series.

> The street vendor sold watches, necklaces, and earrings.
>
> The pitcher adjusted his cap, pawed the ground, and peered over his shoulder.
>
> The exercise instructor told us to inhale, exhale, and relax.
>
> Joe peered into the hot, still-smoking engine.

A. The final comma in a series is optional, but it is often used. If you use a final comma in one series in an essay, use one in all the other series in the same essay.

B. A comma is used between two descriptive words in a series only if *and* inserted between the words sounds natural. You could say:

> Joe peered into the hot *and* still-smoking engine.

But notice in the following sentence that the descriptive words do not sound natural when *and* is inserted between them. In such cases, no comma is used.

> Tony wore a pale green tuxedo. (A pale *and* green tuxedo does not sound right, so no comma is used.)

Activity 1

Place commas between items in a series.

1. The old kitchen cabinets were littered with dead insects crumbs and dust balls.
2. Rudy stretched out on the swaying hammock popped open a frosty can of soda and balanced it carefully on his stomach.

3. The children splashed through the warm deep swirling rainwater that flooded the street.

4. The police officer's warm brown eyes relaxed manner and pleasant smile made her easy to talk to.

5. The musty shadowy cellar with the crumbling cement floor was our favorite playground.

2 Comma after Introductory Material

Use a comma to set off introductory material.

> Just in time, Sherry applied the brakes and avoided a car accident.
>
> Muttering under his breath, Hassan reviewed the terms he had memorized.
>
> In a wolf pack, the dominant male holds his tail higher than the other pack members.
>
> Although he had been first in the checkout line, Deion let an elderly woman go ahead of him.
>
> After the fire, we slogged through the ashes of the burned-out house.

www.mhhe.com/langan

TIP If the introductory material is brief, the comma is sometimes omitted. In the activities here, you should include the comma.

Place commas after introductory material. Once you have completed the activity, review your answers with a partner.

Activity

2

1. As Patty struggled with the stuck window gusts of cold rain blew in her face.

2. His heart pounding wildly Jesse opened the letter that would tell him whether he had been accepted at college.

3. Along the once-pretty river people had dumped old tires and loads of household trash.

4. When the band hadn't taken the stage forty-five minutes after the concert was supposed to begin the audience members started shouting and stamping their feet.

5. Setting down a smudged glass of murky water the waitress tossed Darren a greasy menu and asked if he'd care to order.

www.mhhe.com/langan

3 Comma around Words That Interrupt the Flow of Thought

Use a comma on both sides of words or phrases that interrupt the flow of thought in a sentence.

The vinyl car seat, sticky from the heat, clung to my skin.

Marty's computer, which his wife got him as a birthday gift, occupies all his spare time.

The hallway, dingy and dark, was illuminated by a bare bulb hanging from a wire.

Usually, by reading a sentence aloud, you can hear the words that interrupt the flow of thought. In cases where you are not sure if certain words are interrupters, remove them from the sentence. If it still makes sense without the words, you know that the words are interrupters and that the information they give is nonessential. *Such nonessential or extra information is set off with commas.*

In the sentence

Sue Dodd, who goes to aerobics class with me, was in a serious car accident.

the words *who goes to aerobics class with me* are extra information not needed to identify the subject of the sentence, *Sue Dodd*. Commas go around such nonessential information. On the other hand, in the sentence

The woman who goes to aerobics class with me was in a serious accident.

the words *who goes to aerobics class with me* supply essential information—information needed for us to identify the woman being spoken of. If the words were removed from the sentence, we would no longer know exactly who was in the accident: "The woman was in a serious accident." Here is another example:

Watership Down, a novel by Richard Adams, is the most thrilling adventure story I've ever read.

Here the words *a novel by Richard Adams* could be left out, and we would still know the basic meaning of the sentence. Commas are placed around such nonessential material. But in the sentence

Richard Adams's novel *Watership Down* is the most thrilling adventure story I've ever read.

the title of the novel is essential. Without it the sentence would read, "Richard Adams's novel is the most thrilling adventure story I've ever read." We would not know which of Richard Adams's novels was so thrilling. Commas are not used around the title, because it provides essential information.

Most of the time you will be able to hear which words interrupt the flow of thought in a sentence and will not have to think about whether the words are essential or nonessential.

Use commas to set off interrupting words.

1. A slight breeze hot and damp ruffled the bedroom curtains.
2. The defrosting chickens loosely wrapped in plastic left a pool on the counter.
3. Lenny's wallet which he kept in his front pants pocket was linked to his belt with a metal chain.
4. Mr. Delgado who is an avid Yankees fan remembers the grand days of Mickey Mantle and Yogi Berra.
5. The fleet of tall ships a majestic sight made its way into the harbor.

4 Comma between Complete Thoughts

Use a comma between two complete thoughts connected by *and, but, for, or, nor, so, yet.*

www.mhhe.com/langan

> Sam closed all the windows, but the predicted thunderstorm never arrived.
>
> I like wearing comfortable clothing, so I buy oversize shirts and sweaters.
>
> Peggy doesn't envy the skinny models in magazines, for she is happy with her own well-rounded body.

A. The comma is optional when the complete thoughts are short.

> The Ferris wheel started and Wilson closed his eyes.
>
> Many people left but the band played on.
>
> I made a wrong turn so I doubled back.

B. Be careful not to use a comma to separate two verbs that belong to one subject. The comma is used only in sentences made up of two complete thoughts (two subjects and two verbs). In the sentence

> The doctor stared over his bifocals and lectured me about smoking.

there is only one subject (*doctor*) and a double verb (*stared* and *lectured*). No comma is needed. Likewise, the sentence

> Dean switched the lamp on and off and then tapped it with his fingers.

has only one subject (*Dean*) and a double verb (*switched* and *tapped*); therefore, no comma is needed.

Place a comma before a joining word that connects two complete thoughts (two subjects and two verbs). Remember, do *not* place a comma within a sentence that has only one subject and a double verb. (Some items may be correct as given.)

1. The television sitcom was interrupted for a special news bulletin and I poked my head out of the kitchen to listen to the announcement.

2. The puppy was beaten by its former owner and cringes at the sound of a loud voice.

3. The eccentric woman brought all her own clips and rollers to the beauty parlor for she was afraid to use the ones there.

4. The tuna sandwich in my lunch is crushed and the cream-filled cupcake is plastered to the bottom of the bag.

5. The landlord promised repeatedly to come and fix the leaking shower but three months later he hasn't done a thing.

6. Ruth was tired of summer reruns so she visited the town library to pick up some interesting books.

7. You can spend hours driving all over town to look for a particular type of camera or you can telephone a few stores to find it quickly.

8. Many people strolled among the exhibits at the comic book collectors' convention and stopped to look at a rare first edition of *Superman*.

9. Our neighborhood crime patrol escorts elderly people to the local bank and installs free dead-bolt locks on their apartment doors.

10. Brendan tapped the small geraniums out of their pots and carefully planted them on his grandfather's grave.

5 Comma with Direct Quotations

Use a comma to set off a direct quotation from the rest of a sentence.

www.mhhe.com/langan

The carnival barker cried, "Step right up and win a prize!"

"Now is the time to yield to temptation," my horoscope read.

"I'm sorry," said the restaurant hostess. "You'll have to wait."

"For my first writing assignment," said Scott, "I have to turn in a five-hundred-word description of a stone."

TIP Commas and periods at the end of a quotation go inside quotation marks. See also page 558.

Use commas to set off direct quotations from the rest of the sentence.

Activity

5

1. The coach announced "In order to measure your lung capacity, you're going to attempt to blow up a plastic bag with one breath."

2. "A grapefruit" said the comedian "is a lemon that had a chance and took advantage of it."

3. My father asked "Did you know that the family moving next door has thirteen children?"
4. "Speak louder" a man in the back row said to the guest speaker. "I paid five dollars to hear you talk, not whisper."
5. The zookeeper explained to the visitors "We can't tell the sex of a giant tortoise for almost ten years after its birth."

6 Comma with Everyday Material

Use a comma with certain everyday material.

If you're the last to leave, Paul, please switch off the lights.

Fred, I think we're on the wrong road.

Did you see the playoff game, Lisa?

June 30, 2008, is the day I make the last payment on my car.

I buy discount children's clothing from Isaacs Baby Wear Factory, Box 900, Chicago, Illinois 60614.

> **TIP** No comma is used before a zip code.

Dear Santa,   Sincerely yours,

Dear Roberto,   Truly yours,

> **TIP** In formal letters, a colon is used after the opening:
> Dear Sir: *or* Dear Madam: *or* Dear Allan: *or* Dear Ms. Mohr:

The insurance agent sold me a $50,000 term life insurance policy.

Persons Spoken To

Dates

Addresses

Openings and Closings of Letters

Numbers

Place commas where needed.

1. Would you mind George if we borrowed your picnic cooler this weekend?
2. The enchiladas served at Los Amigos 5607 Pacific Boulevard are the best in town.
3. An estimated 875000 African American men participated in the Million Man March on Washington on October 16 1995.

Activity 6

www.mhhe.com/langan

4. The mileage chart shows Elaine that we'll have to drive 1231 miles to get to Sarasota Florida.

5. The coupon refund address is 2120 Industrial Highway Great Plains Minnesota 55455.

Review Test   1

Insert commas where needed. In the space provided below each sentence, summarize briefly the rule that explains the comma or commas used.

1. "Kleenex tissues" said the history professor "were first used as gas mask filters in World War I."

   _____

2. Dee ordered a sundae with three scoops of vanilla ice cream miniature marshmallows and raspberry sauce.

   _____

3. While waiting to enter the movie theater we studied the faces of the people just leaving to see if they had liked the show.

   _____

4. I had left my wallet on the store counter but the clerk called me at home to say that it was safe.

   _____

5. The demonstrators protesting nuclear arms carried signs reading "Humans have never invented a weapon that they haven't used."

   _____

6. Large cactus plants which now sell for very high prices are being stolen from national parks and protected desert areas.

   _____

7. At the age of twenty-one Tiger Woods won the 1997 Masters Tournament with the highest margin of victory in the golfing tournament's history.

   _____

8. The talk-show guest a former child star said that one director threatened to shoot her dog if she didn't cry on cue.

   _____

9. Tom watched nervously as the dentist assembled drills mirrors clamps picks and cylinders of cotton on a tray next to the reclining chair.

_____

10. Cats and dogs like most animals love the taste of salt and will lick humans' hands to get it.

_____

Review Test 2

Insert commas where needed. Mark the one sentence that is correct with a C.

1. Before leaving for the gym Nikki added extra socks and a tube of shampoo to the gear in her duffel bag.
2. My father said "Golf isn't for me. I can't afford to buy lots of expensive sticks so that I can lose lots of expensive white balls."
3. Clogged with soggy birds' nests the chimney had allowed dangerous gases to accumulate in our house.
4. Oscar took a time-exposure photo of the busy highway so the cars' taillights appeared in the developed print as winding red ribbons.
5. On May 16 2003 my older brother got married and exactly a year later he got divorced.
6. During the summer graduation ceremony students fanned themselves with commencement programs and parents hid in the shade of trees.
7. Leaving seven astronauts dead the space shuttle _Columbia_ broke apart as it returned to Earth on February 1 2003.
8. "When I was little" said Ernie "my brother told me it was illegal to kill praying mantises. I still don't know if that's true or not."
9. A huge side of beef its red flesh marbled with streaks of creamy fat hung from a razor-sharp steel hook.
10. A line of dancing numerals on _Sesame Street_ kicked across the screen like a chorus line.

Review Test   3

In the following passage, there are ten missing commas. Add the commas where needed. The types of mistakes to look for are shown in the box below.

> 2 commas missing between items in a series
> 1 comma missing after introductory material
> 4 commas missing around interrupting words
> 2 commas missing between complete thoughts
> 1 comma missing with a direct quotation

When I was about ten years old I developed several schemes to avoid eating liver, a food I despise. My first scheme involved my little brother. Timmy too young to realize what a horrible food liver is always ate every bit of his portion. On liver nights, I used to sit next to Tim and slide my slab of meat onto his plate when my parents weren't paying attention. This strategy worked until older and wiser Tim decided to reject his liver along with the rest of us. Another liver-disposal method I used was hiding the meat right on the plate. I'd cut the liver into tiny squares half the size of postage stamps and then I would carefully hide the pieces. I'd put them inside the skin of my baked potato beneath some mashed peas or under a crumpled paper napkin. This strategy worked perfectly only if my mother didn't look too closely as she scraped the dishes. Once she said to me "Do you know you left a lot of liver on your plate?" My best liver trick was to hide the disgusting stuff on a three-inch-wide wooden ledge that ran under our dining-room table. I'd put little pieces of liver on the ledge when Mom wasn't looking; I would sneak the dried-up scraps into the garbage early the next day. Our dog would sometimes smell the liver try to get at it and bang his head noisily against the bottom of the table. These strategies seemed like a lot of work but I never hesitated to take whatever steps I could. Anything was better than eating a piece of meat that tasted like old socks soaked in mud.

Review Test   4

On separate paper, write six sentences, one illustrating each of the six main comma rules.

Other Punctuation Marks

40

This chapter will describe other punctuation marks including the colon, the dash, the hyphen, parentheses, and the semicolon.

KEY TERMS

colon: punctuation mark used at the end of a complete statement to introduce a list, a long quotation, or an explanation.

dash: punctuation mark used to signal a pause longer than that of a comma but not as long as that of a period.

hyphen: punctuation mark used with two or more words that act as a single unit or to divide a word at the end of a line.

parentheses: punctuation marks used to set off extra or incidental information from the rest of a sentence.

semicolon: punctuation mark used to mark a break between two complete thoughts or to mark off items in a series when the items themselves contain internal punctuation (such as commas).

Colon (:)

Use the colon at the end of a complete statement to introduce a list, a long quotation, or an explanation.

1. List:

> The store will close at noon on the following dates: November 26, December 24, and December 31.

2. Quotation:

> In his book *Life Lines,* Forrest Church maintains that people should cry more: "Life is difficult. Some people pretend that it is not, that we should be able to breeze through. Yet hardly a week passes in which most of us don't have something worth crying about."

3. Explanation:

> Here's a temporary solution to a dripping faucet: Tie a string to it, and let the drops slide down the string to the sink.

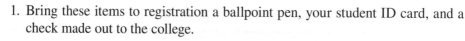

Activity 1

Place colons where needed in the sentences below:

1. Bring these items to registration a ballpoint pen, your student ID card, and a check made out to the college.

2. The road was closed because of an emergency an enormous tree had fallen and blocked both lanes.

3. Willa Cather, the American author, had an insightful comment about plots "There are only two or three human stories, and they go on repeating themselves as fiercely as if they had never happened before."

Semicolon (;)

The main use of the semicolon is to mark a break between two complete thoughts, as explained on pages 475–478. Another use is to mark off items in a series when the items themselves contain commas. Here are some examples:

> Maya's children are named Melantha, which means "black flower"; Yonina, which means "dove"; and Cynthia, which means "moon goddess."

> My parents' favorite albums are *Rubber Soul,* by the Beatles; *Songs in the Key of Life,* by Stevie Wonder; and *Bridge over Troubled Water,* by Simon and Garfunkel.

Working with a partner, place semicolons where needed in the sentences below.

Activity

2

1. Strange things happen at very low temperatures a rose will shatter like glass.

2. My sister had a profitable summer: by mowing lawns, she earned $125 by washing cars, $85 and by walking the neighbors' dogs, $110.

3. The children who starred in the play were Kari Rosoff, nine years old Flora Junco, twelve years old and Ezra Johnson, three years old.

Dash (—)

A dash signals a pause longer than a comma but not as complete as a period. Use a dash to set off words for dramatic effect:

I was so exhausted that I fell asleep within seconds—standing up.

He had many good qualities—sincerity, honesty, and thoughtfulness—yet he had few friends.

The pardon from the governor finally arrived—too late.

TIPS a. A dash can be formed using a keyboard by striking the hyphen twice (--). Computer software also has a symbol for the dash. In handwriting, a dash is as long as two letters would be.

b. Be careful not to overuse dashes.

Place dashes where needed in the following sentences.

Activity

3

1. The victim's leg broken in three places lay twisted at an odd angle on the pavement.

2. The wallet was found in a trash can minus the cash.

3. After nine days of hiking in the wilderness, sleeping under the stars, and communing with nature, I could think of only one thing a hot shower.

Parentheses ( )

Parentheses are used to set off extra or incidental information from the rest of a sentence:

In 1913, the tax on an annual income of four thousand dollars (a comfortable wage at that time) was one penny.

www.mhhe.com/langan

Arthur C. Clarke, author of science fiction books (including *2001: A Space Odyssey*), was inspired as a young man by the magazine *Astounding Stories*.

> **TIP** Do not use parentheses too often in your writing.

Activity

4

Add parentheses where needed.

1. Though the first *Star Trek* series originally ran for only three seasons 1965–1968, it gave rise to a number of spinoff shows that remain popular to this day.

2. Whenever Jack has too much to drink even one drink is sometimes too much, he becomes loud and obnoxious.

3. When I opened the textbook, I discovered that many pages mostly in the first chapter were completely blank.

www.mhhe.com/langan

Hyphen (-)

1. Use a hyphen with two or more words that act as a single unit describing a noun.

> The light-footed burglar silently slipped open the sliding glass door.
>
> While being interviewed on the late-night talk show, the quarterback announced his intention to retire.
>
> With a needle, Rich punctured the fluid-filled blister on his toe.

2. Use a hyphen to divide a word at the end of a line of writing or typing. When you need to divide a word at the end of a line, divide it between syllables. Use your dictionary to be sure of correct syllable divisions.

> Selena's first year at college was a time filled with numer-
> ous new pressures and responsibilities.

> **TIPS** a. Do not divide words of one syllable.
> b. Do not divide a word if you can avoid dividing it.

Working with a partner, place hyphens where needed.

1. The blood red moon hanging low on the horizon made a picture-perfect atmosphere for Halloween night.

2. My father, who grew up in a poverty stricken household, remembers putting cardboard in his shoes when the soles wore out.

3. The well written article in *Newsweek* described the nerve racking experiences of a journalist who infiltrated the mob.

Activity

5

Review Test   1

At the appropriate spot, place the punctuation mark shown in the margin.

1. A bad case of flu, a burglary, the death of an uncle it was not what you would call a pleasant week.   —

2. My grandfather who will be ninety in May says that hard work and a glass of wine every day are the secrets of a long life.   ( )

3. Mark Twain offered this advice to writers "The difference between the right word and the nearly right word is the difference between lightning and the lightning bug."   :

4. The passengers in the glass bottomed boat stared at the colorful fish in the water below.   -

5. Ellen's birthday December 27 falls so close to Christmas that she gets only one set of presents.   ( )

6. The dog-show winners included Freckles, a springer spaniel King Leo, a German shepherd and Big Guy, a miniature schnauzer.   ;

7. I feel I have two chances of winning the lottery slim and none.   —

8. Cold hearted stepmothers are a fixture in many famous fairy tales.   -

9. Some people need absolute quiet to study they can't concentrate with the soft sounds of a radio, air conditioner, or television in the background.   ;

10. A critic reviewing a bad play wrote, "I saw the play under the worst possible circumstances the curtain was up."   :

Word Use

What is it about these signs that makes them funny? How could each one be fixed so that its message is clearer?

Spelling
Improvement

41

This chapter will list six steps towards improving your spelling:

Step 1: Use the Dictionary

Step 2: Keep a Personal Spelling List

Step 3: Master Commonly Confused Words

Step 4: Learn Key Words in Major Subjects

Step 5: Study a Basic Word List

Step 6: Use Electronic Aids

KEY TERM

personal spelling list: a list of words you misspell written on the back page of a frequently used notebook or on a separate sheet of paper.

Poor spelling often results from bad habits developed in the early school years. With work, such habits can be corrected. If you can write your name without misspelling it, there is no reason why you cannot do the same with almost any word in the English language. Following are steps you can take to improve your spelling.

Step 1: Use the Dictionary

Get into the habit of using the dictionary. When you write a paper, allow yourself time to look up the spelling of all those words you are unsure about. Do not overlook the value of this step just because it is such a simple one. By using the dictionary, you can probably improve your spelling by 95 percent.

Step 2: Keep a Personal Spelling List

Keep a list of words you misspell and study the words regularly. Write the list on the back page of a frequently used notebook or on a separate sheet of paper titled "Personal Spelling List."

To master the words on your personal spelling list, do the following:

1. Write down any hint that will help you remember the spelling of a word. For example, you might want to note that *occasion* is spelled with two *c*'s or that *all right* is two words, not one word.

2. Study a word by looking at it, saying it, and spelling it. You may also want to write out the word one or more times, or "air write" it with your finger in large, exaggerated motions.

3. When you have trouble spelling a long word, try to break the word into syllables and see whether you can spell the syllables. For example, *inadvertent* can be spelled easily if you can hear and spell in turn its four syllables: *in ad ver tent*. The word *consternation* can be spelled easily if you hear and spell its four syllables in turn: *con ster na tion*. Remember, then: Try to see, hear, and spell long words in terms of their syllables.

4. Keep in mind that review and repeated self-testing are keys to effective learning. When you are learning a series of words, go back after studying each new word and review all the preceding ones.

Step 3: Master Commonly Confused Words

Master the meanings and spellings of the commonly confused words on pages 588–595. Your instructor may assign twenty words for you to study at a time and give you a series of quizzes until you have mastered the words.

www.mhhe.com/langan

Step 4: Learn Key Words in Major Subjects

Make up and master lists of words central to the vocabulary of your major subjects. For example, a list of key words in business might include *economics, management, resources, scarcity, capitalism, decentralization, productivity, enterprise,* and so on; in psychology, *behavior, investigation, experimentation, frustration, cognition, stimulus, response, organism,* and so on. Set aside a specific portion of your various course notebooks to be used only for such lists, and study them using the methods described above for learning words.

Step 5: Study a Basic Word List

Following is a list of 250 English words that are often misspelled. Study their spellings. Your instructor may assign 25 or 50 words for you to study at a time and give you a series of quizzes until you have mastered the entire list.

absence	believe	conceit	**250 Basic**
ache	beneficial	conscience	**Words**
achieve **25**	bottom	conscious	
acknowledge	breathe	conversation	
advice	brilliant	cruelty	
aisle	bureau **50**	daughter	
all right	business	deceit	
already	cafeteria	definite	
amateur	calendar	deposit	
answer	candidate	dictionary	
anxious	category	disastrous	
appearance	ceiling	disease	
appetite	cemetery	distance	
attempt	chief	doctor	
attendance	choose	doubt	
autumn	cigarette	efficient	
awful	citizen	eighth	
bachelor	college	either	
balance	column	emphasize	
bargain	comfortable	entrance	
basically	committed	environment	
beautiful	completely	exaggerate	

	examine	lightning		people
	existence	likely		perform
	familiar	livelihood		persistent
	fascinate	loneliness		physically
	February	loose		picnic
	financial	magazine		plausible
	foreign	making		pleasant
	forty	maintain		policeman
75	friend	marriage		possible
	furniture	material		precede
	government	mathematics		prefer
	grammar	medicine		preference
	grieve	minute		prejudice
	guidance	mortgage	150	prescription
	hammer	muscle		probably
	handkerchief	naturally		psychology
	harass	necessary		pursue
	height	neither		quantity
	hospital	nickel		quarter
	hundred	niece		quiet
	husband	ninety		quiz
	imitation	noise		raise
	incredible	obedience		really
	independent	125 obstacle		recede
	instant	occasion		receive
	instead	occur		recognize
	intelligence	occurrence		recommend
	interest	omission		reference
	interfere	opinion		region
	interrupt	opportunity		reign
	irresistible	optimist		relieve
	January	ounce		religion
	kindergarten	outrageous		representative
100	leisure	pageant		resistance
	library	pamphlet		restaurant

	rhythm	tendency	vengeance
	ridiculous	**200** tenth	view
	right	than	villain
175	safety	theater	vision
	said	though	visitor
	salary	thousand	voice
	scarcely	through	Washington
	scholastic	tomorrow	wear
	science	tongue	weather
	scissors	tonight	Wednesday
	secretary	tournament	weight
	seize	toward	weird
	separate	transferred	welcome
	sergeant	trousers	whether
	several	truly	which
	severely	twelfth	woman
	shriek	unanimous	women
	siege	until	won't
	similar	unusual	writing
	sincerely	usage	written
	sophomore	used	wrong
	straight	usual	yesterday
	succeed	usually	yolk
	suppress	vacuum	your
	telephone	valuable	**250** you're
	temperature	variety	
	tenant	**225** vegetable	

Step 6: Use Electronic Aids

Several electronic aids can help your spelling. First, *electronic spell-checkers* are pocket-size devices that look much like the pocket calculators you may use in math class. Electronic spell-checkers can be found in almost any electronics store. The checker includes a tiny keyboard. You type out the word the way you think it is spelled, and the checker quickly provides you with the correct spelling of related words. Second, *a computer with a spell-checker* as part of its word-processing program will identify incorrect words and suggest correct spellings. If you know how to write on a computer, you will have little trouble learning how to use the spell-checker feature.

Commonly Confused Words

This chapter will list homonyms and other commonly confused words and provide activities to help you learn to distinguish them.

KEY TERM

homonym: words such as *brake* and *break* that have the same sounds but different meanings.

Homonyms

Some words are commonly confused because they have the same sounds but different meanings and spellings; such words are known as *homonyms*. Following are a number of homonyms. Complete the activity for each set of words, and check off and study the words that give you trouble.

all ready	completely prepared
already	previously; before

It was *already* four o'clock by the time I thought about lunch.

My report was *all ready,* but the class was canceled.

Fill in the blanks: Tyrone was _____ to sign up for the course when he

discovered that it had _____ closed.

brake	stop
break	come apart

The mechanic advised me to add *brake* fluid to my car.

During a commercial *break,* Marie lay on the floor and did fifty sit-ups.

Fill in the blanks: Tim, a poor driver, would always _____ at the last

minute and would usually _____ the speed limit as well.

course	part of a meal; a school subject; direction
coarse	rough

At the movies, I tried to decide on a *course* of action that would put an end to the *coarse* language of the man behind me.

Fill in the blanks: Over the _____ of time, jagged, _____

rocks will be polished to smoothness by the pounding waves.

hear	perceive with the ear
here	in this place

I can *hear* the performers so well from *here* that I don't want to change my seat.

Fill in the blanks: The chairperson explained that the meeting was being held

_____ in the auditorium to enable everyone to _____ the

debate.

hole   an empty spot

whole   entire

> A *hole* in the crumbling brick mortar made a convenient home for a small bird and its *whole* family.

Fill in the blanks: The _____ in Dave's argument wouldn't exist if he

put his _____ concentration into his thinking.

its   belonging to it

it's   shortened form of "it is" or "it has"

> The tall giraffe lowered *its* head (the head belonging to the giraffe) to the level of the car window and peered in at us.
>
> *It's* (it is) too late to sign up for the theater trip to New York.

Fill in the blanks: I decided not to take the course because _____ too

easy; _____ content offers no challenge whatsoever.

knew   past form of *know*

new   not old

> No one *knew* our *new* phone number, but the obscene calls continued.

Fill in the blanks: Even people who _____ Charlie well didn't recog-

nize him with his _____ beard.

know   to understand

no   a negative

> By the time students complete that course, they *know* two computer lan-guages and have *no* trouble writing their own programs.

Fill in the blanks: Dogs and cats usually _____ by the tone of the

speaker's voice when they are being told _____.

passed   went by; succeeded in; handed to

past   a time before the present; by, as in "I drove past the house"

> As Yvonne *passed* exit six on the interstate, she knew she had gone *past* the correct turnoff.

Fill in the blanks: Lewis asked for a meeting with his boss to learn why he had

been _____ over for promotion twice in the _____ year.

peace   calm

piece   a part

    The best *piece* of advice she ever received was to maintain her own inner *peace*.

Fill in the blanks: Upon hearing that _____ of music, my angry mood was gradually replaced by one of _____.

plain   simple

plane   aircraft

    The *plain* box contained a very expensive model *plane* kit.

Fill in the blanks: After unsuccessfully trying to overcome her fear, Selena finally admitted the _____ truth: she was terrified of flying in a

_____.

principal   main; a person in charge of a school

principle   a law or standard

    If the *principal* ingredient in this stew is octopus, I'll abandon my *principle* of trying everything at least once.

Fill in the blanks: Our _____ insists that all students adhere to every school _____ regarding dress, tardiness, and smoking.

right   correct; opposite of "left"

write   to put words on paper

    Without the *right* amount of advance planning, it is difficult to *write* a good research paper.

Fill in the blanks: Connie wanted to send for the CDs offered on TV, but she could not _____ fast enough to get all the _____ information down before the commercial ended.

than   (thăn)   used in comparisons

then   (thĕn)   at that time

    I made more money *then*, but I've never been happier *than* I am now.

Fill in the blanks: When I was in high school, I wanted a racy two-seater convertible more _____ anything else; but _____ my friends pointed out that only one person would be able to ride with me.

their	belonging to them
there	at that place; a neutral word used with verbs like *is, are, was, were, have,* and *had*
they're	contraction of "they are"

The tenants *there* are complaining because *they're* being cheated by *their* landlord.

Fill in the blanks: The tomatoes I planted _____ in the back of the garden are finally ripening, but _____ bright red color will attract hungry raccoons, and I fear _____ going to be eaten.

threw	past form of *throw*
through	from one side to the other; finished

As the inexperienced pizza-maker *threw* the pie into the air, he punched a hole *through* its thin crust.

Fill in the blanks: As the president moved slowly _____ the cheering crowd, the Secret Service agent suddenly _____ himself at a man waving a small metal object.

to	verb part, as in *to smile;* toward, as in "I'm going *to* heaven."
too	overly, as in "The pizza was *too* hot"; also, as in "The coffee was hot, *too.*"
two	the number 2

I ran *to* the car *to* roll up the windows. (The first *to* means "toward"; the second *to* is a verb part that goes with *roll.*)

That amusement park is *too* far away; I hear that it's expensive, *too.* (The first *too* means "overly"; the second *too* means "also.")

The *two* players (2 players) jumped up to tap the basketball away.

Fill in the blanks: The _____ of them have been dating for a year, but lately they seem _____ be arguing _____ often to pretend nothing is wrong.

wear	to have on
where	in what place

Where I will *wear* a purple feather boa is not the point; I just want to buy it.

Fill in the blanks: _____ were we going the night I refused to _____ a tie?

weather   atmospheric conditions

whether   if it happens that; in case; if

> Although meteorologists are *weather* specialists, even they can't predict *whether* a hurricane will change course.

Fill in the blanks: The gloomy _____ report in the paper this morning

ended all discussion of _____ to pack a picnic lunch for later.

whose   belonging to whom

who's   contraction of "who is" and "who has"

> "*Who's* the patient *whose* filling fell out?" the dentist's assistant asked.

Fill in the blanks: _____ the salesperson _____ customers

are always complaining about his high-pressure tactics?

your   belonging to you

you're   contraction of "you are"

> *You're* making a fool of yourself; *your* Elvis imitation isn't funny.

Fill in the blanks: If _____ having trouble filling out _____

tax return, why don't you call the IRS's toll-free hot line?

Other Words Frequently Confused

Not all frequently confused words are homonyms. Here is a list of other words that people often confuse. Complete the activities for each set of words, and check off and study the words that give you trouble.

a, an   Both *a* and *an* are used before other words to mean, approximately, "one."

Generally you should use *an* before words starting with a vowel (*a, e, i, o, u*):

> an orange   an umbrella   an indication   an ape   an effort

Generally you should use *a* before words starting with a consonant (all other letters):

> a genius   a movie   a speech   a study   a typewriter

Fill in the blanks: The morning after the party, I had _____ pounding

headache and _____ upset stomach.

accept   (ăk sĕpt′)   to receive; agree to

except   (ăk sĕpt′)   excluding; but

> It was easy to *accept* the book's plot, *except* for one unlikely coincidence at the very end.

Fill in the blanks: Ved would _____ the position, _____ that it would add twenty minutes to his daily commute.

advice   (ăd vīs′)   noun meaning "an opinion"

advise   (ăd vīz′)   verb meaning "to counsel, to give advice"

> I have learned not to take my sister's *advice* on straightening out my life.
>
> A counselor can *advise* you about the courses you'll need next year.

Fill in the blanks: Karen is so troubled about losing her job that I will _____ her to seek the _____ of a professional counselor.

affect   (uh fĕkt′)   verb meaning "to influence"

effect   (ĭ fĕkt′)   verb meaning "to cause something"; noun meaning "result"

> The bad weather will definitely *affect* the outcome of the election.
>
> If we can *effect* a change in George's attitude, he may do better in his courses.
>
> One *effect* of the strike will be dwindling supplies in the supermarkets.

Fill in the blanks: Scientists have studied the _____ of large quantities of saccharine on lab animals but have yet to learn how similar amounts _____ human beings.

among   implies three or more

between   implies only two

> After the team of surgeons consulted *among* themselves, they decided that the bullet was lodged *between* two of the patient's ribs.

Fill in the blanks: _____ halves, one enthusiastic fan stood up _____ his equally fanatic friends and took off his coat and shirt.

beside	along the side of
besides	in addition to

> *Besides* doing daily inventories, I have to stand *beside* the cashier whenever the store gets crowded.

Fill in the blanks: _____ those books on the table, I plan to use these

magazines stacked _____ me while doing my research paper.

fewer	used with things that can be counted
less	refers to amount, value, or degree

> I've taken *fewer* classes this semester, so I hope to have *less* trouble finding time to study.

Fill in the blanks: This beer advertises that it has _____ calories and is

_____ filling.

former	refers to the first of two items named
latter	refers to the second of two items named

> Sue yelled at her sons, Greg and John, when she got home; the *former* (Greg) had left the refrigerator open and the *latter* (John) had left wet towels all over the bathroom.

Fill in the blanks: Eddy collects coupons and parking tickets: the _____

save him money and the _____ are going to cost him a great deal of

money someday.

learn	to gain knowledge
teach	to give knowledge

> I can't *learn* a new skill unless someone with lots of patience *teaches* me.

Fill in the blanks: Because she is quick to _____ new things, Mandy

has offered to _____ me how to play the latest video games.

loose	(lōōs) not fastened; not tight-fitting
lose	(lōōz) to misplace; fail to win

> In this strong wind, the house may *lose* some of its *loose* roof shingles.

Fill in the blanks: A _____ wire in the television set was causing us to

_____ the picture.

quiet   (kwī;'ĭt)   peaceful

quite   (kwīt)   entirely; really; rather

Jennifer seems *quiet* and demure, but she has *quite* a temper at times.

Fill in the blanks: Most people think the library is _____ a good place

to study, but I find the extreme _____ distracting.

These sentences check your understanding of *its, it's; there, their, they're; to, too, two;* and *your, you're.* Underline the two incorrect spellings in each sentence. Then spell the words correctly in the spaces provided.

Activity

1

_____ 1. "Its not a very good idea," yelled Alexandra's boss, "to tell

_____   you're customer that the striped dress she plans to buy makes

   her look like a pregnant tiger."

_____ 2. You're long skirt got stuck in the car door, and now its

_____   sweeping the highway.

_____ 3. When your young, their is a tendency to confuse a crush with

_____   true love.

_____ 4. After too hours of typing, Lin was to tired to type any

_____   longer.

_____ 5. It is unusual for a restaurant to lose it's license, but this one

_____   had more mice in its' kitchen than cooks.

_____ 6. The vampires bought a knife sharpener in order too sharpen

_____   there teeth.

_____ 7. Your sometimes surprised by who you're friends turn out to

_____   be in difficult times.

_____ 8. When the children get to quiet, Clare knows their getting

_____   into trouble.

_____ 9. There friendship developed into love as the years passed, and

_____   now, in midlife, their newlyweds.

_____ 10. There is no reason to panic if you get a bad grade or too.

_____   Its well known that many successful people were not great

   students.

Review Test 1

Underline the correct word in the parentheses. Rather than guessing, look back at the explanations of the words when necessary.

1. I (know, no) that several of the tenants have decided (to, too, two) take (their, there, they're) case to court.

2. (Whose, Who's) the author of that book about the (affects, effects) of eating (to, too, two) much protein?

3. In our supermarket is a counter (where, wear) (your, you're) welcome to sit down and have free coffee and doughnuts.

4. (Its, It's) possible to (loose, lose) friends by constantly giving out unwanted (advice, advise).

5. For a long time, I couldn't (accept, except) the fact that my husband wanted a divorce; (then, than) I decided to stop being angry and get on with life.

6. I spent the (hole, whole) day browsing (threw, through) the chapters in my business textbook, but I didn't really study them.

7. The newly appointed (principal, principle) is (quite, quiet) familiar with the problems (hear, here) at our school.

8. I found that our cat had (all ready, already) had her kittens (among, between) the weeds (beside, besides) the porch.

9. I (advice, advise) you not to take children to that movie; the special (affects, effects) are (to, too, two) frightening.

10. It seems that nobody will ever be able to (learn, teach) Mario to take (fewer, less) chances with his car.

Review Test 2

On separate paper, write short sentences using the ten words shown below.

1. accept
2. its
3. you're
4. too
5. then
6. principal
7. their
8. passed
9. fewer
10. who's

Effective Word Choice

This chapter will give you practice in avoiding slang, clichés, and pretentious words.

KEY TERMS

cliché: an expression that has been worn out through constant use. Example: *short but sweet*

pretentious language: artificial or stilted expressions that more often obscure meaning than communicate it clearly. Example: *It was a splendid opportunity to obtain some slumber* could be more simply expressed as *It was a good chance to get some sleep.*

slang: nonstandard language particular to a time and often to a specific locale; acceptable in everyday speech, slang should be avoided in formal contexts and, with few exceptions, in writing. Example: *I'm going to have to sweat it out for the next couple of days until the test results are posted* would be more appropriately expressed as *I'm going to have to wait anxiously for the next couple of days until the test results are posted.*

Choose your words carefully when you write. Always take the time to think about your word choices rather than simply use the first word that comes to mind. You want to develop the habit of selecting words that are precise and appropriate for your purpose. One way you can show sensitivity to language is by avoiding slang, clichés, and pretentious words.

Slang

www.mhhe.com/langan

We often use slang expressions when we talk because they are so vivid and color-ful. However, slang is usually out of place in formal writing. Here are some ex-amples of slang:

Someone *ripped off* Ken's new Adidas running shoes from his locker.

After the game, we *stuffed our faces* at the diner.

I finally told my parents to *get off my case.*

The movie really *grossed me out.*

Slang expressions have a number of drawbacks. They go out of date quickly, they become tiresome if used excessively in writing, and they may communicate clearly to some readers but not to others. Also, the use of slang can be an evasion of the specific details that are often needed to make one's meaning clear in writing. For example, in "The movie really grossed me out," the writer has not pro-vided the specific details about the movie necessary for us to clearly understand the statement. Was it acting, special effects, or violent scenes that the writer found so disgusting? In general, then, you should avoid slang in your writing. If you are in doubt about whether an expression is slang, it may help to check a recently pub-lished hardbound dictionary.

Activity

1

Rewrite the following sentences, replacing the italicized slang words with more formal ones.

EXAMPLE

When we told the neighbors to *can the noise,* they *freaked out.*
When we told the neighbors to be quiet, they got upset.

1. I didn't realize how *messed up* Joey was until he stole some money from his parents and *split* for a month.

_____

_____

_____

2. Greg was so *bummed out* the day he got fired that he didn't do anything except *veg out* in front of the TV.

_____

_____

_____

3. Theo was so *wiped out* after his workout at the gym that he couldn't *get it together* to defrost a frozen dinner.

_____

_____

_____

4. When Rick tried to *put the move on* Lola at the school party, she told him to *shove off.*

_____

_____

_____

5. The entire town was *psyched* that the corrupt mayor *got busted.*

_____

_____

_____

Clichés

A *cliché* is an expression that has been worn out through constant use. Here are some typical clichés:

www.mhhe.com/langan

short but sweet	last but not least
drop in the bucket	work like a dog
had a hard time of it	all work and no play
word to the wise	it goes without saying
it dawned on me	at a loss for words
sigh of relief	taking a big chance
too little, too late	took a turn for the worse

(continued)

singing the blues	easier said than done
in the nick of time	on top of the world
too close for comfort	time and time again
saw the light	make ends meet

Clichés are common in speech but make your writing seem tired and stale. Also, they are often an evasion of the specific details that you must work to provide in your writing. You should, then, avoid clichés and try to express your meaning in fresh, original ways.

Activity

2

Underline the cliché in each of the following sentences. Then substitute specific, fresh words for the trite expression. Partner with a classmate and go over your answers together.

EXAMPLE

My boyfriend has stuck with me through thick and thin.
through good times and bad.

1. As the only girl in an otherwise all-boy family, I got away with murder.

   _____

2. When I realized I'd lost my textbook, I knew I was up the creek without a paddle.

   _____

3. My suggestion is just a shot in the dark, but it's better than nothing.

   _____

4. Janice got more than she bargained for when she offered to help Larry with his math homework.

   _____

5. Bob is pushing his luck by driving a car with bald tires.

   _____

6. On a hot, sticky midsummer day, iced tea or any frosty drink really hits the spot.

   _____

7. Nadia thanks her lucky stars that she was born with brains, beauty, and humility.

_____

8. Anything that involves mathematical ability has always been right up my alley.

_____

9. Your chance of buying a good used car from that dealer is one in a million.

_____

10. Even when we are up to our eyeballs in work, our boss wonders if we have enough to do.

_____

Activity

3

Write a short paragraph describing the kind of day you had. Try to put as many clichés as possible into it. For example, "I got up at the crack of dawn, ready to take on the world. I grabbed a bite to eat. . . ." By making yourself aware of clichés in this way, you should lessen the chance that they will appear in your writing.

Pretentious Words

Some people feel that they can improve their writing by using fancy, elevated words rather than simple, natural words. They use artificial, stilted language that more often obscures their meaning than communicates it clearly. Here are some unnatural-sounding sentences:

It was a splendid opportunity to get some slumber.

We relished the delicious repast.

The officer apprehended the intoxicated operator of the vehicle.

This establishment sells women's apparel and children's garments.

The same thoughts can be expressed more clearly and effectively by using plain, natural language, as below:

It was a good chance to get some sleep.

We enjoyed the delicious meal.

The officer arrested the drunken driver.

This store sells women's and children's clothes.

Here are some other inflated words and simpler words that could replace them:

Inflated Words	Simpler Words
subsequent to	after
finalize	finish
transmit	send
facilitate	help
component	part
initiate	begin
delineate	describe
manifested	shown
to endeavor	to try

Activity

4

Cross out the inflated words in each sentence. Then substitute clear, simple language for the inflated words.

EXAMPLE

The ~~conflagration~~ was ~~initiated~~ by an arsonist.

. . . fire was started by an arsonist.

1. Rico and his brother do not interrelate in a harmonious manner.

2. The meaning of the movie's conclusion eluded my comprehension.

3. The departmental conference will commence promptly at two o'clock.

4. A man dressed in odd attire accosted me on the street.

5. When my writing implement malfunctioned, I asked the professor for another.

Review Test   1

Certain words are italicized in the following sentences. In the space provided at the left, identify the words as slang (S), a cliché (C), or pretentious words (PW). Then replace the words with more effective diction.

_____ 1. Losing weight is *easier said than done* for someone who loves sweets.

_____

_____ 2. After dinner, we washed the *culinary utensils* and wrapped the *excess* food.

_____

_____ 3. Bruce is so stubborn that talking to him is like *talking to a brick wall.*

_____

_____ 4. Michelle spent the summer *watching the tube* and *catching rays.*

_____

_____ 5. The fans, *all fired up* after the game, *peeled out* of the parking lot and honked their horns.

_____

_____ 6. The stew I made contained *everything but the kitchen sink.*

_____

_____ 7. That *guy* isn't really a criminal; he's just gotten a *bum rap.*

_____

_____ 8. A company cannot *implement changes and attain growth* without *input from its personnel.*

_____

_____ 9. I failed the test, and to *add insult to injury,* I got a low grade on my paper.

_____

_____ 10. I *perused* several *periodicals* while I waited for the doctor.

_____

44

Editing Tests

This chapter will give you practice in editing, or revising, to correct sentence-skills mistakes.

KEY TERMS

editing: revising to correct sentence-skills mistakes.

proofreading: carefully examining written text to correct typographical mistakes and other related errors.

proofreading symbols: shorthand notation intended to call attention to typographical mistakes and other related errors.

www.mhhe.com/langan

The twelve editing tests in this chapter will give you practice in revising to correct sentence-skills mistakes. Remember that if you don't edit carefully, you run the risk of sabotaging much of the work you have put into a paper. If readers see too many surface flaws, they may assume that you don't place much value on what you have to say, and they may not give your ideas a fair hearing. Revising to eliminate sentence-skills errors is a basic part of clear, effective writing.

In five of the tests, the spots where errors occur have been underlined; your job is to identify and correct each error. In the rest of the tests, you must locate as well as identify and correct the errors.

Editing Hints:

1. Have at hand two essential tools: a good dictionary and a sentence-skills handbook (you can use Chapter 5 and Part Four of this book).

2. Use a sheet of paper to cover your essay so that you will expose only one sentence at a time. Look for errors in grammar, spelling, and typing. It may help to read each sentence out loud. If a sentence does not read clearly and smoothly, chances are something is wrong.

3. Pay special attention to the kinds of errors you tend to make. For example, if you tend to write run-ons or fragments, be especially on the lookout for those errors.

4. Proofreading symbols that may be of particular help are the following:

_℮_	omit	draw two ~~two~~ conclusions _℮_
^	insert missing letter or word	ach_i_eve
cap, lc	add a capital (or a lowercase) letter	(cap) My english ₵lass (lc)

Editing Test   1

In the spaces at the bottom, write the numbers of the ten word groups that contain fragments or run-ons. Then, in the spaces between the lines and in the margin, edit by making the necessary corrections.

¹I remember my childhood as being generally happy and can recall experiencing some of the most carefree times of my life. ²But I can also remember, even more vividly, other moments. ³When I was deeply frightened. ⁴As a child, I was truly terrified of the dark and of getting lost. ⁵These fears were very real, they caused me some extremely uncomfortable moments.

⁶Maybe it was the strange way things looked and sounded in my familiar room at night. ⁷That scared me so much. ⁸The streetlight outside or passing car lights would create shadows in my room. ⁹As a result, clothes hung over a chair taking on the shape of an unknown beast.

¹⁰Out of the corner of my eye, I saw curtains move when there was no breeze. ¹¹A tiny creak in the floor would sound a hundred times louder than in daylight, my imagination would take over. ¹²Creating burglars and monsters on the prowl. ¹³Because darkness always made me feel so helpless. ¹⁴I would lie there motionless so that the "enemy" would not discover me.

¹⁵Another of my childhood fears was that I would get lost. ¹⁶Especially on the way home from school. ¹⁷After school, all the buses lined up along the curb, I was terrified that I'd get on the wrong one. ¹⁸Scanning the bus windows for the faces of my friends. ¹⁹I'd also look to make sure that the bus driver was the same one I had in the morning.

1. _____   3. _____   5. _____   7. _____   9. _____

2. _____   4. _____   6. _____   8. _____   10. _____

Editing Test 2

Identify the five mistakes in essay format in the student paper that follows. From the box below, choose the letters that describe the five mistakes and write those letters in the spaces provided. Then correct each mistake.

> a. Title should not be underlined.
>
> b. Title should not be set off in quotation marks.
>
> c. There should not be a period at the end of a title.
>
> d. All major words in a title should be capitalized.
>
> e. Title should be a phrase, not a complete sentence.
>
> f. First line of a paper should stand independent of the title.
>
> g. One line should be skipped between title and first line of the paper.
>
> h. First line of a paragraph should be indented.
>
> i. Right-hand margin should not be crowded.
>
> j. Hyphenation should occur only between syllables.

	"eating in fast-food restaurants"
	Doing so doesn't have to be terrible for your health. Although I often
	stop at Wendy's or Burger King, I find ways to make healthful
	choices there. For one thing, I order sandwiches that are as plain as
	possible. A broiled hamburger or fish sandwich isn't so bad for you,
	as long as it isn't covered with melted cheese, fatty sauces, bacon,
	or other "extras" that pile on the fat and calories. Another health-
	conscious choice is to skip deep-fat-fried potatoes loaded with salt
	and heavy with cholesterol; instead, I'll order a plain baked potato
	from Wendy's and add just a bit of butter and salt for taste. In
	addition, I take advantage of healthy items on menus. For example,
	most fast-food places now offer green salads and low-fat chicken
	choices. And finally, I order a sensible beverage—ice water or a diet
	soda—instead of soda or a milk shake.

1. _____   2. _____   3. _____   4. _____   5. _____

Editing Test   3

Identify the ten sentence-skills mistakes at the underlined spots in the student paper that follows. From the box below, choose the letter that describes each mistake and write that letter in the space provided. (The same kind of mistake may appear more than once.) Then, in the spaces between the lines, edit and correct each mistake.

a.	fragment	d.	dangling modifier
b.	run-on	e.	missing comma
c.	inconsistent verb tense	f.	spelling mistake

I had a strange experience last <u>winter, I was shopping</u> for Christmas
1

presents when I came to a small clothing shop. I was going to pass it

by. <u>Until I saw a beautiful purple robe on a mannequin in the window.</u>
2

<u>Stopping to look at it, the mannequin</u> seemed to wink at me. I was really
3

<u>startled, I looked</u> around to see if anyone else was watching. <u>Shaking my</u>
4

<u>head I stepped</u> closer to the window. Then I really began to question my
5

<u>sanity, it looked</u> as if the mannequin moved <u>it's</u> legs. My face must have
6   7

shown alarm because the mannequin then <u>smiles.</u> <u>And even waved her arm.</u> I
8   9

sighed with <u>relief, it was</u> a human model after all.
10

1. _____   3. _____   5. _____   7. _____   9. _____

2. _____   4. _____   6. _____   8. _____   10. _____

Editing Test 4

Identify the ten sentence-skills mistakes at the underlined spots in the student paper that follows. From the box below, choose the letter that describes each mistake and write that letter in the space provided. (The same kind of mistake may appear more than once.) Then, in the spaces between the lines, edit and correct each mistake.

a. run-on
b. mistake in subject-verb agreement
c. faulty parallelism
d. missing quotation marks
e. wordiness
f. slang
g. missing comma

It is this writer's opinion that smokers should quit smoking for the sake of
<u>那</u>
₁
those who are around them. Perhaps the most helpless creatures that suffer

from being near a smoker <u>is</u> unborn <u>babies, one</u> study suggests that the risk
₂ ₃
of having an undersized baby is doubled if pregnant women are exposed to

cigarette smoke for about two hours a day. Pregnant women should refrain

from smoking and <u>to avoid</u> smoke-filled rooms. Spouses of smokers are also
₄
<u>in big trouble.</u> They are more likely than spouses of nonsmokers to die of
₅
heart disease and <u>the development of fatal cancers.</u> Office workers are a final
₆
group that can be harmed by a smoke-filled environment. The U.S. Surgeon

General has <u>said</u> "Workers who smoke are a health risk to their <u>coworkers.</u>
₇   ₈
<u>While it is undoubtedly true that</u> one can argue that smokers have the right
₉
to hurt <u>themselves they</u> do not have the right to hurt others. Smokers should
₁₀
abandon their deadly habit for the health of others at home and at work.

1. ____ 3. ____ 5. ____ 7. ____ 9. ____

2. ____ 4. ____ 6. ____ 8. ____ 10. ____

Editing Test   5

Identify the ten sentence-skills mistakes at the underlined spots in the student paper that follows. From the box below, choose the letter that describes each mistake and write that letter in the space provided. (The same kind of mistake may appear more than once.) Then, in the spaces between the lines, edit and correct each mistake.

a. fragment	e. dangling modifier
b. run-on	f. missing comma
c. mistake in subject-verb agreement	g. wordiness
d. misplaced modifier	h. slang

The United States will never be a drug-free society but we could eliminate
                                                  1
many of our drug-related problems by legalizing drugs. Drugs would be sold

by companies and not criminals if they were legal. The drug trade would then
                                 2
take place like any business freeing the police and courts to devote their time
                          3
to other problems. Lawful drugs would be sold at a fair price, no one would
                                                        4
need to steal in order to buy them. By legalizing drugs, organized crime
                                     5
would lose one of its major sources of revenue. It goes without saying that
                                                 6
we would, instead, create important tax revenues for the government. Finally,

if drugs was sold through legal outlets, we could reduce drug problems
         7
among our young people. It would be illegal to sell drugs to people under

a certain age. Just as is the case now with alcohol. And because the profits
                 8
on drugs would no longer be out of sight, there would be little incentive for
                          9
drug pushers to sell to young people. Decriminalizing drugs, in short, could

be a solution. To many of the problems that result from the illegal drug trade.
               10

1. _____   3. _____   5. _____   7. _____   9. _____

2. _____   4. _____   6. _____   8. _____   10. _____

Editing Test 6

Identify the ten sentence-skills mistakes at the underlined spots in the student paper that follows. From the box below, choose the letter that describes each mistake and write that letter in the space provided. (The same kind of mistake may appear more than once.) Then, in the spaces between the lines, edit and correct each mistake.

a. fragment	e. mistake with quotation marks
b. run-on	f. mistake in pronoun point of view
c. mistake in subject-verb agreement	g. spelling error
d. mistake in verb tense	h. missing comma

One reason that I enjoy the commute to school is that the drive gives me uninterupted time to myself. The classes and socializing at college is great,
<u>1</u>   <u>2</u>
and so is the time I spend with my family, but sometimes all this togetherness keeps <u>you</u> from being able to think. In fact, I look forward to the time I have
      <u>3</u>
<u>alone, it</u> gives me a chance to plan what I'll accomplish in the day ahead.
 <u>4</u>
For example, one Tuesday afternoon my history professor <u>announces</u> that a
                                        <u>5</u>
rough outline for our semester report was due that Friday. <u>Fortunatly,</u> I had
                                                           <u>6</u>
already done some <u>reading and I</u> had checked my proposed topic with her the
                        <u>7</u>
week before. <u>Therefore, on the way home in the car that evening.</u> I planned
                                             <u>8</u>
the entire history report in my mind. Then all I had to do when I got home was quickly jot it down before I forgot it. <u>When I handed the professor the outline</u>
                                                    <u>9</u>
<u>at 8:30 Wednesday morning.</u> She asked me <u>"if I had stayed up all night working</u>
                                                                  <u>10</u>
<u>on it."</u> She was amazed when I told her that I owed it all to commuting.

1. _____ 3. _____ 5. _____ 7. _____ 9. _____

2. _____ 4. _____ 6. _____ 8. _____ 10. _____

Editing Test   7

Identify the ten sentence-skills mistakes at the underlined spots in the student paper that follows. From the box below, choose the letter that describes each mistake and write that letter in the space provided. (The same kind of mistake may appear more than once.) Then, in the spaces between the lines, edit and correct each mistake.

a.	fragment	e.	missing capital letter
b.	run-on	f.	dangling modifier
c.	mistake in subject-verb agreement	g.	homonym mistake
		h.	missing apostrophe
d.	missing comma	i.	cliché

Cars can destroy your ego. First of all the kind of car you drive can make
                                        ‾‾‾‾‾‾‾‾
                                           1
you feel like a second-class citizen. If you can't afford a new, expensive car
                                       ‾‾‾‾‾‾‾‾‾‾‾‾‾‾‾‾‾‾‾‾‾‾‾‾‾‾‾‾‾‾‾‾‾‾‾‾‾
                                                        2
and are forced to drive an old clunker. You'll be the object of pitying stares
‾‾‾‾‾‾‾‾‾‾‾‾‾‾‾‾‾‾‾‾‾‾‾‾‾‾‾‾‾‾‾‾‾‾‾‾‾

and nasty sneers. Drivers of newer-model cars just doesn't appreciate it
                                                   ‾‾‾‾‾‾‾
                                                      3
when an '83 buick with terminal body rust lurches into the next parking slot.
           ‾‾‾‾‾
             4
You may even find that drivers go out of there way not to park near you.
                                         ‾‾‾‾‾
                                           5
Breakdowns, too, can damage your self-respect. You may be an assistant

bank manager or a job foreman, you'll still feel like two cents when your
                        ‾‾‾‾‾‾‾‾‾‾‾‾‾   ‾‾‾‾‾‾‾‾‾‾‾‾‾‾   ‾‾‾‾
                              6   7   8
sitting on the side of the road. As the other cars whiz past, you'll stare

helplessly at your cars open hood or steaming radiator. In cases like this, you
                   ‾‾‾‾
                    9
may even be turned into that lowest of creatures, the pedestrian. Shuffling
                                                                  ‾‾‾‾‾‾‾‾
                                                                     10
humbly along the highway to the nearest gas station for help, your car has
‾‾

delivered another staggering blow to your self-esteem.

---

1. _____   3. _____   5. _____   7. _____   9. _____

2. _____   4. _____   6. _____   8. _____   10. _____

Editing Test 8

Locate the ten sentence-skills mistakes in the following passage. The mistakes are listed in the box below. As you locate each mistake, write the number of the word group in the space provided. Then, in the space between the lines, edit and correct each mistake.

1	fragment _____	1	missing comma after
1	run-on _____		introductory material _____
1	mistake in verb tense _____	2	missing quotation marks
1	nonparallel structure _____		_____ _____
1	dangling modifier _____	1	missing apostrophe _____
1	mistake in pronoun point of view _____		

¹The greatest of my everyday fears is technology. ²Beginning when I couldn't master bike riding and extending to the present day. ³Fear kept me from learning to operate a jigsaw, start an outboard motor, or even using a simple tape recorder. ⁴I almost didn't learn to drive a car. ⁵At age sixteen, Dad lifted the hood of our Chevy and said, All right, you're going to start learning to drive. ⁶Now, this is the distributor . . . ⁷When my eyes glazed over, he shouted, "Well, I'm not going to bother if youre not interested!" ⁸Fortunately, the friend who later taught me to drive skipped what goes on under the hood. ⁹My most recent frustration is the digital camera, I would love to take professional-quality pictures, but all the buttons and tiny electronic menus confuse me. ¹⁰As a result, my unused camera is hidden away on a shelf in my closet. ¹¹Just last week, my sister gives me a beautiful digital watch for my birthday. ¹²I may have to put it on the shelf with the camera—the alarm keeps going off, and you can't figure out how to stop it.

Editing Test   9

Locate the ten sentence-skills mistakes in the following passage. The mistakes are listed in the box below. As you locate each mistake, write the number of the word group in the space provided. Then, in the space between the lines, edit and correct each mistake.

1	fragment _____	1	mistake in subject-verb
1	run-on _____		agreement _____
1	missing comma around an	2	missing quotation
	interrupter _____		marks _____ _____
2	apostrophe	1	dangling modifier _____
	mistakes _____ _____	1	nonparallel structure _____

¹I was six years old when, one day, my dog was struck by a car while getting ready for school. ²My mother and I heard the terrifying sound of squealing brake's. ³In a low voice, she said, Oh, my God—Rusty. ⁴I remember trailing her out the door and seeing a car filled with teenagers and a spreading pool of bright blood on our cobblestoned street. ⁵To me, it seemed only a matter of seconds until a police car pulled up. ⁶The officer glanced at the crumpled dog under the car. ⁷And drew his gun. ⁸My mother shouted, "No!" ⁹She crawled halfway under the car and took the dog, like a sack of flour, out from under the wheels. ¹⁰Her housedress was splashed with blood, she cradled the limp dog in her arms and ordered the officers to drive her to the vets office. ¹¹It was only then that she remembered me, I think. ¹²She patted my head, was telling me to walk up to school, and reassured me that Rusty would be all right. ¹³The rest of the story including Rusty's slow recovery and few more years of life, are fuzzy and vague now. ¹⁴But the sights and sounds of those few moments are as vivid to me now as they were twenty-five years ago.

Editing Test 10

Locate the ten sentence-skills mistakes in the following passage. The mistakes are listed in the box below. As you locate each mistake, write the number of the word group in the space provided. Then, in the space between the lines, edit and correct each mistake.

2 fragments _____ _____	2 apostrophe mistakes
1 run-on _____	_____ _____
1 mistake in subject-verb agreement _____	3 missing commas
1 nonparallel structure _____	_____ _____ _____

¹Most products have little or nothing to do with sex a person would never know that by looking at ads'. ²A television ad for a headache remedy, for example shows the product being useful because it ends a womans throbbing head pain just in time for sex. ³Now she will not say "Not tonight, honey." ⁴Another ad features a detergent that helps a single woman meet a man in a laundry room. ⁵When it comes to products that do relate to sex appeal advertisers often present more obvious sexuality. ⁶A recent magazine ad for women's clothing, for instance, make no reference to the quality of or how comfortable are the company's clothes. ⁷Instead, the ad features a picture of a woman wearing a low-cut sleeveless T-shirt and a very short skirt. ⁸Her eyes are partially covered by semi-wild hair. ⁹And stare seductively at the reader. ¹⁰A recent television ad for perfume goes even further. ¹¹In this ad, a boy not older than twelve reaches out to a beautiful woman. ¹²Sexily dressed in a dark room filled with sensuous music. ¹³With such ads, it is no wonder that young people seem preoccupied with sex.

Editing Test   11

Locate the ten sentence-skills mistakes in the following passage. The mistakes are listed in the box below. As you locate each mistake, write the number of the word group in the space provided. Then, in the space between the lines, edit and correct each mistake.

1 fragment _____	2 missing apostrophes
1 run-on _____	_____ _____
1 mistake in subject-verb agreement _____	1 nonparallel structure _____
	1 dangling modifier _____
2 missing commas after introductory material	1 mistake in pronoun point of view _____
_____ _____	

¹Being a waitress is an often underrated job. ²A waitress needs the tact of a diplomat, she must be as organized as a business executive, and the ability of an acrobat. ³Serving as the link between customers and kitchen, the most demanding diners must be satisfied, and the often temperamental kitchen help must be kept tamed. ⁴Both groups tend to blame the waitress whenever anything goes wrong. ⁵Somehow, she is held responsible by the customer for any delay (even if it's the kitchens fault), for an overcooked steak, or for an unavailable dessert. ⁶While the kitchen automatically blames her for the diners who change their orders or return those burned steaks. ⁷In addition she must simultaneously keep straight who ordered what at each table, who is yelling for the check, and whether the new arrivals want cocktails or not. ⁸She must be sure empty tables are cleared, everyone has refills of coffee, and no one is scowling because a request for more rolls are going unheard. ⁹Finally the waitress must travel a hazardous route between the busy kitchen and the crowded dining room, she has to dodge a diners leg in the aisle or a swinging kitchen door. ¹⁰And you must do this while balancing a tray heaped with steaming platters. ¹¹The hardest task of the waitress, though, is trying to maintain a decent imitation of a smile on her face—most of the time.

Editing Test   12

Locate the ten sentence-skills mistakes in the following passage. The mistakes are listed in the box below. As you locate each mistake, write the number of the word group in the space provided. Then, in the space between the lines, edit and correct each mistake.

2 fragments _____ _____	2 missing capital letters
1 run-on _____	_____ _____
2 mistakes in irregular verbs	1 mistake in pronoun point
_____ _____	of view _____
1 misplaced modifier _____	1 mistake in a subject pronoun
	_____

¹The thirtieth-anniversary party of my uncle and aunt was the worst family gathering I've ever attended. ²On a hot saturday morning in july, Mom and I drove out into the country to Uncle Ted's house. ³It had already rained heavily, and the only place left to park was in a muddy field. ⁴Then, you could not believe the crowd. ⁵There must have been two hundred people in Uncle Ted's small yard, including his five daughters with their husbands and children, all the other relatives, all the neighbors, and the entire congregation of their church. ⁶Since the ground was soaked and light rain was falling. ⁷Mom and me went under the big rented canopy with everybody else. ⁸We couldn't move between the tables, and the humidity fogged my glasses. ⁹After wiping my glasses, I seen that there was a lot of food. ¹⁰It was mainly cold chicken and potato and macaroni salads, I ate a lot just because there was nothing else to do. ¹¹We were surprised that Uncle Ted and his wife were doing all the work themselves. ¹²They ran back and forth with trays of food and gathered trash into plastic bags staggering with exhaustion. ¹³It didn't seem like much of a way to celebrate. ¹⁴Mom was upset that she didn't get to speak with them. ¹⁵When we left, I was hot, sticky, and sick to my stomach from overeating. ¹⁶But quickly pushed our car out of the mud and got us on the road. ¹⁷I have never been happier to leave a party.

45

ESL Pointers

This chapter will cover rules useful for speakers of English as a second language (ESL).

INCORRECT:

The ball was thrown by the boy.

The verb is expressed in the passive voice.

CORRECT:

The boy threw the ball.

The action is attributed directly to the boy.

KEY TERMS

active voice: mode of expression in which the subject performs the action expressed by the verb.

count nouns: words that name people, places, things, or ideas that can be counted and made into plurals, such as *teacher, restroom,* and *joke.*

idiomatic: particular to a certain language.

noncount nouns: words that refer to things or ideas that cannot be counted, such as *water, bravery,* and *snow.*

qualifier: a word that expresses the quantity of a noncount noun. Example: *some* water

This section covers rules that most native speakers of English take for granted but that are useful for speakers of English as a second language (ESL).

Articles with Count and Noncount Nouns

Articles are noun markers—they signal that a noun will follow. (A noun is a word used to name something: a person, place, thing, or idea.) The indefinite articles are *a* and *an*. (Use *a* before a word that begins with a consonant sound: **a c**ar, **a p**iano, **a u**niform—the *u* in *uniform* sounds like the consonant *y* plus *u*. Use *an* before a word beginning with a vowel sound: **an e**gg, **an o**ffice, **an h**onor—the *h* in *honor* is silent.) The definite article is *the*. An article may immediately precede a noun: **a** smile, **the** reason. Or it may be separated from the noun by modifiers: **a** slight smile, **the** very best reason.

To know whether to use an article with a noun and which article to use, you must recognize count and noncount nouns.

Count nouns name people, places, things, or ideas that can be counted and made into plurals, such as *teacher, restroom,* and *joke* (*one teacher, two restrooms, three jokes*).

Noncount nouns refer to things or ideas that cannot be counted, such as *flour, history,* and *truth.* The following box lists and illustrates common types of noncount nouns.

TIP There are various other noun markers besides articles, including quantity words (*some, several, a lot of*), numerals (*one, ten, 120*), demonstrative adjectives (*this, these*), possessive adjectives (*my, your, our*), and possessive nouns (*Jaime's, the school's*).

COMMON NONCOUNT NOUNS

Abstractions and emotions: anger, bravery, health, pride, truth

Activities: baseball, jogging, reading, teaching, travel

Foods: bread, broccoli, chocolate, cheese, flour

Gases and vapors: air, helium, oxygen, smoke, steam

Languages and areas of study: Korean, Spanish, algebra, history, physics

Liquids: blood, gasoline, lemonade, tea, water

Materials that come in bulk form: aluminum, cloth, dust, sand, soap

Natural occurrences: magnetism, moonlight, rain, snow, thunder

Other things that cannot be counted: clothing, furniture, homework, machinery, money, news, transportation, vocabulary, work

The quantity of a noncount noun can be expressed with a word or words called a **qualifier**, such as *some, a lot of, a unit of,* and so on. (In the following two examples, the qualifiers are shown in *italic* type, and the noncount nouns are shown in **boldface** type.)

Please have *some* **patience.**

We need to buy *two bags of* **flour** today.

Some words can be either count or noncount nouns, depending on whether they refer to one or more individual items or to something in general.

Certain **cheeses** give some people a headache.
(This sentence refers to individual cheeses; *cheese* in this case is a count noun.)

Cheese is made in almost every country where milk is produced.
(This sentence refers to cheese in general; in this case, *cheese* is a noncount noun.)

Using *a* or *an* with Nonspecific Singular Count Nouns

Use *a* or *an* with singular nouns that are nonspecific. A noun is nonspecific when the reader doesn't know its specific identity.

A left-hander faces special challenges with right-handed tools.
(The sentence refers to any left-hander, not a specific one.)

Today, our cat proudly brought **a** baby bird into the house.
(The reader isn't familiar with the bird. This is the first time it is mentioned.)

Using *the* with Specific Nouns

In general, use *the* with all specific nouns—specific singular, plural, and noncount nouns. Certain conditions make a noun specific and therefore require the article *the*.

A noun is specific in the following cases:

- When it has already been mentioned once

   Today, our cat proudly brought a baby bird into the house.
   Luckily, **the** bird was still alive.
   (*The* is used with the second mention of *bird*.)

- When it is identified by a word or phrase in the sentence

   The pockets in the boy's pants are often filled with sand and dirt.
   (*Pockets* is identified by the words *in the boy's pants*.)

- When its identity is suggested by the general context

    At Willy's Diner last night, **the** service was terrible and **the** food was worse.
    (The reader can conclude that the service and food being discussed were at Willy's Diner.)

- When it is unique

    There will be an eclipse of **the** moon tonight.
    (Earth has only one moon.)

- When it is preceded by a superlative adjective (*best, biggest, wisest*)

    The best way to store broccoli is to refrigerate it in an open plastic bag.

Omitting Articles

Omit articles with nonspecific plurals and noncount nouns. Plurals and noncount nouns are nonspecific when they refer to something in general.

Pockets didn't exist until the end of the 1700s.

Service is as important as **food** to a restaurant's success.

Iris serves her children homemade **lemonade**.

Using *the* with Proper Nouns

Proper nouns name particular people, places, things, or ideas and are always capitalized. Most proper nouns do not require articles; those that do, however, require *the*. Following are general guidelines about when and when not to use *the*.

1. Do not use *the* for most singular proper nouns, including names of the following:

    - *People and animals* (Benjamin Franklin, Fido)

    - *Continents, states, cities, streets, and parks* (North America, Illinois, Chicago, First Avenue, Washington Square)

    - *Most countries* (France, Mexico, Russia)

    - *Individual bodies of water, islands, and mountains* (Lake Erie, Long Island, Mount Everest)

2. Use *the* for the following types of proper nouns:

    - *Plural proper nouns* (the Turners, the United States, the Great Lakes, the Rocky Mountains)

- *Names of large geographic areas, deserts, oceans, seas, and rivers* (the South, the Gobi Desert, the Atlantic Ocean, the Black Sea, the Mississippi River)

- *Names with the format* the _____ of _____ (the Fourth of July, the People's Republic of China, the University of California)

Activity 1

Underline the correct form of the noun in parentheses.

1. (A library, Library) is a valuable addition to a town.
2. This morning, the mail carrier brought me (a letter, the letter) from my cousin.
3. As I read (a letter, the letter), I began to laugh at what my cousin wrote.
4. Every night we have to do lots of (homework, homeworks).
5. We are going to visit our friends in (the Oregon, Oregon) next week.
6. Children should treat their parents with (the respect, respect).
7. The soldiers in battle showed a great deal of (courage, courages).
8. A famous sight in Arizona is (Grand Canyon, the Grand Canyon).
9. My son would like to eat (the spaghetti, spaghetti) at every meal.
10. It is dangerous to stare directly at (the sun, sun).

Activity 2

Underline the correct form of the noun in parentheses.

1. Last night, I went to (a restaurant, the restaurant) with my best friend.
2. (The restaurant, A restaurant) was a more expensive place than we had expected.
3. (The accident, Accident) was caused by ice on the highway.
4. A newspaper reporter is supposed to write a story with (the honesty, honesty).
5. My neighbor's son attends college in (the Chicago, Chicago).
6. Long-distance runners need lots of (determination, determinations) to succeed.
7. A hurricane crossed (Atlantic Ocean, the Atlantic Ocean) before it hit the United States.
8. As the hurricane approached, residents felt a great deal of (fears, fear).
9. (Jupiter, The Jupiter) is the largest planet in our solar system.
10. Computers have been programmed to play (the chess, chess) and can now beat most human players.

Subjects and Verbs

Avoiding Repeated Subjects

In English, a particular subject can be used only once in a clause. Don't repeat a subject in the same clause by following a noun with a pronoun.

Incorrect: The *manager he* asked Dmitri to lock up tonight.

Correct: The **manager** asked Dmitri to lock up tonight.

Correct: **He** asked Dmitri to lock up tonight.

Even when the subject and verb are separated by a long word group, the subject cannot be repeated in the same clause.

Incorrect: The *girl* who danced with you *she is* my cousin.

Correct: The **girl** who danced with you **is** my cousin.

Including Pronoun Subjects and Linking Verbs

Some languages may omit a pronoun as a subject, but in English, every clause other than a command must have a subject. In a command, the subject *you* is understood: (**You**) Hand in your papers now.

Incorrect: The Grand Canyon is in Arizona. *Is* 217 miles long.

Correct: The Grand Canyon is in Arizona. **It is** 217 miles long.

Every English clause must also have a verb, even when the meaning of the clause is clear without the verb.

Incorrect: Angelita's piano teacher very patient.

Correct: Angelita's piano teacher **is** very patient.

Including *There* and *Here* at the Beginning of Clauses

Some English sentences begin with *there* or *here* plus a linking verb (usually a form of *to be: is, are,* and so on). In such sentences, the verb comes before the subject.

There are masks in every culture on Earth.

The subject is the plural noun *masks,* so the plural verb *are* is used.

Here is your driver's license.

The subject is the singular noun *license,* so the singular verb *is* is used.

In sentences like those above, remember not to omit *there* or *here.*

Incorrect: *Are* several chickens in the Bensons' yard.

Correct: **There are** several chickens in the Bensons' yard.

Not Using the Progressive Tense of Certain Verbs

The progressive tenses are made up of forms of *be* plus the *-ing* form of the main verb. They express actions or conditions still in progress at a particular time.

George **will be taking** classes this summer.

However, verbs for mental states, the senses, possession, and inclusion are normally not used in the progressive tense.

Incorrect: All during the movie they *were hearing* whispers behind them.

Correct: All during the movie they **heard** whispers behind them.

Incorrect: That box *is containing* a surprise for Pedro.

Correct: That box **contains** a surprise for Pedro.

Common verbs not generally used in the progressive tense are listed in the following box.

COMMON VERBS NOT GENERALLY USED IN THE PROGRESSIVE

Thoughts, attitudes, and desires: agree, believe, imagine, know, like, love, prefer, think, understand, want, wish

Sense perceptions: hear, see, smell, taste

Appearances: appear, seem

Possession: belong, have, own, possess

Inclusion: contain, include

Using Only Transitive Verbs for the Passive Voice

Only transitive verbs—verbs that need direct objects to complete their meaning—can have a passive form (one in which the subject receives the action instead of performing it). Intransitive verbs cannot be used in the passive voice.

Incorrect: If you don't fix those brakes, an accident *may be happened.* (*Happen* is an intransitive verb—no object is needed to complete its meaning.)

Correct: If you don't fix those brakes, an accident **may happen.**

If you aren't sure whether a verb is transitive or intransitive, check your dictionary. Transitive verbs are indicated with an abbreviation such as *tr. v.* or *v. t.* Intransitive verbs are indicated with an abbreviation such as *intr. v.* or *v. i.*

Using Gerunds and Infinitives after Verbs

A gerund is the *-ing* form of a verb that is used as a noun: For Walter, **eating** is a daylong activity. An infinitive is *to* and the basic form of the verb (the form in which the verb is listed in the dictionary): **to eat.** The infinitive can function as an adverb, an adjective, or a noun. Some verbs can be followed by only a gerund or only an infinitive; other verbs can be followed by either. Examples are given in the following lists. There are many others; watch for them in your reading.

Verb + gerund (admit + stealing)

Verb + preposition + gerund (apologize + for + yelling)

Some verbs can be followed by a gerund but not by an infinitive. In many cases, there is a preposition (such as *for, in,* or *of*) between the verb and the gerund. Following are some verbs and verb-preposition combinations that can be followed by gerunds but not by infinitives:

admit	deny	look forward to
apologize for	discuss	postpone
appreciate	dislike	practice
approve of	enjoy	suspect of
avoid	feel like	talk about
be used to	finish	thank for
believe in	insist on	think about

Incorrect: He must *avoid to jog* until his knee heals.

Correct: He must **avoid jogging** until his knee heals.

Incorrect: The instructor *apologized for to be* late to class.

Correct: The instructor **apologized for being** late to class.

Verb + infinitive (agree + to leave)

Following are common verbs that can be followed by an infinitive but not by a gerund:

agree	decide	plan
arrange	have	refuse
claim	manage	wait

Incorrect: The children *want going* to the beach.

Correct: The children **want to go** to the beach.

Verb + noun or pronoun + infinitive (cause + them + to flee)

Below are common verbs that are followed first by a noun or pronoun and then by an infinitive (not a gerund):

cause	force	remind
command	persuade	warn

Incorrect: The coach *persuaded Yasmin studying* harder.

Correct: The coach **persuaded Yasmin to study** harder.

Following are common verbs that can be followed either by an infinitive alone or by a noun or pronoun and an infinitive:

ask	need	want
expect	promise	would like

Dena asked to have a day off next week.

Her boss asked her to work on Saturday.

Verb + gerund or infinitive (begin + packing or begin + to pack)

Following are verbs that can be followed by either a gerund or an infinitive:

begin	hate	prefer
continue	love	start

The meaning of each of the above verbs remains the same or almost the same whether a gerund or an infinitive is used.

Faith hates **being** late.

Faith hates **to be** late.

With the verbs below, the gerunds and the infinitives have very different meanings.

forget	remember	stop

Esta **stopped to call** home.
(She interrupted something to call home.)

Esta **stopped calling** home.
(She discontinued calling home.)

Underline the correct form in parentheses.

1. The doctor (asked me, she asked me) if I smoked.

2. The coffee is very fresh. (Is, It is) strong and delicious.

3. (Are mice, There are mice) living in our kitchen.

4. The box (is containing, contains) a beautiful necklace.

5. Unless you take your foot off the brake, the car will not (be gone, go).

6. Most basketball players (very tall, are very tall).

7. Many people (enjoy to spend, enjoy spending) a day in the city.

8. The teacher (plans taking, plans to take) us on a field trip tomorrow.

9. Some old men in my neighborhood (play cards, they play cards) every afternoon.

10. When I am happy, I feel like (to sing, singing).

Underline the correct form in parentheses.

1. My grandparents (are, they are) in their nineties.

2. The pizza is two days old. (Is, It is) dry and stale.

3. (Was money, There was money) stolen from the convenience store last night.

4. The manager (owns, is owning) two SUVs: a Honda and a Ford.

5. The package will not (be arrived, arrive) until Friday morning.

6. After a twelve-hour shift, the employees (very tired, were very tired).

7. Most adults need (to sleep, sleeping) at least seven hours each night.

8. Our new puppy (wants to be chewing, wants to chew) all the furniture in our apartment.

9. The library's computer (broke down, it broke down) when I tried to use it.

10. Whenever she hears music, Sara feels like (to dance, dancing).

Adjectives

Following the Order of Adjectives in English

Adjectives modify nouns and pronouns. In English, an adjective usually comes directly before the word it describes or after a linking verb (a form of *be* or a "sense" verb such as *look, seem,* and *taste*), in which case it modifies the subject. In each of the following two sentences, the adjective is **boldfaced** and the noun it describes is *italicized*.

That is a **false** *story.*

The *story* is **false.**

When more than one adjective modifies the same noun, the adjectives are usually stated in a certain order, though there are often exceptions. Following is the typical order of English adjectives:

TYPICAL ORDER OF ADJECTIVES IN A SERIES

1. **Article or other noun marker:** a, an, the, Lee's, this, three, your
2. **Opinion adjective:** dull, handsome, unfair, useful
3. **Size:** big, huge, little, tiny
4. **Shape:** long, short, round, square
5. **Age:** ancient, medieval, old, new, young
6. **Color:** blue, green, scarlet, white
7. **Nationality:** Italian, Korean, Mexican, Vietnamese
8. **Religion:** Buddhist, Catholic, Jewish, Muslim
9. **Material:** cardboard, gold, marble, silk
10. **Noun used as an adjective:** house (as in *house call*), tea (as in *tea bag*), wall (as in *wall hanging*)

Here are some examples of the above order:

a long cotton scarf

the beautiful little silver cup

your new lavender evening gown

Ana's sweet Mexican grandmother

In general, use no more than two or three adjectives after the article or another noun marker. Numerous adjectives in a series can be awkward: **the beautiful big new blue cotton** sweater.

Using the Present and Past Participles as Adjectives

The present participle ends in *-ing.* Past participles of regular verbs end in *-ed* or *-d;* a list of the past participles of many common irregular verbs appears on pages 485–487. Both types of participles may be used as adjectives. A participle used as an adjective may precede the word it describes: That was an **exciting** *ball game.* It may also follow a linking verb and describe the subject of the sentence: The *ball game* was **exciting.**

While both present and past participles of a particular verb may be used as adjectives, their meanings differ. Use the present participle to describe whoever or whatever causes a feeling: an **embarrassing** *incident* (the incident is what causes the embarrassment). Use the past participle to describe whoever or whatever experiences the feeling: the **embarrassed** *parents* (the parents are the ones who are embarrassed).

The long day of holiday shopping was **tiring**.

The shoppers were **tired**.

Following are pairs of present and past participles with similar distinctions:

annoying / annoyed	exhausting / exhausted
boring / bored	fascinating / fascinated
confusing / confused	frightening / frightened
depressing / depressed	surprising / surprised
exciting / excited	

Underline the correct form in parentheses.

1. The Johnsons live in a (stone big, big stone) house.
2. Mr. Kim runs a (popular Korean, Korean popular) restaurant.
3. For her party, the little girl asked if her mother would buy her a (beautiful long velvet, beautiful velvet long) dress.
4. When their son didn't come home by bedtime, Mr. and Mrs. Singh became (worried, worrying).
5. In the center of the city is a church with (three enormous colorful stained-glass, three stained-glass colorful enormous) windows.

Activity 5

Underline the correct form in parentheses.

1. The candies came in a (little red cardboard, cardboard red little) box.
2. The creek is spanned by (an old wooden, a wooden old) bridge.
3. A gunshot left (a tiny round, a round tiny) hole in the car's rear windshield.
4. Many people find public speaking a (terrifying, terrified) experience.
5. The museum acquired (an ancient marble, a marble ancient) statue from Greece.

Activity 6

Prepositions Used for Time and Place

The use of prepositions in English is often idiomatic—a word that means "peculiar to a certain language"—and there are many exceptions to general rules. Therefore, correct preposition use must be learned gradually through experience. Following is a chart showing how three of the most common prepositions are used in some customary references to time and place:

USE OF *ON*, *IN*, AND *AT* TO REFER TO TIME AND PLACE

Time

On a specific day: on Monday, on January 1, on your anniversary

In a part of a day: in the morning, in the daytime (but at night)

In a month or a year: in December, in 1776

In a period of time: in an hour, in a few days, in a while

At a specific time: at 10:00 a.m., at midnight, at sunset, at dinnertime

Place

On a surface: on the desk, on the counter, on a ceiling

In a place that is enclosed: in my room, in the office, in the box

At a specific location: at the mall, at his house, at the ballpark

---

Activity 7

Underline the correct preposition in parentheses.

1. Can you babysit for my children (on, at) Thursday?
2. Please come to my office (on, at) 3:00.
3. You will find some computer disks (in, on) the desk drawer.
4. Miguel will begin his new job (in, at) two weeks.
5. A fight broke out between two groups of friends (on, at) the park.

Activity 8

Underline the correct preposition in parentheses.

1. Tina's husband always sends her flowers (on, at) her birthday.
2. The patients (at, in) the waiting room at the dentist's office all looked uneasy.
3. Let's meet (on, at) the coffee shop after work.
4. The bank is open (in, on) Thursday evenings, but only until six.
5. The Great Depression began when the stock market crashed (in, at) 1929.

Review Test 1

Underline the correct form in parentheses.

1. During the storm, I was startled by the loud (thunder, thunders).
2. (Is, Here is) your new textbook.
3. The ending of the movie was very (surprised, surprising).
4. Many animals that sleep all day are active (at, in) night.
5. (The people, People) in the photograph are my mother's relatives.
6. The city streets were full of (big yellow, yellow big) taxis.
7. My friend and I (are usually agreeing, usually agree) with each other.
8. In the West, New Year's Day is celebrated (in, on) January 1.
9. If the weather is nice tomorrow, let's (think about to go, think about going) to the city ourselves.
10. Most (cheese, cheeses) are made from cow's milk, but others are made from the milk of sheep or goats.

Review Test 2

Underline the correct form in parentheses.

1. Volunteers who gave (bloods, blood) were served coffee and cookies afterward.
2. (Were, There were) only two donuts left in the box.
3. The instructions for the new computer were very (confused, confusing).
4. The snow began to fall (in, at) dawn and continued all day.
5. I stopped at a newsstand to buy (the magazine, a magazine) to read on the train.
6. A (large hairy, hairy large) spider crawled across the basement floor.
7. Susan agreed (marrying, to marry) her boyfriend but then changed her mind.
8. In the United States, Halloween is celebrated (on, in) October 31.
9. After we finished dinner, we (decided to go, decided to be going) to the movies.
10. Most (homes, home) in that neighborhood were affected by the blackout.

Correction Symbols

Here is a list of symbols the instructor may use when marking papers. The numbers in parentheses refer to the pages that explain the skill involved.

Agr	Correct the mistake in agreement of subject and verb (492–497) or pronoun and the word the pronoun refers to (505–508)
Apos	Correct the apostrophe mistake (540–556)
Bal	Balance the parts of the sentence so they have the same (parallel) form (106-107)
Cap	Correct the mistake in capital letters (536–543)
Coh	Revise to improve coherence (80–89, 147–150)
Comma	Add a comma (565–574)
CS	Correct the comma splice (469–481)
DM	Correct the dangling modifier (526–531)
Det	Support or develop the topic more fully by adding details (59–63)
Frag	Attach the fragment to a sentence or make it a sentence (455–468)
lc	Use a lowercase (small) letter rather than a capital (536–543)
MM	Correct the misplaced modifier (522–525)
¶	Indent for a new paragraph
No¶	Do not indent for a new paragraph
Pro	Correct the pronoun mistake (505–508)
Quot	Correct the mistake in quotation marks (557–564)
R-O	Correct the run-on (469–481)
Sp	Correct the spelling error (581–586)
Trans	Supply or improve a transition (83–87)
Und	Underline (561–562)
Verb	Correct the verb or verb form (482–491, 498–502)
Wordy	Omit needless words (115–116)
WW	Replace the word marked with a more accurate one
?	Write the illegible word clearly
/	Eliminate the word, letter, or punctuation mark so slashed
^	Add the omitted word or words
; /: /- /—	Add semicolon (576), colon (576), hyphen (578), or dash (577)
✓	You have something fine or good here: an expression, a detail, an idea

Readings for Writers

Do you agree with writer Amy Tan *(The Joy Luck Club)* about the power of language? What are some other ways language can be powerful? Can you think of a student essay in this book, a fellow student's writing, or a professional reading that affected you in such a way? What was it about the writing that made it powerful?

© Joe Tabacca/AP Photo

"I spend a great deal of my time thinking about the power of language—the way it can evoke an emotion, a visual image, a complex idea, or a simple truth."
Amy Tan, "Mother Tongue"

Introduction to the Readings

The nineteen reading selections in Part Five will help you find topics for writing. (Note that there are also nine professional essays in Part Two.) These selections deal in various ways with interesting, often thought-provoking concerns or experiences of contemporary life. Subjects of the essays include the shame of poverty; the violence of professional sports; the power of family; basic life goals; practical advice on surviving the first year of college; problems with the college lecture system; ways the media influence our attitudes; and the shocks and challenges of everyday life. The varied subjects should inspire lively class discussions as well as serious individual thought. The selections should also provide a continuing source of high-interest material for a wide range of writing assignments.

The selections serve another purpose as well. They will help develop reading skills, with direct benefits to you as a writer. One benefit is that, through close reading, you will learn how to recognize the thesis in a selection and to identify and evaluate the supporting material that develops the thesis. In your own writing, you will aim to achieve the same essential structure: an overall thesis followed by detailed, valid support for that thesis. A second benefit is that close reading will also help you explore a selection and its possibilities thoroughly. The more you understand about what is said in a piece, the more ideas and feelings you may have about writing on an assigned topic or a related topic of your own. A third benefit of close reading is that you will become more aware of authors' stylistic devices—for example, their introductions and conclusions, their ways of presenting and developing a point, their use of transitions, their choice of language to achieve a particular tone. Recognizing these devices in other people's writing will help you enlarge your own range of ideas and writing techniques.

The Format of Each Selection

Each selection begins with a short overview that gives helpful background information as well as a brief idea of the topic of the reading. The selection is followed by three sets of questions:

- First, ten "Reading Comprehension" questions help you measure your understanding of the material. These questions involve several important reading skills: understanding vocabulary in context, recognizing a subject or topic, determining a thesis or main idea, identifying key supporting points, and making inferences. Answering the questions will enable you and your instructor to quickly check your basic understanding of a selection. More significantly, as you move from one selection to the next, you will sharpen your reading skills as well as strengthen your thinking skills—two key factors in making you a better writer.

- Following the comprehension questions are four questions on "Structure and Technique" that focus on aspects of a writer's craft, and four questions on "Critical Reading and Discussion" that involve you in reading carefully and thinking actively about a writer's ideas.

- Finally, several writing assignments accompany each selection. The assignments range from personal narratives to expository and persuasive essays about issues in the world at large. Many assignments provide detailed guidelines on how to proceed, including suggestions for prewriting and appropriate methods of development. When writing your essay responses to the readings, you will have opportunities to apply all the methods of development presented in Part Two of this book.

How to Read Well: Four General Steps

Skillful reading is an important part of becoming a skillful writer. Following is a series of four steps that will make you a better reader—of the selections here and in your reading at large.

1. Concentrate As You Read

To improve your concentration, follow these tips:

- First, read in a place where you can be quiet and alone. Don't choose a spot where there is a TV or stereo on or where friends or family are talking nearby.

- Next, sit upright when you read. If your body is in a completely relaxed position, sprawled across a bed or nestled in an easy chair, your mind is also going to be completely relaxed. The light muscular tension that comes from sitting in a straight chair promotes concentration and keeps your mind ready to work.

- Third, consider using your index finger (or a pen) as a pacer while you read. Lightly underline each line of print with your index finger as you read down a page. Hold your hand slightly above the page and move your finger at a speed that is a little too fast for comfort. This pacing with your index finger, like sitting upright in a chair, creates a slight physical tension that will keep your body and mind focused and alert.

2. *Skim Material before You Read It*

In skimming, you spend about two minutes rapidly surveying a selection, looking for important points and skipping secondary material. Follow this sequence when skimming:

- Begin by reading the overview that precedes the selection.

- Then study the title of the selection for a few moments. A good title is the shortest possible summary of a selection; it often tells you in several words—or even a single word—just what a selection is about. For example, the title "Shame" suggests that you're going to read about a deeply embarrassing condition or incident in a person's life.

- Next, form a question (or questions) based on the title. For instance, for the selection titled "Shame," you might ask, What exactly is the shame? What caused the shame? What is the result of the shame? Using a title to form questions is often a key to locating a writer's thesis, your next concern in skimming.

- Read the first and last couple of paragraphs in the selection. Very often a writer's thesis, *if* it is directly stated, will appear in one of these places and will relate to the title. For instance, in "What's Wrong with Schools?" the author says in his second paragraph that "many students are turned off because they have little power and responsibility for their own education."

- Finally, look quickly at the rest of the selection for other clues to important points. Are there any subheads you can relate in some way to the title? Are there any words the author has decided to emphasize by setting them off in *italic* or **boldface** type? Are there any major lists of items signaled by words such as *first, second, also, another,* and so on?

3. *Read the Selection Straight Through with a Pen in Hand*

Read the selection without slowing down or turning back; just aim to understand as much as you can the first time through. Write a check or star beside answers to basic questions you formed from the title and beside other ideas that seem important. Number lists of important points: 1, 2, 3, and so on. Circle words you don't understand. Write question marks in the margins next to passages that are unclear and that you will want to reread.

4. *Work with the Material*

Go back and reread passages that were not clear the first time through. Look up words that block your understanding of ideas and write their meanings in the margin. Also, reread carefully the areas you identified as most important; doing so will enlarge your understanding of the material. Now that you have a sense of the whole, prepare a short written outline of the selection by answering these questions:

- What is the thesis?

- What key points support the thesis?

- What seem to be other important ideas in the selection?

By working with the material in this way, you will significantly increase your understanding of a selection. Effective reading, just like effective writing, does not happen all at once. Rather, it must be worked on. Often you begin with a general impression of what something means, and then, by working at it, you move to a deeper level of understanding.

How to Answer the Comprehension Questions: Specific Hints

The ten reading comprehension questions that follow each selection involve several important reading skills:

- understanding vocabulary in context

- summarizing the selection in a title

- determining the main idea

- recognizing key supporting details

- making inferences

The following hints will help you apply each of these reading skills:

- *Vocabulary in context.* To decide on the meaning of an unfamiliar word, consider its context. Ask yourself, Are there any clues in the sentence that suggest what this word means?

- *Subject or title.* Remember that the title should accurately describe the entire selection. It should be neither too broad nor too narrow for the material in the selection. It should answer the question What is this about? as specifically as possible. Note that you may at times find it easier to answer the title question after the main-idea question.

- *Main idea.* Choose the statement that you think best expresses the main idea—also known as the *central point,* or *thesis*—of the entire selection. Remember that the title will often help you focus on the main idea. Then ask yourself, Does most of the material in the selection support this statement? If you can answer yes, you have found the thesis.

- *Key details.* If you were asked to give a two-minute summary of a selection, the key, or major, details are the ones you would include in that summary. To determine the key details, ask yourself, What are the major supporting points for the thesis?

- *Inferences.* Answer these questions by drawing on the evidence presented in the selection and your own common sense. Ask yourself, What reasonable judgments can I make on the basis of the information in the selection?

On page 781 is a chart on which you can keep track of your performance as you answer the ten comprehension questions for each selection. The chart will help you identify reading skills you need to strengthen.

Three Passions

Bertrand Russell

PREVIEW

Bertrand Russell (1872–1970), a philosopher and mathematician, was a controversial figure on the world stage. He was imprisoned twice, first in 1918 for his outspoken criticism of British involvement in World War I, and again in 1961 for "inciting civil disobedience" while campaigning for nuclear disarmament. His writings on social, political, and educational issues led to his winning the Nobel Prize for Literature in 1950. "Three Passions" is taken from the prologue to his autobiography.

© Bettmann/Corbis

1 Three passions, simple but overwhelmingly strong, have governed my life: the longing for love, the search for knowledge, and unbearable pity for the suffering of mankind. These passions, like great winds, have blown me hither and thither, in a wayward course, over a deep ocean of anguish, reaching to the very verge of despair.

2 I have sought love, first, because it brings ecstasy—ecstasy so great that I would often have sacrificed all the rest of life for a few hours of this joy. I have sought it, next, because it relieves loneliness—that terrible loneliness in which one shivering consciousness looks over the rim of the world into the cold unfathomable lifeless abyss. I have sought it, finally, because in the union of love I have seen, in a mystic miniature, the prefiguring vision of the heaven that saints and poets have imagined. This is what I sought, and though it might seem too good for human life, this is what—at last—I have found.

3 With equal passion I have sought knowledge. I have wished to understand the hearts of men. I have wished to know why the stars shine. And I have tried to apprehend the Pythagorean power by which number holds sway above the flux. A little of this, but not much, I have achieved.

4 Love and knowledge, so far as they were possible, led upward toward the heavens. But always pity brought me back to earth. Echoes of cries of pain reverberate in my heart. Children in famine, victims tortured by oppressors, helpless old

people a hated burden to their sons, and the whole world of loneliness, poverty, and pain make a mockery of what human life should be. I long to alleviate the evil, but I cannot, and I too suffer.

This has been my life. I have found it worth living, and would gladly live it 5 again if the chance were offered me.

www.mhhe.com/langan

READING COMPREHENSION

1. The word *alleviate* in "I long to alleviate the evil, but I cannot, and I too suffer" means
   a. increase.
   b. tolerate.
   c. enjoy.
   d. relieve.

2. Which of the following would be a good alternative title for this selection?
   a. The Forces Driving Me
   b. The Truth about Love
   c. The Anguish of Life
   d. The Power of Knowledge

3. What sentence best expresses the main idea of the selection?
   a. People's inhumanity to other humans has been a source of great pain in the author's life.
   b. The author wishes he had his life to live over again.
   c. The author sees his life driven by three passions.
   d. The author has found life's struggle to be painful but ultimately rewarding.

4. Russell compares his life's passions to
   a. great winds.
   b. the stars.
   c. a bottomless abyss.
   d. a boundless ocean.

5. Which of the following is *not* a reason that Russell sought love?
   a. It relieves loneliness.
   b. It leads to marriage.
   c. It brings ecstacy.
   d. It provides a glimpse of heaven.

6. *True or false?* _____ Russell believes that he has gained considerable knowledge in life.

7. When Russell uses the metaphor of a "deep ocean" to describe his anguish, he implies that it is

   a. cold.

   b. without life.

   c. almost bottomless.

   d. lacking in color.

8. Russell implies that loneliness, at its core, is

   a. a self-defeating impulse.

   b. impossible to avoid.

   c. a sign of selfishness.

   d. a fear of death.

9. Russell implies that life for him has been

   a. passionately complex.

   b. simpler than he would have imagined.

   c. so troubled that it has increased his faith in God.

   d. more materialistic than he would have wished.

10. We can conclude that the author would agree with which statement?

   a. He regrets that he could not free himself of pity.

   b. Human love is ultimately disappointing.

   c. Heaven is merely a poetic invention.

   d. A loving person naturally wants to relieve the suffering of others.

STRUCTURE AND TECHNIQUE

1. Does this essay follow the traditional one-three-one essay model of introduction, support, and conclusion? How would you outline the essay?

2. This essay primarily is organized in terms of three causes and their overall effect. What is the effect and what are the causes? The essay can also be seen as an exemplification essay. What examples does the author provide to help the reader understand each of his lifelong passions?

3. What kind of transitional signals—time, space, or addition—does Russell employ in the second paragraph? List the transitions you find there.

4. Russell is a master of the use of metaphorical language. For instance, as has already been seen, he compares his anguish to an "ocean." What other examples of metaphorical language can you find? Why do you think Russell chose to use such imaginative language, rather than write in plainspoken terms?

CRITICAL READING AND DISCUSSION

1. Can you identify one or two passions—or at least strong influences—that have, in Russell's words, governed your life? What examples can you provide of how those passions have affected you?

2. Do think that many people are influenced by the same passions as Russell: love, knowledge, then pity? Or do you feel that many people spend their lives influenced by other factors? What other passions or influences do people live by, in your experience?

3. Russell writes, "[I]n the union of love I have seen, in a mystic miniature, the prefiguring vision of the heaven that saints and poets have imagined" (paragraph 2). Most people, whether they believe in heaven in a religious sense or not, have a concept of an ideal place of perfect love and harmony. What on earth—perhaps a place, a relationship, an individual, or a situation—comes closest to giving you a "prefiguring vision" of heaven? What is it about that place, person, or thing that seems heavenly to you?

4. Overall, do you find Russell's statement an uplifting or a saddening one? What elements of each do you find within it? What makes one element outweigh the other, in your mind?

www.mhhe.com/langan

WRITING ASSIGNMENTS

Assignment 1

Write an essay in which you identify three passions that have strongly influenced your life. Like Russell, explain why each of them has been so important to you, and provide examples of how those passions have played out in your life.

Alternatively, select one particular passion, and write about three areas of your life in which this passion has influenced you.

If you choose the first alternative, your thesis statement might be something like this:

> The love of family, a rebellious streak, and affection for the outdoors are three passions that have governed my life.

If you choose the second alternative, this is how your thesis might look:

> My rebellious streak has strongly influenced my family life, my performance in school, and my choice of career.

Assignment 2

Write an essay in which you describe three earthly things you've observed or experienced that have given you something like Russell's "prefiguring vision of heaven." In other words, they have given you a sense of something ideal, pure, perfect, and beautiful. Describe your observations or experiences in rich detail so that your reader will understand why you found them so special, and explain what effect they have had on you. Here is a sample thesis for such an essay:

> In the faces of my newborn niece, my elderly grandmother, and a seriously ill friend, I have glimpsed something like Russell's "prefiguring vision of heaven."

Assignment 3

Clearly, "love" is a multifaceted emotion. People might say they love their spouses, love their children, love their friends, and love humankind in general, but they mean quite different things in each case. Write an essay in which you divide and classify three types of love. Give detailed examples that illustrate how each type of love is demonstrated.

Shame

Dick Gregory

PREVIEW

In this selection, Dick Gregory—the comedian and social critic— narrates two painful experiences from his boyhood. Although the incidents show graphically what it can be like to grow up black and poor, the essay also deals with universal emotions: shame, embarrassment, and the burning desire to hold on to one's self-respect.

I never learned hate at home, or shame. I had to go to school for that. I was about 1 seven years old when I got my first big lesson. I was in love with a little girl named Helene Tucker, a light-complexioned little girl with pigtails and nice manners. She was always clean and she was smart in school. I think I went to school then mostly to look at her. I brushed my hair and even got me a little old handkerchief. It was a lady's handkerchief, but I didn't want Helene to see me wipe my nose on my hand. The pipes were frozen again, there was no water in the house, but I washed my socks and shirt every night. I'd get a pot, and go over to Mister Ben's grocery store, and stick my pot down into his soda machine. Scoop out some chopped ice. By evening the ice melted to water for washing. I got sick a lot that winter because the fire would go out at night before the clothes were dry. In the morning I'd put them on, wet or dry, because they were the only clothes I had.

Everybody's got a Helene Tucker, a symbol of everything you want. I loved   2
her for her goodness, her cleanness, her popularity. She'd walk down my street and my brothers and sisters would yell, "Here comes Helene," and I'd rub my tennis sneakers on the back of my pants and wish my hair wasn't so nappy and the white folks' shirt fit me better. I'd run out on the street. If I knew my place and didn't come too close, she'd wink at me and say hello. That was a good feeling. Sometimes I'd follow her all the way home, and shovel the snow off her walk and try to make friends with her Momma and her aunts. I'd drop money on her stoop late at night on my way back from shining shoes in the taverns. And she had a Daddy, and he had a good job. He was a paper hanger.

I guess I would have gotten over Helene by summertime, but something hap-   3
pened in that classroom that made her face hang in front of me for the next twenty-two years. When I played the drums in high school it was for Helene and when I broke track records in college it was for Helene and when I started standing behind microphones and heard applause I wished Helene could hear it, too. It wasn't until I was twenty-nine years old and married and making money that I finally got her out of my system. Helene was sitting in that classroom when I learned to be ashamed of myself.

It was on a Thursday. I was sitting in the back of the room, in a seat with a   4
chalk circle drawn around it. The idiot's seat, the troublemaker's seat.

The teacher thought I was stupid. Couldn't spell, couldn't read, couldn't do   5
arithmetic. Just stupid. Teachers were never interested in finding out that you couldn't concentrate because you were so hungry, because you hadn't had any breakfast. All you could think about was noontime, would it ever come? Maybe you could sneak into the cloakroom and steal a bite of some kid's lunch out of a coat pocket. A bite of something. Paste. You can't really make a meal of paste, or put it on bread for a sandwich, but sometimes I'd scoop a few spoonfuls out of the big paste jar in the back of the room. Pregnant people get strange tastes. I was pregnant with poverty. Pregnant with dirt and pregnant with smells that made people turn away, pregnant with cold and pregnant with shoes that were never bought for me, pregnant with five other people in my bed and no Daddy in the next room, and pregnant with hunger. Paste doesn't taste too bad when you're hungry.

The teacher thought I was a troublemaker. All she saw from the front of the   6
room was a little black boy who squirmed in his idiot's seat and made noises and poked the kids around him. I guess she couldn't see a kid who made noises because he wanted someone to know he was there.

It was on a Thursday, the day before the Negro payday. The eagle always flew 7 on Friday. The teacher was asking each student how much his father would give to the Community Chest. On Friday night, each kid would get the money from his father, and on Monday he would bring it to the school. I decided I was going to buy a Daddy right then. I had money in my pocket from shining shoes and selling papers, and whatever Helene Tucker pledged for her Daddy I was going to top it. And I'd hand the money right in. I wasn't going to wait until Monday to buy me a Daddy.

I was shaking, scared to death. The teacher opened her book and started call- 8 ing out names alphabetically.

"Helene Tucker?" 9

"My Daddy said he'd give two dollars and fifty cents." 10

"That's very nice, Helene. Very, very nice indeed." 11

That made me feel pretty good. It wouldn't take too much to top that. I had 12 almost three dollars in dimes and quarters in my pocket. I stuck my hand in my pocket and held on to the money, waiting for her to call my name. But the teacher closed her book after she called everybody else in the class.

I stood up and raised my hand. 13

"What is it now?" 14

"You forgot me?" 15

She turned toward the blackboard. "I don't have time to be playing with you, 16 Richard."

"My Daddy said he'd . . ." 17

"Sit down, Richard, you're disturbing the class." 18

"My Daddy said he'd give . . . fifteen dollars." 19

She turned around and looked mad. "We are collecting this money for you 20 and your kind, Richard Gregory. If your Daddy can give fifteen dollars you have no business being on relief."

"I got it right now, I got it right now, my Daddy gave it to me to turn in today, 21 my Daddy said . . ."

"And furthermore," she said, looking right at me, her nostrils getting big 22 and her lips getting thin and her eyes opening wide, "we know you don't have a Daddy."

Helene Tucker turned around, her eyes full of tears. She felt sorry for me. 23 Then I couldn't see her too well because I was crying, too.

"Sit down, Richard." 24

And I always thought the teacher kind of liked me. She always picked me to 25 wash the blackboard on Friday, after school. That was a big thrill; it made me feel important. If I didn't wash it, come Monday the school might not function right.

"Where are you going, Richard!" 26

I walked out of school that day, and for a long time I didn't go back very often. 27 There was shame there.

Now there was shame everywhere. It seemed like the whole world had been **28** inside that classroom, everyone had heard what the teacher had said, everyone had turned around and felt sorry for me. There was shame in going to the Worthy Boys Annual Christmas Dinner for you and your kind, because everybody knew what a worthy boy was. Why couldn't they just call it the Boys Annual Dinner— why'd they have to give it a name? There was shame in wearing the brown and orange and white plaid mackinaw[1] the welfare gave to three thousand boys. Why'd it have to be the same for everybody so when you walked down the street the people could see you were on relief? It was a nice warm mackinaw and it had a hood, and my Momma beat me and called me a little rat when she found out I stuffed it in the bottom of a pail full of garbage way over on Cottage Street. There was shame in running over to Mister Ben's at the end of the day and asking for his rotten peaches, there was shame in asking Mrs. Simmons for a spoonful of sugar, there was shame in running out to meet the relief truck. I hated that truck, full of food for you and your kind. I ran into the house and hid when it came. And then I started to sneak through alleys, to take the long way home so the people going into White's Eat Shop wouldn't see me. Yeah, the whole world heard the teacher that day—we all know you don't have a Daddy.

It lasted for a while, this kind of numbness. I spent a lot of time feeling sorry **29** for myself. And then one day I met this wino in a restaurant. I'd been out hustling all day, shining shoes, selling newspapers, and I had googobs of money in my pocket. Bought me a bowl of chili for fifteen cents, and a cheeseburger for fifteen cents, and a Pepsi for five cents, and a piece of chocolate cake for ten cents. That was a good meal. I was eating when this old wino came in. I love winos because they never hurt anyone but themselves.

The old wino sat down at the counter and ordered twenty-six cents worth of **30** food. He ate it like he really enjoyed it. When the owner, Mister Williams, asked him to pay the check, the old wino didn't lie or go through his pocket like he suddenly found a hole.

He just said: "Don't have no money."   **31**

The owner yelled: "Why in hell did you come in here and eat my food if you **32** don't have no money? That food cost me money."

Mister Williams jumped over the counter and knocked the wino off his stool **33** and beat him over the head with a pop bottle. Then he stepped back and watched the wino bleed. Then he kicked him. And he kicked him again.

I looked at the wino with blood all over his face and I went over. "Leave him **34** alone, Mister Williams. I'll pay the twenty-six cents."

The wino got up, slowly, pulling himself up to the stool, then up to the coun- **35** ter, holding on for a minute until his legs stopped shaking so bad. He looked at me

---

[1]*mackinaw:* a short, heavy woolen coat, usually plaid and double-breasted.

with pure hate. "Keep your twenty-six cents. You don't have to pay, not now. I just finished paying for it."

He started to walk out, and as he passed me, he reached down and touched my 36 shoulder. "Thanks, sonny, but it's too late now. Why didn't you pay it before?"

I was pretty sick about that. I waited too long to help another man.   37

READING COMPREHENSION

www.mhhe.com/langan

1. The words *pregnant with* in "pregnant with poverty" (paragraph 5) mean
   a. full of.
   b. empty of.
   c. sick of.
   d. satisfied with.

2. The word *hustling* in "I'd been out hustling all day" (paragraph 29) means
   a. learning.
   b. stealing.
   c. making friends.
   d. working hard.

3. Which of the following would be a good alternative title for this selection?
   a. Helene Tucker
   b. The Pain of Being Poor
   c. Losing a Father
   d. Mr. Williams and the Wino

4. Which sentence best expresses the main idea of the selection?
   a. Richard felt that being poor was humiliating.
   b. Richard liked Helene Tucker very much.
   c. Richard had to work hard as a child.
   d. The wino refused Richard's money.

5. The teacher disliked Richard because he
   a. was dirty.
   b. liked Helene.
   c. was a troublemaker.
   d. ate paste.

6. *True or false?* _____ Helene Tucker felt sorry for Richard when the teacher embarrassed him.

7. Richard had trouble concentrating and learning in school because he was
   a. poor and hungry.
   b. distracted by Helene.
   c. lonely.
   d. unable to read.

8. Gregory implies that in his youth, he
   a. was not intelligent.
   b. was proud.
   c. had many friends.
   d. and Helene became friends.

9. The author implies that
   a. Mr. Williams felt sorry for the wino.
   b. Richard's teacher was insensitive.
   c. Richard liked people to feel sorry for him.
   d. Richard's father was dead.

10. The author implies that
   a. the mackinaws were poorly made.
   b. Helene was a sensitive girl.
   c. Helene disliked Richard.
   d. the wino was ashamed of his poverty.

STRUCTURE AND TECHNIQUE

1. In paragraphs 1 and 2, Gregory mentions several steps he took to impress Helene Tucker. What were they? Why does he include them in his essay?

2. A metaphor is a suggested comparison. What metaphor does Gregory use in paragraph 5, and what is its purpose? What metaphor does he use in the second sentence of paragraph 7, and what does it mean?

3. In narrating the incidents in the classroom and in the restaurant, Gregory chooses to provide actual dialogue rather than merely to tell what happened. Why?

4. At the end of the essay, Gregory shifts his focus from the classroom to the scene involving the wino at the restaurant. What is the connection between this closing scene and the rest of the essay?

CRITICAL READING AND DISCUSSION

1. When Gregory writes, "I never learned hate at home, or shame. I had to go to school for that" (paragraph 1), he is using irony—an inconsistency between what is expected and what actually occurs. What does he mean by these two statements? What is the effect of his irony?

2. What are Gregory's feelings about his teacher? What were your feelings about her as you read this essay? What could the teacher have done or said that would *not* have made Gregory feel ashamed?

3. Gregory shows how a childhood incident taught him shame. What other important lessons does Gregory learn in this essay? Explain.

4. At the end of his essay, Gregory says, "I waited too long to help another man." Why do you think he waited so long to assist the wino? What are some reasons people do not always help others who are in need (for example, ignoring a homeless person seated on the sidewalk)?

WRITING ASSIGNMENTS

www.mhhe.com/langan

Assignment 1

Dick Gregory tells us in "Shame" that he was ashamed of his poverty and of being on welfare—to the point that he threw away the warm hooded mackinaw he had been given simply because it was obvious proof that he and his family were on relief. Do you think Gregory was justified in feeling so ashamed of his situation? How about other people who are on welfare? Are they justified if they feel ashamed? Choose either of the following thesis statements and develop it in an essay of several paragraphs:

People on welfare are justified in feeling ashamed.

People on welfare should not feel ashamed.

Then develop your thesis by thinking of several reasons to support the statement you have chosen. You might think along the following lines:

Availability of jobs

Education or lack of education

Number of young children at home requiring care

Illness, physical disability

Psychological factors—depression, work habits, expectations, mental illness

Society's attitude toward people on welfare

Assignment 2

At some time in your life, you probably had an experience like Dick Gregory's in "Shame"—something that happened in a classroom, a group of friends or peers, or a family situation that proved to be both embarrassing and educational. At the time, the experience hurt you very much, but you learned from it. Write a narrative essay in which you retell this experience. Try to include vivid details and plenty of conversation so that the incident will come to life.

Assignment 3

Write an essay about three basic things that people must have to feel self-respect. In your thesis statement, name these three necessities and state that a person must possess them to feel self-respect. Here are some ideas to consider:

A certain number of material possessions

A job

A loving family or a special person

A clear conscience

A feeling of belonging

Freedom from addictions

In your supporting paragraphs, discuss the factors you have chosen, showing specifically why each is so important. To avoid falling into the trap of writing generalities, you may want to give examples of people who lack these necessities and show how such people lose self-respect. Your examples may be drawn from personal experience, or they may be hypothetical.

I Became Her Target

Roger Wilkins

> **PREVIEW**
>
> Any newcomer in school often has an awkward time breaking the ice with classmates. For Roger Wilkins, being the only black student in his new school made the situation considerably worse. He could easily have become the focus of the other students' prejudice and fear. Instead, help came in the form of a teacher who quickly made it clear how she saw him—as a class member with something to contribute.

My favorite teacher's name was "Deadeye" Bean. Her real name was Dorothy. She   1
taught American history to eighth-graders in the junior high section of Creston, the high school that served the north end of Grand Rapids, Michigan. It was the fall of 1944. Franklin D. Roosevelt was president; American troops were battling their way across France; Joe DiMaggio was still in the service; the Montgomery bus boycott was more than a decade away, and I was a twelve-year-old black newcomer in a school that was otherwise all white.

My mother, who had been a widow in New York, had married my stepfather,   2
a Grand Rapids physician, the year before, and he had bought the best house he could afford for his new family. The problem for our new neighbors was that their neighborhood had previously been pristine[1] (in their terms) and that they were ignorant about black people. The prevailing wisdom in the neighborhood was that we were spoiling it and that we ought to go back where we belonged (or alternatively, ought not intrude where we were not wanted). There was a lot of angry talk among the adults, but nothing much came of it.

But some of the kids, those first few weeks, were quite nasty. They threw   3
stones at me, chased me home when I was on foot and spat on my bike seat when I was in class. For a time, I was a pretty lonely, friendless and sometimes frightened kid. I was just transplanted from Harlem, and here in Grand Rapids, the dominant culture was speaking to me insistently. I can see now that those youngsters were bullying and culturally disadvantaged. I knew then that they were bigoted, but the culture spoke to me more powerfully than my mind and I felt ashamed for being different—a nonstandard person.

I now know that Dorothy Bean understood most of that and deplored it. So   4
things began to change when I walked into her classroom. She was a pleasant-

---

[1]*pristine:* pure.

looking single woman, who looked old and wrinkled to me at the time, but who was probably about forty. Whereas my other teachers approached the problem of easing in their new black pupil by ignoring him for the first few weeks, Miss Bean went right at me. On the morning after having read our first assignment, she asked me the first question. I later came to know that in Grand Rapids, she was viewed as a very liberal person who believed, among other things, that Negroes were equal.

I gulped and answered her question and the follow-up. They weren't brilliant 5 answers, but they did establish the facts that I had read the assignment and that I could speak English. Later in the hour, when one of my classmates had bungled an answer, Miss Bean came back to me with a question that required me to clean up the girl's mess and established me as a smart person.

Thus, the teacher began to give me human dimensions, though not perfect 6 ones for an eighth-grader. It was somewhat better to be an incipient[2] teacher's pet than merely a dark presence in the back of the room onto whose silent form my classmates could fit all the stereotypes they carried in their heads.

A few days later, Miss Bean became the first teacher ever to require me to 7 think. She asked my opinion about something Jefferson had done. In those days, all my opinions were derivative.[3] I was for Roosevelt because my parents were, and I was for the Yankees because my older buddy from Harlem was a Yankee fan. Besides, we didn't have opinions about historical figures like Jefferson. Like our high school building or old Mayor Welch, he just was.

After I had stared at her for a few seconds, she said: "Well, should he have 8 bought Louisiana or not?"

"I guess so," I replied tentatively.   9

"Why?" she asked.   10

Why! What kind of question was that, I groused silently. But I ventured an 11 answer. Day after day, she kept doing that to me, and my answers became stronger and more confident. She was the first teacher to give me the sense that thinking was part of education and that I could form opinions that had some value.

Her final service to me came on a day when my mind was wandering and I 12 was idly digging my pencil into the writing surface on the arm of my chair. Miss Bean impulsively threw a hunk of gum eraser at me. By amazing chance, it hit my hand and sent the pencil flying. She gasped, and I crept mortified after my pencil as the class roared. That was the icebreaker. Afterward, kids came up to me to laugh about "Old Deadeye Bean." The incident became a legend, and I, a part of that story, became a person to talk to. So that's how I became just another kid in school and Dorothy Bean became "Old Deadeye."

---

[2]*incipient:* about to become.
[3]*derivative:* not original.

READING COMPREHENSION

1. The word *deplored* in "But some of the kids, those first few weeks, were quite nasty. . . . Dorothy Bean understood most of that and deplored it" (paragraphs 3–4) means
   a. supported.
   b. imitated.
   c. often taught.
   d. disapproved of.

2. The word *groused* in "Why! What kind of question was that, I groused silently" (paragraph 11) means
   a. complained.
   b. agreed.
   c. answered.
   d. yelled.

3. Which of the following would be a good alternative title for this selection?
   a. Education in the Forties
   b. A True Teacher's Pet
   c. Eighth Grade
   d. A Teacher's Help

4. Which of the following sentences best expresses the main idea of the selection?
   a. After moving from Harlem to Grand Rapids, Michigan, the author had numerous adjustments to make.
   b. Eighth grade can be a challenging time for a new student.
   c. Using unusual methods, Miss Bean helped her eighth-grade students learn to think for themselves.
   d. A teacher helped the first black student in school to be accepted and to learn to think for himself.

5. After moving to Grand Rapids, Wilkins felt ashamed of
   a. having a stepfather.
   b. being smart.
   c. having lived in Harlem.
   d. being different.

6. By involving Wilkins in class discussion, Miss Bean helped the other students see him as more than a
   a. stereotype.
   b. liberal.
   c. legend.
   d. bigot.

7. Wilkins writes that before entering Miss Bean's class, he held
   a. no opinions.
   b. no original opinions.
   c. opinions based on careful thought.
   d. opinions on various historical figures.

8. The author implies that some of the bigotry in Grand Rapids was the result of
   a. anger about the war.
   b. ignorance about black people.
   c. his youth.
   d. ignorance about physicians.

9. In stating "the teacher began to give me human dimensions, though not perfect ones for an eighth-grader" (paragraph 6), the imperfection that Wilkins refers to is his
   a. different race.
   b. inadequate answers.
   c. becoming a teacher's pet.
   d. coming from another state.

10. We can conclude that Dorothy Bean threw an eraser at the author because she
   a. knew the event would become an icebreaker for him.
   b. wanted to knock the pencil from his hand.
   c. wanted to ask his opinion about something.
   d. wanted him to pay attention in class.

STRUCTURE AND TECHNIQUE

1. Which pattern of development—comparison, narration, or description—does Wilkins use in most of his essay? Explain.

2. Which kind of transition signal—addition, time, or space—does Wilkins use to move his essay smoothly from one event to the next? Find at least four different words that are examples of this signal.

3. In the first paragraph, Wilkins chooses to provide some historical background for his story. Why do you think he chose the specific details mentioned there? What might have been lost if these details had been excluded from the essay?

4. A title can offer interesting insights into an essay, especially if the title acquires unexpected meanings. Before reading this essay, what did you think the title "I Became Her Target" might refer to? What additional meanings do you think Wilkins intended?

CRITICAL READING AND DISCUSSION

1. What does Wilkins mean by the term *nonstandard person* (paragraph 3)? Do you think he later felt more like a "standard" person? Why or why not?

2. Wilkins mentions several ways Miss Bean treated him differently from the way he was treated by the other teachers at Creston. How did her approach differ from theirs? What does this approach reveal about Miss Bean—as a teacher and as a person?

3. Wilkins says that initially he was Miss Bean's "incipient teacher's pet" (paragraph 6). But how did Miss Bean's behavior toward him go beyond mere favoritism? In what way did her treatment of Wilkins affect how his peers regarded him?

4. In paragraph 7, Wilkins says, "Miss Bean became the first teacher ever to require me to think." Before Miss Bean's class, what do you suspect Wilkins—and his classmates—were being taught to do in school? Describe a teacher who gave you "the sense that thinking was part of education." In your opinion, what can teachers do to get students to think?

WRITING ASSIGNMENTS

www.mhhe.com/langan

Assignment 1

Dorothy Bean, Wilkins's favorite teacher, obviously had an important influence on him in more ways than one. She helped him become accepted by the other students, she strengthened his self-image, and she helped him learn to think for himself. Write an essay on one of your favorite teachers and the ways he or she influenced you.

Like Wilkins, dramatize specific incidents to show how this teacher affected you. Provide whatever background is necessary to put the teacher's influence into perspective. Your thesis will be a general statement that summarizes the teacher's impact on your life, such as this one: "Mrs. Croson, my sixth-grade teacher, helped me in ways that strengthened all of the rest of my education." Then go on in your introduction to list three specific ways the teacher influenced you. An example of such a plan of development is "She gave me confidence and taught me the joys of reading and writing."

Alternatively, write an essay on three of your favorite teachers. Your thesis might be about the characteristics the three teachers shared or how they influenced you.

Assignment 2

Wilkins suggests that the students in his new school misjudged him because at first they saw him only as a stereotype, a stranger with no particular personal characteristics. Perhaps we are all subject to prejudging people, if not because of their race, then for another reason. Did a person who made a good impression on you ever turn out to be boring and mean? Did a boss you thought was overly strict ever turn out to be supportive and teach you a lot? Write an essay about someone who was really quite different from what you initially thought he or she would be. You may wish to consider the following characteristics, which often lead people to prejudge each other:

Age

Gender

Race

Sexual preference

Size

Clothing

Job

Begin your essay by explaining in vivid detail your first impression and what caused it. Then go on to narrate some experiences you had with the person and how these experiences changed your mind about him or her.

Alternatively, write about an individual or individuals who have prejudged you. Explain what those people thought of you and why, and describe how they treated you. If they came to change their minds, explain why and how your relationship changed.

Assignment 3

Write an essay in which you contrast your best teacher and your worst teacher. Make a list of the qualities that made one teacher excellent and the other ineffective or worse. Focus on three pairs of contrasting qualities, using either a *one-side-at-a-time* or a *point-by-point* method of development (see pages 288–290). Following are some elements of teaching to consider as you plan your essay:

Grasp of the subject

Ability to communicate

Ability to motivate

Interest in students

Classroom presentation

Sense of humor

In addition, consider what you or other students learned or did not learn, such as the following:

Subject matter

Ways to learn

Ways to think

Self-confidence

Methods of cooperation

Smash Thy Neighbor

John McMurtry

> **PREVIEW**
>
>
> We think of football as one of those all-American things, like baseball or apple pie. Children are encouraged to play football from middle school through college. Hundreds of hours of network TV are devoted to football coverage. And *Monday Night Football* is almost a patriotic ritual. In this selection, however, a former football player says that football games are cruel contests that injure players and bring out the worst in fans.

A few months ago my neck got a hard crick in it. I couldn't turn my head; to look 1
left or right I had to turn my whole body. But I'd had cricks in my neck since I started playing grade-school football and hockey, so I just ignored it. Then I began to notice that when I reached for any sort of large book (which I do pretty often as a philosophy teacher at the University of Guelph), I had trouble lifting it with one hand. I was losing the strength in my left arm, and I had such a steady pain in my back that I often had to stretch out on the floor to relieve the pressure.

Several weeks after my problems with book-lifting, I mentioned to my brother, 2
an orthopedic surgeon, that I'd lost the power in my arm since my neck began to hurt. Twenty-four hours later I was in a Toronto hospital, not sure whether I might end up with a wasted upper limb. Apparently the steady pounding I had received playing college and professional football in the late fifties and early sixties had driven my head into my backbone so that the disks had crumpled together at the neck—"acute herniation"—and had cut the nerves to my left arm like a pinched telephone wire (without nerve stimulation, of course, the muscles atrophy, leaving the arm crippled). So I spent my Christmas holidays in the hospital in heavy traction, and much of the next three months with my neck in a brace. Today most of the pain is gone, and I've recovered most of the strength in my arm. But from time to time I still have to don the brace, and surgery remains a possibility.

Not much of this will surprise anyone who knows football. It is a sport in 3
which body wreckage is one of the leading conventions. A few days after I went into the hospital for that crick in my neck, another brother, an outstanding football player in college, was undergoing spinal surgery in the same hospital two floors above me. In his case it was a lower, more massive herniation, which every now and again buckled him so that he was unable to lift himself off his back for days. By the time he entered the hospital for surgery he had already spent several

months in bed. The operation was successful, but, as in all such cases, it will take him a year to recover fully.

These aren't isolated experiences. Just about anybody who has ever played 4 football for any length of time, in high school, college, or one of the professional leagues, has suffered for it later.

Indeed, it is arguable that body shattering is the very *point* of football, as kill- 5 ing and maiming are of war. (In the United States, for example, the game results in fifteen to twenty deaths a year and about fifty thousand major operations on knees alone.) To grasp some of the more conspicuous similarities between football and war, it is instructive to listen to the imperatives most frequently issued to the players by their coaches, teammates, and fans. "Hurt 'em!" "Level 'em!" "Kill 'em!" "Take 'em apart!" Or watch for the plays that are most enthusiastically applauded by the fans, where someone is "smeared," "knocked silly," "creamed," "nailed," "broken in two," or even "crucified." (One of my coaches when I played corner linebacker with the Calgary Stampeders in 1961 elaborated, often very inventively, on this language of destruction: admonishing us to "unjoin" the opponent, "make 'im remember you," and "stomp 'im like a bug."). Just as in hockey, where a fight will bring fans to their feet more often than a skillful play, so in football the mouth waters most of all for the really crippling block or tackle. For the kill. Thus the good teams are "hungry," the best players are "mean," and "casualties" are as much a part of the game as they are of a war.

The family resemblance between football and war is, indeed, striking. Their 6 languages are similar: "field general," "long bomb," "blitz," "take a shot," "front line," "pursuit," "good hit," "the draft," and so on. Their principles and practices are alike: mass hysteria, the art of intimidation, absolute command and total obedience, territorial aggression, censorship, inflated insignia and propaganda, blackboard maneuvers and strategies, drills, uniforms, formations, marching bands, and training camps. And the virtues they celebrate are almost identical: hyperaggressiveness, coolness under fire, and suicidal bravery.

One difference between war and football, though, is that there is little or no 7 protest against football. Perhaps the most extraordinary thing about the game is that the systematic infliction of injuries excites in people not concern, as would be the case if they were sustained at, say, a rock festival, but a collective rejoicing and euphoria. Players and fans alike revel in the spectacle of a combatant felled into semiconsciousness, "blindsided," "clotheslined," or "decapitated." I can remember, in fact, being chided by a coach in pro ball for not "getting my hat" injuriously into a player who was lying helpless on the ground.

After every game, of course, the papers are full of reports on the day's inju- 8 ries, a sort of post-battle "body count," and the respective teams go to work with doctors and trainers, tape, whirlpool baths, cortisone, and morphine to patch and deaden the wounds before the next game. Then the whole drama is reenacted—injured athletes held together by adhesive, braces, and drugs—and the days following it are filled with even more feverish activity to put on the show yet again at the end of the week. (I remember being so taped up in college that I earned the nickname "Mummy.") The team that survives this merry-go-round spectacle of skilled masochism with the fewest incapacitating injuries usually wins. It is a sort of victory by ordeal: "We hurt them more than they hurt us."

My own initiation into this brutal circus was typical. I loved the game from 9 the moment I could run with a ball. Played shoeless on a green, open field with no one keeping score and in a spirit of reckless abandon and laughter, it's a very different sport. Almost no one gets hurt, and it's rugged, open, and exciting (it still is for me). But, like everything else, it starts to be regulated and institutionalized by adult authorities. And the fun is over.

So it was as I began the long march through organized football. Now there 10 were a coach and elders to make it clear by their behavior that beating other people was the only thing to celebrate and that trying to shake someone up every play was the only thing to be really proud of. Now there were severe rule enforcers, audiences, formally recorded victors and losers, and heavy equipment to permit crippling bodily moves and collisions (according to one survey, more than 80 percent of all football injuries occur to fully equipped players). And now there was the official "given" that the only way to keep playing was to wear suffocating armor, to play to defeat, to follow orders silently, and to renounce spontaneity in favor of joyless drill. The game has been, in short, ruined. But because I loved to play, and play skillfully, I stayed. And progressively and inexorably, as I moved through high school, college, and pro leagues, my body was dismantled. Piece by piece.

I started off with torn ligaments in my knee at thirteen. Then, as the organ- 11 ization and the competition increased, the injuries came faster and harder. Broken nose (three times), broken jaw (fractured in the first half and dismissed as a "bad wisdom tooth," so I played with it for the rest of the game), ripped knee ligaments again. Torn ligaments in one ankle and a fracture in the other (which I remember feeling relieved about because it meant I could honorably stop drill-blocking a 270-pound defensive end). Repeated rib fractures and cartilage tears (usually carried, again, through the remainder of the game). More dislocations of the left shoulder than I can remember (the last one I played with because, as the Calgary Stampeders' doctor said, it "couldn't be damaged any more"). Occasionally broken or dislocated fingers and toes. Chronically hurt lower back (I still can't lift with it or change a tire without worrying about folding). Separated right shoulder (as with many other injuries, like badly bruised hips and legs, needled with morphine for the games). And so on. The last pro game I played—against the Winnipeg Blue Bombers in the Western finals in 1961—I had a recently dislocated left shoulder, a more recently wrenched right shoulder, and a chronic pain center in one leg. I was so tied up with soreness that I couldn't drive to the airport. But it never occurred to me that I should miss a play as a corner linebacker.

By the end of my football career, I had learned that physical injury—giving it 12 and taking it—is the real currency of the sport. And that in the final analysis, the "winner" is the man who can hit to kill even if only half his limbs are working.

In brief, a warrior game with a warrior ethos[1] into which (like almost everyone I played with) my original boyish enthusiasm had been relentlessly conditioned.

In thinking back on how all this happened, though, I can pick out no villains. **13** As with the social system as a whole, the game has a life of its own. Everyone grows up inside it, accepts it, and fulfills its dictates as obediently as Helots.[2] Far from questioning the principles of the activity, most men simply concentrate on executing these principles more aggressively than anybody else. The result is a group of people who, as the leagues become of a higher and higher class, are progressively insensitive to the possibility that things could be otherwise. Thus, in football, anyone who might question the wisdom or enjoyment of putting on heavy equipment on a hot day and running full speed at someone else with the intention of knocking him senseless would be regarded as not really a devoted athlete and probably "chicken." The choice is made straightforward. Either you, too, do your very utmost to smash efficiently and be smashed, or you admit incompetence or cowardice and quit. Since neither of these admissions is very pleasant, people generally keep any doubts they have to themselves, and carry on.

Of course, it would be a mistake to suppose that there is more blind acceptance **14** of brutal practices in organized football than elsewhere. On the contrary, a recent Harvard study argues that football's characteristics of "impersonal acceptance of inflicted injury," an overriding "organization goal," the "ability to turn oneself on and off," and being, above all, "out to win" are prized by ambitious executives in many large corporations. Clearly, football is no sicker than the rest of our society. Even its organized destruction of physical well-being is not anomalous.[3] A very large part of our wealth, work, and time is, after all, spent in systematically destroying and harming human life; manufacturing, selling, and using weapons that tear opponents to pieces; making ever bigger and faster predator-named cars with which to kill and injure one another by the millions every year; and devoting our very lives to outgunning one another for power in an ever-more-destructive rat race. Yet all these practices are accepted without question by most people, even zealously defended and honored. Competitive, organized injuring is integral to our way of life, and football is one of the more intelligible mirrors of the whole process: a sort of colorful morality play showing us how exciting and rewarding it is to Smash Thy Neighbor.

Now, it is fashionable to rationalize our collaboration in all this by arguing that, **15** well, men *like* to fight and injure their fellows, and such games as football should be encouraged to discharge this original-sin[4] urge into less harmful channels than, say, war. Public-show football, this line goes, plays the same sort of cathartic role

---

[1]*ethos:* set of values.

[2]*Helots:* in ancient Greece, people of slave-like status.

[3]*anomalous:* abnormal.

[4]*original sin:* referring to the Christian belief that all humans are in a sinful state because of Adam's disobedience in the Garden of Eden.

as Aristotle said stage tragedy does: without real blood (or not much), it releases players and audience from unhealthy feelings stored up inside them.

As an ex-player in this seasonal coast-to-coast drama, I see little to recom- 16 mend such a view. What organized football did to me was make me *suppress* my natural urges and reexpress them in alienating, vicious form. Spontaneous desires for free bodily exuberance and fraternization with competitors were shamed and forced under ("If it ain't hurtin', it ain't helpin'"), and in their place were demanded armored, mechanical moves, and cool hatred of all opposition. Endless authoritarian drill and dressing-room harangues (ever wonder why competing teams can't prepare for a game in the same dressing room?) were the kinds of mechanisms employed to reconstruct joyful energies into mean and alien shapes. I am quite certain that everyone else around me was being similarly forced into this heavily equipped military precision and angry antagonism, because there was always a mutinous attitude about full-dress practices, and everybody (the pros included) had to concentrate incredibly hard for days to whip himself into just one hour's hostility a week against another club. The players never speak of these things, of course, because everyone is anxious to appear tough.

The claim that men like seriously to battle one another to some sort of finish is 17 a myth. It endures only because it wears one of the oldest and most propagandized of masks—the romantic combatant. I sometimes wonder whether the violence all around us doesn't depend for its survival on the existence and preservation of this tough-guy disguise.

As for the effect of organized football on the spectator, the fans are not so 18 much released from supposed feelings of violent aggression by watching their athletic heroes perform it as they are encouraged in the view that people-smashing is an admirable mode of self-expression. The most savage attackers, after all, are, by general agreement, the most efficient and worthy players of all (the biggest applause I ever received as a football player occurred when I ran over people or slammed them so hard that they couldn't get up). . . . Watching well-advertised strong men knock other people around, make them hurt, is in the end like other tastes. It does not weaken with feeding and variation in form. It grows.

I got out of football in 1962. In a preseason intersquad game, I ripped the car- 19 tilage in my ribs on the hardest block I'd ever thrown. I had trouble breathing, and I had to shuffle-walk with my torso on a tilt. The doctor in the local hospital said three weeks rest; the coach said scrimmage in two days. Three days later I was back home reading philosophy.

© Lucy Nicholson/Reuters/Corbis

Do you consider football to be all-American? Why or why not?

READING COMPREHENSION

www.mhhe.com/langan

1. The word *atrophy* in "without nerve stimulation, of course, the muscles atrophy, leaving the arm crippled" (paragraph 2) means

   a. get stronger.

   b. flex.

   c. weaken.

   d. are unaffected.

2. The word *imperatives* in "It is instructive to listen to the imperatives most frequently issued to the players. . . . 'Hurt 'em!' 'Level 'em!' 'Kill 'em!'" (paragraph 5) means

   a. insults.

   b. commands.

   c. compliments.

   d. questions.

3. Which of the following would be a good alternative title for this selection?

   a. The Violence of Football

   b. Football in the United States

   c. A Man Who Played Football

   d. Football and Corporate Competition

4. Which sentence best expresses the main idea of the selection?
   a. Playing football has caused the author much physical pain.
   b. Most football coaches try to make the game less violent.
   c. Football's popularity is a reflection of some negative aspects of society.
   d. Violence is a central part of organized football both for the teams and for the fans.

5. The author says that organized football is like
   a. all other sports.
   b. philosophy.
   c. war.
   d. football played without coaches and rules.

6. For the author, football was ruined by
   a. people who play without equipment.
   b. adult authorities.
   c. people who dislike its violence.
   d. ambitious executives.

7. According to the author, watching football makes people
   a. believe that "smashing thy neighbor" is good.
   b. realize that football is too violent.
   c. feel a great release from their own violent feelings.
   d. escape from the anxieties of their jobs.

8. The author implies that
   a. society is much less brutally competitive than football.
   b. football players never have doubts about the brutality of the game.
   c. the brutal values of football exist in other parts of society.
   d. many people question the violence in football.

9. The author implies that fans
   a. get rid of unhealthy feelings when watching football.
   b. encourage the violence in football.
   c. are unaware of the violence in football.
   d. discourage the really savage attacks in football.

10. In the last paragraph, the author implies that
    a. his injuries were mild.
    b. the doctor exaggerated the extent of his injuries.
    c. the coach thought that his injuries were mild.
    d. the coach cared more about winning than about his players' injuries.

STRUCTURE AND TECHNIQUE

1. McMurtry uses several patterns of development in his essay: comparison and contrast, cause-and-effect, description, narration, and argumentation. Where does he use each of those patterns?

2. McMurtry uses terms such as "body wreckage," "body shattering," and "skilled masochism" to describe organized football. Find three other phrases the author uses to describe football (beginning with paragraph 9). What effect does McMurtry hope this language will have on the reader?

3. In paragraph 11, McMurtry provides a series of details about the injuries he has sustained playing football. List some of these details. Why do you think he includes these personal details in his essay?

4. In "Smash Thy Neighbor," McMurtry repeatedly describes his own personal experiences with football. What do these anecdotes contribute to the essay? How do they relate to the larger point he is trying to make?

CRITICAL READING AND DISCUSSION

1. What is McMurtry's current profession? How might his present position have influenced his opinions about football?

2. The author makes a comparison between war and football. Do you think this is a fair comparison? Why or why not?

3. According to McMurtry, what qualities of our society are reflected in football? What is your opinion of his analysis?

4. In paragraphs 15–18, McMurtry points out—and then rebuts—the belief that football benefits society. Do you believe that football and sports in general are harmful or helpful to society? Explain.

WRITING ASSIGNMENTS

www.mhhe.com/langan

Assignment 1

Imagine that you are a professional football coach (or if you prefer, the head coach of your school's football team). You have just read "Smash Thy Neighbor" in a national magazine, and you feel angered and hurt by McMurtry's opinion of football. How would you answer his accusations about the sport? Write a letter to the editor of the magazine in which you give three reasons why John McMurtry is wrong about football and its effects on people. You might want to get started with this thesis statement:

I feel John McMurtry is wrong about football for several reasons.

Then continue your letter, describing each reason in detail. Write a separate paragraph for each detail.

Alternatively, imagine that, as a coach, you agree with McMurtry, and write a letter in which you detail three reasons for agreeing.

Assignment 2

Write a narrative essay about a bad experience you had with sports. Among the topics you might write about are

An injury

Not being chosen for a team

Missing an important point or goal

Being pressured by a parent or coach

Being the clumsiest person in gym class

Being embarrassed while trying to learn a sport

You could begin the essay with a sentence or two about your experience with sports in general—whether sports have been an area of pain or pleasure for you. Your thesis should name the particular experience you will write about and tell your readers that this experience was bad (or embarrassing or humiliating or disillusioning or any other word that seems appropriate).

Then organize your supporting paragraphs by dividing your experience into two or three time phases. First, you may want to review Chapter 9, on the narrative essay (pages 203–221).

Assignment 3

Write an essay about a sport you feel is a good one. In each of your supporting paragraphs, give one reason why this sport is good for either players or spectators.

A Hanging

George Orwell

> ### PREVIEW
>
> You are about to attend an execution. In this essay, George Orwell (author of *Animal Farm* and *1984*) recalls a hanging he witnessed when he was an English police officer stationed in Burma. Orwell's sensitivity and vividly descriptive writing will make you see and feel what it is like to take the seemingly endless walk from cell to gallows. You will share the guards' uneasiness and the prisoner's terror. And after you finish the selection, you may also share Orwell's views on capital punishment.

© CORBIS SYGMA

1   It was in Burma, a sodden morning of the rains. A sickly light, like yellow tinfoil, was slanting over the high walls into the jail yard. We were waiting outside the condemned cells, a row of sheds fronted with double bars, like small animal cages. Each cell measured about ten feet by ten and was quite bare within except for a plank bed and a pot of drinking water. In some of them brown silent men were squatting at the inner bars, with their blankets draped round them. These were the condemned men, due to be hanged within the next week or two.

2   One prisoner had been brought out of his cell. He was a Hindu, a puny wisp of a man, with a shaven head and vague liquid eyes. He had a thick, sprouting moustache, absurdly too big for his body, rather like the moustache of a comic man on the films. Six tall Indian warders were guarding him and getting him ready for the gallows. Two of them stood by with rifles with fixed bayonets, while the others handcuffed him, passed a chain through his handcuffs and fixed it to their belts, and lashed his arms tight to his sides. They crowded very close about him, with their hands always on him in a careful, caressing grip, as though all the while feeling him to make sure he was there. It was like men handling a fish which is still alive and may jump back into the water. But he stood quite unresisting, yielding his arms limply to the ropes, as though he hardly noticed what was happening.

3   Eight o'clock struck and a bugle call, desolately thin in the wet air, floated from the distant barracks. The superintendent of the jail, who was standing apart from the rest of us, moodily prodding the gravel with his stick, raised his head at the sound. He was an army doctor, with a grey toothbrush moustache and a gruff voice. "For God's sake hurry up, Francis," he said irritably. "The man ought to have been dead by this time. Aren't you ready yet?"

4   Francis, the head jailer, a fat Dravidian in a white drill suit and gold spectacles, waved his black hand. "Yes sir, yes sir," he bubbled. "All iss satisfactorily prepared. The hangman iss waiting. We shall proceed."

"Well, quick march, then. The prisoners can't get their breakfast till this job's 5 over."

We set out for the gallows. Two warders marched on either side of the pris- 6 oner, with their files at the slope; two others marched close against him, gripping him by arm and shoulder, as though at once pushing and supporting him. The rest of us, magistrates and the like, followed behind. Suddenly, when we had gone ten yards, the procession stopped short without any order or warning. A dreadful thing had happened—a dog, come goodness knows whence, had appeared in the yard. It came bounding among us with a loud volley of barks, and leapt round us wagging its whole body, wild with glee at finding so many human beings together. It was a large woolly dog, half Airedale, half pariah. For a moment it pranced round us, and then, before anyone could stop it, it had made a dash for the prisoner, and jumping up tried to lick his face. Everyone stood aghast, too taken aback even to grab at the dog.

"Who let that bloody brute in here?" said the superintendent angrily. "Catch 7 it, someone!"

A warden, detached from the escort, charged clumsily after the dog, but it 8 danced and gambolled just out of his reach, taking everything as part of the game. A young Eurasian jailer picked up a handful of gravel and tried to stone the dog away, but it dodged the stones and came after us again. Its yaps echoed from the jail walls. The prisoner, in the grasp of the two warders, looked on incuriously, as though this was another formality of the hanging. It was several minutes before someone managed to catch the dog. Then we put my handkerchief through its collar and moved off once more, with the dog still straining and whimpering.

It was about forty yards to the gallows. I watched the bare brown back of 9 the prisoner marching in front of me. He walked clumsily with his bound arms, but quite steadily, with that bobbing gait of the Indian who never straightens his knees. At each step his muscles slid neatly into place, the lock of hair on his scalp danced up and down, his feet printed themselves on the wet gravel. And once, in spite of the men who gripped him by each shoulder, he stepped slightly aside to avoid a puddle on the path.

It is curious, but till that moment I had never realised what it means to destroy 10 a healthy, conscious man. When I saw the prisoner step aside to avoid the puddle, I saw the mystery, the unspeakable wrongness, of cutting a life short when it is in full tide. This man was not dying; he was alive just as we were alive. All the organs of his body were working—bowels digesting food, skin renewing itself, nails growing, tissues forming—all toiling away in solemn foolery. His nails would still be growing when he stood on the drop, when he was falling through the air with a tenth of a second to live. His eyes saw the yellow gravel and the grey walls, and his brain still remembered, foresaw, reasoned—reasoned even about puddles. He and we were a party of men walking together, seeing, hearing, feeling, understanding the same world; and in two minutes, with a sudden snap, one of us would be gone—one mind less, one world less.

The gallows stood in a small yard, separate from the main grounds of the 11 prison, and overgrown with tall prickly weeds. It was a brick erection like three sides of a shed, with planking on top, and above that two beams and a crossbar with the rope dangling. The hangman, a grey-haired convict in the white uniform of the prison, was waiting beside his machine. He greeted us with a servile crouch as we entered. At a word from Francis the two warders, gripping the prisoner more closely than ever, half led, half pushed him to the gallows and helped him clumsily up the ladder. Then the hangman climbed up and fixed the rope round the prisoner's neck.

We stood waiting, five yards away. The warders had formed in a rough circle 12 round the gallows. And then, when the noose was fixed, the prisoner began crying out to his god. It was a high, reiterated cry of "Ram! Ram! Ram! Ram!" not urgent and fearful like a prayer or a cry for help, but steady, rhythmical, almost like the tolling of a bell. The dog answered the sound with a whine. The hangman, still standing on the gallows, produced a small cotton bag like a flour bag and drew it down over the prisoner's face. But the sound, muffled by the cloth, still persisted, over and over again: "Ram! Ram! Ram! Ram! Ram!"

The hangman climbed down and stood ready, holding the lever. Minutes 13 seemed to pass. The steady, muffled crying from the prisoner went on and on, "Ram! Ram! Ram!" never faltering for an instant. The superintendent, his head on his chest, was slowly poking the ground with his stick; perhaps he was counting the cries, allowing the prisoner a fixed number—fifty, perhaps, or a hundred. Everyone had changed colour. The Indians had gone grey like bad coffee, and one or two of the bayonets were wavering. We looked at the lashed, hooded man on the drop, and listened to his cries—each cry another second of life; the same thought was in all our minds: oh, kill him quickly, get it over, stop that abominable noise!

Suddenly the superintendent made up his mind. Throwing up his head he 14 made a swift motion with his stick. "Chalo!" he shouted almost fiercely.

There was a clanking noise, and then dead silence. The prisoner had vanished, 15 and the rope was twisting on itself. I let go of the dog, and it galloped immediately to the back of the gallows; but when it got there it stopped short, barked, and then retreated into a corner of the yard, where it stood among the weeds, looking timorously out at us. We went round the gallows to inspect the prisoner's body. He was dangling with his toes pointed straight downwards, very slowly revolving, as dead as a stone.

The superintendent reached out with his stick and poked the bare body; it os- 16 cillated,[1] slightly. "*He's* all right," said the superintendent. He backed out from under the gallows, and blew out a deep breath. The moody look had gone out of his face quite suddenly. He glanced at his wristwatch. "Eight minutes past eight. Well, that's all for this morning, thank God."

---

[1]*oscillated:* swung back and forth.

The warders unfixed bayonets and marched away. The dog, sobered and con- 17
scious of having misbehaved itself, slipped after them. We walked out of the gallows yard, past the condemned cells with their waiting prisoners, into the big central yard of the prison. The convicts, under the command of warders armed with
lathis,[2] were already receiving their breakfast. They squatted in long rows, each
man holding a tin pannikin,[3] while two warders with buckets marched round la-
dling out rice; it seemed quite a homely, jolly scene, after the hanging. An enormous relief had come upon us now that the job was done. One felt an impulse to
sing, to break into a run, to snicker. All at once everyone began chattering gaily.

The Eurasian boy walking beside me nodded towards the way we had come, 18
with a knowing smile: "Do you know, sir, our friend (he meant the dead man),
when he heard his appeal had been dismissed, he pissed on the floor of his cell.
From fright.—Kindly take one of my cigarettes, sir. Do you not admire my new
silver case, sir? From the boxwallah,[4] two rupees eight annas. Classy European
style."

Several people laughed—at what, nobody seemed certain.   19

Francis was walking by the superintendent, talking garrulously: "Well, sir, 20
all hass passed off with the utmost satisfactoriness. It wass all finished—flick!
like that. It iss not always so—oah, no! I have known cases where the doctor wass
obliged to go beneath the gallows and pull the prisoner's legs to ensure decease.
Most disagreeable!"

"Wriggling about, eh? That's bad," said the superintendent.   21

"Ach, sir, it iss worse when they become refractory! One man, I recall, clung 22
to the bars of hiss cage when we went to take him out. You will scarcely credit,
sir, that it took six warders to dislodge him, three pulling at each leg. We reasoned
with him. 'My dear fellow,' we said, 'think of all the pain and trouble you are
causing to us!' But no, he would not listen! Ach, he wass very troublesome!"

I found that I was laughing quite loudly. Everyone was laughing. Even the 23
superintendent grinned in a tolerant way. "You'd better all come out and have a
drink," he said quite genially. "I've got a bottle of whisky in the car. We could do
with it."

We went through the big double gates of the prison, into the road. "Pulling at 24
his legs!" exclaimed a Burmese magistrate suddenly, and burst into a loud chuck-
ling. We all began laughing again. At that moment Francis's anecdote seemed ex-
traordinarily funny. We all had a drink together, native and European alike, quite
amicably. The dead man was a hundred yards away.

---

[2]*lathis:* long, heavy sticks, usually of bamboo and bound with iron.
[3]*pannikin:* small metal (usually tinned iron) drinking vessel.
[4]*boxwallah:* expert box-maker.

READING COMPREHENSION

1. The word *gambolled* in "[the dog] danced and gambolled just out of his reach" (paragraph 8) means
   a. crawled.
   b. limped.
   c. leaped.
   d. stood.

2. The word *amicably* in "We all had a drink together, . . . quite amicably" (paragraph 24) means
   a. with hostility.
   b. unnecessarily.
   c. quietly.
   d. in a friendly way.

3. Which of the following would be a good alternative title for this selection?
   a. A Burmese Prisoner
   b. Methods of Capital Punishment
   c. The Necessity of Execution
   d. The Difficulty of Taking a Life

4. Which sentence best expresses the main idea of the selection?
   a. Capital punishment is unpleasant to carry out, but it is necessary in some cases.
   b. Executions in Burma were done in an inefficient and amateurish way.
   c. Taking another person's life is morally wrong.
   d. No one cared about the Burmese prisoner who was hanged.

5. Just before he was executed, the prisoner
   a. protested his innocence.
   b. cried out to his god.
   c. tried to escape from the gallows.
   d. said a quiet prayer.

6. *True or false?* _____ The author says that the prisoner had been convicted of murder.

7. After the execution, the author and the other officials
   a. felt relief.
   b. became very depressed.
   c. chased away the dog.
   d. couldn't speak for a long while.

8. The author implies that
   a. the dog that interrupted the march to the gallows belonged to the prisoner.
   b. no one has the right to take another person's life.
   c. the authorities knew the prisoner was innocent.
   d. other methods of execution are more humane than hanging.

9. The author implies that
   a. the prisoner would have escaped if he had not been so heavily guarded.
   b. the prisoner did not die immediately.
   c. the hangman had volunteered for the job.
   d. the superintendent of the jail was nervous and upset about the hanging.

10. The author implies
   a. the people who witnessed the hanging later laughed and joked to cover up the uneasiness they felt.
   b. the native people and the Europeans felt differently about the hanging.
   c. he had become friends with the prisoner before the execution.
   d. Burmese officials were corrupt.

STRUCTURE AND TECHNIQUE

1. Paragraphs 1, 2, and 3 contain vivid descriptions of the people and things surrounding the author on the morning of the execution. What details does he use that appeal to readers' senses of sight, hearing, and touch? What is the effect of all these details?

2. "A Hanging" takes place in Burma, and Orwell occasionally uses regional terms such as *lathis* and *boxwallah* in the course of his essay. Why do you think Orwell chose to include these foreign terms rather than translate them into English?

3. In part, Orwell uses dialogue to tell his story, giving the actual words of numerous individuals. What does the essay gain or lose from this technique? Explain.

4. In paragraph 10, Orwell provides a series of details about the bodily organs of the condemned man. List these details. How do they relate to Orwell's larger point in "A Hanging"?

CRITICAL READING AND DISCUSSION

1. Why does everyone stand "aghast" when the stray dog licks the prisoner's face? Why is this incident important?

2. The author has a moment of understanding when the prisoner steps "slightly aside to avoid a puddle on the path" (paragraph 9). What realization does Orwell come to? How is this insight related to the small incident of avoiding a puddle?

3. The character of the superintendent evolves in the course of this narrative. How do the words he speaks (and the tone of voice he speaks them in) reflect the emotional changes he goes through?

4. The author's thesis is most clearly stated in paragraph 10: "When I saw the prisoner step aside to avoid the puddle, I saw the mystery, the unspeakable wrongness, of cutting a life short when it is in full tide." Do you agree that capital punishment is always wrong? Explain your answer.

WRITING ASSIGNMENTS

www.mhhe.com/langan

Assignment 1

Use examples and details from "A Hanging" to support the following thesis statement:

> In "A Hanging," George Orwell constantly contrasts death with life to show us how wrong it is to kill another human being.

You might organize your paragraphs by showing how death is contrasted with life (1) on the way to the gallows, (2) at the gallows, and (3) after the hanging.

To get started, reread the selection closely, noting words and incidents that seem to be closely related to either death or life. For example, in paragraph 2, Orwell describes the prisoner as "quite unresisting, yielding his arms limply to the ropes." It is as if the prisoner is already dead. In contrast, the guards are filled with life and action: they handcuff the prisoner, lash his arms, and keep a "careful, caressing grip" on him. At many other points in the story, this strong contrast between death and life is described.

Use a point-by-point method of contrast in developing your essay. You may want to look first at the example of this method on pages 289–290.

Assignment 2

Find out (1) if capital punishment is legal in your state, and if so, (2) which method of execution is used. (You could find this information by calling your city or county library.) Then imagine that a statewide vote will soon be taken to find out if voters want to change this law. Decide if you would (or would not) change the law. Give reasons for your decision. For example, if your state does have capital punishment, and you would vote not to change the law, you might give the reasons in the following essay outline:

> Thesis: Our state law allows a jury to vote for "death by lethal injection" for convicted criminals, and I would not vote to change this law.
>
> Topic sentences:
> (a) First of all, the death penalty saves thousands of tax dollars that would be spent to keep criminals in prison for life.
> (b) In addition, the punishment acts as a deterrent to other criminals.
> (c) Most important, death is an appropriate punishment for someone who commits a terrible crime.

To avoid writing in vague, general terms, you may want to use specific examples of cases or crimes currently being discussed in the news. You may also need facts and statistics. You can find these by typing "capital punishment law" and the name of your state into an Internet search engine.

Assignment 3

On the basis of the knowledge you have gained by reading this selection, write an essay with *either* of the thesis statements below:

> Executions today are as brutal as the one described in "A Hanging."
>
> Executions today are humane compared with the one described in "A Hanging."

In your supporting paragraphs, you may want to write about each of the following:

> Methods of execution and atmosphere in which executions are conducted
>
> Kinds of people who are executed
>
> Fairness of the trials and judges

EXECUTION OF REV. STEPHEN BURROUGHS,

How does capital punishment today differ from the hangings that took place during the Salem witch trials in 1692? After doing some research on both, write a comparison or contrast essay. You may refer to Chapter 21 for tips on using the library and the Internet to conduct your research.

A Legendary Moment

Haven Kimmel

PREVIEW

Probably every family preserves the memory of at least one noteworthy argument. Few such arguments, though, are as vividly recorded as the one that appears below. Taken from a widely acclaimed memoir, *A Girl Named Zippy* by Haven Kimmel, it tells of an unforgettable confrontation between two strong personalities.

© Ann Savoy

My mom and dad never fought, not really, which was a good thing, because my 1
dad had a wicked, wicked bad temper, and if he'd married a woman who fought
him they probably would have killed each other. There was a great, legendary moment between them, though, which I'd heard about all my life.

One of the architectural marvels that was in my house in Mooreland was my 2
parents' bedroom door, which was solid wood and heavy, and had a porcelain
doorknob. It opened into the bedroom. At a forty-five-degree angle from the bedroom door was the closet door, which was solid wood and heavy, and had a porcelain doorknob. It also opened into the bedroom. If the closet door was open, the
bedroom door could not be; if they were both halfway open the doorknobs clinked
together like little figurines in a rummage sale. It was possible, I had discovered
through much trial and error, to get the doorknobs stuck together with neither door
open enough to accommodate a grown person. Blocking the door in such a creative way was part of my mental plan for when and if the vampires came.

My mom was nine months pregnant with me, and hugely so, and she and my 3
father were having an actual, vocal argument in their bedroom. My sister's friend
Terri was visiting, and the two of them and my brother were all in the living room.
The argument reached some critical phase and Mom walked out of the bedroom
at the same moment that Dad decided to go in the closet, which caused the bedroom door to smack my mother in the back. She became so instantly enraged (she

claimed it was pregnancy that did it) that she waited just a moment until she was sure Dad was halfway into the closet, and then she threw the bedroom door open, which sent my father flying headfirst into the closet about sixty-four miles an hour, all the way back to where we kept the paint cans. My sister said they could hear him tumbling against the cans, and could actually discern the thick moment when he gathered himself up and prepared to face my mother.

He came out of the bedroom like a bullet, red-faced and with his eyebrows 4 riding up his forehead. Mother was standing in the middle of the living room with her hands on her former hips, waiting for him. Melinda and Danny and Terri fled so quickly, and in so many different directions, that Mom later claimed they must have evaporated into the walls. Dad finally came to a stop right in Mother's face, nose to nose, panting like a bull, with his fists clenched.

"Are you going to *hit* me?!?" my mother asked, pressing her forehead more 5 aggressively into his. And before he could answer, she arced out her own arm and slapped his right cheek, hard. He pulled away from her slightly, stunned.

"I said, are you going to hit me?!" and she raised her left arm, and got him on 6 the other cheek, like a good Christian.

Miraculously, he walked away from her. Looking no less deranged or murder- 7 ous, he backed out of the house without taking his eyes off her, got in his truck and drove away.

It became one of the touchstone moments of their marriage, and afterward, 8 there was never a threat of violence between them again. Mom told me, when I was old enough to ask, that she had learned the lesson from Mom Mary, Dad's mother, who took her future daughter-in-law aside and told her that a woman has got to make herself absolutely clear, and early on. In Mom Mary's own case, she waited until she and my grandfather Anthel were just home from their honeymoon, and then sat him down and told him this: "Honey, I know you like to take a drink, and that's all right, but be forewarned that I ain't your maid and I ain't your punching bag, and if you ever raise your hand to me you'd best kill me. Because otherwise I'll wait till you're asleep; sew you into the bed; and beat you to death with a frying pan." Until he died, I am told, my grandfather was a gentle man.

READING COMPREHENSION

www.mhhe.com/langan

1. The word *discern* in "[they] could actually discern the thick moment when he gathered himself up and prepared to face my mother" (paragraph 3) means

   a. ignore.

   b. laugh at.

   c. detect.

   d. be mistaken about.

2. The word *deranged* in "Looking no less deranged *or* murderous" (paragraph 7) means
   a. calm.
   b. sad.
   c. amused.
   d. crazed.

3. Which of the following would be a good alternative title for this selection?
   a. Fighting
   b. Mother Makes It Clear
   c. Family Memories
   d. Physical Violence in the Home

4. Which sentence best expresses the main idea of the selection?
   a. Because her parents fought so rarely, the author vividly remembers a time that they did.
   b. The author's father had a terrible temper and could have been capable of violence.
   c. The author's mother and grandmother had dealt with the same issue in similar ways.
   d. An argument between the author's parents made it clear that her mother would not be intimidated.

5. *True or false?* _____ The author had personally witnessed this argument between her mother and father.

6. When the bedroom door hit the author's mother in the back, she
   a. slapped her husband.
   b. became instantly enraged.
   c. began to cry.
   d. left the house.

7. The author's mother had been given advice about dealing with her husband by
   a. her husband's mother.
   b. her own mother.
   c. her daughter.
   d. her husband's father.

8. The phrase "when and if the vampires came" implies that, as a child, Kimmel
   a. believed in supernatural beings.
   b. thought that her parents were evil, like vampires.
   c. played a vampire game with other children.
   d. enjoyed reading about vampires.

9. The sentence "Mother was standing in the middle of the living room with her hands on her former hips, waiting for him" suggests that the author's mother

   a. was badly frightened.

   b. was ready to confront her husband.

   c. felt apologetic.

   d. thought the situation was amusing.

10. A reasonable conclusion we can draw from the reading is that

   a. the author was deeply disturbed by the argument between her parents.

   b. the author considers her mother and grandmother to be abused women.

   c. the author thought her mother had gone too far in the argument with her father.

   d. the author admired her mother's spirit in standing up to her father.

STRUCTURE AND TECHNIQUE

1. Find instances in the reading where Kimmel uses (or quotes someone as using) exaggeration. Why might a writer choose to exaggerate? What effect does Kimmel's exaggeration have?

2. What method of introduction—anecdote, question, or broad-to-narrow—does Kimmel use? Why do you think she chose this way to begin her essay?

3. Using Kimmel's description as a guide, draw a sketch that shows what happened if her parents' bedroom door and closet door were opened at the same time. Why does she go into such detail to describe the relationship between the two doors?

4. Kimmel never mentions the subject of her parents' original "actual, vocal argument." Why do you think she chose not to? Would the story have been stronger if she had explained what that argument was about?

CRITICAL READING AND DISCUSSION

1. You might expect a memoir about an author's parents fighting to have a dark, threatening, unhappy tone. But Haven Kimmel presents this incident in quite a different light. How does she seem to feel about what happened? What words or phrases give you clues to her viewpoint?

2. Do you think Kimmel's opinion about what happened between her parents would have been different if her father had slapped her mother? Would your opinion change? Explain your answer.

3. Kimmel uses figurative language to compare her father, first, to a bullet, and later, to a bull. What characteristics of a bullet and a bull does she suggest he shares? Later, why does she say that her mother acted "like a good Christian"? Is that comparison meant seriously or humorously?

4. The author describes this incident as "a great, legendary moment" that she had heard about all her life. Why do you think the incident was so important to the family? Do you have any family stories that people tell over and over again? Why do you think they are important to your family?

www.mhhe.com/langan

WRITING ASSIGNMENTS

Assignment 1

Most families tell and retell certain stories that, for some reason, have become meaningful to them. Write a narrative essay in which you tell of one such memorable incident that occurred in your family.

You might begin your essay with a bit of background about your family—indicating, perhaps, whether the incident you are going to describe was in character or out of the ordinary for the people involved. Your thesis should indicate how you feel about the incident—whether it was, for example, frightening, amusing, touching, or sad.

If appropriate, use bits of dialogue to make the scene come alive for your reader. Add your own comments about why, in your opinion, the story is significant to your family.

Assignment 2

Kimmel refers to her father's "wicked bad temper." Select a person you know who has a very strong personal characteristic—perhaps a bad temper, a great sense of humor, a jealous streak, an optimistic attitude, or some other quality. Write an essay in which you describe three incidents in which the person demonstrated that characteristic. Alternatively, describe three areas of the person's life in which this characteristic is evident.

Your thesis might look like one of these:

My sister's generosity most memorably stands out for me on three particular occasions.

Whether he's at work, at school, or at home, my friend Hal always believes the worst is going to happen.

Assignment 3

Unfortunately, most stories concerning a partner hitting another one are not as lighthearted as Kimmel's. Still, many people remain with abusive partners for many years. Write an essay in which you explore three reasons why a man or a woman might stay with a partner who physically abused her or him. Your reasons might be based on personal experience, observation of people around you, or stories you've heard or read through the media.

Here is a possible thesis statement for this assignment:

A person might stay with a physically abusive partner for one of several reasons.

The Professor Is a Dropout
Beth Johnson

PREVIEW

After being mistakenly labeled "retarded" and humiliated into dropping out of first grade, Lupe Quintanilla knew she wanted nothing more to do with formal education. Life as a wife and mother would satisfy her—and it did, until she saw her own children being pushed aside as "slow learners." Driven to help them succeed, Lupe took steps that dramatically changed her life.

Courtesy of Beth Johnson

Guadalupe Quintanilla is an assistant professor at the University of Houston. She 1 is president of her own communications company. She trains law enforcement officers all over the country. She was nominated to serve as the U.S. Attorney General. She's been a representative to the United Nations.

That's a pretty impressive string of accomplishments. It's all the more im- 2 pressive when you consider this: "Lupe" Quintanilla is a first-grade dropout. Her school records state that she is retarded, that her IQ is so low she can't learn much of anything.

How did Lupe Quintanilla, "retarded" nonlearner, become Dr. Quintanilla, 3 respected educator? Her remarkable journey began in the town of Nogales, Mexico, just below the Arizona border. That's where Lupe first lived with her grandparents. (Her parents had divorced.) Then an uncle who had just finished medical school made her grandparents a generous offer. If they wanted to live with him, he would support the family as he began his medical practice.

Lupe, her grandparents, and her uncle all moved hundreds of miles to a town 4 in southern Mexico that didn't even have paved roads, let alone any schools. There, Lupe grew up helping her grandfather run his little pharmacy and her grandmother keep house. She remembers the time happily. "My grandparents were wonderful," she said. "Oh, my grandfather was stern, authoritarian, as Mexican culture demanded, but they were also very kind to me." When the chores were done, her grandfather taught Lupe to read and write Spanish and do basic arithmetic.

When Lupe was 12, her grandfather became blind. The family left Mexico 5 and went to Brownsville, Texas, with the hope that doctors there could restore his sight. Once they arrived in Brownsville, Lupe was enrolled in school. Although she understood no English, she was given an IQ test in that language. Not surprisingly, she didn't do very well.

Lupe even remembers her score. "I scored a sixty-four, which classified me as 6 seriously retarded, not even teachable," she said. "I was put into first grade with a class of six-year-olds. My duties were to take the little kids to the bathroom and to cut out pictures." The classroom activities were a total mystery to Lupe—they were all conducted in English. And she was humiliated by the other children, who teased her for being "so much older and so much dumber" than they were.

After four months in first grade, an incident occurred that Lupe still does not 7 fully understand. As she stood in the doorway of the classroom waiting to escort a little girl to the bathroom, a man approached her. He asked her, in Spanish, how to find the principal's office. Lupe was delighted. "Finally someone in this school had spoken to me with words I could understand, in the language of my soul, the language of my grandmother," she said. Eagerly, she answered his question in Spanish. Instantly her teacher swooped down on her, grabbing her arm and scolding her. She pulled Lupe along to the principal's office. There, the teacher and the principal both shouted at her, obviously very angry. Lupe was frightened and embarrassed, but also bewildered. She didn't understand a word they were saying.

Guadalupe
Quintanilla today

Courtesy of John Langan

"Why were they so angry? I don't know," said Lupe. "Was it because 8 I spoke Spanish at school? Or that I spoke to the man at all? I really don't know. All I know is how humiliated I was."

When she got home that day, she cried miserably, begging her grand- 9 father not to make her return to school. Finally he agreed.

From that time on, Lupe stayed at home, serving as her blind grand- 10 father's "eyes." She was a fluent reader in Spanish, and the older man loved to have her read newspapers, poetry, and novels aloud to him for hours.

Lupe's own love of reading flourished during these years. Her vocabulary 11 was enriched and her imagination fired by the novels she read—novels which she learned later were classics of Spanish literature. She read *Don Quixote,* the famous story of the noble, impractical knight who fought against windmills. She read thrilling accounts of the Mexican revolution. She read *La Prensa,* the local Spanish-language paper, and *Selecciones,* the Spanish-language version of *Reader's Digest.*

When she was just 16, Lupe married a young Mexican-American dental tech- 12 nician. Within five years, she had given birth to her three children, Victor, Mario, and Martha. Lupe's grandparents lived with the young family. Lupe was quite happy with her life. "I cooked, sewed, cleaned, and cared for everybody," she said. "I listened to my grandmother when she told me what made a good wife. In the morning I would actually put on my husband's shoes and tie the laces—anything to make his life easier. Living with my grandparents for so long, I was one generation behind in my ideas of what a woman could do and be."

Lupe's contentment ended when her children started school. When they 13 brought home their report cards, she struggled to understand them. She could read enough English to know that what they said was not good. Her children had been put into a group called "Yellow Birds." It was a group for slow learners.

At night in bed, Lupe cried and blamed herself. It was obvious—not only was 14 she retarded, but her children had taken after her. Now they, too, would never be able to learn like other children.

But in time, a thought began to break through Lupe's despair: Her children 15 didn't seem like slow learners to her. At home, they learned everything she taught them, quickly and easily. She read to them constantly, from the books that she herself had loved as a child. *Aesop's Fables* and stories from *1,001 Arabian Nights* were family favorites. The children filled the house with the sounds of the songs, prayers, games, and rhymes they had learned from their parents and grandparents. They were smart children, eager to learn. They learned quickly—in Spanish.

A radical idea began to form in Lupe's mind. Maybe the school was wrong 16 about her children. And if the school system could be wrong about her children— maybe it had been wrong about her, too.

Lupe visited her children's school, a daring action for her. "Many Hispanic 17 parents would not dream of going to the classroom," she said. "In Hispanic culture, the teacher is regarded as a third parent, as an ultimate authority. To question her would seem most disrespectful, as though you were saying that she didn't know her job." That was one reason Lupe's grandparents had not interfered when Lupe was classified as retarded. "Anglo teachers often misunderstand Hispanic parents, believing that they aren't concerned about their children's education because they don't come visit the schools," Lupe said. "It's not a lack of concern at all. It's a mark of respect for the teacher's authority."

At her children's school, Lupe spoke to three different teachers. Two of them 18 told her the same thing: "Your children are just slow. Sorry, but they can't learn." A third offered a glimmer of hope. He said, "They don't know how to function in English. It's possible that if you spoke English at home they would be able to do better."

Lupe pounced on that idea. "Where can I learn English?" she asked. The 19 teacher shrugged. At that time there were no local English-language programs for adults. Finally he suggested that Lupe visit the local high school. Maybe she would be permitted to sit in the back of a classroom and pick up some English that way.

Lupe made an appointment with a counselor at the high school. But when the 20 two women met, the counselor shook her head. "Your test scores show that you are retarded," she told Lupe. "You'd just be taking space in the classroom away from someone who could learn."

Lupe's next stop was the hospital where she had served for years as a vol- 21 unteer. Could she sit in on some of the nursing classes held there? No, she was told, not without a diploma. Still undeterred, she went on to Texas Southmost College in Brownsville. Could she sit in on a class? No; no high-school diploma. Finally she went to the telephone company, where she knew operators were being trained. Could she listen in on the classes? No, only high-school graduates were permitted.

That day, leaving the telephone company, Lupe felt she had hit bottom. She 22 had been terrified in the first place to try to find an English class. Meeting with rejection after rejection nearly destroyed what little self-confidence she had. She walked home in the rain, crying. "I felt like a big barrier had fallen across my path," she said. "I couldn't go over it; I couldn't go under it; I couldn't go around it."

But the next day Lupe woke with fresh determination. "I was motivated by love 23 of my kids," she said. "I was not going to quit." She got up; made breakfast for her kids, husband, and grandparents; saw her children and husband off for the day; and started out again. "I remember walking to the bus stop, past a dog that always scared me to death, and heading back to the college. The lady I spoke to said, 'I told you, we can't do anything for you without a high-school degree.' But as I left the building, I went up to the first Spanish-speaking student I saw. His name was Gabito. I said, 'Who really makes the decisions around here?' He said, 'The registrar.'" Since she hadn't had any luck in the office building, Lupe decided to take a more direct approach. She asked Gabito to point out the registrar's car in the parking lot. For the next two hours she waited beside it until its owner showed up.

Lupe enjoys a story with (left to right) her twin grandchildren, Alyssa and Christian, and a visiting friend.

Impressed by Lupe's persistence, the registrar listened to her story. 24 But instead of giving her permission to sit in on a class and learn more English, he insisted that she sign up for a full college load. Before she knew it, she was enrolled in four classes: basic math, basic English, psychology, and typing. The registrar's parting words to her were, "Don't come back if you don't make it through."

With that "encouragement," Lupe began a semester that was part 25 nightmare, part dream come true. Every day she got her husband and children off to school, took the bus to campus, came home to make lunch for her husband and grandparents, went back to campus, and was home in time to greet Victor, Mario, and Martha when they got home from school. In the evenings she cooked, cleaned, did laundry, and got the children to bed. Then she would study, often until three in the morning.

"Sometimes in class I would feel sick with the stress of it," she said. "I'd go to 26 the bathroom and talk to myself in the mirror. Sometimes I'd say, 'What are you doing here? Why don't you go home and watch *I Love Lucy?*'"

But she didn't go home. Instead, she studied furiously, using her Spanish- 27 English dictionary, constantly making lists of new words she wanted to understand. "I still do that today," she said. "When I come across a word I don't know, I write it down, look it up, and write sentences using it until I own that word."

Although so much of the language and subject matter was new to Lupe, one 28 part of the college experience was not. That was the key skill of reading, a skill Lupe possessed. As she struggled with English, she found the reading speed, comprehension, and vocabulary that she had developed in Spanish carrying over into her new language. "Reading," she said, "reading was the vehicle. Although I didn't know it at the time, when I was a girl learning to love to read, I was laying the foundation for academic success."

She gives credit, too, to her Hispanic fellow students. "At first, they didn't 29 know what to make of me. They were eighteen years old, and at that time it was very unfashionable for an older person to be in college. But once they decided I wasn't a 'plant' from the administration, they were my greatest help." The younger students spent hours helping Lupe, explaining unfamiliar words and terms, coaching her, and answering her questions.

That first semester passed in a fog of exhaustion. Many mornings, Lupe 30 doubted she could get out of bed, much less care for her family and tackle her classes. But when she thought of her children and what was at stake for them, she forced herself on. She remembers well what those days were like. "Just a day at a time. That was all I could think about. I could make myself get up one more day, study one more day, cook and clean one more day. And those days eventually turned into a semester."

To her own amazement perhaps as much as anyone's, Lupe discovered that 31 she was far from retarded. Although she sweated blood over many assignments, she completed them. She turned them in on time. And, remarkably, she made the dean's list her very first semester.

After that, there was no stopping Lupe Quintanilla. She soon realized that the 32 associate's degree offered by Texas Southmost College would not satisfy her. Continuing her Monday, Wednesday, and Friday schedule at Southmost, she enrolled for Tuesday and Thursday courses at Pan American University, a school 140 miles from Brownsville. Within three years, she had earned both her junior-college degree and a bachelor's degree in biology. She then won a fellowship that took her to graduate school at the University of Houston, where she earned a master's degree in Spanish literature. When she graduated, the university offered her a job as director of the Mexican-American studies program. While in that position, she earned a doctoral degree in education.

How did she do it all? Lupe herself isn't sure. "I hardly know. When I think 33 back to those years, it seems like a life that someone else lived." It was a rich and exciting but also very challenging period for Lupe and her family. On the one hand, Lupe was motivated by the desire to set an example for her children, to prove to them that they could succeed in the English-speaking academic world. On the other hand, she worried about neglecting her family. She tried hard to attend important activities, such as parents' meetings at school and her children's sporting events. But things didn't always work out. Lupe still remembers attending a baseball game that her older son, Victor, was playing in. When Victor came to bat, he hit a home run. But as the crowd cheered and Victor glanced proudly over at his mother in the stands, he saw she was studying a textbook. "I hadn't seen the home run," Lupe admitted. "That sort of thing was hard for everyone to take."

Although Lupe worried that her children would resent her busy schedule, she 34 also saw her success reflected in them as they blossomed in school. She forced herself to speak English at home, and their language skills improved quickly. She read to them in English instead of Spanish—gulping down her pride as their pronunciation became better than hers and they began correcting her. (Once the children were in high school and fluent in English, Lupe switched back to Spanish at home, so that the children would be fully comfortable in both languages.) "I saw the change in them almost immediately," she said. "After I helped them with their homework, they would see me pulling out my own books and going to work. In the morning, I would show them the papers I had written. As I gained confidence, so did they." By the next year, the children had been promoted out of the Yellow Birds.

Lupe surrounded by her children: Martha, Victor, and Mario.

Courtesy of John Langan

Even though Victor, Mario, and Martha all did well academically, 35 Lupe realized she could not assume that they would face no more obstacles in school. When Mario was in high school, for instance, he wanted to sign up for a debate class. Instead, he was assigned to woodworking. She visited the school to ask why. Mario's teacher told her, "He's good with his hands. He'll be a great carpenter, and that's a good thing for a Mexican to be." Controlling her temper, Lupe responded, "I'm glad you think he's good with his hands. He'll be a great physician someday, and he is going to be in the debate class."

Today, Lupe Quintanilla teaches at the University of Houston, where she has developed several dozen courses concerning Hispanic literature and culture. Her cross-cultural training for law enforcement officers, which helps bring police and firefighters and local Hispanic communities closer together, is renowned throughout the country. Former President Ronald Reagan named her to a national board that keeps the White House informed of new programs in law enforcement. She has received numerous awards for teaching excellence, and there is even a scholarship named in her honor. Her name appears in

Two members of 36 the Houston police department learn job-specific Spanish phrases from Lupe. Lupe also trains the officers in cultural awareness.

Courtesy of John Langan

the Hispanic Hall of Fame, and she has been co-chair of the White House Commission on Hispanic Education.

The love of reading that her grandfather instilled in Lupe is still alive. She **37** thinks of him every year when she introduces to her students one of his favorite poets, Amado Nervo. She requires them to memorize these lines from one of Nervo's poems: "When I got to the end of my long journey in life, I realized that I was the architect of my own destiny." Of these lines, Lupe says, "That is something that I deeply believe, and I want my students to learn it before the end of their long journey. We create our own destiny."

Her love of reading and learning has helped Lupe create a distinguished des- **38** tiny. But none of the honors she has received means more to her than the success of her own children, the reason she made that frightening journey to seek classes in English years ago. Today Mario is a physician. Victor and Martha are lawyers, both having earned doctor of law degrees. And so today, Lupe likes to say, "When someone calls the house and asks for 'Dr. Quintanilla,' I have to ask, 'Which one?' There are four of us—one retarded and three slow learners."

READING COMPREHENSION

www.mhhe.com/langan

1. The word *flourished* in "Lupe's own love of reading flourished during these years. Her vocabulary was enriched and her imagination fired by the novels she read "(paragraph 11) means

   a. grew.

   b. stood still.

   c. was lost.

   d. remained.

2. The word *instilled* in "The love of reading that Lupe grandfather instilled in Lupe is still alive" (paragraph 37) means

   a. frightened.

   b. established.

   c. forced.

   d. forgot.

3. Which of the following would be a good alternative title for this selection?

   a. Difficulties Facing Spanish-Speaking Students

   b. Unfair Labeling

   c. Balancing School and Family

   d. A Courageous Mother's Triumph

4. Which sentence best expresses the main idea of the selection?

   a. Lupe, a first-grade dropout, eventually earned a doctoral degree and created a professional career.

   b. Lupe Quintanilla's experience proves that the educational system must be set up to accommodate non-English-speaking children.

   c. Through hard work and persistence combined with a love of reading and learning, Lupe has created a distinguished career and helped her children become professionals.

   d. In school, Spanish-speaking students may experience obstacles as they aim for professional careers.

5. Lupe realized that her children were not retarded when

   a. they got good grades at school.

   b. she saw how quickly they learned at home.

   c. they were put in the group called "Yellow Birds."

   d. they read newspapers, poetry, and novels to her.

6. Lupe's training for law enforcement officers

   a. teaches them to speak Spanish.

   b. teaches Hispanic literature and culture.

   c. offers a scholarship named in her honor.

   d. brings police, firefighters, and local Hispanic communities together.

7. According to Lupe, Hispanic parents rarely visit their children's schools because they

   a. do not consider schoolwork important.

   b. think doing so would be disrespectful to the teacher.

   c. are ashamed of their English language skills.

   d. are usually working during school visitation hours.

8. "Once they arrived in Brownsville, Lupe was enrolled in school. Although she understood no English, she was given an IQ test in that language. Not surprisingly, she didn't do very well" (paragraph 5). From these sentences, we might conclude that

   a. an IQ test in a language that the person tested doesn't know is useless.

   b. although Lupe was not very intelligent at first, she became more intelligent once she learned English.

   c. Lupe really did know English.

   d. there are no IQ tests in Spanish.

9. We might conclude from the reading that

    a. a school system's judgment about an individual is always accurate.

    b. it is often better for a child to stay home rather than attend school.

    c. by paying attention and speaking up, parents may remove obstacles to their children's education.

    d. working parents should accept the fact that they cannot attend important events in their children's lives.

10. The last line of the reading suggests that

    a. retarded people can become successful professionals.

    b. people should not blindly accept other people's opinions of them.

    c. Lupe's children are smarter than she is.

    d. all of the above

STRUCTURE AND TECHNIQUE

1. Johnson begins the essay by listing Lupe Quintanilla's accomplishments, then revealing that Quintanilla was once classified as retarded. What introductory technique is Johnson employing? Why is it effective here?

2. Paragraphs 3–11 are devoted to the first fifteen years of Lupe's life. But the next decade or so is covered in only two paragraphs (12–13). Why might Johnson have presented Lupe's earlier life in so much more detail? Do you agree with her decision?

3. In paragraph 2, Johnson writes that "[Lupe's] school records state that she is retarded. . . ." But in the next sentence, she writes, "How did Lupe Quintanilla, 'retarded' nonlearner, become Dr. Quintanilla, respected educator?" Why does Johnson put the word "retarded" in quotation marks in the second sentence, but not in the first? What is she implying? Can you find another place where Johnson makes similar use of quotation marks?

4. At one point, Johnson switches from the topic of Lupe's success in college to the topic of the challenges that continued to face her children in school. In what paragraph does she make that switch? What transitional words does she use to alert the reader to her new direction?

CRITICAL READING AND DISCUSSION

1. In the course of the essay, what characteristics and attitudes does Lupe suggest are typical of Hispanic culture? Does she seem sympathetic, critical, or neutral about those qualities or attitudes? How has she dealt with cultural expectations in her own life?

2. How has Lupe handled the question of what language to use with her children? If you grew up in a two-language household, how did your family deal with the issue? How would you approach the issue with children of your own?

3. Do you think Lupe's grandfather was right in allowing her to quit school? What factors do you imagine might have gone into his decision?

4. Lupe credits her fellow Hispanic students with giving her valuable support in college. Is there anyone in your life—a teacher, family member, or friend—who has helped you through challenging times in your education? Explain what obstacles you faced and how this person helped you overcome them.

WRITING ASSIGNMENTS

www.mhhe.com/langan

Assignment 1

Write an essay that takes as its thesis one of the following statements:

Schools need to be prepared to help non-English-speaking students catch up with other students at their grade level.

The responsibility for catching non-English-speaking students up to their grade level rests solely with the students and their families.

Support your thesis with several points, each developed in its own paragraph.

Assignment 2

Lupe Quintanilla is an outstanding example of someone who has taken charge of her life. She has been, to echo the poet whose work she teaches, the architect of her own destiny. Choose a person you know who, in your opinion, has done a fine job of taking charge of his or her own destiny. Write an essay about this person. You might describe three areas of life in which the person has taken control. Alternatively, you might narrate three incidents from the person's life that illustrate his or her admirable self-determination.

Assignment 3

Lupe had to struggle in order to balance her school responsibilities with her duties as a wife and mother. Write an essay in which you identify aspects of your life that you need to juggle along with your responsibilities as a student. They may include a job, a spouse or significant other, children, housekeeping duties, pets, extracurricular activities, a difficult living situation, or anything else that poses a challenge to your academics. Provide vivid, real-life illustrations of how each of those responsibilities sometimes conflicts with your studies.

The Monster

Deems Taylor

PREVIEW

You're about to be introduced to someone you won't like at all. By standards too numerous to count, this individual deserves dislike, disrespect, and dishonor. And yet you will be invited to admire him and overlook his many faults. Can you? Should you? This essay by Deems Taylor, a noted American composer of operas, may challenge your perceptions in suggesting that extraordinary people can't be measured by ordinary yardsticks.

---

1 He was an undersized little man, with a head too big for his body—a sickly little man. His nerves were bad. He had skin trouble. It was agony for him to wear anything next to his skin coarser than silk. And he had delusions of grandeur.

2 He was a monster of conceit. Never for one minute did he look at the world or at people, except in relation to himself. He was not only the most important person in the world, to himself; in his own eyes he was the only person who existed. He believed himself to be one of the greatest dramatists in the world, one of the greatest thinkers, and one of the greatest composers. To hear him talk, he was Shakespeare, and Beethoven, and Plato, rolled into one. And you would have had no difficulty in hearing him talk. He was one of the most exhausting conversationalists that ever lived. An evening with him was an evening spent in listening to a monologue. Sometimes he was brilliant; sometimes he was maddeningly tiresome. But whether he was being brilliant or dull, he had one sole topic of conversation: himself—what *he* thought and what *he* did.

3 He had a mania for being in the right. The slightest hint of disagreement, from anyone, on the most trivial point, was enough to set him off on a harangue that might last for hours, in which he proved himself right in so many ways, and with such exhausting volubility,[1] that in the end his hearer, stunned and deafened, would agree with him, for the sake of peace.

4 It never occurred to him that he and his doings were not of the most intense and fascinating interest to anyone with whom he came in contact. He had theories about almost any subject under the sun, including vegetarianism, the drama, politics, and music; and in support of these theories he wrote pamphlets, letters, books . . . thousands upon thousands of words, hundreds and hundreds of pages.

---

[1]*volubility:* excessive talking.

He not only wrote these things, and published them—usually at somebody else's expense—but he would sit and read them aloud, for hours, to his friends and his family.

He wrote operas; and no sooner did he have the synopsis of a story, but he 5 would invite—or rather summon—a crowd of his friends to his house and read it aloud to them: not for criticism; for applause. When the complete poem was written, the friends had to come again, and hear *that* read aloud. Then he would publish the poem, sometimes years before the music that went with it was written. He played the piano like a composer, in the worst sense of what that implies, and he would sit down at the piano before parties that included some of the finest pianists of his time, and play for them, by the hour, his own music, needless to say. He had a composer's voice. And he would invite eminent vocalists to his house and sing them his operas, taking all the parts.

He had the emotional stability of a six-year-old child. When he felt out of sorts, 6 he would rave and stamp, or sink into suicidal gloom and talk darkly of going to the East to end his days as a Buddhist monk. Ten minutes later, when something pleased him, he would rush out of doors and run around the garden, or jump up and down on the sofa, or stand on his head. He could be grief-stricken over the death of a pet dog, and he could be callous and heartless to a degree that would have made a Roman emperor shudder.

He was almost innocent of any sense of responsibility. Not only did he seem 7 incapable of supporting himself, but it never occurred to him that he was under any obligation to do so. He was convinced that the world owed him a living. In support of this belief, he borrowed money from everybody who was good for a loan—men, women, friends, or strangers. He wrote begging letters by the score, sometimes groveling without shame, in others loftily offering his intended benefactor the privilege of contributing to his support, and being mortally offended if the recipient declined the honor. I have found no record of his ever paying or repaying money to anyone who did not have a legal claim upon it.

What money he could lay his hands on he spent like an Indian rajah.[2] The 8 mere prospect of a performance of one of his operas was enough to set him to running up bills amounting to ten times the amount of his prospective royalties. On an income that would reduce a more scrupulous man to doing his own laundry, he would keep two servants. Without enough money in his pocket to pay his rent, he would have the walls and ceiling of his study lined with pink silk. No one will ever know—certainly he never knew—how much money he owed. We do know that his greatest benefactor gave him $6,000 to pay the most pressing of his debts in one city, and a year later had to give him $16,000 to enable him to live in another city without being thrown into jail for debt.

He was equally unscrupulous in other ways. An endless procession of women 9 marched through his life. His first wife spent twenty years enduring and forgiving

---

[2]*rajah:* prince in India.

his infidelities. His second wife had been the wife of his most devoted friend and admirer, from whom he stole her. And even while he was trying to persuade her to leave her first husband he was writing to a friend to inquire whether he could suggest some wealthy woman—*any* wealthy woman—whom he could marry for her money.

He was completely selfish in his other personal relationships. His liking for **10** his friends was measured solely by the completeness of their devotion to him, or by their usefulness to him, whether financial or artistic. The minute they failed him—even by so much as refusing a dinner invitation—or began to lessen in usefulness, he cast them off without a second thought. At the end of his life he had exactly one friend left whom he had known even in middle age.

He had a genius for making enemies. He would insult a man who disagreed **11** with him about the weather. He would pull endless wires in order to meet some man who admired his work and was able and anxious to be of use to him—and would proceed to make a mortal enemy of him with some idiotic and wholly un-called-for exhibition of arrogance and bad manners. A character in one of his operas was a caricature of one of the most powerful music critics of his day. Not content with burlesquing[3] him, he invited the critic to his house and read him the libretto[4] aloud in front of his friends.

The name of this monster was Richard Wagner. Everything that I have said **12** about him you can find on record—in newspapers, in police reports, in the testimony of people who knew him, in his own letters, between the lines of his autobiography. And the curious thing about this record is that it doesn't matter in the least.

Because this undersized, sickly, disagreeable, fascinating little man *was* right **13** all the time. The joke was on us. He *was* one of the world's great dramatists; he *was* a great thinker; he *was* one of the most stupendous musical geniuses that, up to now, the world has ever seen. The world did owe him a living. People couldn't know those things at the time, I suppose; and yet to us, who know his music, it does seem as though they should have known. What if he did talk about himself all the time? If he had talked about himself for twenty-four hours every day for the span of his life, he would not have uttered half the number of words that other men have spoken and written about him since his death.

When you consider what he wrote—thirteen operas and music dramas, eleven **14** of them still holding the stage, eight of them unquestionably worth ranking among the world's great musico-dramatic masterpieces—when you listen to what he wrote, the debts and heartaches that people had to endure from him don't seem much of a price. Eduard Hanslick, the critic whom he caricatured in *Die Meistersinger* and who hated him ever after, now lives only because he was caricatured in *Die Meistersinger.* The women whose hearts he broke are long since dead; and the

---

[3]*burlesquing:* mocking.
[4]*libretto:* opera text.

man who could never love anyone but himself has made deathless atonement, I think, with *Tristan und Isolde*. Think of the luxury with which for a time, at least, fate rewarded Napoleon, the man who ruined France and looted Europe; and then perhaps you will agree that a few thousand dollars' worth of debts were not too heavy a price to pay for the *Ring* trilogy.

What if he was faithless to his friends and to his wives? He had one mistress to 15 whom he was faithful to the day of his death: Music. Not for a single moment did he ever compromise with what he believed, with what he dreamed. There is not a line of his music that could have been conceived by a little mind. Even when he is dull, or downright bad, he is dull in the grand manner. There is greatness about his worst mistakes. Listening to his music, one does not forgive him for what he may or may not have been. It is not a matter of forgiveness. It is a matter of being dumb with wonder that his poor brain and body didn't burst under the torment of the demon of creative energy that lived inside him, struggling, clawing, scratching to be released; tearing, shrieking at him to write the music that was in him. The miracle is that what he did in the little space of seventy years could have been done at all, even by a great genius. Is it any wonder that he had no time to be a man?

READING COMPREHENSION

1. The word *harangue* in "The slightest hint of disagreement, from anyone, on the most trivial point, was enough to set him off on a harangue that might last for hours, in which he proved himself right" (paragraph 3) means
   a. sarcastic joke.
   b. offended silence.
   c. arrogant speech.
   d. state of depression.

2. The word *caricature* in "A character in one of his operas was a caricature of one of the most powerful music critics of his day. Not content with burlesquing him, he invited the critic to his house and read him the libretto aloud in front of his friends" (paragraph 11) means
   a. mistake.
   b. friend.
   c. flattering description.
   d. exaggerated, mocking portrayal.

3. Which of the following would be a good alternative title for this selection?
   a. Wagner: His Personal Life
   b. Operas and Their Composers
   c. A Selfish Man Who Gave Much
   d. Wagner: A Musical Genius

4. Which sentence best expresses the main idea of this selection?

   a. Wagner's personal failings are less important than the great works he produced.

   b. Although Wagner was famous during his lifetime, very few of his operas are still performed.

   c. Wagner was an unfaithful lover as well as a spendthrift who borrowed money he never intended to repay.

   d. Wagner's operas are still considered among the greatest ever composed.

5. While trying to persuade his best friend's wife to leave her husband, Wagner was

   a. writing *Tristan und Isolde.*

   b. still married to his first wife.

   c. searching for a rich woman to marry.

   d. borrowing money from the husband.

6. *True or false?* _____ Wagner was once thrown into jail for debt.

7. In paragraph 14, the author implies that

   a. the *Ring* trilogy is one of Wagner's less successful works.

   b. Hanslick came to enjoy the character based on him in *Die Meistersinger.*

   c. *Tristan und Isolde* is a magnificent love story.

   d. Wagner had stopped writing music years before his death.

8. The author implies that Wagner

   a. was often able to get the money he desired from others.

   b. neglected the dogs that belonged to him.

   c. despised vegetarians.

   d. was self-conscious about his odd appearance.

9. The author implies that

   a. no one recognized Wagner's talent during his own lifetime.

   b. Wagner was embarrassed to ask others for money.

   c. Wagner thrived on attention.

   d. Wagner may have suffered from a brain disorder.

10. The author implies that Wagner

    a. respected those people who would argue energetically with him.

    b. was chronically depressed, unable to feel pleasure.

    c. was genuinely brilliant about nonmusical subjects as well as musical ones.

    d. profoundly regretted, at the end of his life, his loss of friends.

STRUCTURE AND TECHNIQUE

1. Taylor avoids revealing the name of his subject until paragraph 12. Why do you think he made this choice? And why does he wait until paragraph 14 to balance the negative information about Wagner's behavior with positive comments about his musical works?

2. Why do you think Taylor chose to title his essay "The Monster"?

3. What wording in paragraph 2 is echoed in paragraph 13? How has it been changed when used the second time? What is the effect of this change?

4. Taylor uses unexpected wording in some of his descriptions. What is surprising about the wording in the following excerpts, and how is the meaning affected by that wording?

   "He was almost innocent of any sense of responsibility." (Paragraph 7)

   "He had a genius for making enemies." (Paragraph 11)

   "There is greatness about his worst mistakes." (Paragraph 15)

CRITICAL READING AND DISCUSSION

1. When Taylor writes in paragraph 5, "He had a composer's voice," what is he implying about Wagner's singing? What makes you think so?

2. In what ways, according to Taylor, was Wagner like a six-year-old child (paragraph 6)? Like an Indian rajah (paragraph 8)?

3. From what sources does Taylor imply that he gathered his negative information about Wagner? Why does the author include information about those sources?

4. Do you agree with Taylor's conclusion that Wagner's failings should be overlooked? Do unusually gifted people deserve to be held to different standards from the rest of us? Can you think of any gifted people of our time who are held to different standards?

WRITING ASSIGNMENTS

www.mhhe.com/langan

Assignment 1

Write an essay about a person in your life toward whom you have mixed feelings. Perhaps you enjoy this person's company but do not fully trust him or her. Or you admire the person's family values but find him or her narrow-minded. In your thesis, state both sides of your feelings, as in the following sample thesis statement:

While Mimi is often caring and generous, she can also be too critical.

Then fully describe one side of your subject's personality before you begin describing the other. Throughout your essay, illustrate your points with specific revealing comments and incidents.

Assignment 2

Describe a person you know who has managed to alienate nearly everyone in his or her life. Divide your essay into three sections. Those sections could be about *individuals* the person has alienated, such as any of these:

A parent

A former spouse

A former best friend

A coworker

Alternatively, divide your essay into *categories* of people the person has alienated, such as any of the following:

Family members

Neighbors

Coworkers

Classmates

Describe in what ways your subject has made enemies of these people (or at least lost their friendship). Your thesis statement for this assignment might be like this one:

By being extremely self-centered and unkind, _____ has managed to alienate several people in his life.

Assignment 3

Wagner was a person who had no qualms about taking advantage of the people in his life—by insisting that they listen to him, endlessly borrowing money he never repaid, or having careless affairs. Although most people are not as manipulative as Wagner, most of us know what it's like to have someone take advantage of us for selfish reasons. Write an essay about how it feels to be taken advantage of. Select several specific instances in your life when you felt that someone else was "using" you. In your essay, devote each supporting paragraph to one such anecdote, describing what happened and how you responded. Following is an outline of such a paper.

<u>Thesis</u>: When I was younger, I was taken advantage of by several important people in my life.

<u>Topic sentences</u>:

(a) My sister often borrowed my things and then carelessly damaged or lost them.

(b) A good friend of mine in junior high school took advantage of our friendship to spend time with my brother, whom she had a crush on.

(c) My boss at a shoe store took advantage of the fact that I needed the job by forcing me to do some of his work.

What's Wrong with Schools? Teacher Plays Student, Learns to Lie and Cheat

Casey Banas

PREVIEW

A teacher pretends to be a student and sits in on several classes. What does she find in the typical class? Boredom. Routine. Apathy. Manipulation. Discouragement. If this depressing list sounds familiar, you will be interested in the following analysis of why classes often seem to be more about killing time than about learning.

© Chicago Tribune/Landov LLC

Ellen Glanz lied to her teacher about why she hadn't done her homework; but, of course, many students have lied to their teachers. The difference is that Ellen Glanz was a twenty-eight-year-old high school social studies teacher who was a student for six months to improve her teaching by gaining a fresh perspective of her school. **1**

She found many classes boring, students doing as little as necessary to pass tests and get good grades, students using ruses to avoid assignments, and students manipulating teachers to do the work for them. She concluded that many students are turned off because they have little power and responsibility for their own education. **2**

Ellen Glanz found herself doing the same things as the students. There was the day when Glanz wanted to join her husband in helping friends celebrate the purchase of a house, but she had homework for a math class. For the first time, **3** she knew how teenagers feel when they think something is more important than homework.

She found a way out and confided: "I considered my options: Confess openly 4 to the teacher, copy someone else's sheet, or make up an excuse." Glanz chose the third option—the one most widely used—and told the teacher that the pages needed to complete the assignment had been ripped from the book. The teacher accepted the story, never checking the book. In class, nobody else did the homework; and student after student mumbled responses when called on.

"Finally," Glanz said, "the teacher, thinking that the assignment must have 5 been difficult, went over each question at the board while students copied the problems at their seats. The teacher had 'covered' the material and the students had listened to the explanation. But had anything been learned? I don't think so."

Glanz found this kind of thing common. "In many cases," she said, "people 6 simply didn't do the work assignment, but copied from someone else or manipulated the teacher into doing the work for them."

"The system encourages incredible passivity," Glanz said. "In most classes 7 one sits and listens. A teacher, whose role is activity, simply cannot understand the passivity of the student's role," she said. "When I taught," Glanz recalled, "my mind was going constantly—figuring out how to best present an idea, thinking about whom to call on, whom to draw out, whom to shut up; how to get students involved, how to make my point clearer, how to respond; when to be funny, when serious. As a student, I experienced little of this. Everything was done to me."

Class methods promote the feeling that students have little control over or re- 8 sponsibility for their own education because the agenda is the teacher's, Glanz said. The teacher is convinced the subject matter is worth knowing, but the student may not agree. Many students, Glanz said, are not convinced they need to know what teachers teach; but they believe good grades are needed to get into college.

Students, obsessed with getting good grades to help qualify for the college of 9 their choice, believe the primary responsibility for their achievement rests with the teacher, Glanz said. "It was his responsibility to teach well rather than their responsibility to learn carefully."

Teachers were regarded by students, Glanz said, not as "people," but as "role- 10 players" who dispensed information needed to pass a test. "I often heard students describing teachers as drips, bores, and numerous varieties of idiots," she said. "Yet I knew that many of the same people had traveled the world over, conducted fascinating experiments or learned three languages, or were accomplished musicians, artists, or athletes."

But the sad reality, Glanz said, is the failure of teachers to recognize their 11 tremendous communications gap with students. Some students, she explained, believe that effort has little value. After seeing political corruption they conclude that honesty takes a back seat to getting ahead any way one can, she said. "I sometimes estimated that half to two-thirds of a class cheated on a given test," Glanz said. "Worse, I've encountered students who feel no remorse about cheating but are annoyed that a teacher has confronted them on their actions."

Glanz has since returned to teaching at Lincoln-Sudbury. Before her stint as 12 a student, she would worry that perhaps she was demanding too much. "Now I know I should have demanded more," she said. Before, she was quick to accept the excuses of students who came to class unprepared. Now she says, "You are responsible for learning it." But a crackdown is only a small part of the solution.

The larger issue, Glanz said, is that educators must recognize that teachers and 13 students, though physically in the same school, are in separate worlds and have an ongoing power struggle. "A first step toward ending this battle is to convince students that what we attempt to teach them is genuinely worth knowing," Glanz said. "We must be sure, ourselves, that what we are teaching is worth knowing." No longer, she emphasized, do students assume that "teacher knows best."

www.mhhe.com/langan

READING COMPREHENSION

1. The word *ruses* in "students using ruses to avoid assignments" (paragraph 2) means
   a. questions.
   b. sicknesses.
   c. parents.
   d. tricks.

2. The word *agenda* in "the agenda is the teacher's" (paragraph 8) means
   a. program.
   b. boredom.
   c. happiness.
   d. book.

3. Which of the following would be a good alternative title for this selection?
   a. How to Get Good Grades
   b. Why Students Dislike School
   c. Cheating in Our School System
   d. Students Who Manipulate Teachers

4. Which sentence best expresses the main idea of the selection?
   a. Ellen Glanz is a burned-out teacher.
   b. Ellen Glanz lied to her math teacher.
   c. Students need good grades to get into college.
   d. Teachers and students feel differently about schooling.

5. How much of a class, according to the author's estimate, would often cheat on a test?

    a. One-quarter or less

    b. One-half

    c. One-half to two-thirds

    d. Almost everyone

6. *True or false?* _____ As a result of her experience, Glanz now accepts more of her students' excuses.

7. Glanz found that the school system encourages an incredible amount of

    a. enthusiasm.

    b. passivity.

    c. violence.

    d. creativity.

8. The author implies that

    a. few students cheat on tests.

    b. most students enjoy schoolwork.

    c. classroom teaching methods should be changed.

    d. Glanz had a lazy math teacher.

9. The author implies that

    a. Glanz should not have become a student again.

    b. Glanz is a better teacher than she was before.

    c. Glanz later told her math teacher that she lied.

    d. social studies is an unimportant subject.

10. The author implies that

    a. most students who cheat on tests are caught by their teachers.

    b. most teachers demand too little of their students.

    c. students who get good grades in high school also do so in college.

    d. students never question what teachers say.

STRUCTURE AND TECHNIQUE

1. Which method of introduction—broad-to-narrow, anecdote, or questions—does Banas use in his essay? Why do you think he chose this approach?

2. List the time transitions that Banas uses in paragraph 12. How do they help Banas make his point?

3. Throughout "What's Wrong with Schools?" Banas shifts between summarizing Ellen Glanz's words and quoting Glanz directly. Find an instance in the essay in which both direct and indirect quotations are used in the same paragraph. What does Banas gain or lose from using this technique? (Refer to pages 558–561 for definitions and examples of direct and indirect quotations.)

4. Parallel structures are often used to emphasize similar information. They can create a smooth, readable style. For example, note the series of -ing verbs in the following sentence from paragraph 2: ". . . students **doing** as little as necessary to pass tests and get good grades, students **using** ruses to avoid assignments, and students **manipulating** teachers to do the work for them." Find two other uses of parallelism, one in paragraph 4 and one in paragraph 7.

CRITICAL READING AND DISCUSSION

1. After reading this essay, what do you think Glanz's attitude is? Is she pro- or anti-teacher? Pro- or anti-student? Provide evidence for your position.

2. Banas suggests that many students are in school to get good grades—not to learn. Explain whether or not you agree with this assessment. Do you find that getting a good grade isn't always the same as really learning?

3. The author ends with Glanz's view of "the larger issue": "We must be sure, ourselves, that what we are teaching is worth knowing." What was taught in your high school classes that you feel is worth knowing or not worth knowing? Explain why. Also, what is being taught in your college classes that you feel is worth knowing or not worth knowing, and why?

4. Much of this essay contrasts the behavior of students with that of teachers. In what ways does Glanz see their behavior and views differing? What do you think each group should be doing differently?

www.mhhe.com/langan

WRITING ASSIGNMENTS

Assignment 1

Play the role of student observer in one of your college classes. Then write an essay with *either* of the following theses:

In my _____ class, students are turned off.

In my _____ class, students are active and interested.

In each supporting paragraph, state and detail one reason why the atmosphere in that particular class is either boring or interesting. You might want to consider areas such as these:

> Instructor: presentation, tone of voice, level of interest and enthusiasm, teaching aids used, ability to handle questions, sense of humor, and so on
>
> Students: level of enthusiasm, participation in class, attitude (as shown by body language and other actions), and so on
>
> Other factors: conditions of classroom, length of class period, noise level in classroom, and so on

Assignment 2

Glanz says that students like to describe their teachers as "drips, bores, and numerous varieties of idiots." Write a description of one of your high school teachers or college instructors who either *does* or *does not* fit that description. Show, in your essay, that your teacher or instructor was weak, boring, and idiotic—or just the opposite (dynamic, creative, and bright). In either case, your focus should be on providing specific details that *enable your readers to see for themselves* that your thesis is valid.

Assignment 3

How does the classroom situation Ellen Glanz describes compare with a classroom situation with which you are familiar—either one from the high school you attended or one from the school in which you are presently enrolled? Select one class you were or are a part of, and write an essay in which you compare or contrast your class with the ones Ellen Glanz describes. Here are some areas you might wish to include in your essay:

> How interesting the class was
>
> How many of the students did their assignments
>
> What the teaching methods were
>
> How much was actually learned
>
> How active the teacher or instructor was
>
> How passive the students were
>
> What the students thought of the teacher or instructor

Choose any three of the above areas or three other areas. Then decide which method of development you will use: *one side at a time* or *point by point* (see pages 288–290).

Propaganda Techniques in Today's Advertising

Ann McClintock

PREVIEW

Courtesy of John Langan

Advertisers want your business, and they will use a variety of clever ad slogans to get it. If you've ever responded to ads, you have been swayed by the effective use of propaganda. You may associate the word *propaganda* with the tactics used by strong-arm governments. But Ann McClintock provides evidence that we are the targets of propaganda every day and that it shapes many of our opinions and decisions.

Americans, adults and children alike, are being seduced. They are being brainwashed. And few of us protest. Why? Because the seducers and the brainwashers are the advertisers we willingly invite into our homes. We are victims, content—even eager—to be victimized. We read advertisers' propaganda messages in newspapers and magazines; we watch their alluring images on television. We absorb their messages and images into our subconscious. We all do it—even those of us who claim to see through advertisers' tricks and therefore feel immune to advertising's charm. Advertisers lean heavily on propaganda to sell products, whether the "products" are a brand of toothpaste, a candidate for office, or a particular political viewpoint.

Propaganda is a systematic effort to influence people's opinions, to win them over to a certain view or side. Propaganda is not necessarily concerned with what is true or false, good or bad. Propagandists simply want people to believe the messages being sent. Often, propagandists will use outright lies or more subtle deceptions to sway people's opinions. In a propaganda war, any tactic is considered fair.

When we hear the word "propaganda," we usually think of a foreign menace: anti-American radio programs broadcast by a totalitarian regime or brainwashing tactics practiced on hostages. Although propaganda may seem relevant only in the political arena, the concept can be applied fruitfully to the way products and ideas are sold in advertising. Indeed, the vast majority of us are targets in advertisers' propaganda war. Every day, we are bombarded with slogans, print and Internet pop-up ads, commercials, packaging claims, billboards, trademarks, logos, and designer brands—all forms of propaganda. One study reports that each of us, during an average day, is exposed to over *five hundred* advertising claims of various types. This saturation may even increase in the future, since current trends include ads on movie screens, shopping carts, videocassettes, and even public television.

What kind of propaganda techniques do advertisers use? There are seven basic   4
types:

1. Name Calling.

Name calling is a propaganda tactic in which negatively   5
charged names are hurled against the opposing side or competitor. By using such
names, propagandists try to arouse feelings of mistrust, fear, and hate in their audiences. For example, a political advertisement may label an opposing candidate a
"loser," "fence-sitter," or "warmonger." Depending on the advertiser's target market, labels such as "a friend of big business" or "a dues-paying member of the party
in power" can be the epithets that damage an opponent. Ads for products may also
use name calling. An American manufacturer may refer, for instance, to a "foreign
car" in its commercial—not an "imported" one. The label of foreignness will have
unpleasant connotations in many people's minds. A childhood rhyme claims that
"names can never hurt me," but name calling is an effective way to damage the
opposition, whether it is another car maker or a congressional candidate.

2. Glittering Generalities.

Using glittering generalities is the opposite of   6
name calling. In this case, advertisers surround their products with attractive—and
slippery—words and phrases. They use vague terms that are difficult to define
and that may have different meanings to different people: *freedom, democratic,
all-American, progressive, Christian,* and *justice.* Many such words have strong
affirmative overtones. This kind of language stirs positive feelings in people, feelings that may spill over to the product or idea being pitched. As with name calling,
the emotional response may overwhelm logic. Target audiences accept the product without thinking very much about what the glittering generalities mean—or
whether they even apply to the product. After all, how can anyone oppose "truth,
justice, and the American way"?

The ads for politicians and political causes often use glittering generalities   7
because such "buzzwords" can influence votes. Election slogans include high-
sounding but basically empty phrases like the following:

"He cares about people." (That's nice, but is he a better candidate than his
opponent?)

"Vote for progress." (Progress by whose standards?)

"They'll make this country great again." (What does "great" mean? Does
"great" mean the same thing to others as it does to me?)

"Vote for the future." (What kind of future?)

"If you love America, vote for Phyllis Smith." (If I don't vote for Smith, does
that mean I don't love America?)

Ads for consumer goods are also sprinkled with glittering generalities. Product   8
names, for instance, are supposed to evoke good feelings: *Luvs* diapers, *Stayfree*
feminine hygiene products, *Joy* liquid detergent, *Loving Care* hair color, *Almost*

Home cookies, *Yankee Doodle* pastries. Product slogans lean heavily on vague but comforting phrases: . . . General Electric "brings good things to life," and Dow Chemical "lets you do great things." Chevrolet, we are told, is the "heartbeat of America," and Chrysler boasts cars that are "built by Americans for Americans."

3. Transfer.   In transfer, advertisers try to improve the image of a product by 9 associating it with a symbol most people respect, like the American flag or Uncle Sam. The advertisers hope that the prestige attached to the symbol will carry over to the product. Many companies use transfer devices to identify their products: Lincoln Insurance shows a profile of the President; Continental Insurance portrays a Revolutionary War minuteman; Amtrak's logo is red, white, and blue; Liberty Mutual's corporate symbol is the Statue of Liberty; Allstate's name is cradled by a pair of protective, fatherly hands.

Corporations also use the transfer technique when they sponsor prestigious 10 shows on radio and television. These shows function as symbols of dignity and class. Kraft Corporation, for instance, sponsored a "Leonard Bernstein Conducts Beethoven" concert, while Gulf Oil is the sponsor of *National Geographic* specials and Mobil supports public television's *Masterpiece Theater*. In this way, corporations can reach an educated, influential audience and, perhaps, improve their public image by associating themselves with quality programming.

Political ads, of course, practically wrap themselves in the flag. Ads for 11 a political candidate often show either the Washington Monument, a Fourth of July parade, the Stars and Stripes, a bald eagle soaring over the mountains, or a white-steepled church on the village green. The national anthem or "America the Beautiful" may play in the background. Such appeals to Americans' love of country can surround the candidate with an aura of patriotism and integrity.

4. Testimonial.   The testimonial is one of advertisers' most-loved and most- 12 used propaganda techniques. Similar to the transfer device, the testimonial capitalizes on the admiration people have for a celebrity to make the product shine more brightly—even though the celebrity is not an expert on the product being sold.

Print and television ads offer a nonstop parade of testimonials: here's William 13 Shatner for Priceline.com; here's basketball star Michael Jordan eating Wheaties; a slew of well-known people (including pop star Madonna) advertise clothing from the Gap; and Jerry Seinfeld assures us he never goes anywhere without his American Express card. Testimonials can sell movies, too; newspaper ads for films often feature favorable comments by well-known reviewers. And, in recent years, testimonials have played an important role in pitching books; the backs of paperbacks frequently list complimentary blurbs by celebrities.

Political candidates, as well as their ad agencies, know the value of testimo- 14 nials. Barbra Streisand lent her star appeal to the presidential campaign of Bill Clinton, while Arnold Schwarzenegger endorsed George Bush. Even controversial social issues are debated by celebrities. The nuclear freeze, for instance, starred Paul Newman for the pro side and Charlton Heston for the con.

As illogical as testimonials sometimes are (Pepsi's Michael Jackson, for in- 15 stance, is a health-food adherent who does not drink soft drinks), they are effective propaganda. We like the *person* so much that we like the *product* too.

5. Plain Folks.

The plain folks approach says, in effect, "Buy me or vote for 16 me. I'm just like you." Regular folks will surely like Bob Evans's Down on the Farm Country Sausage or good old-fashioned Countrytime Lemonade. Some ads emphasize the idea that "we're all in the same boat." We see people making long-distance calls for just the reasons we do—to put the baby on the phone to Grandma or to tell Mom we love her. And how do these folksy, warmhearted (usually saccharine[1]) scenes affect us? They're supposed to make us feel that AT&T— the multinational corporate giant—has the same values we do. Similarly, we are introduced to the little people at Ford, the ordinary folks who work on the assembly line, not to bigwigs in their executive offices. What's the purpose of such an approach? To encourage us to buy a car built by these honest, hardworking "everyday Joes" who care about quality as much as we do.

Political advertisements make almost as much use of the "plain folks" ap- 17 peal as they do of transfer devices. Candidates wear hard hats, farmers' caps, and assembly-line coveralls. They jog around the block and carry their own luggage through the airport. The idea is to convince voters that the candidates are average people, not the elite—not wealthy lawyers or executives but common citizens.

6. Card Stacking.

When people say that "the cards were stacked against me," 18 they mean that they were never given a fair chance. Applied to propaganda, card stacking means that one side may suppress or distort evidence, tell half-truths, oversimplify the facts, or set up a "straw man"—a false target—to divert attention from the issue at hand. Card stacking is a difficult form of propaganda both to detect and to combat. When a candidate claims that an opponent has "changed his mind five times on this important issue," we tend to accept the claim without investigating whether the candidate had good reasons for changing his mind. Many people are simply swayed by the distorted claim that the candidate is "waffling" on the issue.

Advertisers often stack the cards in favor of the products they are pushing. 19 They may, for instance, use what are called "weasel words." These are small words that usually slip right past us, but that make the difference between reality and illusion. The weasel words are underlined in the following claims:

"<u>Helps control</u> dandruff symptoms." (The audience usually interprets this as stops dandruff.)

---

[1]*saccharine:* exaggeratedly sentimental.

"Most dentists <u>surveyed</u> recommend sugarless gum for their patients <u>who chew gum</u>." (We hear the "most dentists" and "for their patients," but we don't think about how many were surveyed or whether or not the dentists first recommended that the patients not chew gum at all.)

"Sticker price $1,000 lower than <u>most comparable</u> cars." (How many is "most"? What car does the advertiser consider "comparable"?)

Advertisers also use a card stacking trick when they make an unfinished 20 claim. For example, they will say that their product has "twice as much pain reliever." We are left with a favorable impression. We don't usually ask, "Twice as much pain reliever as what?" Or advertisers may make extremely vague claims that sound alluring but have no substance: Toyota's "Oh, what a feeling!"; Vantage cigarettes' "the taste of success"; "The spirit of Marlboro"; Coke's "the real thing." Another way to stack the cards in favor of a certain product is to use scientific-sounding claims that are not supported by sound research. When Ford claimed that its LTD model was "400% quieter," many people assumed that its LTD must be quieter than all other cars. When taken to court, however, Ford admitted that the phrase referred to the difference between the noise level inside and outside the LTD. Other scientific-sounding claims use mysterious ingredients that are never explained as selling points: Retsyn, "special whitening agents," "the ingredient doctors recommend."

7. Bandwagon.   In the bandwagon technique, advertisers pressure, "Every- 21 one's doing it. Why don't you?" This kind of propaganda often succeeds because many people have a deep desire not to be different. Political ads tell us to vote for the "winning candidate." The advertisers know we tend to feel comfortable doing what others do; we want to be on the winning team. Or ads show a series of people proclaiming, "I'm voting for the Senator. I don't know why anyone wouldn't." Again, the audience feels under pressure to conform.

In the marketplace, the bandwagon approach lures buyers. Ads tell us that 22 "nobody doesn't like Sara Lee" (the message is that you must be weird if you don't). They tell us that "most people prefer Brand X two to one over other leading brands" (to be like the majority, we should buy Brand X). If we don't drink Pepsi, we're left out of "the Pepsi generation." To take part in "America's favorite health kick," the National Dairy Council asks us, "Got Milk?" And Honda motorcycle ads, praising the virtues of being a follower, tell us, "Follow the leader. He's on a Honda."

Why do these propaganda techniques work? Why do so many of us buy the 23 products, viewpoints, and candidates urged on us by propaganda messages? They work because they appeal to our emotions, not to our minds. Often, in fact, they capitalize on our prejudices and biases. For example, if we are convinced that environmentalists are radicals who want to destroy America's record of industrial growth and progress, then we will applaud the candidate who refers to them as "treehuggers." Clear thinking requires hard work: analyzing a claim, researching the facts, examining both sides of an issue, using logic to see the flaws in an argument. Many of us would rather let the propagandists do our thinking for us.

Because propaganda is so effective, it is important to detect it and understand 24 how it is used. We may conclude, after close examination, that some propaganda sends a truthful, worthwhile message. Some advertising, for instance, urges us not to drive drunk, to become volunteers, to contribute to charity. Even so, we must be aware that propaganda is being used. Otherwise, we have consented to handing over to others our independence of thought and action.

READING COMPREHENSION

www.mhhe.com/langan

1. The word *epithets* in "labels such as 'a friend of big business' or 'a dues-paying member of the party in power' can be the epithets that damage an opponent" (paragraph 5) means
   a. courtesies.
   b. descriptive labels.
   c. assurances.
   d. delays.

2. The words *capitalizes* on in "the testimonial capitalizes on the admiration people have for a celebrity" (paragraph 12) mean
   a. reports about.
   b. ignores.
   c. cuts back on.
   d. takes advantage of.

3. Which of the following would be a good alternative title for this selection?
   a. The World of Advertising
   b. Common Persuasion Techniques in Advertising
   c. Propaganda in Politics
   d. Common Advertising Techniques on Television

4. Which sentence best expresses the main idea of the selection?
   a. Americans may be exposed daily to over five hundred advertising claims of some sort.
   b. The testimonial takes advantage of the admiration people have for celebrities, even though they have no expertise on the product being sold.
   c. People should detect and understand common propaganda techniques, which appeal to the emotions rather than to logic.
   d. Americans need to understand that advertising, a huge industry, affects their lives in numerous ways.

5. The propaganda technique in which a product is associated with a symbol or image most people admire and respect is
   a. glittering generalities.
   b. transfer.
   c. testimonials.
   d. bandwagon.

6. The technique in which evidence is withheld or distorted is called
   a. glittering generalities.
   b. bandwagon.
   c. plain folks.
   d. card stacking.

7. The technique that makes a political candidate seem to be just like the people an ad is aimed at is
   a. glittering generalities.
   b. bandwagon.
   c. plain folks.
   d. card stacking.

8. A way to avoid being taken in by propaganda is to use
   a. our emotions.
   b. name calling.
   c. clear thinking.
   d. our subconscious.

9. The author implies in paragraph 16 that
   a. most Americans do not frequently call their grandmothers.
   b. multinational corporations do not have the same values as average citizens.
   c. Bob Evans is an American celebrity.
   d. executives at AT&T and Ford are hardworking and honest.

10. From paragraphs 23 and 24, we can conclude that the author feels
   a. we are unlikely to analyze advertising logically unless we recognize it as propaganda.
   b. propaganda should not be allowed.
   c. if we don't want to hand over to others our independence, we should ignore all propaganda.
   d. we should not support the "products, viewpoints, and candidates urged on us by propaganda messages."

STRUCTURE AND TECHNIQUE

1. In paragraph 1, McClintock's choice of words reveals her attitudes toward both propagandists and the public. What specific words reveal her attitudes, and what attitudes do they represent?

2. What key term does McClintock define in paragraph 2? Why does she define it here? Where else in the essay does she use the technique of definition?

3. McClintock uses parentheses in two lists, the ones in paragraphs 7 and 19. What purpose do these parentheses serve?

4. McClintock provides abundant examples throughout her essay. Why does she provide so many examples? What does she accomplish with this technique?

What propaganda technique (or techniques) does this advertisement use? Is it effective? Why or why not?

CRITICAL READING AND DISCUSSION

1. Some of the propaganda techniques listed in the selection have contrasting appeals. How do name-calling and glittering generalities contrast with each other? Testimonials and plain folks?

2. Why are ads that use the bandwagon approach so effective? What ads have you seen recently that use that approach?

3. The author states, "Americans, adults and children alike, are being seduced" (paragraph 1). What might be the differences between the ways adults and children react to the seductions of advertising?

4. McClintock states, "We are victims, content—even eager—to be victimized" (paragraph 1). Do you agree? Is this article likely to change how you view ads in the future? Why or why not?

WRITING ASSIGNMENTS

Assignment 1

Imagine that you work for an ad agency and have been asked to come up with at least three possible campaigns for a new product (for example, a car, a perfume, a detergent, jeans, beer, a toothpaste, a deodorant, or an appliance). Write an essay in which you describe three different propaganda techniques that might be used to sell the product and how these claims could persuade the public to buy. Be specific about the general looks, the character, and the wording of your ads and about how they fit in with the techniques you suggest.

Assignment 2

Choose three ads currently appearing on television or in print. Show that each ad uses one or more of the propaganda techniques McClintock discusses. Be specific about product names, what the ad looks like, kinds of characters in the ad, and so on. Don't forget that all your specific details should back up your point that each ad uses a certain propaganda technique (or techniques) to sell a product. Your thesis will make some overall statement about the three ads, such as either of these:

Beer advertisements use a variety of propaganda techniques.

Glittering generalities are used to sell very different types of products.

Assignment 3

Do some informal "market research" on why people buy the products they do. Begin by asking at least ten people why they bought a particular brand-name item. You might question them about something they're wearing (designer jeans, for example). Or you might ask them what toothpaste they use, what car they drive, what pain reliever they take, or what chicken they eat—or ask about any other product people use. Take notes on the reasons people give for their purchases.

Then write an essay with the thesis "My research suggests that people often buy products for three reasons." Include in your introductory paragraph your plan of development—a list of the three reasons that were mentioned most often by the people you interviewed. Develop your supporting paragraphs with examples drawn from the interviews. As part of your support, use quotations from the people you spoke with.

Bombs Bursting in Air

Beth Johnson

> ### PREVIEW
>
> Nobody looks forward to the "bombs" of life, to the shocks and even tragedies that blindside us all eventually. After a frightening incident, Beth Johnson muses over the responses that are open to us in the wake of such unwelcome experiences. Is it possible to protect ourselves from the grief and pain that life sends our way? Is it desirable? This essay explores some possible answers.

Courtesy of Beth Johnson

It's Friday night and we're at the Olympics—the Junior Olympics, that is. My son 1
is on a relay-race team competing against fourth-graders from all over the school district. His little sister and I sit high in the stands, trying to pick Isaac out from the crowd of figures milling around on the field during these moments of pre-game confusion. The public address system sputters to life and summons our attention. "And now," the tinny voice rings out, "please join together in the singing of our national anthem."

"Oh saaay can you seeeeee," we begin. My arm rests around Maddie's shoul- 2
ders. I am touching her a lot today, and she notices. "Mom, you're *squishing* me," she chides, wriggling from my grip. I content myself with stroking her hair. News that reached me today makes me need to feel her near. We pipe along, squeaking out the impossibly high note of "land of the freeeeeeeee." Maddie clowns, half-singing, half-shouting the lyrics, hitting the "b's" explosively on "bombs bursting in air."

Bombs indeed, I think, replaying the sound of my friend's voice over the 3
phone that afternoon: ". . . bumped her head sledding. We took her in for an X ray, you know, just to make sure. There was something strange, so they did more tests . . . a brain tumor . . . Children's Hospital in Boston Tuesday . . . surgery, yes, right away . . ." Maddie's playmate Shannon, only five years old. We'd last seen her at Halloween, dressed in her blue princess costume, and talked of Furby and Scooby-Doo and Tootsie Rolls. Now her parents were hurriedly learn-

ing a new vocabulary—CAT scans and pediatric neurosurgery and frontal lobe. A bomb had exploded in their midst, and, like troops under attack, they were rallying in response.

The games over, the children and I edge our way out of the school parking lot, 4 bumper to bumper with other parents ferrying their families home. I tell the kids as casually as I can about Shannon. "She'll have to have an operation. It's lucky, really, that they found it by accident this way while it's small."

"I want to send her a present," Maddie announces. "That'd be nice," I say, glad 5 to keep the conversation on a positive note.

But my older son is with us now. Sam, who is thirteen, says, "She'll be OK, 6 though, right?" he says. It's not a question, really; it's a statement that I must either agree with or contradict. I want to say yes. I want to say of course she'll be all right. I want them to inhabit a world where five-year-olds do not develop silent, mysterious growths in their brains, where "malignancy" and "seizure" are words for *New York Times* crossword puzzles, not for little girls. They would accept my assurance; they would believe me and sleep well tonight. But I can't; the bomb that exploded in Shannon's home has sent splinters of shrapnel into ours as well, and they cannot be ignored or lied away. "We hope she'll be just fine," I finally say. "She has very good doctors. She has wonderful parents who are doing everything they can. The tumor is small. Shannon's strong and healthy."

"*She'll* be OK," says Maddie matter-of-factly. "In school we read about a little 7 boy who had something wrong with his leg and he had an operation and got better. Can we go to Dairy Queen?"

Bombs on the horizon don't faze Maddie. Not yet. I can just barely remem- 8 ber from my own childhood the sense that still surrounds her, that feeling of being cocooned within reassuring walls of security and order. Back then, Mondays meant gym, Tuesdays were pizza in the cafeteria, Wednesdays brought clarinet lessons. Teachers stood in their familiar spots in the classrooms, telling us with reassuring simplicity that World War II happened because Hitler, a very bad man, invaded Poland. Midterms and report cards, summer vacations and new notebooks in September gave a steady rhythm to the world. It wasn't all necessarily happy— through the years there were poor grades, grouchy teachers, exclusion from the desired social group, dateless weekends when it seemed the rest of the world was paired off—but it was familiar territory where we felt walled off from the really bad things that happened to other people.

There were hints of them, though, even then. Looking back, I recall the tiny 9 shock waves, the tremors from far-off explosions that occasionally rattled our shelter. There was the little girl who was absent for a week and when she returned wasn't living with her mother and stepfather anymore. There was the big girl who threw up in the bathroom every morning and then disappeared from school. A playful, friendly custodian was suddenly fired, and it had something to do with an angry parent. A teacher's husband had a heart attack and died. These were interesting tidbits to report to our families over dinner, mostly out of morbid interest in seeing our parents bite their lips and exchange glances.

As we got older, the bombs dropped closer. A friend's sister was arrested for 10 selling drugs; we saw her mother in tears at church that Sunday. A boy I thought I knew, a school clown with a sweet crooked grin, shot himself in the woods behind his house. A car full of senior boys, going home from a dance where I'd been sent into ecstasy when the cutest of them all greeted me by name, rounded a curve too fast and crashed, killing them. We wept and hugged each other in the halls. Our teachers listened to us grieve and tried to comfort us, but their words came out impatient and almost angry. I realize now that what sounded like anger was help-lessness—the inability to teach us lessons we were still too young or too ignorant to learn. For although our sorrow was real, we still had some sense of a protective curtain between us and the bombs. If only, we said. If only she hadn't used drugs. If only he'd told someone how depressed he was. If only they'd been more careful. We weren't like them; we were careful. Like magical incantations, we recited the things that we would or wouldn't do in order to protect ourselves from such sad, unnecessary fates.

When my best friend, a beautiful girl of sixteen, went to sleep one January 11 night and never woke up, I found myself shaken to the core of my being. My grief at the loss of my vibrant, laughing friend was great. But what really tilted my uni-verse was the nakedness of my realization that there was no "if only." There were no drugs, no careless actions, no crimes, no accidents, nothing I could focus on to explain away what had happened. She had simply died. This could only mean that there was no magic barrier separating me and my loved ones from the bombs. We were as vulnerable as everyone else. For months the shock stayed with me. I sat in class watching my teachers draw diagrams of Saturn, talk about Watergate, and multiply fractions, and I wondered at their apparent cheer and normality. Didn't they *know* we were all doomed? Didn't they know it was only a matter of time until one of us took a direct hit? What was the point of anything?

But time moved on, and of course I moved with it. College came and went, 12 graduate school, adulthood, middle age. My heightened sense of vulnerability be-gan to subside, though I could never again slip fully into the soothing security of my younger days. I became more aware of the intertwining threads of joy, pain, and occasional tragedy that weave through all our lives. College was stimulating, exciting, full of friendship and challenge. I fell in love for the first time, reveled in its sweetness, then learned the painful lesson that love comes with no guarantee. A beloved professor lost two children to leukemia, but continued with skill and pas-sion to introduce students to the riches of literature. My father fell ill, but the last day of his life, when I sat by his bed holding his hand, remains one of my sweetest memories. The marriage I'd entered into with optimism ended in bitter divorce but produced three children whose existence is my daily delight. At every step along the way, I've seen that the most rewarding chapters of my life have contained parts that I not only would not have chosen, but would have given much to avoid. But selecting just the good parts is not an option we are given.

The price of allowing ourselves to truly live, to love and be loved, is (and it's 13 the ultimate irony) the knowledge that the greater our investment in life, the larger the target we create. Of course, it is within our power to refuse friendship, shrink from love, live in isolation, and thus create for ourselves a nearly impenetrable bomb shelter. There are those among us who choose such an existence, the price of intimacy being too high. Looking about me, however, I see few such examples. Instead, I am moved by the courage with which most of us, ordinary folks, continue soldiering on. We fall in love, we bring our children into the world, we forge our friendships, we give our hearts, knowing with increasing certainty that we do so at our own risk. Still we move ahead with open arms, saying yes, yes to life.

Shannon's surgery is behind her; the prognosis is good. Her mother reports 14 that the family members are returning to their normal routines, laughing again and talking of ordinary things, even while they step more gently, speak more quietly, are more aware of the precious fragility of life and of the blessing of every day that passes without explosion.

Bombs bursting in air. They can blind us, like fireworks at the moment of 15 explosion. If we close our eyes and turn away, all we see is their fiery image. But if we have the courage to keep our eyes open and welcoming, even bombs finally fade against the vastness of the starry sky.

www.mhhe.com/langan

READING COMPREHENSION

1. The word *faze* in "'*She'll* be OK,' says Maddie matter-of-factly. '. . . Can we go to Dairy Queen?' Bombs on the horizon don't faze Maddie" (paragraphs 7–8) means

   a. surprise.

   b. relieve.

   c. please.

   d. upset.

2. The word *impenetrable* in "it is within our power to refuse friendships, shrink from love . . . and thus create for ourselves a nearly impenetrable bomb shelter" (paragraph 13) means

   a. flimsy.

   b. unable to be entered.

   c. dangerous.

   d. invisible.

3. Which of the following would be a good alternative title for this selection?
   a. Pediatric Tumors
   b. Childhood Tragedies
   c. Life's Lessons
   d. Shannon's Story

4. Which sentence best expresses the main idea of the selection?
   a. Despite all our precautions, sad events will eventually occur in our lives.
   b. Although Shannon's condition was frightening, it turned out well in the end.
   c. The author has experienced a number of unhappy events in her life.
   d. It is worth being truly open to life's joys even though that also means experiencing its sorrows.

5. Shannon's brain tumor was discovered
   a. after she experienced severe headaches.
   b. when she began having seizures.
   c. after she had bumped her head sledding.
   d. during surgery for another condition.

6. The author's best friend had died
   a. after taking an overdose of drugs.
   b. in her sleep.
   c. in a car crash.
   d. as a result of suicide.

7. *True or false?* _____ The author's daughter was alarmed at news of Shannon's illness.

8. The author implies that
   a. most brain tumors prove to be harmless.
   b. her son realized Shannon's condition could be serious.
   c. she had suspected at Halloween that Shannon was ill.
   d. her daughter did not care what happened to Shannon.

9. We can conclude from paragraph 11 that
   a. the author really did know why her best friend died.
   b. the author's teachers didn't care much about her friend's death.
   c. the author's depression led her to take drugs.
   d. her friend's death made the author pessimistic for months.

10. The reader can conclude that the author
    a. thinks her life has been unusually difficult.
    b. believes that the sorrows of life are outweighed by the joys.
    c. thinks people should protect themselves better against pain.
    d. never recovered from the shock of her best friend's death.

STRUCTURE AND TECHNIQUE

1. Johnson begins her essay with a narrative of an evening at her son's sports event. At what point does she make the transition into the body of her essay? Which words or phrases does she use to make this transition?

2. Foreshadowing is a technique an author sometimes uses to hint at something that has not yet been revealed. Find an example of foreshadowing in paragraph 2. Where, later in the essay, does she return to this subject? What is the effect of this foreshadowing?

3. Why do you think the author delays telling about the outcome of Shannon's surgery until the end of the essay? How would the essay be different if she had revealed early on that the surgery was successful?

4. Note the parallel phrasing in paragraph 3: "We'd . . . talked of Furby and Scooby-Doo and Tootsie Rolls. Now her parents were hurriedly learning a new vocabulary—CAT scans and pediatric neurosurgery and frontal lobe." Why might the author have used parallel structure here? What is the effect?

CRITICAL READING AND DISCUSSION

1. The author mentions bombs in the introduction and then uses *bomb* symbolically in other parts of the essay. What are some of the places in which she uses that symbol, and what does she intend it to mean? Do you think it is an effective symbol?

2. In paragraph 12, Johnson mentions incidents involving her first love, a professor, her father, and her marriage. What do these examples have in common? Why do you think Johnson included them?

3. Judging from the rest of the essay, what does Johnson mean by saying that "the greater our investment in life, the larger the target we create" (paragraph 13)?

4. Adults sometimes sentimentally think of childhood as a time of happy, carefree innocence, as the author suggests in paragraph 8, and as depicted in the photograph here. Yet during childhood most of us witnessed events that began to make us aware that life was not always happy or fair. What such events do you remember? What impression did they make on you?

© LWA-Dann Tardif/Corbis

WRITING ASSIGNMENTS

Assignment 1

Johnson writes, "I can just barely remember from my own childhood the sense that still surrounds her [Maddie], that feeling of being cocooned within reassuring walls of security and order."

As a child, what provided you with a sense of security? You might think in terms of people (a grandparent, teacher, pastor), places (your school, the corner store), or situations (lying in bed at night hearing your parents talk) in your life that seemed—at the time, anyway—to be unshakable.

The thesis of your essay might be similar to this:

The sense of security I felt as a child was in large part due to a few important people in my life.

A supporting paragraph about your grandmother, for instance, might begin, "My grandmother's calm personality always made me feel safe and secure. For example, when I broke a dish at her house, she didn't get angry. Instead, she hugged me and said it didn't matter."

Assignment 2

Describe three events in your own life that forced you to recognize the existence of grief and even tragedy. In each case, provide details about how the incident affected you and your outlook on life. You might choose incidents similar to the ones Johnson mentions (there are many examples in paragraphs 9–12) or others.

A topic sentence about one such incident might be something like this:

> My cousin's death at an early age made me realize that adults could not always protect their children.

You would continue by describing the circumstances of the death and how it made you regard the power of adults differently.

Alternatively, write about only one significant tragedy in your life. In your essay, narrate the key events and tell how they affected you and, perhaps, others involved.

Assignment 3

Johnson writes about how her childhood feeling of security eventually changed, first to a "heightened sense of vulnerability" and then to an awareness "of the intertwining threads of joy, pain, and occasional tragedy that weave through all our lives."

Write an essay about a few things that changed for you, or ways that you changed, as you made the transition from childhood to adulthood. For example, after having loved school at first, you might have grown to look down on education and then finally come to realize the importance of education. Below are a few other things toward which people's attitudes often change as they mature.

Birthdays

Family relationships

Relationships with teachers

Career choices

Household responsibilities

Choice of friends

One's own sense of confidence

You might use a thesis statement such as the following for your essay:

> As I made the transition from childhood to adulthood, some of my basic attitudes changed.

Support your topic sentences by contrasting your earlier views with your current views. Consider using examples, narration, and descriptions to help your readers understand the changes you discuss.

An alternative is to write an essay about only one thing in your life that changed. For instance, changes in your relationship with one or more siblings might merit an essay of their own.

Here's to Your Health

Joan Dunayer

PREVIEW

Joan Dunayer contrasts the glamorous "myth" about alcohol, as presented in advertising and popular culture, with the reality—which is often far less appealing. After reading her essay, you will be more aware of how we are encouraged to think of alcohol as being tied to happiness and success. You may also become a more critical observer of images presented by advertisers.

Courtesy of Joan Dunayer

As the only freshman on his high school's varsity wrestling team, Tod was anx- 1 ious to fit in with his older teammates. One night after a match, he was offered a tequila bottle on the ride home. Tod felt he had to accept, or he would seem like a sissy. He took a swallow, and every time the bottle was passed back to him, he took another swallow. After seven swallows, he passed out. His terrified teammates carried him into his home, and his mother then rushed him to the hospital. After his stomach was pumped, Tod learned that his blood alcohol level had been so high that he was lucky not to be in a coma or dead.

Unfortunately, drinking is not unusual among high-school students or, for that 2 matter, in any other segment of our society. And that's no accident. There are numerous influences in our society urging people to drink, not the least of which is advertising. Who can recall a televised baseball or basketball game without a beer commercial? Furthermore, alcohol ads appear with pounding frequency in magazines, on billboards, and in college newspapers. According to industry estimates, brewers spend more than $600 million a year on radio and TV commercials and another $90 million on print ads. In addition, the liquor industry spends about $230 million a year on print advertising, and since 1966 it has greatly expanded its presence on cable and independent broadcast stations. Just recently, NBC became the first network station to accept hard liquor ads for broadcast.

To top it all off, this aggressive advertising of alcohol fosters a harmful myth 3 about drinking.

Part of the myth is that liquor signals professional success. In a slick men's 4 magazine, one full-page ad for Scotch whiskey shows two men seated in an elegant restaurant. Both are in their thirties, perfectly groomed, and wearing expensive-looking gray suits. The windows are draped with velvet, the table with spotless white linen. Each place-setting consists of a long-stemmed water goblet, silver utensils, and thick silver plates. On each plate is a half-empty cocktail glass. The two men are grinning and shaking hands, as if they've just concluded a business deal. The caption reads, "The taste of success."

Contrary to what the liquor company would have us believe, drinking is more 5 closely related to lack of success than to achievement. Among students, the heaviest drinkers have the lowest grades. In the work force, alcoholics are frequently late or absent, tend to perform poorly, and often get fired. Although alcohol abuse occurs in all economic classes, it remains most prevalent among the poor.

Another part of the alcohol myth is that drinking makes you more attractive 6 to the opposite sex. "Hot, hot, hot," one commercial's soundtrack begins, as the camera scans a crowd of college-age beachgoers. Next it follows the curve of a woman's leg up to her bare hip and lingers there. She is young, beautiful, wearing a bikini. A young guy, carrying an ice chest, positions himself near to where she sits. He is tan, muscular. She doesn't show much interest—until he opens the chest and takes out a beer. Now she smiles over at him. He raises his eyebrows and, invitingly, holds up another can. She joins him. This beer, the song concludes, "attracts like no other."

Beer doesn't make anyone sexier. Like all alcohol, it lowers the levels of male 7 hormones in men and of female hormones in women—even when taken in small amounts. In substantial amounts, alcohol can cause infertility in women and impotence in men. Some alcoholic men even develop enlarged breasts.

The alcohol myth also creates the illusion that beer and athletics are a perfect 8 combination. One billboard features three high-action images: a sprinter running at top speed, a surfer riding a wave, and a basketball player leaping to make a dunk shot. A particular light beer, the billboard promises, "won't slow you down."

"Slow you down" is exactly what alcohol does. Drinking plays a role in over 9 six million injuries each year—not counting automobile accidents. Even in small amounts, alcohol dulls the brain, reducing muscle coordination and slowing reaction time. It also interferes with the ability to focus the eyes and adjust to a sudden change in brightness—such as the flash of a car's headlights. Drinking and driving, responsible for over half of all automobile deaths, is the leading cause of death among teenagers. Continued alcohol abuse can physically change the brain, permanently impairing learning and memory. Long-term drinking is related to malnutrition, weakening of the bones, and ulcers. It increases the risk of liver failure, heart disease, and stomach cancer.

Finally, according to the myth, alcohol is the magic ingredient for social suc- 10 cess. Hundreds of TV and radio ads have echoed this message in recent years. In one commercial, for instance, an overweight man sits alone in his drab living room. He reaches into a cooler, pulls out a bottle of beer, and twists off the bottle cap. Instantly dance music erupts, and dozens of attractive young adults appear in a shower of party streamers and confetti. "Where the party begins," a voice says. The once lonely man, now a popular guy with lots of male and female friends, has found the answer to his social problems—beer.

Relationships based on alcohol are unlikely to lead to social success and true **11** friendships. Indeed, studies show that when alcohol becomes the center of a social gathering, it may lead to public drunkenness and violence. The ad's image of the man's new friends ignores an undeniable reality: that alcohol ruins—not creates—relationships. In addition to fighting and simple assault, drinking is linked to two-thirds of domestic violence incidents. Rather than leading to healthy social connections, alcohol leads to loneliness, despair, and mental illness. Over a fourth of the patients in state and county mental hospitals have alcohol problems; more than half of all violent crimes are alcohol-related; the rate of suicide among alcoholics is fifteen times higher than among the general population.

Advertisers would have us believe the myth that alcohol is part of being suc- **12** cessful, sexy, healthy, and happy; but those who have suffered from it—directly or indirectly—know otherwise. For alcohol's victims, "Here's to your health" rings with a terrible irony when it is accompanied by the clink of liquor glasses.

READING COMPREHENSION

www.mhhe.com/langan

1. The word *impairing* in "Continued alcohol abuse can physically alter the brain, permanently impairing learning and memory" (paragraph 9) means
   a. postponing.
   b. doubling.
   c. damaging.
   d. teaching.

2. The word *fosters* in "this aggressive advertising of alcohol fosters a harmful myth about drinking" (paragraph 3) means
   a. avoids.
   b. delays.
   c. promotes.
   d. discourages.

3. Which one of the following would be a good alternative title for this selection?
   a. The Taste of Success
   b. Alcohol and Your Social Life
   c. Too Much Tequila
   d. Alcohol: Image and Reality

4. Which sentence best expresses the main idea of the selection?
   a. Sports and alcohol don't mix.
   b. The media and our culture promote false images about success and happiness.
   c. The media and our culture promote false beliefs about alcohol.
   d. Liquor companies should not be allowed to use misleading ads.

5. According to the selection, drinking can
   a. actually unify a family.
   b. lower hormone levels.
   c. temporarily improve performance in sports.
   d. increase the likelihood of pregnancy.

6. *True or false?* _____ Alcohol abuse is most severe among middle-class people.

7. *True or false?* _____ The leading cause of death among teenagers is drinking and driving.

8. From the first paragraph of the essay, we can conclude that
   a. even one encounter with alcohol can lead to death.
   b. tequila is the worst type of alcohol to drink.
   c. wrestlers tend to drink more than other athletes.
   d. by the time students reach high school, peer pressure doesn't influence them.

9. *True or false?* _____ The author implies that one or two drinks a day are probably harmless.

10. The author implies that heavy drinking can lead to
    a. poor grades.
    b. getting fired.
    c. heart disease.
    d. all of the above.

STRUCTURE AND TECHNIQUE

1. What method of introduction does Dunayer use? What effect do you think she hoped to achieve with this introduction?

2. Dunayer begins her criticism of alcohol with "Part of the myth is . . ." (See the first sentence of paragraph 4.) What addition transitions does she use to introduce each of the three other parts of the myth (in the first sentences of paragraphs 6, 8, and 10)? What is gained by the use of these transitions?

3. The body of Dunayer's essay is made up of four pairs of paragraphs (paragraphs 4 and 5; 6 and 7; 8 and 9; 10 and 11). What is the relationship between the paragraphs in each pair? In which of the two paragraphs does Dunayer present her own perspective? Why do you think she puts her own perspective in that paragraph?

4. In her essay, Dunayer provides vivid descriptions of alcohol advertisements, particularly in paragraphs 4 and 6. What vivid details does she provide? How do these details support her main point?

CRITICAL READING AND DISCUSSION

1. Dunayer presents and then rebuts four "myths" about alcohol. What are these four myths? According to Dunayer, what is the reality behind each myth?

2. Dunayer concludes, "'Here's to your health' rings with a terrible irony when it is accompanied by the clink of liquor glasses" (paragraph 12). What is the "terrible irony" she refers to? How does this irony—already signaled in her essay's title—relate to her main point?

3. Do you think Dunayer's essay is one-sided or balanced? Explain. What additional points could be used to support her point or to rebut it?

4. Advertisers often create myths or use false ideas to get people to buy their products. Besides alcohol ads, what are some other examples of manipulative or deceptive advertising? Do you think advertisers should be permitted to use such tactics to sell products?

WRITING ASSIGNMENTS

www.mhhe.com/langan

Assignment 1

Describe and analyze the print advertisements for beer and liquor on the following page. Argue whether the ads are socially responsible or irresponsible in the way that they portray drinking. Your thesis might be something like one of the following examples:

In two recent ads, ad agencies and liquor companies have acted irresponsibly in their portrayal of alcohol.

In two recent ads, ad agencies and liquor companies have acted with a measure of responsibility in their portrayal of alcohol.

Alternatively, write about what you consider responsible or irresponsible advertising for some other product or service. Cigarettes, weight loss, and cosmetics are possibilities to consider.

Assignment 2

If you have a friend, relative, or classmate who drinks a lot, write a letter warning him or her about the dangers of alcohol. If appropriate, use information from Dunayer's essay. Remember that since your purpose is to get someone you care about to control or break a dangerous habit, you should make your writing very personal. Don't bother explaining how alcoholism affects people in general. Instead, focus directly on what you see it doing to your reader.

Divide your argument into at least three supporting paragraphs. You might, for instance, talk about how your reader is jeopardizing his or her relationship with three of the following: family, friends, boss and coworkers, and instructors and classmates.

Assignment 3

Dunayer describes how alcohol advertisements promote false beliefs, such as the idea that alcohol will make you successful. Imagine that you work for a public service ad agency given the job of presenting the negative side of alcohol. What images would you choose to include in your ads?

Write a report to your boss in which you propose in detail three antialcohol ads. Choose from among the following:

Ad counteracting the idea that alcohol leads to success

Ad counteracting the idea that alcohol is sexy

Ad counteracting the idea that alcohol goes well with athletics

Ad counteracting the idea that alcohol makes for happy families

Sleeping Your Way to the Top

Sora Song

PREVIEW

Are you starving? Not for food; for sleep. If you're like many Americans, you've been sleep deprived so long you no longer know how tired you are. Maybe you even take pride in being able to "get by" on little sleep. But as Sora Song explains in this selection, sleep is not a luxury you can afford to be without.

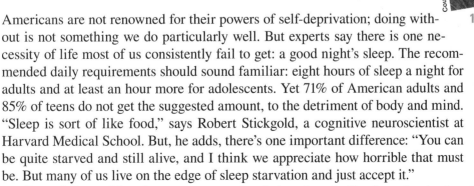

Courtesy of Sora Song

Americans are not renowned for their powers of self-deprivation; doing without is not something we do particularly well. But experts say there is one necessity of life most of us consistently fail to get: a good night's sleep. The recommended daily requirements should sound familiar: eight hours of sleep a night for adults and at least an hour more for adolescents. Yet 71% of American adults and 85% of teens do not get the suggested amount, to the detriment of body and mind. "Sleep is sort of like food," says Robert Stickgold, a cognitive neuroscientist at Harvard Medical School. But, he adds, there's one important difference: "You can be quite starved and still alive, and I think we appreciate how horrible that must be. But many of us live on the edge of sleep starvation and just accept it." 1

Part of the problem is we are so used to being chronically sleep deprived— and have become so adept at coping with that condition—that we no longer notice how exhausted we really are. In 2003, sleep expert David Dinges and colleagues 2 at the University of Pennsylvania School of Medicine tested the effects of restricting slumber to eight, six, or four hours a night for two weeks. During the first few days, subjects sleeping less than eight hours admitted to being fatigued and lacking alertness. But by Day 4, most people had adapted to their new baseline drowsiness and reported feeling fine—even as their cognitive performance continued to plummet.

Over time, the experiment's sleep-restricted subjects became so impaired that 3 they had difficulty concentrating on even the simplest tasks, like pushing a button in response to a light. "The human brain is only capable of about 16 hours of wakefulness [a day]," says Dinges. "When you get beyond that, it can't function as efficiently, as accurately or as well."

In the real world, people overcome their somnolence—at least temporarily— 4 by drinking coffee, taking a walk around the block or chatting with office mates. But then they find themselves nodding off in meetings or, worse, behind the wheel. Those short snatches of unconsciousness are what researchers call microsleep, a sure sign of sleep deprivation. "If people are falling asleep because 'the room was hot' or 'the meeting was boring,' that's not coping with sleep loss. I would argue that they're eroding their productive capability," says Dinges.

What most people don't realize is that the purpose of sleep may be more to rest 5 the mind than to rest the body. Indeed, most of the benefits of eight hours' sleep seem to accrue to the brain: sleep helps consolidate memory, improve judgment, promote learning and concentration, boost mood, speed reaction time and sharpen problem solving and accuracy. According to Sonia Ancoli-Israel, a psychologist at the University of California at San Diego who has done extensive studies in the aging population, lack of sleep may even mimic the symptoms of dementia. In recent preliminary findings, she was able to improve cognitive function in patients with mild to moderate Alzheimer's simply by treating their underlying sleep disorder. "The need for sleep does not change a lot with age," says Ancoli-Israel, but often because of disruptive illnesses and the medications used to treat them, "the ability to sleep does."

If you're one of the otherwise healthy yet perpetually underrested, there's 6 plenty you can do to pay back your sleep debt. For starters, you can catch up on lost time. Take your mom's advice, and get to bed early. Turn off the TV half an hour sooner than usual. If you can't manage to snooze longer at night, try to squeeze in a midday nap. The best time for a siesta is between noon and 3 p.m., for about 30 to 60 minutes, according to Timothy Roehrs, director of research at the Sleep Disorders and Research Center at Henry Ford Hospital in Detroit. He advises against oversleeping on weekend mornings to make up for a workweek of deprivation; later rising can disrupt your circadian rhythm, making it even harder later to get a full night's rest.

According to Dinges' analysis of data from the 2003 American Time Use Sur- 7 vey, the most common reason we shortchange ourselves on sleep is work. (The second biggest reason, surprisingly, is that we spend too much time driving around in our cars.) But consider that in giving up two hours of bedtime to do more work, you're losing a quarter of your recommended nightly dose and gaining just 12% more time during the day. What if you could be 12% more productive instead? "You have to realize that if you get a good night's sleep, you will actually be more efficient and get more done the next day. The more you give up on sleep, the harder it is to be productive," says Ancoli-Israel. "What is it going to be?"

If mental sharpness is your goal, the answer is clear: stop depriving yourself, 8 and get a good night's sleep.

READING COMPREHENSION

www.mhhe.com/langan

1. The word *plummet* in "even as their cognitive performance continued to plummet" (paragraph 2) means
   a. increase.
   b. decline.
   c. remain the same.
   d. change.

2. The word *accrue* in "Indeed, most of the benefits of eight hours' sleep seem to accrue to the brain" (paragraph 5) means
   a. fade away.
   b. accumulate.
   c. disappear.
   d. shift.

3. Which of the following would be a good alternative title for this selection?
   a. Microsleep Is the Answer
   b. New Sleep Disorders
   c. Resting Your Mind
   d. Resting Your Body

4. Which sentence best expresses the main idea of the selection?
   a. Many people are sleep deprived and do not even know it.
   b. Sleep deprivation impairs a person's concentration.
   c. Most people fail to realize that adequate sleep improves mental sharpness.
   d. Chronic sleep deprivation provokes dementia and Alzheimer's.

5. According to sleep expert David Dinges, the human brain is only capable of _____ hours of wakefulness a day.
   a. 6
   b. 10
   c. 16
   d. 26

6. According to psychologist Sonia Ancoli-Israel,
   a. sleep deprivation may mimic the symptoms of dementia.
   b. the need for sleep changes with a person's age.
   c. the ability to sleep is not disrupted by medications.
   d. people with Alzheimer's cannot be treated for sleep disorders.

7. *True or false?* _____ Work is the most common reason people short-change themselves on sleep.

8. *True or false?* _____ Oversleeping can disrupt a person's circadian rhythm, making it more difficult to get a full night's sleep.

9. In paragraph 4, the author suggests that a person who is sleep deprived
   a. can drink coffee or take a walk to maintain productivity.
   b. can engage in microsleep to maintain productivity.
   c. cannot effectively cope with sleep loss for very long.
   d. can effectively cope with sleep loss over a long period.

10. Based on paragraph 7, the author assumes that
    a. people value productivity.
    b. people want to be more efficient.
    c. people spend a lot of time commuting to and from work.
    d. people need a convincing reason to sleep longer.

STRUCTURE AND TECHNIQUE

1. The author uses the second-person approach, which allows her to speak directly to her readers using the pronoun *you*. Why do you think she uses this particular approach? Do you think this approach is effective?

2. What combination of methods—broad statement, contrast, relevance, anecdote, questions, and quotation—does the author use in her introduction? Why do you think she chose this way to begin her essay?

3. Which patterns of development does the author use? Explain.

4. The author provides a number of words and phrases to describe *sleep deprivation*. List at least three of these synonyms.

CRITICAL READING AND DISCUSSION

1. According to the author, many of us do not realize how exhausted we really are. Why do you think people accept sleep starvation but not food starvation?

2. The study at the University of Pennsylvania School of Medicine indicated that sleep-deprived people adapted to less sleep and reported feeling fine. Why do you think these sleep-deprived people did not notice changes in their performance?

3. The author argues: "If mental sharpness is your goal, the answer is clear: stop depriving yourself, and get a good night's sleep" (paragraph 8). Do you agree with this statement? If your answer is yes, why are so many Americans sleep deprived?

4. Are you getting at least eight hours of sleep each night? If not, do you believe that you can "pay back your sleep debt" (paragraph 6)?

WRITING ASSIGNMENTS

www.mhhe.com/langan

Assignment 1

According to Sora Song, "If you're one of the otherwise healthy yet perpetually underrested, there's plenty you can do to pay back your sleep debt" (paragraph 6). Write a process essay that explains how a person can get a good night's sleep. First, brainstorm three or four problems why someone might not get enough sleep. Then, under each area you have listed, jot down some helpful hints and techniques for overcoming these problems.

Each supporting paragraph in this essay would discuss specific techniques for dealing with lack of sleep. Be sure that the advice you give is detailed and specific enough to really help a person in such a situation. You may find it helpful to look over Song's essay.

Assignment 2

According to the 2003 American Time Use Survey, the most common reason Americans go without sleep is work (paragraph 7). Write an essay in which you describe how your sleep is or is not affected by your work. For one week, you may want to keep track of the hours that you sleep and the hours that you work to determine if you sacrifice your sleep to work. You can use several patterns of development, such as exemplification, compare or contrast, or cause and effect.

Assignment 3

As Song discovered while doing her research, 71% of American adults and 85% of teens do not get a good night's sleep (paragraph 1). Do children get the recommended daily requirement? Among adults, which age group is most sleep deprived? Using the Internet, find out what some experts have to say about this matter. Then write an essay about your findings. To access the Internet, use the very helpful search engine Google (*www.google.com*) and refer to Chapter 21, "Using the Library and the Internet."

How to Make It in College, Now That You're Here

Brian O'Keeney

PREVIEW

The author of this selection presents a compact guide to being a successful student. He will show you how to pass tests, how to avoid becoming a student zombie, how to find time to fit in everything you want to do, and how to deal with personal problems while keeping up with your studies. These and other helpful tips have been culled from the author's own experience and his candid interviews with fellow students.

Today is your first day on campus. You were a high school senior three months 1 ago. Or maybe you've been at home with your children for the last ten years. Or maybe you work full time and you're coming to school to start the process that leads to a better job. Whatever your background is, you're probably not too concerned today with staying in college. After all, you just got over the hurdle (and the paperwork) of applying to this place and organizing your life so that you could attend. And today, you're confused and tired. Everything is a hassle, from finding the classrooms to standing in line at the bookstore. But read my advice anyway. And if you don't read it today, clip and save this article. You might want to look at it a little further down the road.

By the way, if this isn't your very first day, don't skip this article. Maybe you 2 haven't been doing as well in your studies as you'd hoped. Or perhaps you've had problems juggling your work schedule, your class schedule, and your social life. If so, read on. You're about to get the inside story on making it in college. On the basis of my own experience as a final-year student, and after dozens of interviews with successful students, I've worked out a no-fail system for coping with college. These are the inside tips every students needs to do well in school. I've put myself in your place, and I'm going to answer the questions that will cross (or have already crossed) your mind during your stay here.

What's the Secret of Getting Good Grades?

It all comes down to getting those grades, doesn't it? After all, you came here 3 for some reason, and you're going to need passing grades to get the credits or degree you want. Many of us never did much studying in high school; most of the learning we did took place in the classroom. College, however, is a lot different. You're really on your own when it comes to passing courses. In fact, sometimes you'll feel as if nobody cares if you make it or not. Therefore, you've got to figure out a study system that gets results. Sooner or later, you'll be alone with those books. After that, you'll be sitting in a classroom with an exam sheet on your desk. Whether you stare at that exam with a queasy stomach or whip through it fairly confidently depends on your study techniques. Most of the successful students I talked to agreed that the following eight study tips deliver solid results.

1. Set Up a Study Place.

Those students you see "studying" in the cafeteria 4 or game room aren't learning much. You just can't learn when you're distracted by people and noise. Even the library can be a bad place to study if you constantly find yourself watching the clouds outside or the students walking through the stacks. It takes guts to sit, alone, in a quiet place in order to study. But you have to do it. Find a room at home or a spot in the library that's relatively quiet—and boring. When you sit there, you won't have much to do except study.

2. Get into a Study Frame of Mind.

When you sit down, do it with the at- 5 titude that you're going to get this studying done. You're not going to doodle in your notebook or make a list for the supermarket. Decide that you are going to study and learn *now,* so that you can move on to more interesting things as soon as possible.

3. Give Yourself Rewards.

If you sweat out a block of study time, and do 6 a good job on it, treat yourself. You deserve it. You can "psych" yourself up for studying by promising to reward yourself afterward. A present for yourself can be anything from a favorite TV show to a relaxing bath to a dish of double chocolate ice cream.

4. Skim the Textbook First.

Lots of students sit down with an assignment 7 like "Read chapter five, pages 125–150" and do just that. They turn to page 125 and start to read. After a while, they find that they have no idea what they just read. For the last ten minutes, they've been thinking about their five-year-old or what they're going to eat for dinner. Eventually, they plod through all the pages but don't remember much afterward.

In order to prevent this problem, skim the textbook chapter first. This means: 8 look at the title, the subtitles, the headings, the pictures, the first and last paragraphs. Try to find out what the person who wrote the book had in mind when he or she organized the chapter. What was important enough to set off as a title or in bold type? After skimming, you should be able to explain to yourself what the main points of the chapter are. Unless you're the kind of person who would step into an empty elevator shaft without looking first, you'll soon discover the value of skimming.

5. Take Notes on What You're Studying.   This sounds like a hassle, but it 9
works. Go back over the material after you've read it, and jot down key words and
phrases in the margins. When you review the chapter for a test, you'll have handy
little things like "definition of rationalization" or "example of assimilation" in the
margins. If the material is especially tough, organize a separate sheet of notes.
Write down definitions, examples, lists, and main ideas. The idea is to have a single sheet that boils the entire chapter down to a digestible lump.

6. Review After You've Read and Taken Notes.   Some people swear 10
that talking to yourself works. Tell yourself about the most important points in the
chapter. Once you've said them out loud, they seem to stick better in your mind. If
you can't talk to yourself about the material after reading it, that's a sure sign you
don't really know it.

7. Give Up.   This may sound contradictory, but give up when you've had 11
enough. You should try to make it through at least an hour, though. Ten minutes
here and there are useless. When your head starts to pound and your eyes develop
spidery red lines, quit. You won't do much learning when you're exhausted.

8. Take a College Skills Course If You Need It.   Don't hesitate or feel 12
embarrassed about enrolling in a study skills course. Many students say they
wouldn't have made it without one.

How Can I Keep Up with All My Responsibilities Without Going Crazy?

You've got a class schedule. You're supposed to study. You've got a family. You've 13
got a husband, wife, boyfriend, girlfriend, child. You've got a job. How are you
possibly going to cover all the bases in your life and maintain your sanity? This
is one of the toughest problems students face. Even if they start the semester with
the best of intentions, they eventually find themselves tearing their hair out trying
to do everything they're supposed to do. Believe it or not, though, it is possible to
meet all your responsibilities. And you don't have to turn into a hermit or give up
your loved ones to do it.

The secret here is to organize your time. But don't just sit around half the 14
semester planning to get everything together soon. Before you know it, you'll be
confronted with midterms, papers, family, and work all at once. Don't let yourself
reach that breaking point. Instead, try these three tactics.

1. Monthly Calendar.   Get one of those calendars with big blocks around 15
the dates. Give yourself an overview of the whole term by marking down the due
dates for papers and projects. Circle test and exam days. This way those days don't
sneak up on you unexpectedly.

2. Study Schedule.

Sit down during the first few days of this semester and 16 make up a sheet listing the days and hours of the week. Fill in your work and class hours first. Then try to block out some study hours. It's better to study a little every day than to create a huge once-or-twice-a-week marathon session. Schedule study hours for your hardest classes for the times when you feel most energetic. For example, I battled my tax law textbook in the mornings; when I looked at it after 7:00 p.m., I might as well have been reading Chinese. The usual proportion, by the way, is one hour of study time for every class hour.

In case you're one of those people who get carried away, remember to leave 17 blocks of free time, too. You won't be any good to yourself or anyone else if you don't relax and pack in the studying once in a while.

3. "To Do" List.

This is the secret that, more than any other, got me through 18 college. Once a week (or every day if you want to), write a list of what you have to do. Write down everything from "write English paper" to "buy cold cuts for lunch." The best thing about a "to do" list is that it seems to tame all those stray "I have to" thoughts that nag at your mind. Just making the list seems to make the tasks "doable." After you finish something on the list, cross it off. Don't be compulsive about finishing everything; you're not Superman or Wonder Woman. Get the important things done first. The secondary things you don't finish can simply be moved to your next "to do" list.

What Can I Do If Personal Problems Get in the Way of My Studies?

One student, Roger, told me this story: 19

> Everything was going OK for me until the middle of the spring semester. I went through a terrible time when I broke up with my girlfriend and started seeing her best friend. I was trying to deal with my ex-girlfriend's hurt and anger, my new girlfriend's guilt, and my own worries and anxieties at the same time. In addition to this, my mother was sick and on a medication that made her really irritable. I hated to go home because the atmosphere was so uncomfortable. Soon, I started missing classes because I couldn't deal with the academic pressures as well as my own personal problems. It seemed easier to hang around my girlfriend's apartment than to face all my problems at home and at school.

Another student, Marian, told me: 20

> I'd been married for eight years and the relationship wasn't going too well. I saw the handwriting on the wall, and I decided to prepare for the future. I enrolled in college, because I knew I'd need a decent job to support myself. Well, my husband had a fit because I was going to school. We were arguing a

lot anyway, and he made it almost impossible for me to study at home. I think he was angry and almost jealous because I was drawing away from him. It got so bad that I thought about quitting college for a while. I wasn't getting any support at home, and it was just too hard to go on.

Personal troubles like these are overwhelming when you're going through **21** them. School seems like the least important thing in your life. The two students above are perfect examples of this. But if you think about it, quitting or failing school would be the worst thing for these two students. Roger's problems, at least with his girlfriends, would simmer down eventually, and then he'd regret having left school. Marian had to finish college if she wanted to be able to live independently. Sometimes, you've just got to hang tough.

But what do you do while you're trying to live through a lousy time? First of **22** all, do something difficult. Ask yourself, honestly, if you're exaggerating small problems as an excuse to avoid classes and studying. It takes strength to admit this, but there's no sense in kidding yourself. If your problems are serious, and real, try to make some human contacts at school. Lots of students hide inside a miserable shell made of their own troubles and feel isolated and lonely. Believe me, there are plenty of students with problems. Not everyone is getting A's and having a fabulous social and home life at the same time. As you go through the term, you'll pick up some vibrations about the students in your classes. Perhaps someone strikes you as a compatible person. Why not speak to that person after class? Share a cup of coffee in the cafeteria or walk to the parking lot together. You're not looking for a best friend or the love of your life. You just want to build a little network of support for yourself. Sharing your difficulties, questions, and complaints with a friendly person on campus can make a world of difference in how you feel.

Finally, if your problems are overwhelming, get some professional help. Why **23** do you think colleges spend countless dollars on counseling departments and campus psychiatric services? More than ever, students all over the country are taking advantage of the help offered by support groups and therapy sessions. There's no shame attached to asking for help, either; in fact, almost 40 percent of college students (according to one survey) will use counseling services during their time in school. Just walk into a student center or counseling office and ask for an appointment. You wouldn't think twice about asking a dentist to help you get rid of your toothache. Counselors are paid—and want—to help you with your problems.

Why Do Some People Make It and Some Drop Out?

Anyone who spends at least one semester in college notices that some students **24** give up on their classes. The person who sits behind you in accounting, for example, begins to miss a lot of class meetings and eventually vanishes. Or another student comes to class without the assignment, doodles in a notebook during the lecture, and leaves during the break. What's the difference between students like this and the ones who succeed in school? My survey may be nonscientific, but everyone I asked said the same thing: attitude. A positive attitude is the key to everything else—good study habits, smart time scheduling, and coping with personal difficulties.

What does "a positive attitude" mean? Well, for one thing, it means avoiding 25 the zombie syndrome. It means not only showing up for your classes, but also doing something while you're there. Really listen. Take notes. Ask a question if you want to. Don't just walk into a class, put your mind in neutral, and drift away to never-never land.

Having a positive attitude goes deeper than this, though. It means being ma- 26 ture about college as an institution. Too many students approach college classes like six-year-olds who expect first grade to be as much fun as *Sesame Street*. First grade, as we all know, isn't as much fun as *Sesame Street*. And college classes can sometimes be downright dull. If you let a boring class discourage you so much that you want to leave school, you'll lose in the long run. Look at your priorities. You want a degree, or a certificate, or a career. If you have to, you can make it through a less-than-interesting class in order to achieve what you want. Get whatever you can out of every class. But if you simply can't stand a certain class, be determined to fulfill its requirements and be done with it once and for all.

After the initial high of starting school, you have to settle in for the long haul. 27 If you follow the advice here, you'll be prepared to face the academic crunch. You'll also live through the semester without giving up your family, your job, or *Monday Night Football*. Finally, going to college can be an exciting time. You do learn. And when you learn things, the world becomes a more interesting place.

READING COMPREHENSION

www.mhhe.com/langan

1. The word *queasy* in "with a queasy stomach" (paragraph 3) means
   a. strong.
   b. healthy.
   c. full.
   d. nervous.

2. The word *tactics* in "try these three tactics" (paragraph 14) means
   a. proofs.
   b. problems.
   c. methods.
   d. questions.

3. Which of the following would be a good alternative title for this selection?
   a. Your First Day on Campus
   b. Coping with College
   c. How to Budget Your Time
   d. The Benefits of College Skills Courses

4. Which sentence expresses the main idea of the selection?
   a. In high school, most of us did little homework.
   b. You should give yourself rewards for studying well.
   c. Sometimes personal problems interfere with studying.
   d. You can succeed in college by following certain guidelines.

5. According to the author, "making it" in college means
   a. studying whenever you have any free time.
   b. getting a degree by barely passing your courses.
   c. quitting school until you solve your personal problems.
   d. getting good grades without making your life miserable.

6. If your personal problems seem overwhelming, you should
   a. drop out for a while.
   b. exaggerate them to teachers.
   c. avoid talking about them.
   d. get help from a professional.

7. Which of the following is *not* described by the author as a means of time control?
   a. Monthly calendar
   b. To-do list
   c. Study schedule
   d. Flexible job hours

8. We can infer that the writer of this essay
   a. cares about college students and their success.
   b. dropped out of college.
   c. is very disorganized.
   d. is an A student.

9. From the selection we can conclude that
   a. college textbooks are very expensive.
   b. it is a good practice to write notes in your textbook.
   c. taking notes on your reading takes too much time.
   d. a student should never mark up an expensive book.

10. The author implies that

    a. fewer people than before are attending college.

    b. most college students experience no problems during their first year.

    c. all college students experience overwhelming problems.

    d. coping with college is difficult.

STRUCTURE AND TECHNIQUE

1. O'Keeney uses a highly structured format in his essay. What are some of the features of this format? Why do you think O'Keeney structured his essay in this way?

2. Does the author clearly state his thesis? If so, where is it stated, and how?

3. What method of introduction does the author use in the section on personal problems (starting with paragraph 19)? What is the value of using this method?

4. Throughout his essay, O'Keeney addresses his audience in the second person—using the word *you*. How does such a technique advance his main point?

CRITICAL READING AND DISCUSSION

1. What, according to O'Keeney, is the secret of getting good grades? Have you used any of O'Keeney's study methods? If so, how useful do you think they have been for you? Are there any that you haven't used but might try? Explain your answer.

2. What does O'Keeney recommend students do to manage their time and responsibilities more effectively? Which of these suggestions are you most likely to use? Which are you least likely to use? Why?

3. What is the secret the author says got him through college? What do you think is the most helpful or important suggestion the author makes in the selection? Give reasons for your choice.

4. Do you agree with the author that Roger and Marian should stay in school? Are there any situations in which it would be better for students to quit school or leave, at least temporarily? Explain, giving examples to support your answer.

WRITING ASSIGNMENTS

Assignment 1

Write a process essay similar to the one you've just read that explains how to succeed in some other field—for example, a job, a sport, marriage, child rearing. First, brainstorm three or four problem areas a newcomer to this experience might encounter. Then, under each area you have listed, jot down some helpful hints and techniques for overcoming these problems. For example, a process paper on "How to Succeed as a Waitress" might describe the following problem areas in this kind of job:

> Developing a good memory
>
> Learning to do tasks quickly
>
> Coping with troublesome customers

Each supporting paragraph in this paper would discuss specific techniques for dealing with these problems. Be sure that the advice you give is detailed and specific enough to really help a person in such a situation.

You may find it helpful to look over the process essays in Chapter 11.

Assignment 2

Write a letter to Roger or Marian, giving advice on how to deal with the personal problem mentioned in the article. You could recommend any or all of the following:

> Face the problem realistically. (By doing what?)
>
> Make other contacts at school. (How? Where?)
>
> See a counselor. (Where? What should this person be told?)
>
> Realize that the problem is not so serious. (Why not?)
>
> Ignore the problem. (How? By doing what instead?)

In your introductory paragraph, explain why you are writing the letter. Include a thesis statement that says what plan of action you are recommending. Then, in the rest of the paper, explain the plan of action in detail.

Assignment 3

Write an essay contrasting college *as you thought it would be* with college *as it is.* You can organize the essay by focusing on three specific things that are different from what you expected. Or you can cover three areas of difference. For instance, you may decide to contrast your expectations about (1) a college dorm room, (2) your roommate, and (3) dining-hall food with reality. Or you could contrast your expectations about (1) fellow students, (2) college professors, and (3) college courses with reality.

Refer to the section in Chapter 13 on methods of developing comparison or contrast essays to review point-by-point and one-side-at-a-time development. Be sure to make an outline of your essay before you begin to write.

College Lectures: Is Anybody Listening?
David Daniels

PREVIEW

College students are doodling in their notebooks or gazing off into space as their instructor lectures for fifty minutes. What is wrong with this picture? Many would say that what is wrong is the students. However, the educator and author David Daniels would say that the lecture itself is the problem. As you read this article, see if you agree with Daniels's analysis of lectures and their place in a college education.

Courtesy of David Daniels

A former teacher of mine, Robert A. Fowkes of New York University, likes to tell 1
the story of a class he took in Old Welsh while studying in Germany during the 1930s. On the first day the professor strode up to the podium, shuffled his notes, coughed, and began, *"Guten Tag, Meine Damen und Herren"* ("Good day, ladies and gentlemen"). Fowkes glanced around uneasily. He was the only student in the course.

Toward the middle of the semester, Fowkes fell ill and missed a class. When 2
he returned, the professor nodded vaguely and, to Fowkes's astonishment, began to deliver not the next lecture in the sequence but the one after. Had he, in fact, lectured to an empty hall in the absence of his solitary student? Fowkes thought it perfectly possible.

Today, American colleges and universities (originally modeled on German 3
ones) are under strong attack from many quarters. Teachers, it is charged, are not doing a good job of teaching, and students are not doing a good job of learning. American businesses and industries suffer from unenterprising, uncreative executives educated not to think for themselves but to mouth outdated truisms[1] the rest of the world has long discarded. College graduates lack both basic skills and general culture. Studies are conducted and reports are issued on the status of higher

---

[1]*truisms:* self-evident truths.

education, but any changes that result either are largely cosmetic or make a bad situation worse.

One aspect of American education too seldom challenged is the lecture system. Professors continue to lecture and students to take notes much as they did in the thirteenth century, when books were so scarce and expensive that few students could own them. The time is long overdue for us to abandon the lecture system and turn to methods that really work.

To understand the inadequacy of the present system, it is enough to follow a single imaginary first-year student—let's call her Mary—through a term of lectures on, say, introductory psychology (although any other subject would do as well). She arrives on the first day and looks around the huge lecture hall, taken a little aback to see how large the class is. Once the hundred or more students enrolled in the course discover that the professor never takes attendance (how can he?—calling the role would take far too much time), the class shrinks to a less imposing size.

Some days Mary sits in the front row, from where she can watch the professor read from a stack of yellowed notes that seem nearly as old as he is. She is bored by the lectures, and so are most of the other students, to judge by the way they are nodding off or doodling in their notebooks. Gradually she realizes the professor is as bored as his audience. At the end of each lecture he asks, "Are there any questions?" in a tone of voice that makes it plain he would much rather there weren't. He needn't worry—the students are as relieved as he is that the class is over.

Mary knows very well she should read an assignment before every lecture. However, as the professor gives no quizzes and asks no questions, she soon realizes she needn't prepare. At the end of the term she catches up by skimming her notes and memorizing a list of facts and dates. After the final exam, she promptly forgets much of what she has memorized. Some of her fellow students, disappointed at the impersonality of it all, drop out of college altogether. Others, like Mary, stick it out, grow resigned to the system and await better days when, as juniors and seniors, they will attend smaller classes and at last get the kind of personal attention real learning requires.

I admit this picture is overdrawn—most universities supplement lecture courses with discussion groups, usually led by graduate students; and some classes, such as first-year English, are always relatively small. Nevertheless, far too many courses rely principally or entirely on lectures, an arrangement much loved by faculty and administrators but scarcely designed to benefit the students.

One problem with lectures is that listening intelligently is hard work. Reading the same material in a textbook is a more efficient way to learn because students can proceed as slowly as they need to until the subject matter becomes clear to them. Even simply paying attention is very difficult; people can listen at a rate of four hundred to six hundred words a minute, while the most impassioned[2] pro-

---

[2]*impassioned:* enthusiastic.

fessor talks at scarcely a third of that speed. This time lag between speech and comprehension leads to daydreaming. Many students believe years of watching television have sabotaged their attention span, but their real problem is that listening attentively is much harder than they think.

Worse still, attending lectures is passive learning, at least for inexperienced 10 listeners. Active learning, in which students write essays or perform experiments and then have their work evaluated by an instructor, is far more beneficial for those who have not yet fully learned how to learn. While it's true that techniques of active listening, such as trying to anticipate the speaker's next point or taking notes selectively, can enhance the value of a lecture, few students possess such skills at the beginning of their college careers. More commonly, students try to write everything down and even bring tape recorders to class in a clumsy effort to capture every word.

Students need to question their professors and to have their ideas taken seri- 11 ously. Only then will they develop the analytical skills required to think intelligently and creatively. Most students learn best by engaging in frequent and even heated debate, not by scribbling down a professor's often unsatisfactory summary of complicated issues. They need small discussion classes that demand the common labors of teacher and students rather than classes in which one person, however learned, propounds his or her own ideas.

The lecture system ultimately harms professors as well. It reduces feedback 12 to a minimum, so that the lecturer can neither judge how well students understand the material nor benefit from their questions or comments. Questions that require the speaker to clarify obscure points and comments that challenge sloppily constructed arguments are indispensable to scholarship. Without them, the liveliest mind can atrophy. Undergraduates may not be able to make telling contributions very often, but lecturing insulates a professor even from the beginner's naive question that could have triggered a fruitful line of thought.

If lectures make so little sense, why have they been allowed to continue? Ad- 13 ministrators love them, of course. They can cram far more students into a lecture hall than into a discussion class, and for many administrators that is almost the end of the story. But the truth is that faculty members, and even students, conspire with them to keep the lecture system alive and well. Lectures are easier on everyone than debates. Professors can pretend to teach by lecturing just as students can pretend to learn by attending lectures, with no one the wiser, including the participants. Moreover, if lectures afford some students an opportunity to sit back and let the professor run the show, they offer some professors an irresistible forum for showing off. In a classroom where everyone contributes, students are less able to hide and professors less tempted to engage in intellectual exhibitionism.

Smaller classes in which students are required to involve themselves in dis- 14 cussion put an end to students' passivity. Students become actively involved when forced to question their own ideas as well as their instructor's. Their listening skills improve dramatically in the excitement of intellectual give-and-take with their instructors and fellow students. Such interchanges help professors do their job better because they allow them to discover who knows what—before final exams, not after. When exams are given in this type of course, they can require analysis and synthesis from the students, not empty memorization. Classes like this require energy, imagination, and commitment from professors, all of which can be exhausting. But they compel students to share responsibility for their own intellectual growth.

Lectures will never entirely disappear from the university scene both because   15 they seem to be economically necessary and because they spring from a long tradition in a setting that values tradition for its own sake. But the lectures too frequently come at the wrong end of the students' educational careers—during the first two years, when they most need close, even individual, instruction. If lecture classes were restricted to junior and senior undergraduates and to graduate students, who are less in need of scholarly nurturing and more able to prepare work on their own, they would be far less destructive of students' interests and enthusiasms than the present system. After all, students must learn to listen before they can listen to learn.

READING COMPREHENSION

1. The word *enhance* in "techniques of active listening . . . can enhance the value of a lecture" (paragraph 10) means
   a. ruin.
   b. ignore.
   c. increase.
   d. claim.

2. The word *atrophy* in "Without [questions and comments], the liveliest mind can atrophy" (paragraph 12) means
   a. waste away.
   b. be unchanged.
   c. compete.
   d. strengthen.

3. Which of the following would be a good alternative title for this selection?
   a. How to Benefit from Lecture Classes
   b. The Necessity of Classroom Lecturing
   c. Problems with Lecture Classes
   d. College Lectures: An Inspirational Tradition

4. Which sentence best expresses the main idea of the selection?
   a. American colleges and universities are being attacked from many sides.
   b. Colleges and universities should offer interactive, not lecture, classes to first-year and second-year students.
   c. College graduates lack basic skills and general culture.
   d. American colleges and universities are modeled on German ones.

5. According to the author, the lecture system
   a. encourages efficient learning.
   b. encourages students to ask questions.
   c. helps professors teach better.
   d. discourages students' attendance and preparation.

6. An example of passive learning is
   a. attending lectures.
   b. writing essays.
   c. doing experiments.
   d. debating a point.

7. To develop their thinking skills, students do not need to
   a. bring tape recorders to class.
   b. question professors.
   c. debate.
   d. attend small discussion classes.

8. The author implies that large lecture classes
   a. require students to have well-developed listening skills.
   b. encourage participation.
   c. are more harmful for juniors and seniors than for first-year students.
   d. are a modern invention.

9. *True or false?* _____ Daniels suggests that small classes demand greater effort from both faculty and students.

10. The author implies that administrators love lectures because
    a. students learn better in lectures.
    b. professors teach better through lecturing.
    c. schools make more money on lecture classes.
    d. professors can show off in lectures.

STRUCTURE AND TECHNIQUE

1. Daniels begins his essay with an anecdote about a former teacher of his. How does this introduction relate to his thesis?

2. Does Daniels directly state his thesis? If so, where is it stated?

3. In describing Mary's classroom experience (paragraphs 5–7), Daniels provides numerous details. What are some of these details? How do they relate to the essay's main idea?

4. Daniels's essay is an argument against the lecture system of education. What argumentation techniques does he employ? (See pages 350–354 for information on argumentation.)

CRITICAL READING AND DISCUSSION

1. Daniels states that "listening intelligently is hard work" (paragraph 9) and "[a]ctive learning . . . is far more beneficial for those who have not yet fully learned how to learn" (paragraph 10). Why might Daniels feel that listening is so hard? And why does he feel that active learning is so good?

2. In paragraph 8, Daniels acknowledges that he has exaggerated Mary's negative classroom experience, saying, "I admit this picture is overdrawn." Does this admission strengthen or weaken his argument? Explain.

3. According to Daniels, the lecture system harms professors by reducing feedback from students to a minimum. What is useful about feedback from students?

4. How do your experiences in both lecture classes and smaller classes compare with Daniels's descriptions? As a student, which type of class do you prefer? Why? If you were an instructor, which type of class would you prefer to teach? Why?

WRITING ASSIGNMENTS

www.mhhe.com/langan

Assignment 1

Write an essay in which you contrast a lecture class with a smaller, more interactive class. First make a list of the differences between the two classes. Following are some possible areas of difference you might consider:

Interest level

Demands on students

Opportunities for asking questions

Opportunities for discussions

Quality of feedback from the instructor

Choose three of the differences you found, and then decide which class you learned more in. You will then have the basis for a thesis statement and three supporting topic sentences. An example of a thesis statement for this essay is

Because of the different approaches to students' questions, class discussion, and feedback from the instructor in grading papers, I learned a lot more in my first-year English class than in my business lecture class.

That thesis statement could be shortened to

I learned a lot more in my first-year English class than in my business lecture class.

The three supporting points for this thesis statement are about

Different approaches to students' questions

Class discussion

Personal feedback on assignments

Change each of the points listed above into a sentence, and you have your three topic sentences. A topic sentence based on the last point above might be "While my English instructor gave me a lot of useful feedback on my assignments, my business instructor put only a grade on papers." Use specific details from your experience to develop your supporting paragraphs.

Here is another possible thesis for this assignment:

While my business principles class was a large lecture class, I learned a lot more in it than in my American literature class because of the quality of the instructor's presentations, time set aside for attention to individual students, and use of audiovisual and computer materials.

If you haven't yet taken any lecture classes, compare any two classes in college or high school.

Assignment 2

In this selection, Daniels has given some disadvantages of lectures. Write an essay on the advantages of lectures. To support your points, use examples from your personal experience and the experiences of others. Begin by jotting down a list of advantages. Then choose the advantages you have the most to say about and develop those in your essay.

Assignment 3

Which teachers or instructors have you had who were not in a rut, who conducted classes that made you glad to learn? Write a description of your idea of a very good teacher or instructor. Your description may be of someone who actually taught you, or it may be of a fictional person who combines all the traits you have enjoyed (or missed) in your teachers and instructors through the years. Be sure to include plenty of specific examples of classroom activities and their effects on students. Here is a list of various aspects of teaching that you may wish to use in your description:

Mastery of subject matter

Ability to excite students about subject

Types of activities used

Relationships with students

Feedback to students

Homework and tests

Seven Ways to Keep the Peace at Home

Daniel A. Sugarman

Courtesy of Daniel A. Sugarman

PREVIEW

We like to think of our homes as havens of peace and security, but they more often resemble battlegrounds. Living together in close quarters, family members must cope with each other's moods, problems, worries, and pressures. The author of this selection presents several helpful suggestions for defusing tense situations in the home. You may discover the underlying reasons for some of your own recurring family quarrels.

Not long ago, the parents of a seven-year-old girl consulted me because their   1
daughter was on her way to becoming a full-fledged hypochondriac.[1] The girl's father was a physician, and both parents were busy, involved people. During an early session with the family, the reasons behind the girl's problems became clear. Dad arrived late and was preoccupied and worried. He started to speak to me when

---

[1]*hypochondriac:* someone who is actually healthy but is convinced he or she is sick.

his daughter interrupted: "My throat hurts a lot. I feel sick." Automatically he produced a tongue depressor and looked into her throat. As he reassured her about her health, I realized the girl's complaints represented the only way that she could engage her father's full attention.

When I pointed out that it was *he* who was unconsciously turning his daughter 2 into a chronic complainer, the father altered his behavior. He began giving her more attention when she was *not* complaining about her health, and treating her physical complaints very lightly when they did occur. The girl began to improve. Soon, she hardly complained about her health at all.

In the course of my clinical practice, I have seen hundreds of families in 3 conflict, and I am astounded at how frequently families unwittingly perpetuate tension-causing behavior. Explosions just seem to happen again and again, until family members can be helped to understand their interactions and learn to meet their mutual needs in less destructive ways.

Although conflicts may be so ingrained for some families that outside profes- 4 sional help is needed, certain principles of Family First Aid can go a long way in reducing friction for most families. Here are seven steps that I have found to be helpful for diminishing family tension.

1. Give Up the Myth of the Perfect Family

A couple of years ago, an unhappy teenager came to my office with her family 5 and announced, "Well, here we are! The *Shady,* not the *Brady,* Bunch!" I find that many people, like this girl, resent their own families for not living up to some ro-manticized notion of family life that can be found only on television. In contrast to TV, real families go through periods of crisis that strain everyone's nerves. During these trying times, most families' feelings and actions bear little resemblance to the sanitized, prepackaged half-hour comedy routines on TV.

Some months ago, for example, Grace and Lew Martin[2] brought their sixteen- 6 year-old son to me. Frank was an angry, sullen boy who had been doing poorly in school and been caught smoking pot there. When Frank took his father's car out and was caught speeding at ninety miles per hour, his parents insisted he come for treatment.

During our first session, it became evident that Frank's problem was certainly 7 not the only one in the family. Mr. Martin had been consistently passed over for promotion at work. Mrs. Martin worked long hours trying to sell real estate, but because of high mortgage rates she was having little success. Frank's fourteen-year-old sister had fractured her leg the previous winter, and several operations had been required before it was set properly. Mr. Martin had become angry and withdrawn, and he was criticizing Mrs. Martin's ability to manage the household. She, in turn, spent more time away from home and began to drink heavily. Family

---

[2]All names in this article have been changed to protect patients' privacy.

fights became more and more frequent. Everyone tried to bolster his or her own tottering sense of self-esteem by shattering the self-esteem of a loved one.

As I listened to this troubled family, I became aware that it wasn't the real problems that were about to do them in. It was their self-hate. Mr. Martin was furious at himself for not having gotten his promotion and because his wife had to work. Mrs. Martin was furious with herself because she wasn't selling houses and because she couldn't stay at home and care for her daughter. Frank was angry at them all, and so guilty about his angry feelings that I suspect his ninety-mile-per-hour ride partially represented an attempt at self-execution. 8

Once the Martin family understood how they were punishing themselves for not being a perfect family, they began to show compassion toward themselves. They rapidly began to solve the real problems. 9

The idea of the typical happy family is becoming an anachronism. As the national divorce rate approaches 50 percent, increasing numbers of people will live in single-parent families. Should these people hate themselves because they aren't part of a typical family? Unfortunately, too many do just that. As high interest rates nibble away at the American dream of owning one's own home, should people hate themselves because they don't have a "typical" single-family dwelling—or because everyone in the family has to work to support this home? Unfortunately, too many do that, too. 10

I often wonder if the perfect American family ever did exist. If it did, I haven't met it often in the past few years. As a matter of fact, research suggests that growing up in a perfectly happy family is not as important as psychologists once thought. In one continuing study of 248 children, Jean Macfarlane at the University of California Institute of Human Development has found that children who grew up in troubled homes do *not* necessarily grow up to be troubled adults. Children who grew up in happy homes are *not* necessarily better adjusted by the age of thirty. 11

When you give up the myth of the perfect family and deal with your real problems in a spirit of compassion, psychological growth begins to take place. 12

2. Tell It Like You Feel It

Have you heard the story of the fifteen-year-old boy who had never said a word in his whole life? He came to breakfast one day and suddenly yelled, "This oatmeal is cold!" His astounded mother replied, "You can *talk!* Why haven't you spoken before?" The boy shrugged and said, "Before this, everything was OK." 13

Funny story. Not so funny when situations like this occur in real families. And they do. All too frequently I encounter people in families who, for one reason or another, feel they must hide their feelings. 14

A few months ago, I saw an unhappy couple. Mrs. Raymond was almost always depressed. Sometimes she couldn't even take care of her home and children. Mr. Raymond was quite protective of his wife—but at the same time he was having an affair. 15

Together in my office, the Raymonds had little to say to each other. Each was 16 very solicitous, but wary of saying something that might upset the other. By not saying what they felt, they managed to upset each other more than if they had communicated their feelings directly.

It's odd how many people believe that when they stop verbalizing, communica- 17 tion ceases. Nothing, of course, is further from the truth, because communication consists of much more than words. Angry silence, sighs, headaches, impotence, and arrests for drunken driving can often be forms of distorted communication.

For his vacation, Mr. Raymond made plans to take his family on a two-week 18 camping trip. Mrs. Raymond told me she *dreaded* the idea of camping. When I urged her to express her displeasure so a mutually satisfying vacation could be ar- ranged, she replied, "But he works so hard. He deserves to go where he wants for vacation." Once at the campsite, she developed headaches and nausea. After two days of misery, she went to a local doctor, who failed to find any physical reason for her discomfort. During the rest of the vacation she tortured both herself and her husband with her physical complaints. It would have been much kinder had she told him how she felt before they left home.

Each time we conceal something from someone close to us, the relationship 19 becomes poorer. So, if you want to reduce family tensions, one of the most impor- tant ways to start is to send honest communications to those you love.

3. Don't Play Telephone

Do you remember the game "Telephone"? A message gets passed from person to 20 person, and everyone laughs at how distorted it becomes. As a game, telephone can be fun. In real life, sending messages through third parties fouls things up. It's important for family members who have "business" with other family members to take it up *directly*.

When tension mounts in a relationship between two people, a frequent way 21 of dealing with this is to send messages through a third person. Family therapists refer to the process as "triangulation." Following a spat, a mother may say to her son, "Tell your father to pass the salt," which may be answered by, "Tell your mother to get her own salt." In many chronic cases of triangulation, the middle- man becomes severely disturbed.

Two years ago, Ruth and Ralph Gordon brought their seventeen-year-old 22 daughter for treatment. Lucille was not doing well in school, using drugs heavily and becoming blatantly promiscuous. When I began to work with her, she was uncommunicative and hostile. After some time, however, she opened up and told me her parents rarely talked to each other—but both used her as a confidante. Mrs. Gordon was sexually unsatisfied and suggested to Lucille that she ask her father to go for marital counseling. Mr. Gordon told Lucille that he was seeing another woman, and he urged Lucille to speak to her mother about improving her grooming. Caught in this tangle of feelings, Lucille became more and more troubled. It wasn't until she refused to play middleman that she began to improve.

When either parent began to send a message through her, she learned to say, "Tell him/her yourself!"

You'll find that when family members learn to dial each other directly, there's 23 rarely a busy signal or wrong number. With direct dialing, a sense of freshness is engendered.[3]

4. Make Your Blueprints Flexible

Almost all parents have a secret master plan for their children. Sometimes this 24 calls for a child to grow up exactly like a parent—or, more often, for the child to become an improved version of the parent. In our culture, with its emphasis on getting ahead and self-fulfillment, it's tempting to hope that our children will realize many of our own desires. Whether we like it or not, though, children have a habit of spinning their own dreams. When a child's plans become different from his parents' blueprint, the family is on a collision course that can be avoided only by understanding and flexibility.

Most parents don't even realize how much they push and pull. I think you 25 would be surprised, too, at how frequently children will say things to their parents only to placate[4] them.

One teenage girl assured her parents that she was going to study harder and 26 prepare for college. This girl told me, "I don't plan to go to college, but I can't tell them yet. They are disappointed enough, and I don't want to rip up any more of their dreams for me." Caught in a web of parental expectations, this girl was miserable, and didn't feel free enough to explore her own potential and channel her abilities into realistic vocational goals.

An experienced parent knows that different children require different han- 27 dling. When we become wise and willing enough to revise our blueprints so that they incorporate the child's realistic needs and aptitudes, we are on the road to a less tension-filled family life.

5. Learn to Use Contracts

Psychologists say that when two people marry, they agree to a contract. Sometimes 28 couples have a strong emotional investment in keeping the not-so-pretty clauses of the contract hidden from everyone—including themselves. Gina and Tom Butler were married twenty-five years before their hidden contract caused problems.

When Tom met Gina, he was a skinny kid from a poor family who had a burn- 29 ing desire to become financially successful. He was, under his bravado,[5] painfully anxious, and he felt very inadequate. Gina was the prettiest girl in town. She was also desperately unhappy at home and couldn't wait to get away from the constant

---

[3]*engendered:* created.
[4]*placate:* please.
[5]*bravado:* false show of courage.

bickering there. When she was sixteen, she had an abortion. At seventeen, she met Tom. As they dated, they unwittingly began to draft their contract. Gina, unconsciously, agreed to make Tom feel adequate to reduce his anxieties. Tom, for his part, agreed never to discuss Gina's abortion, and to remove her from her hostile home situation by marrying her.

For many years their contract worked well. Gina massaged Tom's ego. She **30** encouraged, reassured, supported him. When the children went off to college, however, she felt she needed to grow. She attended a local college, graduated with honors, and accepted a position with a well-known company. As Gina became successful, Tom became irritable and angry. He accused her of not being interested in the family. Eventually, he accused her of having a lover and of being "a tramp, like you were when I met you and like you'll always be." With these words, their contract was breached, and both sought the services of attorneys. Fortunately, Gina's lawyer suggested counseling before divorce. In treatment, the hidden aspects of Gina and Tom's contract were uncovered, and they negotiated a more mature contract based upon mutual respect.

Many family contracts, like the Butlers', tend to disintegrate when one mem- **31** ber of the family begins to grow. And that's really all right, if the family can use the anxiety that inevitably results as a catalyst to promote healthy mutual growth.

I find it helps a lot if you can face up to your hidden contracts and then update **32** them. It's also fruitful when you set clear provisions for the many minor vicissitudes of daily living that can vex the family. Coats not hung up in the closet, hedges left untrimmed—these are the raw materials that fuel family explosions. Frequently, an annoying, persistent source of tension can be cleared away by drafting a new contract, whose terms are clearly understood by all parties.

One teenager agreed to wash the dishes in exchange for transportation to **33** cheerleading practice. One husband agreed not to smoke when he was with his wife, in exchange for her maintaining her weight loss. In these cases, all involved felt they had gotten a good deal, and niggling sources of family tension were eliminated by negotiation.

6. Stop the "Good Guy"—"Bad Guy" Routine

Sometimes, the greatest problems in families arise when people classify children **34** as Good Guys and Bad Guys. These families tend to make a scapegoat of one of their members, who from that point on becomes "it" in a never-ending game of tag.

The Freemonts had four children. Brett, the third child, resembled Mrs. **35** Freemont's uncle Mark, who was serving time for embezzlement. "He's just like Uncle Mark," the Freemonts proclaimed when Brett came home from nursery school with a toy giraffe that he had taken, and again when Brett was eight and got into a fight with another third-grader. By the time Brett was fifteen, he had far more serious problems. "I'm just like my uncle Mark," he told me: the label had become a self-fulfilling prophecy. Brett felt doomed to replicate his uncle's life. But once you realize that no two people are exactly alike, you can free members of your family to be themselves.

Curiously, sometimes the Bad Guy of the family really serves to hold that **36** family together. I once worked with an eighteen-year-old girl who was constantly involved in mischief. As I began to understand her family situation, I realized that this girl's parents were emotionally estranged and the constant turmoil her behavior produced was an attempt to get her parents to form a united front. Indeed, she was partially successful. Her bizarre antics were at times so extreme that her parents barely had time to examine their own problems.

The next time you're in the midst of a family problem, resist your natural urge **37** to think in terms of *right* and *wrong*. Rather, ask yourself, "What is going on here and why?" In our era of no-fault car insurance and no-fault divorce, it makes increasing sense to have no-fault (or all-fault) family problems.

7. Get Rid of Old Emotional Baggage

When people enter into any new relationship, they come to the new with a lot of **38** old fears and unhealed emotional wounds. Unless you look at your own history honestly, you're likely to unwittingly re-create the same unhappy mess that gave you so much pain in the past.

Rachel Dorton grew up in an unhappy household in which her father fre- **39** quently had affairs. When she married, with fidelity her top priority, Rachel chose Mal, a hardworking, earnest accountant. For a time, all went well. After several months of marriage, however, Rachel became increasingly suspicious when Mal did audits in distant cities. She made his life miserable with constant suspicion and pleas for reassurance. After several sessions of counseling, Rachel came to realize that, without conscious intent, she was re-creating the very experiences she had hated so much as a child. As she faced her feelings squarely, she was able to become less provocative, and she came to understand that some men—particularly Mal—could indeed be trusted.

During periods of severe stress, it's astounding how people may treat others **40** the same way they were treated by their parents. Ed Richardson had had a tough childhood. His father, a hardworking train conductor, would often take abuse from passengers and arrive home irritable and tense. Sometimes he would beat Ed severely. "You're no good," his father would proclaim. "You're a nothing."

Ed resolved that he would never hit his own children or call them names. For **41** years his resolve held, but then Ed's company went bankrupt and he was forced to take a job he despised. The family had to retrench and move to a smaller home. During this crisis, Ed's oldest boy cut school and was caught shoplifting. Ed brought the boy home and began to beat him. To his horror he found himself yelling, "You're no good . . . you're a nothing." Shaken by this experience, Ed got professional help. It took him a while to put things back together, but it helped when he realized that, when the chips are down, most people do unto others what has been done unto them.

At its best, a nourishing family serves as a safe haven enclosed by invisible 42 walls of love and concern. In such a family, individuals can replenish diminished feelings of self-esteem.

At its worst, a family can become a red-hot crucible in which ancient con- 43 flicts brew and boil and are reenacted again and again. Most frequently, however, families just seem to bumble along with little emotional insight into how the family itself may be responsible for intensifying or perpetuating a family member's problem.

Solving family problems has never been easy. As a practicing psychologist, 44 I know that good intentions alone are usually not enough. Effective action most often follows accurate understanding. With a little practice, care and use of these seven steps, the chances are good that you'll be able to lower the tension level in the best family of all—your own.

As Sugarman explains, families come in many different forms. What is your idea of the perfect family? Write an essay comparing or contrasting your real family with your idea of the perfect family.

READING COMPREHENSION

1. The word *anachronism* in "The idea of the typical happy family is becoming an anachronism. As the national divorce rate approaches 50 percent, increasing numbers of people will live in single-parent families" (paragraph 10) means

   a. an ideal.

   b. an injustice.

   c. a disease.

   d. something out of its time.

2. The word *catalyst* in "the family can use the anxiety . . . as a catalyst to promote healthy mutual growth" (paragraph 31) means

   a. something that helps bring about change.

   b. an unfortunate accident.

   c. criticism.

   d. a form of destruction.

3. Which of the following would be a good alternative title for this selection?

   a. Creating Family Blueprints

   b. How to Reduce Family Tension

   c. Hidden Contracts

   d. American Families

4. Which sentence best expresses the main idea of the selection?

   a. Believing myths about the perfect family can cause problems.

   b. When people marry, they agree to a contract.

   c. Following certain steps can help keep peace in a family.

   d. Family members play psychological games with each other.

5. The way for a family to stop playing "telephone" is to

   a. get rid of old emotional baggage.

   b. negotiate better contracts.

   c. communicate directly.

   d. create flexible blueprints.

6. *True or false?* _____ Children who grow up in happy homes are not necessarily better adjusted as adults.

7. The "Good Guy"–"Bad Guy" routine means that

   a. family members feel they must be perfect.

   b. family members refuse to communicate with each other directly.

   c. families make scapegoats of one of their members.

   d. parents create secret master plans for their children.

8. The author implies that

   a. "triangulation" can be a helpful way for family members to communicate.

   b. making a scapegoat of a family member can unite a family.

   c. people need to identify their problems before they can act to help themselves.

   d. fidelity is essential in marriage.

9. The author implies that

   a. the perfect American family existed until fairly recently.

   b. creating family contracts inevitably leads to problems.

   c. how a parent treats a child can affect the following generations.

   d. families need "middlemen" to pass along communications.

10. *True or false?* _____ The author implies that all families need professional help at times.

STRUCTURE AND TECHNIQUE

1. For the essay as a whole, what method of introduction—broad-to-narrow, anecdote, or questions—does the author use? What method does he use to begin section 1? Section 2? Section 3?

2. Sugarman supports his main points in several ways. One way is with examples. What examples does he use to support his first step, "Give Up the Myth of the Perfect Family"? How much space is given to each of those examples? What other type of support is used in paragraph 11?

3. How does Sugarman organize and present his main supporting details? What do his methods achieve?

4. Throughout his essay, Sugarman alternates between quoting people directly and reporting indirectly what they said. Should he have used only direct quotations? Should he have used only indirect quotations? Why or why not?

CRITICAL READING AND DISCUSSION

1. According to Sugarman, who is more to blame for family problems: parents or children? Give examples from the selection to support your point.

2. In section 4, what does Sugarman mean by the term "blueprint"? What does he suggest is the way to avoid "a collision course" between parents with a blueprint and a child with different plans for himself or herself? What blueprint did your parents have for you, and how does it compare with your own goals for yourself?

3. Sugarman states that people often "feel they must hide their feelings" from family members. Why do you think it is sometimes difficult for family members to be honest with one another? Do you agree with Sugarman that an important way of reducing family tensions is "to send honest communication"? Or are there times when it is best not to be totally honest? Explain.

4. In section 5, Sugarman discusses family contracts. What does he mean by the word "contract"? Describe any contracts that exist between members of families you're familiar with.

WRITING ASSIGNMENTS

www.mhhe.com/langan

Assignment 1

Write about the three ways that would be most appropriate for keeping peace at your home. Following are examples of how the three supporting paragraphs in your essay might begin.

First supporting paragraph:

One way our family would benefit is if we would stop playing the game of telephone. All too often, one family member uses another to . . .

Second supporting paragraph:

Another step our family should take is "Tell it like you feel it." My mother, for example, sometimes hides her true feelings about . . .

Third supporting paragraph:

Perhaps most important, our family needs to stop the "Good Guy"– "Bad Guy" routine. Two people in my family seem to have been cast in these roles . . .

Develop the ways you choose with specific examples that involve the members of your family.

Assignment 2

Sugarman tells us seven ways to keep the peace at home. However, there are other places where it is important to keep the peace—for instance, at school, at the workplace, in the dormitory room. Choose one of these other places and write your own guide to how to keep the peace there. Use three of the rules discussed in the article or think of other rules, and develop each paragraph by giving specific examples of the rule you are suggesting. Try to include appropriate stories, as Sugarman does, to show what you mean.

Assignment 3

Write an essay-length summary of the selection. Your goal is to write a shortened and condensed—but accurate—version of the selection in about five hundred words. To do this, you should do the following:

In each supporting paragraph of your summary, cover two or three of the peacekeeping methods.

Include only *key* ideas.

Shorten examples (or eliminate extra examples).

Eliminate dialogue and repeated ideas.

Most important, remember that a summary should be *in your own words,* not the original author's. Therefore, don't simply copy material from the selection. You should, instead, put the author's ideas into your own words.

Below is an introduction that you can use to begin your summary:

A Summary of "Seven Ways to Keep the Peace at Home"

<u>Family</u> is a word associated with warmth, affection, caring, love, and peace. In reality, though, family life can be very different. Tension, anger, and frustration take over, at times, in almost every household. In his article "Seven Ways to Keep the Peace at Home," Daniel A. Sugarman describes several techniques people can use to prevent or resolve family conflicts.

In Praise of the F Word

Mary Sherry

PREVIEW

What does it take to get by in high school? Too little, according to the author, a teacher in an "educational-repair shop." In this article, which originally appeared in *Newsweek,* Mary Sherry describes the ways she sees students being cheated by their schools and proposes a remedy you may find surprising.

Courtesy of Mary Sherry

1　Tens of thousands of eighteen-year-olds will graduate this year and be handed meaningless diplomas. These diplomas won't look any different from those awarded to their luckier classmates. Their validity will be questioned only when their employers discover that these graduates are semiliterate.

Eventually a fortunate few will find their way into educational-repair shops— 2
adult-literacy programs, such as the one where I teach basic grammar and writing. There, high school graduates and high school dropouts pursuing graduate-equivalency certificates will learn the skills they should have learned in school. They will also discover that they have been cheated by our educational system.

As I teach, I learn a lot about our schools. Early in each session I ask my stu- 3
dents to write about an unpleasant experience they had in school. No writer's block here! "I wish someone had made me stop doing drugs and made me study." "I liked to party, and no one seemed to care." "I was a good kid and didn't cause any trouble, so they just passed me along even though I didn't read well and couldn't write." And so on.

I am your basic do-gooder, and prior to teaching this class I blamed the poor 4
academic skills our kids have today on drugs, divorce, and other impediments to the concentration necessary for doing well in school. But, as I rediscover each time I walk into the classroom, before a teacher can expect students to concentrate, he has to get their attention, no matter what distractions may be at hand. There are many ways to do this, and they have much to do with teaching style. However, if style alone won't do it, there is another way to show who holds the winning hand in the classroom. That is to reveal the trump card[1] of failure.

I will never forget a teacher who played that card to get the attention of one of 5
my children. Our youngest, a world-class charmer, did little to develop his intellectual talents but always got by—until Mrs. Stifter.

Our son was a high school senior when he had her for English. "He sits in 6
the back of the room talking to his friends," she told me. "Why don't you move him to the front row?" I urged, believing the embarrassment would get him to settle down. Mrs. Stifter looked at me steely-eyed over her glasses. "I don't move seniors," she said. "I flunk them." I was flustered. Our son's academic life flashed before my eyes. No teacher had ever threatened him with that before. I regained my composure and managed to say that I thought she was right. By the time I got home I was feeling pretty good about this. It was a radical approach for these times, but, well, why not? "She's going to flunk you," I told my son. I did not discuss it any further. Suddenly English became a priority in his life. He finished out the semester with an A.

I know one example doesn't make a case, but at night I see a parade of stu- 7
dents who are angry and resentful for having been passed along until they could no longer even pretend to keep up. Of average intelligence or better, they eventually quit school, concluding that they were too dumb to finish. "I should have been held back," is a comment I hear frequently. Even sadder are those students who are high school graduates who say to me after a few weeks of class, "I don't know how I ever got a high school diploma."

---

[1]*trump card:* in bridge, a card of the suit that ranks highest; thus, something powerful, often held in reserve to be used at the right moment.

Passing students who have not mastered the work cheats them and the employ- 8
ers who expect graduates to have basic skills. We excuse this dishonest behavior
by saying kids can't learn if they come from terrible environments. No one seems
to stop to think that—no matter what environments they come from—most kids
don't put school first on their list unless they perceive that something is at stake.
They'd rather be sailing.

Many students I see at night could give expert testimony on unemployment, 9
chemical dependency, abusive relationships. In spite of these difficulties, they have
decided to make education a priority. They are motivated by the desire for a better job or the need to hang on to the one they've got. They have a healthy fear of
failure.

People of all ages can rise above their problems, but they need to have a rea- 10
son to do so. Young people generally don't have the maturity to value education in
the same way my adult students value it. But fear of failure, whether economic or
academic, can motivate both.

Flunking as a regular policy has just as much merit today as it did two genera- 11
tions ago. We must review the threat of flunking and see it as it really is—a positive teaching tool. It is an expression of confidence by both teachers and parents
that the students have the ability to learn the material presented to them. However,
making it work again would take a dedicated, caring conspiracy between teachers
and parents. It would mean facing the tough reality that passing kids who haven't
learned the material—while it might save them grief for the short term—dooms
them to long-term illiteracy. It would mean that teachers would have to follow
through on their threats, and parents would have to stand behind them, knowing their children's best interests are indeed at stake. This means no more doing
Scott's assignments for him because he might fail. No more passing Jodi because
she's such a nice kid.

This is a policy that worked in the past and can work today. A wise teacher, 12
with the support of his parents, gave our son the opportunity to succeed—or fail.
It's time we returned this choice to all students.

READING COMPREHENSION

www.mhhe.com/langan

1. The word *validity* in "[The diplomas'] validity will be questioned only when
   . . . employers discover that these graduates are semiliterate" (paragraph 1)
   means

   a. soundness.

   b. dates.

   c. age.

   d. supply.

2. The word *impediments* in "I blamed the poor academic skills our kids have today on drugs, divorce, and other impediments to concentration" (paragraph 4) means

   a. questions.
   b. paths.
   c. skills.
   d. obstacles.

3. Which of the following would be a good alternative title for this selection?
   a. Learning to Concentrate in School
   b. Teaching English Skills
   c. A Useful Tool for Motivating Students
   d. Adult-Literacy Programs

4. Which sentence best expresses the main idea of the selection?
   a. Many adults cannot read or write well.
   b. English skills can be learned through adult-literacy programs.
   c. Schools should include flunking students as part of their regular policy.
   d. Before students will concentrate, the teacher must get their attention.

5. Sherry's night students are
   a. usually unemployed.
   b. poor students.
   c. motivated to learn.
   d. doing drugs.

6. According to the author, many students who get "passed along"
   a. are lucky.
   b. never find a job.
   c. don't get into trouble.
   d. eventually feel angry and resentful.

7. Sherry feels that, to succeed, flunking students as a regular policy requires
   a. adult-literacy programs.
   b. graduate-equivalency certificates.
   c. the total cooperation of teachers and parents.
   d. a strong teaching style.

8. The author implies that our present educational system is
   a. the best in the world.
   b. doing the best that it can.
   c. very short of teachers.
   d. not demanding enough of students.

9. *True or false?* _____ Sherry implies that high school students often don't realize the value of academic skills.

10. From the selection, we may conclude that the author based her opinion on

 a. statistics.

 b. educational research.

 c. her personal and professional experiences.

 d. expert professional testimony.

STRUCTURE AND TECHNIQUE

1. In current vocabulary, "the F word" usually refers to something other than "fail." Why do you think Mary Sherry used the term in her title, rather than simply using "fail" or "failure"? What effect does her title have on the reader?

2. In which paragraph does the author first mention her thesis? What is her main method of development, and how is it related to that thesis? Where does she use narration to support her thesis?

3. What contrast transition is used in the first sentence of paragraph 10? What ideas are being contrasted within that sentence?

4. In paragraph 11, how many times does Sherry use "mean" or "means"? What might her purpose be for repeating this word so frequently?

CRITICAL READING AND DISCUSSION

1. Sherry writes that "before a teacher can expect students to concentrate, he has to get their attention, no matter what distractions may be at hand" (paragraph 4). What examples of distractions does Sherry mention? Find several in her essay. Can you think of others—perhaps ones that existed in your own high school?

2. What does Sherry mean by calling the program she teaches in an "educational-repair shop"? What does the term tell us about Sherry's attitude toward high schools?

3. Sherry writes, "Young people generally don't have the maturity to value education in the same way my adult students value it." Do you agree or disagree? Support your view with details and observations from your own experience.

4. Do you feel your high school teachers made an honest effort to give you the skills you need—and to make you aware of the importance of those skills? If not, what should your school have done that it did not do?

WRITING ASSIGNMENTS

Assignment 1

Write an essay that has as its thesis *one* of the following statements:

> In my opinion, students have no one to blame but themselves if they leave school without having learned basic skills.

> When students graduate or quit school lacking basic skills, they are the victims of an inadequate educational system.

> Flunking students has more disadvantages than advantages.

Support your thesis with several points, each developed in its own paragraph.

Assignment 2

Sherry proposes using "flunking as a regular policy" as a way to encourage students to work harder. What else might school systems do to help students? Write an essay in which you suggest a few policies for our public schools and give the reasons you think those changes will be beneficial. Following are some policies you may wish to consider:

> More writing in all classes

> Shorter summer vacations

> Less emphasis on memorization and more on thinking skills

> A language requirement

> A daily quiet reading session in elementary grades

Assignment 3

Here are two letters sent to *Newsweek* by teachers in response to Sherry's article:

Letter 1

Mary Sherry's essay advocating the use of flunking as a teaching tool was well intentioned but naïve. In the first place, my local school district—and I doubt it's unique—discourages the practice by compiling teachers' failure rates for comparison. (Would you want to rank first?) More important, though, F's don't even register on many kids' Richter scales. When your spirit has been numbed—as some of my students' spirits have—by physical, sexual, and psychological abuse, it's hard to notice an F. Walk a mile in one of my kids' shoes. Real fear has little to do with school.

Kay Keglovits
Arlington, Texas

Letter 2

Sherry is right: flunking poor students makes sense. But, as she notes, "making it work again would take a dedicated, caring conspiracy between teachers and parents." I once failed a high school junior for the year. I received a furious call from the student's mother. I was called to a meeting with the school superintendent, the principal, the mother, and the student. There it was decided that I would tutor the student for four months so that the F could be replaced with a passing grade. This was a total sham; the student did nothing during this remedial work, but she was given a passing grade. No wonder education is in the condition that we find it today.

Arthur J. Hochhalter
Minot, North Dakota

These letters suggest that if schools want to try flunking as a regular policy, they will have to plan carefully. Write an essay in which you discuss ways to make failing poor students work as a regular policy. Your thesis statement can be something like this: "For a policy of flunking to work, certain policies and attitudes would need to be changed in many schools." As support in your essay, use the ideas in these letters, Sherry's ideas, and any other ideas you have heard or thought of. Describe your supporting ideas in detail and explain why each is necessary or useful.

Is Sex All That Matters?

Joyce Garity

PREVIEW

From the skimpy clothing in ads to the suggestive themes in many of today's TV comedies, our young people are bombarded with sexuality. How does the constant stream of sexual images influence their behavior and dreams? In considering that question, social worker Joyce Garity focuses on one young woman named Elaine, alone and pregnant with her second child.

A few years ago, a young girl lived with me, my husband, and our children for 1
several months. The circumstances of Elaine's coming to us don't matter here;
suffice it to say that she was troubled and nearly alone in the world. She was also
pregnant—hugely, clumsily pregnant with her second child. Elaine was seventeen.
Her pregnancy, she said, was an accident; she also said she wasn't sure who had
fathered her child. There had been several sex partners and no contraception. Yet,
she repeated blandly, gazing at me with clear blue eyes, the pregnancy was an accident, and one she would certainly never repeat.

Eventually I asked Elaine, after we had grown to know each other well enough 2
for such conversations, why neither she nor her lovers had used birth control. She
blushed—porcelain-skinned girl with one child in foster care and another swelling
the bib of her fashionably faded overalls—stammered, and blushed some more.
Birth control, she finally got out, was "embarrassing." It wasn't "romantic." You
couldn't be really passionate, she explained, and worry about birth control at the
same time.

I haven't seen Elaine for quite a long time. I think about her often, though. I 3
think of her as I page through teen fashion magazines in the salon where I have
my hair cut. Although mainstream and relatively wholesome, these magazines
trumpet sexuality page after leering page. On the inside front cover, an advertisement for Guess jeans features junior fashion models in snug denim dresses, their
legs bared to just below the crotch. An advertisement for Liz Claiborne fragrances
shows a barely clad young couple sprawled on a bed, him painting her toenails.
An advertisement for Obsession cologne displays a waif-thin girl draped stomach-
down across a couch, naked, her startled expression suggesting helplessness in the
face of an unseen yet approaching threat.

I think of Elaine because I know she would love these ads. "They're so beauti- 4
ful," she would croon, and of course they are. The faces and bodies they show are
lovely. The lighting is superb. The hair and makeup are faultless. In the Claiborne
ad, the laughing girl whose toenails are being painted by her handsome lover is
obviously having the time of her life. She stretches luxuriously on a bed heaped
with clean white linen and fluffy pillows. Beyond the sheer blowing curtains of her
room, we can glimpse a graceful wrought-iron balcony. Looking at the ad, Elaine
could only want to be her. Any girl would want to be her. Heck, *I* want to be her.

But my momentary desire to move into the Claiborne picture, to trade lives 5
with the exquisite young creature pictured there, is just that—momentary. I've
lived long enough to know that what I see is a marketing invention. A moment after the photo session was over, the beautiful room was dismantled, and the models
moved on to their next job. Later, the technicians took over the task of doctoring
the photograph until it reached full-blown fantasy proportions.

Not so Elaine. After months of living together and countless hours of watch- 6
ing her yearn after magazine images, soap-opera heroines, and rock goddesses, I
have a pretty good idea of why she looks at ads like Claiborne's. She sees the way
life—her life—is supposed to be. She sees a world characterized by sexual spon-

taneity, playfulness, and abandon. She sees people who don't worry about such unsexy details as birth control. Nor, apparently, do they spend much time thinking about such pedestrian topics as commitment or whether they should act on their sexual impulses. Their clean sunlit rooms are never invaded by the fear of AIDS, of unwanted pregnancy, of shattered lives. For all her apparent lack of defense, the girl on the couch in the Obsession ad will surely never experience the brutality of rape.

Years of exposure to this media-invented, sex-saturated universe have done 7 their work on Elaine. She is, I'm sure, completely unaware of the irony in her situation: She melts over images from a sexual Shangri-la,[1] never realizing that her attempts to mirror those images left her pregnant, abandoned, living in the spare bedroom of a stranger's house, relying on charity for rides to the welfare office and supervised visits with her toddler daughter.

Of course, Elaine is not the first to be suckered by the cynical practice of using 8 sex to sell underwear, rock groups, or sneakers. Using sex as a sales tool is hardly new. At the beginning of this century, British actress Lily Langtry shocked her contemporaries by posing, clothed somewhat scantily, with a bar of Pear's soap. The advertisers have always known that the masses are susceptible to the notion that a particular product will make them more sexually attractive. In the past, however, ads used euphemisms, claiming that certain products would make people "more lovable" or "more popular." What is a recent development is the abandonment of any such polite double-talk. Advertising today leaves no question about what is being sold along with the roasted peanuts or artificial sweetener. "Tell us about your first time," coyly invites the innuendo[2]-filled magazine advertisement for Campari liquor. A billboard for Levi's shows two jeans-clad young men on the beach, hoisting a girl in the air. The boys' perfect, tan bodies are matched by hers, although we see a lot more of hers: bare midriff, short shorts, cleavage. She caresses their hair; they stroke her legs. A jolly fantasy where sex exists without consequences.

But this fantasy is a lie—one which preys on young people. Studies show that 9 by the age of twenty, 75 percent of Americans have lost their virginity. In many high schools—and an increasing number of junior highs—virginity is regarded as an embarrassing vestige of childhood, to be disposed of as quickly as possible. Young people are immersed from their earliest days in a culture that parades sexuality at every turn and makes heroes of the advocates of sexual excess. Girls, from toddlerhood on up, shop in stores packed with clothing once thought suitable only for streetwalkers—lace leggings, crop tops, and wedge-heeled boots. Parents drop their children off at concerts featuring simulated on-stage masturbation or pretended acts of copulation. Young boys idolize sports stars like the late Wilt Chamberlain, who claimed to have bedded 20,000 women. And when the "Spur Posse,"

---

[1]*Shangri-la:* an imaginary paradise on earth (the name of a beautiful faraway place in the novel *Lost Horizon*).

[2]*innuendo:* subtle suggestion.

eight California high school athletes, were charged with systematically raping girls as young as ten as part of a "scoring" ritual, the beefy young jocks were rewarded with a publicity tour of talk shows, while one father boasted to reporters about his son's "manhood."

In a late, lame attempt to counterbalance this sexual overload, most schools of- **10** fer sex education as part of their curriculums. (In 1993, forty-seven states recommended or required such courses.) But sex ed classes are heavy on the mechanics of fertilization and birth control—sperm, eggs, and condoms—and light on any discussion of sexuality as only one part of a well-balanced life. There is passing reference to abstinence as a method of contraception, but little discussion of abstinence as an emotionally or spiritually satisfying option. Promiscuity is discussed for its role in spreading sexually transmitted diseases. But the concept of rejecting casual sex in favor of reserving sex for an emotionally intimate, exclusive, trusting relationship—much less any mention of waiting until marriage—is foreign to most public school settings. "Love and stuff like that really wasn't discussed" is the way one Spur Posse member remembers his high school sex education class.

Surely teenagers need the factual information provided by sex education **11** courses. But where is "love and stuff like that" talked about? Where can they turn for a more balanced view of sexuality? Who is telling young people like Elaine, my former houseguest, that sex is not an adequate basis for a healthy, respectful relationship? Along with warnings to keep condoms on hand, is anyone teaching kids that they have a right to be valued for something other than their sexuality? Madison Avenue, Hollywood, and the TV, music, and fashion industries won't tell them that. Who will?

No one has told Elaine—at least, not in a way she comprehends. I haven't seen **12** her for a long time, but I hear of her occasionally. The baby boy she bore while living in my house is in a foster home, a few miles from his older half-sister, who is also in foster care. Elaine herself is working in a local convenience store—and she is pregnant again. This time, I understand, she is carrying twins.

READING COMPREHENSION

1. The word *dismantled* in "A moment after the photo session was over, the beautiful room was dismantled, and the models moved on to their next job" (paragraph 5) means

   a. used.

   b. photographed.

   c. taken apart.

   d. perfected.

2. The word *vestige* in "In many high schools—and an increasing number of junior highs—virginity is regarded as an embarrassing vestige of childhood" (paragraph 9) means
    a. reversal.
    b. activity.
    c. remainder.
    d. error.

3. Which of the following would be a good alternative title for this selection?
    a. Teens and Birth Control
    b. The Use of Sex to Sell Products
    c. An Unbalanced View of Sexuality
    d. The Advantages of Casual Sex

4. Which sentence best expresses the main idea of the selection?
    a. Sexual images have helped our society become more open and understanding about a natural part of life.
    b. We live in a society ruled by Madison Avenue, Hollywood, and the TV, music, and fashion industries.
    c. Sex education courses, required in most states, have not done enough to teach our children about sexuality and responsible behavior.
    d. Nothing, not even sex education, is counteracting the numerous sexual images in our society that encourage irresponsible, casual sex.

5. According to the author, Elaine probably likes to look at sexy magazine ads because
    a. she doesn't have high moral standards.
    b. she wishes she could afford the products being advertised.
    c. they portray the kind of life she'd like to lead.
    d. they remind her of her life before she had children.

6. In contrast to Elaine, the author
    a. understands that most ads portray an unreal world.
    b. finds ads like the Claiborne ad distasteful.
    c. never looks at fashion magazines.
    d. does not have children.

7. Elaine
    a. wanted to become pregnant.
    b. thinks birth control isn't romantic.
    c. never finished high school.
    d. has a healthy fear of AIDS.

8. We can conclude the author believes that
    a. sex is a private matter that should not be discussed.
    b. many young people view sex as an adequate basis for a relationship.
    c. Madison Avenue, Hollywood, and the TV, music, and fashion industries have completely destroyed all morality in America.
    d. virginity is an embarrassing vestige of childhood.

9. The author implies that
    a. sexy ads should be illegal.
    b. schools should teach contraception at an earlier age.
    c. sex should be reserved for an exclusive, loving relationship.
    d. casual sex is sometimes, though not always, a good idea.

10. The author suggests that sex education classes
    a. are a major cause of casual, unprotected sex.
    b. should include the role of sex in a meaningful relationship.
    c. should not include the mechanics of fertilization and birth control.
    d. have taken over a role that rightfully belongs to parents.

STRUCTURE AND TECHNIQUE

1. To support her views about sexuality in popular culture, Garity presents the case of Elaine. Why has the author chosen to focus so much of her essay on Elaine? What would have been lost if Garity had omitted Elaine?

2. List the details that Garity provides as she describes the Claiborne ad. Why does she go to such lengths to describe it? Why might she think it important for the reader to see it so clearly?

3. Garity uses a number of examples to support her claim about the prevalence of sex in popular culture. Cite some of these examples and explain how they support her argument.

4. Throughout paragraph 11, Garity poses a series of questions. What does she gain by using this technique?

CRITICAL READING AND DISCUSSION

1. How do you think Garity felt about Elaine? Affectionate? Scornful? Resentful? Disapproving? Pitying? Explain your answer, pointing out evidence from Garity's text.

2. In paragraph 7, the author says that Elaine is "completely unaware of the irony in her situation." In an ironic situation, there is an inconsistency between what might be expected and what actually happens. What about Elaine's situation is ironic?

3. The author lists numerous examples to illustrate and support her claim that "young people are immersed from their earliest days in a culture that parades sexuality at every turn and makes heroes of advocates of sexual excess." What examples can you think of to add to her list? Describe and explain them.

4. In arguing against the emphasis on sexuality in our culture, Garity focuses on potential dangers to young women. How do you think this highly sexualized culture affects young men? Are they also at risk? Explain.

WRITING ASSIGNMENTS

www.mhhe.com/langan

Assignment 1

Garity accuses the advertising, film, TV, music, and fashion industries of contributing to our sex-saturated society by parading "sexuality at every turn." Choose one industry from that list and write your own essay about how it portrays sexuality.

There is more than one way you can approach this assignment. In an essay on the fashion industry, for instance, you could focus on types of clothing being promoted, ads in print, and ads on TV. In an essay on the music industry, you might discuss three musicians and how their lyrics and their performances promote a particular view of sex. Whatever your choice, include specific, colorful descriptions, as Garity does when discussing ads and fashions. (See, for example, paragraphs 3 and 8.)

Assignment 2

Garity suggests that sex education courses should include more than the "mechanics of fertilization and birth control" (paragraph 10). Write an essay describing several ways you feel sex education classes could incorporate "love and stuff like that." Begin by selecting three general approaches that could be used in a sex education class to get students to think about what a rich, balanced romantic relationship is made of. For example, you might focus on three of the following:

Discussion of what students seek in a relationship

Discussion of a fictional relationship, such as that of Romeo and Juliet or two characters on a TV show

Discussion of the lyrics of a popular song

Bringing into class a psychologist who deals with problems in relationships

Bringing into class one or more couples who have been together for many years

Discuss each method you choose in a separate paragraph. Describe in detail how the method would work, using hypothetical examples to illustrate your points.

Assignment 3

Advertisements represent many elements of our society. Choose an element other than sexuality and analyze the way ads of any kind (in magazines and newspapers, on billboards and buses, on TV and radio and on the Internet) portray that subject. Following are some areas of our lives that are commonly represented in ads:

Family life

Women's roles

Men's roles

Possessions

Looks

Health

In analyzing an ad, consider what images and words are used, how they are intended to appeal to the audience, and what values they promote. Use the conclusion you come to as the thesis of your essay. For example, an essay on men's roles might make this point: "Many of today's TV ads promote participation of fathers in domestic activities."

Support your conclusion with colorful descriptions of several ads. Make your descriptions detailed enough so that your readers can "see" the elements of ads you refer to. Be sure to focus on the parts of the ads that support the point you are trying to make. You could organize your essay by devoting a paragraph each to three significant ads. Or you could devote each supporting paragraph to one of several important points about the subject you've chosen. For instance, an essay about fathers helping at home might discuss child care, cleaning, and cooking. A paragraph on each of those topics might refer to two or more ads.

A Scary Time to Raise a Daughter

Steve Lopez

PREVIEW

If you listen to the radio, watch TV, or surf the Internet, you're likely to come across entertainment and marketing campaigns focused on sex and violence. What concerns author Steve Lopez is the increasing amount that's targeted at teens, and in this selection, he examines the damaging effects this is having on such an impressionable age group.

Three months ago, with my wife's contractions getting closer and closer, we flicked on the TV as a distraction before going to the hospital. 1

Bad idea. 2

No one expects a great deal of enlightenment from the tube these days. But as we switched from one tawdry and vapid reality or dating show to another, I wondered if we should have our heads examined for bringing a child into this world. 3

Especially a girl. 4

It's not just television that scares me. It's the Internet, pop music, radio, advertising. The most lurid elements of each medium now dominate pop culture, and the incessant, pounding message, directed primarily at young people, is that it's all about sex. 5

Sure, some of us boomers had our flower child days of free love, but that was a social revolution, not a corporate-driven campaign. 6

Today, if you haven't just had it, you're a loser. If you don't expect to have it in the immediate future, try plastic surgery, because sex appeal—the one true standard of human achievement—is the only thing worth aspiring to. 7

Yes, I'll admit it: I'm frazzled about all of this because I have a baby girl. Each day, I feel a little more like Dan Quayle, who was once ridiculed for wagging a finger at television's Murphy Brown, an unwed mom. 8

Where's Dan Quayle when you need him? 9

At my daughter's first checkup, our pediatrician mentioned that he routinely has pregnant patients in their early teens. I shook my head and said it's no wonder, given what kids see on TV and the Internet. 10

Forget that, the doctor said. Go for a drive and take a look at some billboards. Belts are unbuckled. Bras are undone. Everyone is on the make. While contemplating these horrors as a new dad, I got an e-mail one day from actress Susan Dey, who has volunteered at the Rape Treatment Center in Santa Monica for 15 years. 11

Dey was America's grooviest teenager in a more innocent media era—she 12 played Laurie on "The Partridge Family." She told me she had gotten an unsolicited e-mail directing her to a Web site with college girls having live sex. Dey checked it out and was horrified at what is essentially a guide for frat boys on how to nail coeds.

"A little alcohol will always loosen up the college chicks!" the site advises, 13 complete with graphic results.

"These are the girls we see at the rape center," Dey said with disgust. Gail 14 Abarbanel, director of the center, said 50% of rape victims are 18 or younger, and the rapists are acquaintances 80% of the time.

"We see a lot of cases where raped women are incapacitated by drugs or alco- 15 hol, sometimes surreptitiously," Abarbanel said. "We even have a few cases where victims have been tagged."

The rapist will use a felt-tip pen to mark his conquest, she said, just as a gang 16 banger leaves his tag on a wall.

When I asked Abarbanel what was going on, she said kids are saturated as 17 never before with marketing and entertainment that's all about sex and violence. Subtlety and restraint are quaint, nostalgic notions, as is attentive parenting.

Another factor, I think, is that very little in the culture encourages independent 18 thinking, and that makes peer pressure all the more powerful. "Look at what's happening with oral sex in the bathrooms of middle schools," Abarbanel said, telling me that, in workshops at local schools, they hear stories about how commonplace it's become.

I've got friends who told me they turn the radio off while taking their kids to 19 school, because it's routine to hear shock jocks carrying on about oral sex. Next time I was in my car, I flipped through the FM dial and, in nothing flat, found that very thing on two stations.

A couple of weeks after we met, Dey called again to say I ought to have a look 20 at the photos in the Abercrombie & Fitch store at the Grove in the Fairfax District. We met there Thursday and took a tour.

On both floors of the store, which markets to a young crowd, the walls were 21 plastered with huge blowups of fresh-faced, great-looking teens who are either nude or nearly nude.

In one, a topless girl is playing the violin while in the clutches of a shirtless 22 boy, and a carefully placed strand of hair is all that keeps her from being completely revealed.

In another, a naked girl is sandwiched by two boys, her breasts completely vis- 23 ible but for a bit of strategic air brushing. The three of them are holding a blanket over what appear to be nude lower bodies.

An odd advertising campaign, you'd have to say—all this nudity being used to 24 sell clothes.

It's all about an image, a clerk explained.   25

Yeah, I gathered as much.   26

"The message is, you should be a sexual object," Dey said outside the store. 27 "Like I've been saying, connect the dots."

She had been telling me the problem isn't the photos in the store, or billboards 28 on the street, or TV shows, or movies, or the Internet. It's all of those things together.

"I taught my daughter to love her body, but that's not what this is about," Dey 29 said. "A boy's not cool if he hasn't just done it. His whole manhood is at stake. I don't think we were ever targeted the way they're targeting this generation, and when does it stop?

"I would love it if parents said, 'No, I'm not putting my credit card down for 30 this.' Can you imagine what would happen if parents said to Madison Avenue, 'I want my 13-year-old to be a 13-year-old'?"

READING COMPREHENSION

1. The word *vapid* in "as we switched from one tawdry and vapid reality or dating show to another" (paragraph 3) means
   a. quick.
   b. uninspiring.
   c. new.
   d. exciting.

2. The word *surreptitiously* in "'We see a lot of cases where raped women are incapacitated by drugs or alcohol, sometimes surreptitiously'" (paragraph 15) means
   a. boldly.
   b. secretly.
   c. suddenly.
   d. illegally.

3. Which of the following would be a good alternative title for this selection?
   a. The Dangers of Date Rape
   b. A Call for Attentive Parenting
   c. Sex and Violence Saturation
   d. Sexy Images in the Media

4. Which sentence best expresses the central point of the selection?
   a. Young people are pounded with messages about sex.
   b. Sex appeal is the only true standard of human achievement.
   c. Everyone needs to fight against the efforts made by marketing and entertainment industries to saturate young people with sex and violence.
   d. Our culture discourages young people from thinking independently.

5. *True or false?* _____ The author is afraid of television, the Internet, pop music, radio, and advertising.

6. As a parent, the author identifies with
   a. Dan Quayle.
   b. Murphy Brown.
   c. Susan Dey.
   d. Gail Abarbanel.

7. According to paragraphs 14–18, which of the following is *not* true?
   a. Rape victims are often incapacitated by drugs or alcohol.
   b. Rape victims are tagged with felt-tip pens by their assailants.
   c. Rapists are strangers 80% of the time.
   d. Half of all rape victims are 18 or younger.

8. Which store did the author find a sexually aggressive advertising campaign?
   a. Diesel USA
   b. The Gap
   c. Abercrombie & Fitch
   d. Banana Republic

9. Based on paragraph 29, we can infer that Susan Dey
   a. does not believe that young people will stop being targeted.
   b. does not believe that her daughter loves her own body.
   c. does not believe that boys are cool.
   d. believes that boys should prove their manhood.

10. Based on paragraph 30, we can infer that Susan Dey
    a. will not use her credit card.
    b. will tell other parents not to use their credit cards.
    c. will not endorse products that exploit sex and violence.
    d. will write a letter to Madison Avenue.

STRUCTURE AND TECHNIQUE

1. The author uses the first-person approach, which allows him to rely on his personal experiences. Why do you think he uses this particular approach rather than the second or third person? Do you think this approach is effective?

2. The author includes a two-word sentence: "Bad idea" (paragraph 2). Why do you think the author is so concise? What effect is the author trying to convey to his readers?

3. How would you describe the author's tone? What clues in the selection lead you to this conclusion?

4. What method—summary, question(s), or predictions—does the author use in his conclusion? Why do you think he chose this way to end his essay?

CRITICAL READING AND DISCUSSION

1. Why do you think "no one expects a great deal of enlightenment from the tube these days" (paragraph 3)? What are your thoughts on television?

2. What are the differences between the social revolution of free love and to-day's corporate-driven campaign to sell sex and violence? What are the similarities?

3. Why was former Vice President Dan Quayle ridiculed for his comments about Murphy Brown? What or whom might Quayle be wagging his finger at today?

4. In paragraph 18, the author argues that our culture does not encourage inde-pendent thinking. Do you agree that young people are not encouraged to think in this way? How might we encourage independent thinking?

WRITING ASSIGNMENTS

www.mhhe.com/langan

Assignment 1

Just like author Joyce Garity in the previous professional essay, "Is Sex All That Matters," Lopez accuses television, the Internet, pop music, and advertising for pounding messages about sex and violence directly at young people. Write an es-say in which you compare or contrast each author's presentation of this topic.

As you develop your essay, think about the following topics:

What is the tone of each essay?

What method of introduction/method of conclusion does each author use?

Which patterns of development do the authors use?

What argumentation techniques does each author employ?

How do the authors each organize and present their main supporting details?

What writing techniques are effectively used by each author?

Is one essay more effective than the other?

Assignment 2

Lopez ends his essay by quoting Susan Dey: "Can you imagine what would happen if parents said to Madison Avenue, 'I want my 13-year-old to be 13-year-old'" (paragraph 32). Write an essay in which you define what a typical 13-year-old girl or boy should be, according to Dey and Lopez.

As you plan your supporting paragraphs, think of different qualities of your term. Support each part of your definition with either a series of examples or a simple extended example.

Assignment 3

Lopez's concern about the blatant sexuality marketed at young people stems from the fact that he recently became the father of a baby girl. This makes the issue relevant and personal to him. Write an essay about a current issue you feel as strongly about. The purpose of your essay will be to bring your issue to the attention of others and to convince your readers of the problem it poses to society.

Reading Comprehension Chart

Write an X through the numbers of any questions you missed while answering the comprehension questions for each selection in Part Five, Readings for Writers. Then write in your comprehension score. If you repeatedly miss questions in any particular skill, the chart will make that clear. Then you can pay special attention to that skill in the future.

Selection	Vocabulary in Context	Title and Main Idea	Key Details	Inferences	Comprehension Score
Russell	1	2 3	4 5 6	7 8 9 10	%
Gregory	1 2	3 4	5 6 7	8 9 10	%
Wilkins	1 2	3 4	5 6 7	8 9 10	%
McMurtry	1 2	3 4	5 6 7	8 9 10	%
Orwell	1 2	3 4	5 6 7	8 9 10	%
Kimmel	1 2	3 4	5 6 7	8 9 10	%
Johnson	1 2	3 4	5 6 7	8 9 10	%
Taylor	1 2	3 4	5 6	7 8 9 10	%
Banas	1 2	3 4	5 6 7	8 9 10	%
McClintock	1 2	3 4	5 6 7 8	9 10	%
Johnson	1 2	3 4	5 6 7	8 9 10	%
Dunayer	1 2	3 4	5 6 7	8 9 10	%
Song	1 2	3 4	5 6 7 8	9 10	%
O'Keeney	1 2	3 4	5 6 7	8 9 10	%
Daniels	1 2	3 4	5 6 7	8 9 10	%
Sugarman	1 2	3 4	5 6 7	8 9 10	%
Sherry	1 2	3 4	5 6 7	8 9 10	%
Garity	1 2	3 4	5 6 7	8 9 10	%
Lopez	1 2	3 4	5 6 7	8 9 10	%

A Writer's Journal

Credits

Text Credits

p. 3: *Have Yourself a Merry Little Christmas*, words and music by Hugh Martin and Ralph Blane. Copyright © 1943 (Renewed) EMI/FEIST Catalog, Inc. All rights controlled by EMI/FEIST Catalog, Inc. (Publishing) and Alfred Publishing Co., Inc. (Print). All rights reserved. Used by permission of Alfred Publishing Co., Inc.

p. 188: Beth Johnson, "Lou's Place." Reprinted by permission. Beth Johnson lives in Lederach, Pennsylvania.

p. 212: Pete Hamill, "The Yellow Ribbon." Reprinted by permission of International Creative Management, Inc. Copyright © Deirdre Enterprises.

p. 218: *You Turn Me On, I'm a Radio*, words and music by Joni Mitchell. Copyright © 1972 (Renewed) Crazy Crow Music. All rights administered by SONY/ATV Music Publishing, 8 Music Square West, Nashville, TN 37203. All rights reserved. Used by permission of Alfred Publishing Co., Inc.

p. 232: "Dad," by Andrew Malcolm. Reprinted by permission.

p. 251: "How to Do Well on a Job Interview," by Glenda Davis. Reprinted by permission of the author.

p. 272: "Taming the Anger Monster," by Anne Davidson. Reprinted by permission of the author.

p. 298: "Born to Be Different?" by Camille Lewis. Reprinted with permission from the author.

p. 320: "Cookies or Heroin?," from *The Plug-In Drug*, Revised and Updated-25th Anniversary Edition, by Marie Winn. Copyright © 1977, 1985, 2002 by Marie Winn Miller. Used by permission of Viking Penguin, a division of Penguin Group (USA) Inc.

p. 339: Tom Bodett, 1987, "Wait Divisions," from *Small Comforts*. Cambridge, MA: Perseus Books. Reprinted by permission of Da Capo Press, a member of Perseus Books Group.

p. 362: Molly Ivins, "Ban the Things. Ban Them All," *The Washington Post*, March 16, 1993. Copyright © Molly Ivins. Reprinted with permission from Pom, Inc.

p. 429: Excerpt from "Cookies or Heroin?" from *The Plug-In Drug*, Revised and Updated-25th Anniversary Edition, by Marie Winn. Copyright © 1977, 1985, 2002 by Marie Winn Miller. Used by permission of Viking Penguin, a division of Penguin Group (USA) Inc.

p. 430: From James Brody, "New Respect for the Nap." Copyright © 2000 by The New York Times Co. Reprinted with permission.

Readings

p. 641: "Three Passions" from *The Autobiography of Bertrand Russell*. Copyright © 2000. Reproduced by permission of Taylor & Francis Books, United Kingdom.

p. 645: "Shame" from *Nigger: An Autobiography*, by Dick Gregory. Copyright © 1964 by Dick Gregory Enterprises, Inc. Used by permission of Dutton, a division of Penguin Group (USA) Inc.

p. 653: Roger Wilkins, "I Became Her Target," *Newsday*, September 6, 1987. Reprinted by permission.

p. 660: John McMurtry, "Smash Thy Neighbor," *Maclean's*. Reprinted by permission of John McMurtry, Ph.D., FRSc., internationally known author and University Professor Emeritus, University of Guelph.

p. 669: "A Hanging," from *Shooting an Elephant and Other Essays*, by George Orwell. Copyright © 1950 by Sonia Brownell Orwell and Renewed 1978 by Sonia Pitt-Rivers. Reprinted by permission of Harcourt, Inc. and by permission of Bill Hamilton as the Literary Executor of the estate of the late Sonia Brownell Orwell and Secker & Warburg Ltd.

p. 678: *From a Girl Named Zippy*, by Haven Kimmel. Copyright © 2001 by Haven Kimmel. Used by permission of Doubleday, a division of Random House, Inc.

p. 683: Beth Johnson, "The Professor Is a Dropout." Reprinted by permission. Beth Johnson lives in Harleyville, Pennsylvania.

p. 693: Deems Taylor, *The Monster*. Copyright © 1937. Originally published by Curtis Brown Ltd. Reprinted by permission.

p. 700: Casey Banas, "What's Wrong with Schools? Teacher Plays Student, Learns to Lie and Cheat," *The Chicago Tribune*, August 5, 1979. Copyright © August 5, 1979, Chicago Tribune Company. All rights reserved. Used with permission.

Photo Credits

Index

Assignments

Assignment	Date Assigned	Due Date	Instructor(s)	Complete	Grade

Assignments

Assignment	Date Assigned	Due Date	Instructor(s)	Complete	Grade

To remove this Langan ASSIGNMENT CHART, detach along the dotted lines!